YO-CEO-630

TEXTBOOK OF PSYCHIATRY
FOR MEDICAL PRACTICE

With the Collaboration of

CHATHAM G. CLEMENTS, M.D., *Assistant Professor in Child Psychiatry, University of Cincinnati College of Medicine*
LOUIS A. GOTTECHALK, M.D., *Research Professor of Psychiatry, University of Cincinnati College of Medicine*
STANLEY M. KAPLAN, M.D., *Assistant Professor of Psychiatry, University of Cincinnati College of Medicine*
JOHN A. MacLEOD, M.D., *Associate Professor of Psychiatry, University of Cincinnati College of Medicine*
JAMES L. TITCHENER, M.D., *Assistant Professor of Psychiatry, University of Cincinnati College of Medicine*

With a Foreword by

MAURICE LEVINE, M.D., *Professor and Director, Department of Psychiatry, University of Cincinnati College of Medicine*

Textbook of
PSYCHIATRY
for
MEDICAL PRACTICE

CHARLES K. HOFLING, M.D.

Assistant Professor of Psychiatry
University of Cincinnati College of Medicine

J. B. LIPPINCOTT COMPANY · Philadelphia and Montreal

Copyright © 1963, by J. B. Lippincott Company

This book is fully protected by copyright and, with the exception of brief extracts for review, no part of it may be reproduced in any form without the written permission of the publishers.

Distributed in Great Britain by
Pitman Medical Publishing Co., Limited, London

Library of Congress Catalog Card No. 63-16325

Printed in the United States of America

To
Othilda Krug, M.D.

Foreword

MAURICE LEVINE, M.D.
*Professor and Director, Department of Psychiatry,
University of Cincinnati*

This book, written by Dr. Charles Hofling and his colleagues, provides an effective and fundamental text for the study of psychiatry. Perhaps its greatest asset lies in the clarity with which it demonstrates repeatedly that the essential problems dealt with by psychiatric patients are universal problems.

Psychodynamics, therefore, is a basic science. Some of its patterns are to be called psychopathologic. Others are to be regarded as less or not at all disruptive or as constructive. But all are related and universal and human.

Such an emphasis upon the universality of psychiatric problems is only one of a large number of emphases in this book. In fact it uses a flexible combination of a number of principles which are basic in the teaching of psychiatry. It interweaves clinical psychiatry with intrapsychic dynamics and with interpersonal dynamics. It makes full use of the multiple etiologic approach. Its thinking is neurophysiologic and psychopharmacologic in part, but these points of view are interdigitated extensively with the crucial concepts of personality homeostasis. The book emphasizes inborn characteristics, developmental processes, and the variety of interactions which take place in the depth and breadth of human personality. It gives attention to usable theory but emphasizes practice as well.

Dr. Hofling's book is an achievement of high value for medical students and for residents in training in psychiatry as well as for interested physicians in other disciplines. It presents contemporary psychiatry clearly and effectively. It deserves great success.

Preface

The devotion of an appreciable portion of time over the past 15 years or so to the teaching of psychiatry to medical students has resulted in the strong impression that a gap exists between the subject as most instructors wish to present it and the assistance which is available through textbooks. There has developed a wide consensus among both students and educators—in which interested practitioners of medicine concur—that the major contribution which psychiatry has to make to nonpsychiatrists is the light it can shed upon problems with which physicians will frequently have to deal. Yet books on psychiatry, whether written primarily for medical students or for practitioners of medicine, have not, by and large, kept pace with this realization—tending, for example, to overemphasize the study of the psychoses and classical neuroses. It is in the attempt to narrow this gap that the publisher's invitation to write a new textbook of psychiatry was accepted by the present writer and his colleagues.

It has seemed to us that there were two principal pitfalls to be avoided. The first was the temptation to slight background material to get quickly to the clinical material; to slight the psychology of the normal and the near-normal, the psychology of development and the psychology of motivation. It has seemed to us that the more a textbook of psychiatry purports to be of value to the practitioner or student of medicine who does not contemplate specializing in psychiatry, the greater its obligation to present a theoretical background of sufficient scope to foster independent thinking about and study of the subject.

The second pitfall was the temptation to substitute the principal research and therapeutic interests of the writers for the legitimate principal interests of the readers. Surely this confusion is at least partly responsible for the fact that so much more psychiatry is "taught" in books than is learned from them.

Accordingly, the first half of the present work is devoted to a leisurely attempt to do two things: to demonstrate the relatedness of psychiatric knowledge to the rest of medicine, and to develop the background that will enable the reader to think psychiatrically when the occasion calls for it.

There follow a number of chapters presenting the chief nosological entities in the field of psychiatry, in which, however, a much more serious attempt is made to enlighten than to be comprehensive. Controversial areas have been given only passing attention.

The book concludes with two chapters on treatment and one on child psychiatry. The authors have the impression that psychiatric treatment, at both the adult and childhood levels, is often glossed over in general works in the field designed for the nonpsychiatrist, a circumstance which may leave the student wondering just what the psychiatrist does and, more importantly, just what he, himself, as a practicing physician, should attempt to do for patients with emotional problems.

The authors share a conviction about the style of much medical textbook writing, a conviction which has especial relevance to books in the field of psychiatry. Medicine in general, and psychiatric medicine in particular, is, of course, full of material of high emotional significance. Yet, perhaps in the attempt to be ultra-scientific, it is the fashion for a textbook to be decidedly prosaic, with one slow-moving, heavily documented statement following another. It is our wish to convey the essentials of the subject-matter without rendering it lifeless in the process. If, in this supplementary contribution to the work of the instructor in psychiatry, we have attempted to teach too little, we yet reserve the hope that what is taught will also, for the most part, be learned.

CHARLES K. HOFLING

Acknowledgments

While this work is in no sense an official publication of the Cincinnati Department of Psychiatry, it is nevertheless a collaborative venture to an even greater extent than is apparent from the title page. Many of the teaching ideas it embodies were drawn from informal conversations with colleagues. Many of the case histories were furnished by members of the department other than those who did the actual writing.

The principal author wishes first to express his gratitude to those colleagues who have shared the actual work of writing: Drs. Stanley M. Kaplan, Louis A. Gottschalk, James L. Titchener, John A. MacLeod, and C. Glenn Clements. In addition to assuming responsibility for particularly important individual chapters, they have offered valuable suggestions pertaining to other portions of the book.

James K. Robinson, Ph.D., Professor of English and Senior Research Associate in the Department of Psychiatry, has given greatly prized assistance to us all in reviewing the entire manuscript and offering both stylistic corrections and pedagogical suggestions.

Special appreciation is due Maurice Levine, M.D., Professor and Chairman of the Department of Psychiatry, for graciously writing the Foreword and for his perceptive scrutiny of a sizable portion of the manuscript. In addition, the Department of Psychiatry has furnished financial assistance to the work, as well as generously freeing periods of time of those engaged in its writing.

Colleagues in the department have kindly served as consultants in the preparation of specific chapters of the book. Thus, Frederick T. Kapp, M.D., and W. Donald Ross, M.D., reviewed the first three chapters; Othilda Krug, M.D., did the same for the chapters on personality development and child psychiatry; Roy M. Whitman, M.D., reviewed the chapter on psychosomatic medicine; Robert Stewart, M.D., those on psychoneuroses and personality disorders; Marshal Ginsburg, M.D., Paul Ornstein, M.D., and Philip Piker, M.D., those on the psychoses; and Glenn M. Weaver, M.D., the sub-chapter on psychopharmacologic agents.

Charles D. Aring, M.D., Professor and Chairman of the Department of Neurology, and J. Park Biehl, M.D., offered helpful suggestions on the chapter dealing with organic brain reactions.

Madelyn L. Hofling, B.S., R.N., kindly undertook the chief responsibility for proofreading the manuscript.

Secretarial assistance of a high order was furnished by Mrs. Frieda DeVaux and Mrs. Laura Parris.

The encouragement and support of the J. B. Lippincott Company in the person of Mr. Brooks Stewart, Medical Editor, is warmly appreciated.

Sincere gratitude is felt toward the many classes of students at the University of Cincinnati College of Medicine, whose fruitful interaction with their instructors has played the greatest part in the development of this work.

CHARLES K. HOFLING

Contents

1. COMMON PSYCHOLOGICAL PROBLEMS IN MEDICINE . . . 1
    STANLEY M. KAPLAN, M.D.
    Preliminaries 1
    The Office Visit 4
    Diagnostic Procedures 6
    Treatment Procedures 17
    Summary 26

2. FUNDAMENTALS OF PSYCHOLOGY FOR THE PHYSICIAN (Part 1) 28
    Basic Psychological Concepts 28
    Mental Health 32
    The Concept of Levels of Awareness 38

3. FUNDAMENTALS OF PSYCHOLOGY FOR THE PHYSICIAN (Part 2) 49
    Motivation: The Basic Drives and Their Manifestation . 49
    Conflict 64
    Organization of the Mind 69

4. PERSONALITY DEVELOPMENT 82
    Human Development: Physiological and Psychological . 82
    Obtaining Data on Early Developmental Periods . . . 83
    Phases of Personality Development 85
    Notes on Family Influences 123
    Notes on Hereditary Influences 127

5. PSYCHIATRIC PROBLEMS SEEN IN THE GENERAL PRACTICE OF
    MEDICINE 130
    LOUIS A. GOTTSCHALK, M.D.
    Grief and Mourning; the Person Suffering From Bereavement or Separation 130
    Some Common Situational Maladjustments 134
    Common Mild Sexual Problems 139
    Malingering 145
    Traumatic Neurosis 151

5. PSYCHIATRIC PROBLEMS SEEN IN THE GENERAL PRACTICE OF MEDICINE—(*Continued*)
    Headache and Head Pain 153
    Backache 158
    Summary of the Mechanisms of Pain Production by Psychological Means 161
    Fatigue and Symptoms of Neurasthenia 162
    Boredom 165
    Addiction or Habituation in Mild or Incipient Form . . 166
    Obesity 176

6. PSYCHIATRY IN THE PRACTICE OF INTERNAL MEDICINE. PSYCHOSOMATIC MEDICINE 182
    Definition of Psychosomatic 183
    Specific Syndromes 186
    Extensions of Psychosomatic Concepts 218

7. PSYCHIATRY IN THE PRACTICE OF SURGERY AND THE SPECIALTIES. SOMATOPSYCHIC SEQUENCES 222
    JAMES L. TITCHENER, M.D.
    Psychiatry and Surgery 222
    Somatopsychic Sequences 255
    Summary and Implications 268

8. INTRODUCTION TO PRINCIPAL PSYCHIATRIC DISORDERS. ORGANIC BRAIN REACTIONS 271
    Introduction 271
    Delirium and Dementia 274
    Specific Organic Brain Reactions 281

9. THE NEUROSES 307
    Traumatic Neuroses 308
    The Psychoneuroses 310
    Prognosis and Treatment of the Psychoneuroses . . . 338

10. THE FUNCTIONAL PSYCHOSES, PART 1: THE AFFECTIVE REACTIONS 341
    Affective (Psychotic) Reactions 341
    Treatment of Affective Psychoses 358

11. THE FUNCTIONAL PSYCHOSES, PART 2: SCHIZOPHRENIC AND PARANOID REACTIONS 360
    Schizophrenic Reactions 360
    Paranoid Reactions: Paranoia and Paranoid State . . . 390

12.	PERSONALITY DISORDERS	397
	Alcoholism	405
	Narcotic Addiction	414
	Sexual Deviation	416
	Neurotic Personalities	422
13.	PSYCHIATRIC TREATMENT MEASURES, PART 1. MEASURES SUITABLE FOR USE BY THE NONPSYCHIATRIST JOHN A. MACLEOD, M.D.	426
	Common Misconceptions About Treatment by the Nonpsychiatrist	426
	Treatment Arrangements	428
	Interviewing	429
	Diagnostic Thinking	430
	Treatment Thinking	435
	The Doctor-Patient Relationship	451
	Commonly Used Psychopharmacological Agents	452
	Collaborative and Ancillary Approaches	460
	Considerations Involved in Psychiatric Consultation	465
14.	PSYCHIATRIC TREATMENT MEASURES, PART 2. MEASURES SUITABLE FOR USE BY THE PSYCHIATRIST	469
	General Remarks	469
	Physical and Chemical Therapies Primarily Symptomatic	472
	Techniques Primarily Psychological	478
15.	PSYCHIATRIC DISORDERS OF CHILDHOOD AND ADOLESCENCE. MENTAL RETARDATION CHATHAM GLENN CLEMENTS, M.D.	516
	The Constitutional Baseline	516
	Symptoms of the First Year (Oral Phase)	517
	Problems of the Muscle-Training (Anal) Phase	521
	Problems of the Oedipal Phase	525
	Problems of the Latency Period	532
	Problems of Adolescence	536
	Psychological Aspects of Mental Retardation	541
INDEX		549

CHAPTER 1

Common Psychological Problems in Medicine

Stanley M. Kaplan, M.D.

Physicians know that a patient is, among other things, a person who has psychological problems. These problems begin as soon as uncomfortable sensations signal to him that some part of his body or mind is not functioning properly. They end, hopefully, with his recovery and full return to family and job, the illness and the inconvenience it caused for the most part forgotten. Sometimes the end is not so hopeful. Illness can lead to severe mental or physical discomfort, serious incapacity, chronic invalidism and death. Because all that's ill does not necessarily end well, illness can be frightening. It usually is, unless it is of a very mild nature.

While the anxious patient turns naturally for care and protection to his physician and others who join in diagnosing and treating his ailment, the physician may just as naturally experience anxiety (usually less than the patient's, of course) in responding to the challenge of restoring the patient's health. The extent to which the doctor can understand and respond to the worries and emotional needs of his patient and the extent to which he can understand his own responses to the patient bear significantly on the course and outcome of the illness.

So many psychological problems may be associated with the diagnosis and treatment of patients that it is neither possible nor practical to consider them all here. What is both possible and practical is to follow the experience of illness through its several phases and to reflect upon a number of the most common psychological issues that confront patient and physician.

PRELIMINARIES

The Presenting Situation

What is it which makes a patient get in touch with his doctor? Why did he telephone for an appointment today rather than yesterday or a month ago? Why didn't he continue to put off telephoning? Though ordinarily only marginally aware of himself, he has had some unusual sensation or some exaggeration of a familiar one which has forced him to act on behalf of his health.

Different patients require different stimuli to induce them to call a doctor. One patient may hurry to report minimal symptoms, while another may have to be dragged to the doctor's office still protesting that a fainting spell or a substernal pain radiating down the left arm is only due to a slight case of indigestion. One patient comes in regularly for a check-up. Another passively watches the progress of a carcinoma which is extensively invading the surface of his body. It is worth considering why patients perceive and act on bodily dysfunction so variously.

Certainly the nature of the stimulus is important. Intense symptoms like severe physical pain or emotional panic will usually lead the patient to call his physician immediately. Any sudden onset of symptoms is more likely to attract attention than their gradual development. For example, an acute abdominal pain more often arouses serious concern than an equal discomfort that has gradually intensified during several weeks.

The appearance and location of the difficulty are also important. A skin rash does not easily evade one's attention, and symptoms in some areas of the body are more alarming than those in others. For instance, a pain in the region of the heart is likely to create considerable anxiety because of the heart's known vital function.

What may not be so generally recognized is that the patient's general attitude toward illness is important. Some patients are constantly aware of their bodily processes, quick to complain about illness. Others, for various reasons, go to extremes to deny even obvious evidences of illness. Some men feel that illness is a sign of weakness or unmanliness and therefore refuse to call a doctor unless symptoms are severe. Some are ashamed to expose themselves physically or mentally to a doctor's examination. There are women, for example, who hesitate to consult a physician because they fear a vaginal examination. A man may hesitate because of shame at revealing that his urinary tract symptoms began after an extra-marital affair. There are many people, indeed, who fear to go to a doctor lest he find something seriously wrong with them.

Even more likely to be overlooked is that attitudes toward doctors carried over from early life can interfere. Though most people have some fear of visiting the doctor, such a visit can be especially painful to those who have had frightening childhood medical experiences or who identify the doctor with a stern or overpowering parent (or a lingering childhood image of such a parent)

When a patient has an emotional upset, still other attitudes may interfere with a decision to visit his physician. Although much has been done, patients and, to some extent, physicians need to be further educated about mental illness. A patient may recognize that his problems are emotional in origin, only to feel that his symptoms are merely "all in my head." He hesitates to offer symptoms which seem (to him) only to reflect weakness. He shrinks from the possibility of being ridiculed, looked upon as queer, accused of being "crazy."

If he actually steels himself to visit his physician, he may do so under the pretext of a minor physical complaint or the need for a general check-up. It will only become apparent to the physician after gentle probing that the patient is actually worried or undergoing some emotional upheaval. He represents the other side of the coin from the patient who, unaware that his physical discomforts are a manifestation of a neurosis, is eager to visit the doctor repeatedly or goes from doctor to doctor in a vain attempt to secure relief from what he considers an organic disorder.

There are, then, opposing forces operating in the patient about to present himself for diagnosis and treatment. Some forces act to encourage him, some to discourage. In general, the greater the pain, the anxiety and the obviousness of pathology, the greater will be the impetus to seek medical assistance. The greater the fear of doctors, the blow to pride, the shame about examination, the greater will be the reluctance to do so. The opposing, counterbalancing forces differ from individual to individual, but there is nearly always some point at which the balance tips and the patient calls for help. Unfortunately, far too many people suffer too much before they decide, too late, to visit the doctor.

Selecting the Physician

A patient chooses his doctor after considering, among other things, the latter's reputation in the community, experiences of friends and family with him, the proximity of his office, and his reputed fee range. Even before he pays his first visit he feels that he knows a great deal about the doctor, although much that he knows may be incorrect. He may have a preconception of his doctor as kindly, warm, understanding or bad-tempered, impatient, even cruel. His very preconceptions, however, are significant to diagnosis and treatment. A patient with a particularly intense need for reassurance and warmth tends often to select a kindly, personable physician. Another, who can only feel secure when excessive protective needs are met, may choose a somewhat authoritarian doctor. Another, with an inner need to suffer, chooses a rather harsh physician. Still another selects a physician in unconscious hopes of sexual satisfaction. Since the motives in selection are so various, it is obviously advantageous for a physician to be psychologically flexible, to be able to recognize the different needs of different patients. Flexibility of response, of course, should not go beyond the boundaries of the genuinely therapeutic.

Making the Appointment

Patients may ask for an appointment in tones ranging from roar to whisper. A particularly aggressive patient calls the office, insists on speaking directly to the doctor, demands an immediate appointment, though there may be no realistic necessity for doing so. Though he may need prompt attention, his aggressive manner may provoke the receptionist into stalling him off until a much later date, or, the demanded appointment made, he may succeed only in so antagonizing doctor and other personnel that he will forever be regarded as a troublemaker. To mix a metaphor, a man who shouts "wolf!" should not drive a doctor to pull the wool over his own eyes. In the face of outrageous or discourteous demand, the doctor should maintain an unruffled disposition and not be blinded to the real presenting situation, a possible illness.

Similarly, the doctor must be alert to the patient who introduces himself not with a roar but with a polite, subdued whimper, the patient who apologizes for bothering the receptionist and asks for an appointment suggesting no urgency for treatment. Conceivably this timid patient may evoke a positive, protective response, but if the doctor is busy and overworked, the receptionist may be encouraged by his docility to fix an appointment some time off. The doctor must look out for the submissive patient as he does for the one who loudly shouts "wolf," must recognize that delay may involve increased discomfort and serious progression of a disease, may precipitate, too, anger and disappointment in the patient, however silently they are borne.

In the first call for an appointment, the patient's is not the only voice heard. At the other end of the line is the voice of the nurse or receptionist. The doctor-patient relationship dervies something from the first voice signals from the doctor's office. Confident and warm, cold, aloof, impatient or even hostile, the voice from the doctor's office means a great deal to the new patient. It may take a doctor some time to undo a thoughtlessly conveyed unfavorable first impression.

THE OFFICE VISIT

It is not too much to say that treatment begins, not in the examining room, but in the reception room. A receptionist who obviously is indifferent to a patient and his feelings can heighten his fear about the symptoms which prompted his coming. The waiting-room, too, matters.

It can depress by the bleakness of its furnishings, the antiquity of its magazines (a copy of *Collier's* on an end table is a bad sign), the inadequacy of its seating facilities, or a general lack of cleanliness. It can depress, too, by too great opulence: a luxuriant office stimulates gloomy speculations about the size of the bills which make such luxuriance possible. Between extremes of drabness and opulence is an appropriate neat, comfortable attractiveness. Interior decorating is not, and should not be, a physician's principal interest, but every doctor should remember that the aspect of his office plays a part in that relationship between doctor and patient that begins with the first call and persists through the balance of the illness.

Waiting in the waiting-room matters, too. Most physicians recognize that their patients have jobs and responsibilities and that unnecessary loss of time in the waiting-room is an imposition on them. There are, happily, only a few doctors who give all their patients the same appointment time and then see them in the order of appearance in the waiting-room (as if they were lining up for shots in the army). With such a system, or nonsystem, the last patient conceivably waits many hours for the doctor, depending how long he spends with previous patients and whether his lunch is a snack or an affair requiring about as much time as that required to shoot nine holes of golf.

The office visit is not solely to be considered from the standpoint of the patient's view of waiting-room, receptionist, and the appointment schedule. The doctor's office forms its view of the patient. The very arrival time is significant. There is a good deal of merit in the axiom that if a patient arrives early he is anxious, if he arrives late he is hostile, and if he arrives exactly on time he is perfectionistic. The early bird may *have* worms, may be particularly worried about his condition, or he may be passive and conforming, fearing to displease the doctor by late arrival. He may also, of course, be early simply because someone driving him to the doctor had had to go on to work. The patient who is late may be so simply because he had a flat tire, but the doctor should not rule out the possibility that his tardiness may reflect, perhaps unconsciously, a depreciating or hostile attitude toward the doctor or a "devil may care" attitude toward illness.

Patients give clues to their natures not only by when they arrive but also how. A patient who is accompanied to the office may reveal fear and a need for support. One expects a child to be accompanied by a parent; one is alerted to possible problems when a 30-year-old married woman is habitually escorted by her mother. He is less likely to be concerned about a patient who comes alone.

Early, late, or on time, accompanied or unaccompanied, a patient inevitably meets his doctor. The handshake provides the doctor with another diagnostic opportunity. The patient's proffer of a clammy palm may convey fright, a desperate appeal for a secure relationship. The proffer of a completely limp one may suggest great inhibition. The complete avoidance of a handshake may suggest problems in interpersonal relationships. A knuckle-breaking or Indian Warrior grip may suggest underlying fears. The physician will be more optimistic at a spontaneous, moderate handshake and a pleasant greeting.

When people shake hands, they quickly appraise one another's dress and grooming. Such appraisal, automatic and frequently aimless in everyday life, is valuable when doctor is meeting patient. Anxious, worried, or physically distressed patients often appear "thrown together" for the visit to the doctor's office. Crumpled clothes and uncombed hair can reflect a temporary disorganization or reduced effectiveness of the patient's personality. A wobbly gait may suggest a neurologic lesion, but it can as well reflect the impact of severe personality stress. Too careful, as well as careless, dress can attract the physician's attention, warning him, for instance, that a fastidiously dressed patient may minimize certain kinds of symptoms in an attempt to look good to the doctor, or that he may find it extremely difficult to follow certain kinds of instructions. Thus an impeccably clean and neat dresser may "forget" to apply nightly the coal-tar ointment the doctor prescribes for his skin ailment.

Not simply dress but the whole appearance of the patient may reflect anxiety, depression, fear, elation or seductiveness. Postures, facial expression, tone of voice, quantity of speech, speed of movement, distractibility—all contribute to the composite picture which the physician forms of the patient's emotional state. They are as useful as much of the information provided by the patient in talking about himself.

How the patient looks and acts and how he speaks give the physician some early guidelines for his response. If the patient's rate of speech is retarded, the physician will wonder if, and how seriously, the patient is depressed. He will also wonder how the depression influences the patient's account of his symptoms. If the doctor asks himself these questions, he will understand the possible meaning of a painfully slow response rather than react with irritation under the impression that the patient is simply delaying medical evaluation. Similarly, if a physician understands that a garbled account of symptoms may be due to fright, he can reduce the patient's apprehensiveness in the interest of an accurate history, a proper diagnosis and treatment.

DIAGNOSTIC PROCEDURES

Obtaining the History

Almost every medical student has had the experience of obtaining what seems to be a completely accurate history from a patient and then, during ward rounds, of standing by, red-faced and dismayed, while the patient gave the instructor an entirely different version of the history of his illness. Variant histories are seldom the student's fault but rather due to the patient's difficulties. He may be feeling great physical discomfort and much anxiety; he responds differently to different interviewers; toxic conditions may be affecting his mentation; he may be editing a first account out of fear of disapproval. History-taking is not to be looked upon solely in terms of the material it uncovers, but in terms of its contribution to the creation of a valuable positive doctor-patient relationship.

There is no set pattern for interviewing to obtain a history of illness. Technics vary with the temperaments of doctors and the personalities and physical conditions of patients. Whatever the variables, it is essential that the interview take place in a setting that affords privacy, since many patients are ashamed of illness and almost all are reluctant to discuss personal matters when others are within hearing or are bustling in and out of the examining room. This care for appropriate interviewing conditions is important because a touchy patient may "forget" to speak of symptoms which are diagnostically important, for example those having to do with excretory or genital function, unless he senses a confidential atmosphere.

The interview must be confidential. It should be comfortable as well for both patient and doctor. Some doctors are most comfortable seated behind a desk. If this arrangement seems to erect a barrier between doctor and patient, the patient's chair may be placed at the side of the desk or the doctor can move from his desk to a chair opposite the patient. Not only seating comfort but leisureliness is at issue: the interview should be conducted in an unhurried manner, especially if it is the initial one, when a great deal of information must be obtained. If the patient is made to feel that every minute he spends with the doctor is begrudged, he is likely to feel irritated or harassed. Yet leisureliness, too, can be overdone: there are limits to the amount of time which profitably can be spent on history during a first appointment. Normally the interview should not go beyond 30 to 40 minutes; additional history-taking can await a later occasion.

During the interview the doctor communicates a great deal nonverbally. His facial expression may convey interest, boredom or anxiety about the patient's symptoms. Of course, he may not really be bored simply because he seems to be staring out the window; he may be thinking deeply about the symptoms presented. Nevertheless, he should be aware how he may appear to the patient and how this appearance will be reflected in the developing relationship or in the attitudes the patient forms toward his illness.

When the doctor does speak, he must be careful what he says. A series of questions fired at a patient can seriously interfere with the process of gathering clear, accurate information. Leading questions can be disastrous. It is the rare medical student who has not read about the symptoms of some exotic and fascinating disease and then, soon afterwards, elicited precisely the symptoms of this disease from an unsuspecting and obliging patient. The following dialogue only slightly exaggerates the technic of rigged interviewing:

> Student: Mr. P., you say you have had fever and have felt quite tired?
> Mr. P.: Yes, sir.
> Student: Joints ever hurt you?
> Mr. P.: Yes, my joints hurt *sometimes*.
> Student: Ever have a rash?
> Mr. P.: Yes!
> Student: On your face?
> Mr. P.: Yes!
> Student: Well, now, did it ever look kind of like a butterfly?
> Mr. P.: You might say that.
> Student: (to himself) Just as I thought; lupus erythematosis, disseminated.

Skillful, as opposed to rigged, interviewing involves a gentle, sensitive leading of the patient over the ground of his case. It enables the patient to speak spontaneously, the doctor to question carefully and systematically. Skillful guidance may be offered in various ways. A nod or the repetition of something the patient has just said may encourage him to proceed in a particular direction. Listening alertly, the doctor may pick up apparently casual information. For instance, if a patient says, "I seem to get this ache more on weekends when I'm at home," the doctor can lead the patient into a discussion of his home life and closest interpersonal relationships. This apparently casual, but sensitively alert, technic reduces the likelihood of overly guarded or defensive responses following from directly phrased questions.

Pointed questions are unfortunate, particularly when one is doing a comprehensive appraisal and wishes to understand whether psychological problems are important, either at the onset of an illness or as a result of it. Psychological manifestations are more likely to come to light if the patient can relate his material freely and with few interruptions. Consider the following example:

> Patient: So I have these headaches, Doctor, that I described to you. Perhaps I should explain again how they are pounding and begin on the left side. It's about then that my husband tells me to go take an aspirin. Then the headache moves to the right side and . . .
> Doctor: Your husband tells you to take an aspirin?

Patient: Yes, that's George for you. Little does he care how much I suffer with them.

The doctor should be interested not only in *what* is related and in *how* it is related, but also in what is missing from the expected history. The *what* is, of course, still the main material. It includes how the patient feels, when he became ill, what influenced his symptoms. The *how* matters too: whether the patient speaks in a childlike, whimpering way or matter-of-factly, boldly or sheepishly. Though one is aware of different manners in patients, often observations are not fully used. Even less often do doctors make full use of obvious omissions. Perhaps a patient has been vague, quickly brushing aside reference to a symptom that would be dealt with directly by most patients. Perhaps he has made a passing comment about the similarity of his pain to that which his father experienced before he died. Though unstressed, such a comment should arrest the physician's attention, make him wonder whether the patient is worried lest he, too, have a fatal disease or whether the pain is a manifestation of a psychological identification (p. 78) with the dead father.

Social and family history should emerge naturally with the history of the present illness. Since the interview situation is optimally an open-ended one, the patient can usually be led rather easily into discussions of pertinent features of his current life, his background and his family history.

The review of systems provides for an orderly check of symptoms that might otherwise be overlooked in a general history-taking period. Some patients answer affirmatively to almost all questions asked, an indication that the patient may be making a bid for attention which he has long sought but infrequently received. It can reflect a need to suffer, or a "hypochondriacal" preoccupation. Other patients may completely deny any of the symptoms in the systems review in something of a show of bravery to the physician, or as a reflection of an inner denial (p. 76) of illness.

In this discussion, no effort has been made to differentiate between interviewing "psychiatric" patients and "other" patients. Generally speaking, no such differentiation is required, but a few comments relating to this matter may be made. When the patient relates his history of illness, one actively follows his account. This procedure may lead to his telling how he slipped and fell on an icy sidewalk and broke his leg, or, in another case, it may lead to a patient's relating how he has felt shaky, nervous, unable to sleep, and unable to concentrate. It is obviously likely to be more important to pursue the details of the life history of the latter patient than of the former. Unless he should spontaneously report them, the nervous patient would be properly guided to discuss such matters as the situation in which his symptoms were most likely to occur, the nature of some of his relationships at home or at work, the way in which he was raised as a youngster, and so on. Another patient, let us say, one with headaches, might spontaneously mention something of the life situations associated with these discomforts.

Some patients are reluctant to discuss personal affairs. The doctor must be willing to look into these matters gradually. Some doctors are hesitant about probing and apologetic when they do so. Actually, investigation of personal affairs is not only legitimate but often essential to the doctor's getting all the information necessary for making a complete diagnosis and developing a proper treatment plan. Any apologies the doctor may make about his interest in personal matters are more likely to add to the difficulties the patient may have than to diminish them.

There are appropriate comments which can be offered unapologetically to help those patients who are reluctant to discuss their personal lives or who seem to feel that the doctor is meddling when he pursues an intimate line of inquiry. The doctor may say, "I think it would help me to understand your symptoms better if I were to know more about you as a person," or, "You are aware that when one is excited his head pounds; when he is frightened, he often has an urge to urinate; when he is embarrassed, his face may become red or feel hot. We know that our emotions can affect us physically in health and in disease. I believe that it would be wise for us to look into your personal life to see what influence it may be having on your symptoms of stomach ulcer." There are many ways of explaining this interest to the patient in an acceptable and positive fashion.

The Physical Examination

Fortunately the physical examination is conducted toward the latter part of the appointment when the relationship has had some time to develop. Being an intimate experience, it can arouse a variety of feelings.

The ordinary sequence of events of the physical examination provides a gradual adjustment to the procedure. A comment announcing the physical examination usually precedes the patient's disrobing, either privately or with the aid of a nurse. Adequate draping is naturally provided. The physician then enters and begins by examining the head and neck and those parts of the body ordinarily exposed in everyday life. Progressively more personal areas are examined; usually the most personal are left until the last, when the patient has adjusted somewhat to the procedure.

The patient's reactions to the physical examination may include embarrassment, fear, anger, even pleasurable stimulation. Here too, the type and the intensity of the response depends considerably upon the personality of the patient. There is commonly a feeling of embarrassment when standing naked before another person, a feeling which does not automatically vanish because the other person happens to be a physician. Such a reaction can, of course, be reduced by providing adequate draping for the undressed patient and by exposing only those areas of the body being examined. However, a matter-of-fact attitude on the part of the physician about bodily exposure is usually more helpful than marked concern about draping or overzealous reassurance, which only intensifies self-consciousness. It is well to maintain the realistic attitude that, after all, the patient is there to be examined by a professional person, whose purpose it is to restore the patient's health.

Shame or embarrassment may be felt particularly by the patient when certain parts of the body are inspected. This is frequently so with the pelvic examination. The practice of having a nurse present at this time serves to minimize embarrassment and also to reduce any unintentional erotic stimulation that may occur if the procedure is carried out when doctor and patient are alone. A word should perhaps be said about frequent well-intended comments, such as "This won't hurt," or "Relax!" or "Just breathe in and out," provided in a somewhat harried voice by the physician or nurse during the examination. If these comments are not offered well, they tend to increase the patient's tension. It is well to consider here the merit of a calm, reasonably quiet, and confident attitude on the part of the physician and nurse in attendance.

Fear may be aroused during the examination, particularly if unfamiliar medical instruments are used. It may also occur when a painful area is examined. If there is a reasonably good chance that pain will be experienced, it is a good idea to tell the patient what is planned and what discomfort he may expect.

Some patients seem overly ready to exhibit their bodies. It is probably best not to engage in any struggle to keep them covered, but instead to complete the examination in the ordinary manner and at the ordinary pace. A few patients seem to derive sensual pleasure from examination. It is worth recognizing that this response is usually something of which the patient is unaware.

The physician might also periodically inspect his own reactions to doing physical examinations. For example, he may find that he has been overly squeamish or possibly overly curious. If so, he might ask himself why this is the case, and how it may be influencing his examinations. Adequate draping, as mentioned earlier, is desirable, but if the physician does not feel sufficiently free to uncover completely the area of the patient's body to be examined, and instead attempts awkwardly to examine through or around clothing, he may find himself at a distinct disadvantage diagnostically. Somewhat similar is the response that can occur in a physician with a patient who is irritable during examination. (This, of course, is not infrequent if the patient is uncomfortable.) In such a case, the physician will certainly keep in mind the patient's feeling and will do all that he can to make him as comfortable as possible, but he will also not be threatened by this circumstance and will not respond by doing a cursory examination out of unnecessary concern over provoking the patient.

Any persistent patterns the physician may have developed in connection with this phase of his work, such as repeatedly forgetting to do vaginal or rectal examinations, bear scrutiny. They may reflect an unrealistic attitude toward certain body parts, and could have the unfortunate effect of denying the patient a reliably thorough examination.

Perhaps it scarcely needs to be pointed out here that the doctor can gain additional impressions of the patient's psychological make-up by observing the latter's reactions to the physical examination. Observing whether or not the patient is experiencing shame, fear, or some other emotion can lead to a clearer interpretation of the physical findings. For example, moderate abdominal muscular tension can be a manifestation of shame as well as a response to intra-abdominal pathology. Quick withdrawal from a painful stimulus can be due to fear as well as hyperesthesia resulting from a neurologic lesion.

The following example illustrates several of the observations just made:

Miss K. G., a tall, thin, 39-year-old, unmarried woman, came to the doctor for a general check-up. She was not feeling as well as she ordinarily did, and she had lost about 8 pounds in the preceding several months.

Miss G. visited her physician somewhat infrequently, even though the physician had the distinct impression that she was often concerned about her health. Unmarried, she seemed to lead a rather lonely life in an apartment with her older sister, like her a somewhat prim schoolteacher.

The doctor completed his history-taking and virtually all of the physical examination during the first visit. Since he was a bit rushed, after reflecting a moment he suggested that the vaginal examination be deferred until the next visit, a week later.

The patient looked momentarily affected, but said nothing. She failed to appear for the next appointment. The doctor, somewhat concerned, elected to pursue the matter by having his nurse telephone Miss G. and arrange another appointment.

This time the patient came to the office. When doctor and patient discussed the reason for the failed appointment, it became apparent that Miss G. was embarrassed and ashamed at the prospect of a vaginal examination, and so she had "forgotten" the appointment.

The vaginal examination revealed that the patient had vaginitis and that she had been scratching the vaginal area vigorously. Fortunately, the physical and laboratory studies were completed, since they revealed that the patient was mildly diabetic.

Laboratory Procedures and Their Implications for Patients

The physician's routine activities involve a variety of procedures that are usually strange to the patient. The commonplace aspect of laboratory procedures to the doctor is frequently responsible for his overlooking how frightening these procedures may be for patients. The problem is compounded by the rapidly multiplying number of procedures available to physicians through recent technologic advances. Even those few chronic patients whose illnesses seem to have subjected them to virtually every type of procedure, now have to adjust to new ones.

Patients often misunderstand what is to be done to them and why it is being done. Yet many patients approach dreaded tests with stoically sealed lips. Others seek information from fellow patients who, though misinformed, are often willing to provide inside information which frightens and confuses rather than reassures. It can be surprising to learn from patients what they thought would happen to them during a procedure or as a result of it. A test as simple and seemingly well known as the electrocardiograph can arouse, in patients who have not had this test before, the fear of electric shock. A lumbar puncture terrifies those who believe that if the doctor blunders slightly while doing the test they will experience severe pain, impairment of sexual potency, or even paralysis. A simple venipuncture or "pin prick" for a blood count can often arouse much more fear than the ashamed patient is willing to admit.

Consider the following examples:

A 40-year-old man was obviously anxious during and after a spinal tap. Several hours after the procedure he complained of back pain. He said that he was worried that he might develop a paralysis of the lower extremities. He had understood from a previous conversation with a friend that this could occur if the patient moved when the needle was inserted. He was certain that he had jumped while the needle was in. Actually no difficulties were experienced by the physician who did the procedure. The patient had jumped when the local anasthetic was introduced into the skin.

A 38-year-old man was brought to the receiving ward because of an acute myocardial infarction. He was apprehensive about leaving his wife and entering the hospital, since he was quite dependent upon her. His most anxious moment occurred, however, during the taking of an electrocardiogram. He became frightened when the electrodes were applied, since he expected an electrical shock. His apprehension was particularly undesirable inasmuch as the patient had so recently experienced a coronary occlusion.

Many procedures are conducted in completely unfamiliar surroundings. While the patient may be relatively free of tension when exposed to a test conducted by his own physician, he may become quite anxious if he is sent to a strange laboratory where the same procedure is conducted by an unknown technician. The stillness of the electroencephalographic laboratory, added to the strangeness of the application of wires to one's head, or the darkness of an x-ray room where the unsuspecting patient may be raised or lowered on a mysteriously moving table, can arouse all kinds of frightening fantasies.

A 14-year-old boy with gastric disturbances was sent to the x-ray department for a gastrointestinal series. It was apparent that a struggle for control of his deeper angry impulses was important in his personality organization. When he returned to the ward he said, "The big machine bothered me. It was spooky. It made me think of movies like Frankenstein. Frankenstein was on a table that stood him up like that. He broke the straps and stomped off and killed people." The darkness was "frightening" and "the red light that went off and on was spooky." He said that he was originally afraid of the dark and always had left the light on when he went to sleep.

Another consideration is the effect of the patient's emotional reactions on the *results* of the tests. A relatively routine blood pressure determination can be influenced appreciably by the manner of the examiner and by the circumstances under which it is made. Fear of the test can influence heart rate as recorded by the electrocardiograph, or the activity of the barium-filled stomach or colon as viewed during fluoroscopy.

Tests can be influenced by the doctor's expectations of his patient's performance as well as by the patient's attitude toward the doctor and the test. A subjective test, for example one with an end-point of pain or weakness, may be influenced by what the doctor wishes his patient to accomplish or experience. For instance, a physician may be interested in the analgesic effects of a new drug, especially in its influence on the pain threshold. Although the medication may actually have very little pharmacological effect, the pain threshold, as measured, may change on the basis of the patient's deep needs to comply with the physician's expectations and thereby win his praise. On the other hand, there are tests that require the consistent motivation of the patient to insure a correct evaluation. For example, measurements of pulmonary function often require the patient's fullest cooperation in forcefully expelling the breath. This cooperation may or may not be forthcoming, depending upon the patient's attitude when the test is conducted.

It is evident that the physician-patient relationship is influenced by many circumstances. Certainly the manner in which the physician handles test procedures is among them. A striking example of this is the responses of those hospitalized patients who entirely judge the competency of the house physician on his ability to do a venipuncture. If it is done expeditiously and (relatively) painlessly, the doctor is a good one. Office patients also have intense feelings about laboratory procedures. They respond most favorably and are the most cooperative when they are familiarized with the tests beforehand.

A 45-year-old man with a peptic ulcer discussed his relationship with his doctor, who was transferred to another service. "I was pretty much attached to Dr. B.—I miss him a great deal." When asked to describe this relationship, he said, "Well, every morning he'd be up and cheerful—for my money he was a good doctor—explained what he done and what tests I got and what was going to happen—like when I went to be gastroscoped I was upset—he talked to me about it and he was right, it wasn't as bad as I thought it would be—I pictured it to be quite a job."

Disclosing the Diagnosis

It has been noted that a patient may seek clues to the nature of his illness rather than question the doctor directly. He may be attuned to the type of question the doctor asks during history-taking. He may watch the doctor's facial expression during the physical examination. He may place some importance on the kinds of laboratory studies that are ordered. He may even try to glance at notes on the doctor's desk. Of course, sometimes the diagnosis is clear and as evident to patient as to doctor. Yet the fishing for clues is not uncommon, for there may be a lengthy interval before the physician is able (or feels it correct) to reveal the diagnosis with certainty to the patient.

Disclosing the diagnosis may arouse anxiety in the patient as well as create a dilemma for the physician. It is pleasant to be able to tell a patient with complete honesty that he is absolutely well. It is not so pleasant if the physician discovers that the patient has a serious or fatal condition. Often the question is raised in medical discussions, "Should the patient be informed when he has little or no chance to live beyond a certain time because of a malignancy?" Some physicians advocate informing all dying patients of their plight. Others advocate informing none.

To give a stock answer to this question is quite unsound. Every situation raises particular questions. How well integrated psychologically is the patient? What is his life situation? How will his death affect the lives of others in the family? What has been the patient's attitude toward illness and death?

The physician has also to inspect his own thinking and behavior in these trying situations. Is he withholding information from the patient (who might want to know his future) because of his own sensitivities and an inclination to avoid the usually difficult task of discussing bad news? If the doctor chooses not to inform the patient, he must reckon with the difficulties consequent upon keeping up a story he has concocted as a substitute for the authentic one. As this becomes more complicated and difficult to do, unfortunate things can happen. The patient may learn or sense that the physician, whom he has trusted and depended upon during this desperate period of his life, can no longer be considered reliable. If the patient's reactions are added to the doctor's discomfort about a loosely made falsification, doctor and patient may drift emotionally farther and farther apart at precisely the time when the patient most needs a secure relationship.

If the doctor has been honest with himself and has concluded that frankness is appropriate for his patient, how does he advise his patient that he has a fatal illness? There is no simple formula. Often the patient *knows* even though he does not know. That is, he has an awareness which he has hidden from himself. Frequently the disclosure may be effected gradually, at a rate at which the patient is able to gain emotional and intellectual mastery over the disturbing information. A series of discussions may be necessary to provide the patient with the opportunity to become aware of his condition. Often the patient will suggest the diagnosis which the physician can then confirm. Sometimes it is best for the doctor to state the truth before the patient does, particularly when such a statement will convey to the patient a willingness on the doctor's part to bear a full share in the difficulties to come.

It is usually easier to disclose the presence of a serious or chronic, but not necessarily fatal, illness. Once again, the doctor-patient relationship, invariably important, has to be safeguarded. It can be disrupted by inconsistencies on the doctor's part. Profuse but unjustified reassurance may seem kind, but is inappropriate in the long run. But hope is important for all human beings.

A more difficult problem arises when the diagnosis is in doubt. Not infrequently the physician exhausts all possible means for arriving at a diagnosis without result. He may wonder whether the chest pain radiating down the left arm signifies coronary artery disease when repeated electrocardiograms are negative, whether there is organic pathology behind abdominal pain the patient describes but for which there are no positive findings. At times the patient may have to be told that no definitive diagnosis can be made. On other occasions the doctor may feel that, even though he is uncertain about the diagnosis, it is best for the patient that a positive stand be taken and a flat statement made to the effect that there is no (organic) disease process. Such situations on occasion require the physician's courage and willingness to put aside concerns about his own reputation and to consider chiefly the patient's own needs.

How far does the doctor go with his patient in this type of exchange?

> Dubious doctor: Mr. X., I have examined you completely—from head to toe—and I am of the impression that there is nothing wrong with your heart.
> Mr. X.: Gee, that's fine, doctor. I feel much relieved.
> Dubious doctor: Yes, you're as sound as a dollar. Of course, I think it might be a good idea to come in at least once a month, for a while, to get repeat electrocardiograms.
> Mr. X.: (in altered tone) You do? Oh . . .

Clearly, this type of hedging, while it safeguards the doctor's reputation, is apt to do the patient more harm than good.

Often a physician is amazed at what the patient indicates a preceding physician has said about the patient's illness. He wonders how the other doctor could have been so ignorant, confused, irresponsible, or even unethical. Before passing judgment, however, the physician might do well to talk frankly with those physicians who are now seeing some of his ex-patients. Patients find it difficult to understand the physiological and psychological implications of a diagnosis. Often distortions creep into their conceptions out of an inner need to see their illnesses in some particular manner. For example, a patient with morbid feelings of guilt (unrecognized) may exaggerate the severity of an illness. An ambulatory psychotic patient with hypochondriacal fears may understand what the doctor has to say about his illness entirely differently from an emotionally healthier patient. Ample discussion of diagnosis with the patient is an important means of diminishing such distortions.

TREATMENT PROCEDURES

Aspects of Office Treatment

With the disclosure of diagnosis, the physician usually discusses the treatment plan with the patient. A physician is naturally as interested in the process of tracking down the clues that lead to accurate clinical diagnosis as he is in prescribing and observing the effects of treatment. The diagnostic process can be looked on as the cream of the doctor's job. But it is the treatment and its results that primarily interest the patient. He is wondering what medicine he will be given, how long he will have to take it, whether he will need surgery or hospitalization, and whether there is an effective treatment for his disorder.

Treatment usually requires the active cooperation of the patient. If he continues as an out-patient, that is, is not hospitalized, he may be entrusted with his own medication, diet, periodic application of salves, or recording of temperature according to a program outlined by the doctor. The type of therapeutic plan offered by the physician will depend upon the sophistication of the patient and the complexity of the program outlined. It will be recalled that, in the discussion which dealt with laboratory procedures, a point was made that physicians may wrongly assume, on the basis of the commonplace role of such matters in their own medical lives, that patients readily understand these procedures. Similarly, it may be wrongly assumed that patients will understand the treatment program without efforts on someone's part to explain it. It is often necessary to devote considerable time explaining to the patient the rationale of treatment and explaining instructions for taking any prescribed medication.

Patients naturally vary in their attitudes toward taking medicine. An anxious or a perfectionistic patient who is told to take his medicine at 8, 12, 4, and 8 o'clock may stand poised with pill and glass of water in hand, virtually waiting for the second hand to sweep around to the exact instant for him to pop the pill into his mouth and reassuringly wash it down with a swallow of water. A very passive person, or one who has some need to deny illness, on the other hand, may wonder at 4 o'clock whether he has been reminded by anyone to take the noon dose. He may have to rely completely on another person to hand the pill to him. It is important to consider the intellectual as well as the emotional competence of the patient. Consider, for example, an elderly person with generalized arteriosclerosis and a moderate degree of cardiac failure. Only careful appraisal will, perhaps, reveal evidence of the patient's mental confusion. The well-intending physician may carefully explain the dosage and frequency with which the patient must take his digitalis, only to have the patient forget the instructions by the time he has reached home. In such cases, the outcome can be serious, if not fatal, unless a second person in the home helps the patient to remember when and how to take the medication. One might ask, in such a case, which was the more important of the doctor's duties, to make the correct cardiac diagnosis or to make certain that the digitalis was taken properly?

Additional problems are posed when the physician recommends surgery. (See Chap. 7.) Certainly most patients accept the physician's recommendation, but others, for a variety of psychological reasons, use all kinds of rationalizations to delay or avoid such a course. Discussion leading to a clear understanding of the reasons for following through with such a recommendation improves the chances of gaining patient cooperation.

What if the patient refuses to accept the treatment plan? Additional discussion often provides the physician with the motive behind what may seem on the surface to be stubborn, foolhardy, or defiant behavior of the patient. It may relate to shame over illness (equated with weakness), to marginal suspicious fears of being harmed by medication, to near-suicidal self-destruction as atonement for some feeling of guilt, and so on. Once the reason is discovered, the physician has at least the opportunity to deal with it and then to gain the satisfaction of successfully helping another patient along the road to good health.

Whenever medication is dispensed (or, for that matter, whenever a specific treatment measure is being used), it is a good idea to try to evaluate both the psychological and the pharmacological effects of the drug being used. The placebo effect is by now familiar to all physicians —although not always kept in mind. What are the effects of the size, shape, taste, price, and other features of the medication? The beneficial placebo effects of any pharmacological agent should not, of course, be underestimated, but they should be recognized.

A brief comment may be made here about the use of consultants. Some patients feel that their family physicians handle too few of their problems and that they act in the manner of a clearinghouse, routing them from one consultant to another depending upon the prevailing physical complaint. Others are concerned but fearful of hurting the doctor's feelings should they ask for another medical opinion. Moreover, physicians vary in their attitudes towards consultation. Unfortunately, to some it represents defeat or humiliation. This is another of those situations where the physician advisedly should try to understand not only the feelings of the patient and the patient's family, but also his own in the matter. The consultant system offers the advantages of the opinion of a person who may have more knowledge *in a specialized area* than most physicians have, someone who can provide a fresh viewpoint of a case, and a person who can share the responsibility in difficult decisions. Consultation can provide the patient and his family with a feeling (when it is appropriate) of confidence that their doctor has left no stone unturned in his attempts to restore the patient's health. At times, this also provides the members of the family with the feeling that they have been completely faithful in their efforts to assist their loved one.

Sometimes the patient goes from one doctor to another or from one clinic to another in a vain attempt to find the nonexisting "cure." This, at times, is understandable but can lead to frantic and unconstructive behavior. It can result in physical and emotional exhaustion of the patient as well as useless financial depletion. There is, additionally, the possibility that the patient may unsuspectingly fall into the hands of quacks or "healers." This kind of situation calls for an open discussion of the problem with the patient and frequently, more importantly, with the well meaning family or friends.

Psychological Aspects of Hospitalization

Usually the physician has reasonably clear guide-lines for determining whether or not the patient should be hospitalized. There are, however, some borderline situations, when the doctor asks himself whether hospitalization in the long run may not prove more harmful than helpful to the patient. He may consider the psychological effects of this maneuver, particularly in patients with recurrent or chronic illness. A variety of conditions may make the decision concerning hospitalization a difficult one. Not all can be considered here, but a few examples may serve.

Consider first this situation:

A 28-year-old patient experienced recurring abdominal discomfort for a period of approximately 5 years. The patient related that his symptoms occurred periodically, though not with great frequency, and that they caused mild to moderate discomfort. During the history taking, the doctor found that the patient had always made a somewhat marginal life adjustment. He had lived with his parents, but, perhaps for the first time, in the past year or so he had shown some signs of learning to adjust more effectively to society. He had joined social groups and had finally held a job for longer than a few months.

Certainly the decision regarding hospitalization versus office visits, to pursue further the investigation of this patient's abdominal pains, would take into consideration the possible harmful effects of removing him from his everyday life at a time when he was making his first attempts to adjust socially. Hospitalization would not only remove him from the normal stream of social activity, but would also foster the more dependent role he had been trying desperately to escape for the first time.

On the other hand, consider the problems involved in deciding whether or not to hospitalize a person who had adjusted to society reasonably well but who revealed periodic intense needs for care and attention. Perhaps it is a patient with a peptic ulcer the physician has followed for a long time. The physician has learned during this time that the patient experiences severe exacerbations of his ulcer syndrome under certain types of life stress. In this case, the physician may decide to hospitalize this patient prophylactically (even though he has minimal symptoms), should there be evidence that life stresses have sharply increased and threatened to impose too much of an emotional strain on him.

How will a patient react to the recommendation of hospitalization?

This too will depend upon the patient. It will be a welcomed relief to the patient in severe physical distress. It will often be reassuring to the patient who is frightened because of the seriousness of his illness. Patients who have strong wishes to be removed from life's responsibilities and prefer a sheltered life may also find hospitalization inviting. Whether or not the person has had previous hospitalization will affect his response. Most patients, however, will experience some anxiety over leaving homes and familiar surroundings to enter the somewhat strange and awesome medical environment. Patients often have frightening misconceptions of hospitals. In this connection, it is particularly striking to see the surprise of many patients when they are admitted to a psychiatric unit and find pleasant surroundings rather than the madhouse they had anticipated.

Once admitted to the hospital, the patient ordinarily has to make a number of adjustments. While in some ways his life is more relaxed there, in others it is more regimented. He usually has to remain in bed or confined to an area much smaller than that to which he is ordinarily accustomed. Meals may be different in type and served on a schedule different from that of his usual life. His role changes from the active provider to the passive, often helpless, recipient. He is removed from the interesting stimuli and challenges of life, and his interest turns instead to his bodily processes.

The patient comes in contact with many unfamiliar people. These include house physicians, nurses, attendants, orderlies, dieticians, and others. He has to depend upon them for care while his own familiar physician is away. At times, he will feel thrust upon these people before he has had a chance to develop confidence in them. This adjustment is made easily by normally gregarious persons who are able to cope with new people well, but not by the more withdrawn, inhibited person who has avoided close interpersonal contact during his lifetime.

A number of comments could be made here. Every effort should be made to ease the patient into the hospital situation with a minimum of stress and a maximum feeling of safety and security. Hopefully the admitting clerk is pleasant and understanding. Optimally the nurse meets the patient, guides him through the initial anxiety-provoking moments, shows him to his room or bed, and briefly introduces him to the key personnel who will be taking care of him.

At best, however, it is impossible to eliminate all of the potentially stressful situations that may arise for the patient during his hospital stay. Often the hospital environment is mistakenly looked upon as a place of complete refuge and security where all needs are immediately provided. This is not the case entirely. The variety of events of the ordinary day in the hospital can have its impact upon the patient. For example, the death of a patient on an open ward or in a nearby room can be disturbing. The admission of other patients, interestingly enough, can stir anxieties in hospitalized patients. Friction between patients or between patients and staff, as well as interpersonal problems between members of the staff, may have their effect upon the patient.

What are these effects? The patient may become emotionally upset. Exacerbations of his physical disease process may become evident. Often otherwise unexplained setbacks in the patient's progress can be traced to some disturbance in the hospital environment. The stimulus or triggering event can be obvious or subtle. Here are two examples:

An 18-year-old boy with very labile diabetes was progressing satisfactorily on the ward, maintained on his usual dosage of insulin. Then an elderly patient with whom he had had only moderate contact died of an extensively metastasizing carcinoma. Over the next several nights the young diabetic slept poorly. He frequently shouted out in his sleep, "Mr. S. (the deceased patient)! Hold him! Don't let him go!" His diabetes went completely out of control for the following ten days.

A 39-year-old Negro woman with tuberculosis was placed in a single room in an effort to accomplish necessary isolation precautions during treatment. Though the patient had been a mild alcoholic for many years, since the death of her mother two years before admission she had markedly increased her alcoholic intake. On admission, she was jaundiced, febrile, cachectic, and obviously seriously ill. A liver biopsy revealed cirrhosis and hepatic tuberculomas, and treatment with antibiotics was instituted. Over the following several months clinical signs slowly remitted, and it was believed that her general response was good. However, she kept losing weight so that death from inanition seemed likely. Occasional spikes in fever occurred. During an interview one day with the patient it became apparent that she was quite depressed. Prolonged bedfastness in a single room, removal from human contacts and personnel's decrease in interest in this chronic case seemingly contributed to the patient's depression and despair of recovery.

Fortunately, isolation was no longer necessary, and the patient was transferred to a five-bed ward. In the larger room a relationship was encouraged between this patient, who had a need to receive support and attention, and another patient, who needed to indulge others. The ward personnel were stimulated to revive interest in the patient, and within a short time the depression lifted. Her appetite improved, her weight increased for the first time since admission, and fever spikes disappeared. The patient gradually became ambulatory and slowly but definitely recovered.

Unpredictable events in the hospital are not always damaging to the patient; sometimes they favor the patient's recovery. A patient may have a particularly compatible roommate. A nurse may be identified unconsciously with a needed mother. A particularly congenial group of patients may encourage a patient to enter into unfamiliar social relationships.

Predictable events can be damaging. Antagonism between the patient's physician and staff can be reflected in patient care; impairment of communication can lead to errors or to failure in properly carrying out the doctor's orders. Furthermore, the patient will feel the tension and become insecure in reaction to the disharmony in staff relations.

If disharmony in the staff is predictably disturbing to the patient, a patient's behavior may predictably disturb the staff. When a person is ill, anxious, uncomfortable with pain, or bored, he is likely to behave in other than his usual manner. At times he can irritate those taking care of him. Another patient, distinctly not annoying, should alert the staff to possible trouble. Though he may take his medicine and undergo diagnostic tests compliantly because he is a pleasant, intelligent person, it is worth considering that his superficially admirable behavior may reflect an emotional disturbance such as an apathetic depressive response to illness, a schizoid withdrawal as the result of stress or an emotional retreat to a form of childish obedience. Like the submissive patient mentioned early in the chapter who was unable to assert himself when he called for an office appointment, this patient risks neglect in favor of a more obviously difficult one.

The difficulties of the obviously difficult patient may not really be obvious either. One may automatically dislike him, but a doctor exists not to like or dislike but to understand and to treat. Actually any number of problems may be concealed beneath the difficult patient's exterior. He may be frightened and therefore use aggressive behavior to hide his fears from himself and others. He may be simply uncomfortable. Whatever the patient may appear to be, the doctor is not behaving professionally if he reacts to him (or allows his staff to react) with harshness and anger. Here are two examples of uncomprehending treatment:

Nurses complained about the grumbling and altogether mean attitude of an elderly Negro man on a medical ward of a general hospital. The resident physician was annoyed by the patient's uncooperativeness whenever he attempted to examine or treat him. The personnel finally found themselves avoiding him. The patient had a malignant intra-abdominal growth, but the staff felt that he had no knowledge of this. After a staff member spent some time quietly talking to the patient, it became clear that the patient's actions resulted from the fact that he indeed strongly suspected that he had cancer and that he was very concerned about his own life and especially about his family which would be impoverished if he died. Such worries accounted for his uncooperative behavior.

A 43-year-old man was admitted to a medical ward because of a mild heart attack. This was the first time in his life that he had been hospitalized. After being put on bed rest he experienced no further pain and seemed to be progressing satisfactorily, but he was constantly making requests of the nurses when they passed his bed—especially during the night—to bring him fresh water, or a urinal, or anything he could think of. When the item was brought, he engaged the nurse in lengthy conversation and seemed very reluctant to let her leave. In desperation, the nurses moved him to the far end of the ward to keep him from monopolizing their time. Soon after, he became quite obviously anxious, agitated and depressed, and he complained of chest pains. An interview quickly revealed that he was afraid he might have another heart attack and die. His motive in seeking the constant presence of the nurse was to have a protective person nearby. Recognizing his fear, the staff moved him to a bed close to the nurse's desk, and his recovery progressed uneventfully.

Problems of Discharging the Patient from the Hospital

While most patients become somewhat childlike during the more serious phases of illness, they begin to grow up again as they enter convalescence. The period of recovery has been compared to adolescence, since the hospital patient moves out of a dependent position similar to that of childhood, where all needs are met and protection and security offered, and gradually adapts himself to living independently in the active world. This growth is to be fostered. A recuperating patient should be expected gradually to take over his own care, encouraged to broaden his range of interests and physical activity. Ultimately he should be able to resume all previous responsibilities of life.

Pressures from the patient to be discharged from the hospital at an inappropriately *early* time may arise from several sources. Some patients feel ashamed of illness and hospitalization. Those who have spent a great deal of their lives in vocations and hobbies that prove to others and themselves that they are real men are particularly likely to deny illness and press for early discharge. Some patients count heavily upon relationships with spouses or parents and find it exceptionally painful to be separated from them. Others are concerned about being away from home because they fear marital infidelity or neglect of their children.

There is more likely to be pressure to defer discharge, particularly if the patient has been in the hospital very long or has been seriously ill. Even those who put pressure on the doctor to discharge them may be anxious when the appropriate time comes to leave. Pressure may vary from a mild question about whether a patient has regained sufficient strength to an indignant protest against being kicked out. Frequently patients will experience exacerbations of the physical symptoms of illness from which they seem to have recovered, or new complications will appear. These physical or emotional reactions can be as severe as the symptoms which necessitated hospitalization. An asthmatic patient may have another attack. A hypertensive patient may experience a marked blood pressure elevation. A patient with neurotic symptoms may have an exacerbation of his neurosis.

Whether they are aware of them or not, a number of considerations lead patients to want to remain in the hospital. One of the most common is that the hospital offers security and protection, particularly when the patient is, or even has been, very ill. To give up the hospital can be emotionally tantamount to giving up one's parents if confinement in the hospital has been lengthy. Other considerations, too, may be important. There may be stresses in the home or at work which the patient wishes to avoid. He may fear that the heart attack, stroke or other frightening illness could recur at home, where there would be no physicians or nurses in the event of an emergency.

A 56-year-old spinster had had a mild agitation and depression several months prior to being admitted to the hospital. These symptoms intensified when it was later discovered that she had chronic lymphocytic leukemia. The patient had been living alone, supporting herself well for the previous 14 years as a typist. She had had one previous bout of depression when she was 16 years old, following her mother's death. She always had said, "When Mother dies, I want to die." The patient's mother was 56 years old when she died, which was the patient's age when she was admitted to the unit.

In the hospital, the patient clung to the nurses, constantly sought reassurance, and often felt others disapproved of her. However, with the protection of the hospital, sedation, and supportive psychotherapy, her depression subsided. After 6 weeks on the unit, it was thought that her recovery was adequate and plans were made for her to return to work. She was afraid to leave the hospital and return to her job, since she did not feel self-confident and feared she would make a number of errors at work and be dismissed. These prospects of failing seemed quite frightening to her, and the therapist postponed discharge. It was then decided that she should remain in the hospital while going out to work for initially brief, then increasingly longer periods of the day. Her employer agreed to this plan without hesitation. The first day at work, the patient had an attack of nausea and returned immediately to the hospital. With gentle urging, she went back to work the next day and met with some success. With increasing success each day, she gradually reorganized and ultimately resumed her previous mode of adjustment to life.

It is psychologically beneficial for the patient to have an opportunity to discuss some of his feelings about leaving the hospital. The physician can often dispel unnecessary concerns or arrange the transition from hospital to home in a manner least painful to his patient.

The professional staff is also to be considered in connection with the discharge of the patient. For example, unnecessary delay in discharging the patient may reflect the staff's guilt over neglect or dislike of the patient. It may reflect, too, the physician's response to the patient's childish, plaintive or seductive attitudes.

An unnecessary sense of urgency to discharge the patient before he is prepared for it may reflect reactive anger at an "uninteresting" patient or at one who subtly provokes and taxes the patience of the physician. It is well to recognize that a sign-out without recommendation of the staff, a decision seemingly made by the patient, has sometimes been fostered for a variety of reasons by the physician in charge, who may not be aware of his own motivations.

Patients Receiving "Correct" Treatment but Not Getting Well

There are times when diagnosis of the physical disorder seems correct, the mode of treatment appropriate, and yet the patient remains ill. In other instances, the patient gets well only to fall victim soon after to another and then another disease. Still others are subjected to endless operative procedures. Finally, some patients remain invalids for unusually long periods or even permanently. Such patients pose an exasperating problem for the physician. They comprise a large percentage of the inmates of chronic disease hospitals.

Some patients seem to have a need to be ill. Since illness serves an important psychological function for them, they are willing to pay what would appear to well people to be an enormous price. Their willingness may stem from a wish to escape a sexual role which seems frightening or dangerous, a need to remain in a dependent role free of responsibilities and mature social demands, a need to use illness in a self-punitive way, to experience constant pain or suffering because of deep feelings of guilt. Others fail to respond physically to treatment because of severe psychological depression. Some use illness not only in a hostile way toward themselves, but to control others or make miserable the lives of those close to them with whom they are angry.

Sometimes when the patient is unresponsive to treatment, the difficulty lies with the doctor-patient relationship. The patient has angry feelings which he does not feel free to express openly, and the doctor is distant. In other instances, the doctor has paid insufficient attention to prevailing psychological stresses in the patient's life which are affecting his physiologic state.

When, for whatever reason, the patient persistently fails to respond, a reinspection of the patient's psychological state and the doctor's own frame of mind is called for. Perhaps a fresh opinion from a consultant can be very helpful here.

SUMMARY

The purpose of this chapter has been to present a panoramic view of the emotional experiences of the patient and, to some extent, of the physician during the course of illness. Extensive comment on illness situations and thorough discussion of the psychology of the individual are left to subsequent chapters.

Summary

It should have been made evident that a medical disorder cannot be considered in isolation. Medical disorders occur in people, who are in a society composed of people. The sick person must be viewed in a broad and dynamic way with recognition that the course of his illness will be influenced by a host of stimuli arising both from within himself and from his social and physical environment.

Considerable attention has been given to the meaningfulness of the doctor-patient relationship, a relationship with few parallels in adult life. It has meaning in terms of its influence both upon the emotional suffering the sick person may be spared and upon the actual course of the illness, whether physical or psychological in nature.

The medical student's educational endeavors can be hectic and complex in this age of rapidly expanding scientific knowledge. There is so much to be learned about the pathophysiologic mechanisms and pharmacologic treatment of illness which often seem the essentials of medicine that psychological concepts may be relegated, almost out of desperation, to secondary importance. Sometimes, unfortunately, they are considered of no importance. However, the practicing physician, relaxed and confident in his ability, is usually very much aware of the significance of psychological influences on his patients, on himself and on the doctor-patient relationship. A reasonable goal for the student might be to develop an ability to recognize psychological problems and to achieve a basic understanding of the principles by which they may be diagnosed and treated.

CHAPTER 2

Fundamentals of Psychology for the Physician (Part 1)

BASIC PSYCHOLOGICAL CONCEPTS

Mind

Unless one makes a point of reviewing, in some such fashion as that of Chapter 1, the many aspects of medical practice in which psychological factors play a critical part, one is inclined to take the workings of the mind rather for granted much of the time. Indeed, the field of medical knowledge has become so large and so complex that one naturally wishes to take certain things for granted, and one may even find it a bit disconcerting when the evidence indicates that this is unwise.

Clinical pathology, for example, requires such an extensive understanding of biochemistry and microbiology, that one willingly assumes that mental factors are irrelevant to the test results. Yet, as we have seen, this may not be the case (p. 14). Therapeutics requires such an extensive knowledge of physiology and pharmacology that failure to obtain an expected effect leads one naturally to seek a purely physicochemical explanation. Yet there are other possibilities (p. 26).

Because the student of medicine tends to take *mind* for granted—unless the patient or the setting in question is unmistakably psychiatric—his concept of it may be blurred or fragmentary. Mind may be equated with its purely intellectual functions or with its purely conscious functions. It may, at times, be equated with brain, or, on the other hand, it may be thought of as something quite separate from the body, as an entity which may come into reaction with the body—perhaps only under special circumstances.

Ideas of this sort, however common, can be very misleading and cannot contribute significantly to an understanding of situations such as many of those described in Chapter 1. What is needed at this point is a confrontation of this elusive concept, *mind*, and an attempt to render it less vague. An inquiry into the nature of mind can, of course, raise profound questions, ultimately of a philosophical kind. It is beyond the scope of this book to go deeply into such questions; what is sought here is an operationally useful definition. Perhaps the most direct route to such a definition is through consideration of two familiar and closely related ideas: *homeostasis* and *adjustment*.

Homeostasis and Adjustment. Definitions of Mind

As the student will have learned in physiology, *homeostasis is the general tendency to uniformity and stability in the normal (physicochemical) body states of an organism.* The term was given its modern medical significance by the great physiologist, Walter B. Cannon. In the human being, such processes as the maintenance of a relatively constant pH of the circulating blood and a relatively constant supply of oxygen to the brain are matters of homeostasis. If life is to be sustained, this tendency must somehow win out over the ceaseless changes in which the living organism is involved.

As one considers the situation further, it becomes apparent that these changes are of two sorts: those taking place within the organism (the constant alterations which comprise metabolism) and those taking place externally to the organism (the constantly changing environmental conditions). Both sets of changes increase in number and complexity as one ascends the evolutionary scale, reaching their maximum in man. For example, the environmental changes of relevance to a human being range from such simple physical alterations as those of temperature, gaseous composition of the atmosphere, and degree of illumination, through changes in significant material objects, including man's countless artifacts, to the most subtle and complex changes of all, those in human relationships. The inner changes cover an equally wide range. There are physical changes, such as the increase in stature with normal growth, a near infinity of chemical changes, changes in the instinctual drives, changes in mood, in the emotions, and in thought.

To preserve life, to avoid pain, to seek comfort, it is necessary that the human being maintain not just a series of equilibria, but *an equilibrium*, a balance between the totality of inner and outer changes. In psychology, *the series of techniques or processes by which the individual strives to meet these changes, strives to maintain a satisfactory equilibrium between himself and his world, is termed adjustment.* Thus the concept of adjustment may be thought of as a direct extension of the concept of homeostasis, an extension which involves a shift in emphasis from parts to the whole. *Parts* of the organism (cells, tissues, organs, organ-systems, interlocking organ-systems) utilize homeostatic mechanisms; *the whole organism adjusts.*

As a tentative answer to the question, what is mind? one may say that *mind is the means by which the human organism adjusts.*

The difference between organ-responses and organism-responses upon which such a definition rests is implicit in our ordinary speech. Thus one says: "The *pulse rate* is 80 per minute." "The *liver* is secreting glycogen." "The *wound* heals." Yet one says: "The *patient* is late for his appointment." "*He* looks distressed." "*He* presents an unusual complaint." All of the first three statements concern matters of homeostasis; all of the last three statements concern matters of adjustment; they concern *mental* activities. Exceptions to this usage can be found, but, in general, whenever it feels correct to use a personal subject, the resulting sentence will refer to a mental activity.

It is not that the one set of statements is somehow "more physical" than the other; all of the latter statements clearly involve physical activities. It is that the latter activities are performed by the organism *as such,* i.e., as a unit. Thus one can frame another (working) definition of mind: *mind is the body in action as a unit.**

In our theoretical framework, where does this leave the *brain*? It is certainly true that the brain is the central integrative organ of the mind; without it, mental activity is impossible; if it is injured, mental activity is usually impaired. Yet it would be a serious mistake simple to *equate* brain with mind, and it would be something of a mistake even to equate brain function with mind.

It is easy to see this in the case of most activities involving gross motor components. If an individual is hurrying to keep an appointment, is playing golf, or even playing bridge, one can readily see that *all of him* is hurrying or playing. That is to say, the total, unified activity is composed of numerous coordinated activities which add up to the fact that the organism, the person, is doing something. It is not just his brain which is functioning, but his muscles, his circulation, his respiratory apparatus, and so on. Even in such a quiet activity as that described when one says, "He looks distressed," one can make out a number of coordinated aspects which add up to the total phenomenon. The facial muscles assume a certain typical configuration; the postural muscles are affected; there may be altered respiration, agitated movements of the hands, the secretion of tears.

Study of the central nervous system, and particularly of the brain, can certainly form one quite legitimate *approach* to an understanding of mental phenomena. One can begin with the sound biological principle that all activity of the human organism (whether considered as a whole or in any of its parts) involves physical changes. These changes

---

* Jules Masserman used "body in action" as a definition of mind in his book, **Principles of Dynamic Psychiatry,** Philadelphia, Saunders, 1946.

may, in the aggregate, be quite gross, as, for example, the movements of the lower extremities in running. They may be submicroscopic, as, for example, the electrophysical alterations which accompany the activity of a few neurons in the brain. But they do occur. All activity of the human organism, therefore, may be studied—at least in theory—from a physiological point of view.

Mental functions are no exception to this statement. They may be studied as highly integrated functions of the body, under the direction, so to speak, of the central nervous system, and particularly of the brain. In a significant sense they are manifestations of a general property of living tissue and especially of central nervous system tissue, the property of irritability. A simple physiological pattern, upon the basis of which one can approach the study of mental phenomena is the reflex arc. Stimuli, either impinging upon the body from without or generated within the body by metabolic processes, bring about a state of heightened tension. There follows a tendency to discharge resulting in effector activity (motor or secretory). In any pattern more elaborate than a simple reflex, factors opposing immediate discharge play a part.

The study of the inhibiting forces, their origin and their effect on the discharge tendency, is the immediate subject of psychology. Without these counterforces there would be no psyche, only reflexes.*

As the pattern becomes elaborate, as the organism begins to function *as such*, as a unit, or, in other words, *as the activity becomes part of an effort at adjustment*, one can speak of it as mental activity. Such activity can be studied through either of two approaches: the physiological and the psychological. While still being able to make certain objective physical and chemical measurements, one can also communicate directly with the subject to ascertain what is going on. The more complicated the activity becomes, the greater is the value of the psychological methods of study. As extreme examples, one might consider such activities as the playing of a difficult hand at bridge or the writing of a musical composition. However great the advances of neurophysiology may become, it is highly unlikely that one will ever be able to learn as much about activities such as these through physical and chemical methods of study as through talking with the subject about them.

Personality

Closely related to the concept of mind, yet more limited and specific, is that of *personality*. Personality refers to *the whole group of adjustment techniques and equipment which are characteristic for a given individual in meeting the various situations of life*. The description of

---

* Otto Fenchel: The Psychoanalytic Theory of Neurosis, New York, Norton, 1945.

an individual's personality is the answer to the question, what is he like?

Personality attributes—techniques and equipment with which adjustment is effected—are relatively stable. If one knows a person well, one can frequently predict, in a general way but with considerable accuracy, how he will react in a given situation. On the other hand, personality has a developmental history. Over an extended period of time, modifications do occur. The personality of an adult is apt to be recognizably similar to that of the same person as a child, but the two are clearly not identical.

It is therefore necessary to consider personality from two standpoints. The first is often called the "cross-sectional" point of view; it is the one in which one attempts to assess the equipment and the techniques of adjustment that are currently characteristic of an individual. The other may be called the "longitudinal" point of view, in which one attempts to ascertain how a given personality came to be what it is. The present chapter and Chapter 3 deal primarily with aspects of the personality seen in cross-section. Chapter 4 will be largely devoted to a presentation of personality development. In the study of an individual patient, one uses both points of view.

MENTAL HEALTH

A thoughtful reading of Chapter 1 will doubtlessly have raised other rather fundamental questions. One of these may well have to do with the concepts of mental health and mental illness. In the introductory chapter attention was repeatedly drawn to the variety of ways in which persons may respond to seemingly simple and standardized situations. Some of these ways were surprising, some "eccentric," and some downright unhealthy. But where does one draw the line between mental health and illness? Is it meaningful to attempt to draw such a line?

These questions are, of course, parts of the larger question as to the nature of health in general. Before discussing attempts to define mental health, it may be of value to review some aspects of the larger question.

General Criteria Applied to Health in General

It would all be relatively simple if the physician could simply define health as "the absence of disease." Yet it would not be easy, even then, since disease can certainly be obscure. But still, if one could rely upon such a definition, he could feel that he was quite far on his way to being able to designate a given individual as "well," if he had eliminated from consideration the numerous well-established disease entities. "John Jones is well because he does not have pneumonia, peptic ulcer, arteriosclerosis, etc., etc."

Unfortunately, as nearly every practicing physician would agree, the matter is not so simple. There is clearly more to a state of buoyant good health than the absence of conventionally diagnosable disease. One may make an analogy with the functioning of an electronic device, say, a radio or television set. Every tube and condenser may be in good condition, the wiring may be intact, and yet a set may not be functioning perfectly. Free from gross defect, it may nevertheless need a series of delicate adjustments for best performance.

OBJECTIVE (STATISTICAL) CRITERIA. Faced with this problem, the physician has often turned to a statistical approach. In effect he says, "Never mind about an ideal definition. Let us determine what is the average condition and call that normal." And, indeed, such a procedure has often proved of considerable value. For example, consider the matter of weight. Given the statistical fact that the average weight of a North American adult male of average height is 160 pounds,* one can say with assurance that for such a subject to weigh 100 pounds or 220 pounds is abnormal, unhealthy. With the matter of height, it is true, one is on slightly less solid ground, since the average height has undergone remarkable changes in recent years, yet average figures are still of some value. In a great many other determinations—about four pages of them in tabular form in most textbooks of clinical pathology—a statistical approach has largely been used in establishing the normal.

Yet seldom does one find a clear dividing line. For a man of average height, a weight of 100 pounds or of 220 pounds is abnormal, but what of a weight of 130 pounds or of 190 pounds? A red cell count of approximately 5 million per cu. mm. is normal; one of 3 or 7 million is abnormal; but what of one of 4.2 or 5.8 million?

In using a statistical approach there is the further problem of being led astray if one does not take environmental factors thoroughly into account. Thus, in certain large areas of Asia, Africa, and Latin America one might do extended statistical surveys of red cell counts and arrive at an average of, let us say, 4 million. Clearly it would be rash to call this figure normal or healthy merely because it was average. The truth is, of course, that one would be dealing with populations of which large segments were chronically ill with one or another endemic disease (avitaminosis, protein deficiency, malaria, hookworm). On the other hand, if the population base for the statistics were to be the natives of the Andes Mountains, one might find an average red cell count of above 6 million. In this case one would be rash to assume some widespread disease, since the figure merely represents a healthy compensatory mechanism brought into play by the rarefied atmosphere.

---

* An approximation.

A well-known example from our own country illustrating the potential fallacy of relying overmuch on statistics in the determination of the normal resulted from surveys of oral hygiene made in the armed services. It was the rule, rather than the exception, for untreated dental caries to be present; yet no physician or dentist would, on this basis, consider the condition to be a healthy one.

SUBJECTIVE CRITERIA. It scarcely needs to be added that if there are pitfalls in an undue reliance on the objective data of statistics, there are also pitfalls in relying heavily on essentially subjective data. A sense of well-being is surely a fundamental attribute of good health, but it is by no means a guarantee of it. To cite a single example, one need only refer to the experience of cancer detection clinics to establish the fact that many a person who feels completely well is, in fact, dangerously ill.

Still another aspect of making the diagnosis of good health or normality has to do with the matter of degree of maturity. One need look no further than the previously mentioned laboratory determinations to see that, in a great many instances, what are perfectly normal findings at one stage of development are indicative of pathology at another.

From this brief discussion of the problem of ascertaining and defining the essence of health in general, it appears that several reservations or qualifications are indicated. It appears useless to look for one touchstone or criterion by which to establish such a diagnosis. It appears that neither objective nor subjective data alone can be completely relied upon to determine the condition of health. Furthermore, it seems clear that even the combination of some objective and some subjective data is inadequate unless the subject's environment and degree of maturity are given full consideration. In fact, one is strongly led in the direction of regarding health or normality as a relative, rather than an absolute, concept.

Nevertheless, there is no need to conclude that, because of these difficulties, the concept of good health is to be abandoned. There are some shadows, but the idea of a state of good health retains substance. It is clear, for example, that a state of good health is to be regarded as incompatible with the existence of definable disease. It is clear that good health conforms to certain statistical norms; in fact, to most statistical norms that do not involve a violation of the first principle (no diagnosable disease). It is clear that good health involves both objective and subjective features. It is clear that good health involves adaptation to the subject's environment and maturational features appropriate to the subject's age.

Psychological Criteria Applying to Mental Health

If one turns now to the narrower question of defining mental health, one finds that both the useful criteria and the difficulties mentioned in the discussion of general health apply. Certain forms of psychiatric illness are well understood and clearly described, and it is perfectly sound to say that such conditions are incompatible with a state of health. Indeed, certain psychiatric *symptoms* are quite clear-cut and therefore indicative of mental illness, even if the precise nature of the illness eludes immediate definition.

Similarly, the statistical approach to concepts of health and illness is of established value in psychiatry. Perhaps the clearest example of this fact is offered by the determination of intelligence. As the student will recall, to say that a subject "has a normal I.Q." means simply that he has been shown to be able to perform a number of carefully selected intellectual tasks with an efficiency which is not significantly less than average for members of his age group. However, just as in the tests of clinical pathology, this approach has its limitations. For one thing, there is again the absence of a clear dividing line. An I.Q. of 100 is normal; one of 60 is obviously abnormal; but what of an I.Q. of 80? For another, statistical deviations from the average have (in this case) significance for the determination of health when in one direction only. An I.Q. of 160 is certainly unusual, but not in the least unhealthy.

The need to take environmental factors into account in forming an appraisal of a subject's mental health is, if anything, even greater than it is in determining his physical health. For example, many beliefs and patterns of behavior which have constituted quite acceptable ways of perceiving, evaluating, and reacting to one's world in other times and places would, if present in a twentieth century American, be indicative of serious mental illness.

The case is similar with the matter of psychological maturity. While psychological maturity may be more difficult to define than physical maturity, it is quite imperative that any estimate of a subject's mental health take this factor into full consideration. Psychological phenomena which are universal and entirely normal features of childhood are frequently indicative of illness if they persist into adult life. To the points mentioned above (absence of definable illness, a degree of conformity to statistical norms and to the general environment) must therefore be added the principal characteristics of psychological maturity. What are these characteristics? The finer theoretical details may be open to debate, but there is considerable agreement as to the larger features. These include: (1) the ability to appraise reality with reasonable accuracy; (2) the ability to love others; (3) the capacity to work productively (and comfortably); (4) possession of an effective conscience; and (5) the ability to find gratifications for basic personality needs. These several points may be briefly elaborated.

1. THE ABILITY TO APPRAISE REALITY WITH REASONABLE ACCURACY. Probably no individual is so mature as to be able to determine the realities of his situation in a fashion quite uninfluenced by his own wishes and fears, yet the popular mind agrees with scientific psychology in giving some such capacity a high place in any list of the criteria of maturity. Nowhere is the value of this attribute more clearly demonstrated than in the practitioner of medicine. If the student will think, for a moment, of any admired and respected physician with whom he has had the opportunity to work, it will be apparent that such a man's decisions are primarily based upon realistic evaluations of the medical problems with which he deals. No matter how strong his wishes for a patient to make a prompt recovery, his continued appraisal of the physical and laboratory findings is not (for the most part) seriously affected by these wishes. No matter how disturbing his fears of some possible complication, he does not, as a rule, close his eyes to evidence suggestive of it.

By contrast, the behavior of children is often not at all realistic, being based upon an appraisal of their situation which is heavily influenced by their emotions. For example, a child who has seen a frightening television show may, for a while thereafter, be quite frightened of being alone or of being in a darkened room, despite the objective harmlessness of such situations. For another example, a child, because of the urgency of his wishes, may perceive the week preceding Christmas or his birthday as being almost endless.

One of the significant corollaries to a well-developed sense of reality (also brought out by contrasting the behavior of mature adults with that of children) is the tendency to be influenced by long-term, rather than short-term, values. If one sees himself and his situation realistically, he will often be able to make a constructive long-range decision even though it entails temporary discomfort. On the other hand, if unrealistic fears and wishes impair one's view of things, such a course may be impossible.

2. THE ABILITY TO LOVE OTHERS. Since "love" is a much abused term, it may not be immediately apparent how very greatly the capacity to love correlates with psychological maturity. In the present discussion, the capacity to love is intended to mean the capacity for sustained affectionate relationships with other persons in which their happiness and well-being are taken into account, while the legitimate self-interest of the one who loves is not ignored. It is thus to be distinguished from

unelaborated sexual desire, from mere ingratiating behavior, and from masochism (p. 416).

To the observer, the principal confusion is likely to be that between a capacity for loving and an intense need for love. The latter is, of course, fully present from the moment of birth, while the former is acquired (under favorable circumstances) during childhood and adolescence. Since both the capacity and the need for love can give rise to all sorts of winning, affectionate, ingratiating behavior, it may not be an easy matter to distinguish between the two. A principal touchstone by which love may be identified is its willingness to do what is best for the loved one even if the action is temporarily provocative of his displeasure.

3. THE CAPACITY TO WORK PRODUCTIVELY. The ability to work productively, as a criterion of mental health, perhaps needs less elaboration than some of the other points. What should be emphasized is that the mature individual derives a functional pleasure from his work (at least in some of its principal aspects). He works not because he is compulsively (p. 329) driven to do so and not (to any great degreee) as a means of nourishing his pride, but from a natural inclination and for the realistic benefits that accrue to himself and others from his activities.

4. POSSESSION OF AN EFFECTIVE CONSCIENCE. The characteristics of an effective adult conscience are often subject to misunderstanding. It should be stressed that the effectiveness is better measured by the *timing* than by the *severity* of conscience activity. As an illustration, one may consider the frequent remorse of the alcoholic on "the morning after." In such instances, conscience activity may cause the individual considerable suffering, but it is not likely to contribute to a healthy adjustment, since it occurs after the fact. The function of a mature conscience is largely a preventive one; it guides the healthy adult in such a way as to keep him out of trouble (not merely in the limited sense of avoiding punishment, but in the broader sense of avoiding behavior which would be destructive to himself or others).

As contrasted with the conscience of a child (p. 73), that of an adult should be more consistent, more independent, and more realistic. A mature conscience is relatively immune to threats or bribes, whether these come from figures in the environment or by some process of self-deception. The reality-orientation of a mature conscience involves its ability to distinguish between the "rules of the game" for an adult and those for a child, as well as between those making for a constructive life in adult society as a whole and those which may have obtained in the original family circle. Thus, as an individual matures, the prohibitions of conscience should relax in certain directions and (quite often) tighten in others. For example, the prohibitions against heterosexual activity, appropriate to childhood, must relax if the individual is to achieve a healthy adult adjustment. On the other hand, if there has been a childish indifference to social problems, this needs to be replaced by conscience pangs in the presence of various forms of injustice.

5. THE ABILITY TO FIND GRATIFICATION FOR BASIC NEEDS. As will be discussed in the succeeding chapter, certain fundamental, biologically derived strivings form the wellspring of human motivation. While it is characteristic of a mature adult—as indicated in (1)—to be able to dispense with immediate gratification of some of these strivings for the sake of long-range achievements, it is also characteristic to be able to obtain ultimate satisfaction of them. The pleasurable meeting of the demands of hunger and thirst, sexuality, certain aggressive urges, etc., has decidedly a place in an adult scheme of life. Yet, in line with (4), it is typical of maturity that such needs are satisfied in ways which entail a minimum of suffering to oneself and others.

THE CONCEPT OF LEVELS OF AWARENESS

A third quite fundamental question raised by a consideration of Chapter 1 derives from those incidents in which it appeared that patient or doctor was acting under the influence of mental forces of which he was completely or not at all aware (pp. 12, 16, and 25).

Resistance to This Concept

It has become commonplace nowadays to speak of unconscious or "subconscious" mental activity.* One sees or hears references to unconscious forces or to "the unconscious" in stories, in cartoons, at the theatre and on television programs. Laymen are quite as apt to use such expressions as are physicians. It would be easy to assume from these circumstances that there is a widespread, genuine understanding and acceptance of the significance of mental phenomena of which the subject is not conscious, but the assumption would be essentially false. The fact is that there exists a considerable natural resistance to the idea, so that acceptance tends to be superficial rather than thorough, sporadic rather than constant, and, quite often, limited to inferences about *other persons* rather than about oneself. (There is the further complication that this inner resistance is itself in some measure unconscious.)

It is not in the least strange that there should exist a strong tendency

---

* A preliminary word about terms may be in order here. The word "subconscious" is not an accepted scientific term and should be avoided. Furthermore, when the word "unconscious" is used in its usual psychological sense, it does not refer to a major alteration in the physiological state of the brain (as in "he was knocked unconscious"), but to the fact that some aspect of the subject's mental life is not within his sphere of awareness.

not to believe fully in the influence of unconscious mental processes, a tendency which may interfere with the task of learning about them. At the outset there can very easily be something disquieting about the idea that one does not know himself nearly as well as he had supposed. It is really quite a different matter from the superficially similar recognition that one has at the outset of his studies in anatomy and physiology. The idea that there is a great deal about the structure and function of the human body which he does not know and must strive to learn may, of course, involve some anxiety, but, in the main, the prospect is stimulating. The idea that there are complex and powerful hidden forces in one's *mind*, however, is apt to have a more threatening impact. One is apt to feel, "if I cannot be sure of myself, what can I be sure of?"

The difference between learning about the intricacies of the body and learning about the hidden forces of the mind is implicit in the distinction referred to on page 30 between the customary way of speaking about organ-responses and that of speaking about organism-responses. One can rather easily consider his pancreas, lungs, or the small muscles of the fingers in a detached, impersonal, unemotional fashion which facilitates learning; one can scarcely think about *himself* (his mind) in this fashion.

Evidence of Levels of Awareness

There are several ways in which one may set about lessening the resistance and acquiring a set of working convictions about the existence and the significance of unconscious mental forces. The first of these is to make a careful survey of the evidence.

SLIPS AND ERRORS OF EVERYDAY LIFE. The body of evidence which lies closest to hand, within the range of everyone's observation, involves a consideration of certain common mistakes or "slips of behavior," as they are often called. Here are a few examples from real life. Doubtless the reader can add others from his own experience.

A young physician, just getting started in practice and somewhat limited financially, receives a letter from the alumnal association of his medical school requesting a contribution. He had enjoyed his studies, is proud of the school, and would like to do something for it. After a brief hesitation, he writes a check. . . . Several days later he discovers the envelope containing the check in his coat pocket.

A college boy, serious about his work but somewhat behind in his studies, considers how he will spend a weekday evening: calling on his girl friend or going to the library to study. He decides that, everything considered, the latter is much the wiser course. He gets in the family car, drives a few blocks absent-mindedly . . . and finds that he has pulled up in front of the girl's house.

Early in the week, a businessman, who customarily spends Saturday afternoons on the golf course, becomes aware of a mild toothache. He is a bit apprehensive about seeing his dentist, but makes an appointment for one o'clock on Saturday. . . . As it turns out, he has almost completed his round of golf before twinges of pain make him realize that he has forgotten the appointment.

A student nurse, at a school whose dean was considered an unpleasant tyrant, inadvertently parked her car in the space reserved for the dean's use. She returned to find attached to the windshield wiper a sharply worded note from the dean, advising her to be more careful in the future. Although she disliked the dean, this feeling seemed to be quite outweighed by the fear that she might have jeopardized her school standing. She decided to call up and apologize. . . . Only after she had hung up the receiver did the girl realize that her roommate had been giggling because she had said, "Dean ———, I'm terribly sorry that I parked in your *plot* this afternoon."

Minor slips and errors of this sort are sufficiently common and innocuous that they are usually passed off with little reflection. Often they seem rather humorous, particularly when they happen to someone other than oneself. Comedians frequently make use of this technique to create amusing situations.

If one considers these four examples of things that were "unintentionally" done (or omitted), one can make out a pattern. The young doctor wishes to be generous, but also wishes to save his money for personal needs. The student realizes that he should study, but also wishes to enjoy his girl friend's company. The business man wants to look after his health, to be freed of the toothache, but he fears the pain of the dentist's drill and wants the recreation of his golf game. The young nurse wants to reestablish herself in the good graces of the dean, but also has some need to express her anger. In each case there are opposing strivings and there is a brief period in which both strivings are in the subject's awareness. Then one tendency appears to gain the upper hand, and the other is dismissed. While the second tendency is completely out of the subject's sphere of awareness, it nevertheless exerts the deciding influence upon his behavior. Then some circumstance occurs which reintroduces the hidden motive into consciousness (feeling the letter in the pocket; the sight of the girl's house; the recurrence of the toothache; the giggling of the roommate). Notice that in each case the idea or impulse which was put and kept out of awareness is quite understandable in itself, quite meaningful. None of these happenings was an accident in the true sense of the word.

Notice also that in each case the idea or impulse which was put or kept out of awareness was one of which the subject's "better judgment" did not really approve (under the circumstances). It was deemed selfish or shortsighted or cowardly or rash, as the case might be. In other words, it is not only that the hidden idea or impulse is in itself meaningful; *it is equally true that the processs of its being hidden is meaningful.*

It is not to be thought that behavioral "errors" of this sort are limited to relatively inconsequential matters; far from it. The following examples illustrate the same mechanism at work in graver situations.

An intern on a medical ward has had considerable difficulty with a certain patient who is ill-tempered, querulous, and constantly complaining of pain and of lack of attention. It is the intern's belief that the patient is not actually in pain but is merely using this complaint as a technic of enforcing his numerous requests. The resident, having examined the patient thoroughly, comes to the conclusion that the pain is caused by an actual physical lesion. He explains the basis for his belief to the intern and instructs the latter to write a p.r.n. order for aspirin and codeine, pending the attempt at definitive treatment. The intern respects the resident's judgment, accepts the recommendation, and believes that he has mastered his irritation with the patient. A day later, when the order book is reviewed, it is noticed that the p.r.n. order has been written for aspirin alone. The patient has experienced needless distress during this period.

A doctor is consulted by an old and admired friend with whom he has been on very close terms. The friend complains of a chronic cough. He is known to be somewhat allergic and to be a heavy smoker. The doctor examines his friend, has him cut down his smoking, and then treats the allergy. The cough persists. The doctor suddenly realizes that he has neglected to have a chest roentgenogram made. When this procedure is done, the presence of lung cancer is revealed. In reviewing the case at this point, the doctor comes to the painful recognition that his uncharacteristic omission of the roentgenologic examination at the first examination was based on dread of what might be found and of the implications for himself. The doctor is himself a heavy smoker.

A careful consideration of the last example reveals that the psychological events here were not precisely the same as in the other examples. In this case there is no reason to believe that the physician's fear of cancer was in his awareness *at any phase* of the episode until the final jarring moment of the x-ray report. That the fear existed there can be no doubt, but it had been banished from awareness before the episode in question; the power of the hidden fear was increased by the circumstance that the patient was a close friend, but it operated from below the threshold of the doctor's awareness until the final moment of realization.

There is a shorter and more scientific expression for the psychological mechanism which has been hitherto referred to as "putting or keeping out of awareness"; it is *repression.*

It is important to realize that this mechanism goes into action automatically; it is independent of ordinary volition. The various instances just cited illustrate this point quite clearly. There can, for example, be little question but that the young physician really intended to contribute to the alumnal fund; he was chagrined to find later that he had almost failed to carry out his intention. Similarly, the college boy's judgment had really indicated to him that it would be in his best interest to spend the evening in studying. And it is the same with the other illustrations. Perhaps the last example is the clearest of all on this score. There was no doubt but that the doctor was characteristically a conscientious person, or that he genuinely wanted to offer his friend the best possible treatment.

A comparison of these illustrations indicates another point. The *degree* of repression going into effect in the several situations is variable. In the example of the student nurse making the telephone call, the repression was so slight that the girl realized merely from her perception that her friend had been amused—and before the latter had said anything to her—not only what she had said to the dean but the reason for the slip. On the other hand, in the last example, the repression was powerful enough to hide the fear motive from consciousness until the strong shock of the x-ray report.

To take such differences into account, two terms are used. Mental material that is not in the subjective's awareness nor immediately accessible to it, but which can be brought into awareness with sustained effort or with some mild reminder is said to be *preconscious*. Material which is not accessible to awareness with any amount of voluntary effort, but which requires a sudden shock or the use of special psychological techniques (p. 44) if it is to enter the field of awareness is termed *unconscious*.

EXPERIMENTS WITH HYPNOSIS. A second body of evidence for the existence of mental processes which are excluded from the subject's awareness comes from experiments with hypnosis.* This evidence is not, of course, a matter of everyday experience, but, carefully considered, it is, perhaps, logically the most convincing of all. Here is the report of an experiment of a sort which has been performed many times.

H.S., a psychology student, having consented to be a hypnotic subject, is placed in a deep trance. He is known not to drink coffee and to smoke only on rare occasions. While he is in the trance, it is suggested to him by the hypnotist that, at the conclusion of his lunch that day, he will have an irresistible urge to try a cup of coffee and then to ask for a cigarette and light it. It is further suggested that, from the moment the trance is ended until he has lit the cigarette, he will have absolutely no knowledge of the source of these impulses, but that, at the moment

---

* A brief discussion of the subject of hypnosis is given on pp. 489 to 492 in the chapter on methods of psychiatric treatment (Chap. 14).

he has begun to smoke, a full recollection of the suggestions will enter his field of awareness. He is asked to repeat the suggestions and does so readily. He is then gradually awakened from the trance state. On his full awakening, he is asked to describe the events of the trance. He attempts to do so, but can remember nothing of them.

An hour later, as he is finishing lunch, H.S. gets himself a cup of coffee, quite to his own surprise. He drinks it, and then asks a friend for a cigarette and lights it. With the first puff, a puzzled expression comes over his face, succeeded by one of amusement. He then describes the hypnotic suggestions in detail.

In this example, a set of ideas is first—that is, during the trance—given to the subject. He demonstrates that he is quite aware of the ideas by repeating them. Then, in response to the final hypnotic suggestion, the ideas become completely inaccessible to his conscious mind, and cannot be summoned up by voluntary effort. While still below the threshold of his awareness, they act powerfully enough to cause him to break with his habitual pattern of behavior. When the subject is released from the suggested amnesia by beginning to smoke, the ideas again enter consciousness.

Another sort of hypnotic experiment affording evidence as to the existence of unconscious mental material has to do with the recovery of (spontaneously) forgotten memories. In such an experiment one may, for example, question a cooperative adult subject in detail about some very specific period in his early life, noting the points on which he is no longer able to give information. Questions on these points are then repeated with the subject in a state of "hypnotic regression," i.e., with the subject in a deep trance in which it has been suggested that he return psychologically to the time in question. As a general rule, quite a bit of additional information is then recalled. As a specific instance, one may have asked an adult subject in the waking state to name the day of the week on which his tenth birthday occurred. Very likely one would have found that the subject was unable to give this information, since such a fact is rarely retained in consciousness. (Yet, at a time just prior to the event, when the birthday was being eagerly looked forward to, such a fact would be considered of great importance and carefully noted.) Quite often, the correct answer* can be obtained from the same subject through the technique or hypnotic regression. The unavoidable inference is that the fact has been unconsciously retained over a considerable span of years.

RESULTS OF PSYCHOANALYSIS OR INTENSIVE PSYCHOTHERAPY. A third body of evidence comes from the treatment of patients with psychoanalysis or intensive psychotherapy.† In such situations, the

---
* Which can be corroborated through the use of a so-called "perpetual calendar."
† These therapeutic procedures are discussed in Chapter 14.

therapist endeavors to provide a relaxed atmosphere and to develop a relationship of mutual trust and confidence, and (particularly in psychoanalysis) he asks that the patient use the method of *free-association*. (In this method, the patient reports verbally his thoughts, emotions, and sensations, making no effort at deliberate organization, censorship, or control.) Under these several conditions the return into consciousness of buried memories is greatly facilitated.

While the material obtained in such situations is highly relevant to the therapy, its value as evidence in the present discussion is entirely independent of the presence of any emotional illness in the subject.

A young doctor, in generally good health both emotionally and physically, has noticed and, on occasion, remarked to his friends, that all of his life he had felt an automatic, "instinctive" dislike of older men with certain physical characteristics: a swarthy complexion and dark body hair. In several individual cases in which he got to know such a person reasonably well, he was able to assure himself that no objective grounds whatever existed to account for his unfavorable and unpleasant emotional reaction. Even here, the feeling did not entirely disappear, and his knowledge of it was a source of embarrassment.

At a somewhat later period, in connection with his psychiatric training, the doctor underwent a personal psychoanalysis. This experience involved the release of many long-forgotten memories, one of which threw light on the unwanted reaction just described. The doctor recalled that, at the age of four years, during a family crisis, he had spent several days in the home of a cousin of his father's, a man with a swarthy complexion and dark hair, who had treated him in a cruel and frightening fashion. The doctor had not seen this man in 20 years, and for most of this time he had completely forgotten the disturbing episode.

Although the young doctor, after regaining awareness of this memory, continued to feel that the older man's treatment of him as a small boy had been wrong, he found that his automatic dislike of persons with similar body characteristics came to an end.

This example brings out with special clarity the important fact that mental material which is unconscious may exert *a greater influence* upon an individual's emotions and behavior than the same material could do if it were conscious. The principal reason for this is not at all mysterious; it is simply that material which is excluded from the sphere of awareness is not accessible to the ordinary processes of evaluation, reason, and judgment.

The various illustrations offered in the course of this discussion of mental material existing below the threshold of awareness give an idea not only of the influence of such material, but also of its richness and variety. Any sort of impression, thought, or emotion, singly or in combination, may continue to be an active part of an individual's mind although not in consciousness.

It should also be apparent that, with respect to any given idea or feeling, the attribute of being-in-consciousness is not a fixed one. Under one set of conditions, the thought or feeling may be in full consciousness; under another set, it may not be in consciousness although accessible with effort (it may be preconscious); under still another set, it may be quite inaccessible to awareness (unconscious).

Applications of the Levels of Awareness Concept

APPLICATIONS TO PATIENTS. However convincing the evidence for the existence and significance of unconscious mental forces may be, one still has to deal with one's emotionally based reluctance to accept and utilize this concept fully. It is here that the gradual lessons of clinical experience can prove of value. If one makes a practice of keeping the levels-of-awareness concept in mind and of applying it to one's consideration of the behavior of patients, that is to say, if one looks in a thoughtful and unhurried fashion for the possible operation of unconscious forces, one finds that much behavior which has seemed puzzling, unpredictable, and therefore often annoying, becomes comprehensible. With comprehension comes the possibility of the doctor's being more effective in his management of the patient.

The following case history illustrates this principle; it involves the not uncommon problem of obtaining permission to operate.

Mrs. J. W. was a patient on a woman's surgical ward of a university hospital. She was a quiet, very neat, and rather dignified woman in her early 40's. She had been admitted for evaluation of obscure but persistent abdominal complaints. Both during the formal history-taking and in casual conversations, Mrs. W. tended to be rather reserved and, in general, to minimize her difficulties. It was fairly clear, however, that she was attempting to conceal a good deal of inner tension beneath her polite, composed exterior.

During the diagnostic period, Mrs. W. was visited twice by her husband and her vivacious teen-age daughter. It was noted by the intern and the nurses that, in the daughter's presence, the patient made a particular effort to maintain an appearance of relaxed good humor.

After several days a diagnosis was reached. The surgical resident and the intern took the patient aside during morning ward rounds and informed her that she had cancer of the rectum. They went on to tell her that the tumor had not spread far and that, with prompt treatment, her chances of recovery were good. The operation that was proposed would involve resection of the involved bowel and adjacent tissue and the construction of a colostomy. The patient listened in silence. She appeared shaken by the information—more so at reference to the operative procedure than at reference to the diagnosis—and finally said that she would have to think over the matter before making a decision.

The following day, during the staff surgeon's visit, the patient was again asked for her consent to the procedure. She flatly refused, offering only superficial rationalizations for her decision.

The surgical resident was disappointed and somewhat irritated by the refusal. He had not expected it, having evaluated the patient as intelligent and reasonable, not at all "flighty" or "hysterical." As a matter of fact, the patient's mood at this point did not appear to be frightened in the usual sense so much as subdued and low-spirited.

While the resident was pondering what, if anything, he could do next, he had an enlightening conversation with one of the nurses. The nurse told him that, the previous afternoon, in a rare moment of candor, the patient had referred to her mother, now dead for a good many years, whom she had taken care of through a lingering final illness. During this period the patient's mother had been confined to bed with a stroke. Mrs. W. had intimated that her mother had been incontinent of urine and feces during much of this time.

The puzzle did not become entirely clear at this point, but the resident had seen and heard enough evidence to be convinced that the patient's refusal was based upon deep-seated and highly personal motives. Further, he grasped the probability that, since the patient seemed in general to be reasonable and "cooperative" and yet had not yielded to logical arguments, the motives behind the refusal were not fully conscious ones. The resident acted upon this understanding by getting the patient's consent to remain in the hospital a few days longer and by arranging for a psychiatric consultation.

The psychiatrist saw Mrs. W. several times. He was able to win the patient's confidence. He confirmed the data noted by the resident and the nurse and was able to elicit some additional relevant information, allowing an evaluation of the emotional forces involved in the patient's refusal of the operative procedure.

During these conversations it was gradually revealed that the patient had had very mixed feelings toward her mother, who appeared to have been a demanding and possessive woman. Mrs. W. had been in her teens (approximately the present age of her daughter) when her mother had become a bedfast invalid. She had had to assume the entire nursing responsibility and had done so very conscientiously. The mother's incontinence demanded almost constant efforts on Mrs. W's part to keep her physically clean. Although her strict conscience would not allow her to recognize the fact, Mrs. W. had experienced intense resentment toward the sacrifices demanded of her by her mother at this time.

The psychiatrist realized that Mrs. W. had developed severe feelings of guilt because of her anger, feelings which were intensified by her mother's eventual death. *Although she had not permitted herself to become fully aware of it, Mrs. W. felt—in the current situation—that she would occupy her mother's position.* She was facing a period of invalidism, which would be in connection with a disease of the bowels. More specific still were the implications (to the patient) of the proposed colostomy: Mrs. W. felt that she would have the same (to her, disgusting) problem with incontinence that she had had to face with her mother. The patient feared that her daughter would come to hate her as she had hated her mother. Mrs. W. could not have put all of these thoughts into words, but her unrecognized inner conviction was that death would be preferable to such an intense reactivation of the old conflicts and a deserved punishment for her hatred of her mother.

It was quite clear that, generally speaking, Mrs. W. had been in reasonably good emotional health during her adult life. There now existed a crisis in which, so to speak, circumstances had conspired against the patient to strike her where she was most vulnerable. The psychiatrist's objective was not to conduct an extensive psychotherapy, but simply to free the patient sufficiently from the inner pressures to enable her to accept the surgeon's potentially life-saving recommendation.

Some progress in this direction was made through the process of ventilation, i.e., through the patient's being encouraged and helped to voice her thoughts more thoroughly than she had ever done before. The similarity between the old situation and the current one was brought into the patient's consciousness more clearly than before. More importantly, this step allowed the *differences* to be stressed (the shorter period of invalidism, the likelihood of a favorable outcome, the availability of nursing assistance). Insofar as these could be recognized, reassurance was offered the patient about the harmlessness of her long-standing angry feelings toward her mother. Reassurance could also be offered to the effect that there would be little basis for similar feelings in the patient's daughter.

As a result of these conversations, Mrs. W. came to understand one aspect of her personality better than she had been able to do previously, and she came to realize that her refusal of the operation had been irrational. She changed her decision and allowed the course of treatment to proceed.

APPLICATIONS TO ONESELF. Experience tends to confirm the value of acceptance of the levels-of-awareness concept when applied to self-scrutiny fully as much as when applied to the study of other persons. *The realization that one's mood, one's way of approaching problems, one's efficiency, may be affected by factors which are not in full consciousness can lead one to cultivate the ability for a heightened self-awareness, an ability which can, at times, be of decisive help in the practice of medicine or the pursuit of one's private affairs.* Let us, in imagination, rearrange the case-history of J. W. slightly, along lines which are common enough in hospital experience, to illustrate this point.

Suppose that the problem had been essentially the same, but that the patient had been more provocative in manner and had refused operation in a fashion which cast doubt upon the doctor's diagnostic acumen or technical skill. The doctor's first reaction in such a case might well have been one of more serious annoyance. Whether or not he then would have persisted in his efforts to help the patient and whether or not he then would have been able to think through the problem to the extent that he did, would have depended in large part on his ability to become aware of his own emotions, to have some understanding of their sources, and so to discount them in evaluating the situation and planning the course of action.

It is only the realization that one's own adjustment to life can be made more effective by an acceptance of the levels-of-awareness concept that makes such an acceptance possible.

Suggestions for Further Reading

Freud, S.: The Psychopathology of Everyday Life, Chapters I, V, VI, X, and XII *in* The Basic Writings of Sigmund Freud, New York, Modern Library (Random), 1938.

―――: A General Introduction to Psychoanalysis, pp. 29-83, Garden City, New York, Permabooks (Doubleday), 1953.

Levine, M.: Psychotherapy in Medical Practice, pp. 283-302, New York, Macmillan, 1942.

Menninger, K. A.: The Human Mind, ed. 3, pp. 21-34, New York, Knopf, 1945.

Saul, L.: Bases of Human Behavior, ed. 2, pp. 99-104, Philadelphia, Lippincott, 1960.

CHAPTER 3

Fundamentals of Psychology for the Physician (Part 2)

MOTIVATION: THE BASIC DRIVES AND THEIR MANIFESTATION

Both in the introductory chapter and in the preceding chapter dealing with some theoretical concepts, frequent reference was made to the *motivation* of human beings, with no attempt to define the term or to clarify the origins of the various motivational forces. Yet obviously one of the most pressing questions in the study of any organism is, what makes it go? This chapter will be devoted to an attempt to develop a partial answer to this question as it applies to human beings. (As is the case with *mind* and *consciousness,* anything like a complete answer exceeds the boundaries of psychiatry, as these are usually understood.) The inquiry assumes additional interest as an illustration of how deeply psychiatry is rooted in basic biological principles.

Motivation may be defined quite simply, for present purposes, in terms of the discussion at the beginning of Chapter 2, as *the tendency to effect adjustment.* One can add that *a motivated activity is one which is theoretically capable of being perceived by the (human) subject as a part of his efforts at adjustment.* (One says, "theoretically capable of being perceived" rather than simply "perceived" to allow for the fact, brought out in the latter portion of Chapter 2, that a great deal of human motivation takes place below the threshold of awareness.)

When considered from the conventional, surface point of view, there appear to be almost countless motivations operative, at one time or another, in any human being. Any given motivational state appears to become increasingly complex as one begins to inquire into it. If one selects any specific activity in which he happens to be engaged and begins to probe its motivation, begins to ask the question, Why? he comes, as a rule, not upon one but a series of interlocking answers that seem to spread out and to deepen, involving many considerations. If, however, one were to persist and if he were able to penetrate into the further recesses of his mind (i.e., into the less conscious or unconscious aspects), he would ultimately reach a point at which a certain simplicity re-enters the picture.

As an example, consider the following introspective material (incomplete and highly condensed) derived from a report given by a premedical student as part of an elective course in psychology. (Details of the student's life are, for the most part, not requisite to following the train of thought, but one point may be mentioned. The student had lost his maternal grandfather, to whom his mother was devoted, when he was a very small boy.)

The student leaves the dinner table promptly, goes to his room, and begins to read a subchapter on the humors of the mammalian eye in a textbook of physiology. Why is he doing this? *To acquire some knowledge of the subject.* Why? Actually it happens to be from no deep interest in the immediate subject, but *to get a good grade in the next physiology quiz.* Again, why? *To do well in the course as a whole, to complete the requirements for graduation from college* Why? *To be able to go to medical school and become a doctor.* Why become a doctor? *To study and treat the sick.* And why is this important to him? More than one motive here. From preliminary experiences, he knows that *the gratitude and respect of those he helps make him feel good. The practice of medicine ensures a good living.* But there are other ways to obtain gratitude; there are easier ways to earn a good living, are there not? . . . *Understanding the inner workings of the human body is very interesting* . . . Anything else? . . . *His mother's father was a doctor; his mother loved and admired his grandfather very much, as did he.* She has been in many ways a good mother, kind and affectionate. He loves her and wants her admiration; eventually he wants to be loved and admired by a wife who will be like her. To achieve this, *he has felt that he must be like the person whom mother loved and admired so greatly* . . . In a basic sense, *he reads about the humors of the eye because he loves and wants to be loved.*

The late Logan Clendenning, Professor of Medicine at the University of Kansas, has stated a similar general idea in very strong terms.

When a man is no longer under the grinding necessity of acquiring food for his next meal, he will turn to other things—to the operations of the stock exchange, to politics, racehorses, or the gathering of first editions. When a woman no longer needs to exert any . . . fascination of limb or lip to capture a sugar-broker, she turns to lyric poetry or to dyspepsia. But in none of the variegated depravities of the mind or soul—the plan of the battle of Austerlitz, the Fifth Symphony . . . the organization of the Standard Oil Company, the "Ode on a Grecian Urn," or Rob Hazelton's collection of postage stamps—can I discern anything but a weak disguise either of the means to acquire food and shelter that they may be converted into energy and tissue, or of the means to acquire a mate in order that another individual may be reproduced.*

Clendenning has unquestionably overstated the case (in all likelihood, deliberately so). The overstatement lies, of course, in the "nor can I discern *anything but* . . ." Notice that, in the example of the premedical student, the uncovering of each successive motivational element in no way invalidates the preceding elements. It remains quite true, for example, that the student wishes to acquire some knowledge of the immediate subject in order to get a good grade in the next quiz. Yet it is clear that the more superficial motivations are, in some fashion, dependent upon the deeper ones, rather than the other way round (and rather than being free of all connection with them).

The example could, of course, have been entirely different—it contains nothing unique or strange—but the principle of its analysis would remain the same. In one important sense, motives are rarely as simple as they may at first seem: this everyone knows. As one pursues these motives to their ultimate sources, however, one finds that they are all refinements, derivatives, or combinations of a relatively small set of fundamental urges of the human organism, the *basic drives*.†

As the student probably realizes, the field of the study of instinctual behavior (*ethology*) has been a very active one in recent years.[2] One of the greatest problems has been to sort out from the complicated mass of human behavior the small group of urge-response units which are essentially automatic, built into the organism from the beginning, genetically determined. This fundamental group—eating in response to hunger, drinking in response to thirst, copulation in response to sexual desire, etc.—comprises the true *instincts*. The problem becomes so difficult and complex in man because here the capacity for *learning* has become so great. This capacity is, on the one hand, correlated with the development of the human brain (which is the largest of any species, not only relative to the size of the body but also relative to the size of the rest of the nervous system). On the other hand, it is correlated with the development of *culture*, the repository of learning, in human society.

There is no reason whatever to suppose that man's progenitors were in any way deficient in instinctual endowment; quite the reverse seems to have been the case. But with the development of the equipment for extensive learning and of a repository of items to be learned, while the instincts remained, the patterns of behavior became complex and *increasingly modifiable*. In man, therefore, it is rather less meaningful

---

* Logan Clendenning, The Human Body, New York, Knopf, 1935.

† Or, as will be described in the present and succeeding chapters, resultants of the simultaneous operation of drives and certain inhibitory forces.

to speak of *instincts* (meaning drive plus automatic pattern of behavior) and more meaningful to speak merely of *basic drives* (genetically determined "urges to action"). These drives form the ultimate substratum of all motivated behavior.

Self-preservative Drives: Hunger as a Model

Rather than to pursue this essentially theoretical discussion further at this point, it may be well to consider a concrete example. Let us review the physiological basis and fundamental course of the drive, *hunger*—one which is given a place in nearly every system of classification.

As the student will recall from physiology, the need for a relatively constant food intake is referable to the metabolic processes going on in all of the cells of the body. The energy source for these processes is supplied through the blood stream, primarily in the form of glucose. The relatively constant level of blood sugar is a matter of homeostasis, of which the immediate effector organ is the liver. Through breakdown of stored glycogen and its release into the blood stream, the liver can maintain an adequate blood sugar level, under average demands, for some five hours. After this, in the absence of food ingestion, gluconeogenesis is utilized.

That the phenomenon called hunger is affected by the level of blood sugar is attested by the fact that insulin injections (lowering the level) augment hunger contractions in the stomach, whereas the intravenous administration of glucose inhibits them. In ordinary experience, however, hunger is more closely related to the phases of stomach activity. It is as if, during evolutionary development, a safety factor has gotten built into the organism so that hunger and (when possible) the relief of hunger normally occur before the blood sugar level becomes critically low.

As a matter of fact, the only period when no hunger contractions are taking place in the fundus of the stomach is during the half hour or so right after a full meal. As the stomach empties itself, the waves of contraction approach nearer the cardiac end, and, by about four hours after eating, they assume the typical characteristics associated with hunger. Along with the muscular activity there is increased secretory activity on the part of the cells of the gastric mucosa, producing pepsinogen and hydrochloric acid. Within the lumen of the stomach the pepsinogen becomes pepsin, and the acid-enzyme solution accumulates.

These phenomena involve the direct participation of the central nervous system. Hunger contractions have been shown to occur when the stomach has been isolated from the central nervous system, but they are less frequent and less vigorous. The sensory nuclei of the vagus nerve in the medulla oblongata appear to be the primary "hunger center," mediating both influences affecting the hunger contractions and those involved in hunger sensations.

Along with these several activities, there is a degree of subjective awareness of them. Hunger is thus a particular kind of tension state, a state which, if unrelieved, rather quickly becomes one of considerable discomfort. With this state, there comes a general readiness for action (as indicated by a heightened reflex irritability) and a particular readiness and inclination for a specific kind of action—the eating of food—which will bring relief, will lower the tension.

One can discuss the basic drive, hunger, from at least three standpoints: the *source* (which has just been reviewed); the *aim*, the sort of action toward which the drive impels the subject, in this case, the act of eating; and the *object*, a potentially satisfying something in the environment which the aim must involve, in this case, the class of substances called food. The same three standpoints can be used in a consideration of any of the basic drives.

Notice that the ultimate source of a basic drive is purely a matter of physiology and biochemistry; it is, furthermore, essentially fixed and constant, not varying appreciably with time or circumstances, and not varying from one member of a given species to another.

It is different with the aim and the object; everyone becomes hungry in the same way, but he does not eat in quite the same way, nor does he eat the same things. The aim and the object of a drive involve an interaction between the organism as a unit and portions of his environment; they are thus matters of adjustment, matters for psychological consideration.*

Aims and objects become more complex than sources. For example, the aim of eating may involve a number of preliminary, subordinate, or complementary aims, such as locating, taking possession of, and preparing food, as well as a number of derivatives and refinements showing a very heavy influence of learning, such as table manners. The object, also, while limited to a certain general class of substances, may be considerably influenced by learning: what is considered perfectly edible by one group may be considered poisonous or evil by another.

On the basis of the characteristics discerned in the basic drive, hunger, one may attempt to generalize and to compose a list of the other human phenomena which belong in the category, basic drives. Unfortunately, there is by no means a full consensus among psychologists, psychiatrists, and ethologists as to the components of this category. The

---

* Not instead of, but in addition to, other sorts of consideration.

following table, however, would probably meet with considerable agreement among psychiatrists. For the most part, such disagreements as exist have to do with possible additions to the list rather than with subtractions from it.

Basic Drives*

 Hunger—eating†
 Thirst—drinking
 Breathing
 Urination
 Defecation
 Libido—sexual activity (sexual-social activity)
  autoerotic activity
  courtship
  mating
  jealously; sexual fighting
  parental, especially maternal, activity
  social activity
 (Aggression—exploratory activity, aggressive activity, destructive activity)

The principal question involves the last item on the list, the one set in parentheses. Some psychiatrists consider that aggression has a derivation which is not strictly comparable to that of the other items and therefore would not include it in a list of the basic drives. Some psychiatrists consider aggressive urges fundamental in the hereditary make-up of man. This question will be considered in the discussion beginning on page 61.

It can readily be seen, in a general way, that the first five drives in the list—hunger, thirst, breathing, urination, and defecation—have more characteristics in common with one another, as biological phenomena, than they share with sexual or aggressive urges. This circumstance is sometimes given recognition by grouping them together as "the self-preservative drives." Having considered hunger in some detail, it will not be necessary to give individual consideration to the other members of this group.

---

 * Some ethologists would also list temperature-regulating activity, the sleeping-waking cycle, and "an urge to general motor activity" (very similar to, if not identical with, "aggression"). Some psychiatrists would list a so-called "death instinct" (*Thanatos, destrudo*) instead of merely "aggression," and some psychiatrists might also list "dependency needs." These last two motivational states will be discussed at a later point in this chapter.

 † In three cases—hunger-eating, thirst-drinking, and libido-sexual activity—there exist generally accepted names for the drive or drive state in addition to names for the instinctually determined behavior.

Libido: the Sexual-Social Drive

It is a matter of widespread knowledge, as generally disseminated among laymen as among physicians, that psychiatry is particularly interested in the development and manifestations of the sexual (or, better, the sexual-social) drive. What is not nearly so well understood is the scientific rationale for this interest. A discussion of the sexual-social drive follows presently, but before giving details, it is pertinent to state concisely the fundamental similarities and the significant differences between this drive and the drives of the self-preservative group.

SIMILARITY TO THE SELF-PRESERVATIVE DRIVES. Like the other basic drives, the sexual drive has its source in the biochemistry and physiology of the body, and is, at the core, genetically determined. In the healthy adult human being, the sexual drive, like the others, is related to an *object* in the environment, in this case a person of the opposite gender; like the others, the drive leads the human being to experience a characteristic *aim* toward that object, copulation.

DIFFERENCES FROM SELF-PRESERVATIVE DRIVES. The differences between the sexual-social drive and the other basic drives, though less fundamental than the similarities, are perhaps of even greater significance in understanding the role of this force in affecting human behavior. First, it should be clear that the sexual-social drive has a considerably *less imperative* character than do the other drives. For example, in the ordinary case, gratification of hunger may be postponed for only a matter of days, or, at most, for a few weeks, until collapse and ultimately death intervene. Gratification of the breathing-drive can, at most, be postponed for only a couple of minutes. The others lie somewhere in between in this respect. By contrast, a human being may experience great frustration of his sexual drive continuing over long periods of time without danger to life.

Other points of difference between the sexual-social drive and the other basic drives have to do with *the vastly greater variability of the former with respect to aims and objects*. The reader has perhaps noticed that, in the statement of the similarities, two qualifying adjectives were used with respect to the person experiencing the sexual drive, namely, "healthy" and "adult." No such qualification was necessary in discussing hunger; nor would it have been necessary in discussing any other of the self-preservative drives. Unlike the other drives, the sexual drive has *a complicated developmental course*.

A very small child, when under the influence of hunger, has essentially the same aim and the same object as an adult. A sick person, when under the influence of hunger, has essentially the same aim and object as a well one. (There may be, it is true, quantitative differences in hunger during illness, i.e., a person may then experience hunger less intensely than he ordinarily would, but the nature of the aim varies not at all and the object varies only within an extremely limited range.) On the other hand, the sexual drive in a child may have quite a different aim from that in an adult; for example, the aim may be to be cuddled and caressed as an end in itself. Similarly, the object of the sexual drive in a child may be completely different from that in an adult; for example, when a small child masturbates, the object of his libido is his own body, not that of a person of the other sex. The effect of certain kinds of illness is equally marked. For example, an adult male, suffering from the perversion called *voyeurism* (p. 416), may have, as his principal sexual aim, the looking at the body of a woman, rather than sexual intercourse. An example of a radical alteration in object is afforded by *homosexuality*, in which the desired sexual object is a person of the same sex as the subject.

Still another difference between the sexual drive and the other basic drives is that the object of this drive is ordinarily another *person*. This is literally true in normal adult sexuality and in most of the perversions; in the case of masturbation, it is usually true in fantasy; i.e., masturbatory activity is usually accompanied by fantasies of another person, once the individual is old enough to fantasize.

This list does not exhaust the points of difference between the sexual-social drive and the self-preservative drives, but it may suffice to explain the special place occupied by the course and manifestations of the sexual-social drive in the development of the personality and in influencing behavior, both in sickness and in health.

A cardinal feature in the production of emotional disturbances is the existence of chronic conflicts, of chronic tensions and frustrations. The subject of conflict will be discussed in detail in a later portion of this chapter, but it can doubtless be understood at this point, that whereas a serious frustration of one of the self-preservative drives can lead to an *intense* conflict, it is well-nigh impossible for it to lead to a *chronic* conflict.* If one of the self-preservative drives is blocked, the individual either solves the situation rapidly or perishes, but he rarely develops an emotional illness. Moreover, the essentially fixed character of the aims and the objects of the other basic drives limits the behavioral patterns to which they can give rise. Frustration of these drives will certainly lead to an intensification of efforts to gratify them, but only under the most unusual circumstances can it lead to a deviate or pathological pattern of behavior.

Now, what of the source and developmental history of the sexual-

---

* An exception to this statement, although the situation is rare in our culture, is chronic, *partial* frustration of the hunger drive.

social drive? As has been mentioned, the source, like that of the other drives, is multiple and derives from the chemistry and physiology of the body. There are hormonal components: the gonadal hormones, certain adrenocortical and pituitary hormones, and perhaps others. There are also components deriving from the periphery of the body, from the so-called "erotogenic zones." These areas are the portions of the body which from the beginning are natural sources of physical pleasure. They include the lips (and, to a lesser extent, the tongue and the rest of the mouth) the nipples, the anorectum, and portions of the external genitalia. The skin, itself, functions diffusely in this way. While not, strictly speaking, considered erotogenic zones, the special sense organs, particularly the eyes, function as mediators of physical pleasure, and hence may be mentioned in this connection.

If one studies the responses of infants, one can make out the pleasure-role of all of these portions of the body quite clearly. Obviously the mouth, and particularly the lips, are a source of great pleasure. Sucking, mouthing, and, later, chewing are eagerly indulged in, not merely in the function of eating, but for the sensations thus produced. The skin is a great source of physical pleasure, as shown in the responses to caresses and fondling. Functional stimulation of the anorectum is pleasurable; every mother or nurse has noticed the pleased expression which often accompanies evacuation of the bowel. Stimulation of the external genitalia is discovered by all normal infants as a source of pleasure. Certain kinds of visual stimulation are clearly pleasurable, as indicated by the fixing of vision on shiny objects.

Two questions—interrelated—naturally arise in the student's mind on first consideration of this material. (1) On what grounds are all these experiences considered parts of a single phenomenon? (2) Why speak of this phenomenon as the "sexual" or "sexual-social" drive, rather than speaking simply of, let us say, "pleasure drives?" The answer to both questions lies in a consideration of the developmental history of the drive in the course of normal maturation, plus a consideration of what has taken place in the production of those deviate expressions of sexuality known as the *perversions*.

Whereas, during the first years of life, neither the hormonal influences nor the pleasure-yielding capacity of any of the erotogenic zones is such as to establish a long-lasting primacy of any one mode of physical gratification, by the time normal adulthood is reached, such a primacy is clearly established, and it is accorded to heterosexual genital activity leading to orgasm and the release of tension. Nearly all of the original modes of physical gratification are retained and they play a part in love-making, but a preliminary and subordinate part. That is to say, looking, kissing, fondling, caressing, etc., are important not so much as ends in themselves but as parts of a total experience (actual or anticipated), of which the genital experience is the most significant.

The various perversions (p. 416), deviate modes of gratification which are nevertheless unmistakably sexual, are, in essence, instances in which the normal developmental fusion of the various components of the sexual drive (under genital primacy) has not taken place, or, once having taken place, has been undone. In such cases, some pleasure experience other than genital union leading to orgasm has assumed the greatest functional significance, while nevertheless revealing its essentially sexual character. Thus, in the perversion of (male) *homosexuality*, it may happen that the mouth or the anus becomes the principal pleasure zone. In some instances of *masochism* (a condition in which erotic pleasure is experienced in receiving threatening or painful stimuli), the skin may be the site of gratification. In *voyeurism*, the eyes become the organs of sexual pleasure. And so on.

In the normal person, it is obviously not the case that *all* of the pleasure-yielding capacity of the original erotogenic zones is, so to speak, absorbed by or integrated with genital strivings. That pleasurable aspect of eating which occurs in addition to the satisfaction of nutritional needs is a prime illustration of the persistence of "oral pleasure." So are smoking and chewing tobacco or gum. (When talking occurs largely for the purpose of relieving tension, rather than for communication, it, too, may be considered an oral pleasure.) Similarly, the comfort of a warm bath or the stimulation of a brisk rub-down ("skin pleasure") may normally be indulged in for its own sake, having no direct connection with genital activity. Many visual activities (the enjoyment of nature, the visiting of art galleries) may be pursued in some measure for their own sake. Yet the persistence, in the normal adult, of the pleasure-potentialities of these various experiences does not, by reason of their relatively moderate intensity, invalidate the pattern described above, one in which these elements are integral components of the individual's erotic life.

In the table listing the basic drives it was indicated that libidinal activities include a group of closely interrelated phenomena. Up to this point, the discussion has been largely confined to a consideration of the simplest and most direct of these, "mating activities." A more detailed and extensive consideration of "libido theory," as it is called, is appropriately reserved for the specialist, but it is necessary at this point to give some indication of how libido comes to supply the basic motivational force underlying activities that are properly described as "social."

At first thought, it may well seem that the social bonds, the bonds that link human beings in a variety of positive relationships, are far removed from what can be considered sexual. In one sense, this is quite true. Yet, despite the removal, there is a direct linkage between the one and the other. As a starting point, it may be remembered (p. 56) that libido is the only one of the basic drives (apart from aggression) having the characteristic of usually requiring another *person*, rather than some inanimate substance, as its object. What is needed at this point to bridge the conceptual gap is some explanation of the psychological process, the *mechanism* by which an elemental biological force becomes modified and refined so as to furnish the basis for a sizeable number of relationships in which a sexual element is not ordinarily recognized by the participants or detected by others.

As a matter of fact, more than one mechanism is operative—this aspect of the subject will be further clarified in the chapter on development—but the most important mechanism is the one termed *sublimation*. Consider the following examples, none of them rare and some of them of universal application.

Example 1. A young writer loses his sweetheart to a rival. He is left in a state of frustration and tension since his principal libidinal object has been removed. Eventually he writes a romantic novel and finds that this activity relieves much of the tension.

Example 2. A young woman loses her lover in battle. She becomes a nurse's aide in the Red Cross, and finds release in caring for wounded soldiers.

Example 3. An elderly, widowed professor experiences an erotic attraction to a talented girl, one of his graduate students. The circumstances make the pursuit of a romance inappropriate. The professor is able to obtain considerable satisfaction from unstinted giving of his time and knowledge toward a development of the girl's professional abilities.

Example 4. A happily married man has, in the natural course of events, a number of attractive women friends: business associates, women relatives, wives of men friends. He responds to these women with such feelings and behavior as courtesy, friendliness, tenderness, and occasional good-natured teasing.

Example 5. An orphaned youth is reared by his uncle, a warm, kindly, and generous person. In their deeper levels, the young man's feelings toward the uncle involve an erotic component. This aspect, however, is completely repressed. The young man's motivations toward his uncle find expression in considerate attention to the uncle's interests and well-being.

Example 6. During his year of internship, a doctor is separated from his fiancee. He finds that the writing of love-letters, the sending of various small gifts, and the making of plans for their future together afford a measure of relief from his immediate frustration.

What has taken place in these various examples? In examples 3, 5, and 6, the libidinal object has been retained, but the aim has been altered, altered in a way which affords appreciable relief from the tension of the frustrated drive. In examples 1 and 2, both object and aim have been altered, but some reduction of tension, some gratification, has nevertheless been achieved. Sublimation, then, may be defined as *a technique or mechanism of adjustment through which a drive is, as it were, deflected into other channels of expression (discharge), channels affording a sufficient release of tension to facilitate the maintenance of the individual's state of equilibrium.*

Notice that sublimation occurs with varying degrees of deliberateness, but that it need not involve repression. (Example 5 is perhaps the only one of the list in which the basic drive, in its original form, is kept entirely below the level of consciousness.) Notice also that sublimation of some libidinal impulses may come into play even when the subject has unrestricted access to his principal love object (Example 4). The point here is that every healthy adult has more libidinal energy at his disposal than can be absorbed by any one object.

Finally, it is important to realize that Example 5 is a particular case of what is actually a very general situation. This point will be further clarified in the chapter on personality development, but it may be simply presented here. There is ample evidence to believe that all human beings are, to a degree, bisexual. Anatomically speaking it is a fact that each sex possesses, in rudimentary (homologous) form, the reproductive organs of the other (e.g., the prostate in the male and the clitoris in the female). Physiologically speaking, certain of the sexual hormones are nonspecific in the sense that they are conducive to sexual behavior but not to specifically male or female behavior. Psychologically speaking, the libido, in its elemental, original form is not entirely restricted, in its investments, to persons of the opposite sex. What normally happens, however, is that the portion which turns toward persons of the same sex as the subject is very largely sublimated: the aim is altered. Furthermore, considerable repression is involved, with the result that the subject ordinarily remains unaware of the erotic origin of these feelings (of friendship and comradeship).

Thus it is that the libido comes to supply energy not merely for the individual's love life in the narrow sense, but for most of the friendly, constructive relationships which have made the development of human society and the acquisition of human culture possible.*

---

* There are, of course, intellectual (logical) considerations, as well as instinctual or emotional ones, which have influenced human beings to cooperate with one another, but, without the latter, the former would probably never have been given the time to come into play.

Hostility and Aggression

When one considers the plight of the world in this latter half of the twentieth century, with large coalitions of nations hostilely arrayed against one another, able, ready, and almost willing to unleash immeasurable destruction upon mankind, one is strongly tempted to postulate the existence of another basic drive, one whose primary aim would be activity of a hostile, destructive nature. Further seeming evidence in this direction is afforded by the crime and "delinquency" rates that receive so much publicity. When one reads in the newspaper, for example, of an elderly gentleman being severely beaten by a gang of young hoodlums to whom he was unknown, or of the proprietor of a fruit stand being shot and killed in a robbery which netted the robber but a few dollars, the motivation of the criminals seems so obscure as to make the idea of some built-in destructive instinct seem more plausible than any other postulate.*

Furthermore, a consideration of history indicates that man has always devoted a large proportion of his energies to fighting or otherwise injuring his own kind. Our present age, by reason of modern technology, may be the most critical that the world has ever known, but the psychological forces involved in the danger are in no sense new; they seem to have existed as long as the species. *No longer (or wider) than the existence of the species, however.* That is to say, no species other than man fights and injures its own kind so persistently.[2] Fighting occurs, of course, in a great many species, but it is, for the most part, highly restricted as to the circumstances. Indeed, among mammals, fighting between males for a sexual object and occasional fighting for a limited food supply comprise almost the only examples. Even in these cases, fighting to the death is decidedly the exception, rather than the rule; the weaker combatant "surrenders" and the fight is over. Furthermore, as indicated by the work of Tinbergen and others, interspecies fighting among mammals, apart from the obtaining of food, is still less common than intraspecies fighting.

This circumstance—that the ethologists have found so little evidence of intraspecies destructive behavior (and of interspecies destruction apart from hunting) in species other than man—is rather a strong argument against postulating a basic drive of a hostile, destructive nature, since all of the basic drives previously listed have their clear counterparts in all mammalian and many other species.

---

* Also relevant in this connection are the many ways in which human beings act destructively toward themselves. Not merely suicide in the limited (acute) sense, nor the chronic long-drawn-out types of suicide such as severe alcoholism, but the subtler, more attenuated ways in which many persons are continuously bringing unhappiness upon themselves (see p. 422).

Among other arguments against the existence of a "hate drive" or "death drive," one of the more significant derives from the seeming absence of any chemical or physiological source at all comparable to those of the (other) basic drives.

If, then, one maintains reservations about listing an urge to destroy as a basic drive, how is one to explain hatred as a motivational state and destruction as a mode of behavior? To a considerable extent, the answer appears to be that the *hostile, destructive pattern of response is a learned one*. In essence, it appears to be the *principal response to frustration* of the (other) basic drives.[1] This point will be further clarified in the chapter on personality development. However, it should be apparent that such frustrations are early, in some measure unavoidable, and hence universal in human life. Hostile, destructive impulses are therefore present in every human being from infancy onward. Quantitatively there is, however, tremendous variation from one individual to another (variation with respect to the force of these impulses), depending largely upon the type, timing, and outcome of the frustrations he has experienced during his earliest and most formative years.

Whereas the "urge to destroy" appears to be acquired, it seems likely that there is a basic drive upon which destructive tendencies are, so to speak, grafted, and from which they derive their energy.[5] This is the one placed in parentheses in the Table on page 54, which psychiatrists term "aggression" and which is probably equivalent to what ethologists term "the urge to general motor activity." Insofar as it is unmodified by hatred born of frustration, this drive appears to have as its aim the making of exploratory contact with and the gaining of a sense of mastery over objects in the environment. When the contacts are made and the mastery exerted for destructive purposes, one may then speak of this drive as being in the service of anger or hatred.

This dual significance of aggression is reflected in the ambiguity of the term in popular usage. Sometimes the word is used synonymously with hostility-destructiveness, as in the expression, "aggressor nations." Sometimes it is used praisingly, synonymously with "initiative," as in the expression, "an alert, aggressive businessman."

The biological source of the aggressive drive is thought ultimately to lie in the physiology of the motor apparatus of the body (muscle and, perhaps, nerve physiology). The details are, however, not as thoroughly understood as are those of libido.

More remains to be said about aggression, and, in particular, about the hostile-destructive urges to which it lends force. In addition to their omnipresence and their very early acquisition—characteristics which make it of practical, clinical value to treat hostile impulses as if they constituted a basic drive, whatever one may conclude with respect to their origin—these urges have two other characteristics in common with libido, but differing from other basic drives. Firstly, they have a *developmental course*, and secondly, they are capable of *sublimation*.

A few examples may clarify the significance of the first point. There are, in short, modes of expression of hostility, each one appropriate to a particular developmental level. Thus, an infant of two months discharges hostility through a particular type of crying; one of seven months, through biting; a child of two years, through soiling; one of seven years fights with his arms and legs; an adult may do this also, but he is likelier (at least in our culture) to be destructive in less physical ways.

With respect to the second point, that of sublimation of hostile, destructive impulses, consider the following examples.

A soldier receives a severe dressing-down from his sergeant. Prudence dictates that he not respond with overt hostility. During the next several hours he is aware of a sustained tension. After he has been able to work out with the heavy punching bag during a recreational period, the tension vanishes.

A mathematics teacher is severely provoked by the repeated and insolent negligence of a student in doing his assignments. He has an impulse to do something destructive to the student, but instead, he requires the student to spend a number of hours after school working problems in the neglected area. The angry tension subsides as a result of his enforcing this relatively constructive disciplinary measure.

Dependency Needs

There is little serious thought that the group of strivings which, in clinical psychiatry, are often referred to as "dependency needs" should be considered a true basic drive. Yet rather primitive strivings of this sort often stand in a similar relationship to a conscious motivational state as that occupied by the basic drives; hence it is of some practical value to consider them briefly at this point.

Clinically speaking, the term "dependency needs" ordinarily refers to a set of deep-seated cravings to be taken care of, provided for, and ministered to in a fashion appropriate to a small child. These cravings arise naturally on the basis of the helplessness of the infant; as is the case with destructive urges, they persist and are made stronger on the basis of frustrations, frustrations of the nutritional and erotic needs of infancy. Like destructive urges, dependency needs are capable of sublimation.

Many a peptic ulcer patient (p. 186) may be said to be suffering from ungratified (often unconscious) dependency needs. To a point, a sublimatory type of gratification of these needs may be achieved through an activity such as saving money. In such cases, the deeper significance of the money is that it represents the means to achieve the desired state of being looked after and waited upon.

CONFLICT

Everyone knows that human life is not merely a series of gratifications of drive states. Nor is it merely a series of preparatory activities leading to gratifications, a series of easily performed behavioral patterns serving to keep the individual in a continuous state of full adjustment. Quite the contrary; one of the characteristic and significant features of human life is that it is fraught with *conflict*. (Surely this is one of the most interesting features also, as is attested by all great dramatic literature.) Even more specifically characteristic of human life—as contrasted with the lives of members of other species—are the variety and complexity of the conflicts.

If one were to arrange in a list the various types of conflict which can be experienced by human beings, going from the most obvious and overt to the subtlest and most complex, one might use such headings as the following: (1) conflict between an individual and some inanimate feature of his environment; (2) conflict between one individual and another (interpersonal conflict); (3) conflict between opposing motivations within a single individual (intrapersonal conflict). This third category can be further subdivided into: (a) instances in which the conflicting motivations are largely conscious; (b) instances in which only one of the conflicting motivations is conscious; (c) instances in which none of the conflicting motivations is conscious.

At one time or another in the course of his practice, it is the role of the physician to attempt to assist his patients in the handling of all these types of conflicts. When a cardiac patient is "fighting for air" and the doctor orders oxygen, he is assisting in the resolution of a conflict of type 1. When a young wife is becoming irritable and "run down" because of too frequent contact with a nagging mother-in-law and the doctor suggests a change of residence to lessen the contacts, he is assisting in the handling of a conflict of type 2. If a patient with a mild chronic illness knows that he should decrease his activities but delays doing so out of conscious shame and the doctor then offers various persuasive considerations to lessen the shame, he is assisting in the handling of a conflict of type 3 a.

If the conflict is of type 3 b, and, to an even greater extent, if it is of type 3 c, the patient's problems may well require the attention of a psychiatrist. Yet the odds are that the patient will first come to the attention of his family doctor or a nonpsychiatric specialist, and ultimately effective treatment will therefore depend in most instances upon the ability of the doctor first consulted to perceive the nature of the situation. For example, the successful outcome of the case of the woman with cancer of the bowel (p. 45) depended upon the recognition by the surgical resident and the nurse that the patient was experiencing an inner conflict without being aware of all of its components (type 3 b).

Forces Opposing the Basic Drives

Another way of classifying conflicts of an intrapersonal (also called "endopsychic") nature is on the basis of a careful delineation of the conflicting forces. Here the simplest type is a conflict arising between one basic drive and another.

A draftee, during basic training, puts in a hard day's work. He gets a brief pass and finds that he has two dollars to spend. Should he buy himself a good meal, or should he make a long-distance call to his girl friend?

Conflicts of this general type are fairly frequent, but they are usually quickly solved one way or another and rarely come to a physician's attention. It is when one force in an intrapersonal conflict derives from libidinal, hostile, or dependency strivings and the other force has a quite different (noninstinctual) origin that the conflict becomes more difficult and may be productive of illness. It now becomes necessary, therefore, to consider the nature of the forces within the personality which may come into opposition to the basic drives.[1]

Fear

Of these forces, the most elemental is certainly *fear*. Everyone has experienced this emotion at one time or another and so has some understanding of its several aspects. There are the various physiological elements (many of them objectively measurable): heightened activity of the sympathetic division of the autonomic nervous system and of the adrenal glands and a number of phenomena secondary to this activity, including an increase in cardiac and respiratory rates, a decrease in circulation time, a generalized hyperreflexia, an inhibition of gastric function, etc. If the fear is marked, there are characteristic changes in general appearance and particularly in facial expression, partially but not entirely due to sympathetic and adrenal activity. The eyes are widely opened and the pupils dilated; the eyebrows are elevated and the forehead may show a transverse wrinkling. There may be contractions of the smooth muscle tissue in the skin ("goose flesh") and the hair, where naturally short or close-cropped may show a tendency to "stand on end" (*erectores pilae*). Often there is a generalized skin pallor. There may be sweating of the palms of the hands and soles of the feet. There may be trembling of the extremities and of the lips.

There are also strong, deeply disturbing, subjective elements. These derive in part from the subject's perception of the physiological alterations, in part from perception of the external danger, and in part from the functions of memory and fantasy. (The essence of the subjective experience is scarcely capable of being expressed in words without resort to tautology.)

When fear reaches an extreme degree, the condition is termed one of *panic* (or, in less scientific usage, one of *terror*). In such instances, all of the characteristics just listed are usually present to a very considerable extent, and, in addition, there is an element of confusion and irrationality.* When severe disasters strike—such as major fires, earthquakes, hurricanes, or, in wartime, bombing raids—this element is frequently responsible for a majority of the casualties.

The stimulus for the fear response is, of course, the perception (or, at least, the impression) that the environment has become dangerous in some fashion. A very few stimuli (loud noises, falling, perhaps the sudden appearance of something strange) are seemingly responded to with fear by infants from the first; most fear stimuli become operative through conditioning or more complicated forms of learning.

The origins and development of the fear response are shrouded in evolutionary history. It is clear, however, that the ability to experience fear has definite adaptive value. So long as the fear is only of mild or moderate intensity, it has primarily an energizing effect upon the subject, preparing him, in Cannon's famous phrase, "for fight or flight." Under the influence of fear, many a person has performed feats of which he would not ordinarily have been capable.

Anxiety

Closely related to fear, but psychologically distinguishable from it, is the phenomenon of anxiety. The physiological components of anxiety are probably the same as those of fear. (Whether or not there are subtle biochemical—hormonal—differences is a disputed question.) The subjective components are similar to those of fear, but they have a more "diffuse" quality since the perception of a specific, dangerous feature in the environment is lacking. Anxiety may, in fact, be defined as *a fear-like emotion not referable to an external danger*. Anxiety is a universal human experience, and (unlike fear) it comes close to being an uniquely human experience; except under rare and somewhat artificial conditions, such as laboratory experiments, members of other species appear not to experience anxiety.

---

* For this reason, one may properly speak of *panic state* as a psychosis.

Like fear, anxiety is a very uncomfortable state; like fear, it is capable of many gradations of intensity; like fear, in its extreme forms anxiety may result in a condition indistinguishable (clinically) from panic and usually given the same name. Like fear, in its milder forms anxiety has a clear-cut adjustment value, influencing the subject toward a greater intensity (or a different type) of adjustment effort than he might otherwise have made.

A medical student, during his first weeks on the psychiatric service of a general hospital, experienced mild feelings of anxiety. (There was essentially no *fear*, since the patients were not grossly destructive and the staff appeared competent.) The student's natural curiosity and inclination to learn were reinforced by the anxiety feelings, and he made an exceptionally vigorous effort to master the didactic material and to understand his own reactions and those of the patients to whom he was assigned. By the end of this period on the service, the student found that his anxiety had begun to diminish, and his instructor considered him to have become one of the most effective students in his section.

Anxiety is probably best considered as a learned way of responding, ultimately traceable to fear-producing experiences, i.e., to fearful experiences in the individual's past, usually his remote past.

An adolescent is brought to the receiving ward of a hospital in an acute attack of anxiety, with palpitation, rapid pulse, sighing respiration, and excessive perspiration. He is tense and somewhat hyperalert. He knows that he feels "frightened," but he cannot explain the source of the feeling even to himself.

Psychiatric interviews gradually bring to light what the boy has been unaware of, namely that he has been experiencing sexual tension and has had the impulse to masturbate. He "fears" this tension and its impulse, because of the unconscious conviction that to yield to such an expression would bring about various dire consequences.

At the time of the attack, there was no basis for actual fear, inasmuch as no one was aware of his sexual impulses and, with discretion on his part, no one need have become aware of masturbatory gratification. However, during the course of psychotherapy the patient eventually was able to recall having been terribly—and quite consciously—frightened by real threats of drastic punishment from his father in connection with some tentative masturbatory activity much earlier in his childhood.

It would not be correct to say that anxiety is merely repressed fear. On the one hand, the anxiety experience itself—the actual sensations—is fully conscious. On the other hand, even though repression (p. 41) has often been heavily involved in the background stages leading up to the anxiety, a complete removal of the repression still does not reveal any actual danger in the environment. What one can say is that in anxiety some aspect of the personality is responding *as if* something dangerous were happening *within* the organism. (In the example cited, the "something dangerous" would be the mounting pressure of libido.) One can say further that, if one can investigate the psychological situation thoroughly, the "dangerous" inner force has usually come to be thus regarded on the basis of old, repressed experiences linking it with an external danger. (In the example cited, sexual feelings had become linked with the likelihood of punishment by father.)

There is yet more to be said about anxiety (further clarification of its role in human behavior will be offered in the clinical sections of this book) but it is necessary now to go on to discuss briefly two other emotional states which, like fear and anxiety, may come into conflict with motivations deriving from the basic drives. These are feelings of *guilt* and feelings of *shame*.

Guilt Feelings

Not so much is known physiologically about the state of guilt as about fear and anxiety. There is some indication that gastric function may be reduced, and there may be alterations in posture and gait, such that the carriage is less erect and the step less resilient. Subjectively there is generalized discomfort akin to that in anxiety and, more specifically, there is *a feeling of self-condemnation*.

There is no evidence to indicate that infants (or, for that matter, animals other than man) are capable of experiencing a sense of guilt. On the other hand, children past the age of about six years evidently experience guilt in much the same fashion as do adults. As will be described in Chapter 4, it is during the time between these two periods that events take place in the course of human development which result in the formation of *conscience*.* Guilt feelings may properly be called the disapproving function of conscience. (To anticipate the developmental story, it may be said that ultimately guilt feelings are traceable to an *internationalization* of parental authority, to an unconscious, self-administered punishment or expectation of punishment which is deemed justified.)

Feelings of Shame

A sense of shame is similar to a sense of guilt in many respects. A significant point of difference appears to be that it is far less related to the disapproving function of conscience and more related to some disfigurement of the idealized image which an individual tends to hold of himself and which he wishes others to hold of him. Thus a sense of shame is more readily influenced by the responses of other persons than

---

* The technical term for that aspect of the mind which exercises conscience-functions is *superego*. (See pp. 73 to 74.)

is a sense of guilt. (Ultimately, feelings of shame are traceable to an unconscious expectation of abandonment by parental figures, because one is not living up to what is expected of him.)

To summarize what has been said about the opposing forces in intrapersonal conflicts: (1) Conflicts between two (or more) of the basic drives, while not uncommon, are not, as a rule, of much psychological significance. (2) Of the basic drives and related motivational states, libidinal strivings, hostile strivings, and dependency strivings are of the greatest importance in the production of conflict. (3) The principal inner forces which come into opposition to the drives are fear, anxiety, guilt, and shame.*

TYPES OF CONFLICT

An additional way of classifying intrapersonal conflicts—one which is of great clinical significance—is to divide them into *realistic conflicts* and *(psycho)neurotic conflicts*. A realistic conflict is one into which an individual is drawn on the basis of objective considerations, consciously and accurately perceived and interpreted. Such a conflict may involve a clash between two of the basic drives; more significantly it will involve a clash between one of the basic drives and fear or a realistic (socially accepted) sense of guilt or shame. A neurotic conflict is one into which the individual is drawn on the basis of highly subjective considerations, and it invariably involves unconscious components. It involves a clash between libidinal, hostile, or dependency strivings, on the one hand, and anxiety or feelings of guilt and/or shame, often unrealistic, on the other.

It is essential to distinguish between *(psycho)neurotic conflict* and *(psycho)neurosis* (cf. pp. 74 and 75 and Chap. 9). The vicissitudes of human development are such that no individual reaches maturity with a perfect capacity for adjustment. No one is able to deal with every situation realistically; thus everyone is beset to some degree with neurotic conflicts. On the other hand, a neurosis is, by definition, an illness; it is marked by rather well defined clinical symptoms. Obviously, then, it is by no means true that everyone has a neurosis.

ORGANIZATION OF THE MIND

For a very long time, philosophers and religious thinkers have endeavored to conceptualize the organization of the mind, to visualize some grouping of its several principal types of functioning which would furnish the basis for deeper understanding. More recently, psychologists and psychiatrists have contributed their efforts to this undertaking.

---

* Some authorities find it useful to distinguish a fifth inner force which operates against drives, namely, *disgust*.

Scientifically speaking, none of these attempts has proved thoroughly satisfactory; very likely all of them have involved a degree of arbitrariness, of oversimplification, of undue objectification.

In this book, for the most part, no attempt will be made to place a heavy reliance upon any scheme of "mental structure"; in the main, the discussions will attempt to remain rather close to matters of direct observation or immediate inference. Yet, since it is impossible to do much in the way of collateral reading without encountering references to the hypothetical organization or "structure" of the mind and since brief portions of the more theoretical discussions to follow will make use of such references, a brief presentation will be offered of the model which deservedly enjoys the widest acceptance in modern psychiatry, the psychoanalytic conceptualization of the structure of the mind as consisting of three aspects or components: *id, ego,* and *superego.*

Id

Considering the range of mental phenomena in man, with their refinements and complexities, one realizes that the basic drives are much more like one another than they are like other aspects of mental life. They are universal. They are built in (or, in any case, acquired very early in infancy). They have a primitive, elemental character. To put it simply, they have an animal character: counterparts of the basic drives are to be found in most of the animal kingdom. Above all, they are forces: they stand in somewhat the same relationship to the organism-as-a-whole as do various forms of fuel to an engine.*

If one is to use some device or model to represent the different functional groupings or aspects of the mind, the drives (with all of their component and derivative impulses) seem naturally to belong to the same aspect and to be in some fashion distinct from other aspects. The name that has been given to the functional grouping of the instinctual forces is the *id*. This term (the Latin word for *it*) was adopted to indicate the primitive, rather impersonal nature of the forces clustered there.

It is held that, under normal conditions, these forces remain for the most part unconscious. However, they exert a continuous pressure upon the rest of the mental apparatus, making their presence known through specific sensations, desires, feelings, and thoughts, which are consciously perceived.

---

* It is not quite correct to say that the drives are *energy*. Rather they are *forms* by which energy is transmitted to the mental apparatus. The ultimate *sources* of "psychic energy" are essentially the same physicochemical changes which yield energy to other functions of the organism.

Ego

At the outset of life, the mind of the infant has not yet had the opportunity to acquire faculties. All that is working are the built-in elements. At one time it was said that the mind of the young infant is all id. Since then, it has been recognized that the statement was an oversimplification. It is more accurate to say that the mind of the young infant is quite undifferentiated. The infant mind is, however, in general, more like the id portion of the adult mind than like any other portion (see Chap. 4). It follows from the undifferentiation that the conflicts of earliest infancy are not *internal* (intrapersonal, endopsychic) conflicts. They do not take place between one functional agency or aspect of the mind and another, but between forces of the id-mind and environmental forces. In terms of the discussion on page 64, they are all conflicts of type 1 or 2.

Since the adaptive techniques of the infant mind are few and inadequate, the forces of the environment impinge upon it with an intensity almost never equaled in later life. Furthermore, inner stimuli, manifestations of the basic drives, are very strong and compel it to contact its environment, seeking relief of tensions. In consequence of this interaction between the id-mind and the environment (especially other human beings), a portion of the mind gradually becomes altered, taking on new characteristics and eventually acquiring a certain autonomy. This altered portion is called the *ego* (the Latin word meaning I).[4]

As a result of the circumstance that the ego is not built in,* as is the id, but is developed, it is the most "personalized" portion of the mental apparatus, the portion of one's mind that is most nearly unique. (One's environment plays a critical part in this development, and no two environments are ever exactly alike.)

Earlier in this book (p. 30) it was said that the function of the mind was adjustment. It should now be added that capacities for adjustment come to localize, so to speak, in the ego. The ego consists of the *executive faculties of the mind*. It controls perceptive activity, integrative activity (memory, interpretation of stimuli, etc.), and motor activity.

With this picture of the nature of the ego, one can understand that, *once having become differentiated from the id, the ego frequently comes into conflict with it*. This statement is merely a specific, technical way of indicating that, once a portion of the mind has been altered by the environment (by experience), the possibility exists for conflict *within* the mind and no longer only between the mind and the external

---

* One might say, however, that a *capacity* for ego formation is built in.

world. This fact deserves elaboration, for it underlies much of human progress, much of human distress, and all of the functional (non-organic) mental illnesses.

To speak a bit figuratively, one may say that, once the ego has begun to form, the forces of the id have no direct contact with objective reality, but are "buried" deep within the mind. The ego, on the other hand, is in continuous contact with reality; it has been shaped by reality; and it maintains recognition of certain facts of reality. Considerations such as those of time and place, safety and danger, possibility and impossibility, are all functions of the ego. Figuratively speaking, the id can only say: "Want this! Need that! Satisfy!" All too often, if the organism were to yield unreservedly to the promptings of the id drives, the result would be suffering or danger, far outweighing in the long run the pleasure of immediate instinctual gratification. Since the ego, as the "executive of the mind," has control of the motor apparatus, to a great extent it can determine whether or not a basic drive is to obtain gratification. That is, approaching and making use of an object of a given drive is usually dependent upon motor activity, which is controlled by the ego. Furthermore, since the ego is the agency of the mind in closest contact with the environment, i.e., in control of the sensory apparatus, it can exercise a selective action on sensory stimuli coming to the individual from the outside. The ego can direct *attention* toward one object and away from another; if necessary, it can *repress* (p. 41) certain perceptions altogether and in this way exercise a further blocking effect on gratification of drives. If a person cannot perceive an object suitable for a given drive, the drive is blocked as effectively as if the object were recognized but motor activity were prevented.

As everyone knows, however, such inhibition of instinctual demands is not a simple or a painless affair. The ego is closer to reality, but the id is closer to the fundamental biology of the organism. If the id's demands are frustrated (blocked), the result is apt to be tension and discomfort.

It is now possible to return to the phenomenon of anxiety and to express with somewhat greater precision the nature of this experience. In the small infant, anxiety, like the other emotions, is experienced by the mind in a general way (diffusely): it is not, so to speak, localized in any one aspect or agency of the mind. As soon as the ego has begun to develop, however, anxiety (like the other emotions) becomes primarily an ego experience.

Anxiety was described (p. 66) as a reaction to the perception of something within the subject regarded as dangerous. Now, an inner, like an outer, danger is a relative matter; i.e., it is a factor which exceeds or threatens to exceed the adaptive capacities of the individual.

Hence another way of describing anxiety would be to say that it signifies a threatened loss of ego control, an inadequacy of the ego to cope with whatever conflict the personality may be struggling with.

For a while in the early history of the individual, anxiety is merely something which happens *to* the mind; then it is something which localizes in the ego, but is still passively experienced. Another step may now be mentioned. In the course of time, the ego acquires the capacity actively to summon up small amounts of anxiety (through its control over the function of memory) and to use them. In effect, the ego uses mild anxiety as a warning to itself and to the personality in general, as a warning and as a weapon in the ego's struggle against the id forces. Anxiety is utilized as a means of subduing instinctual drives, of reminding the personality, so to speak, that the gratification of a given drive would be, in some sense, dangerous. An example may serve to clarify the point.

A patient revealed to his psychiatrist that he became anxious whenever he was in a situation that offered an opportunity to steal. In the course of a number of interviews it was brought out that, in a setting of considerable emotional deprivation, the patient had, as a young child, developed impulses to steal the property of other children. When these impulses were gratified, severe punishment resulted. In such situations, the developing ego of the young child experienced fear.

The emotional deprivation continued for a number of years, and the impulses to steal also persisted. As the patient grew older, his ego resisted these impulses, even in the absence of any direct threat from the environment, by summoning up a feeling of anxiety.

The adolescent boy who was brought to the receiving ward in an acute attack of anxiety (p. 67) also illustrates this process. Here the id impulses were not hostile, but sexual. As in the case above, they were combated by the boy's ego through the use of anxiety. However, in this instance, a further development occurred, inasmuch as severe *symptoms* were in evidence.

In this case the anxiety itself became so great, once it had been called up, that it ceased to act in the service of the ego and, in fact, caused a temporary breakdown of ego function. As a result, the boy's behavior became less adaptive and was overtly symptomatic.

Superego

To round out this picture of the mental apparatus, it is necessary to introduce a third aspect of the mind, used in modern psychology along with the id and ego concepts, the *superego*. (Latin for "higher self.") The idea of this functional grouping is, perhaps, more readily understandable than those of the id or ego, since it has a considerable degree of correspondence to the popular idea, *conscience*. The scientific view of this mental agency is that, like the ego, it is not built into the organism; it is not transmitted by the genes; it is developed.*

The superego is considered to be a further differentiation of a portion of the ego. As mentioned above, the ego develops out of the id-mind of the infant under the influence of the environment. The superego also develops under the influence of the environment; not, however, of the entire environment, but, rather, of quite specific portions of it. The environmental objects that are of the greatest importance in shaping a person's superego are the authority figures with whom he first comes in contact, his father and mother. Further aspects of the development of the superego will be brought out in the next chapter, but it should be added at this point that authority figures other than parents also play a part in shaping the superego, figures such as older relatives, teachers, and religious leaders.

The principal difference between the concept, *superego,* and the popular concept, *conscience,* is that, whereas the latter almost always refers (in ordinary speech) to standards, promptings, and prohibitions of which the individual is conscious, the former is more extensive, involving mental activity which may be conscious, preconscious, or unconscious.† In this book, the term, conscience, will, for the most part, be retained, but it will be used as synonymous with the term, superego; i.e., it will be used to refer to inner standards and warnings and to self-approval and self-disapproval at any of the three levels of awareness.

Defense Mechanisms (of the Ego)

The expression, "defense mechanisms," or "defense mechanisms of the ego," is widely used in psychoanalytic psychiatry to designate *certain specific adjustment techniques,* an understanding of which is of fundamental importance to an understanding of inner conflicts and thus of the behavior that springs therefrom (including those forms of behavior considered to be symptomatic of illness).[3]

The word, "defense," is used in this expression because these technics are devices whereby a portion of the mind defends itself against experiencing those disturbing emotions—fear, anxiety, guilt, and shame—which, as we have seen (pp. 65 to 69), often arise in opposition to the

---

* Again, as in the case of the ego, it probably would be more nearly accurate to say that it is not built into the organism as a finished product, ready to unfold; it is probable that a *capacity* for superego formation is built in.

† Strictly speaking, psychoanalytic literature makes a further distinction, as follows: *superego* is used to refer to the prohibitions of the parents which become a part of the child's mind, and the term, *ego ideal,* is used to indicate the standards and ideals of the parents which become a part of the child's mind. The portion of the ego ideal which is conscious is much larger, relative to the whole, than is the portion of the superego which is conscious. For the sake of simplicity, the term, ego ideal, will not be used in this book.

demands of the basic drives. The phrase, "of the ego," is frequently used in the expression to indicate that, once it has begun to coalesce, *it is the executive aspect of the mind (the ego) which utilizes these mechanisms.*

As a matter of fact, in view of the last-mentioned circumstance, *a neurotic conflict* may be re-defined (in terms of the schematic representation of the mental structure) as *a conflict, largely unconscious, between the ego and the id.*[1] (The ego is, however, in most instances, acting largely under superego pressure.)

Although it is not implied in the expression, "defense mechanisms of the ego," it should be stated, before going further, that *all of these technics can be brought into action unconsciously.* (In fact, all but one of them—sublimation—are regularly utilized thus.)

Various authorities have delineated these mechanisms in slightly different ways; thus the *number* of distinct mechanisms which appear in discussions of this topic varies, as, to a lesser extent, do the *names* given to the mechanisms. The following brief discussion relies primarily on the presentation of Anna Freud,* the first author to give the subject full and systematic treatment. The list of mechanisms which will be referred to in the present book are as follows: (1) sublimation, (2) regression, (3) repression, (4) denial, (5) reaction-formation, (6) projection, (7) introjection, (8) isolation, (9) undoing, (10) turning against the self, and (11) displacement. These technics will now be considered in turn.

1. SUBLIMATION has already been illustrated and discussed (p. 59), and also defined as follows: *a technique of adjustment, through which a drive is, as it were, deflected into other channel(s) of discharge, channel(s) affording a release of tension facilitating the maintenance of the individual's state of equilibrium.* It should be added that, in a great majority of instances, the activity which constitutes the sublimation will be one which is socially approved. More importantly, it should be stated that *sublimation is the sole mechanism of the list whose utilization is never pathogenic* (psychologically speaking). The aim and/or the object of the sublimated drive has been altered, but release is not blocked. Sublimation may or may not offer a thoroughly adequate solution to the problem with which the personality is confronted, but it never leads to symptom formation.

2. REGRESSION may be defined as *a psychological process whereby the personality (or portions of it) retraces developmental steps, going back to earlier interests, modes of gratification, and problems.*

An example of regression would be the resumption of infantile atti-

---

* Freud, A.: The Ego and the Mechanisms of Defence, New York, Internat. Univ. Press, 1946.

tudes and behavior in a child of three years upon the birth of a sibling. Another example would be the child-like enthusiasm and temporary shift in values, sometimes voluntary and sometimes involuntary, which is often a feature of an adult's recreational activities (games and sports). The latter instance would usually be relaxing, invigorating, and therefore beneficial; if kept within reasonable bounds, it would not be pathogenic. On the other hand, unless carefully handled, the former instance could be distinctly pathogenic. Yet one assumes (and, when adequate investigative technics can be applied, one finds the assumption confirmed) that, even in instances such as the former, the process gets under way as a means of attempted adjustment. That is to say, the child in the example sought (unconsciously) to avoid certain problems of his age—including the problems of being an older sibling—by becoming a baby again. The trouble is that the psychological cost of attempting to turn the clock back in this way is usually excessive, resulting in further frustrations and maladjustment.

It should, perhaps, be mentioned that, of all the defense mechanisms, regression (when pathogenic) gives the strongest appearance of *happening to the personality*, rather than having been actively (albeit unconsciously) brought into play by the ego. The significance of this observation is not, however, really clear.

3. REPRESSION has been multiply illustrated and briefly defined in Chapter 2 (pp. 39 to 41). The definition may be rephrased as follows: *repression is the psychological technique whereby thoughts, emotions, and/or sensations are thrust out and kept out of awareness.*

4. DENIAL has strong similarities to repression, but differs in that it is directed, not against unwanted stimulation from within the personality, but against some disturbing aspect(s) of the environment. It may be defined as *the technique whereby the ego refuses to allow awareness of some unpleasant or threatening aspect(s) of external reality.* The following anecdote illustrates this mechanism.

A small child has been promised that he will be taken to the zoological gardens to see the animals. The automobile breaks down, and the family is obliged to stay at home. All afternoon the child keeps saying, "Bobby going to zoo now. Bobby going to zoo now."

Whereas the use of denial is perfectly normal in the above illustration, in which it is made possible by the subject's immaturity, this mechanism clearly involves a defective or incomplete appraisal of reality ("reality testing"). Hence it is a sign of illness if used to any great extent by an adult, as in the following example.

A mother lost her son in battle. The young man had been almost her exclusive interest in life. Despite having received official confirmation of his death, she continued to deny this fact in words and actions. She went about, speaking of him as if he were alive and making preparations for his return.

5. REACTION-FORMATION may be defined as *the mechanism whereby an original attitude or set of feelings is replaced in consciousness by the opposite attitude or feelings.* As will be further clarified in the following chapter, reaction-formation plays a part in normal personality development. For example, in the course of learning socially approved habits of elimination, the child must alter his original attitudes toward excretory processes and products. Although reaction-formation can thus be of adaptive value, when it is used to any considerable degree by an older child or an adult, it imparts a certain *rigidity* to the personality, since it involves a rather forcible wrenching of the personality make-up. Here are two examples of its use by adults as a major technique of defense.

Troubled by various severe conflicts, a young man became a chronic alcoholic. When intoxicated, he became very aggressive and provoked fights with his companions. He experienced a series of reverses, losing his friends and his job, and becoming estranged from his wife and his children, whom he antagonized and humiliated. Eventually, the man dropped out of sight for several years.

When he returned to his native city, he had become a preacher of a small and radical sect, and he was a teetotaler. He acquired a pulpit and became known for his fiery, aggressive sermons. His favorite theme was the description of the severe punishments to be visited in the world to come upon any of his congregation who touched a drop of liquor.

Although the stern and forbidding nature of the man's personality prevented him from having many close friends, his wife and his children returned to him, and he came to be held in considerable esteem in the community.

A young matron was a leading figure in the local S.P.C.A. (Society for the Prevention of Cruelty to Animals). She suffered from certain neurotic symptoms (obsessions) and for this reason was led to enter psychoanalytic treatment. In the course of her analysis, she recalled a number of situations in her early childhood in which she had derived pleasure from tormenting small animals.

6. PROJECTION is illustrated in the following examples.

A tired and fretful little child is taken to bed by his mother and told that he must take a nap. The child's instantaneous inner feeling is one of anger at his mother, but awareness of this emotion would be productive of too much anxiety, so the child's conscious feeling, which he promptly expresses, is, "You're mean, Mommie! You don't like me!"

A student is constrained to spend an evening studying a subject that is very difficult for him. He finds the work quite unpleasant, and, rather than recognizing his own inadequacy, he *projects* the blame wherever he can—to the uncomfortably hot weather, to the inconsiderate person playing the radio in the next room, to the excessively strict instructor giving the assignment.

A married man in early middle age begins to experience strong impulses toward infidelity. His conscience is sufficiently strong to prevent his acting directly upon these impulses or even to be fully aware of them. After a time, he begins to develop the idea that his wife is uninterested in him. Eventually, he comes to believe that she is entertaining other men. He spends much time and effort in an attempt to establish the validity of this completely false idea.

The first illustration is, of course, of no pathological significance (although it would probably have to be considered pathological if it were the invariable response to nap-time), in view of the subject's immaturity. The second illustration is sufficiently mild that it, too, would be considered to be within normal limits of experience. As can readily be seen, however, the third illustration is decidedly pathological, and, in fact, represents a *paranoid reaction* (pp. 390 to 395).

From these examples, one can arrive at a definition of *projection: it is the mechanism whereby feelings, wishes, or attitudes, originating within oneself, are attributed to other persons or to features of the environment.*

7. INTROJECTION is, in some respects, the opposite of projection, and it may be defined as *the mechanism whereby a quality or attribute of another person is taken into and made a part of the subject's personality*. Introjection may be regarded as the psychological counterpart of the biological mechanism of eating: in both phenomena something is taken in from the outside and made a part of oneself. (Indeed, the expression, "oral incorporation" is sometimes used synonymously with introjection.) Introjection is obviously similar to ordinary *imitation*, but it occurs automatically, involuntarily, and unconsciously, and is therefore much deeper-going than imitation.

Introjection of parental characteristics has a great deal to do with the shaping of a child's personality (and thus, indirectly, even with certain aspects of his appearance, as, for example, habitual types of facial expression, of gait, and of posture). On the other hand, the same technique or something very like it is, on occasion, used in later life. The popular notion that a husband and wife who have been married for a long time, particularly if the emotional attachment is quite strong, "grow to look like one another" probably contains an element of truth. This element rests upon a process of mutual (partial) introjection. (Some authorities prefer the term, *identification*, for the process of "growing like" someone, once early childhood is past, i.e., once an appreciable amount of ego development has taken place. In this book, however, no distinction will be made between the two terms.)

8. ISOLATION is the *psychological process whereby the actual facts of an experience are allowed to remain in consciousness, but the associative linkages between these facts and the related emotions or impulses are broken, with the latter becoming lost to consciousness.* The adaptive value of this mechanism can be clearly seen from the following example.

A medical student, working for the first time in an anatomy laboratory, will often "wall off" some of the emotional responses elicited by the bodies, thus being able to concentrate his full attention (while in the laboratory) and his full capacity of memory (when reviewing anatomical facts later) on the intellectual aspects of the situation.

On the other hand, since the technique blocks expression or even recognition of powerful feelings, it prevents any sort of release and thus can lead to a build-up of inner tensions.

9. UNDOING is illustrated in the following famous examples.

When, in the biblical narrative, Pontius Pilate washes his hands in the presence of the crowd (Matthew 27:24), it is his intention to divest himself of the guilt connected with the trial of Jesus.*

When Lady MacBeth rubs her hands endlessly, as if washing them, she is attempting to undo the crimes which she and her husband have committed.*

This mechanism may be defined as *the psychological process in which a specific action is performed that is (unconsciously) considered to be in some sense the opposite of a previously occurring unacceptable action or wish and thus to "neutralize" or "erase" it.* In scientific usage, the term, undoing, does not refer to an efficacious righting of a wrong or correction of an error.

10. TURNING AGAINST THE SELF—a cumbersome but almost self-explanatory phrase—*is the psychological process whereby a drive or an emotion (usually aggressive-hostile) is diverted from its original object and made to operate against the subject, in whole or in part.*

Consider again the second example used to illustrate reaction-formation (p. 77). Suppose that the young woman had had both a slightly stronger *sadistic* drive (urge to gain pleasure through tormenting other creatures) and a more punitive superego. In such a case, the defense against the anxiety and guilt which would attend indulgence of the

---

* It might be argued that these examples are not quite apt, since the subjects made certain *conscious* connections between the ritualistic acts and their offenses. Yet, what was presumably in their minds without being conscious was the wishful belief that the acts might really undo or mitigate the offenses in some fashion.

cruel impulses might have been to turn the drive around, so to speak, so that it operated against her own person. The result would have been that the young woman would have become a *masochist* (one who takes pleasure in being hurt or humiliated).

11. DISPLACEMENT is the *psychological process whereby certain drives or certain emotions are (unconsciously) transferred from one object, activity, or situation to another (which has been given a similar meaning)*. This mechanism is fairly often recognized by the layman, and it is sometimes used in the theatre for either comic or tragic effects (depending upon the intensity and the nature of the drive or emotion which is displaced). An example would be an individual who perforce accepts a reprimand from a superior and then releases his anger by abusing a subordinate or, perhaps, by kicking his dog or an inanimate object (without seeing the connection between the two episodes).

A little reflection will indicate that there is considerable overlapping among these mental devices. Thus, for example, sublimation can well be considered to be based upon displacement in some instances. Repression has features in common with isolation and with denial. As a matter of fact, one could perhaps say that there is an element of repression in all of the other mechanisms, inasmuch as they operate unconsciously.

Other Ego Techniques

It is also true that there are other operations which the ego undertakes in an effort to reduce or to avoid inner distress, operations which might be thought to have some claim to inclusion in a list such as has just been surveyed. For instance, there is the technique called *suppression* and defined as *the voluntary denial of attention to an emotion, impulse, or thought*. There are also some rather complex, although commonly used, technics, such as *rationalization* ("the grapes were probably sour anyway").

Suppression is not included in the list of "defense mechanisms" because it does not fulfill the criteria of being unconscious and involuntary. Rationalization is usually not included because it is held to be analyzable into simpler components (projection, denial, etc., as the case may be).

Thoughts along these lines do not invalidate attempts to categorize and describe the devices by which the ego participates in or attempts to deal with endopsychic conflicts. They do suggest, however, that, helpful as such attempts are, it is a bit arbitrary and, by comparison with nature, a bit clumsy to make separate (let alone, hard-and-fast) categories of mental subtleties such as we have been considering.

At one time of life or another, under one set of circumstances or another, any of the defense mechanisms may be used—at least to some degree—without giving rise to psychopathology. On the other hand, as has been indicated, every one of them except sublimation has a price-tag attached. The price takes the form of a surrender by the personality of a portion (sometimes small, sometimes large) of its ability to appraise and its freedom to deal rationally with the situations it confronts. If any of the mechanisms except sublimation is used extensively, the personality quite often finds itself in a more difficult or a less satisfactory situation than the one which it attempted to solve in the first instance.

Further references to these technics will be made in the following chapter on personality development and in the chapters on psychiatric disorders. A working knowledge of them is of high value to the physician in the evaluation and treatment of psychiatric illness and in any appraisal of human nature. It is suggested that the student review the list carefully.

Bibliography

1. Fenichel, O.: The Psychoanalytic Theory of Neurosis, New York, Norton, 1945.
2. Fletcher, R.: Instinct in Man, New York, Internat. Univ. Press, 1957.
3. Freud, A.: The Ego and the Mechanisms of Defence, New York, Internat. Univ. Press, 1946.
4. Freud, S.: The Ego and the Id, London, Hogarth, 1927.
5. Hartman, H.: Comments on the psychoanalytic theory of the drives, Psychoanal. Quart. *17*:368-388, 1948.

Suggestions for Further Reading

Brenner, C.: An Introductory Textbook of Psychoanalysis, New York, Internat. Univ. Press, 1955.
Fletcher, R.: Instinct in Man, New York, Internat. Univ. Press, 1957.
Freud, S.: New Introductory Lectures on Psychoanalysis, Chapter 3, New York, Norton, 1933.
———: A General Introduction to Psychoanalysis, Chapters 20-22, Garden City, New York, Permabooks (Doubleday), 1938.

CHAPTER 4

Personality Development

Chapters 2 and 3 have been devoted to a presentation of certain fundamentals of the (adult) human mind, certain principles of its function and organization. A thorough understanding of psychiatric disorders requires that this information be supplemented by a developmental account. The question, "What is this patient like?" can best be pursued against the background of the question, "How did he get to be the way he is?" Anatomy and pathology can be better understood in the light of embryology; psychology and psychiatry can be better understood in the light of developmental psychology.

HUMAN DEVELOPMENT: PHYSIOLOGICAL AND PSYCHOLOGICAL

For convenience in discussion and comprehension, it is customary to divide the developmental history of the human personality into seven phases, as follows: *the period of infancy* (birth to about age 1½); *the muscle-training period* (1½ to about 2½); *the family triangle period* (2½ to about 6); *the latency period* (6 until puberty); *puberty* (11 or 12 to 13 or 14); *adolescence* (from the end of puberty until 18 or 20); and *adulthood*.

There are two other periods of life, which, while not, strictly speaking, developmental, are very generally characterized by specific features of their own: *the period of involution* ("change of life") and *the period of old age*. These stages will also be considered in the course of the present discussion.

As is true of almost all types of biological development, one personality phase blends into the next; hence a division such as the one just outlined is, to a degree, arbitrary. Certain strivings and certain personality characteristics and techniques of adjustment come into existence in connection with the maturational and experiential features of a portion of the developmental story. They do not disappear abruptly with the transition to the next phase, but fade into the background, where they may remain alongside of other strivings, characteristics and techniques which are currently being developed. Nevertheless, there are certain nodal points of development which form the core of each period, distinguishing it from the others and thereby making this theoretical arrangement a suitable one.

OBTAINING DATA ON EARLY DEVELOPMENTAL PERIODS

A question which naturally arises in the student's mind has to do with the obtaining of psychological data on the earlier developmental periods. The point at which a child becomes willing and able to use introspection and to communicate the results of introspection to an observer in a comprehensible fashion varies considerably from one individual to another, but obviously it comes after a number of the very important early phases. Furthermore, the ordinary memory span of an older child or of an adult does not include events of the first couple of years of life. Yet this information is of very great theoretical importance. How, then, is it obtained?

There are four principal lines of approach to this objective: direct observation, often supplemented by special techniques; experimental regression; naturally occurring regression (mental illnesses); and psychotherapeutic techniques. These will be briefly discussed.

Direct Observation

Direct observation of infants and small children has, of course, always been available as a means of study. Until relatively recent times, however, scientific interest in such observation has been rather limited. The observers were principally parents and those entrusted with the care of children; in other words, the observers were subjectively involved to an extent which often precluded the gathering of reliable data and, to an even greater extent, the correct interpretation of the data. For instance, who would blame a young mother for insisting that the random smiling of her infant of one month was meant especially for her? Who, indeed, would wish her to think otherwise? And yet, of course, the truth is that at this age the infant is incapable of recognizing stimuli to an extent that would make possible such a specific response. Just as some inferences were made for which there were inadequate objective grounds, so other inferences were missed for which there were substantial grounds. For example, the sensuality of infants and small children was, until the present century, in large part, misinterpreted or ignored.

The principal element, then, which has made direct observation of infants and small children of greater scientific value in recent times has been in the observers themselves. If they are impartial, unprejudiced, and skilled, and if certain kinds of apparatus are available (such as the one-way vision screen and various recording devices), much useful data can be obtained. Simple experimental situations can be set up, and the responses of the subjects can be studied. Very likely the student will have had some introductory experiences of this sort in pediatrics.

Certain types of questions lend themselves to study through the supplementary use of various laboratory techniques, such as the electroencephalograph (a device for measuring very small changes in electrical potential of the brain or major portions of it) and the electromyograph (a device for measuring similar changes in muscles). If, for example, one wished to learn whether or not visual stimulation of a given sort would produce activity in the occipital cortex of the newborn, an electroencephalographic tracing from this area would establish the answer.

Experimental Regression

Another means of investigation depends upon the procedure called "experimental regression." This approach ordinarily involves the use of hypnosis. While the subject (an older child or an adult) is in the hypnotic trance, the suggestion is given that he will return (psychologically) to some time in his past life that it is desired to examine. It can be further suggested that, when the subject has "come back" from the regressed phase to his current status, he will recall his experiences and will be able to talk about them. In this way, the subject can use his mature powers of verbal communication to give the examiner his impressions of an earlier—sometimes even of a pre-verbal—period.

Study of Mental Illnesses

Another approach to the problem is offered by the study of adults (or older children) afflicted with certain severe types of mental illness, such as schizophrenia (p. 360). An emotional retreat from current realities (i.e., a *regression*) is characteristic of all forms of psychiatric illness, but it is especially marked in schizophrenia and certain other psychoses. At times the clinical situation may be similar to that of an experimental regression, insofar as the patient may be using the verbal facility of an adult to express some of the problems and conflicts of infancy.

As a matter of historical fact, this line of investigation was one of the first to yield extensive material about the inner workings of the infant mind. Of course, in using such an approach it is imperative that the investigator remain aware of two qualifying factors: (1) some of the infantile experiences being recalled may be quite atypical for infantile experiences in general, and (2) the illness frequently produces distortion both in recall and in reporting.

Psychotherapeutic Techniques

Finally, one may approach the problem through utilizing the increase in memory span that is a regular feature of a patient's experience in psychoanalysis or in an "uncovering" type of psychotherapy. In such a setting, the process of free-association* taking place under conditions of mutual trust and confidence, along with the spontaneous partial regression which is part of intensive psychotherapy or psychoanalysis, produces a heightened ability to recall experiences from the remote past, often including some experiences taking place before the (full) acquisition of speech. The same reservations as those mentioned in the preceding paragraph apply to this method of investigation, but less stringently, since the personalities of the subjects have, as a rule, large healthy components, not appreciably affected by the condition for which treatment is undertaken.

After infancy, but during the earlier years of childhood, there is, of course, an additional period during which the individual is still not able to use introspection and verbalization as can an adult. Considerable information regarding this developmental stage has been obtained through the method of observation last mentioned above. More recently, the direct psychoanalytic study of children has confirmed and expanded, and in some instances corrected the material thus obtained. Through various modifications in technique, such as the encouragement of expressive play, the child analyst can make it possible for the child to reveal a good deal about himself despite his inability to participate in an adult type of interview.

PHASES OF PERSONALITY DEVELOPMENT

Infancy†

As the student will realize from his work in the pediatric nursery, an outstanding characteristic of the newborn human infant is his helplessness. At first, one is apt to think of this characteristic very largely in motor terms, but it is far more pervasive than that. The mental intake is under as inadequate a control as the output.

---

* A description of psychoanalysis and other psychotherapeutic technics will be given in Chap. 14. *Free-association* is the process whereby the patient communicates to the therapist whatever thoughts emotions, and sensations pass through his mind, making no conscious effort to direct, edit, or organize these phenomena.

† The material in this and the following three developmental subdivisions is largely based upon the work of the Freuds, father and daughter and of Erik Erikson. See items 2, 5, and 6 in bibliography.

It must be remembered that the newborn has abruptly moved from his intra-uterine situation, one in which every need was satisfied automatically and continuously, to one in which, no matter how loving the attention, needs are met imperfectly, and in which there is a relatively enormous amount of stimulation. The young organism is bombarded with stimuli from without: visual, auditory, thermal, tactile, olfactory, gustatory, and painful. It is also bombarded with stimuli from within: hunger pains, the pangs of thirst, muscle sensations, etc.

It must be further realized that what we have called "the executive functions of the mind" have not yet developed, let alone been linked together into an operating mental system (the *ego*). In other words, the infant mind has only a very limited repertoire of technics available with which to cope with the excessive stimulation. For example, the active direction of *attention*—concentrating on certain stimuli and excluding others—is not yet possible. Nor is the infant mind capable of *organizing* the impressions it receives. Finally, although the infant is capable of a number of motor responses, at first it does not have sufficient control over the motor apparatus to make these responses adaptive.*

In pediatrics the student will have learned that the baby's first response to noxious stimuli, whether internal or external, is apt to be the so-called "mass reflex" response (crying and jerky movements of all extremities) that is usually recognized as a distress signal by those in attendance but is otherwise very largely nonadaptive. Somewhat later, the components of this response can be produced separately, but for some time the only voluntary acts of adaptive value of which the young infant is capable remain sucking, crying, and kicking.

It was mentioned earlier that the phylogenetic development of fear—and of anxiety—is not thoroughly understood. However, the ontogenetic development of these emotions (which are at first indistinguishable) is considered to begin in the experiences of the process of birth and of the earliest days of extra-uterine life. Not only is the stimulation intense, but insofar as the individual's control is concerned, things are never more "out of hand" than during and immediately after birth.[3]

It is generally understood by physicians that during the early weeks of life the infant is incapable of recognizing objects in his environment, animate or inanimate. What is equally important but somewhat less well understood is that the infant is also quite incapable of recognizing himself, in whole or in part. Yet these two abilities are so completely

---

* There is a neurological, as well as a psychological basis for this inadequacy of control over the voluntary musculature. At birth, the process of myelinization of pyramidal tract fibers is very incomplete. Myelinization proceeds rapidly at first and is largely complete by about age 5, but not entirely so until age 15.

interdependent that it is inevitable that they develop simultaneously. To know what constitutes one's self, one must know what is not-self.

Specific examples, illustrating the contrast in the process of perceiving-and-recognizing between an adult and a small infant, may make this important point clearer. The contrast is of clinical significance, for in certain forms of serious mental illness, the patient perceives in an infantile way and loses track of the boundary between self and not-self.

An adult looks at a shiny object such as a silver teaspoon. Physiologically speaking, the process begins with the stimulation of certain cells of the retinae, but the full process is quite a complex matter. It involves the *translation* of the stimulation into something *meaningful*. The quality of brightness or shininess is localized; that is, it is attributed to the exact region occupied by the silver. It is refined; that is, discrimination is made between the brightness of silver and other kinds of brightness, such as that of a mirror. Certain other attributes of the object, as for example, that of its spacial configuration, are also noted. On the basis of similar impressions stored in the memory, the whole group of closely related impressions deriving from the piece of silver is recognized, almost instantaneously and as a unit, as constituting one specific object, a silver spoon.

In the case of a young infant, whose eyes happened to turn in the direction of the spoon, the process would begin in exactly the same way, but the mind would not yet be capable of integrating and interpreting the stimuli. Not only would there be no memory, no recognition of the object, *but there would be no localizing of the source of the stimulation*. All that the infant would experience psychologically would be a generalized sensation of brightness.

It is much the same with stimuli arising from within. Consider the case of an adult with colitis. Sensory messages coming from the bowel are received, integrated, and interpreted. The distress is recognized as a cramping type of pain, differing in significant ways from other types of pain. Localization occurs; the individual is able to say (in at least a general way) what portion of his body is affected.

In a similar situation, the very young infant experiences intense distress but has no awareness of its meaning or source.

At a slightly later time, the infant begins to have vague perceptions of objects and of himself, but he cannot yet distinguish between the two. There is reason to believe, for example, that at this phase the infant regards the mother's breast (or the bottle held by the mother) as part of his own body. Certainly the mother's breast becomes important to the baby and is recognized by him before his own fingers and toes.[2]

Ordinarily the environment is favorable to the infant's growth and comfort. A cycle is repeated over and over: sleep, mounting inner tension from biological drives, wakefulness, crying, satisfaction of needs in the mother's arms and at the mother's breast, relaxation, and sleep again. At the same time that the infant receives bodily nourishment from the mother, he receives her love in other forms: warmth, closeness, caresses, fondling, and gentle voice. Indeed, food and love are at first, indistinguishable.

Soon a new phase makes its appearance. After immediate needs have been satisfied and before recourse to sleep, the infant continues to be active. He plays; he explores. In short, the baby begins to "catch up" with the stresses of existence and finds a gradually increasing amount of energy at his disposal.

Whereas the position of the young infant is actually one of complete dependence, the prompt satisfaction of his needs, taking place repeatedly before there is adequate recognition of objects, allows the infant to form a vague impression, *not of helplessness but of a kind of omnipotence* (given general recognition in the expression, "His Majesty, the baby"). Thus the sequence of biological need, wish for satisfaction of the need, and actual satisfaction, occurs often enough for the impression to be gained that the wish ensures its own satisfaction with as yet no understanding that an outside, independent agent is a necessary link in the chain of events. The existence of this phase—sometimes referred to as that of "infantile omnipotence"—is of great importance in the understanding of certain aspects of the psychoses, for in such conditions, the patient may return in various psychological respects to this very early stage and regain a feeling of this kind.

Under the pressure of urgent inner needs and in the absence of a firm grasp of reality, the normal infant has at times a satisfaction-producing experience of a sort not possible for older children or adults except in dreams or in serious mental illness: *hallucinations*. This phenomenon—*a sensory type of experience for which there is no external stimulation*—will be discussed more fully in the clinical portions of the book (see especially, p. 279). For the moment, the simplest way to regard the phenomenon is as a kind of vivid, waking dream. In other words, under the influence of a strong wish, the infantile personality is unable to distinguish the mental image of that which is desired from the actual object itself. Of course, the satisfaction thus produced can be only a temporary one. In the course of time, if real gratification of the need continues to be lacking, the inner tension mounts to a point at which it must be recognized. The following example is illustrative of this sequence.

An infant awakens under the stimulation of mild hunger. An observer can detect such indications of tension as restlessness and an unhappy expression with sporadic whimpering. After a few moments—there having been no relief—the infant is seen to assume a more relaxed position and to lie quietly, making sucking movements. This phase persists for several moments. Then, rather abruptly, the infant again shows that he is distressed. He moves his arms and legs and cries vigorously.

Another way of allaying oral tensions, somewhat closer to reality, is thumb-sucking. This maneuver can be regarded as a primitive kind of *sublimation* (p. 75). It can be seen that the act of suckling in the young infant serves both the self-preservative drives (p. 54) and the sexual-social drive. Insofar as it is the means of taking in nourishment and fluid, it is in the service of the drives, hunger and thirst. Insofar as it is in itself a source of physical pleasure to the infant, it is in the service of the sexual-social drive, As one would expect, thumb-sucking is a more successful technique in the relief of the infant's oral pleasure need than it is in the relief of the needs for food and fluid. Thus, when thumb-sucking is carried on in later developmental stages, the phenomenon is referable to ungratified pleasure needs much more than to ungratified nutritional needs (p. 519).

In time, the infant's recognition of the mother comes to include her entire person. The baby looks upon the mother as the source of relief of all unpleasant tensions. At first, the gratifications are fused; the baby takes in milk and love at the same time and indistinguishably. Gradually he learns to differentiate the two necessities and to appreciate them separately. As a rule, it is at about four months that the infant can distinguish clearly between his mother (or mother-figure) and any other person who may occasionally be in attendance upon him.

As was mentioned, the infant receives a very early impression of being omnipotent (if the ministrations of those caring for him are reasonably effective). In the natural course of events, however, this impression cannot long persist, since, even in the most considerate homes, there are periods of frustration. As a matter of fact, such experiences, if they are not excessive, are beneficial from a long-range point of view, inasmuch as it is largely through various incidental frustrations that a sense of reality can develop.

As the infant begins to become aware of his mother as a figure separate from himself and to lose his impression of being omnipotent, he tends naturally to attribute this quality of being all-powerful to the mother (and then to the father and perhaps to other adult figures as well).

This shift in perspective involves a loss of what, in an older person, would be called self-esteem. Inevitably the infant experiences a yearning somehow to regain the original feeling of omnipotence. The yearning cannot, of course, be fully or lastingly gratified, but a temporary and partial gratification is achieved through the psychological technique of *introjection* (p. 78). Insofar as the infant can feel himself to be, in some sense, one with the mother or other parent-figure, the feeling of omnipotence is restored for the moment and the self-esteem is enhanced.[3] The developmental significance of the use of the technique of introjection does not, however, lie in this partial and artificial restoration of the feeling of infantile omnipotence, but in the fact that the use of introjection results in the establishment of lasting identifications with various characteristics of the parents, i.e., it enriches the infant's personality. (As will be seen in the course of the ensuing discussion, the use of introjection is by no means limited to this very early period.)

The illusion of omnipotence is not given up easily. In diminishing degree, it persists for some time. In pathological cases, it is never given up entirely. As a rule, the child is able to give it up in large measure only because his ability for real, objective mastery over his environment steadily increases. The more his sense of security comes to be based upon actual ability, the more readily can the child accept the lesson presented by the inevitable further frustrations of life, namely, that neither he, nor his parents, nor yet any other human being, is omnipotent.

Mention of infantile frustrations leads to the point (previously referred to on p. 62) that these experiences are widely considered to be the source of human hostility. The sequence, *frustration* → *hostility*, appears to be automatic and inevitable. Whereas, in theory, the immediate gratification of every infantile and childhood need might preclude the development of hostile strivings, such a situation cannot exist in real life. And, indeed, this is just as well, for a child so reared would have a very imperfect grasp of reality and be totally unprepared for the vicissitudes of adult life. It is but the truth that there are some things about which a well-adjusted adult finds it natural and right to get angry. There are some things worth fighting for.

From the parents' standpoint, therefore, the problem of the infant's and child's frustrations is one of compromise, of seeing that the infant encounters a reasonable minimum of frustrations and that the young child encounters a carefully graded series of frustrations. In other words, the parents should offer maximum care and protection at first, and thereafter should keep their expectations in line with the child's capabilities. In this way, the child's aggressiveness and his capacity for hostility will develop normally.

A good bit more remains to be said about the instinctual, the emotional, and the beginnings of the social development of the infant. As it happens, all of these features come together in the act and situation of suckling.* It was noted above that this act procures for the infant

---

* They are not, of course, confined to this situation. Appropriate stimulation of the skin, for example, is an important factor in the growth of the infant's responsiveness and sense of identity. The latter is also dependent upon **proprioceptive stimulation.**[2]

Phases of Personality Development 91

the simultaneous satisfaction of both some of the drives of self-preservation and the sexual-social drive. At the outset, the self-preservative component is stronger and more evident, and it is as if the sexual-social component borrows strength from it. However this may be, the mouth is clearly the most significant part of the infant's body at this time, the most highly charged instinctually and emotionally.

As indicated in Chapter 3, although the mouth as a part of the body and oral types of gratification in general are, in the normal course of events, superseded in significance by other body areas and other types of gratification, the impact of this early period is never lost. A certain amount of the libidinal tension in older individuals continues to find release through oral channels. The *proportion* (as well as the absolute quantity, although this cannot be measured) of libido that retains oral objectives varies considerably from one individual to another. It is commonly known that, not only the basic pleasures of eating and drinking, but the derived pleasures, such as smoking and chewing gum, are more highly valued by some persons than by others. Within limits, such variations are of no psychopathological significance, although they are reflections of somewhat different experiences during the oral (infantile) period of development. They do contribute to the phenomenon of individual personality differences in later life (see Chap. 12). Moreover, if this stage is attended by unusual circumstances, the subject's oral needs may vary in kind or in degree beyond "normal limits."

The "fat lady" in the carnival side-show is much more likely to be suffering from a severe disorder in the development of her basic drives than from a primary disorder of her endocrine functions. Her daily diet of 6,000 calories is apt to be a manifestation of her excessive oral needs. (See discussion of obesity in Chap. 5.)

The special circumstances which produce such inordinate needs (aside from constitutional variations, which evidently exist, but of which not a great deal is yet known) may be grouped under three headings: excessive frustration, excessive gratification, or, more commonly, a combination of both. The third case would be exemplified by a situation in which the nutritional needs of the infant were met bounteously, while the related emotional needs were being severely frustrated.

An infant fed from a bottle-holder with a large nipplehole would receive his full nutritional requirements but no (attendant) gratification from his mother's presence and insufficient gratification of his sucking needs.

In such instances, the problems of the oral period are apt to become so severe that a relatively large portion of the libido cannot, so to speak, free itself with the passage of time to become available for other aims and other objects. This state of affairs is referred to as a *fixation*. As a definition, one may say that *fixation is that state in which personality development is arrested in one or more of its aspects at a level short of maturity.* Typically, the term is used to designate the condition in which the intellectual and physical aspects of development have continued, more or less on schedule, but the sexual-social and aggressive drives, in their various components, have retained the aims and objects of an early period of life. (So much depends upon the stage of development of these drives, however, that fixation may involve other aspects of the personality as well.)

We have spoken of emotional deprivation of the infant, and this usage may require further clarification. In the newborn infant, it is scarcely possible to speak of emotions in the ordinary sense. The stimulation impinging upon the infant mind, from within and without, induces painful tensions, and the infant desires to rid himself of these tensions. As we have seen, he does so through the use of a series of techniques of increasing complexity. Yet, as we have also noted, it is these very tensions that gradually force the infant mind to recognize objects.* It is only through objects—the mother's breast, the mother's arms—that the tensions can ultimately be relieved. There is no initial love of objects; they are only a means to the peaceful oblivion of sleep, the nearest possible approximation to the peace of the womb.[3]

Gradually, however, as the gratifying release from inner tension and the positive libidinal pleasure become closely associated, through repetition, with these objects—and with other manifestations of the mother's love, subtler and more difficult to specify—an answering feeling begins to be awakened in the infant. Although this feeling is, for a while very close to its instinctual sources, is still quite "selfish," it gradually begins to assume the characteristics of trust and of love.

For all mankind, therefore, the mother (or mother figure) is the first love object. Since there is usually no other object at this very early period, and since the infant is almost entirely dependent upon her, this relationship assumes an intensity that is seldom or perhaps never equaled. The precise nature of this relationship, the course it takes, and its eventual outcome are, therefore, of tremendous significance for the entire future pattern of the developing personality.

---

* The term, object(s), is a very broad one in much psychological and psychiatric discussion. In this book, it will be used to include inanimate objects, parts of human beings, and human beings themselves. The last-mentioned usage is becoming uncommon in ordinary speech, and hence may sound a bit strange though it is retained in a few expressions such as "the object of his affections."

Up to this point, the discussion has concerned itself largely with the normal course of events. Nevertheless, with an understanding of the significance of the mother-infant relationship, one can realize quite readily that any serious flaw in it will almost inevitably have far-reaching consequences with respect to the mental health of the individual, Thus it may not be surprising to learn that all of the more serious psychologically caused illnesses of human beings have a basis (not necessarily the only one, of course) in a disturbed mother-infant and/or mother-child relationship. This point will be again encountered in the clinical chapters of this book, where it will receive further discussion.

Period of Muscle Training

As indicated earlier, there is nearly always an overlapping of developmental stages. During the period of infancy, the new human being has not only learned to recognize his own body and to differentiate it from outside objects, but he has also begun to use the parts of his body in a meaningful fashion. His developing ego has started to coordinate both sensory impressions and motor responses and to integrate the two sets of activities. At six or eight months an infant will reach for and grasp a bright-colored object lying nearby, will turn it over with his hands, inspect it, and very likely put in into his mouth. At six to eight months, the infant has sufficient strength and coordination to sit upright unsupported; at eight to ten months, the development of the neuromuscular apparatus of speech has become sufficiently advanced to allow the infant to say monosyllables. At this age, the infant has evolved a means of moving about rather effectively, first creeping and then crawling. The first attempts at standing are also made at about ten months; at 11 to 12 months the infant stands with slight support, and soon thereafter he stands unsupported. The first few steps alone and the use of words for common objects have, as a rule, occurred by the end of the period of infancy.

In summation, a fair amount of motor development has thus taken place during infancy. It is, however, in the second developmental period (of the scheme outlined at the start of this chapter) that muscle training becomes the focus of adjustment efforts. All portions of the neuromuscular apparatus are involved in these efforts, but—in our culture at least—it is the learning of specific control of the bladder and bowel sphincters ("toilet training") that is the most highly charged emotionally and so the most significant with respect to personality development.

The reader will recall from anatomy and physiology that there is a tripartite control of the bladder and bowel sphincters: a reflex tendency toward evacuation in response to mild pressure (distention), a semivoluntary inhibition of the original evacuation tendency, and finally, a voluntary "inhibition of the inhibition" which, in older children and adults, allows the evacuation tendency to operate.

The development and mastery of this control apparatus takes place in an emotional setting of considerable intensity. As any student with small brothers and sisters, with pediatric experience, or with small children of his own knows, the attitude of the infant and the very young child toward excrements is far different from that of older children and adults. Not only is the infant free of such negative feelings as embarrassment, shame, and disgust, but he gives unmistakable evidence of positive feelings toward these bodily products and the acts that bring them forth.

In the discussion of the sources of the sexual-social drive, mention was made of the expression of pleasure that infants often assume while in the process of having a stool. Other examples of a similar nature will easily come to mind in anyone at all familiar with babies. For example, it is quite usual for an infant to play with his feces in various ways (or to attempt to do so). Similarly, it has often been noted that an infant is more apt to urinate while in the arms of someone he knows and is fond of than in those of a stranger or someone he dislikes—a circumstance with the implication that the bodily product, urine, is originally connected with positive rather than with negative emotions.

Apart from this natural pleasure in excreting and excrements, there is the matter of freedom. The infant voids and defecates whenever these drives exert the slightest pressure; he is not required to endure any sustained tension in connection with these drives.

Perhaps it can now be seen why it is that bladder and bowel training are sources of greater stress—and potentially of greater conflict—to the small child than are the other varieties of muscle training. In the matter of standing and walking, for example, the infant's developing impulses and the wishes of the parents coincide almost perfectly. The infant is normally eager to stand and to walk, and his eagerness is matched by that of the parents. It is much the same with articulation and talking. The healthy baby begins to vocalize and then verbalize spontaneously. The parents are pleased with such behavior, and ordinarily do everything possible to encourage the trend. Not only do the parental wishes coincide with the child's impulses in these matters, but the developmental trend is perceived by the child as being in the direction of greater freedom, greater mastery over his environment.

Sphincter-training—and other types of habit-training, such as table manners and "deportment"—that block or restrain the normal physical outlets of the child are a quite different matter, different on at least three counts: (1) the impulses of the child and the wishes of the parents are usually in opposition. (2) The child is called upon to alter not merely his *behavior*, but also his natural *attitude*, to conform to his parents' wishes. (3) The alterations appear to be in the direction of a *loss*, rather than a *gain*, of freedom. (It is true that, in the long run, a *greater* degree of freedom and motility is achieved through the mastery of bladder and bowel control and of other social conventions, but the small child does not grasp this truth.) The first and second of these points require further consideration.

The natural antagonism between child and parent in this matter is of especial significance for a number of reasons. To an extent, it is a function of the child's development. Whereas in the nursing period, the child's ego has barely begun to develop, in the muscle-training period, ego formation is much more advanced. The child has a better recognition of objects and has begun to develop "a mind of his own." Thus there is a greatly increased possibility of a clash of wills over a matter such as toilet training. Moreover, the situation is such that if motivated to do so, the child now has it in his power to thwart the mother—by refusing to use the toilet or by soiling and bed-wetting—more effectively than ever before. At the same time, if their relationship has been a reasonably good one, there is naturally a strong desire on the child's part to please the mother.

Thus in connection with the process of learning to regulate the bladder and bowel sphincters in accordance with social usage, the child feels two ways about one and the same thing. He desires to retain his infantile freedom with regard to urination and defecation, and yet he wishes to please his mother and win her approval through cooperation. He resents his mother for her attempts to control his bodily functions, and yet he loves her as the source of affection and support. Such a combination of positive and negative feelings toward the same person or situation is called *ambivalence*.[3]

In the normal course of events, the positive feelings win out after a time, and the child begins to conform to the accepted pattern. For love of his parents, the child also begins to take on their *attitudes* toward excretory products and acts. The original pride and pleasure become replaced, consciously, by a certain amount of shame and disgust. As these feelings develop, they are of some assistance to the child in producing a further degree and a more automatic type of conformity. The mechanism at work, whereby an original attitude or set of feelings is replaced in consciousness by the opposite attitude or set of feelings, will be recognized as *reaction-formation* (p. 77). The shift in attitude with respect to bladder and bowel activities and products is the first clear example of the personality's use of this defense technique.

If reaction-formation were the sole or even the principle defense mechanism available to the child during the stress situations of the muscle-training period, the personality could scarcely come through this developmental phase without acquiring serious limitations. Since such an outcome is the exception, it is clear that other mechanisms must be utilized. Of these, the most important is *sublimation* (p. 75). Starting with the original situation in which the small child takes pleasure in smearing and otherwise manipulating his bodily excreta, one can list a series of sublimatory activities, in which the aims and the objects of these "anal impulses" become progressively modified in the direction of greater social acceptability. Such a series might include the following activities: making mud pies, playing in wet sand, manipulating clay or plasticene, finger painting, sculpturing, and painting with a brush. In one sense, writing itself might be considered the last term in such a series. Such activities as these afford sufficient instinctual gratification to allow the child, in most instances, to accept the restrictions imposed by the parents in the course of sphincter training without the necessity of developing symptoms or morbid character traits.

In mentioning such a list, one runs the risk of conveying the false impression that sculpture, or oil painting, or writing involves nothing more than sublimated smearing impulses. Such a notion is, of course, convincingly refuted by the fact that, whereas nearly everyone has learned to control his excretory products and interests, and whereas a sizeable minority have sustained character limitations thereby, few persons are able to become successful sculptors, painters, or writers. In other words, impulses from the muscle-training period furnish a portion of the *motivation* of many an artist, but have relatively little to do with his *ability*.

We have said that the positive incentive of the young child in learning to control his sphincter apparatus (and in learning "good manners" in general) is the need for parental love and approval. This need is normally greater than is the strength of the infantile impulses, and the satisfactions that come in the form of caresses, praise, rewards, and enhanced prestige outweigh the satisfactions of evacuating bladder and bowels freely and of messy table manners.

If the parents handle the problem lovingly and well, the result to the child of this developmental phase will be a gain in self-control without a loss in self-esteem and, in fact, with "a lasting sense of autonomy and pride." (Erikson)

If, however, certain factors alter this favorable balance, the developmental course may be correspondingly changed. Such factors can be of two general sorts: those making the original impulses stronger, and those making the environment less conducive to progress. An example of the first sort would be any organic disease having the effect of stimulating bowel or bladder activity, as, let us say, a prolonged bout of infectious diarrhea. Examples of the second sort are much commoner, and they derive chiefly from parental (especially maternal) attitudes toward training in general and bowel training in particular.

These destructive attitudes are of several types. One such attitude is that of the insecure and hence overambitious mother who seeks to bolster her own self-esteem by fostering premature accomplishment in her children. Another disturbing attitude, also the product of character difficulties in the mother, is that of a preoccupation with neatness, cleanliness, and fastidiousness as ends in themselves. Still another such attitude is that of domination, the excessive need on the mother's part to control the behavior of others. Finally, there may be the opposite kind of situation, in which the mother is overpermissive and obtains a vicarious gratification through rearing her children with no sense of shame or guilt and no need to conform to social usage.

In the last-mentioned situation, the child may be relatively free of inner conflict for a time, but he is destined for serious difficulties later on in life since his character will not have been tempered to adjust to realistic demands of the environment.

In any of the other three situations, the conflict between mother and child, and quite soon, *within* the child himself, may become intense. Even today, pediatricians often hear mothers relate in detail the measures that they have used to bring about mature bowel habits precociously: placing the infant on the toilet (or a miniature toilet) regularly at the age of several months; using suppositories, laxatives, and enemata, and various bribes, threats, and punishments.

In struggling with such conflict situations, the child may respond in a number of ways. Almost invariably the personality suffers as a result. Some of the long-term effects will be considered in the clinical portions of this book. Some of the shorter-term effects will be noted in Chapter 15.

One kind of attempt at adjustment is of such far-reaching significance as to warrant illustration here; it is through the mechanism of *regression* (p. 75).

A child of two and one-half years was brought to the pediatrician by his mother, with complaints of markedly infantile behavior. The child sucked his thumb a great deal, would rarely go to sleep without a bottle, and spoke only in the monosyllables of a year-old infant. He was enuretic and often incontinent of feces.

The history revealed that hereditary and congenital factors were normal and that the child's development had proceeded at a normal pace during the first six or seven months. At about this time, the mother, who was a dominating, controlling woman with an inordinate passion for cleanliness, had begun attempts at toilet training, attempts which eventually came to include strenuous measures. After an initial, very tense effort at compliance lasting several months, the child appeared to have given up. Thereafter, although he continued to grow physically, his behavior altered in a retrograde fashion. In some respects, the child's behavior at two years of age was more infantile than it had been at the age of one, and his mood continued, for the most part, to be one of fretful irritability.

In this particular instance, both parents had become genuinely concerned about the child's condition, and they were able largely to accept the pediatrician's advice which included calling a truce in the muscle-training conflict, offering the child more acceptance, and devising various low-pressure inducements to resume the task of growing up. Within the space of six months, the child had abandoned the infantile position.

As has been mentioned, regression can occur at any developmental level. Although it is always a sign of trouble, it is to be distinguished whenever possible from a similar clinical picture existing on the basis of *fixation* (p. 92). The point is of considerable significance with respect to prognosis and therapy since it is almost always easier (though not necessarily easy) to help a patient regain a level of maturity which he has once reached than it is to help him attain such a level for the first time.

While the development of sphincter control is the principal stress-center of the muscle-training period, other highly significant developments are taking place at the same time. Of these, control of the "long muscles" and control of the speech apparatus are the most important.[2]

These developments are, in the main, sources of pleasure to the small child; self-confidence increases with the increasing degree of mastery of the body. Manipulation of the arms and legs affords an outlet for normal aggressiveness and curiosity. However, motor facility rapidly outstrips judgment: a small child can run across a busy street long before he realizes that it is unsafe to do this. It is necessary for the parents to set limits on the child's motor expression. The manner in which this is done is apt to have important consequences with respect to personality development. A proper compromise between a dominating over-protectiveness and a laissez-faire attitude will allow ample scope for the expression of inquisitiveness and reasonable aggression, while fostering the necessary minimum of trustful compliance. Excessive efforts at control tend to favor the metamorphosis of healthy aggressivity into hostility, whether the overt response is one of meekness or rebelliousness. On the other hand, excessive casualness fosters imperfections in the developing abilities at self-control.

The acquisition of speech—which has begun before this period—now makes a great advance, providing new means of expression which are uniquely human. Whole books have been written about this aspect of development alone. Here it merely may be pointed out that this facility has several key aspects. It is a means of communication par excellence and thus favors socialization. It is a means for the discharge of tensions without gross bodily involvement; by thus interposing a delay between perception of inner (drive) stimulation and action, it favors ego development. It affects thought processes, facilitating the development of conscious, rational thinking.

Period of the Family Triangle

If the period of muscle training has proceeded normally, the child emerges from it with greatly increased perceptual, intellectual, and motor abilities. At two years, the child can speak in sentences of three or four words, can run with only occasional falls, and can identify many of the parts of his own body by pointing. At three years, the child can give his first and last names, as well as the names of most objects around the house. He can execute simple errands and make crude "pictures" with chalk or crayon.

All of these accomplishments are, of course, executive (ego) functions, and it is correctly inferred that the child's ego has experienced considerable expansion and development during the muscle-training period. Physical growth and development have occurred as well and the sexual-social drive has increased in strength, so that the child of three looks and acts like a little boy or girl rather than like a baby.

Whereas the problems, the conflicts, and the achievements of the child during the first two developmental periods have been much the same for boys as for girls, the differences now become marked. The child's increased awareness of his own body, his increased awareness of the physical, emotional, and cultural differences between his father and mother (and brothers and sisters, if he has them), and perhaps above all, the increasing differentiation which the parents make in their responses to the child in accord with his gender all combine to bring about a set of problems, conflicts, and achievements which is not the same for boys and girls alike. From this point on in the discussion, therefore, it often becomes necessary to trace separately the course of personality development in boys and girls.

ACHIEVEMENTS OF THE FAMILY TRIANGLE PERIOD. To anticipate this portion of the developmental story for a moment, one may summarize the family triangle period by saying that its greatest achievement is a decisive shift from the self-centered (narcissistic) position of the very small child to a position in which love and desire for other persons *begin* to approximate their adult meanings. Some presentations of personality development reflect the significance of this alteration by dividing the period into two phases, one preceding and one following the first clear indications of this shift. For our purposes, it may be sufficient to indicate that the material which immediately follows is concerned with what is often called the "self-centered sexual phase."

CHANGES IN THE BOY. In the case of the little boy, the first and simplest change to occur, as infancy recedes and the problems of the muscle-training phase begin to be surmounted, is that the penis starts to supplant the mouth and the sphincter areas as the bodily region of chief emotional significance, the region upon which the libido begins to be focused. Masturbatory activity can be noted during the earlier developmental periods, but it is of a more random, less purposeful nature, as well as of a rather sporadic occurrence. Beginning at about age two and one-half, the purposeful seeking of a sexual type of pleasure through manipulation of the external genitalia is an almost universal occurrence in the normal child.

Such activity is not only harmless in itself, but it is of definite survival value for the human species, inasmuch as it links the libido with the organs of reproduction. That is to say, it is the first behavioral link in the chain of events which place the libido in the service of reproduction. Nevertheless, as every family physician knows, masturbatory activity on the part of the child customarily arouses more or less vigorous opposition on the part of the parents. In some respects the conflict that ensues is actually more stressful than the one which arose in connection with excretory activity. Whereas the parents accepted the naturalness of excretion and strove merely to regulate the time and place for the exercise of these functions, it is still quite common for parents not to accept the naturalness of childhood masturbatory activity and to strive to block this function altogether.

It is worth mentioning that negative parental attitudes (and the attitudes of some physicians) have several sources. At the present time, ignorance, misinformation, and tradition have decreased in importance as sources for such attitudes in parents (as they had for physicians at least a generation ago). However, almost certainly, these were never the most important sources. The most significant sources have been and remain the fears and resentments, largely unconscious, deriving from the time when the parents themselves were children.

In their efforts at suppression of the child's masturbation, parents often resort to various threats and punishments. In their mildest form, such measures may be merely implicit, as in the tone of voice with which a parent attempts to redirect a child's attention away from his genitals. In intermediate form, they may consist of explicit verbal prohibitions and, perhaps, the statement that the child will injure himself physically if the masturbation persists. In more extreme (but not actually rare) forms, the suppressive measures on the part of the parents include threats of cutting off the penis and such punitive acts as tying the child's hands at night. In addition, since masturbation is considered sinful in a number of theologies, parents often resort to various threats of a supernatural nature that are apt to be interpreted in a primitive and overconcrete fashion by the child.*

As a result of these various measures (plus other factors to be mentioned presently), the little boy comes to fear the loss of the very organ he has begun to value so highly. This fear acts to inhibit the masturbatory activity. Another important motive which conflicts with the masturbatory impulse derives from the child's affection for and dependence upon his parents, with his strong need for their affection and approval. Ordinarily, the eventual outcome of the conflict is similar to that of the previous conflict regarding excretory functions: the child conforms more or less to the parents' wishes and either discontinues the practice of masturbation or continues it with diminished frequency and greater discretion. Before this outcome is reached, however, other elements in the developmental story have appeared and exerted their influence.

During the "self-centered sexual phase," the pride taken by the little boy in his genitals and the generally heightened interest of children of both sexes in anatomic features is plainly disclosed (see also material on p. 525). Great pleasure is derived from running about naked (as, for instance, at bath time and bedtime), and the child will go out of his way to exhibit his body and to see the bodies of others. Various personality (behavior) disorders of later life, e.g., *exhibitionism* and *voyeurism* (see Chap. 12) have a basis in fixations to this phase.

As was mentioned in the discussion of infancy, the first object of emotional significance to the baby is the mother's breast and, shortly thereafter, the mother herself. In the case of the boy, the mother ordinarily remains the principal love object throughout most of development. However, the precise nature of the feelings that come together and are experienced as "love" undergoes a series of modifications. These changes are, in part, the result of the processes of maturation: the child's increasing powers of perception, memory, and integration of impressions, as well as increasing endocrine activity that is thought to be characteristic of the period under discussion. The changes lead into the central aspects from which this period gets its name.†

Originally, the infant responds positively to the mother's breast, the

---

* Various questions involved in the management of sexual education and sexual behavior in children are frequently referred to the physician. This problem is discussed in Chapters 5 and 15.

† In psychoanalytic literature, this developmental stage is often called "the Oedipal period." As the student may recall, Oedipus is a character in ancient Greek legend and in a remarkable trilogy of plays by Sophocles, who unknowingly kills his father and marries his mother, subsequently punishing himself with blindness.

source of nourishment, warmth, and comfort, and then to her arms and her voice, *as pleasure-giving things*. Somewhat later, the mother is perceived as a unit. At the same time, the infant's (and then the small child's) positive responses begin to assume some of those qualities known in older children and adults as love. By the muscle-training period, one can say that the small child loves his mother *as a person*. The developmental step which next occurs (during the family triangle period) in connection with the child's growing capacities involves further discrimination: the little boy now begins to love his mother *as a woman*. Up to this point, the mother has naturally been *quantitatively* favored as the love object by children of both sexes. Now, as all of the differences, obvious and subtle, that mark off a man and his behavior from a woman and hers, begin to register and become integrated in the little boy's mind, a *qualitative* difference (tenderness, possessiveness) makes its appearance in the positive feelings directed toward the mother, as contrasted with those directed toward the father.

This development is greatly facilitated by both the deliberate and inadvertent behavior of the parents toward the child. As the small infant does not recognize differences in gender among the persons in his world, so the parents ordinarily differentiate only slightly between a boy and a girl infant, insofar as their overt responses are concerned. At some time during the muscle-training period, however, the parents begin to respond more and more clearly to the little boy *as a boy* and to the little girl *as a girl* (differences in verbal shadings and in those of physical contact, differences in the activities suggested and the expectations expressed, etc.). In fact, the parents make it quite clear, as a rule, that the attitudes and responses of the little boy and the little girl are not to be the same.

Moreover, since the father and mother cannot do otherwise than react in ways characteristic of their own total personalities, there is a further differentiation. The father responds to the son *as a man to a boy*, and the mother, *as a woman to a boy*. (The reverse is, of course, also true: the father responds to a daughter as a man to a girl, whereas the mother responds as a woman to a girl.)

The rationale for the designation of this developmental phase as "the family triangle period" now becomes clear. As a result of the biological development and the differentiation of attitudes just described, the little boy finds himself in a triangular situation in which he seems to be "the other man." His wishes to possess the mother and to stand first in her estimation and favor are blocked by an established and more powerful rival.

During the earlier portions of this developmental period, the little boy's efforts to "win" his mother are often obvious.

When Jim was about three, his father brought his mother flowers for her birthday. Jim disappeared from the house for a few minutes and then he ran into the room with a bouquet picked from a neighbor's garden. "Look, Mommy! For you! Prettier than Daddy's."

Jim was, as a rule, quite affectionate to his mother, but he also enjoyed being masterful on occasion. If he had built something with his blocks, he would (with her help) drag his mother from her chair and lead her in a confident, masculine way to see what he had done.

On evenings when his father worked late at the store, Billy, aged four, would usually insist on sitting at the head of the table. "Now I'm Daddy," he would say, "and I'll take care of you, Mommy."

The exhibition of masculine prowess takes different forms at different ages.

At three and one-half years, Bobby's "Look, Mommy!" summoned his mother to the bathroom to see him urinating into the toilet from a distance of a couple of feet. A few years later, on a new scooter-bike, it was "Look, Mommy! No hands!"

Even in a healthy, tolerant, and affectionate home atmosphere, this first "love affair" is doomed to disappointment. Even where competitive masculine strivings such as those in the examples above are fully accepted, there are natural limits beyond which the little boy cannot go. The father, for example, retains certain prerogatives beyond those permissible to the boy. He alone sleeps with the mother, and he remains (as a rule) the principal disciplinarian of the household. In time, as the boy comes to perceive his father's invincibility and his own relative inadequacy, he begins to give up the struggle *on its original terms* and to move toward the next developmental phase.

There is a period before this, however, during which the father is, in some ways, a very threatening figure to the little boy (insofar as he is perceived as a dangerous rival). The reader may naturally wonder how this picture of the father develops, since in the ordinary household he is secure enough in his relationship with the mother that he need not respond seriously to the little boy's activities. As a matter of fact, what is taking place in the child's mind at this point is, in considerable measure, unconscious. The little boy wishes to dispossess father, wishes him out of the way, but this attitude clashes both with his awe, based on his father's superior power, and with his (conscious) love and admiration for his father. The wish is largely handled through the mechanism of *projection* (p. 77), i.e., it is transformed into the feeling that the father is the hostile one and desires to harm the little boy in some way. Thus it comes about that a father who is no more than normally aggressive temporarily assumes a more formidable posture in the deeper level of the child's mind.

It is at about this point that the line of developments having to do with masturbatory activity ordinarily connects with the family triangle developments. On the one hand, the boy is in conflict with parental authority, particularly that of the father, over his biologically derived impulses to masturbate. On the other, he feels himself to be in conflict with his father over possession of his mother. Furthermore, his love for his mother includes a sensual component, although the extent and manner of conceptualization of this feeling vary considerably. The little boy feels threatened in both situations; the threats merge (in his mind) and assume a physical character: that he will lose his penis.

An additional element in the situation usually contributes in an important way to the strength of this fear. It is the boy's recognition of the anatomical differences between the sexes and, specifically, the absence of the penis in the female. The infant cannot recognize such details as sex differences, and the very small child finds them of little significance. During the family triangle period of development, however, when the little boy is acutely concerned about his own body, physical differences assume great significance. At this point, the sight of the genital region of a female (sister, girl playmate, mother, female statue or picture) makes a considerable and troublesome impression. Seeing an individual who does not possess a penis brings home the idea that the loss of this organ is a real possibility. That is to say, the boy's initial interpretation of the girl's body at this point—based on the understandable assumption that all human creatures were originally made as he is—is that here is a person who has actually *lost* the organ that is so important to him.*

Under the influence of this variously derived *castration fear*,† as it is called, the boy feels compelled to renounce his possessive, sensually tinged love for his mother, and to limit his feelings for her to those of a tender, affectionate, and, perhaps, playful nature.

It is important to understand thoroughly the position of the father, as seen by the little boy, during the family triangle period. There is no question but that the father is perceived (with varying degrees of consciousness) as an increasingly formidable rival for the possession of the mother. But from the very first, and usually from an even earlier point

---

* It should not be inferred from this material that the child should be artificially shielded from such observations. If the relationship between the boy and his parents is fundamentally sound, his anxiety can be adequately met, in time, by explanation and reassurance appropriate to his ability to understand and through his general sense of security in the home.

† Actually the term *castration fear* is inaccurate. The literal meaning of castration is, of course, removal or destruction of the testes or ovaries, whereas what the little boy fears is loss of the penis. However, the term has the sanction of tradition and is the one generally employed in technical works in the field.

than the period under discussion, the father is also seen *as a model.* Consider again the examples on page 103. In the first and third anecdotes, the boy was doing exactly what he had seen the father do; in the second and fourth, he was doing childish approximations of what he considered the father's activities to be.

Now, there is a well-known tendency on the part of human beings to *become* in some respects *like* strongly frustrating figures. Sometimes this process is quite conscious, as indicated in the old saying, "If you can't fight 'em, join 'em!" Sometimes this process is quite unconscious; and sometimes, as in the present instance, it involves both conscious and unconscious elements. In the one case, it is called *imitation,* and in the other, *introjection* or *identification* (p. 78). Imitation is usually based very largely on positive feelings for the model; identification is based on *strong* feelings, which may be positive, negative, or a combination of both. Thus, as his sense of frustration increases, but also on the basis of his admiration and love, the little boy tends to become more like his father.

In the course of normal development, the family triangle period comes to a close when the little boy stops trying to displace father and directs his primary attention to the task of learning how one becomes a man.

In the discussion of the *superego* (pp. 73-74), it was mentioned that this aspect of the mind receives its principal developmental impetus after infancy but before the age of about six years. It was also stated that the influence of the parents is of major significance in superego formation. The key point may now be made more explicit. The core components of the superego are (normally) the introjected characteristics of the like-sexed parent which are added to the child's personality toward the end of the family triangle period.

The sequence that has just been sketched in the case of the little boy* is the normal one. As can readily be understood, it is a stressful period, taxing the adjustment capacity of the young ego severely. It does not take a great deal in the way of additional stress—from whatever source —to exceed the capacity of the child's ego to effect a successful adjustment, with the result either that neurotic symptoms develop at this time or the maturation of the personality is interfered with in a way predisposing to the development of symptoms at a later date.

Several of the numerous possibilities that, singly or in combination, may constitute such stress, may be considered here. The first possibility is that the preceding developmental periods may not have gone

---

* This paragraph and the two succeeding ones may also be taken to apply to the little girl, if the reader will make the appropriate alterations ("mother" for "father," "femininity" for "virility," etc.).

smoothly, with the result that the child approaches the problems of the family triangle period at a time when he has not yet solved earlier adjustment problems (i.e., while retaining certain *fixations*), and therefore must operate at a serious disadvantage. Other possibilities have to do with the personalities of the father and mother and with their responses to the child. If the father is nonloving and unduly aggressive, the little boy's anxiety may become so great as to bring about a *regression* (p. 75). A somewhat similar result may be produced, even if the father's responses are essentially healthy, if the mother's behavior (whether voluntarily or not) is seductive, or oversolicitous in a way which is interpreted by the child as seductive.

On the other hand, if the father's personality is perceived by the child as being weak and lacking in virility, other difficulties may ensue, for then the little boy lacks the appropriate model and the control which he so greatly needs. Similarly, if the mother appears to be lacking in femininity, the child's subsequent relationships with women will have been given a disadvantageous beginning. Finally, whatever their individual personalities, if the relationship between the father and mother is not basically one of love and trust, the little boy is inevitably placed under additional stress. Despite the original fantasies of coming between the father and mother, and of winning the mother for himself, his own healthy development requires, most of all, a home atmosphere of affection and security.

CHANGES IN THE GIRL. Turning now to the experiences of the little girl during this period, one notes some close counterparts to those which have just been described. The external genitalia supplant the mouth and the sphincter areas in emotional and instinctual significance, and clitoral masturbation regularly occurs. A conflict between the child and parents ensues (with regard to masturbatory activity) which is very like that described in the case of the boy.

Emotionally speaking, however, the girl's situation is, in two important respects, quite different from that of the boy. One of these has to do with the little girl's perception of herself, and the other with her choice of love object.

Whereas the boy's heightened awareness of the anatomical differences between the sexes adds to the intensity of his castration fear, the girl's interpretation of the anatomical facts is either that she has been defectively formed or that she has already somehow been mutilated. Thus, in their natural ignorance of the internal organs of generation in the female, *both* the little boy and the little girl assume the latter to be anatomically inferior, but the *effects* of the assumption are markedly different in the two cases, depending upon the point of view.

As a matter of fact, the little girl feels inferior anatomically not only to her brothers and to other male figures but also to her mother and to other adult women, since she finds herself lacking in physical equipment (breasts) possessed by the others. As a natural result of the dependent position of infancy and earliest childhood, the girl tends to hold her mother responsible for what she regards as her deficiencies, and a temporary period of disillusionment with the mother ensues. (The reasons for this are usually not fully conscious.) Though unpleasant at the time, this feeling is actually of considerable importance in setting the stage for the next step in the little girl's emotional development.

This step—a turning to the father, making him the principal love object—may at first seem to be merely the female counterpart of the boy's heightened interest in the mother during this period. In a biological sense it is, yet there is an important difference. Whereas the boy *retains* a single principal love object (the mother) throughout childhood and merely learns to respond to her in increasingly mature ways, the girl *must make a change* in her chief love object, from mother to father, if her subsequent development is to proceed normally. To do this, a good bit of energy is required, and the little girl is, so to speak, both pulled and pushed into making the change. She is pulled by the positive attraction naturally existing between father and daughter, and pushed by the feeling of disillusionment with the mother that was mentioned above.

Once the change has been accomplished, the girl finds herself in a triangular situation which is the counterpart of the one faced by the boy, and which works itself out in an analogous fashion although more gradually and perhaps less completely.

It should be made clear that the girl's "disillusionment" and subsequent rivalry with the mother—like the boy's negative feelings toward the father—are normally only temporary (except for minor residuals). Toward the end of the family triangle period, the girl stops looking upon the mother as having slighted her physically, stops regarding her as a rival for the father's love, and regards her more and more as a model.

Certain experiences of this period are, however, thought to have a lasting effect upon the typically feminine attitude toward the body and its adornments. While it is true that certain of the secondary sex characteristics, such as the beard and the muscular development, are apt to become physical sources of pride in men, the external genitals remain by far the most significant area of the body for them emotionally. In women, on the other hand, pride in the body—which may be quite strong—is more diffuse. That is largely why attention to the figure and the many different aspects of grooming and the selection of clothing and ornaments become so important for them.

Reflecting upon the foregoing discussion of experiences of the family triangle period and considering that the span of time during which these experiences take place extends up to the age of about six years—a time when the mental faculties have become quite well developed—the reader may well be wondering why relatively few of these deeply significant feelings and events can later be voluntarily recalled. There is no question but that memory function has begun considerably before this, since most persons can recall a number of events from as early as about age three without difficulty. Does the absence of recollections of the family triangle experiences then mean that they are not universal, perhaps not even very common? No; it cannot mean this, for psychoanalytic research has shown that roughly comparable experiences are the common lot of all human beings and closely comparable ones are the common lot of human beings of our Western culture. What happens is a selective (although largely automatic and involuntary) forgetting of some of the principal elements. This forgetting is ordinarily of adaptive value, inasmuch as it frees the child's conscious mind from the more trying aspects of the period through which he has just passed. (The mechanism involved here is the one which has previously been identified as repression [p. 76].)

There is good reason to believe that for most human beings, normal as well as neurotic, the family triangle period is of greater significance than any other in shaping the personality. Because its conflicts are so highly charged emotionally, it is also the period that is the most difficult to write about in a manner that is both accurate and effective. In a scientific account, such as the one just presented, there is always the risk of making the child's experiences seem dry or mechanical. Of course, they are not; they are full of life, full of simple drama. In a textbook of psychiatry, there is also some risk of emphasizing what might be called the tragic aspects of these experiences—since, when things go wrong, they do predispose to tragedy in various forms in later life. The truth is that, oftener than not, things go essentially right and that whereas there is a tragic aspect to the frustration of the child's first romance, it is a tragedy with a future. It is the end of the first act, not the end of the play, and it is, furthermore, a play in the writing of which the principal actor, the individual, will have a large share.

Latency

Science agrees with common sense that one's earliest years are one's most impressionable years, a view which has medical implications. For example, there is good reason to believe that an individual who has experienced an emotionally healthy childhood up to the age of three years or so will only under very unusual circumstances develop a functional psychosis (p. 271) at any later period of his life. Similarly, given an emotionally healthy first six or seven years, it is highly unlikely that an individual will develop a serious psychoneurosis at any time in later life.

Aside from the degree of vulnerability to mental illness, the individual's personality in many ways has taken on its rough outline by the end of the first six years. In line with what was said in the last paragraph of the preceding section, it should be added that the personality has not yet acquired much of its content nor its sense of direction: innumerable impressions are still to be received, and the personality will be affected by many of them. Yet, with the exception of certain superego features, these modifications and additions tend to affect details (especially of adjustment techniques) rather than fundamental structure.

The developmental phase called the *latency period* extends from the end of the family triangle period to the beginning of puberty, thus lasting for about six years. It should not be assumed from the word "latency" that this is a quiet, inactive period. On the contrary, it is (potentially) a time of great activity and accomplishment, particularly in the intellectual and social, but also in the motor, spheres. Whereas the child of six will exercise his intellectual capacity in making such differentiations as those between morning and afternoon, right and left, summer and winter, the child of 12 will have advanced to the point of defining such abstractions as charity, revenge, justice, and mercy. Whereas a child of six can socialize for a limited extent, can carry on unsupervised play for brief periods, and can participate in such cooperative activities as decorating a classroom under supervision, the child of 12 is ready for such complicated social situations as group scouting projects or a dancing class. Given the opportunity, the child of six can have learned to swim well enough to be left at the deep end of the pool; the child of 12 has the ability to have achieved considerable perfection of form. So striking are these developments that the latency period has been called the period of the acquisition of skills (Erikson).

The term "latency" refers to the *relative* quiescence, emotionally and instinctually, of the phase which follows that of the family triangle. That which is relatively latent is the child's sexual interest. As noted in the previous section, the earlier period is quite conflict laden. It draws to a close with a partial *resolution* of the conflicts: the child abandons or diminishes his masturbatory activity in return for the parents' approval and help, and renounces his desire for possession of the parent of the opposite sex, putting in its place the wish to become like the parent of the same sex.

It is this resolution of conflicts which makes possible the accomplishments of the latency period. The child is enabled to function in a less anxious, more relaxed way, and from a stabler emotional position. The child's ego, during this phase, is less taxed in the effort to find some working compromise between id impulses and environmental pressures. A great saving in energy results, energy which the personality is free to invest in other enterprises.

Then, too, the mechanism of *sublimation* is, on the one hand, of great value in making possible the temporary resolution of family triangle conflicts (in the boy's case, seeking manly accomplishments in general, rather than possession of the mother), and on the other, directly responsible for some of the latency period achievements. Consider again the examples of sublimation presented on page 59. Notice the similarity of the emotional position of the novelist and that of the child at the close of the family triangle period. Like the novelist, the child finds himself unable to possess an important love object and thereupon enters a period of relatively great intellectual achievement.

Sublimation is used by the child to re-channel instinctual energy and thus reduce inner tension. More diffuse, intellectual curiosity, for example, takes the place of sexual curiosity; real social achievement takes the place of fantasied sexual achievement. The individual is never more educable than during the latency period—a fact which has long been given recognition by educators, who usually set the age of six as the time to begin formal schooling.

The child's heightened identification with the parent of the same sex has been mentioned. This process now extends to include other children of the same sex, an important development. This is, of course, the period when boys usually seek the company of boys, and girls that of girls. Friendship becomes, probably for the first time, an intensely meaningful experience. Group feeling begins to develop, and identification thus comes to involve not only individuals but groups. The little boy, for example, comes to think of himself not only as a boy, but as part of a Cub Scout den and pack, part of a school class, part of a church group, part of an inner circle of neighborhood chums.

The relationships among children of the same sex are developed and sustained, not merely on the basis of mutual identifications, but on the basis of affection (investment of libido). For this reason, the period is sometimes referred to as that of "normal childhood homosexuality." This phrase does not ordinarily refer to overt acts or conscious thoughts of a homosexual nature (although transient, minor episodes may occur), but to a sublimated homosexuality. In some instances of adult homosexuality, however, it has been shown that an emotional fixation to this period exists (see case history on pp. 417 to 420).

In the course of the discussion of the muscle training period, it was mentioned that a certain portion of the child's character is shaped on the basis of *reaction-formation*. Conformity to social usage in matters of bladder and bowel function, table manners, and certain other aspects of deportment clearly originate in this way, as do the attitudes upon which the conformity comes to rest. Similarly, it is typical for a number of personality traits to have been developed prior to the latency period. Thus, cleanliness may have been substituted for the natural messiness of the small child, kindness for occasional impulsive cruelty, industry for a proneness to gratifying fantasies, modesty for exhibitionism.

However, it has been pointed out (p. 77) that reaction-formation, if extensively used, gives the personality a rigidity incompatible with the high degree of adaptability characteristic of a healthy maturity. Freely speaking, one might say of many children entering the latency period that they are "doing the right things for the wrong reasons."

As it turns out, the experiences of latency ordinarily offer the child new sources of strength that foster the development of greater flexibility of character. Prior to latency, the relationships of the child have been primarily (in some cases, almost exclusively) with adults. Even in the early school situation the child tends to relate primarily to the teacher rather than to the other children. For example, in instances in which the child feels that one of his classmates is getting the better of him or treating him unfairly, there is a strong tendency for him to complain to the teacher, to "tattle on" the offender, rather than attempt to straighten things out directly with the other child. With the development of group feeling, however, the child comes to feel more secure, and therefore to have less need for attitudes or performance based ultimately on fear of adult displeasure. At the same time, the social (as well as the personal) value of such characteristics as neatness, kindness, and modesty becomes apparent. The usual result is that the child relaxes or discards some of the reaction-formations, thus acquiring a more mature type of superego. Thereafter he will tend to behave in socially acceptable ways less because he must (or feels that he must) and more because he wants to do so.

Puberty

The period of puberty—from 11 or 12 to 13 or 14 years of age—is marked by a burst of hormonal activity, particularly gonadal activity, which results in the individual's becoming able to participate in reproduction. At this time the secondary sex characteristics begin to be acquired: growth of pubic and axillary hair; breast development in the girl; enlargement of penis and testes in the boy; deepening of the voice, particularly in the boy, but, to a lesser extent, in the girl. The major biological events of the period are the onset of menstruation in girls and of nocturnal emissions of semen ("wet dreams") in boys.

It is an interesting fact that this period resembles that of the family triangle in several ways. The individual's sexual development (in the narrow sense), which has been largely side-tracked during latency in favor of intellectual and social development, now resumes its course. This means, in effect, that the child must now return to the very problems which had previously been dealt with in the family triangle period. (This time, however, as a result of the developmental advances made in the interim, the way begins to open for a different, and ultimately a definitive set of solutions—solutions that are fully achieved at the end of the next period, adolescence, and mark the onset of maturity.)

Ordinarily masturbation is resumed at this time, or if the practice has not been entirely discontinued, its tempo is increased. In contrast with the situation during the family triangle period, pubertal (and subsequent) masturbation normally is remembered, not requiring repression. On the other hand, whereas the fundamental love object at puberty may again be the parent of the opposite sex, such ideas are repressed throughout puberty (and thereafter). As a matter of fact, the two contrasts go together: the *facts* of pubertal masturbation escape repression *because the fantasies*, in their more tabooed aspects, are not any longer allowed into consciousness.

Masturbatory activities during puberty and later ordinarily is accompanied by *conscious* sexual-romantic fantasies involving persons of the opposite sex other than the parent: glamorous-seeming adolescents, movie stars, or other romanticized figures, or more rarely, favorite classmates. This alteration in the conscious object(s) is made possible by the greater socialization which has taken place during latency.

As in the family triangle period, guilt feelings are mobilized by this activity. These feelings have two principal sources: one is the conscious recognition of the (continuing) disapproval of the parents and of other authority figures; the other is the superego's disapproval of the unconscious persistence of the old incestuous desires. (Since the superego has a large unconscious component [p. 74], it is quite possible for this aspect of the mind to go into vigorous action despite the subject's lack of awareness of the nature of his "misdeed.") The guilt feelings are, however, normally of lesser intensity than in the late family triangle period, both because the personality in its executive aspects (i.e., the ego) is now stronger and because the unconscious incestuous fantasies are, so to speak, diluted by the less stringently forbidden conscious romantic fantasies.

The parental responses to the child in his situation of conflict are of great importance. If the attitude of the parents is fundamentally one of kindness and casual understanding, the child is helped toward the eventual achievement of a mature sexual adjustment. If it is cold, suspicious, threatening, or overtly punitive, the child's sexual development may be blocked, stunted, or diverted into some deviant pathway (via regression). If it is hypocritical or inappropriately stimulating, the child's sexual development may be shunted in the direction later called *psychopathic* (p. 402).

If the relationship between the child and his parents has been a good one, with relatively free-and-easy communication, the child's factual knowledge regarding the sexual aspects of life will have become reasonably complete and accurate by the time the definitive bodily changes of puberty begin to take place. Of even greater importance to the child than knowledge, however, is the child-parent relationship, per se, as is the relationship of the parents to one another. If the latter is clearly one of love and mutual respect, the child is guided and helped by the parental models more than by their words. The attitude of each parent toward himself, particularly with respect to acceptance of his own gender, is similarly significant.

MENARCHE; PSYCHOLOGICAL ASPECTS OF THE MENSTRUAL CYCLE. The last-mentioned point is well illustrated in connection with the young girl's experience of menarche. Regardless of the books she may have read or the intellectual soundness of the advice she may have received, and even, perhaps, transmitted, if a mother does not enjoy a fundamental acceptance of herself as a woman, if she cannot take a normal pleasure in her erotic and reproductive functions, she is very apt to pass on to her daughter fears, inhibitions, and tensions in this area of life. As a result of such feelings, functional menstrual difficulties may develop. As is well known, this type of disability seems to "run in families." Severe menstrual cramps, headaches, moodiness, and partial incapacitation at the time of menstruation usually have an emotional causation and are not often seen in girls whose mothers have accepted their sexuality in a healthy fashion.

Although it is getting a bit ahead of the developmental story, it may be well to indicate at this point, apropos of the comments above, certain cyclic alterations in mood and in the strength of various needs which, in mild degree, are typical of normal women and which are related to hormonal changes of the menstrual cycle.* (It is suggested that the student review the material from his physiology course pertaining to the menstrual function.)

The sexual cycle in women is usually considered to "begin" with the

---

* This portion of the discussion is based upon the work of Drs. T. Benedek and B. Rubenstein of Chicago.[1]

phase immediately following menstrual bleeding, the phase in which the next Graafian follicle is ripening and estrogenic hormones are being produced in increasing amounts. During this phase, the woman's basic drive toward heterosexual activity becomes increasingly intense. In situations in which direct expression of these impulses is not feasible and sublimation is utilized, there is ordinarily a period of increasing, outwardly directed, constructive activity. This phase reaches its height at the time of ovulation, when estrogen production has reached its peak and progesterone secretion has begun. If the external situation *or the woman's inner conflicts* are such as to preclude adequate gratification on either a direct or a sublimated basis, there is a period of considerable tension and distress. If there are deep-seated conflicts regarding sexuality, the woman's behavior may be primarily a reflection of defenses against sexual or other creative activity.

Normally, a period of relaxation follows ovulation. During the phase beginning at this time, progesterone secretion steadily increases. The maternal component of the libido gains the ascendency. Essentially mature women tend to become more motherly at this time. Women with significant conflicts about motherhood may utilize a variety of defenses against such impulses. Women who have remained emotionally fixated at a quite early developmental phase may reveal (in one way or another) wishes to be taken care of and ministered to, as if they themselves were babies.

In the commoner form of the cycle, in which conception does not occur, hormone production abruptly drops almost to zero about twelve days after ovulation. In response to—or at least parallel with—this hormonal deficiency, the personality experiences a mild regression and a transient lowering of self-esteem. Some degree of fatigue, irritability, and low spirits is quite common at this point. Normally the onset of menstruation brings prompt relief from such feelings. If there is an unconscious (perhaps neurotically enhanced) need to be pregnant, however, the depression may persist and even deepen.

Adolescence

The period of puberty may be looked upon as the beginning of adolescence, and the resolution of the major problems mobilized at puberty typically occupies a considerable portion of adolescence. Like puberty proper, adolescence, particularly in its early phases, is normally rather a stormy time. Cultural factors as well as biological and psychological ones seem to be involved here, but, at least under current circumstances, there is good reason to believe that an adolescence which presents no overt indications of turbulence is one in which some important developmental steps are being postponed or omitted.

Characteristic of the adolescent are changeability and inconsistency. It is rather natural that parents (and other adults) find the adolescent hard to understand, since he behaves like a child one moment and like an adult the next. (Usually the adolescent finds himself almost equally hard to understand.) Giving up the attitudes of childhood for more independent ones is accompanied by a real struggle, one feature of which is this rapid alternation between childish and mature ways of looking at things and reacting to them. This shifting point of view includes the adolescent's attitude toward his parents: one day the father and mother appear to be wise and wonderful, and the next they appear stupid and insensitive. (The oscillations can, however, be somewhat reduced by the parents, if they are not unduly affected by either.)

A workable set of solutions to the problems characterizing this period is ordinarily reached in time, but in early adolescence, some of the defense mechanisms of the family triangle period are heavily relied upon. One of the most useful of these is sublimation. Beginning in early adolescence, the individual is apt to show a fresh burst of intellectual activity. It is, indeed, quite typical of the adolescent (if of normal intelligence or better) to become interested in questions of a rather searching, deep, and often abstract nature: questions of philosophy, of religion, and of science. Often such inquiries constitute the beginning of the individual's major career interest. (A circumstance which may not be perceptible to an observer since the inconsistency of the adolescent may obscure such trends. It is not unusual for an adolescent to react in a seemingly negative way to the very subject which may later engross his interest.) A good bit of the motivating force behind such interests derives from sublimated libido—as well as sublimated aggression. The postpubertal individual desires to realize himself fully, i.e., to express his various drives, but realistically he is not yet quite able to do so, with the result that a great deal of his restless energy may be diverted into intellectual channels.

Sublimation also plays a significant part in the development of a new and different type of solution from those possible in previous developmental periods. Whereas the adolescent is not at first emotionally capable of finding, let alone sustaining, a complete, mature sexual relationship, he is capable of beginning to develop emotionally gratifying relationships with members of the other sex. Such relationships cannot, of course, be considered merely as sublimations since they afford various kinds of direct gratifications from the desired objects (affectionate companionship, sharing of experiences, preliminary phases of love-making). Nevertheless, since the complete sexual aim is, as a rule, relatively inhibited, sublimation clearly plays a part in such relationships. These adolescent "affairs" are of great importance, inasmuch as they lead in the direction of eventual freedom from the bonds of the family triangle situation.

As is generally realized, the establishment of such contacts often does not come easily in the beginning. It is typical for the adolescent to be rather shy and awkward in many situations, particularly those in which he is called upon to relate to someone of the other sex. (Although he naturally tries his best to dissemble the difficulty.) Numerous illustrations of these qualities will doubtless come to the reader's mind upon reflection. Here is one such episode, quite common in real life, which is occasionally portrayed on television or in the movies for its comic effect.

A boy and girl, secretly somewhat interested in each other, approach from opposite directions along a sidewalk or school corridor. Each one moves slightly aside to allow the other to pass freely, but the boy moves to his right and the girl to her left, so that their relative positions are maintained. Each one glances up, sees the mistake, and "corrects" it by a move to the opposite side, still keeping their paths in the same line. As they pass in some confusion, they brush against each other.

To an observer, the preconscious motivation is perfectly clear. Adolescent shyness and awkwardness of this sort are primarily manifestations of the ego's attempt to keep firm hold on the resurgent sexual impulses, an attempt that often carries somewhat beyond the mark, inhibiting appropriate social responses. To some extent, such characteristics may be thought of as based upon reaction-formations since the underlying wishes and fantasies are just the opposite.* However, unless the shyness and awkwardness are extreme, they are not to be deplored in early adolescence. As a matter of fact, in mild degree, they may be viewed positively as evidence of ego and superego strength.

The adolescent is certainly capable of sincere friendships, but it should be understood that, until quite late in this period, what passes for "love" is usually quite different from the cluster of interrelated feelings called by the same name in the mature adult (p. 36). The difference derives in large part from the fact that, in the very nature of things, the adolescent is not yet free from certain insecurities and dependency needs of earlier childhood. His own abilities are still only partly developed, and his own self-esteem has not yet reached a comfortable, stable level. As a result, much oftener than not, when the adolescent believes himself to be strongly attached to someone of the other sex, even when he believes himself to be devotedly "in love," he is actually seeking to strengthen his self-esteem (without knowing it). Frequently this bolstering of the self-esteem has more to do with the

---
* Various sorts of mechanisms may be employed to handle conflicts of the sort just illustrated. Cf. discussion of *blushing* on p. 312.

way in which the adolescent's sexual-social status and activities are recognized by members of his own sex than with the emotional responses of the alleged love object in themselves.

As has often been pointed out by sociologists, this principle is reflected in adolescent dating customs and objectives in which the achievement of conquest is so often desired.[6] Typically, the adolescent girl wishes to have many invitations, to be much sought after, to be conspicuously popular. It is a mark of her success if she can achieve such a status without allowing her dates to go very far in the way of physical intimacies. Often the most enjoyable part of her success lies in the knowledge of the admiration and envy of her girlfriends. The adolescent boy wishes to feel irresistible to "women," and often makes it one of his aims to go as far as possible in the way of intimacies as a proof of his masculine prowess. He is counted a success by his male friends if he can "make out" with a number of girls, or even if he can manage to give such an impression.

It is typically a part of growing up to "fall in love" a number of times, usually beginning at about age 16, and usually with someone a bit older than oneself. The differences between such an experience and the experience of mature loving are rather profound,* but they may be summarized quite simply: being "in love" primarily involves a wish to receive, whereas mature loving is based upon the capacity to give. The person "in love" idealizes the love object (hence the saying, "love is blind") and thereafter makes his happiness completely dependent upon demonstrations of his love object's approval. If these evidences are not forthcoming, the individual's self-esteem is markedly lowered so that he becomes depressed. Mature loving, on the other hand, is a function of a personality already comfortable and reasonably sure of itself. Idealization of the love object may take place nevertheless, but it is not essential. Whereas a return of affection is certainly desired, the individual's self-esteem is not devastated if such a return is blocked. Loving involves feelings of tenderness as well as desire, and it involves the wish to do what is in the best interest of the loved one. Therefore it is capable of a certain amount of expression and gratification even in the absence of a loving response.

As a rule, a series of infatuations (occasions of being "in love") precedes the development of a truly loving relationship, and if these experiences are not too distressing, they tend to lead the adolescent toward the eventual formation of a mature love relationship (or at least toward the capacity to form such a relationship).

This development, when it comes, offers the long-term answer to the

---

* A generally mature adult may "fall in love" also, but in such a case, the process is usually transformed into the state of loving in the sense described above.

sexual conflicts having their origin in the family triangle period. The two principal prerequisites for a satisfying mature love relationship are: (1) the change in the nature of "love" from the predominantly possessive feeling of childhood to one in which genuine giving becomes of equal importance with receiving, and (2) the change in the love object from the parent (or parent substitute) to a person of one's own generation.

In some instances the personality does not mature beyond the stage of early adolescence, and a healthy love life never develops. In such cases, the individual is often constrained to go from one infatuation to another. Since he is unable to give emotionally in a sustained way, the relationships do not last. The only remedy for the lowering of self-esteem that follows each failure seems to be to repeat the experience with someone else. This immature pattern of behavior is familiar to everyone through reading of the marital misadventures of various celebrities. The superficially comic effect hides real tragedy, as is occasionally indicated by suicide attempts and other kinds of destructiveness which may accompany this behavior.

In other instances the personality may mature in most respects well beyond the state of early adolescence and yet, for various reasons, may not find a situation in which the direct satisfaction of sexual needs is feasible. In such cases, as in the earlier phases of everyone's development, sublimation may be of great value; it can go far toward the maintenance of reasonable comfort and well-being. Because they offer the opportunity for direct expression of certain aspects of loving and for the expression through sublimation of certain other aspects, the medical and nursing professions are apt to be of particular value to those of their members in this position.

Maturity

The principal characteristics of the mature personality were sketched in Chapter 2, and it will be worthwhile for the reader now to review this material (pp. 35 to 38). As noted then, complete emotional maturity, like the perfect health of which it is such an important component, is a rare phenomenon. Nearly everyone has certain partial *fixations* (p. 92), certain aspects or "quirks" of his personality which indicate a lack of advancement along some lines beyond earlier developmental levels. Fortunately, it is within the capacity of most persons to gain, in time, a sufficiently close approximation to maturity to afford the basis for a comfortable and worthwhile life. (Perhaps, the accent should fall upon the second adjective since health is not a guarantee of happiness.)

Probably the most significant test of an individual's degree of maturity is parenthood. An immature person is rarely capable of being a generally adequate parent (although he may manage satisfactorily in particular situations), whereas a mature person tends naturally to be a good parent. The reasons for this state of affairs are not obscure. Actually, the advent of children places very heavy demands upon the emotional stability of the parent—so much so, that it is often the precipitating circumstance for the outbreak of a psychiatric disorder.

If the emotional development of the adult has not reached the point at which he has a reasonably stable self-esteem and a considerable capacity for "unselfish" loving, the advent of children is seriously threatening (whether or not it is consciously thus perceived) since exclusive possession of the marital partner is no longer possible. If the adult has not been able to free himself from the original attachment to his own parent of the opposite sex, the fact that the mate is now a parent may mobilize the old conflicts to a disturbing degree. To speak in terms of the man's position, he may now react to his wife with the jealousies, guilty feelings, and/or inhibitions which he had experienced toward his mother.

If the adult has serious early fixations, the advent of children will mean that his childish and even infantile needs will be further stimulated, and frustrated, through witnessing the appropriate gratification of these needs in the children. Furthermore, the appearance of the various natural conflicts of childhood among his own children will be a source of stress to the adult who has never quite succeeded in mastering these conflicts himself. As a result of these circumstances, the immature adult often finds himself in a position of rivalry and competition with his own children, to his distress and theirs.

On the other hand, emotionally mature parents are sufficiently secure in their own love relationship (with one another) and sufficiently comfortable in the knowledge of their own worthwhileness and abilities, that neither envy or jealousy becomes a serious problem. It has been mentioned before that the libido of a healthy adult typically exceeds the amount which can be invested in a single object; hence it is that such an individual takes naturally to parenthood.

Involutional Period

This period of life is the one in which reproductive—as distinct from erotic—capacity is lost. It is, of course, quite definitely marked in women, first by alterations in and then by cessation of the menstrual function. These changes typically occur over a timespan of several years, beginning, on the average, during the middle forties. (There is some impression that the healthier and more firmly established the woman's erotic—including maternal—life is, the later the menopause comes, although this has not, as yet, been scientifically confirmed.) In men, the stage of involution is much less clearly marked, and in some instances, may never reach completion, but some changes of an involutional nature usually do take place, commonly some 10 to 15 years later than in women. In both sexes, the involutional phase is brought on by hormonal alterations within the gonads which are approximately the reverse of those occurring at puberty.

Psychological disturbances at this period are rather frequent, ranging in intensity from mild spells of melancholy or such alterations in behavior as isolated episodes of infidelity to severe reactions, reaching psychotic proportions. (The latter are commoner in women.) Much has been written about such disturbances, a large proportion of it impressionistic and probably incorrect. Among women, the commonest syndrome is one marked by such symptoms as menstrual irregularities, "hot flashes," feelings of inner tension, restlessness, and irritability. The combination of known physiological alterations with observable psychological disturbances led earlier psychiatrists and gynecologists to believe in the existence of a straightforward cause-and-effect relationship between the two. Even today, it is rather common for symptoms at this period to be treated primarily with large doses of various hormones.

While there is no reason to doubt that hormonal alterations during the period of involution may act as a kind of stress, it appears altogether unlikely that such stress is (psychologically) specific, or in itself adequate to account for the varied symptom picture. (See discussion of *involutional depressive reaction* on p. 357).

There are several reasons for doubting that psychiatric reactions during the involutional period—or even any special group of them—constitute a separate disease entity. For one thing, involution, like puberty, is a period through which everyone must pass, yet many persons go through it with no (psychiatric) symptoms whatever and many others experience only very mild symptoms. Secondly, it has been found by numerous physicians that treatment with barbiturate sedation or tranquilizers, suggestion, and reassurance is quite as effective as treatment with massive doses of estrogens, androgens, or other hormones ("replacement therapy"). On the other hand, hormonal treatment is often quite inadequate to afford the patient relief of symptoms. (So also is the case with the more conservative type of treatment.) Finally, there is the fact that the clinical picture of involutional symptomatology varies tremendously even among severe cases. One patient may present a clinical picture of profound *depression* (p. 341); another, a *schizophrenic* picture (p. 360); another, a *paranoid* picture (p. 390); while still another may present predominantly *hysterical* symptoms (p. 312).

It is known that these conditions have differing etiologies. Therefore it seems highly probable that the hormonal changes of the involutional period can be no more than contributing factors to the illnesses.

There is every reason to believe that the *meaning* of involution to the individual is a far more significant source of stress than are the biochemical alterations, and if clinical symptoms develop they are primarily a result of this meaning. The experience of involution is differently interpreted by different individuals—a circumstance which, together with their antecedent problems, accounts for the variety of reactions noted.

Among women, it is quite clear that one of the most significant feelings experienced at "change of life" is a threat to the self-esteem. The realization that the reproductive function is being lost may have the implication (whether consciously or unconsciously) that one is of less value as a person and less desirable as a woman. Ordinarily the children are no longer small at this time and so are less dependent upon the mother than in previous years. This change may also contribute to the feeling of being less needed and less worthwhile than before.

In men, the period of involution is apt to be a less stressful experience for several reasons: it is less clearly marked; it comes later in life (when the ability to reproduce may have assumed a lesser significance); and the reproductive function (as distinguished from the sensual-erotic) has always been of somewhat less emotional importance. Nevertheless, the feeling of an impending loss of virility is occasionally present to a disturbing degree, and in such cases the disturbance is again primarily a matter of lessened self-esteem. Much of the philandering of older men, either actual or in fantasy, has its basis in the quest for reassurance that they can still be found attractive by women, and not in the sudden development of a new and genuine love relationship.

For the middle-aged adult, man or woman, who has made a basically good adjustment to life, including a sound sexual and marital adjustment, for the person who is sufficiently mature to find parenthood a continuing source of gratification (through an unselfish pleasure in the development and the achievements of the children), the period of involution presents no critical problems. In fact, as new interests rise to supplement the old and old interests long deferred can claim attention, the period of middle age can become one of the most gratifying of life.

Old Age

In evaluating the period of old age, it is of major importance to realize what its stresses are. First may be mentioned certain purely physical changes that may or may not be present, but that, when present, can affect the personality as a whole. These changes involve specific disabilities, such as a reduction in visual or auditory acuity, and also those of a more diffuse nature, such as a diminution in speed of reaction, in vigor, and in the capacity for physical endurance. Some physical alterations may involve the central nervous system directly, as alterations in the caliber of the cerebral blood vessels or in the condition of the neurons themselves. This aspect of the subject will receive attention in the clinical section of this book (especially in pp. 287 to 291), but it can readily be understood that pathology of the central integrative organ of the mind can, in itself, act as a source of stress.

Second, and usually of greater importance, there are almost invariably significant changes in the environment. A number of these changes are likely to be of such a nature as to pose threats, either actual or potential, to the self-esteem of the aging or aged person. For example, the individual's children will now have reached full (relative) maturity and independence. Even when this development is welcomed by the parent, it is rather likely to arouse a feeling of lessoned status vis-à-vis the children, of being less needed and less useful than before. (Under the conditions of Twentieth Century western culture, it is also rather likely to mean that the aged parent will see a good bit less of his children than before.) Similarly, the aged person is apt to find himself in complete or partial retirement from his job, a circumstance which, at least for members of the middle and lower classes, is likely to involve a similar feeling (often accurate) of reduced importance. In addition to these elements, the aged individual will inevitably have lost through death a number of figures who had been sources of emotional gratification and support to him: his own parents, of course, older brothers and sisters, some of his close friends, perhaps his spouse, perhaps even younger relatives.

Loneliness is an increasingly frequent problem in old age and it can be a very serious one, particularly if the individual has been somewhat shy and diffident by temperament. The old person is apt to feel unsure that he is wanted—or even likeable—and therefore may well find it difficult to make friendly overtures. The resulting partial isolation may bring about further complications, since it favors the development of mistaken impressions about other persons (and, in others, about him).

The environmental changes are, of course, not merely losses of one kind or another, nor are they all of a personal nature. They also involve the advent of new situations and new conditions, to which the aged person is, more or less, required to adjust: different economic conditions, new means of transportation and of communication, perhaps different (and less pretentious) living quarters. Such changes may or may not be of a sort which would have constituted stress at any time of life, but in old age they are very apt to do so since they all require some expenditure of energy in adjusting to them, and the supply is now limited.

In fact, the crux of the emotional problems of the aged person may be summarized (in many instances) by saying that he is called upon to make an increased effort of adjustment at a time when his abilities for such an effort are decreasing. In the face of a diminution of the habitual sources of libidinal and aggressive gratifications and a diminution of ego strength (which may, in this situation, result from mild organic changes in the central nervous system), the personality usually experiences a certain amount of regression. Hence it is that older individuals, even those in generally good physical condition, are frequently described as "childish." The fewer the unsolved inner conflicts and the stronger the ego during maturity, the less pronounced will be the regression during old age. In the individual who has enjoyed a healthy maturity, it is not likely to progress, even in quite advanced years, beyond a mild and acceptable eccentricity.

NOTES ON FAMILY INFLUENCES

The preceding discussion of personality development has involved repeated references to family interrelationships. The chapter to follow will include some further material along this line. In later chapters of this book, devoted to the principal psychiatric syndromes, there will be additional references to ways in which interaction among members of a family affects the individuals in it. So important is the influence of the family upon the destinies of its members (as well as upon the larger society of which it is the most fundamental unit) that numerous books have been devoted to the subject, of which one of the best is Bell and Vogel's *A Modern Introduction to the Family*.*

It is impossible for a medical textbook, such as the present one, to explore this subject with appropriate thoroughness, and such an attempt will not be made here. However, it may be of value to draw attention to certain features, often ignored or misunderstood, which have particular relevance to the degree and the problems of adjustment of those individual members of families who are seen as patients (and to their recognition by the physician).

1. On the one hand, there are the truisms that healthy adults, when they marry, tend to form healthy families, and that healthy families offer their children the best opportunities for healthy individual development. On the other hand, since complete health is an ideal, for the most part an abstraction, there is the fact that the equilibria within a family usually depend upon both healthy and neurotic interactions

---

* Bell, N. W., and Vogel, E. F. (eds.): A Modern Introduction to the Family, Glencoe, Ill., Free Press, 1960.

among its members and between any individual member and the family as a unit. Insofar as the family is "a going concern," these equilibria possess a certain stability. Changes in the fortune of the family as a whole impose adjustment problems on its individual members, and changes in the manner of adjustment of individual members impose adjustment problems on the other members and on the family unit.

Thus it does not always follow that a personality alteration of a given member of a family in the direction of health will contribute to an increased stability of the family; in fact, the initial effect may be the reverse. Consider the cases in which the bonds between a father and mother include an important interdigitation of neurotic elements. Here are some examples at random: (a) the father has a relatively strong sadistic orientation (p. 416) and the mother has a masochistic one (pp. 416 and 423); (b) the father has a relatively strong feminine component of his personality, which is compensated by the mother's having some masculine inclinations and aptitudes; (c) the father has a pseudo-masculine need for intellectual dominance, and the mother a need to be somewhat passively ingratiating, making her a good listener. If, in any of these instances, either member of the couple were to seek psychiatric assistance for reasons perhaps not closely related to the characteristics just mentioned, to move in the direction of greater general emotional health and thus to modify the characteristic involved in the interdigitation with the spouse, the immediate result would often be a disequilibrium. This disequilibrium would be apt to affect not only the spouse, but the other members of the family.

As an analogous problem, consider the instances in which one member of a family—one of the children or a dependent relative—has the status of invalid or semi-invalid, whether from organic or psychogenic illness. The other members of the family will have come into some form of adjustment to this individual who may, indeed, be the center of the family in a sense. This form of adjustment may be far from ideal, but nevertheless it may be not without certain gratifications (e.g., a feeling of noble self-sacrifice or a feeling of superiority), and it may afford a basis of operation to individual family members and even to the family as a whole. It is generally recognized that the removal of such an invalid member through death or permanent hospitalization may produce a disequilibrium in the family. What is somewhat less widely recognized but equally true is that the *recovery* of the invalid member may also produce a disequilibrium, through creating a different set of adjustment problems. (Indeed, one even finds that certain members of the family, without conscious intention, may behave in ways which interfere with the process of recovery.)

In either of the types of situation cited (change in father-mother relationship or change in health status of a dependent member of the family), the net gains to the individual from treatment may be masked, limited, or even outweighed by the secondary and tertiary effects.

Since the physician—with the psychiatrist being no exception—traditionally has tended to focus his interest on an individual, his patient, these effects mediated through the family may surprise, disappoint, and even anger him.

2. Another aspect of influences within the family which may be taken into insufficient account by the physician has to do with the differences in status and in role of the children of a given family. Let us consider as a hypothetical case, a family with four children: a girl of 12, a boy of nine, a girl of eight, and a boy of six. Let us say that the family, in its individual members and as a whole, is a reasonably healthy one, but the parents, for cultural reasons, have a slight preference for boys. The family is moderately well-to-do and has not been subject to unusual stresses; however, in connection with the father's job, two changes of residence have been necessitated, one of them six and one five years ago.

At first glance one is tempted to say that the influences which have been at work on the four children have been quite similar and that the personality assets and liabilities of the four children should therefore be similar, apart from constitutional variations and the differences in gender.

A closer consideration, however, will indicate that each child has, in fact, a unique position and thus unique adjustment problems.

Starting with the 12 year old, one finds these "special" features about her situation (at a minimum). She is the first and oldest child; she is the older of two girl children; she is the only girl (and one of the two children) to have had the birth of a sibling occur during her family triangle stage of development; she is the only child to have been of school age at the time of the family moves. There are a number of concomitants to these features; for example, the birth of this child, though welcome, was tinged with a slight disappointment at her sex (which was less evident at the birth of the second girl). The joy at the birth of the first boy was not lost on the oldest child and was a special experience for her. The initial efforts of this girl at effecting a social adjustment, including a school adjustment, were influenced by the family moves when she was six and seven years of age. Being the first child, she was the child of her mother's (natural) maternal insecurity. Being the oldest child, she has had to assume more responsibility for the other children than they have had to assume for her or for one another.

The nine-year-old's situation has its special features also. He is the first boy, the older boy, a boy "sandwiched" in between two sisters, the only child to have a sibling arrive during his infancy. As a result of being the first boy, he enjoys from the day of his birth a certain prestige all his own. Yet, due to his younger sister's prompt arrival, he has had to experience a diminution of his mother's attentions during late infancy, an experience not shared by any of the other children.

The eight year old is a girl, closely preceded and followed by boys, and peculiarly tempted to be competitive with her older brother since she is so close to him in age, more tempted to emulate him than her sister who is separated from her by four years. Yet, in general, she has an easier time of it than her older sister, since the family's desire for a boy is fulfilled and since she has the year-older brother to "break the ice" for her socially.

The six year old is the youngest and last child. As the youngest, he sees all of his siblings enjoying privileges not yet open to him; as the last child, he is somewhat "babied"; less pressure is put upon him to grow up in his ways than was placed upon the other children. He has an auxiliary mother figure in the older girl.

This consideration of varying adjustment problems is, of course, merely skimming the surface. It has not taken into account many other features of the circumstances of each child which combine to make the experience of each one decidedly different from the others: features such as rate of physical maturation, special aptitudes, physical illnesses, resemblances to one or another member of the family (including the "extended family": grandparents, uncles, aunts, and cousins). Nor has it indicated the further complexities introduced when one or other (or both) of the parents is expressing definite neurotic traits in the family situation. Yet it may be enough to expose the extreme naïveté of remarks such as, "Knowing Miss Y., I was surprised to find that her sister (brother) was so different in temperament."

3. Despite these intrafamilial differences, there are as a rule strong points of similarity in outlook of the family upon society as a whole and its larger forces. Here the question is one of interfamilial differences. Since the physician is himself the product of a family, he is not exempt from these differences. In evaluating the position of the patient and the patient's family, he may err in either direction: underestimating them or overestimating them. If he underestimates them, the physician may mistakenly assume that a given (current) experience of the patient may have a similar meaning for the patient as it has for the physician. If, for example, the physician has come from a large family and has four or five children of his own, it may be difficult for him to empathize with (sense the true feelings of) a young father who is dismayed at his wife's third pregnancy and experiencing symptoms of one kind

or another in response to what is for him an appreciable and unfamiliar stress.

If he overestimates the differences, the physician may have an unnecessary sense of distance between himself and certain of his patients (or may give the patients such a feeling). If, for example, the physician in his youth has been strongly embued with middle class American standards, he may be unduly impressed with the great wealth of a patient, failing to see the many facets of the patient's situation which are disturbing or troublesome in ways to which the physician may have been accustomed. Or, at the other extreme, he may fail to appreciate the innate dignity and intelligence of a patient from a low socioeconomic stratum, being misled by the patient's questionable taste and poor grammar.

There has developed a professional discipline, that of the social worker (and particularly the subdivision of the psychiatric social worker) who is especially suited by education and training to assist in matters involving an extensive appreciation of, and efforts to work with, the families of patients. Something of the functions and scope of this discipline will be discussed in Chapter 13. No amount of assistance, however, can replace a conscientious effort on the physician's part to learn more about the family influences and to take full cognizance of them in his work with patients.

NOTES ON HEREDITARY INFLUENCES

Both because more is known about experiential than about hereditary and other congenital influences* upon mental health and illness and because, up to the present time, study of experiential influences has been more fruitful in pointing the way to therapeutic possibilities than has study of hereditary and congenital influences, the former will receive considerable more emphasis than the latter in the discussions to follow. (See, however, material on p. 264, pp. 356 to 357, pp. 375 to 377, and fn. p. 218.)

This circumstance should not be interpreted to mean that congenital and, particularly, hereditary factors are deemed unimportant. They are, at the present time, under widespread and promising investigation, but even apart from these efforts the relevance of hereditary factors in questions of mental health and illness is unmistakable. It is unfortunately possible for an individual with no known hereditary flaws to

---

* As the student with some acquaintance of genetics will realize, the contrast of "hereditary" with "experiential" factors, while a common one, involves an oversimplification which would be out of place in any extended discussion. Neither set of factors operates in a vacuum. The basic drives, for example, which are considered to be "built in" personality elements, require certain kinds of experiential stimulation if they are to attain recognizable development and expression.

become psychiatrically ill (even seriously so), but if it is possible, it is certainly not common for the reverse to be true, i.e., for an individual with known hereditary flaws to develop psychologically in a fully healthy fashion (apart, in some instances, from medical intervention).

The specific psychiatric* disorders which are known beyond question to be gene-determined are not numerous. Among them may be mentioned *amaurotic familial idiocy, hepatolenticular degeneration, gargoylism, galactosemia, Huntington's chorea, phenylpyruvic oligophrenia,* and a handful of others.

Hereditary factors are strongly suspected of being of significance in some instances of *manic-depressive psychosis* (Chap. 10), some instances of *schizophrenia* (Chap. 11), and some instances of *mental deficiency* (in addition to the conditions included in the previous paragraph; see pp. 541-546).

There are other instances, of which *diabetes mellitus* is the commonest example (p. 264 and fn. p. 218), in which gene-influenced metabolic disorders are thought to exert an indirect influence upon the development of personality difficulties. In the case of diabetes, it is considered likely that the inborn metabolic alterations can enhance the "oral needs" of the subject to a point at which a greater than usual frustration of these needs is almost inevitable. This frustration, in turn, can seriously affect the pattern of personality development.

Of great and increasing interest are the informal observations and scientific studies of built-in individual differences of a psychological nature (broadly speaking). Such differences as the rate of development of perceptual and motor systems, subtle differences in the mode of perception, differences in the inclination to motor activity, differences in the initial strengths of the basic drives—all of these must inevitably influence the development of personality.

Many of these individual differences need have little to do with the specific question of health versus illness, although a great deal to do with the fascinating variety in human personalities. It is not difficult to understand, however, how certain of these differences could affect the probability of the development of certain psychological disorders. For example, an individual with a built-in tendency toward a strong and precocious libidinal drive could quite likely have a more stressful family triangle experience than one in whom libidinal development was less intense or more gradual. In an analogous way, an individual with a built-in tendency toward vigorous and precocious motor expression

---

* The designation of the conditions which follow as *psychiatric* is, of course, not to say that they are not in the legitimate fields of interest of other disciplines, but merely to indicate that they produce syndromes of mental disturbance.

might find the experiences of the muscle-training period more significant than would the average child.

There is, indeed, reason to suspect that a complementary relationship exists between certain details of hereditary endowment (and limitation) and the experiences of childhood in determining which inner conflicts will be relatively prominent and which relatively insignificant in any given individual.

Bibliography

1. Benedek, T., and Rubenstein, B. B.: The Sexual Cycle in Women. Psychosomatic Medical Monographs, Vol. III, Nos. I and II. Washington, D.C., National Research Council, 1942.
2. Erikson, E. H.: Identity and the Life Cycle, Chapter 2. Vol. I, No. I, Psychological Issues, New York, Internat. Univ. Press, 1959.
3. Fenichel, O.: The Psychoanalytic Theory of Neurosis, Chapters IV and V, New York, Norton, 1945.
4. Freud, A.: The Psychoanalytical Treatment of Children, London, Imago, 1946.
5. Freud, S.: Three contributions to the theory of sex, *in* The Basic Writings of Sigmund Freud, New York, Modern Library (Random), 1938.
6. Gorer, G.: The American People, New York, Norton, 1948.

Suggestions for Further Reading

Bell, N. W., and Vogel, E. F.: A Modern Introduction to the Family, Glencoe, Ill., Free Press, 1960.
Erikson, E. H.: Childhood and Society, New York, Norton, 1950.
Freud, S.: Three Contributions to the Theory of Sex, *in* The Basic Writings of Sigmund Freud, New York, Modern Library (Random), 1938.
Gesell, A., *et al.:* The First Five Years of Life, New York, Harper, 1940.
Gorer, G.: The American People, New York, Norton, 1948.

CHAPTER 5

Psychiatric Problems Seen in the General Practice of Medicine

Louis A. Gottschalk, M.D.

From being a medical specialty that concentrated principally on the diagnosis and treatment of the mentally ill, the discipline of psychiatry has moved during the past two or three decades toward providing useful insights in the evaluation and management of emotional problems of people who are not necessarily mentally ill. These insights have evolved from applying psychodynamic* and etiologic knowledge about the psychoses, neuroses, and neurotic character disorders (personality disorders) to the task of comprehending the psychology of the normal personality and to the psychopathology of everyday life.

In this chapter, a range of examples will be considered of common emotional difficulties that often come first to the attention of the nonpsychiatric physician, particularly the general practitioner. No attempt will be made to include here an exhaustive coverage of these kinds of emotional or psychiatric problems, but rather some typical illustrations will be given.

GRIEF AND MOURNING; THE PERSON SUFFERING FROM BEREAVEMENT OR SEPARATION

From studies of the psychodynamics of mental depression, some interesting similarities and differences have been learned with respect to normal grief reactions, pathological grief, and neurotic (p. 333) and psychotic (p. 341) depressive reactions. Acute grief is a natural reaction to the loss of a love object. A love object is usually a person but may be an inanimate object or a situation or activity which has been asso-

---

* *Psychodynamic* means "pertaining to or concerned with motives and other causative factors in mental life."

ciated with a person. A grief reaction is typified by feelings of sadness, loss of general interest, decrease in initiative, and some mild changes in physiological functioning such as constipation, loss of appetite and decrease in sexual activity. Grief and mourning feel painful to the patient, but the process is a self-limiting one. There is convincing evidence that it is a necessary emotional process toward accepting the loss of a love object and in increasing the capacity to continue to live productively and to replace the relationship to the lost object with appropriate substitutes. In fact, many psychiatrists believe that the absence of an acute grief reaction signifies that the mourning process is being inhibited, for one reason or another, and that the complications of this inhibition, often labelled as a "delayed grief reaction," can be of psychopathological consequence. The complications include true depressive reactions or, sometimes, functional somatic disturbances or tissue changes. When somatic disorders appear to be substituting for the expression of deep or intractable grief (or for an actual depression) they have been called "depressive equivalents," particularly if the expression of sadness is inhibited.

Depressive reactions are similar to grief reactions symptomatically, but in depressive reactions the symptoms have reached psychopathological proportions as evidenced by a serious interference with the individual's effective functioning. Also, in depressive reactions, to various degrees, the process of mourning with its usually salutary emotional release and catharsis is blocked or is incapable of helping the patient give up a lost love object or restore a patient's injured self-esteem or allay his feelings of guilt. In fact, in depressive reactions there are a variety of additional symptoms, such as loss of self-esteem, self-depreciation, feelings of guilt, sometimes feelings of persecution and suicidal feelings. These symptoms stem largely from unresolved, often unrecognized, hostile reactions the patient is experiencing toward frustrating objects or people in his world. In some instances, the depressed patient has also lost a love object, real or symbolic, but this is not always so readily apparent as in grief reactions, for the lost object may be some habit, some value orientation or some other aspect of the self which the patient has renounced. The psychodynamic factors in depressive reactions will be more fully elaborated in Chapter 10.

The general physician needs to know how grief manifests itself, that the expression of acute grief with the loss of or separation from a love object is a normal reaction, and that the absence of a grief reaction in such situations may presage a delayed grief reaction or a depressive equivalent. When the patient begins to become persistently self-disparaging and evince suicidal preoccupations, psychiatric referral is usually indicated.

The general physician may avoid referral by first trying to help such patients in their work of grieving, and this is not difficult psychotherapy to do if the physician has no personal aversion to the manifest expression of such emotions as grief, resentment, and affection. A patient's process of grieving can be facilitated by a physician's telling the patient of the natural and medically healthy aspects of open mourning and by his seeking to decrease the patient's personal and social taboos about expressing the complete range of mourning reactions, no matter how contradictory to one another these emotional reactions may seem to be. Then the physician must get the patient to review, step by step and over and over again, even the small details of his associations with the love object and all his emotional feelings and fantasies experienced in every event shared with the love object. The physician should be prepared to give the patient plenty of time to unravel his life story and encouragements to exhibit emotion freely must often be reiterated from psychotherapeutic session to session. Expressions of sympathy and generalizations that everyone has to face such things before the patient has had an opportunity to express his feelings should be used sparingly. Such responses by the physician tend to discourage the psychotherapeutic process called "working through," which refers in this instance to overcoming the patient's resistance and inertia to talking about and manifesting the mixed emotional ties to the absent love object. When the mourning reaction appears blocked by underlying, guilt-ridden, resentful and hostile feelings toward the lost object, attempts should be made to facilitate expression by the patient of such feelings. A casual, matter-of-fact, nonjudgmental attitude of the physician about such current and past feelings of the patient tends to break up the emotional blocks damming up the grieving process. Often the self-recrimination and depreciation are an unrecognized expression of guilt feelings by the patient over old or recent hostile urges the patient has felt toward the lost love object. Alleviation of these symptoms is facilitated by helping the patient to talk about such pathogenic emotional logic and by helping the patient to discriminate the lack of actual cause and effect relationship between his past destructive thoughts or wishes toward the love object and the actual loss of the love object. Some patients are ashamed of the rage they are marginally aware of at the loss of a loved one on whom they were more dependent than they realize. Such negative feelings are so incompatible with their genuine love for the departed person, that they feel bewildered and ashamed of themselves and are unable to communicate with anyone else about their inner conflicts. A sensitive physician, who detects this rather common emotional reaction in his patient, can help his patient feel more comfortable about himself, by helping the patient bring these conflicting feelings out into the open, and then indicating to the patient that such reactions are actually consistent with love and mutual dependence and are not blameworthy.

During the period in which memory images of the lost object are being revived and dwelt upon by the mourner, the doctor can often make out another phenomenon. If one has been sufficiently well acquainted with the mourner and with the one who has died, one can often detect the acquisition by the person grieving of certain of the mannerisms, behavior features and even medical symptoms of the deceased. This phenomenon has been called *introjection* or *incorporation*, and it is considered to be an adaptive psychologic mechanism by which, in the case of a grief reaction, a mourner attempts to cope with the sense of loss by making a quality or attribute of the departed person part of his own personality (see also fn., p. 346).

The early detection of grief reactions by the physician is important for the purpose of differential diagnosis. Grief reactions are sometimes associated with symptoms of physiologic dysfunction. As just mentioned, some grieving patients, without realizing it, develop medical symptoms similar to those suffered by the loved one who departed. Moreover, in patients who have suppressed the expression of grief, there is sound evidence that the loss may precipitate medical disease in which there is tissue change or damage.

The physician, thus, has to decide whether the patient with vague somatic complaints, who has had a recent object loss, may be spared needless and tiring medical examinations and tests, as is likely to be the situation with the patient having an acute grief reaction, or whether more extensive diagnostic medical studies need to be carried out, as in the equivocal situation with nongrieving patients who have undergone object loss.

A physician is usually familiar with these complicated choices in his decision-making. Obviously, his usual, careful clinical judgment must be followed regarding which of his patient's somatic complaints to investigate with further diagnostic tests and procedures. When there is the least suspicion that a serious organic process is present in a patient with psychiatric symptoms, thorough diagnostic assessment should be considered. Certainly, openly grieving patients are not immune to medical disease which has no casual relationship with their grief. The recommendation being made here is to make some psychiatric diagnostic efforts as well as general medical ones; for example, to pursue inquiries about the temporal relationship of the onset of the patient's symptoms to the loss of the love object and also to find out about the complaints and symptoms of the departed person.

With the advent of the antidepressive or energizing drugs (p. 459), many physicians are dispensing these agents with the idea that they can avert or abort grief reactions or even obviate the necessity of an individual's having to go through this emotional suffering. Even though transient inhibition of a grief reaction may occur with the administration of antidepressive medication, there is no evidence whatsoever that the use of such a short term physiochemical approach to acute grief is warranted. At the present time, it appears to be psychologically inadvisable, because it only postpones or avoids adaptive mourning reactions.

SOME COMMON SITUATIONAL MALADJUSTMENTS

Vocational Maladjustments

The study and treatment of vocational maladjustments has become a prominent area of activity in recent times. The importance of this area of assessment and service is attested to by the growth and development of vocational counselling centers at many universities or as a fee-supported service available in the larger cities. Another mark denoting the importance of this area of professional functioning is the advent of a new medical specialist, the industrial physician.

Vocational maladjustments often initially come to the attention of the general physician. Frustrations at one's place of employment may, of course, stem from many sources, some of them principally external to the patient. But some vocational maladjustments may be brought on by the unique needs, expectations, reactions and conflicts of the individual patient. The onset of vocational maladjustment may, in fact, be the initial sign of an impending psychiatric illness. Or recurring or persisting occupational maladjustment may be evidence of an active, ongoing emotional disorder.

Occupational maladjustment may manifest itself quite obviously in complaints referable to the patient's work situation and be directed toward people in the work environment or to various other aspects of the work milieu. On the other hand, the evidence of an occupational maladjustment may be quite indirect. Only by inference from various types of attitudes or behavior may the physician begin to surmise that a vocational maladjustment is involved. The clues for such an inference are varied and include absenteeism, repeated accidents at work, feelings of fatigue or decreased output at work, the onset or aggravation of psychophysiological reactions such as skin disorders, cardiovascular, gastrointestinal, and neuromuscular reactions, and episodes of alcoholism.

To detect occupational maladjustment and to determine what proportion of the symptoms is due to situational factors and what proportion to an underlying personality disorder disabling the patient requires that the physician be interested in and willing to take time to listen to the patient.

SITUATIONAL FACTORS. There are a number of situations at places of employment which commonly precipitate emotional disturbances in mentally healthy people. One of these is a physically unhealthy or dangerous work milieu. Another is an unwarranted rebuke, repudiation or demand of the employee by a foreman or by a senior or fellow employee. Yet another situation is the promotion or increase in salary or some other benefit or favor given other employees, but not made available to the patient. These are only a few examples of emotionally disrupting occupational situations which could provoke emotional disturbances in individuals who have no neurotic potential or symptoms.

On the other hand, work conditions may be disturbing and disrupting enough—without, perhaps, being obviously so—that an otherwise quiescent psychoneurotic or psychotic reaction or transient emotional disorder may be activated. Mildly unhealthy work situations, unreasonable or unfair demands by an employer or employee, mild frustrations in receiving promotions or other benefits can be stresses sufficient to evoke pathological emotional and physiological symptoms and signs in patients so predisposed.

The examining physician needs to realize that in some individuals both situational factors and personality vulnerabilities are necessary to evoke symptoms of vocational maladjustment rather than one type of factor or the other being solely responsible.

PERSONALITY DISORDERS. One kind of vocational maladjustment is a "job phobia." The patient with a job phobia complains of feeling uncomfortable, tense or anxious at the job situation. A job phobia is related to conflicts about working and to repressed aggressions which no longer have a constructive outlet in occupational activity. To understand the psychopathology of a job phobia, it is necessary to know what a phobia is.

A phobia is an irrational fear, and the psychological mechanism of a phobia is one of attributing the source of anxiety to some external situation, e.g., open spaces, heights, streets, and so forth, rather than to the actual precipitant of the anxiety, which is an inner conflict (see pp. 325 to 329). One's place of work may become the site of such a displacement of anxiety.

Hence, the general physician, in his work of assessing etiological and psychodynamic factors involved in a vocational maladjustment, should look for irrational motives for avoiding going to work in the process of history-taking from a patient who is staying away from work purportedly because of obnoxious personnel or physical circumstances at the job. However, to detect that a phobic mechanism is involved in a vocational problem is often quite difficult because of the patient's convincing rationalizations or because of other psychologic defenses the patient may be using. Most job phobias, as seen by general physicians, are masked by some symptoms which provide a rationalization for avoiding work. That is to say, the patient presents a somatic complaint which, he says, prevents him from working, rather than recognizing his fear of or anxiety about the job. (See case history on p. 147 ff.) In instances where a phobia is suspected but its presence cannot be demonstrated, referral for psychiatric evaluation is appropriate.

An underlying phobia is only one of the many intrapersonal factors which lead to occupational maladjustment. Major mental illness, an impending schizophrenic (p. 360) or manic-depressive reaction (p. 354), or an organic mental disorder (p. 271) are likely to impair one's adjustment at work. The minor mental illnesses, the psychoneurotic disorders (p. 307) and neurotic character disorders (p. 397) likewise may be involved.

There is one other general type of problem which can be classified among vocational maladjustments which require some attention here. This is the situation in which a person can find no vocation which is of sustaining interest. A variant of this is the situation in which the person discovers—after spending many years pursuing a specific vocation or profession—that he is emotionally or temperamentally unsuited for what he thought might be his life work. Such people occasionally present themselves to the physician with minor physical complaints and mild depressive symptoms.

The physical findings relevant to medical illness are usually of minor significance and have no relevance to the patient's vocational dilemma, which may be mentioned by the patient only cursorily. The factors involved in this type of vocational problem are highly individualized, and special diagnostic studies are often required to clarify these factors and point toward the remedy. Vocational counselling, a specialized field in which clinical psychologists have made major contributions, is helpful. Such counselling involves psychologic diagnostic procedures, including the use of standarized psychological tests. Therapy may require intensive psychotherapy or psychoanalysis.

Marital Maladjustments

When to classify instances of marital discord as acceptable phenomena of ordinary domestic life and when to categorize them as chronic or pathologic maladjustments is an issue which defies simple formulation. Since the general physician traditionally has established himself as the avuncular confidant of the family, patients readily tend to tell him, often quite spontaneously, about their political, recreational or financial differences with their spouses. In longer standing doctor-patient relationships, more personal and intimate marital conflicts are discussed by patients, and the wise physician intuitively knows that good rapport with his patient is catalyzed by his listening, sometimes dispassionately and sometimes sympathetically, to these confidences. The physician who knows his patient well can sometimes tell whether the patient is likely to be exaggerating symptomatic complaints to gain sympathy and possibly undue reparations of some sort from the physician for the reported wrong-doings of the patient's spouse. He is likely to be discerning as to how the current status of the marital relationship is influencing the patient's feelings of illness or well-being.

In marriages where there are recurring signs of maladjustment, a physician needs to be alert to a number of facts which relate to the pathogenesis of symptom formation.

1. Chronic marital maladjustment may be the manifestation of an underlying emotional disorder of one or both of the partners.

2. The personality disorders of each of the marital partners may interdigitate in such a way that the two partners may provoke one another to frustration and aggression; in fact, they may have unconsciously chosen one another with something like this in mind, and, though the partners to the marriage are not able to live satisfactorily together, they cannot live comfortably apart. Why some people need such miserable relationships is difficult to understand. Sometimes a need for punishment, usually unconscious, is a factor. Sometimes an urge to be hurt and to atone is involved. Sometimes an inveterately cynical viewpoint about human relationships is involved. The need for people to suffer in their relationships with one another and to misunderstand and to hurt one another has been depicted by novelists and dramatists the world over; the discipline of dynamic psychiatry has systematically investigated and discovered many of the factors that lead to such unhealthy needs.

3. Acute or chronic marital discord may be the final stress precipitating a psychophysiological malfunction, such as migraine, peptic ulcer, certain dermatoses, neuromuscular disorders and so forth.

4. When a physician decides to try to intervene in marital maladjustment by counselling or psychotherapy, he should avoid making the common error of generalizing from his own marital experience and background and making recommendations that fit his personality, orientations, and value-commitments. Such an approach may not apply to a patient or to the patient's spouse.

A third party in two warring factions may only spread the battle lines and add confusion. Unless he is prepared to take time to listen to both sides of the problem and be a tolerant and neutral counsellor, the physician had better assign the patient and spouse for help elsewhere, such as a clinical psychologist, social service agency, or psychiatrist.

5. The sexual relationship in marriage is a delicate indicator of compatibility, for successful and gratifying sexual relationships require mutual interest and affection and a nice understanding of each other's individuality. Mild to major personality deviations are usually soon reflected in some disturbance of this aspect of married life. Thus, information about the sexual adjustment in the marriage can help the physician decide, in general, whether or not serious marital discord is present.

Family Maladjustments

The physician will often find that, in addition to some of the marital problems that are presented to him, there are family conflicts generated by the patient's associations with other members of the family besides the spouse. The physician is in a strategic position to offer help with such problems, for patients may be willing or become willing to try to evaluate and modify a situation which is tied to the preservation of health. Patients are often less willing to work on their social and emotional problems in many other contexts.

A few examples of some family maladjustments will be briefly discussed to illustrate the range of these problems.

1. A spouse who is finding that the children are interfering with the regularity and quality of the supplies of attention and support from the partner. Such a problem is very common in married life, but it is usually not voiced directly because of shame about having such feelings. It may involve either partner. There is sound evidence from systematic studies, that, much more than is generally realized, men experience feelings of frustration and rejection with the birth of children, especially of the first child, and that reactions to such a newcomer appear frequently while the offspring is being carried in the mother's womb. Studies of symptom formation or neurotic behavior in men soon after a wife becomes pregnant have revealed that as high as 40 per cent of men, in one study, become emotionally upset. The emotional disturbance may be expressed directly or inhibited by suppression or repression. Such symptoms as gastrointestinal symptoms, headaches, insomnia, anxiety attacks, depression may occur (see pp. 314 to 316). Alternatively, various kinds of overt behavior may be provoked, such as the seeking of extramarital relationships (with derivative complications of this maneuver ensuing: for example, guilt, remorse, separation, and impending divorce), unfounded rages at the wife, overprotectiveness and unreasonable fears of harm coming to her, and so forth.

Some men even develop all of the symptoms of pregnancy—morning nausea, abdominal discomfort and swelling, going to bed like the wife when she prepares to deliver the baby; this syndrome has occurred in prospective fathers often enough to acquire a name: "couvade."

2. A parent may seek undue vicarious satisfaction through a child's achievement. Quite frequently a mother whose career aspirations or activities have been interrupted for any reasons whatsoever may, consciously or unconsciously, try to make up for earlier frustrations by grooming an offspring for the special role she herself wanted. The physician may have the occasion to observe the patient when she is complaining of her daughter's stubborn recalcitrance over fitting into the role which the patient has set for her without consideration of the child's own individuality. Or perhaps the patient will find some reason to see the physician when her child, who has become a success in the area the mother desired, now wants to go her own way, to live her own life and differentiate from the mother.

3. A comparable conflict and disruption of the personality integration of an offspring occurs when a father decides that a daughter born to him should have been a son and proceeds to indicate to the child (in various ways) his preference for a boy. The daughter's sexual identification may become confused, especially if the girl's mother herself has serious reservations and doubts about the desirability of being a woman.

It is the child who suffers most in this family problem. The confusion she has regarding her sexual role and the disparaging view of femininity inculcated by such parents are likely to lead to symptom formation or inappropriate, i.e., neurotic, behavior at periods of time when she is called upon to be a woman. Menarche, the menstrual period, dating, heterosexual love making, marriage, pregnancy, childbirth, having to be a mother—any of these situations—may evoke psychiatric manifestations and, in some patients, even physiological dysfunctions, such as dysmenorrhea, lack of fertility, dyspareunia.

COMMON MILD SEXUAL PROBLEMS

The last-mentioned parental conflict capable of causing far reaching family maladjustment leads us quite naturally to consider the broad scope of common sexual problems that come to the attention of the physician for evaluation and constructive resolution. These can be surveyed here from the perspective of the usual chronological order of their presentation to the physician in his practice.

Problems of Sexual Education

Patients frequently seek advice from physicians on how to give their children well-balanced, factual sexual instruction. The modern psychiatric viewpoint about this is that children's questions about the origins of human life, procreation, and childbirth should be answered casually and directly, but that the parent should not offer details beyond the scope of the child's questions and that the questions should be answered fully, in language completely comprehensible and consistent with the child's level of intellectual development. Sometimes a parent requests, possibly out of neurotic embarrassment or anxiety, that the physician be the person to give the information to a young child. This is hardly necessary for a teenage child or younger, for it is preferable if the parents take the responsibility to discuss these matters with their own children, unless a key parent is absent from the family or is not qualified to do the job because of some not readily modifiable emotional disturbance.

To obtain expert information on feminine physiology, however, a young girl may benefit from some instruction from the physician on the physiology of the menstrual cycle and on some aspects of hygiene during the menstrual period which the parents cannot provide authoritatively. Moreover, it is customary for physicians to provide advice and instructions on birth control measures, in harmony with the religious conviction of the patient.

A physician should be prepared to recommend, on request, reading material on sexual education for children and adults. There are many excellent pamphlets and books on this subject at all levels of comprehension. Some of these books are listed in the footnote below.* Just as he makes it his business to know the ingredients of his prescriptions, the physician recommending such reading material should be acquainted with the contents of this bibliographic matter so that he can intelligently estimate its effect and discuss any questions that may arise when his patient reads it. If the reading material is sought by a parent for a child, the parent should be advised to become acquainted with the contents first before turning the literature over to the child. The parent may also need to be advised that literature should not, in any event, be used to the exclusion of personal conversational interchanges and discussions, for giving a child a book to read on the subject and not discussing the matter could quite likely signify to the child

---

* Corner, G. W.: Attaining Manhood, New York, Harper, 1938; Corner, G. W.: Attaining Womanhood, New York, Harper, 1939; Duvall, E. M. and Hill, R.: When You Marry, Boston, D. C. Heath & Co., 1945; Duvall, E. M.: Facts of Life and Love for Teenagers, New York, Association Press, 1956; Gruenberg, B. C.: Parents and Sex Education, New York, Viking Press, 1923; Levine, M. I., and Seligmann, J. H.: A Baby is Born, New York, Simon & Schuster, 1949; Parker, V. H.: For Daughters and Mothers, Indianapolis, Bobbs-Merrill, 1940; Peterson, J. A.: Toward a Successful Marriage, New York, Scribner, 1960; Stone, H. and Stone, A.: A Marriage Manual, New York, Simon & Schuster, 1935.

that the subject matter is something that the parent, hence by extension perhaps everyone, finds too delicate or forbidding to speak about.

Transient or Situational Impotence

A not uncommon problem presented by an anxious young or middle-aged male is fear of waning sexual potency based on several episodes of unexpected impotence or recurring impotence in certain specific situations. The physician who lets himself become myopically preoccupied with oversimplified etiologic formulae may focus no further than structural disease involving the genitourinary system. The function of the central nervous system is important in regulating erection and ejaculation in the male, and inhibitory effects from the cerebral cortex may occur by a number of means.

Mild systemic physical illness, physical exhaustion and fatigue, and especially pain, as is well known, can cause transient impotence. But subtler threats, symbolic more than real, to the individual's health or feeling of well-being may also cause temporary impotence. Some examples of such symbolic threats are: an injury to the nose, a discouraging setback at one's job, a note of indifference or derision from the spouse during foreplay, unresolved resentment toward the sexual partner, guilty fear about the sexual act, acute grief over the impending loss of a loved one.

The wise physician will explore whether some physically or emotionally stressful event of this sort has occurred which might account for the impotence. Depending on what he discovers during careful history taking along these lines, he will find himself in a more knowledgeable position to counsel or reassure. His therapeutic tactics must be tailored specifically to the patient's psychodynamics. There is, however, general information about sexual readiness and performance which is reassuring to most patients. Many patients are reassured, for instance, about fluctuations they anxiously notice in their sexual interest or performance and about such variations in their sexual partner when they are told by the physician that physical illness, emotional stress, and certain biological rhythms (e.g., the menstrual cycle) do affect the intensity of sexual desire, degree of sexual gratification, and sexual performance. This kind of information is especially welcome to men who have some deep-seated doubts about their masculine prowess and their capacities to deal with life's challenges and adversities. Knowing this, they are not so inclined to panic over the false belief that they have now found some further evidence they lack virility. The unknown, the misunderstood, the incomprehensible, the unpredictable has always been an anxiety-provoking phenomenon to man, especially the man with self-doubts and insecurities. Facts help to allay the anxiety.

A middle-aged man had an auto accident sustaining minor injuries and a fractured nose. He quickly recovered from his minor injuries and returned to his employment as machine shop foreman. His nose had been badly disfigured, and he made arrangements to have rhinoplastic surgery with an otolaryngologist. He felt too ashamed to tell the doctor that he had become unable to maintain an erection in sexual relations with his wife since the accident. But the physician was alerted to this possibility by previous experience with such instances and by the fact that the patient asked repeated questions about whether his nose would remain straight after the operation and whether the airways would function as well as they once had. The physician sensed the patient could not bear, at that time, to verbalize his fears of permanent loss of potency. In this case, the physician carried out the operation, and when the patient was discharged from the hospital with his nose still bandaged, the physician showed him an x-ray picture of the repaired nose and told him: "Now your nose is perfectly straight and it is going to stay like that from now on and work perfectly." When the patient visited the doctor a week later, he told the doctor with obvious relief and pride, the whole story of his impotence and how he had regained complete sexual potency since the nasal operation.

A husband and wife argued frequently over how their three-year-old son should be reared and disciplined. The father wanted to institute physical punishment and the hurrying of independent and self-sufficient behavior. When the husband was unable to maintain an erection during sexual intercourse, after a heated argument with the wife earlier in the evening, he became anxious that his manhood was waning. He consulted a psychiatrist who pointed out that he was expecting too much of himself to mitigate so quickly the hostile feelings towards his wife which he experienced a few hours before and that his difficulty having an erection merely meant he was not ready to make love to his wife and did not reflect upon his virility. The patient felt reassured by this information and was able to function satisfactorily soon after with his wife. More long lasting improvement in his shaky concept of himself in the masculine role did not occur until he realized that, for personal reasons dating back to his feelings about a younger brother, he was begrudging the attention and time his wife gave to their little son.

A woman, feeling deserted, bitter, and repudiated by her wastrel husband, successfully and with a vengeance seduced a married man to make love to her. In the sexual act, the married man was unable to maintain an erection. Later, he told her frankly that he had become aware of two reasons for his impotence with her. For one thing, he had been unable to put out of his mind the sense of being disloyal to his wife. Secondly, he had been frightened by her aggressive manner of seduction.

Persisting functional impotence and premature ejaculation are symptoms usually requiring more thorough and intensive psychotherapy; such symptoms are sufficient to warrant psychiatric referral.

It should be noted, in these times when psychoactive pharmacologic agents are being used profusely, that certain tranquilizers (p. 457), for example, Mellaril (thioridazine), have been found to produce inhibition of ejaculation or decreased sexual drive. Consequently, the physician should not overlook obtaining a history as to what medicaments the patient has been taking that might conceivably contribute to impotence.

Transient or Situational Frigidity

Just as certain conditions may lead to transient impotence in men, so similar circumstances may lead to reversible, self-limiting frigidity in women.

Whereas, in males sexual potency is culminated definitely by an orgasm associated with ejaculation of sperm, the female orgasm has no clear-cut physiological concomitant, and hence its occurrence is somewhat difficult to establish with objective certainty. This has resulted in controversial opinions as to what constitutes a true orgasm in the woman. Some experts on these matters hold that only a vaginal orgasm, accompanied by paroxysmal contractions of involuntary muscles deep in the vaginal vault, is equivalent to the male orgasm.[3] Others claim that the clitoral orgasm, accompanied by more voluntary paroxysmal muscular contractions around the vaginal orifice, is sufficient evidence of the arousal to the zenith of sexual excitement in the woman. These details and controversial views are mentioned here merely so that the reader will realize that, on reading more exhaustive discussions of sexual frigidity than is being presented here, the conclusions drawn and recommendations made will depend, to some extent, on which view one holds with respect to what constitutes the female orgasm. In the discussion of sexual frigidity here, this issue is being side-stepped and frigidity is being regarded as the absence of any climax whatsoever, either vaginal or clitoral.

With this definition in view, it is nevertheless correct to say that no woman can be expected to have an orgasm with every coitus. (To spare her husband's feelings or for other reasons a woman may feign sexual excitement with coitus when she has none whatsoever, or she may not complain of lack of pleasure.) The absence of an orgasm is usually not brought to the attention of the physician unless the patient has developed a great deal of frustration and resentment over a relatively long-standing lack of sexual gratification. Only then may a complaint be made to the physician directly or an allusion be made to some problem in the area of sexual functioning during the voicing of many complaints of a somatic or interpersonal nature, the significance of which will be missed by the busy physician. A woman patient who does not tell her sexual partner about her frigidity is not likely to discuss this personal matter spontaneously with her physician. The reasons are likely to be similar in either case, namely, shame, prudishness, guilt, pent-up resentment that the patient fears may explode too destructively, or lack of realization that such an unsatisfying sexual relationship may contribute to symptoms. One way to give the patient an opportunity to discuss such problems is to ask routinely that the patient tell about her sexual life and interests, and her lack of satisfactions, if any. Patients who are uncommunicative about their sexual problems on such occasions are not usually well enough motivated at the moment to follow through on the appropriate therapeutic recommendations that the physician would make. Those who can discuss their sexual frustrations should have a thorough interview focussing on their sexual life including development in early childhood, experiences, memories, and fantasies which bear on concepts of sexual role, reactions to menarche and menses, identifications with the feminine role, attitudes toward childbirth and childrearing, and reactions to sexual intercourse. Such information will provide the physician with sufficient data to decide whether his patient has been experiencing transient frigidity or chronic frigidity, each of which requires a somewhat different therapeutic program.

In women with transient frigidity, it is very helpful and supportive if the physician explains some of the natural variations occurring in the ebb and flow of sexual desire and feelings of gratification.

For instance, it affords some comfort and understanding if the patient is told that mild—and, of course, more severe—medical illness, such as a respiratory infection, may temporarily decrease the level of sexual arousal. Furthermore, different phases of the female sexual cycle are associated with different degrees of sexual receptivity and reactivity. It has been demonstrated, as mentioned in the preceding chapter, that heterosexual interests and desire to have sexual relations are more prominent, in the nonneurotic woman, during the preovulatory phase of the sexual cycle, when estrogen levels are relatively high, than during the postovulatory period when progesterone levels are high.[2] To some extent, this pattern is physiologically and biochemically determined, as in the oestrus cycle of the subhuman animals, but the psychological and social components of sexual behavior in the human animal are so overriding that sexual receptivity, though probably not the capacity for sexual arousal, can occur at any time during the female sexual cycle. It is impossible in human beings, in women as well as in men, to differentiate precisely and separately the relative magnitudes of the physiological and psychological components to sexual arousal.

Some examples of the psychological factors which are capable of temporarily inhibiting sexual arousal in women are grief reactions, the reactions occurring during periods of withdrawal from alcohol or some other drug in women who have been addicted to them, acute anxiety states of any kind, acute guilt feelings due to the participation in sexual activities that the individual, consciously or unconsciously, feels are forbidden.

Women, as well as men, are capable of having transient states of decreased sexual responsiveness in reaction to an acute illness, medically or psychologically determined. This fact must be realized by the physician, for such frigidity disappears upon recovery from the acute illness. Often the physician can ameliorate or remedy the disturbing illness or emotional conflict by giving sympathetic support.

In contrast to such relatively modifiable states of frigidity are those in which the woman has been and remains sexually frigid. Unless there are anatomical or structural factors causing the frigidity—and frigidity caused by these factors is comparatively rare—the treatment of sexual frigidity requires intensive psychotherapy.

MALINGERING

Definition and Initial Implications as to Mental Illness

Malingering is the simulation of symptoms of illness or injury in order to attain a particular deceptive objective. The severity of mental illness in the malingerer may range all the way from none (quite unusual) to the frankly psychotic.

Malingering in war time, by military personnel or refugees, is common. It is used for purposes of escape from military duty, survival when in the hands of an enemy, or for other ends. Under certain of these circumstances, malingering is not necessarily a manifestation of mental illness, and indeed, it may constitute a constructive adaptive measure from the viewpoint of one of the combatants. Malingering in such situations, however, does present a diagnostic problem for the military physician, but these details need not occupy our further attention here for we are interested principally in the situations confronting the civilian physician.

Differential Diagnosis

Malingering, when it occurs in everyday-life situations, is considered to be the reflection of a personality disorder (Chap. 12) and usually of an antisocial attitude. It can be one manifestation of a mental disorder of psychotic proportions. But when this is so, other personality features typifying a psychosis (see full discussion in Chap. 8) are so prominent that little question remains about the underlying disorders. These leads, taken altogether, help considerably in the detection and evaluation of the significance of the counterfeit symptoms or signs of malingering.

More difficult for the physician, with respect to making a differential diagnosis of malingering, is the problem of *conversion reactions* (p. 312). In conversion reactions, the patient unconsciously develops symptoms of dysfunction of organs or parts of the body innervated by the sensorimotor nervous system in order to prevent or decrease any consciously felt anxiety. The bodily dysfunction not only defends against or allays anxiety, but its very nature also usually symbolizes the underlying mental conflict which is potentially productive of anxiety. There is usually a more obvious objective, as in malingering, which is gained by the conversion illness, for example, getting attention and sympathy or avoiding participation in an interpersonal activity. This phenomenon is called "secondary gain" (see also Chap. 9).

How can malingering be distinguished from conversion reactions? It may be helpful to think of the conceptual difference between a lie and a mistake, and to regard malingering as similar to the lie and conversion reactions as being more comparable to the mistake in the sense of being an unintentional, dissociated, erroneous simulation of medical illness. There are imperceptibly graded degrees of awareness and hence many types of reactions ranging between malingering, consciously adopted to resolve some clearly defined external difficulty, and conversion reaction, unconsciously utilized to satisfy unrecognized inner needs and conflicts. Sometimes the degree to which the subject is conscious of his motivations is difficult to determine. In such cases, the decision as to where the line should be drawn between malingering and conversion is arbitrary.

There are a number of useful aids in differentiating between malingering and conversion reactions. First of all, there are a number of features to which it is profitable to pay attention in the mental status examination (p. 430). The general attitude of the malingerer is often hostile, suspicious, and unfriendly, especially if he is challenged about the causes of his symptoms, and he presents himself as quite concerned about them. In fact, there are often medicolegal implications in his illness, such as compensation awards for injuries. The patient with a conversion reaction is more inclined to be appealing, clinging, and friendly with relative unconcern about his bodily dysfunction. The malingerer is less likely to give a history of recurring episodes of loss or change of sensorimotor function throughout his life time. The patient with a conversion reaction is more likely to be suggestible and to be "fooled" by diagnostic tricks than is the malingerer. Anatomical diagnosis is important in the neurological differentiation between physically determined disease and malingering or conversion reaction. Paralysis of localized muscle groups or anesthesia in discrete sensory nerve distributions is typical in physical disease; whereas, paralysis of an entire limb or a stocking or glove type of anesthesia is characteristic of malingering or conversion reaction (p. 321). When in doubt about these distinguishing features, referral to a specialist (neurologist, ophthalmologist, otolaryngologist) is often of assistance in differential diagnosis. Psychological testing by a clinical psychologist may also be very helpful in arriving at a diagnosis, for such tests can point out the relative importance of sociopathic and delinquent trends in the patient as well as the importance of other psychiatric diagnostic entities, such as psychoneurotic or psychotic reactions.

As has been indicated, an attempt at solution of a problem through malingering very often has, at least in the ordinary civilian situation, an emotionally unhealthy (neurotic) basis. In some instances, as in the example below, a malingered complaint serves to hide a true psychoneurosis, in this case, a phobia.*

Miss E. H., an attractive and intelligent young airline hostess, aged 24, was referred to the company physician for the evaluation of recurring complaints of low back pain. The history, of several weeks' duration, was of sporadic episodes of pain, not entirely characteristic of any recognized syndrome and not clearly related to stress, although the patient maintained that she could not perform her duties when experiencing an attack.

The patient was found to be physically very fit; no organic or postural basis for the pain could be discovered. There was no evidence of muscle spasm. X-ray examination and routine laboratory studies were negative.

Miss H's recent work record indicated that she appeared to be using the complaint to avoid assignment to certain specific (night) flights which were a part of her intended schedule and on which she had previously worked for a period of two years. The patient was not seeking compensation, and she had no wish to resign from employment at the airline. She had indicated a preference for a schedule of all daytime flights and a hope for a promotion to a supervisory position, for neither of which changes did she have the requisite seniority.

When the physician questioned the patient about the material on the work report, Miss H. said that she thought that she could manage to work on any flight which carried two stewardesses, since then the amount of physical work was less and she need not be on her feet so much of the time. The patient became somewhat confused when questioned about the avoidance of night flights, offering only the partial truth that these flights often carried only one stewardess.

The personnel physician wavered between a diagnosis of conversion hysteria (p. 312) and one of malingering, but he was concerned about

---

* For definition, see p. 135. Phobic reaction is discussed in detail in Chapter 9.

his failure to disclose any real clues as to the motivating forces. He made the interviews (before and after the laboratory work) as relaxed as possible and managed to convey his sincere interest in being of help to the patient. At one point, Miss H. made a slip of the tongue, seeming to indicate that she had not been suffering from pain in her back. This circumstance inclined the physician to place greater credence in the diagnosis of malingering. However, the patient had, in general, a good record with the airline and was an appealing, likeable person, so the physician was unwilling to let the evaluation rest merely with making the diagnosis.

A third interview was scheduled, in the course of which, after obvious hesitation, the patient decided to take the physician into her confidence and made the following enlightening disclosures (not, however, in the connected fashion in which they are here presented, but piecemeal).

Although the practice was actively discouraged by the airline, Miss H., like many another hostess, had frequently accepted dates with prosperous male passengers. She said that she had become very popular in this respect and implied that the relationships thus achieved frequently included physical intimacies. Her way of alluding to this subject conveyed the clear impression that the situation had never been conflict-free for her. About six months ago, the patient had met—not in connection with her job—a sincere, hard-working, and virtuous young man, with whom she had gradually fallen very much in love. One month before the present evaluation, this man had proposed marriage, and the patient had accepted. For financial reasons, the couple had agreed upon a year's engagement.

Shortly afterward, the patient had recevied a whispered proposition from a passenger on a night flight. To her surprise, Miss H., who had expected to respond merely with a prompt, discouraging sally, experienced a severe attack of anxiety, which left her so shaky that she was barely able to fulfill her duties during the rest of the flight.

The next time the patient boarded the plane, she began immediately to experience the same sensations. In fact, they had invariably been felt on all of her flights since that time, and seemed somehow to attach to the experience of flying itself. There was some variation in the intensity of the symptoms, however; the anxiety was just bearable on daytime flights and on flights with another stewardess.

Miss H. did not understand the basis for her fear of being on the plane, nor why the experience should be especially severe at night and when working alone. She was very ashamed of herself, since fear of planes or of flying was derided in her circles. Having on one occasion felt a twinge of back pain in connection with lifting a heavy carryingcase from an awkward angle, she had hit on the plan of trying to get a change in assignments on the basis of complaints of a sore back.

The company physician did not attempt to make the patient see the above correlations, but he did recommend psychiatric treatment for the phobia. This was carried out, with eventual full relief from the anxiety symptoms. The patient had given up her back complaints after the third interview with the company physician.

Compensation Problems and the Question of "Secondary Gain"

In evaluating the problem of the malingerer, medicolegal issues are commonly involved. For example, the objective of a malingerer may be to avoid punishment for an antisocial act. The general physician does not very often become involved in making assessments in cases where criminal charges are involved. A patient's trying to obtain financial compensation is, on the other hand, a common situation in which the physician finds himself participating.

In reaction to a physical injury or severe emotional stress, where financial compensation is known to be available, certain complications may ensue. A latent phobia for work may be activated or self-sufficiency may be renounced in favor of depending on unearned income. These reactions are more likely to occur in individuals with neuroses or neurotic character disorders. Continuing compensation or a disability pension may serve as a powerful inducement in the neurotically disabled worker or veteran to assume that his condition, whether presumptively physical or mental, is irreversible. Furthermore, the individual is provided with a socially convenient rationalization that encourages dependency and permits him to give up his need for a conventional self-respect.

In this connection, psychologists have delineated many of the underlying principles of a type of learning they call "operant conditioning," in which behavior, followed by some type of reward, tends to increase in frequency and furthermore, to persist indefinitely. Compensation and disability pensions, in a general way, appear to evoke responses in a manner that is predictable according to the principles of operant conditioning theory. There is evidence that the longer compensation dependency is in existence, the more difficult it is to modify. There is consensus among medical experts[5, 6] on the subject, on the basis of empirical data, that compensation for neurosis or damages for injury should be abolished or that changes in the administration of such compensation should be brought about.

Workmen's compensation laws have valuable features which need to be preserved and these include the protection of workers from loss of livelihood due to injury or disease arising in the course of employment and the protection of employers against suits at common law. And pensions for disabled veterans serve the necessary purpose of preventing loss of income to those who have experienced a decrease in earning capacity in the service of their country. Some of the excellent suggestions that have been made toward the management of compensation problems are as follows:[7] (1) more emphasis in compensation practices on "rehabilitation" and less on "compensation" and "disability benefits," (2) more financing of active treatment rather than on disability support, (3) the termination of the secondary gain phenomenon through lump sum settlement, and (4) individual and group psychotherapy.

Reactions of the Physician which Interfere with His Effectiveness

A person in the helping role, such as a physician, may have difficulty maintaining a neutral attitude toward the patient who may be a malingerer, especially one who may be the beneficiary of some disability compensation. Many people, in fact, react strongly to the malingerer and their attitudes tend to be of two kinds: (1) repudiation and hostility stemming from suppressed envy that the patient may be able to get something the observer would like but could never allow himself; (2) excessive sympathy, based on identification with the patient and on the neurotic concept that pain and suffering should be rewarded rather than relieved.

Both of these attitudes, usually stronger and more impelling to action than is realized, are understandable when one pauses to consider that attitudes are acquired after many years of parental training and social acculturation. The child renounces, bit by bit, his wishes to receive love and attention without effort on his part, only after continual parental exhortation and coercion and evidences of disapproval and threats of withdrawal of love. The assumption of self-sufficient attitudes and behavior and of earning one's own way are reinforced by parental and extraparental attitudes. Initial attempts to master and overcome one's infantile mode of relating to parents are often associated with overcritical and intolerant attitudes toward younger individuals who appear to be still in the lap of bountiful care. The self-righteous indignation that wells up in some people when confronted with a possible malingerer who is seeking compensation benefits is reminiscent of the older child's intolerance and envy of the younger child's special privileges with the mother (and indeed, may be related to such an early experience).

Parenthetically it may be remarked that an equally strong feeling of intolerance is very often experienced toward the patient with a conversion reaction. If the physician misunderstands the psychopathology and psychodynamics of this disorder and attributes the patient's bodily dysfunction to conscious simulation and feigning of illness, he may be inclined to react with all the impatience and rejection that he might fell toward a malingerer. When some doctors learn that such patients are not consciously feigning an illness, a few of them may have a disparaging attitude toward the patient for having what they regard as a weakness, that is, a mental illness that masquerades in such a way that it confuses diagnostic efforts and, most disturbing, frustrates routine medical therapeutic efforts.

Conversely, a person who has an oversympathetic attitude toward the patient with a problem involving compensation is often reacting vicariously, that is, in the way he would like to be treated when he feels hurt. (It has been suggested that this oversympathetic reaction is similar to and is probably ingrained by a mother's kissing the hurt place to make it well.)

Realizing the range of attitudes that one may be capable of experiencing in these situations can help physicians deal with patients of these kinds with more equanimity. Expected and understood events and emotions are easier to cope with than the unpredictable and unexpected.

TRAUMATIC NEUROSIS*

The physician frequently sees a patient who has been involved in a recent accident and who has sustained only minor or trivial injuries or who may have major injuries. Whatever the circumstances with respect to physical injuries, the patient is almost certain to have a very thorough physical examination, roentgenograms, and other diagnostic procedures to detect all of the traumatic effects of the accident on the anatomy and physiology of his body. Insurance and prepaid medical care programs, in fact, generally make provision for paying the cost of hospitalization and diagnostic and therapeutic procedures necessitated by the accident.

What is not provided is the appropriate attention by the doctor, as well as the insurance coverage for the cost of treatment, to the mental effects of the accident. Psychiatric studies have shown that individuals who have been in auto accidents when there has been a close brush with death, and even when the threat of a fatal outcome has been minimal, have powerful emotional reactions to this exposure to potential destruction. These emotional reactions are usually so evanescent in duration and yet so disrupting to the person's self-integration that he notices them only subliminally or rapidly forgets or represses them. These reactions can be characterized as various degrees of death- or mutilation-fear or anxiety. All accidents or near accidents arouse the fear of dying. The majority of patients do not speak up spontaneously to other people, such as the doctor, about this disturbing fear, either because they have repressed it or if they are aware they experi-

---

* See discussion of this disorder and a case presentation of it in severe form at the beginning of Chapter 9.

enced it, they often do not mention it because they feel ashamed about their fear. Or they have not considered it was important for them to verbalize about the matter to anyone.

Systematic studies have shown that these subliminal fears of death can provoke cripping reactions of a psychological type: a "traumatic neurosis." Such a neurosis begins to manifest itself insidiously and gradually after the accident. In many instances, the psychological disability precipitated by the accident is more disabling in the long run than any of the physical injuries sustained.

In this connection, an investigation of personality changes in individuals three to six months after being discharged from a hospitalization for a traumatic injury revealed that impairment of personality adjustment had often appeared.[10] The personality changes were not of the kind due to brain damage. Most of these patients had not discussed any fears of dying or being killed by the accident with their physician while in the hospital, and their physician had generally never broached the subject to them. Typically, expert medical attention was turned toward efficient management and treatment of manifest physical damage. On the follow-up study of these patients, it was found that even the characteristic style of their personal reactions had sometimes changed, that is, impulsive, sociopathic types of individuals had become anxious and inhibited, obviously neurotic individuals had become more so or had developed new psychophysiologic complaints, and so forth.

Such disrupting and potentially disabling delayed reactions to the "emotional shock" of an encounter with the threat of dying can be attenuated. Giving the patient an opportunity to verbalize all of his emotional reactions during and soon after the traumatic experience seems to dissipate the likelihood of a traumatic neurosis. Since such a neurosis also develops in individuals who block out of awareness their deeper fears and anxieties, the physician interested in protecting a patient against crippling consequences of a traumatic neurosis must also pursue his inquiries with those patients who claim they are not aware of any emotional reactions to an obvious threat to their physical well-being or existence. Occasionally, the physician may have to supply the missing emotional counterpart to the patient's memory of the traumatic event. (The psychologic defense mechanism being employed by such a patient may actually be "isolation," "denial," or "repression." (See Chap. 3, section on *The Organization of the Mind*, for fuller details about these psychological mechanisms.) Remarks that may help such a patient verbalize his emotional reactions are: "You must have felt scared to death about what happened or could have happened," or "You were probably more anxious about getting killed (or killing someone) than you realize." It is just as important and salutary to elicit the patient's fears of injuring or killing others as it is to have him articulate his fears of getting hurt. Only after the patient has verbalized the range of his emotional reactions to the traumatic situation, is it appropriate and supportive for the physician to tell the patient that other people feel the same ways in such situations and that it is natural to have such reactions. When the physician is reassuring before the patient has verbally expressed his emotional involvement and reactions, the patient tends to become blocked from telling his own personal experiences and feelings.

HEADACHE AND HEAD PAIN
Incidence, Pathogenesis, and Diagnostic Features

Headache is a major complaint of more than one half of the patients who seek attention of the physician. It is a symptom which may be associated with a large variety of disorders of physiological and psychological origin.

The most commonly encountered headaches are the "tension headaches" from sustained muscular tension and vascular constriction; these are frequently associated with disturbing emotional conflicts. Migraine headaches rank next in frequency followed by the headaches associated with fever and septicemia. Then come those due to nasal and paranasal, ear, tooth, and eye disease. The headaches of meningitis, intracranial aneurysm, brain tumor, and brain abscess, though important and dramatic, are much less common.

A physician should have a working knowledge of the physiological mechanisms of headache and the role that psychological factors play in the production of this symptom. Harold Wolff and his co-workers were largely responsible for demonstrating that the cerebral cortex and the nerve cells of the brain were not primarily involved in the pathophysiology of headache, but that the symptom was likely to arise from fatigued or irritated muscles, from dilated blood vessels, from inflamed meninges, from stretched dura or distorted venous sinuses. Whenever there is distortion of these pain-sensitive structures, headache may be precipitated. This distortion may be effected by the changing of intracranial spinal fluid pressure, cranial skeletal muscle tension, inflammation about the ears, teeth, and paranasal sinuses, or systemic disease involving organ systems located elsewhere in the body than the head and neck.

The diagnostic evaluation of headache is difficult because of the many ways in which the symptom may vary and the fact that multiple etiologic factors, acting separately or in causal chains, may contribute to the symptom. In approaching the task, the physician should prepare himself with knowledge of the distinguishing characteristics of the different kinds of headaches as well as with the range of tests and techniques useful in differential diagnosis. There are several texts available which deal thoroughly with these matters.*

The focus here will be on clarifying the personality factors which can play a part in precipitating head pain. It is, of course, as much an error to diagnose a physiologically determined headache as psychological and to treat it only by psychological means as it is to diagnose a psychogenically determined headache as completely physiological and to use only such a means of treatment.

The varieties of headache associated etiologically with personality disorders may be categorized as follows: (1) migraine, (2) tension headaches, (3) "psychogenic" headaches (conversion reactions and malingering).

Migraine

Migraine and its variants will be discussed in detail in Chapter 6. The psychological factors as a trigger mechanism in migraine appear to be the least obvious to the uninitiated physician. The personality features and reactions dominant in individuals suffering from migraine have been carefully studied. These individuals have been found to be affable but inflexible, emotionally self-controlled, ambitious, meticulous and perfectionistic, tending toward the intellectualized mode of relating to others, inhibited in the easy expression of emotions, especially rage, and fitting frequently into the psychiatric nosologic group called obsessive-compulsive personality (p. 400). When these individuals become frustrated in their unremitting attempts to gain approval through hard work, they become resentful and anxious and feel fatigued. This emotional setting is the one which commonly sets off the labile physiologic mechanisms leading to the dilatation of cerebral arteries and their stimulation of afferent nerves of pain.

An attractive 27-year-old mother of three young children suffered from severe migraine headaches. These had developed gradually during the first three years of her marriage when she found that her husband was hypercritical of her as a housewife, demanding that she be extremely fastidious and orderly, that he was indifferent to participating in mutually interesting activities with her, and that during sexual intercourse he usually had premature ejaculations. She bristled with severe resentment, frustration, and feelings of rejection.

---

* Wolff, H. D.: Headache and Other Head Pain, New York, Oxford Univ. Press, 1948; Ryan, R. E.: Headache, Diagnosis and Treatment, St. Louis, Mosby, 1954; Friedman, A. S., and Merritt, H. H.: Headache, Diagnosis and Treatment, Philadelphia, Davis, 1959.

When a young man, also unhappy in his marriage, made romantic overtures towards her, she not very reluctantly submitted to the seduction. This clandestine liaison lasted for three years, during which the patient had no migraine headaches. She was able to rationalize away any feelings of guilt about this adulterous affair by emphasizing to herself her husband's indifference and hypercritical attitude toward her. When her lover moved out of the city, she began to consider whether or not she wanted to divorce her husband or accept a different lover. At this time, apparently by chance, her husband transiently showed some slight signs of more interest in her feelings and welfare as a person, and she developed an acute anxiety attack followed by vaguely conscious guilt feelings. Now she suffered the first migraine headache she had had for several years, and she could understand why.

In this setting, she returned to her family physician for advice and consultation. He recognized the complicated interplay of her life situation, emotions, and her migraine. He decided to interview the patient's husband, promising his patient to maintain her confidences, and to consider referring both of them eventually to a marriage counsellor or psychiatrist.

Tension Headache

As has been demonstrated by electromyography, tension headaches result from prolonged contraction of the muscles of the face, scalp, neck, and shoulders. Reduced blood supply to these muscles, due to their contraction, plays a role in maintaining the pain. If the muscle is continually contracted for hours or days, the pain and tenderness may outlast the period of muscle contraction and be experienced as stiffness.

Tension headaches may be precipitated by any stimulus provoking increased muscular tension. Head injury, refractive errors of the eye, a cold draft, or faulty posture are generally known to be capable of precipitating tension headaches. Less widely known is the fact that emotional reactions are probably the commonest cause of increased skeletal muscle tension, in the head or elsewhere in the body, and hence of tension headache.

A number of different emotional states are capable of triggering tension headaches. Anxiety or mild depressive states are frequently associated in some individuals with these headaches. More specifically, resentment or hostility that the individual feels inhibited from expressing, for any reason whatsoever, is one of the most common emotional conflicts capable of producing tension headaches. There is some evidence that the inhibited resentment associated with tension headaches is resentment which the patient is often aware of but considers inappropriate or futile to express and so suppresses. The inhibited anger of migraine, on the other hand, is only marginally if at all within the migraine patient's awareness, and the psychodynamic factors involved as well as the object of his anger is something of which he is not conscious.

The symptoms of tension headache may be experienced as discomfort over the whole head or as a feeling of fullness or tightness as if the person were wearing a tight cap. Most of the patients locate the center of discomfort in the back of the head and neck.

The aching may be bilateral or unilateral and be experienced in the occipital, temporal, parietal, or frontal regions of the head. Feelings of dizziness may occur, but usually not nausea, vomiting, or visual disturbances, as in the classical migraine type. Some tension headaches may last for weeks or months.

Treatment of these headaches is usually within the province of the general physician. The physical contact of a careful examination as well as thorough history-taking together help provide the climate of rapport and reassurance that may enable the patient to verbalize relevant resentments and anxieties. Psychotherapy of this kind, with further opportunities for the patient to relieve pent-up feelings, is as necessary a part of the therapeutic regimen for such patients as the judicious use of medication. Single episodes of tension headache respond well to aspirin. Sedatives, muscle relaxants, and tranquilizers to lower the threshold of arousal are of avail in some individuals, but should not be given indiscriminately. Massage and heat are helpful, not only for their relaxing effect on skeletal musculature, but their supportive psychotherapeutic value.

A college student complained of episodic headaches over a period of three months which were experienced across the forehead and at the back of the head. He reported that they were usually relieved about 30 minutes after he took 10 grains of aspirin, but that if he failed to take such medication for them he simply could not study or work in class.

Further inquiry by his physician about his life situation led the student to relate that he had been involved for many months in throes of indecision about changing his career plans, after having found that he could not really sustain interest in his course work. He further related that he had recently taken vocational aptitude tests at the college counselling center which had been interpreted to show that he had low aptitude levels for the career in which he was training. He said that he knew he was going to change his academic course work and shift to a program he found more to his liking and also one in which he had been found to show substantial aptitude. But he had decided for a number of reasons to complete the college courses for which he had already signed up, even though he had lost interest in them and had different plans for his future.

Further history and careful physical examination substantiated that his headaches were tension headaches. His difficulty studying or working in class was found to be due more to his loss of interest in his courses than to his tension headaches. His tension headaches diminished and disappeared after he discussed with his doctor over several interviews his mixed feelings about his academic plans and after he distinguished the valid from the neurotic reasons for completing the college courses he did not like.

"Psychogenic" Headache

In a small percentage of patients, the headache cannot be understood in terms of "end-organ" mechanisms, and it has features that indirectly indicate that it is initiated at a cortical level of the central nervous system. Such headaches previously have been loosely designated as "psychogenic" and this classification generally has not been taken to include those many kinds of headaches, e.g., migrane and tension headaches, that are precipitated by personality disturbances which initiate vascular and muscular physiological changes in the pain-sensitive structures of the head. In the latter types of headaches, psychological factors are also necessary but not sufficient factors in the pathogenesis.

The so-called "psychogenic" headaches are composed of two broad groups of emotionally determined headaches. One is the type of headache conventionally called hysterical; this type of symptom is part of a conversion reaction (p. 312). (See also, p. 162 on "psychogenic" pain.) The other type of "headache" is that affected by the malingerer; it involves the feigning of pain to achieve consciously planned ends.

Headaches as conversion reactions are accompanied by subjectively experienced pain which is not deliberately feigned. The pain usually is localized to the top of the head or it shifts from area to area. At times the patient seems to be relatively unconcerned about the head pain. The pain may be protracted and disabling, continuing as long as the patient is converting anxiety to somatic symptoms in this way. As with other conversion symptoms the headache represents, symbolically, some forbidden urge and the attendant punishment, for example, a wish to hit someone else on the head and the atonement for this wish. The pain may be described as a sense of pressure, as band-like, as pricking, or burning. Responses of the headache to diagnostic tests are equivocal and vary from day to day. The intensity of the headache is likely to be unaffected by simple analgesics; whereas drugs which alter reactions to pain—such as tranquilizers, sedatives, opiates—may provide temporary relief.

The diagnosis of conversion headache cannot be made simply after medical diagnostic procedures have proved equivocal or negative. To make the diagnosis, the psychologic meaning of the headache and associated complaints should be clarified (p. 322) and the hysterical character structure of the patient should be established, including evidence that the psychological mechanism of conversion probably has been used in the past as well as in the present.

The preferred treatment of conversion headaches is psychotherapy. Medication should be used sparingly for it is only of transient avail and it may lead to habituation.

BACKACHE

Backache is as difficult a syndrome to assess as headache, and it is as common as a chief complaint. In general, backache can be caused by mechanical difficulties, systemic disease, or psychological disturbances. The mechanical causes are perhaps the most frequent and they include postural defects, obesity, injuries from lifting or falling, fractures and dislocations, anatomical anomalies. All of these mechanical factors, except the somatic anomalies, in turn may be the outcome of some emotional conflict or stress. Systemic illness as a cause of backache includes metastatic carcinoma, tuberculosis, gall bladder disease, and duodenal ulcer (posterior wall); kidney disorders and uterine displacement are actually relatively rare causes of backache. Psychological disturbance as an etiological factor in backache, on the other hand, is much more important than it has been recognized or understood to be.

Estimates of the relative importance of various etiological factors in backache are quite varied. Most investigations are colored by the source of the patients studied. In other words, most studies of this matter are affected by sampling bias. The findings are also probably affected by experimenter bias; that is, the findings probably tend to be skewed in the direction of the observer's etiological predilections and expectations. For example, in one study of patients at an Air Force convalescent hospital, it is reported that no more than 4 per cent of backache cases were found to be caused only by organic disease.[8] In another study it is reported that among individuals who complained of back injuries developed during working in an industry, 90 per cent were incorrectly diagnosed as intervertebral disc syndromes; moreover, almost 50 per cent were found to be malingerers, almost 20 per cent had a definite neurosis, and 11 per cent had a frank psychosis.[1] Many orthopedic specialists report[4, 9] that mechanical factors, such as faulty adaptation to the upright posture, are the primary factors leading to backache. They reason that these mechanical factors produce increased muscle tension and localized vascular ischemia which can eventuate in the pain of acute or chronic backache.

These sample studies illustrate that in the general population the relative importance of the various etiological factors in backache is difficult to assess. However, the fact that personality factors have been found to play such a predominant part in some studies points up the necessity of the physician's knowing the types of psychiatric illnesses that may be associated with the manifestation of backache. These are: (1) psychosis or borderline psychosis with a somatic delusion of something wrong in the spine or in the back of the body, (2) conversion reactions (see also the discussion of headaches), (3) anxiety or depressive reactions with the psychophysiological reaction of increased muscular tension, and (4) malingering. It is important to note first that these same psychiatric entities may be associated with pain experienced in most other parts of the body besides the back.

The problem of evaluating the underlying causes of backache is complicated by the fact that emotional factors may provoke pain without pathological structural or functional intervening variables being involved, as is the situation with "psychogenic" headache. Moreover, emotional conflicts can aggravate and prolong pains initially originating from other somatic processes by increasing muscular tension or vascular constriction, physiological processes which, in themselves, can stimulate pain nerve endings.

Treatment of Backache When Due to Increased Muscle Tension (Psychophysiological)

Some orthopedic specialists may not recognize that mechanical factors such as poor posture or obesity (see p. 176) may be the result of emotional stress or emotional attitudes about one's position in the world. Furthermore, though they often recognize the prevalence both of the somatopsychic and psychosomatic sequences in the pathogenesis of backache, they are inclined to treat the mechanical factors involved in the back pain, rather than the emotional factors, because they understand mechanical factors better and have an optimistic view that the pathogenic emotional reactions will subside spontaneously or as a result of the patient's maintaining a mechanically correct posture. Such a happy outcome does not regularly occur. The psychological factors contributing to the pain usually also require attention and direct treatment.

To restore comfort, productivity, and self-respect, the physician should not think of the backache syndrome in terms of either an orthopedic or a psychiatric disease, but should consider that both factors are, as a rule, inseparably involved in the production of the clinical picture. Treatment of the patient with emotional disturbances should include attempts to deal with the personality characteristics that contribute to the backache, whether the backpain is mediated by a psychogenic or psychophysiological mechanism. In either case, the principal psychotherapeutic maneuver should be to let the patient express his feelings of frustration and resentment, his guilt or shame, and to help him understand something about his typical emotional reactions and attitudes.

Measures to relieve pain, induce muscular relaxation, and improve blood flow are also important in the management of backache. Physiotherapeutic measures are helpful. Bed rest, confinement, and immobility, though affording relief transiently in some acute ailments, may make some backache patients worse because no outlet for aggression is provided and the muscle tension and, consequently, the pain, increase. Muscle relaxants and mild analgesics are helpful. Local infiltration of tender areas with 1 per cent procaine may be of value for its placebo effect as much as for any muscular relaxation it may directly induce.

Sometimes treatment for backache is complicated by litigation for compensation. Here again, the wish to become well may be outweighed by the secondary gain coming from continued compensation and the satisfaction of covert dependency urges. There is evidence that an early cash settlement, in such instances, facilitates rehabilitation.

Management of Backache Due Primarily to Psychologic Factors

Such problems, if mild, can be helped considerably by the general physician who is interested and has had some experience in supportive psychotherapy. For the more complicated problems, where uncovering and insight therapy is appropriate, the assistance of the psychiatrist should be requested.

A sophisticated, tense 35-year-old woman complained to her physician of steady dull pain in the upper lumbar area of her spine. She was apologetic about this complaint, saying it was probably on a "neurotic" basis. Then she added that both of her children, a ten-year-old boy and an eight-year-old girl were getting psychiatric treatment, and this proved that she was "not only neurotic but incompetent as a mother."

The physician thought that, though she was at times an emotionally disturbed person, her self-criticism was exaggerated. He did a thorough physical examination and he found that the woman had some point tenderness over an upper lumbar vertebra. While the patient was being questioned further, she mentioned casually that she had burned the skin on her left leg recently in the shower bath and that she had found she could not discern temperature differences with this leg as well as the other. The physician, thereupon, started complete neurological studies, which eventually revealed a spinal cord tumor.

A neurosurgical operation was successful in removing a small intraspinal neoplasm. The physician reflected that a neurosis or a personality disorder does not immunize a patient against organic disease.

A somewhat obese, 65-year-old grandmother sought psychiatric consultation by self-referral, complaining of relentless pain in the region of the lower cervical and upper thoracic vertebrae. She winced with pain and held her head very stiffly, as she related that she had been suffering from this pain in the neck and back for three and a half months and that she had been unable to get relief for more than 24 hours at a time. She was afraid she was "going out of my mind" from the continual dull, steady pain, which was sometimes accompanied by paresthesias down the right arm and into the index finger. Her internist and orthopedic surgeon had found on x-ray studies that she had a degenerated cervical disc. They provided her with every form of treatment they claimed they knew—short of surgery—and the pain persisted. She had had bed rest, traction, hot packs, postural exercises, analgesics, muscle-relaxants, aspirin, antidepressant medication, ultrasonic vibration to the region of the degenerated nucleus pulposus, and so forth. Though her pain had abated, perhaps, it still recurred. Her other doctors had told her that the pain might eventually leave, but that it might not because they thought she was hypersensitive to pain.

Physical examination of the neck and shoulders did show increased tension of the muscles of her shoulders and back of her neck.

The interview revealed that her husband had died over 30 years ago and that she had reared her own three sons, then had nursed and otherwise assisted her mother-in-law and her own father until their deaths up to four years ago. Now she felt she lacked companionship. She felt that her contemporaries did not seek after her because she did "not have much to offer intellectually or socially." She said that her own children, now grown up and with families of their own, liked her for what she could do for them rather than what they might to do for her. In other words, she was used to being wanted and useful and now she felt undesirable and unwanted because friends and relatives did not seek after her company. Her feelings of depression and isolation and her unbending expectation that friends and relatives should customarily initiate social relationships with her rather than letting this be a bilateral arrangement, were found to be psychologic factors aggravating her back pain. Discussing her frustrated needs and unhappy feelings appeared to break the tension-pain cycle, so that she became backache-free for a long period of time.

SUMMARY OF THE MECHANISMS OF PAIN PRODUCTION BY PSYCHOLOGICAL MEANS

We will pause here briefly to review the two different kinds of mechanisms leading to the complaint of pain, whether in the head, back, or other areas of the body. Pain is, of course, always a subjective experience. It does not result only from the stimulation of the peripheral sensory portion of the nervous system. It may be mediated directly from the central nervous system. Developmentally, the capacity to experience pain is first acquired from many peripherally induced experiences. But in early childhood, pain experiences—like dreams or other visual or auditory hallucinations or vivid memories—begin to occur without corresponding stimulation of the end-organs as memory experiences accumulate and are stored in the brain. That is, painful experiences may be vividly recalled, and like the memories of other sensory experiences, they may actually be hallucinated (p. 279), for example as in phantom limb pain. Such pain is mediated within the central nervous system, and it may or may not correspond nicely in its localization with the peripheral nerve distribution. Furthermore, its very quality, intensity, and frequency can have the symbolic significance and representations that typify the kinds of complex associations and generalizations which the human forebrain makes possible.

Peripherally mediated pain can be precipitated by intense emotions, such as anger, anxiety-fear, guilt, and shame, which provoke various physiological changes in the body. Some of these changes are increased muscular tension, vasoconstriction, tachycardia, variations in gastrointestinal activity and so forth. These physiological changes, if sufficiently prolonged, can stimulate peripheral pain nerve endings. Such pain is localized, diffusely or precisely, to the area of peripheral nerve stimulation.

Centrally mediated pain is sometimes called "psychogenic pain" and it commonly occurs in such psychiatric syndromes as conversion reactions, hypochondriasis, depressive reactions, and schizophrenia. It is also precipitated by the mobilization of the strong emotions mentioned above. But more complicated psychologic configurations are involved. The pain is more likely to have some symbolic significance in relation to various contexts of the patient's life. The location of the pain may be determined, for example, by an unconscious identification with some loved person, the pain being either one suffered by the patient himself when in conflict with this person or a pain suffered by this loved individual, in fact or in the patient's fantasy. These types of pains may be associated with plaguing feelings of guilt, the pain being a means of atonement. The pain may result from the frustration of strong, aggressive impulses, pain being experienced instead of the sense of effectively discharged aggression or the sense of accomplishment. The pain may serve as a replacement for a real or threatened loss of a relationship. The pain may be an experience sought for by a patient (with a masochistic character structure) who is intolerant of success and who because of faulty rearing and misconceptions arising in childhood, has the idea that pleasure and human warmth is permissible, if at all, only through suffering, self-denial, or humiliation.

FATIGUE AND SYMPTOMS OF NEURASTHENIA

"Neurasthenia" is a term that was once used to describe almost any psychiatric condition. The expression was taken literally to mean weakness or exhaustion of the nervous system.* Today, it is not included in the official psychiatric nomenclature; when it is used informally, it is limited in denotation to conditions characterized by continuous fatigue. Many people experience this symptom in a minor degree; in fact, temporary feelings of fatigue and exhaustion are among the most common of all symptoms. But in the so-called syndrome of neurasthenia, feelings of easy fatigability and exhaustion are predominant. There is usually a wide variety of other symptoms, including aches, pains, and tingling sensations, dizziness, insomnia, diminished potency, and complaints of inadequate functioning of any organ system or systems of the body.

When confronted by a patient with such a syndrome, the physician is likely to think first of a somatic illness, such as an endocrine deficiency, a chronic infection (tuberculosis or brucellosis were formerly favorite initial diagnostic possibilities considered) or a neoplasm. A not uncommon clinical working principle is to rule out all organic etiological possibilities, and, if no definite pathological physical process can be established, then the syndrome is regarded as psychologically determined. Here again, it must be remembered that psychiatric illness cannot be safely diagnosed by exclusion of physical illness. Otherwise, psychiatric illness in medically ill patients will be overlooked, emotional illness may be believed to account for the symptoms when it does not, or the psychiatric patient may be subjected to many unnecessary and expensive diagnostic procedures. Hence, it is important to describe here the distinguishing characteristics of fatigue states due to psychologic stress and conflicts.

Such fatigue syndromes may be acute (as in military life, associated with severe emotional stress) or chronic. The aches, pains, easy fatigability, and weakness do not appear to follow any well-defined pattern from the viewpoint of body anatomy or structure. The complaints of organ dysfunction are vague, inconsistent, and an unvarying symptom-complex is a feeling of continuous exhaustion and easy fatigability.

By itself, these symptoms do not enable the physician to make the diagnosis of a psychoneurotic basis for a patient's illness. At least several of the following personality or experiental factors need to be established: (1) History of onset of these symptoms of exhaustion in temporal relation to a life stress or crisis. (2) Long-standing experiencing of these symptoms, with evidence that complaints of weakness or exhaustion were of value early in the patient's life as ways of getting support or attention or a family history that at least one parent or key parent surrogate used such means to cope with stressful life situations.

---

* See, for instance, the description of "neurasthenia" in Sinclair Lewis: Arrowsmith, Chap. 28: III, 1925.

(3) The presence of amnesia as to the time of onset of these symptoms. (4) Evidence of conflictual interpersonal relationships associated with emotional conflicts. Some examples of the kinds of emotional conflicts involved are as follows: (a) wishes to be rid of or free of a burdensome obligation to a loved person and conflicts over these urges with feelings of guilt, (b) sexual impulses that the patient has not been able to gratify because of reality factors or inner restrictions, (c) feelings of loneliness and frustrated dependency and a need to escape from the despair with one's self, (d) hostile urges toward someone which conflict with fears of retaliation, loss of love, or feelings of guilt. Emotional conflicts of these kinds consume an individual's energy, and the less conscious these inner struggles are, the less likely will any resolution and constructive decisions be arrived at in quieting the emotional turmoil. (5) Evidence of an underlying mild to moderately severe depressive reaction, with feelings of lowering of self-esteem, self-criticism, anhedonia,* loss of appetite, loss of weight, constipation, and the other vegetative signs that are described in detail elsewhere (see Chap. 10). There should be the history of the loss of a love object or the experiencing of an injury to one's pride or esteem, such as the failure to gain an expected promotion. (6) Evidence of a grief reaction or delayed grief reactions. Various combinations of these factors are associated with the personality make-up of the individual suffering from the symptom-complex of exhaustion and easy tiring.

Treatment of "Fatigue" States

The first therapeutic efforts of the physician should obviously be attempts to improve the precipitating situation if it can be ascertained. Helping the patient to raise his self-esteem by actual achievement, to secure love in a legitimate way, or to find substitutes for lost love objects are the environmental manipulations that may be appropriate. Whatever changes are sought should be tailored to the specific problems in the patient's life.

The form of neurasthenic syndrome seen in war time, "combat fatigue," is usually manageable by temporary environmental change and emotional support.

In everyday life, chronic fatigue states usually have a more persisting psychoneurotic component, which does not respond in a lasting way to environmental changes or to tranquilizing or energizing medicaments. Psychotherapy involving attenuation of the inner psychological conflicts is necessary. Focal psychotherapy of specific psychological conflicts may suffice to relieve substantially the symptoms of fatigue.

---

* *Anhedonia* is the inability to experience pleasurable feelings.

Sometimes psychoanalysis is necessary, and this type of treatment is usually entirely successful.

BOREDOM

Boredom is a complaint not infrequently confided to the family doctor, but one that is too often accepted by him at face value. Like the term "nervousness," it may satisfy a hurried clinician who does not realize that it may connote anything from a to z, at a subjective level, and certainly at an etiological level. Clinical psychodynamic studies have shown that the complaint of "feeling bored" or being in a state of "boredom," are cues to a number of kinds of psychological states which the patient usually does not recognize or cannot, at first, express more accurately.

For one thing, saying that one felt "bored" may be a very polite, socially acceptable way of reporting, with a minimum of guilty fear or embarrassment, that one was enraged with some state of affairs. It may acknowledge relatively mild resentment about a situation, as when one says "I was bored with my company" and this in turn may mean, when translated into inner psychodynamic experience, "I resented my company's discussing subjects I do not know or care much about, for I wanted to show myself off and have them pay more attention to me."

On the other hand, the complaint of boredom may signify an impending or actual state of mental depression with all of the potentially serious ramifications of this type of psychiatric illness. The term is used more often by patients to describe an affect or mood disorder than a schizoid or schizophrenic type of subjective experience. Adolescents and adults who are undergoing a slow change in their sense of identity, that is, in their awareness of who they are and who they want to be or who are dissatisfied with some aspects of their value system or their role in society or in their family, frequently feel "bored" and tell others they feel this way.

All of these underlying emotional aspects of the state of boredom can be accompanied by physiological concomitants, such as various gastrointestinal, genitourinary or neuromuscular changes. These are usually of more immediate interest to the physician. But focusing on the assessment of complaints referable to these physiological changes without evaluating the mood and affect associated with the state of boredom can handicap the physician's diagnostic work. An illustrative case may help emphasize the attention due and further inquiry merited by the complaint of boredom.

A 59-year-old woman complained of boredom, recurring attacks of disrupting anxiety and frequent nausea and vomiting on arising in the morning. She was a small woman, whose frail beauty was fading. Her husband, a successful entrepreneur, had recently retired and was now spending much time at home. The morning nausea and vomiting were symptoms that the patient had had periodically since childhood in situations where she felt under pressure to face some event, family situation, desire or emotion that was unacceptable to her. Her physician had looked after her for years, had assured himself that this latest episode of morning vomiting was not due to an organic disease; he requested psychiatric consultation to evaluate her overwhelming feelings of boredom and episodes of panic.

Psychiatric clinical evaluation, corroborated by psychological testing, revealed that this patient characteristically dealt with disturbing life situations, fears and resentments by putting the upsetting thoughts and emotions out of her mind or by avoiding becoming involved in any situations which might conceivably arouse unpleasant mental experiences. She was quite depressed under her façade of boredom and tension.

Her feeling of boredom was found to be the resultant subjective experience remaining when she suppressed and repressed more disturbing emotional conflicts, namely: (1) her sadness and sense of loss that the physical beauty for which she had long been admired and sought after was irretrievably going; (2) her anxiety about aging and eventual ill health, the prospect of which had been recently unavoidably brought to her attention by the illness and death of several of her friends; (3) her resentment at her husband, now that he was home and retired, that he was spending very little time with her doing things or talking with her, but instead was very busy developing and running several business enterprises from the home. The patient's anxiety attacks and nausea were symptoms occurring whenever she partially recognized the discrepancy between the bland and honeyed dream-world she wanted life to be and the way life really turned out to be.

After a period of psychotherapy—during which she relaxed her vigilant attitude of avoidance and denial—her symptoms decreased and disappeared. In the process she found new zest for living and was able to broaden the base on which she gained her personal security and self-respect.

ADDICTION OR HABITUATION IN MILD OR INCIPIENT FORM

The physician is in a position, by the very nature of his profession, to witness the incipient or ongoing habitual use by patients of drugs and related substances. The excessive use of a drug is always a matter of professional concern and it may become an indication for a patient's hospitalization if the problem of effecting his withdrawal from physiological (or severe psychological) dependence on the addiction is an issue.

Definition of Drug Addiction

Drug addiction has been described by a World Health Organization committee as "a state of periodic or chronic intoxication, detrimental to the individual and to society, produced by the repeated consumption of a drug (natural or synthetic). Its characteristics include: (1) an overpowering desire or need (compulsion) to continue taking the drug and to obtain it by any means, (2) a tendency to increase the dose, and (3) a psychic (psychological) and sometimes a physical dependence on the effects of the drug." By *physical dependence* is meant an altered physiological state brought on by repeated ingestion or administration of a drug in order to prevent the appearance of abstinence symptoms. The term, *habituation,* is ordinarily used to indicate a psychological dependence on the use of a drug because of the relief it provides from emotional tension.

Patients who disclose their addiction often readily provide the history of how they became addicted. This may be instructive in terms of indicating what not to do when providing analgesic medication to a patient suffering prolonged discomfort or pain. Such hindsight is clearer than foresight, but it scarcely tells one how the addiction might have been detected or even avoided earlier. What are some of the situations and personality factors leading to addiction problems, both major and minor?

Before embarking on a discussion of these points, it should be clarified that addictions are considered to be pathological and a health problem—hence of medical and psychiatric interest—when they are of a magnitude sufficient to cause irreversible deleterious biological changes, reversible physiological changes that seriously impair the body's defenses against disease or when they interfere with the culturally acceptable performance of a person's occupational, social, or domestic activities.

Contrary to popular opinion, the prolonged use of certain stigmatized drugs, such as morphine, cocaine, and marijuana, has comparatively little (direct) adverse effect on the physical health of the addict. The adverse effect of these drugs is more in the ethical and social areas of the addict's life, and these are not a direct effect of the narcotics, but rather a social consequence of the life of addiction, or in some instances, a way of life that was already typical of the addict.

Tobacco, alcohol, and even food of various kinds, while less stigmatized, can produce deleterious effects on the physiology of the body when used for long periods of time in excessive amounts. At the same time, there are many kinds of eating and drug ingestion habits that are innocuous or nearly so, and are at the margin of the domain of conventional medical interest. Between these extremes of habitual use of drugs or other substances are more moderate types of addictions or habituations which the physician inevitably observes, but for which he does not customarily try to enforce withdrawal treatment. On the other hand, patients with incipient to moderate addictions may ask for a physician's opinions and therapeutic advice about the possible deleterious nature of their addictive habit. These are the occasions when the physician should have some specialized information in order to perform his professional function.

Psychodynamic Factors in Addiction and Habituation

The use of the mouth and the upper end of the alimentary canal to relieve tension and induce a sense of inner security—though a temporary one—is probably inborn and certainly reinforced from infancy to old age. Serenity is induced not only by the ingestion of food, but also by putting chemically inert substances into the mouth: the thumb, the pacifier, chewing gum, and later a placebo pill. The power of the thing-in-the-mouth (or elsewhere in the gastrointestinal system) to alleviate distress is attested to by the many experimental and clinical observations that the "powerful" placebo is capable of relieving the discomforts and pains of 40 to 50 per cent of surgical and medical patients in hospitals. Small wonder that chemicals that do have a physiological action on the body or a noticeable taste or smell often have an even more persisting and persuasive alleviating effect on a patient's feelings of illness, anxiety, and pain.

Careful personality studies of patients with addictions to opiates have revealed that these patients experience euphoria and feelings of contentment when they receive their drugs, whereas individuals not addicted to opiates do not experience such feelings when opiates are given; instead they feel sedated and drowsy. Furthermore, patients addicted to opiates have been shown often to have underlying depressive reactions (Chap. 10) in contrast to patients who are not addicted. The use of the drug provides an escape from their inner unhappiness and tension. The drug seems to provide the sense of security and well-being that a nursing child gets from the mother. The attraction of such a gratifying and, in a sense, convenient substitute for the feeling of a mother's protection and comfort probably accounts, in part, for the unrelenting psychological dependence of the patient on the drug. Chronic addicts who have gone through withdrawal symptoms usually have symptoms and signs of strong anxiety and depression for rather long (sometimes interminable) periods of time after discontinuing the drug. It is these symptoms which they seek to allay when they return to the habit of taking the drug. (The discussion of narcotic addiction is continued in Chapter 12 on Personality Disorders.)

With those pharmacologic agents (such as certain sedative drugs) where the physiological dependence is much less marked than with the opiates or altogether absent, the psychological dependence has a psychodynamic basis similar to the one described, but it, too, is of lesser magnitude.

The physician may find that he has contributed to the establishment of an addiction. Sometimes this situation develops when a patient complains of intractable pain in a setting where his illness appears to be incurable and possibly fatal. In such a context, a certain number of patients, who would otherwise not do so, become addicted with the collaboration of their doctors. Those patients who survive the illness are left with a complication of the therapeutic program for their sickness, a complication in the form of an addiction to an analgesic or soporific drug. Such situations are fairly common and the medical profession is not generally critical of such an occurrence, for the relief of pain and discomfort is known to be a life-saving measure during some illnesses (e.g., myocardial infarction) and pain relief is considered a positive value of humane dimensions if prolonged suffering or death appears to be likely. Sometimes the physician discovers a patient has become addicted under different circumstances, usually one in which the patient is addiction-prone, and the physician realizes he has unwittingly aided in the process of addiction by supplying the necessary amounts of medication. Situations of this sort are likely to occur when the physician has not taken time to inquire about and evaluate the patient's personality or has not found some other means to provide for the interpersonal needs that have led to the addiction.

What can the doctor do if he suspects that he has contributed to the development of an addiction? Enlisting the patient's cooperation in withdrawing the drug is of initial importance. Determining, with the patient, the factors promoting the need for the drug and hence for sometimes inordinate solace, comfort, and escape, and evolving other avenues to take care of these needs is essential. During first attempts to withdraw the drug, the physician should not be discouraged or resentful if he discovers that the patient has obtained supplies of the drug from other sources than himself. Such desperate techniques to maintain the status quo are frequent among patients who are being weaned from a drug. Hospitalization and psychiatric consultation should be seriously considered for problem cases.

Habituation to Tobacco

The excessive use of tobacco is growing, probably because of persuasive advertising and in spite of suggestive medical evidence that this often soothing and pleasant pastime probably has deleterious though transient effects on cardiovascular and gastrointestinal functioning and more gradual but longlasting effects in the direction of contributing to the growth of neoplasms in the respiratory airways.

The physician may have to decide whether he should advise a patient to discontinue the use of tobacco. The physician's views on such an issue tend to be swayed not only by the medical condition of the patient but also by the physician's own indulgence, or lack of it, in the tobacco habit.

Tobacco smoking serves as a means of discharging emotional tension and as a substitute gratification for various emotional needs. The movements of the hands, the respiratory inhalation and exhalation, the involvement of the lips or teeth may simultaneously serve as brief outlets for aggression or substitutes for intimacy and closeness. The mild physiological reactions to smoking, for example, increased heart rate and peripheral vasoconstriction, may provide a short-lived stimulus toward wakefulness or relative alertness for a drowsy or fatigued individual. A person who is ashamed of an insatiable hunger for love or nurture may partially gratify and concomitantly punish the self through the ororespiratory system by smoking until tongue, oropharynx, and larynx are actually hurting. The emotional use that smoking is put to, of course, varies to some extent with each individual and depends on the unique personality structure of the person. No simple psychodynamic formula applying to every smoker is possible.

The shortcomings of tobacco as a relief of emotional tension are several-fold: (1) Though smoking is a relaxing and tension-decreasing habit, its effect in these respects is weak and evanescent. Nevertheless, for the reasons given above a strong psychological dependence and a very mild physiological dependence on smoking may develop. (2) There is evidence that continual and heavy smoking do have mild deleterious biological effects. The advantages of the tobacco habit are that it has such broad social and cultural approval and that in extreme moderation the habit has minimal, if any harmful effects on the body.

All these considerations are ones which the physician must weigh before attempting to change a patient's tobacco habit.

Two examples are given here to illustrate some of the factors involved in the strength of the smoking habit. The first example emphasizes the contribution of the impetus of associated events as a stimulus evoking the wish and need to smoke. The second example illustrates the deeper psychological needs and emotional ramifications that are involved in the smoking habit. The psychologist, E. R. Guthrie, famed as a contributor to conditioning and learning theory, in illustrating how strength of habit depends crucially on feedback from a current situation or response, told the following story about himself.

"Drinking or smoking after years of practice are action systems which can be started by thousands of reminders. . . . I had once a caller to whom I was explaining that the apple I had just finished was a splendid device for avoiding a smoke. The caller pointed out that I was at that moment smoking. The habit of lighting a cigarette was so attached to the finish of eating, that smoking had started automatically."

An inveterate smoker, who was a patient in psychoanalysis, was told by his internist that he had to stop smoking for medical reasons. He reluctantly complied with his doctor's advice. The psychoanalyst noted that his patient's first reaction to the total abstinence from smoking was increased tension, anxiety, and restlessness. Then he began to have florid nightmares of starvation, being involved in a plane crash, being in the midst of atomic warfare, and dying slowly from cancer of the stomach. Later, he began to fall asleep transiently on the couch and then he would awaken with a start and feel briefly disoriented. A month after discontinuing smoking the patient was severely depressed and had suicidal ideas. He was experiencing keenly every past grief reaction, separation experience, and loss that he had ever had. Hospitalization was considered. He managed to pull through the withdrawal from his dependence on tobacco without hospitalization, after he lived through and clarified the multiple emotional ramifications and substitutions involved in his smoking habit.

When medical factors dictate that tobacco smoking should, without question, be given up, as in coronary artery disease, chronic lung disease, peripheral vascular disease, the physician must remind himself that the psychological dependence on tobacco fulfills a need, albeit neurotic in some instances, and that the patient may well develop some new symptoms in the process of or following withdrawal. Provision for taking care of these needs should be considered. Sometimes more adequate means of providing relaxation or alleviation of tension may be prescribed. The wisdom to do this, however, requires sound knowledge of the emotional structure and needs of the patient.

Habituation to Alcohol

Alcohol is another substance, like tobacco, the use of which is sanctioned by most modern societies, and hence its ingestion, even to the point of occasional inebriation, is more often looked upon by others with humor than with disfavor. No wonder, then, with all the so-called social drinking being done and casually discussed, that the physician may easily overlook the circumstance that a patient has an unrelenting psychological dependence on alcohol.

Alcohol has been facetiously described as "the poor man's psychiatrist," but this is an inadequate delineation, for alcohol makes no economic or social distinctions when it comes to trying to do the psychiatrist's job. It is probably true that alcohol has been one of the favorite and most successful means mankind has found of cushioning the immediate impact of life's cruelest and most painful facts. It is probably true that disabling acute mental illness has been repeatedly averted by the anesthetic effect of alcohol. But it is also true that frequently alcohol, as a remedy, produces mental disability (in the form of addiction) or somatic complications (in terms of peripheral neuritis, chronic central nervous system dysfunction, or liver disease) that far outweigh in seriousness the initial emotional disturbance for which the alcohol was supposed to provide a cure.

In reciting here these psychopharmacologic characteristics of alcohol, the attempt is not so much to present new knowledge about alcohol but rather to select pertinent data among those generally well-known facts about alcohol and to synthesize a common-sense approach useful to the physician in his over-all evaluation of the patient who indicates he takes a drink. (See extended discussion of alcoholism on pp. 405 to 414 in Chap. 12.)

The physician's major problem is to determine whether his patient is using alcohol to excess or in such a way that, in the long run, the patient is more likely to be harmed than helped. Many persons are reluctant to acknowledge to themselves or certainly to someone else that they are becoming or have become addicted to alcohol. With studious omission by the patient of pertinent information, including amount and frequency of drinking, a physician may have absolutely no grounds for suspecting addiction to alcohol. In such cases, there is nothing he can actually do until several alcoholic indiscretions of the patient are recognized by the patient's family and the physician's attention is directed to the problem. Such signs as tremors of the hands, sores at the corners of the mouth, weight loss, peripheral neuritis, brain syndrome, liver disease are rather far-advanced signs of alcoholism, and these should certainly evoke this possibility in the physician's mind. The history of absenteeism from work or "lost weekends" and the witnessing of slurred speech, ataxia, and alcoholic breath are all additional cues for the physician that the patient has a problem of alcoholism.

The actual treatment of the addiction, once it has been detected, requires some fair degree of experience in psychiatric medicine. Methods of simple exhortation or authoritarian threats do, indeed, suffice to discourage some alcoholics from continuing their habituation. But such a result is an exception rather than a rule. In any event, for any long-lasting benefit, the patient's cooperation with the treatment usually needs to be obtained. The precipitating and continuing emotional factors leading to drinking need to be clarified and the better ways of relating to others and oneself have to be learned. These steps take time (see p. 412).

The clinician needs to be reminded that abrupt withdrawal from alcohol or other sedative drugs may lead to convulsions in some individuals. The administration of tranquilizing agents and anticonvulsant drugs during the period of withdrawal from the alcohol can prevent these complications.

Sedatives and Tranquilizers

Patients may become addicted to sedatives and tranquilizers because of the same kinds of personality factors that lead to addiction to other drugs, including alcohol. In fact, many of the people who are severely addicted to sedatives were once chronic alcoholics, and they have substituted one sedative for another (the alcohol). Patients do develop some tolerance to sedatives and can develop physiological and psychological dependence on them, as well as having withdrawal symptoms when their use is discontinued. Irreversible central or peripheral nervous system damage is relatively rare in reaction to sedatives and tranquilizers but instances of such complications have been reported. Side effects of these medicaments are quite common. They may involve any body system, and these seem to be the principal deterrent to their indiscriminate administration. In spite of side effects, these medicaments are prescribed much too freely and carelessly by physicians, and their habitual use by some patients can be ascribed to overenthusiasm by the medical profession as to their value. Apparently sedatives, tranquilizers, or antidepressive drugs may be administered to psychiatric patients for long periods of time—as much as several years—without grossly noticeable complications appearing, except for the occasional obvious side effects. No one, however, has yet done careful and systematic studies to determine whether these patients do develop any permanent impairment of central nervous system functioning as a result of these psychoactive drugs. The principal reason for this is that most of our measuring techniques are not precise or sensitive enough to discriminate between the various kinds of impairment of higher nervous system functioning. At this time, it is not safe or scientifically justifiable to assume that prolonged use of these drugs is without physiological harm. This is a question which needs serious and careful investigation.

The psychological dependence that can develop on these drugs merits attention here. Many physicians are unaware that on introducing patients to their use they are indirectly and tacitly suggesting to the patient that he is certainly in need of support, that he should not rely on his own personality resources to master his disturbing fears or impulses, and that he should trust some outside force, the medication, which the physician will kindly prescribe for him. This message is, of course, appropriate generally for acute stresses and emotional upsets.

But many patients are typically prone to rely heavily and protractedly on such supports. The psychological crippling by such dependence on psychoactive drugs is marked. The medical profession has contributed to this state of affairs, spurred perhaps by lack of knowledge with respect to how else to relieve a patient's neurotic tensions and emotional distress, by working under the pressure of time, and by "medical articles" in popular magazines and national advertising which induce patients to ask physicians for "that new nerve medicine." A plea to the doctor to exercise caution and moderation in introducing patients to psychoactive drugs cannot be too strongly voiced. Prevention of unnecessary habituation to them is called for on a nation-wide scale.

Stimulants and Antidepressants

The physician must exercise the same precautions in prescribing stimulating and antidepressant drugs that he uses in prescribing sedatives and tranquilizers. Furthermore, many of these drugs have adverse side effects.

The psychomotor stimulants, such as the amphetamines, pipradrol, methylphenidate, are drugs which act as energizers to the thought processes, mood, and behavior of both depressed and normal persons. They are used in the treatment of some mild depressive syndromes, neurotic reactions in which fatigue is a prominent symptom, and in states of lassitude such as those which might follow a protracted viral infection. The use of these drugs is limited because of their side effects of irritability, restlessness, anorexia, and insomnia. In moderate or severe depressive syndromes the psychomotor stimulants are contraindicated because they tend to promote more tension and deeper depression.

The antidepressants are administered to elevate the mood of depressed patients. They can be divided into two groups; those that are monoamine oxidase inhibitors and those that are derivatives of iminodibenzyl. They seem to have little effect on the mood of normal people, but this point has not yet been adequately studied. Some of these, especially some of the more potent monoamine oxidase inhibitors, have been found to cause hepatitis.

The antidepressive drugs have been found to be effective pharmacological agents in the treatment of depressive reactions, particularly endogenous and involutional depressive reactions. Their intensive use in large mental hospitals for depressive reactions has made large inroads on the use of electroshock therapy, which was formerly the most common type of psychiatric therapy for these psychoses. Now the use of the antidepressive drugs, as well as the use of various even newer psychoactive drugs having both antidepressive and tranquilizing actions, has spread from their administration by psychiatrists to inpatients, to their administration by nonpsychiatric physicians to outpatients.

These antidepressive drugs have not been used long enough to determine whether addiction to them can take place. In any event, physiological dependence on these drugs—in the usual sense of the phrase—is difficult to assess. There is no doubt, however, that certain kinds of patients, namely, those who are anxious, suggestible, and looking for a magical panacea for their life problems and feelings, are the kinds of patients readily susceptible to popping an antidepressive pill into their mouths whenever they feel moody and merely sad at the moment. These kinds of patients are capable of becoming psychologically dependent on antidepressive drugs as well as other stimulating drugs, tranquilizers, or hypnotics. Such patients are likely to report to their physicians that the medicament, whatever it may be, has ameliorated their symptoms. Such patients are likely to be positive placebo-reactors and the physician should not let himself be lulled into complacency that he has discovered just what his patient has needed. Not uncommonly a patient has developed a psychological dependence on a drug—as some patients may do on a laxative—which has little, if any, directly beneficial pharmacological therapeutic action. The physician must weigh the risk of side effects or more deleterious drug reactions in patients who develop a psychological dependence on a drug, such as one of the antidepressive type, which is providing symptomatic relief on the basis of a placebo effect. He, of course, is equally obligated to avoid fostering psychologic dependence to an antidepressive medicament when the drug does pharmacologically contribute to symptomatic relief. The doctor should be alert to other therapeutic procedures which can also bring about the same therapeutic result, for example, the recommendation of psychotherapy or a change in the patient's milieu or life situation.

The stimulants, for example, the amphetamines, are known to be addicting to psychologically predisposed individuals. Brain syndromes with psychosis (toxic psychoses) have occurred in individuals habituated to amphetamines. There is some suggestive evidence that increased tolerance to the amphetamines is possible; at least, in some of the individuals who have developed psychotic reactions to the amphetamines, unusually large doses of the substance were being taken for a sizeable period of time before the onset of the toxic psychosis.

A patient who has habitual urgency to take stimulant drugs or antidepressive drugs regularly should not be allowed to take such drugs for a period of more than a month without having a psychiatric consultation. A severe neurotic character disorder or psychotic depressive reaction might be underlying the complaints for which this kind of medication was prescribed. The pharmacologic therapy of psychiatric patients is not well enough mapped out or understood at this point that treatment of symptoms or signs alone is a sufficient guide for adequate and safe therapy. The personality syndrome and psychodynamics underlying the patient's complaints need thorough assessment before a definitive and appropriate therapeutic regimen—including pharmacotherapy, if necessary—can be carried out.

OBESITY

The problem of obesity is one which continues to plague and confound the medical sciences. Etiological formulations appear to be plausible and therapeutic programs appear to be effective on one group of individuals; entirely different kinds of etiological formulations and therapeutic regimens seem to be appropriate in another group of obese people. The principle of multiple causation undoubtedly applies to the obesity syndrome; and this fact, coupled with the characteristic that there are many degrees of severity of the condition, precludes the development of a unified etiological formula and a simplified and workable therapeutic program. Experienced medical and psychiatric practitioners are quick to express humility when discussing their treatment of obesity due to emotional disturbances in early childhood. Each kind of practitioner, on the other hand, has valid suggestions to offer to the other, based on experiences with patients whose overeating and obesity have proven to be reversible.

What are some of the current theories and facts about obesity? And what are some psychiatric insights that are useful toward the understanding and the medical management of the overweight patient?

There is evidence that centers for hunger and for satiety exist in the central nervous system, in infrahuman animals and presumably in man, in the region of the hypothalamus. Also, there is evidence that impulses from the cerebral cortex play upon these subcortical centers or way stations. The functional intactness of these areas of the nervous system is necessary to maintain an equitable balance between a person's food intake and body weight in order to maintain an optimal performance of his activities as a human organism and for the kinds of adaptations to his environment that he has genetically inherited by natural selection. Cellular damage involving one of these crucial centers or way stations in the brain may upset the neurohumoral balance so that one continues to feel hungry or unsatiated after a full meal. Brain tumors and encephalomyelitis have been reported to lead to obesity in some individuals. Various pharmacological agents, for example, chlorpromazine (p. 456), have been noted occasionally to stimulate overeating and obesity. Frontal lobotomy—a neurosurgical procedure in which corticothalamic pathways are severed—also tends to lead to obesity. Obesity stemming from all such factors can be classified as "neurogenic" obesity.

Apparently, no kind of psychotherapy is sufficient to ameliorate the symptom of overeating when it is based on a cellular change or toxic factor affecting these brain centers. Fortunately, obesity due to such causes is quite uncommon. Anorexic drugs, which presumably depress the appetite centers, appear to be the only therapeutic avenue in the direct handling of these problems and these drugs are of quite variable effectiveness. The patient's emotional reaction to his change in body habits and appearance and to how people react to his obesity cannot be disregarded, however, by the doctor, for this emotional reaction can have a more disabling effect on the patient's over-all efficiency and healthy functioning than the obesity itself. Accordingly, the doctor should give the patient plenty of time to air his feelings of frustration, resentment and anxiety about his obesity.

Relatively infrequently, obesity is caused by metabolic factors and such obesity may be etiologically classified as "metabolic" obesity. The obesity problem is not greatly simplified by this or any other attempt to classify and give names to presumptive etiological groupings. One can readily discern that, on the one hand, a metabolic disorder might lead to obesity through provoking overeating via a toxic effect on a subcortical appetite or satiety center. On the other hand, a metabolic disorder might induce overeating at a cerebral cortical level of mediation. Furthermore, the activity level of an organism is another avenue by which body weight might be influenced, and changes in activity level of an individual can be initiated by neurogenic, metabolic, or even psychological means. And finally, there are investigators of the obesity problem who have the theoretical persuasion that, at least in some instances, obesity is not due simply to overeating but to some fault in carbohydrate and fat metabolism. These various pathways by which body weight may be metabolically affected illustrate the complexity of the pathophysiology of obesity.

Nevertheless, if by "metabolic" obesity one understands that any single one or combination of these pathophysiological routes is involved, it is not incorrect to assert that patients whose obesity is primarily due to a metabolic disorder can usually be helped by treatment of the underlying metabolic disorder. Dietary restriction, anorexic drugs, and supportive psychotherapy are useful principally as ancillary measures.

Now we come to the question of "psychological" obesity (by far the commonest variety), that is, obesity initiated principally through personality and emotional disorders and not via any known or established neurogenic or metabolic abnormality. Again this classification is more useful to organize one's thinking and approach to the obese patient than to demarcate a clearly separate and distinct etiological factor in obesity. There is evidence that the psychological factors in obesity may act directly on eating habits to change body weight or may first upset neurohumoral homeostatic mechanisms which then lead to the addition of excessive body weight.

Some of the kinds of personality and emotional disorders leading to obesity will be listed here and briefly discussed.

1. Certain psychotic reactions, such as the manic-depressive or affective disorders, are associated with wide swings in weight in some individuals. The periods of obesity usually occur in temporal relationship to the resolution and upward swing of a depression cycle. Sometimes the psychotic depressive episode has included schizophrenic manifestations and the patient begins to overeat as improvement occurs. Patients may report having insatiable appetites or no appetite whatever but simply a compulsive need to fill up their "stomach" or "insides" which feel empty.

The use of anorexic drugs with such patients may be hazardous, for patients such as these may have idiosyncratic personality reactions to anorexic pharmacological agents because these agents are also psychomotor stimulants. Primary attention should be paid to treatment of the personality disorder and not to the obesity, for usually the patient's weight stabilizes at an appropriate level after the patient has fully recovered from the mental illness.

2. Some patients begin to overeat in reaction to various life situations or intrapersonal conflicts. Some of these are as follows:

Overeating to allay one's sense of loss of a love object. In other words, the individual copes with the loss of a loved person, animal, inanimate object, or social or professional position by overeating. Some psychiatrists would call the obesity occurring in such a context a "depressive equivalent" and they would mean by this that the patient is avoiding experiencing the painful emotions associated with loss by overeating.

Overeating as a substitute for sexual love. Individuals who have strong feelings that sexual pleasure is bad or forbidden have been known to use eating as a substitute for sexual love. In cases of this sort, the obesity may serve as an additional barrier to becoming sexually involved, for the unattractiveness of the obesity may discourage sexual approaches.

Patients with this type of emotional problem react relatively favorably to psychotherapy. Unless a physician is particularly gifted and well trained as a psychotherapist, however, this kind of psychological problem usually requires the attention of a psychiatrist.

Overeating as an expression of covert rage or suppressed resentment. The biting, tearing, and masticating aspects of chewing may be used as auxiliary outlets for pent-up destructive aggressive urges. Individuals, for example, who have had embittering and agonizing life experiences in situations which, moreover, suppressed expression of frustration and anger have sometimes used overeating as an outlet for these pent-up feelings. Actually, psychological processes of this sort usually proceed below the patient's level of full awareness. The pent-up aggression continues to accumulate—often faster than it is discharged by indirect outlets—for people who have suffered traumatic experiences tend to behave and emote in ways which were often necessary during the stressful life periods but which currently foster repudiation by and alienation from other people. These latter experiences in turn generate new hostilities and frustrations in the traumatized individual.

Psychotherapy is necessary to break up this kind of psychological and behavioral self-defeating cycle. Dietary restrictions tend to aggravate the patient's frustration and aggression and eating under these conditions may occur in voracious binges. Anorexic drugs are generally of little avail.

Overeating to avoid provoking envy in others. Overeating may occur as a deliberate means to detract from one's appearance so that friends or relatives will not envy, and hence dislike, one for being physically attractive. To go to such ends to make oneself likeable is, in itself, a sign of a deep sense of insecurity, especially if this is a motivating force in an obese adult. In puberty and adolescence, such an urgent need to be nonthreatening towards people whose love one wants is not uncommon; at this age range, such a self-sacrificing motivation, though pathological, may not have such serious psychiatric implications.

Psychotherapy is usually very helpful with personality problems of this sort.

Overeating due to deprivation of love, warmth, respect, and physical contact in childhood. Overeating may be a means of supplying the self directly with the basic requirements of parental protection, nurture, and security. Maternal and paternal deprivation—of an emotional more than a physical kind—can promote a deep sense of emptiness, lack of personal worth, and distrust of the authenticity of the parents' love. A primitive adaptative mechanism of loving oneself through feeding oneself may ensue. People who develop obesity on the basis of this kind of psychological orientation usually become overweight before puberty and are fat all their lives. They affect an outward appearance of superficial sociability, even approaching the jovial, but the intensity and depth of their relationships with others is limited. The sociability is conditional and it appears only when these patients are eating or feel well-fed.

Obesity based on this specific psychogenesis is extremely difficult to ameliorate by any kind of psychotherapy, including psychoanalytic therapy. The psychologic damage was usually done so early in the patient's formative years that nothing can be done to induce the patient to change his view of himself vis-à-vis the world. Gratifying emotional experiences with other individuals are insufficient to encourage the patient to give up his overeating, which seems to occur almost on a conditioned reflex basis. Dietary restrictions and anorexic drugs are of temporary value but rarely of continuing efficacy. Group psychotherapy, like individual psychotherapy, has been reported to have only a temporary beneficial effect on patients with this kind of emotional problem.

The general physician sooner or later becomes the doctor responsible for patients with this kind of obesity problem. Generally, these patients may or may not come for treatment of the obesity itself, but for medical treatment of some other condition, not infrequently a condition aggravated or caused by their obesity. The usual medical procedures are of limited avail in modifying this obesity. These patients may resent the doctor's interest in their obesity and his recommendations to lose weight, although they may not express this view openly. Treatment of medical problems which the patient is interested in tackling proceeds more successfully. A relationship with the physician which has been built up over a number of years seems to be the type in which this kind of obese patient becomes better motivated to tackle the obesity problem. At the present time, most psychiatrists admit that such patients are more effectively helped and handled by internists and general practitioners than by psychiatric therapy in its present state of knowledge and know-how.

Bibliography

1. Baro, W. Z.: Industrial head and back injuries. The neurological and psychiatric viewpoint, Industr. Med. *19*:69, 1950.
2. Benedek, T., and Rubenstein, B.: The Sexual Cycle in Women, Washington, D.C., National Research Council, 1942.
3. Bergler, E., and Kroger, W. A.: Kinsey's Myth of Female Sexuality, New York, Grune, 1954.
4. Cave, E. F.: Back pain caused by conditions other than intervertebral disc injury, Med. Clin. N. Amer. 42:1589, 1958.
5. Hellebrandt, F. A.: Disability, rehabilitation and the law of damages, Industr. Med. 22:558, 1953.

6. Parkoney, A. R., and Moore, F. J.: Neuroses and compensation, Arch. Industr. Hyg. Occup. Med. 8:547, 1953.
7. Ross, W. D.: Practical Psychiatry for Industrial Physicians, Springfield, Ill., Thomas, 1956.
8. Sargent, M.: Psychosomatic backache, New Engl. J. Med. 234: 427, 1946.
9. Sypher, F.: Pain in the back: a general theory, J. Int. Coll. Surg. 33:718, 1960.
10. Titchener, J., *et al.*: Consequences of surgical illness and treatment, A. M. A. Arch. Neurol. Psychiat. 77:623, 1957.

CHAPTER 6

Psychiatry in the Practice of Internal Medicine. Psychosomatic Medicine

Despite the vigor and originality which have been manifested in the area of psychosomatic investigations during the past three decades, the term *psychosomatic* continues to be used with a good bit of imprecision by physicians as well as laymen. Sometimes it is used to refer to a small collection of specific diseases, such as peptic ulcer, essential hypertension, and bronchial asthma, in which emotional factors are generally considered to be of definite etiological significance. Sometimes it is described as being merely "a return to the *art* of medicine." Sometimes it is used as if it were synonymous with psychoneurotic, as when one hears it said, "Mr. Smith's illness can't be psychosomatic, since he shows no signs of nervousness." Sometimes it is used to designate patients having what is vaguely called "an emotional overlay" to some organic process. Sometimes it is even used as a sort of euphemism for malingering, as when one hears it said, "I think Mr. Jones' symptoms are largely psychosomatic; in fact I don't think they would have to be so severe unless he wanted them to be." Perhaps the greatest confusion is shown in remarks such as, "I can't believe that disease X is a purely psychosomatic disorder."

Now, with the exception of the last two examples, none of these references is absolutely wrong. The student will no doubt realize, in the course of the present chapter, the extent to which psychosomatic concepts have entered the body of knowledge which is the property of internal medicine and some of the specialties. Yet it may correctly be inferred from these differences in usage that a thorough-going assimilation of psychosomatic concepts is not an easy matter and, in fact, must encounter some widespread doubts and reservations. In the first example cited (peptic ulcer, etc.), the reservations take the form of implying that psychosomatic medicine makes its contribution only within exceedingly narrow limits. In the second example, it is implied that there may be wide application of the ideas clustering around the term, "psychosomatic," but that these ideas contain nothing really scientific. In the last example, the implication is that "psychosomatic" is a kind of label which seeks to exclude relevant data of some sort.

DEFINITION OF PSYCHOSOMATIC

Perhaps it would be best, at this point, to submit a definition of psychosomatic, in the light of which the discussion may be pursued. Above all else, psychosomatic refers to *an orientation in medicine,* a point of view, based upon certain convictions and leading to a certain methodology. "In the present phase of our investigative techniques, certain body functions and their disturbances can best be studied by psychological methods, while other functions can be approached only by physiological methods. In studying the totality of organic processes, both methods must be applied *at the same time** in order to account for the whole phenomenon."†

As the student well knows, the strongest trend in medicine since the Renaissance, and particularly during the last 100 years, has been toward the rational, the material, the scientific, toward that which can be explained completely by application of the laws of physics and chemistry, toward that which can be weighed and measured. This trend continues vigorously at the present time. For example, even during the past decade, the proportion of time at a typical medical "grand rounds" devoted to direct examination of the patient has grown progressively less and the proportion of time devoted to an evaluation of a list of figures on the blackboard (expressing various biochemical data) has grown progressively greater.

Furthermore, despite occasional disappointments (and certain other limitations, which, unless they are sought, may not be noticed), the trend has "paid off" and continues to do so. The knowledge represented by the figures on the blackboard is absolutely vital, containing the key to an understanding of many processes in health and illness. Since the turn of the last century, the infectious diseases have given way in very large measure wherever a concentrated and sustained application of such knowledge has been made. Deep inroads have been made into the areas of metabolic and degenerative disease, and there is reason to

---

* Italics mine. C.K.H.
† The quotation is from Franz Alexander: Studies in Psychosomatic Medicine, p. 34, Ronald, New York, 1948, who has been an outstanding contributor to knowledge in this area.

hope that even neoplastic disease will not remain impervious to knowledge being gained in the laboratory and expressible in the figures on the blackboard.

In view of all this—and despite the fact that much of the data and some of the contentions offered from the psychosomatic point of view are in themselves quite plausible—it is understandable that there should exist reservations among nonpsychiatrists as to whether or not these data and contentions possess sufficient clarity and scientific usefulness to affect one's fundamental orientation and one's methodological approach. Granted, let us say, that Mr. Smith's arthritis manifested itself shortly after his mother-in-law came to live with the family, or that Mr. Jones's headaches seem to have begun at about the time of the birth of his son, how can one fit this material into the orderly marshalling of the figures on the blackboard? How can one express the relationship of mother-in-law trouble to a sedimentation rate of 25 mm./hr., or a response to certain aspects of parenthood to a prescription of ergotamine tartrate? In a case of pneumonia, one aspect of etiology and of treatment can be brought out clearly on the blackboard by stating the sensitivity of the specific microorganism(s) to various antibiotic agents, but what is one to do with the fact that the patient's resistance had been lowered by a reckless indifference to matters of personal hygiene?

Questions of this nature lead one to a consideration of another aspect of the difficulty. The psychological observations may seem not only imprecise, difficult or impossible to quantify, but also disturbingly *nonmaterial*. To a listener who has not had the opportunity or who has not had the inclination to master the appropriate background material, the psychological data may seem positively esoteric, involving—if they are to be brought into logical relationship with the patient's overt and often measurable symptoms—what even the greatest psychiatrist once called "the mysterious leap from the psychic into the physical."*

In informal interdisciplinary discussions, even within the field of medicine, the participants—let us say, a psychoanalytic psychiatrist and an internist specializing in rheumatology—may often, although perhaps unintentionally, contribute to this seeming mystery. The psychiatrist may speak almost as though the patient had no body, and the internist as though he had no mind. The medical student or even the general practitioner is left with the sense of an awkward gap between the two.

Now the truth is that this seeming gap is a man-made illusion.

---

* Sigmund Freud: In A General Introduction to Psychoanalysis, New York, Permabooks (Doubleday), 1953.

Definition of Psychosomatic 185

Nature knows nothing of it. (It is suggested that the student review, at this point, the discussions of mind and brain on pp. 28 to 32 and of the state of fear on pp. 65 to 66.) Let us take one sequence of closely related phenomena in a human being and trace it through, however laboriously, for the sake of demonstrating this truth. Our subject, let us say, is in an automobile which has stalled on a railroad track; he is returning home after having heavily indulged at a banquet.

A stream of light quanta impinge upon certain modified neurons deep within his retinae and there institute a self-propagating series of electrophysical changes, nerve impulses, which are relayed through a series of retinal cells until they reach the ones whose fibers constitute the optic nerve. The impulses continue through the fibers of the optic nerve and tract, reaching the lateral geniculate bodies. At this point, some of the impulses are transferred to neurons forming the brachium of the superior colliculus and reaching the nuclei of the oculomotor nerve. From these nuclei impulses are transmitted back to the eye, effecting pupillary adjustments. Other of the impulses pass to the nucleus of the posterior commissure and the nucleus of the medial longitudinal fasciculus, whence they are transmitted to influence various ocular and postural movements.

The main stream of impulses passes through the fibers constituting the optic radiation to the cells of the visual cortex, lying alongside the calcarine fissure of the occipital lobe of the brain. Certain neurons mediate between this incoming stimulation and impulses taking efferent pathways and ultimately influencing processes of accommodation and of binocular vision. Other neurons relay the afferent impulses to various centers of association in the cortex, including centers in the pre-frontal area. An elaborate interplay of intracortical neuronal impulses ensues, in the course of which the stream of excitation is influenced by neurons bearing traces of similar previous excitations. There is also a massive exchange of impulses between cortical areas and thalamic nuclei and between thalamic and hypothalamic nuclei.

Within a short space of time, impulses reach the motor cortex and the cerebellum. Efferent impulses pass down the pyramidal and cerebellospinal tracts. These impulses reach the muscles of the extremities, which go into action in a coordinated fashion.

At the same time, other impulses go out from the hypothalamic nuclei, primarily over fibers linking with the peripheral fibers of the sympathetic branch of the autonomic nervous system. These impulses produce widespread effects, including an increase in heart rate and in blood pressure, a redistribution of blood volume, a release of epinephrine and of blood sugar, and a cessation of gastric muscular and secretory activity. The last-mentioned effect persists for some time.

The gastric musculature becomes relatively atonic. The gastric lumen remains overdistended and its contents relatively achlorhydric. Eventually muscle tone is restored, but the emptying of the stomach is delayed. Afferent impulses from receptors in the gastric muscles ascend in the fibers of the vagus nerve to its nuclei. A portion of these impulses are relayed through the fibers of cells lining the solitary tract to a variety of efferents from the cervical and thoracic spinal cord. The preliminary motor activity of vomiting ensues.

In speaking of the same sequence of events, one might, alternatively, have said:

The subject sees a bright light down the track, focuses on it, and realizes that a train is approaching rapidly. He becomes frightened, leaves his automobile, runs for safety, and experiences a severe "attack of indigestion" shortly thereafter.

A very clear case of "psychosomatic" illness! The most important point here is that the two ways of speaking refer to aspects of *the same phenomena*. There is no "leap" except the one the subject executed in leaving his car. The "mind-body problem," as it is called, is not free of mystery, but the mystery is largely confined to the profound question of just what consciousness is, and it does not in any way interfere with the multiple close correlations existing between the first way of describing the phenomena and the second.

In discussing psychosomatic sequences, there is thus no suggestion that nonphysiological events are causative agents in the production of physiological (or pathophysiological) events. It is merely that certain complex physiological phenomena are at the same time psychological phenomena, and often lend themselves better to a description in psychological terms. As a major corollary to this statement, it should be said that many examples of deranged physiology, i.e., many disease states, are best studied and treated by the simultaneous application of physiological and psychological techniques.

SPECIFIC SYNDROMES

To go more deeply into the subject of psychosomatics, it will be helpful to discuss a number of clinical entities in the pathogenesis of which psychological phenomena frequently play a significant part.

Peptic Ulcer

The following case history, while unusual in respect to the age of the patient, reveals some aspects of the etiology of this condition with especial clarity.

Mr. R. M., an 89-year-old, white widower, a retired mailman, was admitted to the hospital vomiting red blood. The present illness dated back only six weeks, having begun with marked dyspepsia and anorexia. Tarry stools had been noted for about four weeks, and moderate epigastric pain, coming on within 15 to 30 minutes after the ingestion of food, for two weeks. Massive gastric hemorrhage with transient loss of consciousness occurred on the morning of admission.

Direct examination showed an alert, pleasant, well-preserved old man. His temperature was 99°; pulse-rate was 80 per minute; and blood pressure was 130/80 mm. of mercury. The physical findings were essentially normal with the following exceptions: edentia, a soft apical systolic heart murmur, a slightly enlarged liver, epigastric tenderness, and an enlarged prostate.

Several of the laboratory studies were contributory. The hemoglobin was 7.5 Gm. per 100 cc. The red cell count was 3.2 million, and the white count was 13,600 per cu. mm. A stool guaiac test was strongly positive (showing blood). Emergency roentgenography of the upper gastroenteric tract showed a large penetrating ulcer on the lesser curvature of the stomach.

A tentative diagnosis of gastric carcinoma was made (in view of the patient's age and the location of the ulcer). At the operation, however, Mr. M. was found to have a large but benign ulcer, probably of recent origin.

The patient's hospital course was very favorable. Because of his age and his spry, friendly manner, he was a great favorite with the nurses and received an unusual amount of care and attention. Medical and surgical management was routine, except for digitalization, which was instituted because of minimal postoperative signs of cardiac decompensation. Mr. M. was discharged from the hospital after one month.

The patient's personal history was of particular interest. R. M. had enjoyed exceptionally good health, having seen a physician only once in his entire life (for a urinary ailment) prior to the present illness. Epigastric pain, melena, and hematemesis had never previously been noticed. There had been occasional mild dyspepsia, but the patient had had, for the most part, an unusually keen appetite. Mr. M. had noted a tendency to obesity, kept in check by the activity his occupation had required. The patient had never been an alcoholic, but his consumption of beer and whiskey had been above average. He had also been a steady smoker.

Mr. M. was the oldest of three siblings surviving infancy, and he had, from rather an early age, contributed to the family income by selling newspapers and doing odd jobs. His parents had both lived to an old age; the father died at 87, and the mother at 76. The patient had lived at home until his marriage at the age of 27. This marriage, a basically happy one, had lasted for 58 years, terminating with the wife's death four years before the patient's admission. There had been two children, one of whom had died some 15 years earlier. Immediately after his wife's death, the patient went to live with his son and daughter-in-law, with whom he remained until hospitalized for the present illness.

The situation in the son's home was not a happy one. The patient's daughter-in-law had at first been willing to "humor" the old man, but had steadily become more and more tired of this role. There had been arguments about the quality of the meals. The patient stated that his daughter-in-law made no effort to please him in this respect (as his wife had done).

Six weeks before admission, there had been a quarrel, with a subsequent attempt to patch things up. Four weeks before admission the daughter-in-law laid down the ultimatum—following further differences —that the only condition on which she would permit the patient to continue living at the house was that he would obtain his own meals, either preparing them himself or eating at a restaurant. Having no other surviving children, the patient tried to accept these terms. (It will be recalled that the former date corresponded with the onset of the patient's anorexia and dyspepsia, and the latter with the onset of melena.)

Mr. M. lived for one year, following the admission just described. He rented a small apartment of his own, being too proud to try to resume getting along with his son and daughter-in-law under the conditions laid down. He prepared some of his meals and obtained others in restaurants. He had a few old friends, but did not confide to them very extensively the difficulties of his situation.

During this period there were two other admissions. On both occasions the presenting complaints were of epigastric pain and vomiting blood. The first time the patient responded well to conservative medical management. On the patient's final admission, he was found on x-ray examination to have a perforation of his gastric ulcer into the lesser peritoneal sac. A jejunostomy was performed, and the usual supportive measures were taken. The patient's condition on admission, however, was very poor. He was uremic and anemic, and he survived the operation by only two days. The portion of the necropsy relevant to the patient's gastric condition noted chronic peptic ulcer with recent acute exacerbation and extensive erosion of the wall of the stomach.[9]

Aside from the unusual instances in which peptic ulcer develops rather quickly following some form of direct trauma to the epigastric region, the occurrence of this lesion is generally considered to be primarily the result of a sustained increase in the production of acid gastric juice, continuing during periods (such as at night) when this secretion is ordinarily at a low level.*[16] This hypersecretion is typically accompanied by a general increase in gastric motility.

As the student knows, the cells of the gastric and upper duodenal mucosa are protected from the digestive action of the acid-enzyme solution by a coating of mucus (secreted by specific cells of the mucosa). It is not certainly known precisely how the first tiny lesion in the mucosa, the precursor of an ulcer, is formed. In the ordinary course of events, however, it appears likely that the thin mucous lining is transiently worn off of various small areas from time to time by the mechanics of digestion. In the absence of a hypersecretion of gastric juice, no lesion is produced, and the mucous lining is quickly replaced. If, on the other hand, there is a more or less constant, round-the-clock hypersecretion of the acid-enzyme solution, there is always the possibility that, in some small area, the mucosa will itself be destroyed by the digestive processes. Once such a tiny lesion has started, there is a

---

* Auxiliary factors may be a lack of local cellular resistance or a diminished secretion of protective mucus, but there is little direct evidence to support these ideas.

tendency for it to be self-perpetuating since the protective coating of mucus cannot be immediately reformed. In this fashion a penetrative process can get under way.

It appears highly probable that, in most instances, the chronic hypersecretion of gastric juice and hypermotility of the gastric musculature are the result of excessive stimulation mediated through the gastric branches of the vagus nerve. An etiological inquiry into peptic ulcer thus involves the very important question, whence comes this intensification of vagal activity?

In seeking an answer, one's first thought might well be that constitutional variations (between one individual and another) are involved. This idea seems quite likely to be correct.[16, 20] Precisely wherein the variations lie is not certainly known: whether it is a matter of a general and spontaneous readiness for overactivity of certain parasympathetic centers or whether the vagal innervation is excessive merely relative to an over-readiness of response of the end-organs or whether there are still other factors.

Further reflection indicates, however, that constitutional factors alone cannot account for an illness such as that of Mr. M. Whatever his constitution may have been, there is no reason to suppose that it had undergone marked changes just prior to the onset of his ulcer. The same line of evidence holds for most instances of this disease.

One's next thought might naturally be that hunger must be involved in the (relatively) excessive vagal activity. In a sense, this idea also proves to be correct, but a moment's additional thought will indicate that it must be an unusual kind of hunger.[20] For one thing, it may not be complained of, yet would have to be well-nigh insatiable. For another, it appears to be relatively independent of any deficiency of gross caloric intake, and of any kind of nutritional deficiency. For example, old Mr. M. at no time—even in giving his past history—complained of not getting enough to eat or of being continually hungry in the usual sense. Nor do most peptic ulcer patients. What he did complain of was not getting enough of a certain kind of attention, not receiving a certain consideration, in connection with the pattern of life at his daughter-in-law's, and in particular, in connection with the preparation and serving of meals. It is clear that *for him* such attention and consideration were equated with being loved; he "hungered for love."

How does this equation in the mind come about? To understand this point, it is necessary to understand thoroughly certain aspects of early human development. (The student should review the material on pp. 85 to 93.) There is a period during infancy when the baby's emotional life centers around the experience of nursing. While receiving the mother's milk, the baby is also receiving her love. Two cardinal needs and two gratifications, at first indistinguishable. In the ordinary course of events, this linkage weakens and is forgotten, but it never ceases to exist. The forgetting tends to be universal, but the weakening varies considerably from one individual to another and from one set of circumstances to another.

Emotionally speaking, if an individual remains at (is *fixated* to) the infantile phase of development, whenever in later life he encounters frustration of his need to be in a particular kind of dependent-affectionate relationship, *his total response tends to include innervations of a sort appropriate to hunger but having very little correlation with his nutritional intake*. If, having progressed emotionally beyond the infantile stage, the individual responds to circumstances of his later life by making an emotional retreat (by *regressing*) back to this phase and then encounters frustration of his dependency needs, the same physiological response tends to occur. In the case of Mr. M., it appears likely that the situation was intermediate between these two possibilities. The patient's having been the eldest of 11 siblings suggests that he may well have experienced ungratified dependency needs (thereby increasing the force of such cravings); his marrying rather late, remaining at home with his parents, is also suggestive of dependency. His tendency toward obesity and his having been an habitually heavy drinker and smoker are further indications of strong "oral needs." On the other hand, a degree of regression is almost universal in extreme old age. It is possible that this particular patient could have faced widowhood and readjustment to a less sympathetic environment without developing such severe symptoms if he had been called upon to do so 20 years earlier.

The case history of Mr. M. illustrates a number of further points in connection with the pathogenesis of peptic ulcer. One of these is that the central emotional conflict of such patients is typically (at least in part) unconscious. Mr. M. knew, of course, that his life in his son's home was not happy. He could say to the doctor that his daughter-in-law did not treat him well. He knew that the trouble had something to do with his meals. He could even make an unfavorable contrast of his daughter-in-law with his wife (and possibly with his mother). *But he could not have said, for he was unaware of it, that he was in a state of tension and distress because he needed and was not receiving a kind of affectionate consideration primarily appropriate to an infant, because in fact, he desperately wanted "to be babied."* This recognition was blocked by repression; the motivating force requiring the repression was pride (more accurately, the avoidance of shame). Despite the repression, it was relatively easy for observers to sense this need; the nurses understood it immediately without being told, and the old man warmed to their mothering.

A second point strongly suggested by the history of Mr. M. is that the pathogenic conflict involved in the production of the ulcer was quite *specific*. During his exceptionally long life, Mr. M. had had ample occasion to encounter many sorts of stress situations, and his history indicates that he had done so. Helping the family at an early age, courtship and marriage, parenthood, carrying on his job for many years under markedly changing conditions, the loss of his parents, the urinary ailment, the loss of a child: all of these vicissitudes, and doubtless others besides, he had withstood. Yet, as fortune would have it, the vulnerable aspect of his personality was very largely shielded until his last years. (On the other hand, it appears to have been not merely the occurrence of a specific conflict situation, but its occurrence under the special circumstance of his lessened adaptational powers which led to the development of the ulcer. There is the further possibility—although this was denied in the history—that, in recent months the old man's diet was in some fashion inappropriate.)

The question of the degree of specificity of the central conflict initiating various psychosomatic sequences is an important one and one about which there exists some difference of opinion among experts in the field. Further data will be presented in connection with essential hypertension (p. 193) and bronchial asthma (p. 200), and the question will be discussed in general terms on pages 207 to 209.

Aside from the patient's age, there is a feature in the story of Mr. M. which is not typical for a great many peptic ulcer patients, namely, that the frustration of his dependency needs was primarily imposed from without. In ulcer patients seen in private practice, one may frequently look in vain for serious external frustration of this sort. While the layman's stereotype of the ulcer victim as a hard-driving, materially successful executive with many responsibilities and several telephone lines is clearly overdone, it is not without an element of truth. Many an ulcer patient may, indeed, be in very comfortable material circumstances, may have considerable ability, an attractive home, plenty of well-prepared food, an outwardly successful marriage, etc.

One may well ask if it is really possible that the physiological derangements leading to ulcer formation in such prosperous patients take their starting point in an emotional conflict similar to that of the old man. Yet intensive study of such persons, using psychoanalytic techniques, indicates that it is entirely possible and that a quite similar conflict is involved oftener than not. The point of difference is this: whereas in the case of Mr. M. the conflict was between certain dependency strivings on the one hand and an unfavorable environment on the other, in the "successful" type of patient the conflict is *purely internal*, taking place between dependency strivings and feelings of shame and guilt. There may be no external hindrance to the gratification of the infantile cravings, but there are powerful internal hindrances.*

In such cases, *the conflict is, to a larger degree, unconscious*; as a rule, the patients are not able (at first) to express as much of their dissatisfaction and distress as was Mr. M.

In addition to a certain amount of repression, the psychological mechanism by which such persons have striven to deal with their dependency needs is that of *reaction-formation* (p. 77). Thus it is quite frequent for an ulcer patient of this type, who has deep-seated wishes to be taken care of, fed, and ministered to, nevertheless to be aware of and to manifest outwardly only the reverse attitudes, i.e., a tendency to work excessively hard and to assume responsibility for other persons. In this way he maintains his self-esteem, but his physiological mechanisms are not deceived, and they respond in accordance with his basic (unconscious) motivational state.

It can be seen, as a natural corollary to the fact that the central conflict is largely unconscious, that such patients, although often endowed with high intelligence and good judgment, may be unable, without professional assistance, to apply this intelligence and judgment toward effecting a more comfortable adjustment. Insofar as they are not aware of what they are basically seeking, they are not able to modify their life situations in such a way as to bring adequate gratification and relaxation of tension. Furthermore, if the situation is modified for them—if, for example, the physician strongly recommends a long vacation and the recommendation is accepted—they often become restless and lowspirited, since they are then assailed by the very feelings of shame and guilt which caused the dependency strivings to be buried in the first instance.

What are the implications of these various psychophysiological correlations for the management of patients with peptic ulcer? In a certain number of cases, of course, the conventional medicinal, nursing, dietary, and perhaps surgical measures will suffice to produce a long-lasting or even a permanent remission of symptoms. These instances are to be explained in either of two principal ways: (1) They are cases in which psychological factors are of relatively slight significance. (2) They are cases in which psychological factors are of great significance, but in which (a) the conflict was largely environmental and some favorable environmental change occurs either coincidentally or in con-

---

* In many instances, both types of hindrances may be in operation at the same time.

nection with the illness, (b) the knowledge that he is ill lessens the patient's shame and guilt over "taking it easy" to the point at which the inner conflict lessens in intensity, or (c) the oral gratifications received through the doctor (pills, special diet, etc.) are sufficient to meet the hitherto unsatisfied needs to an appreciable extent.

There are, however, a considerable number of cases in which the conventional measures will produce only a quite temporary remission, and in which further measures are indicated. With respect to such measures, the indications for the two (psychological) types of patients differ. With the first type, it then becomes a part of the physician's job to attempt to affect some modification of the conflict through *environmental manipulation* (p. 513). For example, in the case of Mr. M. there would be two possibilities: (a) to establish a good professional relationship with the son and daughter-in-law and then attempt to educate them as to what was at stake and to counsel and persuade them to adopt a more constructive approach to the old man's problems; (b) to utilize social agencies (p. 461) in the attempt to effect a more congenial living arrangement for the patient outside his children's home.

With patients of the second type, the physician's task is to attempt some lessening of the inner conflict by moderating one of the conflicting forces. Theoretically it might seem not to matter which side of the conflict was approached, the dependency strivings or the shame-guilt motivations. Practically, however, it makes a great deal of difference. Since the dependency strivings are entirely or very largely unconscious, while the shame and (to a lesser extent) the guilt over "taking it easy" are to a considerable degree conscious, it is the latter with which the physician may more reasonably hope to deal. Through a series of discussions, beginning while the patient is in active conventional treatment for his ulcer, he should strive first to increase the patient's recognition of these reactions and then to help him to see that they are unrealistically severe. If these measures do not suffice, the patient should be referred to a psychiatrist for intensive psychotherapy in collaboration with the medical management.

Essential Hypertension

Although productive of numerous and grave complications, this syndrome is characterized clinically by a single primary pathological feature, diastolic hypertension, at first fluctuating and later sustained.

Mr. F. N., a 43-year-old, married, semi-skilled laborer, was admitted to the hospital in an episode characterized by severe headache, vomiting, convulsive twitching of the extremities, and confusion. Physical examination was not remarkable except for blood pressure of 210/125, and eye grounds showing marked arterial narrowing and spasm, with a few small hemorrhages and bilateral papilledema. A spinal tap revealed an initial pressure of 380. Clinical studies disclosed a bundle branch block on EKG, minimal cardiac enlargement, but no evidence of decompensation. Renal studies were entirely negative; urine negative. The BUN was 14, concentrating capacity 1.035, PSP normal. An intravenous pyelogram was negative.

By two weeks after admission, the papilledema had receded, and ten days later all evidence of hemorrhage of the eye grounds had disappeared, leaving the patient with a Grade 2 hypertensive retinitis. During the patient's hospital stay, the blood pressure showed considerable lability, varying between extremes of 220/120 and 130/85. (The patient did not care for the ward atmosphere, but liked that of the research laboratory in which he was being studied. On two occasions it happened that blood pressures were taken on the ward immediately before and after brief visits to the laboratory, where the pressure was also determined. The findings on these two occasions corresponded very closely, being approximately as follows: 170/100, 130/80, and 190/120.)

The patient's general attitude on the ward was outwardly pleasant and cooperative. Nevertheless he appeared rather tense, and at times when he was unaware of being observed his expression was characterized as "moody and sullen."

During his hospital stay, the patient was seen in a series of interviews, giving the following information. The patient was an only child. His parents separated when he was two years old, sending him to another city to be raised by his mother's older sister and her husband.

(He was subsequently told that upon arrival he was very disturbed, refused to eat for an entire day and to talk for a week.) His mother very seldom visited. His aunt and uncle were very strict in their discipline; unruliness or a show of temper was punished with switching.

F. N. was of average intelligence, but was never more than a passing student. His main outlet was athletics. He got in a good many fights and won most of them. In his late teens he considered becoming a professional fighter, but was told by a trainer that he lost his temper too easily and would be an easy mark for any smart fighter.

The patient went to work at 18. His work history consisted of a long series of unskilled and then semiskilled jobs, no one of which lasted more than three or four years. He showed little ambition and received few promotions. During a number of years, he continued to fight at the drop of a hat.

F. N. married in his early twenties. During the early years of the marriage, he was rather promiscuous sexually. At the same time he developed a strong dependent type of attachment to his wife. When the patient was 31, his wife nearly died in connection with the birth of their third child. Following this episode, Mr. N. abruptly discontinued all of his extramarital activities. He also made a great, and successful, effort to bring his temper under control and to stop fighting. However, concurrent with these changes, the patient began drinking more and more heavily. At one period his consumption of whiskey reached an average of a quart per day. His appetite remained good, and his drinking seldom interfered with his work. His libido decreased markedly during this period, and did not subsequently return to normal. The patient never fought when he had been drinking heavily; all that he could say on this score was that the whiskey usually "made him feel good; feel like taking it easy."

The patient's wife had always done a good bit of nagging, and her tendency in this direction increased considerably over the years of the patient's heavy drinking. Because of this pressure, and because he became frightened at contracting lobar pneumonia after overexposure when he had been drinking heavily, the patient resolved to give up drinking. At this time he was 39 years of age.

At about the same time, Mr. N. followed his wife's lead in becoming very seriously interested in religion. The couple joined a radical Protestant splinter sect, having strict prohibitions against drinking, swearing, gambling, and fighting. The patient became a very conscientious church-goer, attending services several times each week. Despite this change on the patient's part, Mrs. N. continued to be rather difficult to live with.

At age 40, Mr. N. took the job which he held at the time of his hospital admission. It was the most responsible position that he had ever occupied, and the responsibilities were increased by the circumstance that he was elected to union office. As it happened, there were serious problems which his local had to face during the ensuing three years, involving differences both with the company and with the parent union. On several occasions, Mr. N. was required to participate in negotiations. The patient experienced repeated trouble in controlling his temper, but always managed to do so. Mr. N.'s hypertension was first discovered in the course of a routine physical examination by the company doctor, made two years before the present admission.

As in the case of peptic ulcer there is good reason to suppose that some type of constitutional predisposition is involved in the pathogenesis of essential hypertension.[15] The nature of the predisposition is not certainly known, nor the proportion in which psychological and nonpsychological factors have combined, long before the illness, to produce it.

To elucidate the condition as far as is at present possible, one may begin with a consideration of the emotional state of *anger*. Like fear (p. 65) and other emotional states, anger involves a built-in pattern of response to a particular situation, in this instance, environmental frustration of some basic drive. The pattern varies from one species to another, and the intensity of the response varies, to an extent, from one individual to another within the same species. In human beings, anger involves an uncomfortable and quite distinctive subjective state and a number of bodily changes. Teleologically speaking, the bodily changes are of a nature which prepares the subject to take vigorous action against the frustrating object, i.e., to fight (or, if necessary, to flee).

Omitting finer details, the typical sequence of events is as follows:

visual, auditory, etc., activity (perception of the object), associative cortical activity (evaluation of the object as "enemy"), hypothalamic activity (the essentially affective component), sympathetic nervous system activity, and adrenal cortical activity. As a result of the latter two phases, there are numerous bodily alterations, including an increase in tone of the voluntary musculature and *a widespread increase in tone of the smooth muscle fibers of the arteriolar walls*. This increase in tone causes a constriction of the arteriolar lumina and thus an increased peripheral resistance to the circulation of the blood. Partially as a result of direct stimulation, but more significantly as a compensatory reaction to the increased resistance, the cardiac effort increases. With the maintenance of the circulation against the heightened resistance, there is inevitably an increase in the arterial pressure.

It should be added that in human beings the initial stimulus, the environmental frustration, need not be physically present. It may be evoked symbolically, as when in conversation reference is made to some inimical figure or situation.

In a somewhat vague way, all of this is common knowledge, and it may be tested in the laboratory. If a sphygmomanometer is attached to a relaxed subject, one who is not on guard against the experience of emotion, and if repeated measurements of the blood pressure are made during the course of a detailed and vivid personal conversation, it will be found that transient blood pressure elevations often occur with the discussion of topics arousing anger.

Both in naturally occurring situations and in the laboratory situation, the reaction of anger is typically self-limited. Sometimes the angry tension is directly discharged (one fights, either in a gross physical way or with words); sometimes it is discharged through *sublimation* (p. 75); sometimes it is relieved by getting away from the stimulus (one leaves the provocative situation). In all of these cases, the physiological responses die down and the bodily states return toward a basal condition. There are no sequellae.

Now suppose, for the sake of discussion, that through some unusual combination of circumstances all avenues of solution—fighting, sublimation, fleeing—were completely blocked or nearly so. (Under natural conditions, such a situation could happen to no other species than man.) The state of anger then becomes *chronic*. Certain physiological mechanisms which, speaking teleologically, were designed for emergency use, are kept in operation continuously.

After a considerable (and varying) period of time, the arteriolar walls tend to lose some of their natural elasticity, presumably as a result of the sustained constriction and the stress of the continuously elevated arterial pressure. In the face of the persisting, abnormally high peripheral resistance, the heart must continue to work harder than its normal capacity allows. Gradually this sustained workload brings about a hypertrophy of the cardiac musculature. Gradually the arterial, particularly the diastolic, pressure rises. Sooner or later, the abnormal circulatory state produces complications in various organs of the body. (In essential hypertension, it is these complications which ultimately prove fatal.)

For a psychophysiological sequence of events of this nature to be of value in elucidating the pathogenesis of essential hypertension, it is necessary to establish some natural basis for its coming into play. Specifically, the questions are: How, in general, can one account for the existence of a chronic, unresolved state of anger? and, What is the evidence that such a state frequently exists in patients with essential hypertension and correlates with the development of the disease?

One might rephrase the first question to ask, What set of circumstances would tend to block all avenues of solution theoretically available for the relief of angry tensions? Reasoning by analogy with the situation in some peptic ulcer patients, one might think of two possibilities: (a) the existence of some peculiar and highly unfavorable environmental conditions, conditions which would be both provocative of anger and highly restrictive of its motor expression, and (b) the possibility that the subject was largely unaware of his anger (had repressed it) and was therefore unable to relieve it. As a matter of fact, one can find examples in which such situations have contributed, in all probability, to the pathogenesis of essential hypertension, but they are exceptional cases. (An example of the first possibility is the occasional development of hypertension in apparent response to harsh prison conditions.)

Actually, a commoner answer to the first question is often found in pursuit of an answer to the second. If one examines hypertensives using merely a cursory interview or one confining itself largely to the elicitation of physical complaints, the patient is not likely to disclose his anger. As a matter of fact, the superficial demeanor of many hypertensives is often perfectly affable and may even be gentle. If, however, one uses a more relaxed and yet more thorough interviewing technique, one finds that a high percentage of such patients are consciously (and chronically) angry persons. If one adds to the investigative techniques, the use of projective psychological studies (p. 542) and periods of free association (p. 486), the percentage is found to be still higher and the intensity of the anger still greater.

Putting this information together, one can say that a great majority of essential hypertensives are struggling with the emotion of anger.[17, 18] While it is very often true that the hypertensive is repressing his anger to some extent, the greater portion of his control of the anger is by the exercise of suppression (p. 80), i.e., it is a conscious control.

If it is extensive and sustained, suppression can block any primary, direct expression—and hence any relief—of the angry tension almost as completely as can repression. The effect of suppression in choking off the other two relief-affording possibilities—sublimation and flight from the external stimulus—is less marked than it is upon channels of primary expression, yet there is some such blocking effect, probably because really extensive use of such techniques would be considered by the subject as an undesirable admission of his anger. Be that as it may, one often finds the subject making a degree of use of both sublimation and avoidance. Sometimes the two are combined, as in the not unusual example of a male hypertensive who was an ardent hunter and fisherman; his periods in field and stream not only afforded some discharge of the angry tensions, but took him away from his wife, in this instance the source of much of the provocation.

As one pursues further an understanding of the emotional position of the hypertensive, deeper questions arise. Why is there so much anger? Why is it so rigorously suppressed? It is not possible to answer these questions in detail in the present context, partly because the answers become highly individual, but a few general considerations may be offered.

In the first place, one can see that the rigor of the suppression is, in part at least, explicable in terms of the intensity of the anger. The simplest of the factors causing the suppression is fear of the results of a thorough-going expression, fear of causing injury to others which would be later regretted per se or which would be to the subject's long-term disadvantage. Further, it may be said that very often the hypertensive has a strong and restrictive type of conscience, one which does not allow a normal play of emotional expression. One can also see that a vicious cycle can be readily set up between the anger and the suppressive efforts; the more rigorous the suppression, the more the angry tensions build up; the more the tensions build up, the more the subject feels the necessity of suppression. The situation is something like that of building a dam without an adequate spillway. The bigger the dam, the greater the water pressure becomes; the greater the water pressure, the bigger the dam needs to be.

The basic conflict between expression of hostile impulses on the one hand and inhibitory forces on the other has usually had its origin in stress situations of the subject's early childhood. For example, the parental response to any show of hostility may have been so retaliatory as to have inspired great fear in the subject, or so martyrlike as to have aroused unreasonable feelings of guilt. In addition, one quite regularly finds that features of the patient's current environment are of significance in keeping the conflict alive. Typically, the hypertensive is struggling not only with residual anger toward figures of his past but also with similar impulses toward key figures in the present.

The most thorough elucidation of the psychological sequence of events involved in the pathogenesis of essential hypertension has come from the study of those patients who have been psychoanalyzed. Here reconstructions have been possible of the whole life history. Here, too, derives proof of the etiological significance of the inner conflict. That is to say, the therapeutic effect of psychoanalysis—when instituted very early in the course of the disease—is strong evidence that the relationship between the inner conflict and the rising blood pressure is one of cause-and-effect. If the conflict can be truly resolved before the physiological disorder has progressed to the point of histological alterations, it appears that the course of the disease can be halted.[1]

Unfortunately, for a variety of reasons, this favorable outcome does not occur often. Since early hypertension is usually asymptomatic, it frequently does not come to medical attention. When it does come to medical attention, the emotional aspects are often overlooked. When they are taken into consideration, it is still often impossible, highly impractical, or for various reasons unacceptable, for the patient to follow a recommendation for psychoanalysis or intensive psychotherapy.

Let us, therefore, consider a commoner situation, one in which the patient comes to the physician with his hypertension still in a fairly early stage, but with some symptoms. Let us say further that the patient is not in a position to receive intensive psychoanalytic or psychiatric help, and that the original physician must do what he can. In addition to conventional measures, what further help can be offered, based on an understanding of the emotional aspects of the disease?

A psychotherapeutic approach to the patient could include several aspects. (1) Spending sufficient time in conversation with the patient to develop an understanding of the current provocations and of the possibilities inherent in the patient's personality for sublimations. (2) Working with the patient and often with some key figures in his current life to reduce the provocation. (3) Encouraging the patient to exploit the possibilities of sublimation to the fullest extent. (4) Attempting to achieve a lessening of internal pressure by encouraging the patient to express his hostile feelings verbally in conversations with the doctor. The degree of success of this measure is, however, a variable and highly individual matter. Sometimes a "blowing off steam" in this fashion promotes subsequent relaxation. Sometimes it mobilizes more hostility than it releases. If judicious experimentation indicates that ventilation does not appear to lead to subsequent relaxation, or if the question remains in doubt, this technique may best be left for the psychiatrist to consider in those cases which are referred to him.

Before leaving the subject of essential hypertension, it may be well to point out that here, as in the case of peptic ulcer, there appears to be a considerable degree of specificity with respect to the emotional conflict contributing to the development of the disease. Various sorts of stress may play a part in creating tensions leading eventually to the increase in blood pressure, but the available evidence suggests quite strongly that the tension of unrelieved anger is far and away the most significant. (Again as in the case of peptic ulcer, the psychological situation may be rather a complex one. The question as to what degree of unexpressed anger can be "absorbed" by the personality without leading to a physiological disturbance depends for its answer upon a variety of factors.)

Bronchial Asthma

Here, to begin with, is a case history illustrative of this condition.

On a day about the middle of December, Mrs. L. C., aged 26, the wife of a young business executive and the mother of two small children, was brought to the hospital in the course of an episode of severe respiratory difficulty, which had then persisted for approximately six hours.

The patient was in serious and obvious distress, being close to exhaustion. She was unable to walk without assistance and unable to lie down. She was pale, perspiring freely, and faintly cyanotic. Breathing was very labored, particularly on expiration. The chest was in an expanded position; all of the auxiliary muscles of respiration were in use, but the volume of respiratory exchange was considerably reduced. Breathing was accompanied by wheezing which was audible throughout the room, being most marked on expiration. The pulse rate was 115 per minute. The temperature (taken rectally) showed an elevation of 0.8°.

Aside from findings related to the acute respiratory embarrassment, the physical examination was essentially normal. The patient was clearly underweight, but showed no evidence of malnutrition.

Laboratory examination of the sputum revealed elongated gelatinous casts of the small bronchi as well as traces of blood. Examination of a sample of venous blood showed mild hemoconcentration plus an increase in the proportion of eosinophils amounting to 6 per cent. A chest roentgenogram was essentially negative.

A diagnosis of severe bronchial asthma was made. The patient was placed in bed in the Fowler position. She was given an oxygen-helium mixture, subcutaneous injections of epinephrine, 1:1,000, and slow intravenous injections of aminophylline. A single dose of 50 mg. of Demerol was also given.

The attack yielded to these measures. By the following day, the patient was completely free from respiratory distress. Physical examination at this time was negative except for faint wheezing rales on auscultation of the chest. On the third hospital day, even these had disappeared. Laboratory findings also returned to normal except for a slight eosinophilia.

The patient was then discharged from the hospital, but entered upon a period of study in the out-patient division. According to the medical history, the attack which had resulted in the hospital admission was by far the most severe the patient had experienced. There had been two previous attacks within the past three months plus several minor episodes which sounded like abortive attacks. Prior to this three-month period, there was no history of asthma for some 20 years. There had been a few transient attacks in childhood. Mrs. C. added that, during the past three months, she had frequently experienced a sense of oppression in the upper chest.

The patient was known to have several allergies; to giant and small ragweed and to "house dust." Since early adolescence she had experienced mild hayfever in the late summer, which was adequately controlled with antihistamine preparations taken orally. The medical history indicated that she had contracted upper respiratory infections with something above average frequency, but these had never been severe. Her tonsils and adenoids had been removed at the age of seven.

In giving her recent history, Mrs. C. mentioned that the family had moved from New York State to their present location (the Midwest) three months before the recent admission. Although a native of the city in which the hospital was located, she had lived away from it for a period of eight years, including five years of college and three of marriage. The history of a series of asthmatic attacks coming so shortly after a major geographical move prompted a re-evaluation of her allergic status. On cautious testing, it was found that the three substances previously mentioned still constituted her only sensitivities among the inhalants. She was also tested for bacterial allergies, but there were no strikingly positive findings.

It was clear to all observers during this period that Mrs. C., even when completely asymptomatic so far as her chest was concerned, was decidedly tense. Moreover, while perfectly gracious and cooperative, she did not seem happy; on one or two occasions she appeared to be on the verge of tears, although she never actually wept. She, herself, complained of "nerves," saying she had been irritable and "jumpy" during recent months. Accordingly a psychiatric referral was made. The patient accepted the referral with some reservations, but once started, it became clear that she had a considerable need to talk. In the course of a number of interviews, the following material was obtained.

The patient was the only child of wealthy parents, the product of an unhappy marriage which ended in divorce when she was six years of age. From that time until going away to college at the age of 18, she had lived with her mother and grandmother (the latter now deceased). The atmosphere of the household was rather formal. Feelings were not, as a rule, expressed very openly; there was an attitude of "noblesse oblige." The patient was, generally, quite shy and reserved. Although very attractive personally and with a flair for clothes, the patient had few dates while in high school, her social activity being largely confined to large, relatively formal affairs. She was quite "overprotected," and, in addition, her mother appeared to dislike men in general and was sarcastically critical of her occasional escorts.

The patient's experiences at college, rather to her surprise, turned out to be very favorable ones. She was fortunate to make a permanent friendship with a girl who was her roommate for two years, a lively, warm-hearted, and rather mature person. Summer vacations were usually spent visiting at the homes of college friends or travelling abroad. The contacts with her mother were few and transient. Under these circumstances, the patient became more relaxed, more confident, and gradually more sociable. During her senior year, she met the man she later married. He was quite a virile person, a football hero, but also warm and considerate. In deciding to marry him—a decision which was not made easily, and was finally taken in quite an impulsive fashion—the patient was largely influenced (as far as she knew) by the latter qualities. At the time of the marriage, the patient's mother was out of the country. The mother's subsequent reaction was rather negative, but for a while the young couple saw little of her.

The marriage was essentially a good one. Mrs. C. had not anticipated the sexual aspect of marriage, and she was sexually frigid at first, but by degrees she relaxed somewhat in this relationship also. She found that she had become romantically interested in her husband; she came to enjoy the preliminary phases of love-making, and occasionally was able to experience mild orgasm.

The two pregnancies were planned and were essentially uneventful. Mr. C. was a good father, and the couple were able to afford domestic help. The experience of motherhood was seemingly more stressful for the patient than for the average young woman, but, under the favorable circumstances, she had been able to accept the stress without appreciable ill effects. She was a very conscientious mother.

About six months before the patient's hospital admission, the large corporation for which the husband worked indicated that he would be transferred to the patient's native city. With the transfer went a promotion, and so the husband was desirous of accepting. The patient had mixed feelings about this prospect. On the one hand, she wanted to please her husband and had an inclination to see more of her mother; on the other, she sensed deep but vague misgivings. For her husband's sake, she suppressed the latter feelings, and three months before the hospital admission the family made the move.

All the material arrangements were satisfactorily effected, but from that time on things began to go emotionally wrong for the patient. There occurred a blend of disturbing elements, which Mrs. C. had not been able to sort out consciously to any great degree, but which received some clarification in the conversations with the psychiatrist. One element was that Mr. C., could spend less time at home than had been his custom. His love for his wife was, of course, perfectly unchanged, and the sexual aspect of their relationship assumed, if anything, a greater significance since the element of comradeship was somewhat decreased.

More disturbing was the developing pattern between the patient and her mother; it was, in essence, the old pattern given added intensity by the new elements in the situation. On the one hand, the patient's mother began to lavish her own brand of attention on the two small children, spending a good bit of time with them and giving to them in needless (and sometimes obstructive) material ways. On the other, the mother displayed a thinly-veiled opposition to Mr. C., viewing the patient's loyalty to him with a chilly skepticism and any hints of the patient's sexual emotions with a disapproving disdain.

On the surface, the relationship between the mother and the patient and her husband was, for the most part, correct. The patient could rarely bring herself to criticize her mother. Mr. C. was ordinarily somewhat distantly polite. The older woman was "generous"; she gave the young couple a membership in an exclusive country club, entertained for her daughter, etc.

Mrs. C.'s inner tension mounted rapidly; she began losing the emotional ground that she had gained over the preceding eight years (she regressed). In fact, her conflicts became in a sense more active than they had been in later childhood and adolescence because of her newfound position as wife and mother (see below). The sense of oppression in the chest began within two weeks of the move and gradually increased. The first asthmatic attack began in the course of an argument between the patient and her husband in which Mr. C. expressed opposition to the mother's exerting such an influence in their affairs. The attack ended abruptly when the patient burst into tears—the only time during the whole three months in which she actually wept—and the husband gave ground. The second attack immediately followed an extended telephone conversation between the patient and her mother, in which Mrs. C. had refused to fall in with some plan being advocated by the mother.

The patient was quite reticent in speaking about the events immediately preceding the third attack. Eventually she allowed herself to reconstruct them as follows: Mr. C. had managed to come home relatively early one afternoon. The children were taking naps, and no one else was at home. On impulse, the patient and her husband had retired to the bedroom. They were in the act of love-making, when the doorbell rang. The ringing persisted. Finally unable to ignore it, Mrs. C. had thrown on a housecoat and answered the door. It was her mother, arriving with two friends to show them her grandchildren. The asthmatic attack developed within a matter of minutes and gained rapidly in severity.

In considering the role of emotional factors in the pathogenesis of bronchial asthma, it is valuable to note the connections between an asthmatic attack and ordinary crying. It has long been noted by clinicians that the sounds made in asthma resemble those of a whining cry or a repressed sobbing. In this connection, the fact that a great many asthmatics, like Mrs. C., report that they often feel like crying but seldom do so, assumes further interest. There is the additional clinical point that (again as in the case of Mrs. C.) if a patient does begin to cry while experiencing an asthmatic attack, the attack often ceases or ameliorates.

The relationship between crying and an asthmatic attack is particularly clear in the case of young children. If a small child is frightened or hurt and feels like crying, but nevertheless, because of pride or for any other reason, struggles with all his might against the impulse, a series of choking sobs usually ensues and is not infrequently followed by a temporary wheezing.

In such instances, the organs of the respiratory tract are clearly under the simultaneous influence of antagonistic innervations. The stimulatory impulses come largely over the fibers of the phrenic nerve and intercostal nerves in the cervical and upper thoracic segments of the spinal cord, and the inhibitory ones come largely over the fibers of the vagus nerve. Both sets of impulses are clearly being initiated by higher centers; in such cases, they are ultimately referable to cortical (psychic) centers.

Intensive study of patients with bronchial asthma by psychoanalytic techniques indicates that, in a large proportion of cases, the emotional situation immediately underlying an asthmatic attack is precisely that of wishing to cry and yet being unable to do so.[6] (In the case of Mrs. C., who, following the psychiatric evaluation, entered a period of intensive psychotherapy, the evidence offered by the first asthmatic attack and its cessation was repeatedly confirmed by episodes within the therapeutic hours in which sudden, mild attacks of asthma were aborted when the patient wept freely.)

More profound questions about the psychological contribution to the pathogenesis of bronchial asthma have to do with the nature of the basic conflict or conflicts giving rise to the emotional state which calls forth the symptoms. Here again, as in the case of peptic ulcer and essential hypertension, there appears to be a considerable degree of specificity with respect to the conflicting forces. The most typical situation is one in which sexual and/or hostile impulses conflict with anxiety and feelings of guilt, with the particular feature being that the anxiety has to do with the potential loss of a source of (desperately needed) dependency gratification.[1, 22] The stifled crying is a plea for forgiveness and continued help. It is stifled partly from anger, partly from shame, and in considerable measure because the basic elements of the situation (in their deeper implications) are largely unconscious.

In the case of Mrs. C., several elements may be identified which fit closely into this configuration. Although these elements were, in themselves, discrete, they ran together to form the key situations. First, there was the conflict between the recently acquired sexual attraction to the patient's husband and the remobilized feelings involving the patient's mother: dependency, the need to conform to her point of view, and the fear of losing her support. Then there were angry feelings toward the mother, arising partly out of the mother's attitude toward the patient's husband and partly out of envy of the mother's solicitous attentions to her grandchildren. These angry feelings were in conflict with the same set of factors which opposed the patient's sexual expression. Finally, there were angry feelings toward the husband over his increased involvement with his work. This emotion, in turn, was in conflict with the need to depend upon him as a source of affection and support. None of these feelings was entirely conscious, and the major portion of the dependency needs was quite unconscious.

It should be mentioned that Mrs. C. was, *emotionally speaking*, fundamentally less ill than is the case with a large proportion of bronchial asthmatics. Although her approach to an emotional maturity, at the time of her asthmatic attacks, was still a partial and tentative one, she had nevertheless gone further in this direction than have many other patients with the asthmatic syndrome.

It should also be made clear that somatic factors, related less directly or not at all to the psychological factors, described, were in all probability of significance in the production of Mrs. C.'s illness: the various mild allergies, the respiratory infections,* and undetermined constitutional factors. Similar elements are very likely involved in most cases of bronchial asthma. There appears to be considerable variation in bronchial asthmatics with respect to the relative importance of the various factors: variation among the set of somatic elements as well as between them and the set of psychological elements. In some cases of asthma, the disproportion is so great that one looks in vain for identifiable somatic elements; in other cases, one looks in vain for identifiable psychological elements.

The place of psychological measures in the treatment of bronchial asthma naturally varies also. The variation depends not merely upon the relative importance of psychological factors, however, but upon the refractoriness of the condition to physical methods of treatment (desensitization procedures, anti-infection measures, avoidance of allergens) and upon the accessibility of the patient to a psychological approach. In the case of Mrs. C., an extended period of psychotherapy was used. In the course of this treatment, the current conflicts were considerably clarified; the patient received, through the therapeutic relationship, some immediate gratification of her dependency needs, allowing her to become less dependent upon her husband and, more importantly, upon her mother; she was given reassurance as to the legitimacy of some of her aggressive and sexual needs. Eventually the therapy succeeded in bringing about a permanent, though partial, reduction in her dependency strivings, allowing greater confidence and

---

* See, however, the discussion on p. 219.

greater personal freedom. As a result of these happenings, the key conflicts were very appreciably lessened. During the first six months of therapy there were several attacks of asthma, but after this period the patient remained free of chest symptoms.

To achieve symptom remission in patients with bronchial asthma, it is usually sufficient to bring about a clean break in the psychophysiological chain of events in *either* segment, the one best described in psychological terms or the one best described in physiological terms. In cases in which the specific allergens are limited in number and can be clearly identified, desensitization procedures, reinforced with antihistamine preparations, will usually suffice. In more complicated cases, or cases in which the chemical aspect cannot be clarified, psychological measures are called for (in addition to whatever conventional measures can be established as useful). Here, one's first thought would be to study the patient and his life situation thoroughly, attempting to discover what the possibilities are of helping the patient through some form of environmental manipulation. If, for example, Mrs. C. had lacked the personality assets to make her a good candidate for intensive psychotherapy, the most helpful measure would probably have been to recommend to the patient and her husband—and to work with them to accept the recommendation—that the patient's physical and emotional well-being be given top priority in family planning and that, accordingly, the family arrange to move to another location.

In a number of patients not responding satisfactorily to medication alone, yet for whom intensive psychotherapy may not be feasible and clear-cut environmental change not discernible or not achievable, a period of supportive psychotherapy (p. 440) by the family physician is indicated. Asthmatic patients often derive considerable benefit from the process of ventilation of thoughts and feelings in the presence of a friendly, understanding, and nonjudgmental listener. In addition to partial relief of emotional tensions, such a brief psychotherapy gives a certain amount of direct and legitimate gratification to the patient's dependency needs.

Summary and Implications

Having now considered three disease states—peptic ulcer, essential hypertension, and idiopathic bronchial asthma—in the pathogenesis of which psychological factors are very often of fundamental significance, it is time to review the data and note some generalizations and implications.

In all of these cases, a relationship has been noted between a physiological derangement and an underlying emotional state. Essential hypertension correlates with chronic, suppressed (and repressed) anger. Peptic ulcer correlates with chronic frustration of an oral type of dependency needs. Bronchial asthma correlates with a chronic conflict between a type of dependency needs (to be protected and taken care of) and sexual and hostile impulses. But how are the correlations best expressed? A great deal of the activity of a healthy human being correlates with underlying motivational states. As we shall see (pp. 316 to 320), all psychoneurotic symptoms do so as well. What are the special features of the correlations in the case of disease syndromes such as those we have just considered? Most human behavior, for example, has an adaptive value, involves an attempt at adjustment. This is even true of nearly all psychoneurotic and much psychotic behavior. Is it, in any sense, true of "psychosomatic" diseases?

First it is well to note that in the disease states considered the pathogenic innervations (the final neural pathways) involved the autonomic system, either solely or primarily. Unlike activity of the voluntary and sensory components of the nervous system, activity of the autonomic division is generally considered to be inaccessible to consciousness, directly and per se.* Therefore, in these cases, the patients were not only to a significant degree unconscious of their basic conflicts, but also unconscious of the pathogenic innervations. That is to say, a hypertensive is apt to be unaware of his hypertension for a considerable period of time; an ulcer patient may be unaware of the initial (microscopic) stages of ulcer formation; an asthmatic is unaware of the preliminary innervations which set up the asthmatic attack proper.

Furthermore, it is clear that, even when gross symptoms have developed, these symptoms in themselves have no homeostatic and no adjustment value (see p. 29). (It is true that *the responses of the environment*—specifically, the responses of physicians, nurses, etc.—have a considerable value to the patient, but this is not due to any *inner* significance of the symptoms for the patient, but to their scientific significance as perceived by professionals.) To express this fact in technical terms, one may say that the symptoms of diseases such as essential hypertension, peptic ulcer, and bronchial asthma, have no *primary gain* (p. 319).

Thus it is quite incorrect to say—as one sometimes hears it said, even by physicians—that "Mr. Jones's hypertension is expressive of his angry disposition." In such a case, the disease does not afford expression of anything; it effects no discharge of motivational tensions; it is merely "the physiological concommitant of an emotional state" (Alexander).

Another point of consideration has to do with the previously men-

---

* It appears possible that this idea may require partial revision, but the revision would not alter the main lines of argument here advanced.

tioned question of specificity. Despite the television and radio commercials, it is evidently not very meaningful and certainly not very constructive to ascribe numerous quite specific disease states to something as vague and amorphous as "stress and strain." There is, as has been described, evidence to believe that the psychological contribution to the pathogenesis of disease states such as those we have been considering is *typically* of a rather specific nature. For example, sustained frustration of a certain kind of anger (anger of a sort which would ordinarily lead to fighting) tends to produce hypertension, not peptic ulcer. Or, to put the relationship in perhaps a more significant form, if one is seeking to elucidate the emotional pathogenic components in a case of early essential hypertension, it is profitable to begin the search by looking for factors which provoke and factors which inhibit the expression of anger-leading-to-fighting.

It is, however, also important to note that the concept of specificity has limitations—a delineation of which is the objective of considerable research effort at the present time. While it appears correct to say that *typically* a certain disease state A is based in part upon a certain variety of emotional conflict X, it is usually not a difficult matter to find exceptions, and it is important to recognize them when they occur. The cases taken to be exceptions can be of either of two sorts: true exceptions and pseudo-exceptions. The true exception is the case, disease state A without emotional conflict X; the pseudo-exception is the case, emotional conflict X without disease state A.

The latter circumstance is not at all difficult to understand. Since there is no question but that, in the diseases which we have been considering, the psychological factors do not constitute the whole etiology, since there is no question but that a somatic "predisposition" (either inherited or acquired) and/or somatic "precipitants" are involved, emotional conflict X without disease state A is precisely what one would at times expect, and would often indicate merely that the somatic prerequisites were not present. In some instances, there is the further possibility that the absence of disease state A is because emotional conflict X has not yet been operating over a sufficiently long period of time. There is the third possibility that whereas the somatic prerequisites are, in some measure, present, and whereas the emotional conflict has also been present, the conflict has been handled in some other (pathological) fashion. For example, given a high degree of chronic anger and given also motivational forces blocking the direct motor expression of the anger as well as a clear awareness of it, a possible result might be the development of a *paranoid psychotic* reaction (p. 390). In such a case, the effect of the original anger upon visceral and somatic innervations could be radically altered.

The true exceptions, the cases in which disease state A exists without evidence of emotional conflict X, are probably less common. (Sometimes, when such a case is presented it turns out that evidence of the emotional conflict has not been carefully sought.) When this situation does exist, one explanation can be that the purely somatic etiological elements are so severe as to have produced the disease state without a significant emotional contribution (of any sort). A very simple example would be the production of attacks of bronchial asthma by the repeated inhalation of an irritant gas, such as chlorine. Another example could be the existence of a purely seasonal hayfever in response to a single potent allergen, let us say, giant ragweed. (Even in cases such as this, however, it is of interest to note evidence indicating the possible influence of psychogenic elements. It is possible, for instance, through the use of hypnotic suggestion, both to bring on a typical attack in the absence of the allergen and to inhibit an attack in the presence of the allergen.)

Another explanatory possibility has to do with the fact that with frequent or sustained production of a response the response tends to become increasingly easy to elicit. In a sense, it becomes a *habitual* response and may come to be elicited by stimuli which would originally have been inadequate. Thus, if a patient suffering from a disease based on disturbed psychophysiological responses is examined late in the history of his disease, the original specificity may have been very largely washed out. In such instances, there may be some meaning to the "stress and strain" type of explanation.

Finally, the possibility cannot be excluded—such is the complexity of organization of the human personality—that atypical cause-and-effect sequences do assume real significance at times, i.e., that disease state A is based in part upon emotional conflict Y.

It has been noted, perhaps, that in all of the present discussion, very little has been said about so-called "disease types" ("ulcer type," "hypertensive type," etc.). This is because the evidence for the significance of personality "types" in the production of somatic illness is very weak. In fact, as usually expressed, disease types are little more than a figment of the popular imagination. What has happened is that some secondary correlations have been mistaken for primary ones. For example, it is true that many a successful, hard-driving business executive suffers from peptic ulcer. His business success, however, does not correlate in any direct way with the ulcer; it correlates with his ability and with his use of the psychological mechanism of reaction-formation (p. 77). In his efforts to hide his excessive dependency needs (particularly from himself), he assumes ever widening responsibility; this assumption of responsibility, in the natural course of events, is rewarded with promotions. Yet the assumption of responsibility can derive from any of several motivations, the others of which are unrelated to the occurrence of peptic ulcer. And, on the other hand, as we have seen in the case of Mr. M., the central conflict contributing to the development of peptic ulcer need not involve an appreciable degree of reaction-formation or assumption of responsibility.

Having considered some important pathophysiological reactions in detail and having derived some generalizations from this consideration, we may now review more briefly some other medical conditions in the pathogenesis of which emotional factors tend to be significant.

Mucous Colitis (spastic colitis, irritable colon)

In its most typical form, this distressing condition is characterized by sensations of abdominal fullness and discomfort, transiently relieved by defecation or flatus, by belching and bouts of nausea, by abdominal rumblings, and by small, frequent (sometimes extremely frequent) bowel movements. More often than not, the presenting complaints will include reference to constipation. Objectively speaking, this condition is rarely present; the complaint is referable to the patient's preoccupation with his eliminative tract. The history will often indicate that the stools tend to be loose and watery; this condition is usually to be considered as an artifact, being related to the self-administration of unnecessary laxatives and/or enemas.

Mucous colitis has long been thought to involve a neurotic component. Before considering the following abbreviated case history, it is suggested that the student re-read that portion of Chapter 4 which deals with the muscle-training stage of personality development (pp. 93 to 99).

Mr. J. D., aged 31 years, had presented with all of the features just listed. On the basis of a thorough diagnostic evaluation, it was determined that his condition, which had persisted (and worsened) over a period of some six years was one of mucous colitis. For 18 months, the patient was treated by reassurance, regulation of diet, (partial) control of his laxative habit, and the prescription of tincture of belladonna. On this regimen, the patient's illness ameliorated only slightly. Mr. D. was therefore referred for psychotherapy, while the original measures were being continued. In the course of the psychotherapy, which was both intensive and prolonged, a considerable elucidation of the patient's condition was achieved.

Mr. D. had come from a moderately prosperous farm family in Virginia; his parents, however, were immigrants from Central Europe, neither seeking nor achieving "social standing." The patient's developmental history revealed that great stress had been placed upon toilet training, which had been early and rigorous with as much emphasis having been placed upon rewards for conformity as upon punishment for lapses. In general, much emphasis had been given to certain "old fashioned virtues," cleanliness and orderliness, and later thrift, making good grades in school, and material achievement. A relaxed approach to living was considered "slothfulness" and a serious vice.

The patient somehow developed the beginnings of an academic and scholarly turn of mind although his attitude tended to be dilettantish rather than practical. Against his inclinations, he was sent to an agricultural college, but he later persuaded his parents to allow him to transfer to a fashionable southern university, where he studied liberal arts.

Through social activities while at the university, Mr. D. met his future wife. This woman, who was three years his senior, was a member of the native aristocracy. Her parents were dead, and she was the heiress to a large estate near the university town.

About eight months after graduation, Mr. D. married the heiress and became the manager of the estate, being then 23 years of age. The marriage was, to an extent, one of convenience, but certain misrepresentations were involved on both sides. The woman had represented herself as being wealthier than she actually was; as it turned out, the estate was run down and in need of vigorous management. For his part, the patient had created the impression of being more energetic and resourceful than he actually was able to be.

There existed a certain amount of mutual affection between the two, and the patient remained essentially symptom free during the first two years of the marriage. The revenues of the estate continued to dwindle, however, and the family's financial situation became more critical with the birth of three children during the ensuing five years. The onset of the patient's colitis coincided with the advent of the first child (when he was 25).

Mr. D.'s efforts to direct and supervise the agricultural activities upon which the family's fortunes rested held an element of pathos. To all outward appearances, he remained steadily at work, taking vacations but seldom and seeming to put in long hours. As a matter of fact, his work was extremely distasteful to him, and he wasted a great deal of time in contemplation of nature, in covert periods of recreation, and in daydreaming. He often attempted to rationalize matters, saying to himself that a farmer's material success depended upon many factors which were beyond his control; and he attempted to conceal from his wife that her inherited wealth was continuing to dwindle. The rationalizations were, however, quite inadequate for his peace of mind, and the efforts at concealment were only partially successful.

On the basis of this material, a formulation of the patient's psychophysiological disturbance can be made. One sees that Mr. D. was in severe conflict between wishes to "take it easy," not to compete, to enjoy life in a rather passive way, and emotions of anxiety, shame, and guilt. This conflict was only partially unconscious; Mr. D. had some awareness of it and could have partially expressed it in words even prior to the therapy. The next link in the chain was, however, entirely unconscious. This link depended upon the circumstances of the patient's early training and the atmosphere of the home in which he was reared. As a small child, he had equated bowel function with giving (to his mother), with doing the expected, the constructive thing. His experiences during this early period were of unusual intensity. Hence, although the old equation came to be completely repressed, it continued to exist in the unconscious regions of his mind. When, in young adult life, he entered a situation calling for vigorous, productive, masculine efforts of a sort for which his potentialities had never been developed,* his psychophysiological state became chronically that of a small child striving to please mother by producing stools. His lower bowel received excessive, more or less continuous, motor and secretory innervations of a sort appropriate to the old situation although completely inappropriate to the new. Since the old pattern contributed not in the slightest to reaching an equilibrium in the new situation, the inner tensions persisted and the innervations became chronic—as they had not been in the situation of early childhood.

Although the particular life history and current situation of Mr. D. have highly individual features, the key conflict and its physiological concommitants are typical for a great many patients with mucous colitis.[21] As can be seen, there are similarities to the situation of peptic ulcer patients. There is, however, a significant and distinguishing difference. Whereas the ulcer patient characteristically rejects or is unable, for external reasons, to achieve gratification of his oral-dependent needs, the colitis patient characteristically accepts considerable dependency gratification, but thereby enters a peculiar state of guilty anxiety which is contributory to the disturbed physiology.

Patients whose mucous colitis does not respond to conventional measures (including reassurance and advice) and who are referred for psychotherapy, usually respond symptomatically to the mere institution of this measure, deriving a sense of emotional support and also some measure of relief from the sense of guilt through the confessional aspects of the treatment. However, the sort of thorough-going personality modification required to provide assurance against redevelopment of the syndrome may be extremely difficult to achieve.

Hyperthyroidism (thyrotoxicosis, Graves' disease)

The syndrome produced by an excess of circulating thyroid hormone may be the result of any of three situations: Graves' disease proper (diffuse hyperplasia and hypertrophy of the gland), hypersecretion by the discrete nodules of toxic nodular goiter, and the inadvertent over-

---

* The basis (in early life experiences) for this stunting is not germane to the development of the compensatory measures contributing to the pathogenesis of the colitis.

administration of thyroid hormone. The discussion which follows is confined to the first of these situations.

The etiology of Graves' disease is not thoroughly understood; nor need it be precisely the same in all cases. The familial incidence of the disease is sufficiently marked to make it appear likely that an hereditary factor is often of significance. Some type of somatic predisposition is probably always present. It appears highly probable that the site of the basic disorder is not the thyroid gland itself; the gland is seemingly an end-organ under disturbed control.

The evidence suggests that a variety of factors may initiate this disturbed control, thus precipitating the disease, but that the commonest of these factors are of an emotional nature. For example, there is the widespread and long-standing clinical recognition that patients with this disorder frequently relate the onset of symptoms to a single event of high emotional stress or to an emotionally stressful period. In a pioneering study, one investigator (Moschowitz) reported a number of situations in which an emotional stress operating upon a large group of persons had simultaneously triggered the development of hyperthyroidism in several members of the group.[14] Another investigator (Conrad), attempting to quantify impressions of the triggering effect of emotional trauma, reported evidence of such trauma in 94 per cent of a series of 200 patients.[3]

The diagram on the following page illustrates mechanisms which are thought frequently to be involved in the production and maintenance of hyperthyroidism.

The fundamental biological significance of the thyroid appears to derive from its function of aiding the organism in adaptational efforts to master sustained environmental and internal stresses (including such normal phases of special stress as puberty and pregnancy). The thyroid hormone thus appears, to an extent, comparable to epinephrine with which it is a synergist. Speaking teleologically, one may say that a principal difference is that epinephrine is designed to rally the body mechanisms very quickly for an emergency situation, whereas the thyroid hormone exerts its tonic effect "for the long haul."

Here are excerpts from the case history of a hyperthyroid patient.

Miss L. E., a 19-year-old girl was admitted to the hospital for medical observation. The patient had had many sore throats during the preceding year, and, on admission was complaining of aching in various joints. She was found to have a fever, a leukocytosis, an elevated sedimentation rate, and a somewhat elongated P-R interval on the electrocardiogram. A tentative diagnosis of rheumatic fever was made. Penicillin and salicylates were given. The fever, leukocytosis, abnormal sedimentation rate and joint pains disappeared, although some complaint of weakness remained. On the eighth hospital day, the patient

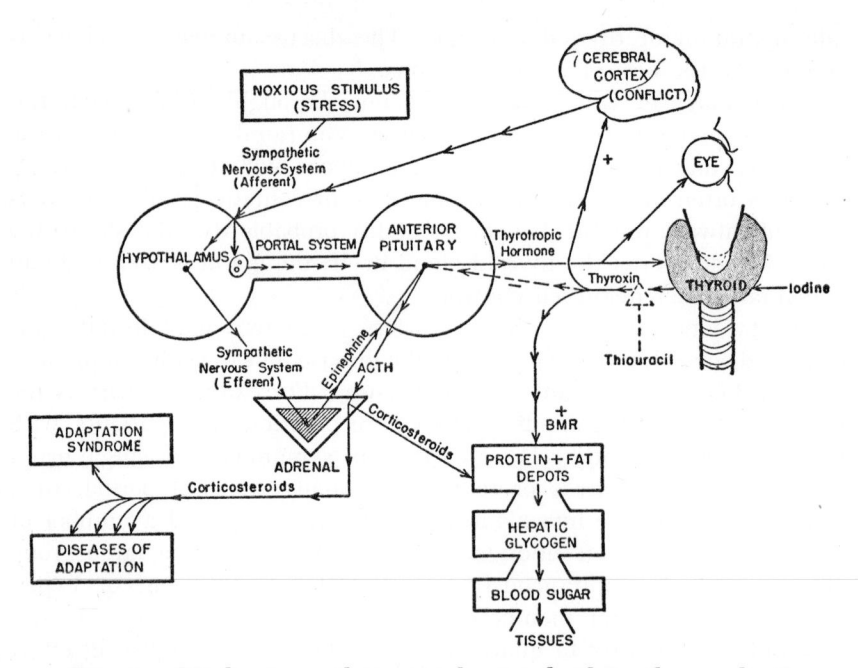

FIG. 1. Mechanisms that may be involved in the production and maintenance of hyperthyroidism are illustrated schematically. Activation of the hypothalamus may result in (1) an increased secretion of epinephrine and a subsequent stimulation of the anterior pituitary by the increased circulating epinephrine, and/or (2) the secretion of some humoral agent by the hypothalamus which is then transported to the anterior pituitary. Stimulation of the anterior pituitary results in increased production of thyrotropic hormone with a subsequent stimulation of the thyroid gland. The reciprocal relation between the thyroid and anterior pituitary is illustrated. (After Mirsky, from Alexander, F., Psychosomatic Medicine: Its Principles and Applications, New York, Norton, 1950.)

developed a tachycardia without corresponding temperature elevation or leukocytosis. The thyroid had been considered questionably enlarged, and at this time a determination of the basic metabolic rate was made; it was found to be +52. Further laboratory studies indicated a significant depression of the serum cholesterol and an increase of approximately 60 per cent in the uptake of radioactive iodine.

Miss E. was quite shy and reticent and, at the time of admission, a reliable outside informant had not been available. When the diagnosis of hyperthyroidism was made, a further attempt at obtaining history revealed the information that the patient's admission to the hospital had followed that of her mother (who had an acute bowel obstruction) by a single day. More striking still, it was discovered that the mother had died of postoperative complications on the afternoon of the patient's seventh hospital day, and that this information had been unintentionally conveyed to her by a relative who had come to the hospital to visit both mother and daughter.

Aside from indications of mounting "nervousness," irritability, and hints of muscular weakness during the preceding six months, the conventional medical history was not contributory. The patient's personal history was, in brief, as follows.

Miss E. was the eldest of four children, having a brother 17, and twin sisters 14 years of age. She came of a family of very limited means. Her father was a housepainter who became an alcoholic and was divorced by the mother when the patient was eight. The patient's mother went to work and with some help from relatives was just able to support the family. Much of the care of the younger children devolved upon L. E.

The patient was hard-working and conscientious. She was a good student, but quit school at the age of 16 to go to work and supplement the family income. The situation had worsened during the half-year preceding admission, inasmuch as the patient's mother experienced abdominal complaints for which she would not seek proper medical attention; she was often unable to work and occasionally had required nursing.

The patient was asked about her dreams, and she said that they were usually unpleasant or frightening. She often dreamt of being chased by something she could not see or of running on a treadmill.

To generalize from patients who (as was eventually true of Miss L. E.) have received intensive psychological study, one may describe a rather typical development of the basic situation of conflict as follows. The individual has sustained serious threats to his security—or, less often, threats merely to his sense of security—in early childhood, under circumstances making it difficult or impossible to turn to parents (or other protective older figures) for help, support, and reassurance. Under this stress, the individual makes a desperate and premature attempt to behave like a parent, himself. The psychological mechanism involved at this point appears to be that of *identification* (p. 78), but it is an identification which is premature in its scope and intensity, both physiologically and psychologically.

This defense orientation persists, although the real life situation may undergo a phase of amelioration (unlike the case of L. E.). In later life, the patient appears driven to assume excessive responsibilities of a parental, and especially of a maternal sort, responsibilities which cannot be sustained except by functioning on a quasi-emergency basis. (This assumption of excessive responsibility differs from that seen in the "typical" peptic ulcer patient both in its precise motivation—the hyperthyroid patient is, so to speak, "running scared"—and in its characteristic form—the hyperthyroid patient is not overly "ambitious" in the conventional sense of the word.) The manifest clinical disease may develop in response to the accumulated stress of the situation, but often it is triggered by some sort of "last straw," such as an additional pregnancy, a sudden financial loss, or (as in the case of L. E.) the illness or death of a key figure.

Recent work by Alexander and his associates indicates that hyperthyroid patients can be differentiated experimentally from normal controls on the basis of their physiological and psychological responses to a standardized stress situation (a motion picture involving threats to survival). The data thus far gathered by this method tend to substantiate the more impressionistic material obtained from therapeutic work with patients.[2]

TREATMENT OF HYPERTHYROIDISM. As the student is doubtless aware, the choice of treatment of patients with thyrotoxicosis lies primarily between the use of radioactive iodine and surgery. Apart from its theoretical interest, an understanding of the possible role of emotional factors in the pathogenesis of the disorder may be of value in any of four ways: (1) In some instances, early recognition of the state of affairs may enable the physician to recommend some environmental changes which will lessen the possibility of the development of the full-blown condition. (2) After the use of surgical or radiation treatment, some modification of the patient's situation may lessen the chance of a recurrence (which is ordinarily given as five to ten per cent). (3) Despite permanent alleviation of the patient's thyroid disease, if the basic, emotionally disturbing situation goes unaltered, it may be productive of other sorts of maladjustment; hence it is often deserving of attention on preventive grounds. (4) In connection with any efforts at suggesting a modification of the patient's situation, or if no such efforts are possible, a supportive psychotherapy (p. 440) is often indicated, with the aim of helping the patient effect a less taxing life adjustment.

Migraine Headache

The migraine syndrome may be defined as being typically a periodic, severe hemicrania, preceded by various prodromata and associated with nausea and a tendency to vomit (see pp. 154 to 155). Both the prodromal period and the attack itself vary markedly as to duration, ranging from minutes to days. Symptoms of the prodromal period may include feelings of inner tension, facial flushing or pallor, episodes of dizziness, and transient visual difficulties, such as scintillating scotomata. The headache itself may be extremely severe; it is frequently described as "throbbing" or "pounding." If it persists for some length of time, it may become generalized although it is almost invariably unilateral in onset. Swelling of the nasal mucosa and injection of the conjunctiva are common. As noted, the patient is apt to vomit, but the vomiting does not bring appreciable relief. A prolonged attack is often accompanied in its latter portion by an uncomfortable degree of contraction of the neck muscles.

The immediate cause of the symptoms of migraine is a series of vascular phenomena. The early portion of the prodromal phase is characterized by excessive fluctuations in the degree of contraction of the cranial arteries. Shortly before the onset of the headache there is often a period of sustained constriction of the cerebral arteries. The headache itself is the result of the ensuing phase, one of marked dilatation of the cranial arteries, typically more pronounced on one side than the other, and affecting the adjacent tissues which become edematous and tender.

A fundamental understanding of the etiology of migraine is still incomplete. There is a rather well marked familial tendency of the disorder, a fact that is suggestive of the possibility of subtle hereditary differences in the mechanisms governing the cranial blood flow. However this may be, there is widespread agreement that emotional factors are of great significance in the production of the migraine syndrome.

Psychoanalytic study of patients with migraine[1, 7] indicates that the central emotional conflict relevant to the development of the headaches is one involving resentment and hostility on the one hand and the inhibiting forces of anxiety and guilt feelings on the other. There are thus important similarities between the emotional problems of the patient with migraine and those of the hypertensive. There is, however, at least one significant difference. Whereas the hypertensive is to a considerable extent aware of his hostile impulses, the patient with migraine typically is not. In other words, whereas the hypertensive dares not *act* on his hostile impulses, the migrainous patient dares not even *think* of them. In the migrainous patient, the mechanism of repression is brought into use more promptly and more extensively. (In addition, there may well be differences between the two groups as to the precise nature of the principal hostile impulses, but an elucidation of this point is beyond the scope of the present account.)

The treatment of patients with migraine has two aspects, chemical and psychotherapeutic. The less severe attacks often respond to a sizeable dose of aspirin plus a brief period of rest and quiet. More severe episodes require the administration of a vasoconstrictor drug, such as ergotamine tartrate, which is most promptly effective when given intramuscularly, but which may also be given orally or rectally.

Except in the milder cases, the treatment of patients with migraine should usually involve a psychotherapeutic component. This is true even if it turns out that attacks can be quite successfully aborted with the use of drugs. The patient with severe migraine is characteristically tense, rigid, vaguely aware of a good bit of inner pressure, and not leading a very happy life (although it may be a very responsible and productive one).

The psychotherapy should afford the patient an opportunity for ventilation of feelings, for some heightened awareness of his current needs and anxieties, for support and reassurance of a sort favoring relaxation, and for a reappraisal of his current life situation, with encouragement to seek ways of reducing provocations and aggravations.

EXTENSIONS OF PSYCHOSOMATIC CONCEPTS

Whereas an understanding of the psychophysiological sequences most likely to be involved in the production of certain specific disease states, such as those which have been considered in this chapter,* is of high value in the study and management of these conditions, a realization of the possible role played by emotional factors in the pathogenesis of whole classes of disease may ultimately be of even greater significance.

Consider, for example, the whole matter of resistance to infection. If asked how he contracted his severe cold, Mr. Jones is likely to say that he sat next to someone in the theatre or in church or on the bus who was sneezing or coughing. Or he may say that he went out in the rain without his overshoes or in the cold without his overcoat. Or he may say that he has had to go without much sleep, or with an inadequate diet, for several days. Yet the truth is that he has probably done all of these things numerous times without "catching" a cold. Not unlikely, he has even done all of them together, on occasion, without developing an infection.†[8]

A similar puzzle exists with respect to the morbidity in epidemics. No matter how virulent the infectious agent nor how widespread the epidemic, there is usually an appreciable number of persons who have been exposed, but who do not contract the disease. In past ages, this mystery was often explained by reference to supernatural agencies. (Cf. Exodus: 9 and 10; Daniel Defoe's *A Journal of the Plague Year.*)

---

* The conditions cited by no means exhaust the list of specific organic disease states in the pathogenesis of which emotional factors, largely unconscious, appear to play a significant and identifiable part. Rheumatoid arthritis, ulcerative colitis, certain cardiac conditions, and certain of the dermatitides could have been discussed. In addition, there are other conditions, such as diabetes mellitus (p. 264) and possibly pernicious anemia in which constitutional factors play a more complicated role. In diabetes, for example, as mentioned in Chapter 7, it is thought that oral needs are congenitally of abnormal force due to the metabolic disturbance. These needs inevitably encounter frustrations, and the resultant conflict hastens the course of the illness.

† Of course, if he has done all of them together, it would probably become pertinent to inquire into the motivation for such carelessness, since the situation would suggest the presence of an unconscious need to court ill health.

More recently, a number of scientific speculations have been advanced, involving such possibilities as constitutional variations in physiological defense mechanisms, mutations affecting the virulence of the microorganism, and the existence of subclinical cases of the disease in question, with the production of specific immune bodies. As the student knows from bacteriology, these explanatory ideas have been substantiated in a number of instances by the results of carefully conducted immunological studies.

Yet the explanation is still far from complete. Returning to the example of the common cold with its various complications, one knows that the variety of infectious microorganisms is so great (and constantly changing) that specific immunities could scarcely account for all of the great discrepancy that exists among individuals with respect to susceptibility. One knows, further, that an individual's susceptibility varies from time to time in a way which is not compatible with a very complete explanation along the lines of constitutionally based, permanent, individual differences in the body's defenses against infection. Evidently the general defense mechanisms of the body vary, within the individual and from time to time, in a way which is not fully explicable by any of the factors thus far mentioned.

That these differences may at times be due to emotional factors was recognized in Frank Loesser's comic hit song in the musical comedy, *Guys and Dolls*, "A Person Can Develop a Cold." The popularity of the song indicates the audience's response to its truth.

Particularly within the past 15 years, evidence has gradually accumulated to indicate that emotional factors can produce a variety of alterations in the physiology of the body which can have an effect upon susceptibility to infection. Experiments have, for example, indicated that changes in vascularity, in secretions, and in swelling of the nasal mucosa may correlate with changes in the subject's state of personal adjustment.[11] Other experiments have shown that the pH of nasal secretions and of saliva can be affected by changes in the subject's emotional state.[4, 5, 9, 19] Now it is well known that for every species of microorganism there exists a set of optimum physicochemical conditions with respect to growth and reproduction, and, further, that relatively slight alterations in these conditions may exert a decisive effect upon the fate of the microorganisms. Hence it is a rather direct inference that emotional changes can effect susceptibility to respiratory tract infection.

The existence of this sequence has, in fact, begun to be removed from the area of inference. Kaplan and his associates have, within the past few years, reported variations in the bacterial population of the oropharynx of a patient that have been closely correlated with changes in emotional status.[12, 13] Indeed, the correlations were sufficiently close and consistent that the bacterial variations could be correctly predicted from a determination of the emotional status alone.

It is also being recognized that emotional factors may contribute significantly to the developmental course of a number of surgical conditions. This subject will be discussed in the following chapter.

In all of the material of the present chapter, emphasis has been placed on a particular kind of interweaving of psychological and physiological data, an interweaving in which psychological factors were considered primarily in the etiological phase of the inquiry and physiological factors primarily in the diagnostic phase. As a glance back at the definition of "psychosomatic" (p. 183) will indicate, however, this orientation involves a field of interest broader than the area in which psychological factors influence the pathogenesis of disease. The area of disease states in which organic lesions of various parts of the body exert an influence upon the personality (so-called "somatopsychic" sequences) is also of great interest. It, too, will be discussed in the chapter which follows.

Bibliography

1. Alexander, F.: Psychosomatic Medicine: Its Principles and Applications, New York, Norton, 1950.
2. Alexander, F., Flagg, G. W., Foster, S., Clemens, T., and Blahd, W.: Experimental studies of emotional stress: 1. Hyperthyroidism, Psychosom. Med. 23:104-114, 1961.
3. Conrad, A.: The psychiatric study of hyperthyroid patients, J. Nerv. Ment. Dis. 79:505, 1934.
4. Fabricant, N. D.: Effects of emotions on the hydrogen ion concentration of nasal secretions in situ, Arch. Otolaryng. 43:402, 1946.
5. Fabricant, N. D., and Perlstein, M. A.: pH of nasal secretions in situ in infants and children, Arch. Otolaryng. 48:67, 1949.
6. French, T. N., and Alexander, F.: Psychogenic Factors in Bronchial Asthma, Psychosomatic Medicine Monograph IV, National Research Council, Washington, D.C., 1941.
7. Fromm-Reichmann, F.: Contributions to the psychogenesis of migraine, Psychoanal. Rev. 24:26, 1937.
8. Gohd, R. S.: The common cold, New Engl. J. Med. 250:687, 722, 1954.
9. Grossman, L. I., and Brickman, B. M.: Some observations on the pH of saliva, J. Dent. Res. 16:409, 1937.
10. Hofling, C. K.: Psychosocial factors in the pathogenesis of a peptic ulcer in an 89-year-old man, Ohio M. J. 46:1064, 1950.
11. Holmes, T. H., Goodell, H., Wolf, S., and Wolff, H. G.: The Nose: An Experimental Study of Reactions Within the Nose of Human Subjects During Various Life Experiences, Springfield, Ill., Thomas, 1950.

12. Kaplan, S. M., and Gottschalk, L. A.: Modifications of the oropharyngeal bacteria with changes in the psychodynamic state: a validation study, Psychosom. Med. 20:314, 1958.
13. Kaplan, S. M., Gottschalk, L. A., and Fleming, D. E.: Modifications of oropharyngeal bacteria with changes in the psychodynamic state: a preliminary study, Arch. Neurol. Psychiat. 78:565, 1957.
14. Moschowitz, E.: The nature of Graves' disease, Arch. Int. Med. 46:610, 1930.
15. Pickering, G. W.: High Blood Pressure, New York, Grune, 1955.
16. Portis, S. A.: Diseases of the Digestive System, ed. 3, Philadelphia, Lea & Febiger, 1953.
17. Reiser, M. F., Rosenbaum, M., and Ferris, E. B., Jr.: Psychologic mechanisms in malignant hypertension, Psychosom. Med. 13:147, 1951.
18. Reiser, M. F., Ferris, E. B., Jr., and Levine, M.: Cardiovascular disorders *in* Whittkower, E. D., and Cleghorn, R. (eds.): Recent Developments in Psychosomatic Medicine, Philadelphia, Lippincott, 1954.
19. Starr, H. E.: Studies of human mixed saliva, J. Biol. Chem. 54: 43, 1922.
20. Weiner, H., Thaler, M., Reiser, M. F., and Mirsky, I. A.: Etiology of duodenal ulcer: I. Relation of specific psychological characteristics to rate of gastric secretion (serum pepsinogen), Psychosom. Med. 19:1, 1957.
21. White, B. V., Cobb, S., and Jones, C. M.: Mucous Colitis, Psychosomatic Medicine Monograph I, National Research Council, Washington, D.C., 1939.
22. Whittkower, E. D., and White, K. L.: Psychophysiological aspects of respiratory disorders *in* Arietit, S. (ed.): American Handbook of Psychiatry, New York, Basic, 1959.

Suggestions for Further Reading

Alexander, F., and French, T. M.: Studies in Psychosomatic Medicine, New York, Ronald, 1948.

Alexander, F.: Psychosomatic Medicine: Its Principles and Applications, New York, Norton, 1950.

Grinker, R. R., and Robbins, F. P.: Psychosomatic Case Book, New York, Blakiston, 1954.

Lidz, T.: General concepts of psychosomatic medicine *in* Arieti, S. (ed.): American Handbook of Psychiatry, New York, Basic, 1959.

CHAPTER 7

Psychiatry in the Practice of Surgery and the Specialties. Somatopsychic Sequences

JAMES L. TITCHENER, M.D.

PSYCHIATRY AND SURGERY

There is at least one moment in the practice of medicine when the relationship between doctor and patient is *not* highly relevant to treatment and to the patient's well-being. This moment comes in the operating room when the surgeon is alone with the highly technical task of operating, and the patient's well-being is in his hands and those of the anesthetist. This exception is especially remarkable when one considers that well before and long after the operation, while waiting for and recovering from surgery, the patient is undergoing an intense emotional experience. During the operation he is unconscious, as a rule, and there is no personal relationship with his doctor. But before and afterward the surgical patient is exquisitely sensitive at all levels to all of the major and minor vacillations in his relations with his physician, surgeon, nurses, attendants, and technicians.

Though the surgeon, anesthetist, and surgical nurses do not need to understand human nature to do their expert work in the operating room—apart from the necessity of being able to communicate with one another—the whole remainder of the course of illness is affected by the interaction, intensely meaningful, between patient and surgical personnel. In this chapter evidence will be presented demonstrating that swings of emotion in reaction to events in the course of surgical illness and treatment are remarkably common and often of considerable magnitude. In addition, evidence will be offered indicating that the patient's needs in certain relationships are augmented in the surgical situation, and that the relationship between patient and doctor is apt to involve (for the patient) an intimacy and a degree of expectation, hope and fear, reminiscent of feelings of a very early period in life.

Some of the essential qualities of the modern surgeon, his willingness and capacity to bear responsibility and his skill, knowledge, and expertness, as conveyed through his reputation, have powerful emotional significance in the surgical experience. One would not, of course, change the feelings of respect and trust engendered in the patient, and, very likely, one could not change the countervailing, less conscious tendency to fear the power of surgery, but one can describe and comprehend these emotional forces and then seek ways to help patients toward better balanced and more realistic reactions to their surgical experience.

Forces in the Surgeon-Patient Relationship

What are the forces active in the surgeon-patient relationship? On the doctor's side, there are likely to be authority, knowledge, self-assurance, and the power (at least from the patient's point of view) to do good or ill. On the patient's side, there are likely to be submission, doubt, feelings of uncertainty, and helplessness. Often patients try valiantly to overcome each of these contrasts in the relationship in a *compensatory* fashion. It is easy to be fooled by these compensatory efforts, as one is when he interprets them literally, thereby missing their true motivation, the attempt to make up for a sense of inadequacy or uncertainty.

Let us consider the relationship between the surgeon and his patient with regard to the authority and submission aspects of their respective roles. For example, take a fast-moving, hard-driving, and tight-lipped businessman who *knows* that he can leave the hospital two days earlier than scheduled to do so by the doctor. He has compensated for doubts of his well-being and for feelings of submission by taking over the management of his treatment. At the opposite pole of the same axis, one finds a usually hard-driving businessman who has completely lost initiative in the hospital and needs direction and assurance regarding everything he does. He has adapted by attributing absolute competence to the surgeon and is infinitely cooperative because he fears offending the doctor by even seeming to object to anything that is done.

Among the possibilities on the knowledge-ignorance axis of the relationship, one finds the patient who suggests a "sampling of my cholesterol; I think the old thyroid may be kicking up." At the other extreme one finds a patient whose questions can become querulous and demanding as they wear upon surgeons, nurses, and attendants alike. One of these patients identifies with the doctor to compensate for his uncertainty; the other tells the doctor over and over that he knows absolutely nothing.

The third imbalance in the doctor-patient relationship, the doctor's self-assurance contrasted with feelings of inadequacy in the patient, may be compensated for by some businessmen with telephones humming and secretaries hurrying to their bedsides or by women who cannot relinquish the cares of their households. At the other extreme there is the experienced and faithful employee who doubts suddenly and unreasonably that he will ever be useful again.

Finally, patients affected by the surgeon's appearance of great power to do good or ill may respond with absurdly tough independence or fearlessness, or at the other extreme, become utterly helpless, unable to void, pass flatus, cough, turn over, or assist in any way toward recovery.

Perceptions of the surgeon-patient relationship, made more intense by the surgical experience, appear repeatedly in the fantasy-life of a majority of patients. They are evoked by some of the realities, but they are based upon the patient's presurgery personality, his particular store of memories, his ways of perceiving and dealing with the world. Many surgical patients live through the relationship with an adaptation which does not require compensatory devices, even though most patients experience inner feelings about the relationship and have barely conscious fantasies which have some of the quality so far described.

It is not only the surgeon-patient relationship which influences the psychology of a person approaching surgery. One must inquire more extensively into the channels of reaction to the surgical experience before going more deeply into the motivations of surgical patients and considering their management.

A great many persons have had tonsillectomies and can remember them. The details of these memories illuminate the problem of psychological reactions to impending surgery in two ways. First, they demonstrate the impact of the idea of surgery upon the human being and help to explain his adult responses. Second, the details of these memories can suggest the childhood experience with trauma, how the adaptive system of the individual has responded to this stress, and therefore how the person will respond again. The way the subject describes early surgery is more informative than the facts about the event.

This writer's methods of collecting such memories have not been systematic (nor has he found in the literature a description of any extensive series). However, the memories collected have been rich in detail, quite vivid, and they have been remembered by patients until late in life, though a tonsillectomy is seldom a major procedure.

It is not difficult to grade the memories with respect to the degree of fear (or anxiety) experienced, the source of the fear, and the person most closely associated with the fear. It is also possible to discover the defenses which were employed to deal with the feeling aroused by the experience.

For example, a 34-year-old, well-educated man retains the following strong impression of his tonsillectomy at about age 7. His head had a turban of bandages and the room was always dusky and empty, but the night nurse slept under his bed. We can sketch in a tentative formulation that the danger was magnified and strange, that he felt lonely and depressed, and that a woman posed an uncertain threat to him, perhaps because of his own unadmitted desires, since she hid like an old-maid's imagined rapist, under the bed. Note that there may be a kernal of reality in the man's impression. Perhaps the nurse's cot was stored under his bed, but did she *sleep* there?

An eight-year-old girl dreamed during anesthesia that "there was a coral reef curving out from a beach into some still water. Two sparkles, one a man, the other a woman, ran back and forth over the reef. Suddenly they joined, becoming one sparkle, the coral reef parted, and the water flowed in." This more progressive response to a tonsillectomy, a looking forward to the development of femininity, to the relief the operation may bring and to the gratifications in store, touches upon deeply emotional, personal and developmental issues of wide importance in the girl's life. One can be sure she had a positive and supportive relationship with her surgeon and anesthetist.

This discussion of everyman's tonsillectomy serves to point out the intensive and extensive impact of the surgical experience. Tonsillectomy, a relatively minor and safe procedure, has impact because it happens to the young. The major surgical procedures affect both the young and old in widespread fashions that we shall spend most of the remainder of this chapter discussing. In preparation, the reader might pause to recall and reflect a while on his own tonsillectomy. This will provide him with a higher level of empathy in reading about the varieties of reaction to the surgical experience.

Modifying Effects of Surgical Experience

Just as the surgeon's knife and suture cut into reactive tissues, just as the anesthesia interacts in a dynamic way with complex biochemical and respiratory systems, so the whole surgical experience has a definitely modifying effect upon the way of life, the adaptive processes of thinking and feeling, of the human being. The depth, the extensiveness, the acuteness, the duration, and the significance of these modifications depend upon a variety of factors, but they are still comprehensible and should not be considered inevitable consequences or "side effects" of surgical treatment.

First, these modifications depend upon the defensive styles and flexibility of the patient's personality before the illness or the surgical experience. Second, psychological adaptation depends upon the personal meaning of the illness and operative procedure as well as upon the degrees of suffering, discomfort and danger encountered during the experience. Third, the nature and extent of change in personal adjustment depend upon the effectiveness of physical recovery and upon the outcome of the surgical treatment.

One can determine the consequences of surgery by a process of *triangulation*, using information about previous adaptation, about the impact of the illness and operation, and about the outcome of the treatment. This comprehensive approach to surgical practice is the one most important from the patient's point of view. For instance, a duodenal ulcer, causing the head of a family pain and absence from work, might be relieved without recurrence by a subtotal gastrectomy. The patient could expect to be a more effective and comfortable person as a result of treatment. However, it is not uncommon that with surgical treatment there is a shift in the complex balance of forces leading not to further pain or discomfort from the ulcer, but stimulating the development of a new symptom or group of symptoms to replace the old trouble. From the comprehensive point of view, the patient is not improved, although his ulcer has been removed. For example, the impact of the surgical experience in combination with some unresolved factors in the pre-existing personality could lead to an aggravation of a tendency toward alcoholism. Indeed, this sequence of an operation for duodenal ulcer followed by increase of alcoholism is not uncommon.[1] The man may be without his ulcer but even less effective, more often absent from work and less happy. Therefore a comprehensive point of view in medicine, surgery or psychiatry calls for a total balance sheet which attempts to answer the questions: "How is the patient doing with respect to his *whole* way of life before and after the surgical, medical, or psychiatric treatment? How is he doing at work, at home, and with respect to his concept of himself as an individual?" One cannot always answer these questions in the clinical situation. Omissions in the evaluative balance sheet must be accepted. Nevertheless, this comprehensive concept of the natural history of surgical illness, treatment and recovery is an ideal toward which we can work.

Beginning of the Surgical Experience

The late Robert Benchley once wrote about his fantasies on the way to a dental appointment. Among other adventures he pictured himself battling hordes of Communists on the steps of City Hall. He triumphed impossibly and heroically over the invaders, but his major victory was avoidance of his dental appointment. His fantasy ends with a cruel awakening at the door of the dentist's waiting room. We are nearly all procrastinators, rationalizers, evaders, or deniers when it comes to seeking diagnosis and treatment of the symptoms or signs of an illness. Large-scale studies of patient populations indicate that a *significant* procrastination occurs with 30 to 50 per cent of those patients surveyed. In a study at the Cincinnati General Hospital Surgical Service in 1952-53,[5] delay was considered to be "significant" when it made the illness substantially worse or when it put the patient in greater jeopardy. Thus, very brief delay with gastric bleeding could be more significant than much more prolonged delay with a less dangerous condition. Patients with illnesses requiring surgery are more likely than others to delay seeking diagnosis and treatment. Not even doctors and medical students are immune to this weakness.

An important understanding of the phenomenon of significant delay in seeking diagnosis and treatment of surgical illness (or medical and psychiatric illness, for that matter) may be grasped from a comparison of the methodology of several studies of the problem. Some public health surveys have asked the patient why he waited so long before getting help, or questionnaires have been used to determine reasons for the length of the period between the appearance of a sign or symptom and calling a doctor. This type of clinical research study has revealed that the modern citizen in the U.S.A. or the British Isles is remarkably ignorant of the meaning of signs or symptoms, in spite of vigorous educational campaigns in both countries. Another type of clinical research on the same problem has involved a different method with quite different findings. In this research the aim of investigation, as far as the patient knows, is not directed at the problem of delay. Rather, the method consists of nondirective interviews with the patient during his hospital stay. In such studies the delaying behavior can be seen in the whole context of motivation, personality pattern, reaction to illness, feelings about surgery and attitudes toward medicines, physicians, and surgeons. When the patient's confidence has been gained through this technique, it will soon become evident that *in almost all cases* ignorance of the general significance of a sign or symptom has *not* been a factor in the delay. Lack of knowledge, or deficient awareness of the meaning of signs or symptoms is usually the reason the patient gives to the inquiring doctor and often the patient is convinced of his ignorance himself, but he has this conviction for psychologically defensive purposes, not because of actual lack of information or the opportunity to use education. The patient most often claims that he "doesn't know" what the symptoms or signs are about as a means of protecting against his fears or for reinforcement of his defensive wall against feelings about illness and surgery, or for adjustment in the relationship with the doctor, who may be seen as an angry parent if delay has been the consequence of any *motive* on the patient's part. When the clinical investigator can acquire information in the indirect manner and through the relationship developed in consecutive psychiatric interviews, he will find the delaying behavior to be a complex phenomenon with important implications for comprehending patients' attitudes toward illness. The cause of delay is not principally the ignorance the patient claims. The investigator will find that in almost every case the procrastination is a result of motivation, controlled by forces at work on both conscious and unconscious levels of the patients' personalities. The researcher finds a varying balance of these motivational forces at work in both the delayers and the nondelayers. The difference is determined by which way the balance shifts. Nearly everyone wishes at least briefly to avoid recognition of signs or symptoms and so the required treatment, but too often these wishes triumph over the conflicting hopes for relief of discomfort and better health. The main difference between the delayers and those who report promptly for diagnosis and treatment lies in the ability that some patients have for solving problems.

When there is a perception of some change in body function a series of intricate interactions occurs in capacities for rational judgment, irrational defense mechanisms and psychic drives. Let us illustrate some of these sequences.

A large, muscular fireman, 45 years of age, was quietly and stoically depressed during his preoperative period while awaiting surgery for carcinoma of the bladder. In bedside interviews he tended to be taciturn, but patience rewarded the interviewer with an occasional parting of the curtain hiding the fireman's feelings. Cystoscopy had found the cancer to be well advanced and invasive of the bladder wall. Everyone felt he had been unfortunate that some sign or symptom had not appeared earlier.

His distaste for bed rest and his nervousness about the attentions of nurses were the first strong feelings elicited in talks with him. He had never required medical care before, he claimed, shaking his head ruefully. How had he discovered the illness and brought it to a physician's attention?

"Hematuria," he said.

"Hematuria?"

"Yes, blood in the urine, you know, it got real red a few days before I saw the doc."

Sometime later he added incidentally that he had had a "cold in my bladder" six weeks before admission. The "cold" in the bladder was the *actual* first appearance of the hematuria, tragically ignored and heavily rationalized before he finally gave in to the recognition of the need for diagnosis. In further interviewing we found the hematuria had recurred episodically during a six-week period prior to his first consultation. Clearly, he did not fully know that hematuria would indicate cancer but he did know that it meant *something*, something he did not want to know. His masculine pride, his virile independence of needs for attention and care, and his even greater fear of the meaning of the blood in the urine from his penis combined to defeat his rational judgment that this "something" needed medical attention. He had the knowledge but he had to deal with it in an irrational manner, because his concept of masculinity seemed to be threatened by the possibility of illness requiring hospital care. His behavior was influenced also by the idea of blood from his penis which was too shocking and too overwhelming to be integrated into purposeful judgment. He was forced by these motivations to evade the truth rather than to be deprived of it by ignorance.

The idea that delay is hardly ever a consequence of ignorance alone and that the actual causes lie in fears, evasions and denial can be underlined by pointing out that people in our Western culture, at least, are actually deeply and extensively concerned about *any* changes in bodily function or configuration. The adolescent, for example, watches his body change with great concern, searches his skin, his musculature, and his genitals to be sure that the changes conform to the expected. In times only recently past, fraternity boys would administer to their pledges a drug which would turn their urine blue. What a frantic worry this temporary alteration in body function would bring about! The adult has acquired defenses and an adaptation which keep him more stable than the adolescent, but the tension about the body remains at less conscious levels. The tension is kept quiet by defense mechanisms which will present as lack of awareness.

The seriously delaying patients experience these initial conflicts about surgical illness and treatment so acutely that their good sense concerning their needs is overcome. Many potential delayers have the good fortune to have their conditions discovered by family, friends, or physician, in spite of their own motivation to ignore the problem.

A 52-year-old German housewife of incredible strength had been carrying the burden of an invalid husband and demanding children. She reported to her physician for treatment of a cough. He treated the cough and found a small lump in a breast. She did not return for reexamination and possible biopsy. A family friend happened to be a woman physician who heard from the first doctor that the patient claimed she did not "have the time to come back and it seemed to be getting smaller anyway." This woman physician quickly and simply made arrangements for hospitalization and drove her car to the patient's door, refusing to take "No" for an answer.

The patient was severely depressed before surgery and worse for a time after the operation. She claimed tearfully that she had been promised she would not lose her breast. We found later that the loss of a breast meant to this woman a giving up of an important means of adaptation. Her way of life had been so devoted and dedicated to caring for her husband and children that she figuratively, but almost literally, suckled everyone around her. Incidentally, her husband suffered a depression during his wife's hospital stay. He had unwittingly reinforced the denial which nearly caused fatal delay in this woman's case.

This illustration of delay illuminates the underlying and everyday thought about surgical treatment in *all* patients, that is, the more general feelings about surgery encountered consistently.

Motivational Factors Underlying Delay in Seeking Treatment

What are the more general motivational factors underlying delay in seeking diagnosis and treatment, and how do these same factors appear in the over-all population of surgical patients who do not delay but might?

First of all, there is the "everyday psychopathology" of being a surgical patient or a potential one. That is to say, there is the inevitable distress, uncertainty, daily horror and confusion of having to approach a clinic, a doctor's office, or a hospital. The most frequent form of encounter with the inexorable mystique of medicine and surgery is in the dentist's chair. Is there anyone who does not peer furtively and anxiously as the dentist turns to his precisely drawered cabinet to pull out yet another gleaming instrument? "What the devil is he getting now; what will he do with that? What does it mean; how much and how long will that tiny, weird instrument hurt me?" Bound by our sense of duty and need to do the Right Thing according to all good sense about dental health, we are all cowards, helpless to fend off aversion to pain and fearful of what is coming next. The truly surprising part of the usual reaction is that there is no arguing with the anticipation of pain or the fear of uncertainty, even though previous experience should have taught us that the pain is usually minimal and the feeling of helplessness unnecessary.

Ascribe this commonplace set of reactions to the surgical patient and double or triple it to discover the types and intensity of feelings that he has in anticipation of diagnosis and treatment. Clinics, offices, and hospitals can be made quite pleasant by modern architecture and decoration, but they have lost little of their power to make a man or woman feel smaller, more helpless, shamefully subject to pain, and terribly uncertain about what is to happen next. Even the immaculateness, the whiteness, the rustling of starched uniforms, and the gleaming of the instruments stir a feeling that the hospital, clinic, or office is strange and beyond comprehension. To be assured nothing bad will happen requires a major act of faith in doctors and nurses.

The mystery and fear continue after hospitalization. It is induced by the talk of the professionals, the odd things required for diagnostic testing, by the remarks of other patients, and by the difficulty of understanding physiology and the diagnostic process. Take the hospital at night. There are yellow and black signs on the street outside which ask the passing motorists and others to respect the need for quiet. There are pictures on the wall of pretty nurses with fingers to puckered red lips saying, "Sh-sh-sh." To the average, hyperalert surgical patient whose mental apparatus is extremely vigilant there is no place in the world noisier than a hospital. Some patients could sleep better in a steel mill. A nurse patters by, her hose whispering clamorously. In the distance a bedpan slams. A door swishes open and swings squeakily shut. Voices can be heard from the nurse's station, as an intern and a resident chuckle over ward experiences. The whole din, the clamor, the noise of a hospital at night, is not great when measured in decibels, but it is great when considered as echo of the patient's anxiety, his wonder about what his experience will mean and how far it will go.

There are reasons for *everybody's* fear of surgical diagnosis and treatment. A physician can reduce its intensity by openness and by relative freedom in giving information. But doubt will persist because no patient can be absolutely certain about the outcome of diagnostic and treatment procedures. Some of the fear of pain, death, and loneliness and some of the unknowns will perhaps always be associated with the surgical experience in spite of progress toward enlightenment of physicians, surgeons, and patients.

Neurotic Reactions

There are certain feelings which are not explainable on the basis of inevitable threat and uncertainty. These are the *neurotic* reactions to the surgical diagnostic work and treatment. Reactions to the surgical experience may be classified as "neurotic" when they are based less upon dangers of the operation and the illness than upon inner feelings and attitudes arising from conflict between drives and other agencies of the personality (see p. 75). The truth is that in the stressful surgical situation every individual's disposition to "neurotic" difficulty is greatly enhanced. In fact, it may be doubted if anyone escapes the manifestation of some symptom or other neurotic reaction at some time during the course of diagnostic operation, and convalescence. There are so many opportunities during the whole experience that at least once some conflict acquired in earlier years will have its resolution partly overthrown by one or many of the forces brought to bear upon the surgical patient. Neurotic reactions to the stress of admission, diagnosis, operative treatment, recovery, and convalescence vary almost infinitely in nature and degree. The extent of neurotic difficulty in surgical treatment depends upon how much various elements of the experience threaten psychological defenses, how much of the previous adaptation is unbalanced, how much the stresses are specific for exciting pre-existing conflict, and finally, how much the reaction to the experience is that of anxiety rather than that of (realistic) fear.

As will be discussed in detail in Chapter 9, neurosis is essentially caused by trauma, remote and recent. Traumatic overstimulation through deprivation and/or overindulgence of various sorts at an early time requires a compromise solution of the conflict between impulses and counteracting forces in the mind. The neurosis usually occurs at a later time when the compromise solution breaks down in the face of a new conflict (in some fashion related to the childhood one) and the pressures of the old conflict and the new lead to a new compromise in the form of symptoms. This formula for neurosis will be borne in mind during consideration of the minor and major neurotic reactions to surgery in which some element of the surgical situation may be seen to match in content or force the trauma of earlier experience, thereby releasing anxiety and the need for more extensive and costly defensive maneuvers.

The appearance of these reactions on surgical wards is widespread, as found by repeated clinical research studies.[3, 4] The mechanisms underlying the phenomena are complex. In order to describe with some clarity the intricate course of neurotic reactions to surgery, the following basic assumptions are made. (1) The intensity and pervasiveness of neurotic reactions will depend in part upon the strength, the form, and the flexibility (or rigidity) of the previous adaptation. (2) The form of the neurotic reactions will depend in part on the *meaning* of the whole surgical experience to the inner perceptions of the individual. (3) The depth of breakdown of adaptation will depend upon the difference between the amount of stress suffered and the capacity of the adaptation to deal with the stress. In summary, these assumptions relate to the importance of the individual's past history, to the meaning of the current experience (for him), and to the amount of excitation in excess of the subject's capacity to adapt.

The variety of neurotic developments arising from and during the surgical experience is immense, and the mechanisms brought into play are involved, overlapping, and numerous. Some organizing principles are needed with which to consider these sources of anxiety and conflict. What follows is designed for a consideration of the neurotic problems of surgical patients (and is not necessarily the best approach for more general comprehension of neurotic conflict or neurosis).

The reactions and disturbances will be surveyed from the following points of view:
1. The body and the body-image.
2. The self and the self-image.

3. Emotions: love and hate.
4. Survival and death; anxiety and depression.

These elements of approach to the problem are not distinct categories, but one or another of them may give a clearer view of an individual case.

1. THE BODY AND THE BODY-IMAGE. Illness and operation endanger the intactness of the body's configuration and function. Concern over this threat to the body and its activities may be adjusted to realistically by some individuals, but in others, the worry inflames buried memories from periods of very early and delicate mental development. These memories, in moving closer to the surface of awareness, arouse anxiety. The idea that a cutting of the flesh is to take place, even if the part to be cut will be restored to its former size and shape, is often too forceful a reminder of fears of mutilation, or even annihilation, in childhood. Then the child was surrounded by a very large-scale world with powerful and often threatening figures in it. (The reader will recall, for example, that during the family triangle period, pp. 99 to 108, genital mutilation seemed a real possibility.) Now, in the surgical experience, the fears are literal again; hence deeply repressed original fears may come close to consciousness, particularly if a weak or brittle defense had been devised to contain them. The current state of fear is made intense by the unconscious memory and by the releasing from repression into awareness of the idea that action arising from an inner impulse will result in retaliation from the environment. This anxiety has the further property, partly because it has been so long locked in reservoirs of unconscious memory, of being freely *displaceable* (p. 80). That is, instead of fear for the genitals and mutilation of those parts, the fear may become attached to other body parts, such as the extremities, the nose, and so on. Hence this old sense of vulnerability may be mobilized by the psychic reactions to surgical illnesses affecting many areas of the body.

A 39-year-old brewery foreman repeatedly refused a recommended herniorrhaphy claiming he could not spare the time and could get along without treatment for his hernia anyway. But in dreams his fear of unmanning was quite impressive. In one of these he pictured a man with a finger so limp he could not dial a telephone.

Some patients fear bodily harm; much of the force of this fear is derived from residues of partly resolved infantile and childhood conflicts remaining in the unconscious. These conflicts were concerned with fears of bodily harm and mutilation associated with aggressive and sexual wishes for which the child expected retaliation.

In addition to simple, direct fears of bodily harm, there is the important problem of the relation of *body-image* to surgical illness. Even the strongest person will experience, when he is sick, an intense investment of feeling and mental energy in his image of the body. This phenomenon of withdrawing investment of energy in business or social pursuits or from relationships with other persons and redirecting it toward interest in the intactness and function of the body is technically termed *body narcissism* (a hyperinvestment of interest in the image of one's own body). It is an extremely common and in that sense, a "normal" reaction to threatened physical change. The reaction becomes pathogenic under two conditions: when it is carried too far, or when it is resisted too strongly. Unrealistic refusal of treatment for the purpose of denying that there is reason for physical concern is an example of strong resistance to the tendency to invest in the body-image. The housewife described on page 229, who delayed seeking surgical attention, is an example of this type, and she shows the depressive reaction to an enforced change in the body-image from the loss of a breast after surgery. These reactions to change from outward-directed interests to bodily preoccupations are ubiquitous in people who are sick, but they vary widely in degree and form. One may expect to see the greatest reactions in people who are most "extraverted," because they must change the most, and the least reactions in people whose interests have, for a long time, been invested in one or several organs of the body. Effective treatment of this phenomenon of heightened concern over the body-image will depend upon understanding it, expecting it, and then reducing, rather than enhancing, the shame and injured pride which may result from surgery.

Practical problems in body-image psychology arise in patients whose surgery results in a colostomy, the loss of a breast, a hysterectomy, or an amputation. These changes in body shape and function will require sizeable alterations in psychological adaptive measures (defenses) as well as in organic functions. Often, the need for such major alterations in the ways of maintaining psychic equilibrium will end in neurotic reactions. The colostomy, for example, not only affects appearance and external behavior, but also forces a change in one's idea of his body, making necessary changes in elementary functions and rhythms which were acquired and structured very early in life. (See case history on pp. 45 to 47.)

To recapitulate: (a) Surgery means cutting, opening, and perhaps removal of body parts. An operation revives fundamental fears of severe injury implanted in infancy and early childhood. These unconscious conflicts concerned with retaliation are often reactivated by the expectations of a surgical procedure. (b) When awareness of an illness impinges upon the personality, an increasing portion of the available mental energy flows, so to speak, toward concern with the body and the mental image of it. This inexorable change, in which feelings of affection and fondness for outer objects turn to bodily concern, may lead to intense shame and fear of loss of love and respect. (c) Stability of psychological equilibrium depends in part upon intactness of the body and consistency of its functions. When intactness must be altered or the consistency of function is interrupted, an adjustment must occur to maintain psychological equilibrium.

2. THE SELF AND THE SELF-IMAGE. The previous section dealing with reactions to surgery from the viewpoint of feelings about the body, its intactness, consistency of function, and the mind's picture of it, has an obvious and profound connection with biological adaptation. In this section on the *self* and the *self-image*, it is necessary to speak of matters of slightly greater psychological complexity. The term, *self*, is used here to refer to the whole psychic integration of the person, i.e., in the approximate sense of *personality* (p. 31). The self is thus different from the *ego* (p. 71) in that the ego is an agency or aspect of the self, participating in maintaining the consistency of the self as well as in carrying out the executive functions of perception, motility, thinking, memory, and judgment. By *self-image* is meant the partly conscious, partly idealized, partly critical *sense of the self*. (*Sense of identity* is a nearly synonymous, more popular term for *self-image*.)

One may safely assume that the self, the personality, as a system, will strive to maintain its current integration, and that, when stimulations impinge from without or arise from within, adjustments will be made to retain the intactness, the consistency, and the inertia of the system. The successful maintenance of integration will depend upon the amount of excitation (e.g., knowledge of need for surgery for lung disease) and the capacity of the self for making adjustive changes.

Consideration of the integration or adjustment of the self may be concluded with mention of the special working, in the surgical situation, of those psychological techniques designed to cope with conflict, *the mechanisms of defense* (pp. 74 to 80). One tends to see in surgical patients combinations of defenses and coping mechanisms the individual patient has adopted through a history of responding to other situations. However, there are three defense mechanisms which the surgical experience appears to elicit with especial frequency. These defenses are *denial* (p. 76), *projection* (p. 77). and *reaction-formation* (p. 77). If a person is at all likely to employ one of these defensive techniques, he will be especially prone to do so while enduring the stresses of surgery, and, if denial, projection, or reaction-formation are parts of the armamentarium of the patient, one will find them used forcefully during an admission for surgery.

As will be recalled, denial is a relatively crude defense, in which the perception of a fact is altered so that it is no longer perceived. A great deal of psychic energy must be used to maintain the block against perception: one lie (to the self) requires another, and then another. Thus denial, beyond its most temporary, everyday forms, indicates a point of tenderness in the personality, a weakening of integration with very crude and costly efforts to contain the anxiety. The particular stresses of the surgical experience will bring out potentials for the use of this mechanism, and its appearance warns of serious underlying trouble. Further, denial is dangerous for the patient, since it may interfere with diagnosis or force refusal of the indicated treatment.

Reaction-formation, it will be remembered, is a turning away from expression of a surging inner impulse by behaving in an opposite fashion. The extensive appearance of this defense seems prompted by peculiarities of the surgeon-patient relationship. It is inevitable that the frustrations of the illness mobilize anger, and soon the anger is felt toward the surgeon, as though he were responsible for the illness, rather as a child's anger is often directed toward parents, who are held responsible for all manner of frustrations. The involuntary defense mechanism against possible discovery of this anger (by the object, the doctor, or even by the subject, the patient) is to behave in a fashion which reverses the inner impulse.

It may be fine to have a supremely cooperative, uncomplaining and helpful patient, and some patients can afford, even in a stressful setting, to manifest all of these qualities realistically, but very often cloying sweetness and ostentatious self-sacrifice are factors in the attitudes of those who initially seem to be in the helpful category. When the uncomplainingness and the helpfulness are overdone, one is dealing with the defense of reaction-formation, a mode of coping with stress which can be helpful to patient and doctor only when used rather sparingly. A heavy use of reaction-formation does, after all, allow the release of some hostility, since family, friends, and doctor are made to feel guilty by the patient's "sweet" self-sacrifice. Sometimes the extreme cooperativeness can make a mockery of the doctor's instructions. Such expressions of underlying anger, however, do not truly help the patient; they only complicate his situation. Reaction-formation is a disadvantage to the patient by obscuring the emotional side of communication with the doctor, even to the point where essential information about signs or symptoms will be withheld because the patient "did not want to complain." Also, the over-use of this defense in the hospital and with doctors has a damming-up effect upon emotions which should have some realistic discharge. This damming-up will take its toll later because the personality has been made rigid to support its defensiveness. The anxiety may be reserved for the postoperative phase when energies are needed for recovery. (See section on postoperative anxiety below.)

The mechanism of projection may be frequently observed in surgical patients. Frustrations and fears of harm in the surgical situation are adjusted through projection of these feelings to people in the environment including nurses, attendants, doctors, and members of the family. Any of these persons may be seen as cruel, indifferently sadistic, unfair, malicious, and hateful toward the patient. Accusations may be kept to the self and brooded over or they may be loudly voiced in the form of exaggerated though legitimate complaints or of fully developed delusions. These projections may attain at least temporary delusional status although the patient is not otherwise or continuously psychotic. Projection with such a degree of distortion may arise only when the patient is affected by exceptionally forceful surges of aggression in response to some of the threats of the encounter with surgical illness and treatment. Once again, the projection of aggressive impulses, their disavowal by attributing them to others, not only makes a patient difficult and unpleasant to manage, but also the disposition of aggressive energy in this unrealistic fashion will lead to secondary adaptive formations based upon these distortions. These changed ways of viewing reality will not be easily relinquished; they will demand further distortion of the ego's attitudes toward inner impulses. Such adjustments can affect surgical recovery too. When a patient feels bitterly that the doctors and nurses are neglectful of him, thus projecting his rage in response to fears of harm from the surgery, he is likely to respond with both gross or subtle resistances and interferences with treatment. Signs of growing or extensive use of projection as a defense mechanism in surgical patients deserve early attention and even postponement of an operation, if possible. The sources of the anxiety and anger should be deftly approached to make this defense less necessary.

These three mechanisms for defending the self against the threat of overwhelming anxiety or actual disintegration are especially meaningful signs of disturbance arising from the stress of surgery. They should be looked for in the doctor-patient relationship, particularly in instances of change in personality make-up. When a fairly candid and reasonable person becomes too compliant, too anxious to please, supremely cooperative, and too even in temperament during the turmoil and upheaval of illness and surgical treatment, the doctor should look for the possibility that there has developed a need to protect the self against feelings about the illness and treatment. One should not make a hero or saint out of the rare patient who has no complaints, no fears, and completely stoic reactions to pain, for in such instances one may be reinforcing the use of reaction-formation and be doing the patient a disservice with respect to later adaptation.

These three mechanisms, which require energy and much reshaping of ego functions to accomplish their purpose of protecting against personality disintegration, are designed to remove feelings and attitudes from the (conscious) self. They form an interesting parallel to the patient's common concept of surgery, that it is to remove "bad" and diseased parts of the body.

Whatever defense mechanisms may be involved, the effect of surgical illness and treatment upon the organization of ideas, memories, and fantasies included in one's view of himself (self-image) may vary from the unpleasant sense of exposure and nakedness of the self in a medical setting to drastic fears of disfigurement, fragmentation, or even obliteration of the idea of oneself. Another set of problems in the area of the relation of self-image to surgery is the stimulation of magical wishes for change in one's feelings toward himself, i.e., that there can be a miraculous making-over and rebirth of the self-image through the vaunted powers of surgery.

It should be admitted that one of the most intense initial anxieties of any patient entering any medical setting, be it dermatologic, medical, psychiatric, or surgical, is that of realizing a fear of exposure, just having to undress and be looked at, probed, and palpated. It is mostly unrealistic but almost always true that a person feels some of his or her secret self is out in the open. Some exposure to discomfort is unavoidable if one is to do diagnostic examinations. The doctor's, nurse's, and attendant's sensitivity to the strength of this feeling, without indulging it, is an important element of a patient's treatment (see p. 11).

The more serious self-image reactions arise from the real or imagined effects of the illness and treatment. Though they often conceal such feelings, many patients feel their illness and the signs and symptoms of it constitute a stigma, an indication that the flesh is weak and the person less worthy. These suspicions are only partly conscious and usually irrational, but they can be intense. The inability to continue work or the maintenance of family, home, and household contributes to the deterioration of self-esteem and increases the supposed discrepancy between the candid appraisal of the self and the built-in (ideal) picture of what the self should be. This diffuse but persistent idea of stigma, the weakness of being sick, is most often based upon shame over the unconsciously perceived *wishes* to be passive, to be helped, to be made over, and so forth. These are human wishes, especially justified in such times of discomfort and worry, but unacceptable to the self-image of many patients. Resistance to this disturbance of self-image will often involve cantankerousness, refusal of medication, and other struggles for rugged independence.

The sense of completeness as a person, a psychobiologic necessity, can be profoundly dependent upon the presence of procreative capacity. Man seems to need to feel that he *can* reproduce though he may rationally decide to control this function. Studies of the psychological correlates of menstrual cycles (pp. 113 to 114) have revealed that the woman's sense of emptiness during menstruation expresses unconscious disappointment at the failure to become pregnant, even though for some the actual realization of a pregnancy would seem catastrophic. The relevance of this sexual component to a man's or a woman's self-image is that surgical treatment may involve the excision of reproductive organs. An unsophisticated woman may speak rather openly about her fears when inquiry is made regarding her objections to a hysterectomy. She may tell the interviewer of the persistent feeling that she is to be scooped out, deprived, made less desirable and less a woman. The more sophisticated woman will understand these fears are mostly groundless and she will therefore be more reticent, but she will have the fears nevertheless. Both women will be subject to some degree of shame, fear of abandonment and depression before or after a hysterectomy or ovariectomy. Both women will very likely view themselves as less complete, less feminine, and with less capacity to be maternal or desirable to men.

These changes in self-image are not rational but they are nearly universal and inexorable in their association with operations on the genitalia or reproductive systems of men and women. Before and during treatment, explanation and time are required for an emotional working-through of the change. Readaptation may require, in addition, some special psychiatric assistance.

Most patients waiting for surgery spend some of their time contemplating the changes in self-image after surgery. The factors molding this anticipation of self-image after an operation include the clarity and endurance of previous ideas of the self, the type of bodily change expected, pessimism or optimism about the recovery from the illness, and a total feeling about the surgical experience including the relationship with the doctors. So many factors enter the change in self-image and the degree of hopefulness about how one will be accepted at home, by loved ones, and at work that a complete discussion is impossible here.

There comes a time during nearly every person's surgical experience when he tries to see himself as he will be after he has been through it, and to anticipate the degrees of assurance he will have about himself, especially if he knows there is to be some limitation or disability imposed by the surgical treatment. The clarity and reality of this image on the other side of the experience can be very relevant to the degrees of anxiety felt before and after the operation.

Some patients heading toward a postoperative depression acquire a self-despising quality in their anticipated self-images. Others experience a shaky uncertainty about their expected selves, and they grow anxious that they will be liked less, even abandoned. One also finds in some patients, however, a stable realism in anticipations of the self-image, in which changes are accounted for, adjustments are made, limitations are accepted, and the surgical treatment is viewed as an effort toward relief or amelioration of a condition.

The problems of plastic surgery for cosmetic, reparative, or rehabilitative purposes present special cases of the more general interactions of self-image and body-image with the surgical experience. In most respects the reactions before and after plastic surgery are similarly determined by concerns about the strength, attractiveness, and masculinity or femininity of the patient's image of himself. The major difference from the general problem described above is that the anxiety and the distortions involved are more consciously and obstinately expressed by the plastic surgery patient.

3. AFFECTS (EMOTIONAL FORCES): LOVE AND HATE. The surgical situation evokes and is affected by strong feelings of two principal kinds in patient and doctor. Ambivalence (p. 95), the disturbing mixture of love and hate, makes for most of the trouble and leads to most of the psychologically expensive and exhausting attempts to defend against and repress feelings toward the doctor, the patient, friends, and family (depending upon the subject).

Why should such elemental forces as love and hate be involved in surgery? Why should ambivalence motivate some patients to avoid diagnosis and treatment at all costs and motivate others to seek surgical treatment for relief of the inner conflict? Finally, why should these feelings affect the course and outcome of illness and treatment?

Perhaps the reader tires of these questions and mutters, "I'll ask you one. Why can't at least one of the fields of medicine be considered *objectively*? Love and hate are good for opera and movies, but in surgery we need light, precision, endurance, ingenuity, and science. Run along back to your desk; chew your pencil and dream of 'love and hate.' We have work to do, and the patient's love and hate can wait for someone else's leisure."

Yet it is not indulgence in a fuzzy kind of magic to bring in love and hate as part of an objective approach to surgery. They are as objective and vital as the warmth, color, and turgor of the flesh to be incised in an operation. The doctor who *neglects* consideration of them is actually being subjective, because his personal needs require inattention to certain elements of his patient's illness and treatment—just as some persons who consider medicine as a career forsake it because they cannot stand the sight of blood.

There are two especially useful approaches to questions about the interactions of love and hate with the surgical experience. The first lies in an understanding of emotional development, and the second in a formulation of the internal psychic responses to the impulses of love and hate, the responses which lead to conflict over these feelings.

Let us consider first the connection between psychological development and the problem of ambivalence during the course of a patient's surgical illness and treatment. As will be recalled from the discussions in Chapters 3 and 4, the feelings of love and hate mature through the early phases of development, from infancy through childhood; they become elaborated, become associated with various types of experience, and almost from the beginning, they are engaged in conflict with the counterforces of guilt and shame (p. 68). The hostile component of aggressive feeling in childhood encounters the threat of punishment. The intense nature of the threat and its inevitability enter memory and become structured as an anticipation of punishment if hostility is expressed. This structured response to a feeling within the self acquires gradually a wider and deeper base as it sinks into the unconscious. Finally, the hostile feeling and a responding fear of punishment become (as a rule) an automatically operating system. No *conscious* perception of anger and guilt feeling is necessary for the operation of defense mechanisms which keep both feelings from entering awareness. The meek clerk at the water cooler who feels his boss's eyes on his back spills the cup all over his trousers without realizing his wish to rebel and to be punished for rebellious thoughts. He thinks it is an "accident."

Feelings of love develop even more intricately (see pp. 101 to 102). They also encounter, almost from the beginning, a fear of punishment from the rival for the object of the affection and (often) fear of derision or rejection by the loved one. These anticipations and guilt and shame become structured and implanted as permanent systems in the unconscious regions of the mind, to be activated by feelings of love in later relationships. A young woman is nauseated following her necking dates with an older man whom she admires. She believes the response means fatigue and tension, but does not recognize the sexual excitement which shames and disgusts her.

As will be recalled, in children the first and most crucial experiences of love and hate, and the first encounter with the conflicting feelings of guilt and shame, take place in the family and especially with the parents. The intensity, quality, and balance of these complex feelings in the child-parent-family relations determine the modes of impulse regulation and the nature of the child's spontaneity. The manner of integrating these forces heavily influences the style of later relationships.

Then a person acquires an illness; it is diagnosed, and he is sent to see a surgeon. Enough has already been said about the emotional impact of this sequence; in nearly every case it is considerable, perhaps momentous. The next step involves the recognition that, in moments of high emotional charge, more primitive emotions (less refined, less civilized) come out; the feelings of childhood are revived with an intensity close to that which they originally possessed. *The surgeon is the likely object of these feelings, and he becomes the center of the guilt and shame conflicts about them.* This fundamental sequence accounts for much of the peculiar behavior of surgical patients. It accounts (in part) for the reverence certain patients have for surgeons, a kind of reverence which just conceals anger and which may be transformed (in these patients) into scorn or contempt, given certain frustrations. It largely accounts for the fanatic attachment of some patients and for the unreasoning flight of others. The surgeon takes the place of the parent in the unconscious motivations of the patient because of the patient's needs and because the surgeon, like the parent, is viewed as capable of great good or harm, reward or punishment.

Though most patients evince a feeling of respect and trust toward their surgeons—which, in most cases, has a large genuine component—there is also a varying but omnipresent ambivalance. Hardly any child feels pure love or hate for a parent; nearly always the emotions are mixed. The impact of a surgical experience elicits this ambivalence, and it is directed toward the surgeon. The facade of the adult, the civilized temper, is lost, and the more fundamental feelings are closer to the surface. This ambivalence of love and hate tends to draw some patients toward surgery as a treatment for their difficulties and drives others away.

At one end of this continuum there is a classical group of patients who seek surgical procedures for a variety of neurotically determined signs and symptoms. Frequently the symptoms are in the abdominal area, and they may become confused with other illnesses, such as varieties of gall bladder or pancreatic disease. However, almost any body area may be the focus of the patient's concern and may serve to incline the diagnostician to recommend surgical exploration or treatment. The area or the part of the body involved in the symptoms has a symbolic or personal psychological meaning to the patient (p. 317), although other factors, such as the presence of other surgical or medical illnesses, may also influence the "choice."

The technical term for such a patient is *polysurgical addict*.[2] In this expression, "polysurgical" means a need for repeated surgical intervention for emotional reasons, and the word "addict" refers to the predilection for surgery. (Incidentally, it is not uncommon for drug addicts to present symptoms of a sort usually associated with surgical intervention for the purpose of having narcotics prescribed as an interim measure.)

Discussion of the problem of those who seek operations for the mitigation of unconscious conflict is included in this section because it is so close to the association of the feelings of love, hate, shame, and guilt with surgery. One cannot, of course, generalize for *all* of the patients who seek to involve surgical treatment in their emotional illnesses, but one can describe some of the important motivations and the dynamic sequences they cause.

Often the person who presents a diagnostically confusing symptom with the underlying motive of seeking surgery looks upon the surgeon (unconsciously) as a powerful lover who also fulfills a parental function, and he or she views the operation as an ultimate love affair for which great sacrifice is asked and given. It is important to understand the drama involved and the willingness for, or actual seeking of, self-injury, because both of these conditions help to distinguish this type of patient from those who need surgery for other reasons. The feelings of love in such cases are desperately unrequited because they arise from unmet childhood needs still sought from the parent of the same or opposite sex. The object of the feeling of love is unattainable in real life; desires have never been resolved, so they have not shifted to more maturely selected objects. Such patients have often tried to find a person meeting the qualifications of the unconscious guilty and/or shameful fantasy, but none has sufficed. Wishes for parental care and support are combined in the fantasy with incestuous drives. Both elements of the fantasy-quest, which is unconscious but nevertheless powerfully motivating, are in conflict with the counteracting forces of shame and guilt over such wishes. The latter conflicts explain why a surgeon, a remote, immaculate, potent and authoritative figure, the perfect material for fantasy, becomes the object of the love seeking: pain can be allayed, punishment administered in the very expression of love. In one wish, in one (fantasied) acting-out of the wish, in one dramatic playing out of the search, the patient is accepted into the surgeon's (loving) care, and something is done to the body involving pain, finally relieving the guilt. The surgery has sexual significance to such persons *because* it is perceived as painful and possibly dangerous or injurious. The unattainable is attained for the moment *because* of the sacrifice, sometimes of a body part. Submitting to surgery as an act of loving, as an act of sexual gratification, is made possible by the extreme degree of passivity in being a surgical patient. The feeling of being helpless is really gratifying to an intense degree because that is the only manner of sexual pleasure open to such a patient (in view of his inner conflicts). Surgery offers sexual pleasure because it combines punishment with the pleasure, because the relationship with the surgeon has imputed dramatic and magical qualities which make it desirable for men or women with profoundly unresolved conflicts regarding sexuality. The emphasis on asepsis and avoidance of contamination and the formal nature of the relationship help also to conceal even from the patient the sexual nature of the wish.

Having an operable illness can be, for some very troubled people, an indirect, guilt-expiating way of exploring the catastrophe of sexual relations with a parental figure. However, such a seeking is an addiction. What is sought turns out to be not severe enough or not pleasurable enough. The conflict is not excised with the surgical excision, and soon the symptoms return requiring diagnosis and "treatment" again, usually with a different doctor, a new object of the mixed and conflicted feeling. Soon after convalescence, disillusionment returns, and a new dose of the pleasure-pain, love-hate mixture is required.

Clinical manifestations of such ambivalence are extremely varied. The dramatic, longing quality of the person's life and current expressions may be the most impressive sign. A history of repeated surgery for vague reasons is another. Some patients present symptoms of a conversion reaction (pp. 312 to 322) and may be diagnosed positively by the psychiatric methods advised for such patients.

There is reason to believe that the true and classical "polysurgical addict" is disappearing from the clinic and emergency room, to be replaced by newer examples of neurotic disorder. Diagnostic methods and the modern clarity and strictness of criteria for surgery seem to have been important factors in controlling this form of behavior. Particularly does this seem to be true at hospitals with a strong teaching emphasis. (For example, in the 200 randomly selected patients studied at the Cincinnati General Hospital, there was not a single patient of the classical and pure type which was repeatedly described in earlier articles on this problem.)

A less readily discernible psychopathological motive for placing oneself in line for surgical treatment is found in the melancholic patient whose depression (pp. 341 to 351) is expressed somatically. In clinical terminology, such symptoms are called *depressive equivalents*. Not infrequently a man or woman in the involutional period of life (pp. 119 to 121) will present physical symptoms of a nagging, persistently uncomfortable type, difficult to define precisely and not responsive to conventional treatment measures. Such patients will usually be taciturn, perhaps irritable, and rather uncommunicative although not clearly depressed. They will report that the symptom is very wearing, that work is difficult or impossible, and they will attribute withdrawal from or difficulty in personal relationships to deteriorating health.

Since these patients have a special capacity for making physicians feel guilty and inadequate, the doctor will often overreach himself in trying to diagnose and treat these stubbornly reproachful people. The doctor is sorely tried by the refractoriness of the problem and the misery it creates in the patient and his family. The symptoms are often in the chest and lower abdomen and in an age group in which cancer and circulatory problems are frequently a danger. One can be misled if he is too easily persuaded by the patient's interpretation of his melancholy as a reaction to his physical complaint. One needs to recognize the possibility that a depressive response to a life situation preceded the development of the intransigent physical complaint.

How many times does one read that Mr. X, aged 53, fatally wounded himself with a bullet in the head and that he had been "concerned over ill health"? One must ask how many times the Mr. X's have been suffering from an involutional depression (p. 357) in which melancholia was not manifest. One cannot know how many of these cases presented to a doctor a depressive equivalent in the form of a somatic symptom, a nagging chest pain, joint symptoms, or deep-lying abdominal pain for which no definite diagnosis could be established.

The point here is that depressions taking a somatic form may frequently appear in surgical practice with a special urgency for treatment. Diagnostic and treatment efforts may have been exhausted in the attempt to find relief. The physician-patient relationship may have become tense and hostile. Finally, the depressed patient (who does not always *seem* very depressed) communicates a positive need for operative surgery. He is dealing with a sequence of frustration and lowered self-esteem leading to shame. He suffers anger at people close to him, which is followed by guilt and a fear of even greater loss of affection and esteem. He turns to surgery hoping all of this will be excised. He actually wishes that the toxic feelings, the deep bitterness, which are presented as the somatic symptom, will be removed as diseased body parts can be removed for relief of pain and for renewed strength. When there is guilt, expiation is seen as a means of relief. Through the suffering, the risk, and the long, uncomfortable recovery, the patient may hope to regain the sympathy and then the love and esteem of a wife, husband, or son and daughter. Surgery means *change*, and what other medical means of treatment can offer that? The trouble, of course, is that the change is not of the right kind. The surgery may or may not relieve the symptoms, but is not likely to relieve the basic depression or the causes of it. Occasionally melancholia itself becomes more evident and replaces the somatic depressive equivalent as the main presenting symptom.

This problem of the depressive patient presenting a somatic symptom to surgical treatment is probably a good bit commoner than the previously described surgical addiction, a different form of neurotic disturbance. It belongs in a section on love and hate, because a depression or its somatic equivalent is, to a large extent, a product of intensified ambivalence and because the patient often turns to surgery for definitive relief of the guilt and shame reactions in his inner conflicts.

Certain other psychotic or quasi-psychotic patients occasionally seek surgical relief for somatic manifestations which are actually unrelated to organic processes. In these cases, a positive diagnosis of schizophrenia (pp. 360 to 390) or hypochondriasis* (pp. 336 to 338), combined with medical and surgical work-up will usually prevent unnecessary or psychologically injurious operations.

From the previously mentioned series of surgical patients studied psychiatrically (p. 227), it can be estimated that about 10 per cent of the patients admitted to a surgical service have been seeking relief of psychological problems as a primary motivation for surgical treatment. Many others may hope for psychological change *as a by-product* of surgical intervention. (In the 10 per cent is included a large number of patients with chronic illnesses, for whom surgery *is* indicated.) These people have made their illnesses a way of life. For example, there are older diabetic patients who have begun to have circulatory complications which they alternately aggravate and then nurse through operative procedures and lengthy recovery only to start again with aggravation of the difficulty. Gallbladder and pancreatic sufferers and some duodenal ulcer patients are in this group of people who have a way of life partly forced upon them and partly welcomed as an adjustment to difficult life circumstances. This way of life includes partial or total invalidism, multiple clinic or office visits and recurrent surgery.

On the other hand, the bulk of surgical patients are involved in conflicts causing fear of surgical treatment in excess of what the actual suffering or risk warrants. These patients have conflicts about feelings of love and hate which are excited, revived, or are breaking through because of the emotional interpretations they have made of the meaning of the illness and anticipated operation.

---

* The term, hypochondriasis, refers to a near-delusional (p. 279) conviction of illness or to hallucinatory (p. 279) pain or feelings of strangeness (p. 368) and other excitations in body parts. These chronic disturbances verge on psychosis and are often monosymptomatic, i.e., involve one severe and persistent complaint.

Near the beginning of the chapter mention was made of tonsillectomies and the vividness of the memories engendered by them. It was added that from the form of the memories, figuring what fantasy had added, one could determine the attitude and conflicts to be met in the adult experience with surgery. In the context of childhood, the tonsillectomy is interpreted by the child as an attitude of the parents or the outside world toward the child patient who feels helpless to resist. The attitudes, as was suggested earlier, could be punitive, harmful, rewarding, helpful, with promise of better health, and so on. In the child facing tonsillectomy these feelings are more obvious and closer to the surface. It would be uncommon to find an adult who feels directly and consciously that the anticipated surgery is, for example, a punishment for bad thoughts, *but it is not uncommon for such an attitude to reach a motivating degree of intensity in the unconscious from the excitation of previously repressed conflicts.* A view of surgery as punishment, for instance, can be an unconscious, motivating attitude if an abiding fear of personal harm had been only partly resolved when the childhood conflicts of aggressive feelings versus guilt were repressed. The feelings of love, hate, guilt, and shame in incompletely resolved conflicts from an earlier period of life can be similarly involved in conflicts brought to a supra-threshold level by the surgical experience.

A 28-year-old, delicate and pretty, married Negro woman entered the hospital for surgical treatment of mitral valve disease. Her cardiac symptoms were moderately incapacitating and were getting more serious. She suffered nightmares about her coming operation from which she would awake screaming. She was terrified in the dream by the masked and white-gowned surgeon. The mask covering the face and the surgeon's penetrating gaze seemed mainly responsible for the terror in the dream.

The patient was a happily married, intelligent, high school-educated woman. Her family had been ambitious. Her father was an upright, moralistic person, and her mother, an acidly sharp, fervently proud woman, who demanded much from herself and her children. The family's pride and the striving atmosphere left little room or time for communication of feeling or admission of moral or emotional weakness.

Twice the patient had to be returned from the operating room because of severe tachycardia and rising systolic blood pressure. A third attempt with a careful program of preoperative medication failed, and a fourth attempt at anesthesia beginning on the ward produced the same results. The patient was discharged, to begin psychiatric treatment, but she moved from the city before her first appointment.

This patient, being one of those in the 200-patient survey, was interviewed several times by a psychiatrist during her hospital stay. From the material thus obtained, a tentative interpretation of her problems may be offered. In summary, the masked figure of the surgeon represented, in the deeper layers of this woman's mind, the feelingless parents, both the remote and moralizing father and the demanding mother. She could see only the doctor's cold eyes in her dream, and they told her nothing of his intention. How did he *really* feel toward her, and what might he do as a consequence of knowing her feelings? From an appreciation of the terror in her nightmare, it appears that love and anger had been very questionably acceptable by her family even as thoughts of a child. What rage or indignation and what punishments would be forthcoming, if they were known to the parents? The patient's childhood had been secure as far as shelter, food, education, and guidance were concerned. But she had always felt uncertain with regard to the reception of strong feeling of any kind. Would it be met with scorn or stern condemnation? She had to wonder what would happen if one of her inner feelings called for more than verbal reproof and what harm the wrath of either parent could bring upon her. This lack of confidence and fear of an almost supernatural vengeance centered upon her anticipation of surgery. The fears were expressed in the dreams, and (it was thought) culminated in the neurocirculatory response to the preparations for anesthesia. She suffered a basic lack of trust, though in her everyday expressions she was quite accepting of the surgical plans for her.

Surgery is quite definitely one of the stimuli in human life which can break through well-tried and long-used defenses to bring forth repressed conflict. The feelings on both sides of the conflict, the love-hate ambivalence and the reactive feelings of guilt and shame will attach themselves to one or many of the facets of the complex illness-surgery experience. As a matter of fact, almost any kind of psychopathology can appear, superficially or deeply, briefly or at length, during the surgical course.

In other words, it is very likely that a patient's reactions will not be wholly realistic, that he will somehow be influenced by the stirring of old conflicts over the experience, and that the total behavior of the person will resemble in important ways his responses when the conflicts were first engendered in childhood. This is not to say that all surgical patients will act childishly. Most of them will *act* like adults, but they will have to struggle with problems which are reactivated from childhood, and this struggle may be even more difficult than it was the first time, when they had parental support.

Let us now try to be specific about the breaking through of repressed conflict. Usually the first sign in the surgical setting is a change in personality. This change, subtle at first and then more noticeable to those who have known or are getting to know the patient, indicates the mobilizing of defenses against the anxiety given off by the inner stirrings of conflict.

A 43-year-old mother of four children with an open, free, and generous personality became fretful, distracted and uninterested in her surroundings during preparation for a hysterectomy for fibromatous tumors. She developed some minor symptoms which could not be clearly associated with the tumors or with reaction to medication. The previously mastered neurotic conflict had to do with ambivalent feelings toward both parents and toward her own fitting into feminine roles. This patient had developed a reasonably healthy adjustment to these problems, in fact a way of enjoying femininity. A breakdown in this adaptation was threatened by the hysterectomy. The disturbance early in the hospital course, with some frank anxiety, seemed to precipitate a working-through of the problem. Her adjustment after surgery soon returned to its previous balance with the same durability.

We shall see in a later section how the trend might have been toward a less flexible and less satisfactory adjustment if her initial reaction in the hospital had been more rigid and more stoutly defended (if, for example, she had had to use denial and projection to handle the anxiety). In other words, *some* early disturbance and recovery may have prepared her for the restructuring of the former balance.

Occasionally the early repressed conflicts with associated neurotic problems are so opened by the surgical experience that a return to a previously effective balance is not possible.

A 42-year-old man, who was dependent for his living and his self-esteem upon his mobility—he was a telephone lineman—suffered acute back pain. A ruptured intervertebral disk was diagnosed, and surgery was advised. He was quiet about the pain and discomfort and did not reveal concern about resuming the work he enjoyed. However, his convalescence was prolonged, and he suffered symptoms of muscular weakness and pain which interfered with his work. His interests in sexual and other gratifications died down. He had previously mastered his doubts of personal adequacy, but the pain, the operation he inwardly feared, and the limitation of mobility impaired his confidence, which had depended upon maintenance of a virile and agile image of himself.

The most complicated forms of emotionally unhealthy reactions to surgery based upon reawakened conflict consist of chain-reaction sequences in which the psychopathology affects the surgical illness either through physiologic pathways or through the patient's behavior, including his ability to cooperate with the treatment. Then the effect upon the surgical condition may, in turn, affect the patient further emotionally.

Several ways have been described above in which emotional responses influence and are affected by the charged relations with doctors and other personnel in the hospital. At this point it can be added that the "unreal" elements in these relations arise from tendencies to impute to current significant figures the attitudes felt about *previous* significant figures (see p. 487). This intellectually inaccurate but emotionally valid tendency to attribute to the physician or surgeon such characteristics of a parent or other figure from the past is reinforced by the reactivated conflicts involving love and hate. The flow of feeling to and fro in these hospital relationships can excite the neurotic conflicts or can calm them.

The type of illness and the nature of the surgery, the meaning of the surgical experience, can elicit the particular type of conflict to which the patient is disposed. The course of events in the treatment, the complications that arise, and the end-result can influence the nature of current conflict, its means of expression, and the ways the person elects for coping with it.

To take an obvious example, an appendectomy from which a young man awakens with a feeling of relief and a surge of "that wasn't as bad as I thought!" can have a remarkably progressive effect upon solving conflicts over the value of virility and ability to master fears of harm.

An orthopedic problem which requires demobilization for treatment may lead to some complications. Frustration and anxiety may arise from reawakened conflicts over feeling submissive to others but fearful of them. The frustrations in such patients may rise dangerously, though not expressed, and may lead, especially in older people, to serious depression or patterns of resigned invalidism which are very difficult to reverse.

People who sustain head injuries very often present a special problem with respect to the expression of psychological conflict (see pp. 303 to 306). Of course, all of us are potential victims of head injury in this high-speed age. However, any survey of the patients who actually do sustain head injuries will reveal that the largest portion of these patients consists of those who behave in ways that make such injuries more likely. There are many such types, but the largest subgroup consists of the hard-driving, hard-fighting, hard-drinking set. To over-simplify, these individuals behave in a way which denies danger (technically speaking, they behave *counterphobically*). They unconsciously use a special form of magic in which risks are constantly taken to prove to themselves that they are not really so fearful after all. They feel they must live under an anvil suspended by a hair to be worthy at all, but occasionally (or often) the anvil does fall. When it does, there is a vast recharging of all the old conflicts and there is often a major change in character which can be very painful. The fears, which had been concealed beneath the rationalizations regarding the values of bravery and toughness, which were in turn protected by the allegedly fearless behavior, come to the surface in an intensified form when the trauma actually does occur. The person has found that he *is* vulnerable and that the magic does not work when he awakens from the severe concussion and finds himself in a hospital ward with perhaps some concomitant injuries. One often observes a change then from a person with a self-protecting belief in invulnerability to a more frankly anxious and worried individual. Frequently there will be sequelae in the form of somatic and neurological symptoms including headache, dizziness, diplopia, and a great variety of others. These patients are probably psychologically treatable in these early post-traumatic days, but they are much less treatable by the time that the symptoms have set in severely or by the time there is a shift to a facade of bravado again.

The exact nature of conflicts regarding love, hate, guilt, and shame is never obvious in the patient's reactions to the surgical experience and to his relationship with the physician and surgeon. The conflicts are so closely bound to the wide variety of psychic defense structures to contain the pressure and so entangled with the realistic attempts people make to cope with current stresses that one does not see the conflicts in pure culture. However, it seems best when confronting the multiple problems and difficult feelings of surgical patients that one keep in mind the concept of reawakened conflict brought out of its dormant, repressed state by the events of the illness-surgery-convalescence sequence. With this concept in mind, one can search for the cause of the difficulty within the patient and within the relationships most important to him. One is thereby enabled to avoid a wish to argue the patient out of his illogical position. Recognition of old problems brought out by the stress of surgery does not do away with the technical difficulties in a patient's treatment. However, this etiological recognition gives one a start toward aiding the patient to find an adjustment to the current stress.

4. SURVIVAL AND DEATH; ANXIETY AND DEPRESSION. Feelings of tension, apprehension and dread, with the neurocirculatory concomitants of pounding heart, sweating, tremor, increased respiration, coldness of the extremities, and other signs typify the condition of the patient waiting for surgery. Of course, in most cases these discomforts are not experienced continuously but only during the crises, major or minor, of the hospital stay. This discomfort and its timing vary widely from patient to patient.

Terms for feelings such as those experienced before surgery are often confused; *anxiety, tension, apprehension,* and *dread* are not full synonyms. The broad term, to be used here as comprehending all these feeling states, is *tension*. By tension is meant the feeling that what is about to happen is beyond enduring, that capacities have been stretched to the breaking point. The source of tension can be *fear,* a stimulus from the outside,* or *anxiety,* a stimulus from the inside, a surge of unresolved conflict. Surgical patients, because they have conflicts and because they are usually facing some risk, experience mixtures of anxiety and fear. (Cf. Mrs. J. W. in Chap. 2.) It is difficult to weigh one against the other and to measure the relative intensity of each. The anxious and fearful patient will attempt to cope with these feelings by using methods characteristic of him.

Studies of surgical patients at the Cincinnati General Hospital and elsewhere have led to a classical finding which correlates well with a more basic and theoretical understanding of tension states. This finding, that there is a pattern in the appearance of anxiety, also appears to facilitate a better grasp of the factors responsible for chronic adverse psychological reactions to the stress of surgery.

First of all, it has been frequently observed that preoperative anxiety or fear is common in surgical patients. However, anxiety-fear and their physiological concomitants are not observable in every surgical patient. Also, these feelings may vary in intensity without a strong correlation with the type of operation the patient is going to have. The amplitude of the feeling may range from near-panic to a negligible degree of intensity.

Consider the following study undertaken by the writer and his associates.[3]

Objectives:
1. Evaluate effectiveness of psychological adaptation prior to surgery.
2. Assay average levels of tension during the preoperative phase of the surgical experience.
3. Assay average levels of tension during postoperative phase.
4. Evaluate effectiveness of psychological adaptation three to six months after discharge from the hospital.

The question: What prediction can be made preoperatively with respect to effectiveness of adaptation three to six months after discharge from the hospital?

Hypothesis:
1. The amount of psychological trauma as a consequence of the surgical experience will be correlated with the average levels of preoperative anxiety. Levels of preoperative anxiety serve as a predictor of the disturbance accruing from the operation.

---

* Some things inside the body may be felt as an outside force, such as awareness that something is going wrong with a body part or function.

2. The degree of trauma or disturbance will be directly proportional to the average levels of preoperative anxiety.

Actual observation of a number of patients through the surgical experience supports the first hypothesis that there *is* a correlation between consequences and preoperative anxiety. The second hypothesis that the changes are directly proportional is *not* supported.

A *moderate to severe* level of anxiety appearing *pre*operatively is significantly predictive of an improved or restored psychological adaptation after convalescence. In fact, it appears that patients who do *not* evince tension prior to stress are more likely to manifest an *aggravation* of psychological adaptive difficulties after discharge from the hospital. The most difficult predictions are in those who have very severe levels of anxiety before surgery. The number of patients in this group is the smallest and thus statistical results cannot be as meaningful, but these patients seem able to turn in either direction, toward an improved or aggravated status.

Moderate to high levels of *post*operative anxiety, like the absence of preoperative anxiety, correlate with a deterioration in adjustment after convalescence. Our study of randomly selected surgical patients disclosed that about a third were psychologically impaired after convalescence.* Some of this impairment correlated directly with illnesses which were progressive or too severe to have been significantly ameliorated by the treatment.

There are many possible explanations for this association of moderate-to-severe preoperative anxiety with the postconvalescent psychiatric condition of the patient. The definitive research has not yet been done. It is the writer's opinion that preoperative anxiety may be interpreted, in large measure, as a *signal* given by the organism to itself to prepare for stress in all fronts (see p. 73). The patient who evinces this tension has a better working, more flexible adaptive system, which can be mobilized and can shift its resources to deal with the stress. The anxiety signal is *used* by these patients, rather than stifled or shunted, as it must be in those patients who do not manifest tension. *Post*operative anxiety seems not to be a signal to mobilize, but a sign of breaking down of adaptive capacity. The stress of surgery, not anticipated consciously as very great, has actually been greater than the psychic resources available to meet it.

To support the point well, clinical illustration would have to be too extensive for inclusion here. It can be said, however, that experience indicates that those displaying brittle types of adaptation, those who stifled their tension before surgery, were likely to show anxiety after

---

* This does not include organic brain disorders.

the peak of (external) stress had passed and an increase of psychological difficulty at the end of the whole surgical course. The most differentiating underlying variable in this study of the responses to stress appears to be not the *severity of psychopathology* but the *flexibility of the personality* with respect to its capacity to shift and mobilize its various adaptive devices.* That is, patients could suffer high, medium, or low levels of anxiety and fear prior to surgery and then show psychological improvement or relapse in their convalescence, to some extent irrespective of whether their overt neurotic difficulties were minimal, moderate, or severe to begin with. Those patients showing moderate anxiety-fear preoperatively seemed significantly different from the others in the flexibility of their adaptive systems. These qualities were associated with psychological improvement or maintenance of the psychological status quo ante, whether or not the patients entered the hospital with a chronic and troubling neurotic illness.

Depression following the operation is also closely correlated with aggravation of the psychiatric condition as an outcome of the operation. Postoperative depression, when the operation has been a success, most likely indicates that some hoped-for neurotic need has not been met. Postoperative depression and postoperative anxiety are strong indicators that some sort of psychiatric follow-up is advisable to prevent worsening of psychological difficulty or to help the patient make best use of the surgical treatment he has had. There is little doubt that the surgical condition itself will be affected during the convalescence by its interaction with the emotional factors at work.

Tension arises before operative surgery from excitation of partly resolved conflicts acquired in early development and from aspects of the surgical experience itself. The most effective adjustment to tension is possible when anxiety-fear is permitted into awareness and is allowed some expression. In this area of expression and awareness of the pressures of anxiety-fear, the relationship with the physician or surgeon can be very useful. The surgeon's capacity for empathy, his ability to sense another's feelings without having to feel his feelings,† is extremely valuable. It is impossible to do more than estimate or have global impressions of the types of unconscious conflicts the patient feels, but it is possible to get a fairly refined impression of the patient's realistic fears. For example, it is almost axiomatic that patients fear endless sleep in anesthesia and mutilation or pain from surgery. The first fear is a good reason for the patient to be made fairly well acquainted with the anesthesiologist before the operation. However, the

---

* There is a correlation between these two factors, but it seems not to be a one-to-one correlation.

† This is one way of expressing the difference between empathy and sympathy.

axiomatic fear has many versions: each patient has his private fantasy. The skillful doctor can bring some of these fantasies to light and do it in a way that greatly reduces shame or embarrassment as well as the load of pent-up anxiety the patient carries. For instance, an appendectomy patient has told postoperatively of his picture of the surgeon searching through a sea of pus to sort out the coils of intestine and in his confusion and frenzy being unable to find the offending organ. This anxious daydream, experienced in the hour or so before going to the operating room, has echoes of the patient's personal psychology, including some hints of conflicts over sexuality, but at its surface level it represents a distortion of the actual operative procedure. One should not laugh at the fantasy or pat the patient benevolently; one should listen and explore a bit, and let some clear light fall upon it to reduce the distortions involved.

Fear of surgery, as was said, tends to center on not waking from anesthesia and mutilation or death from the operation itself. Depression is somewhat more complicated. It arises from separation, from being away from home and familiar surroundings, and also from choking back of feelings of frustration and resentment toward the doctors and nurses. Dejection may (also) be a reaction to the knowledge that the treatment cannot ameliorate or cure as one had hoped, or it may be a reaction to an aggravation or advancement of the disease. In its most complicated and severe forms, it occurs when a patient has a deep wish not to survive, when the surgery has been seen as a partial or complete suicide, and when the expiation of guilt and expression of in-turned hostility has not been sufficient (see Chap. 10).

Anxiety is seen in patients who fear that they will not survive, and depression in patients who fear that they will survive. This somewhat dramatic summary is an oversimplification, of course, but its application to surgical patients is highly relevant.

SOMATOPSYCHIC SEQUENCES

Beginning students of chemistry learn a concept of great importance for the understanding and practice of medicine. This concept goes beyond purely chemical principles. It is an idea relevant to the whole of medical practice and especially relevant to the relations between psychologic and somatic systems.* Reference is intended to the symbol $\rightleftharpoons$ which appears in the middle of many chemical equations to indicate that the process can go in either direction. The double arrows convey an essential idea in biology, a concept which should be conscientiously applied to the practice of medicine. In its original application, the

---

* I.e., between systems best described in psychological terms and those best described in somatic terms.

symbol means that chemical substances are not just stirred up to make a new combination, but that there is an interactional *process* in which the quantities on one side of the equation are in dynamic equilibrium with the quantities on the other. Looking imaginatively into a vat or flask, one can almost see the ions busily fleeing from one side to the other and back.

The double arrows indicating an interactive process should be drawn between the psychological and somatic systems to remind us that there is a constant interaction and that all processes between the two systems may go in either direction. Thus far in this chapter we have considered in the surgical experience an example of a primarily somatopsychic sequence. We have made observations about people who have acquired an illness, and we have attempted to understand their psychological reactions to it. We have followed them through their experience with treatment and we have sought to understand the effect upon psychological adjustment of changes in the body and alterations in the mind's image of the body. There has been an effort to keep in mind that there is a *double* arrow in the equation, that the systems are in constant interaction. The best example is perhaps that of a postoperative depression. The patient has reacted to his illness and operation with melancholy. As a result of his melancholy and the concomitant psychic retardation (p. 343), the patient may be unable to cooperate with some of the essentials of postoperative treatment. He may be very still and neither cough nor roll over, so that a stasis pneumonia is made more likely. He may refuse or subtly resist taking nourishment. It even seems in such cases that the general torpor of a seriously depressed surgical patient is reflected physiologically so that recovery is sluggish and prolonged.

Let us turn now to some somatopsychic sequences outside of the surgical field (in the narrow sense) to consider some further effects of somatic illness upon psychological adjustment, while keeping in mind the double arrow symbol indicating interaction between systems. The general principles of this sequence have been discussed in the description of the surgical experience. We can apply these principles to the additional instances to be considered. We need not consider each of the somatic conditions from the standpoint of body and body-image, self and self-image, and the effects of anxiety and depression. We need only remember that each of these conditions *could* be discussed from each of these points of view.

Cardiovascular Disease

Feelings about the heart and the vascular system and the reactions to heart disease have been extensively and closely studied by a great number of clinical investigators. The findings of this line of research have brought us understanding of the treatment and clinical problems of cardiovascular patients, and also have provided insights into fundamentals of human psychology. Even so, it is not wise to comment in tones of finality upon the clinical problems of cardiology and their relation to emotional responses, because of the major breakthroughs occurring throughout the field at an accelerating rate. The writer recalls the excitement attending the design and testing during World War II by Blalock and Taussig of a procedure to treat the tetralogy of Fallot. Following the established success of this surgery upon the heart's interior, there has occurred a proliferation of more and more ingenious procedures for the definitive treatment of a widening variety of cardiovascular diseases. Also, the breakthroughs in the fields of electronics and communication have led to applications in cardiovascular research, diagnosis, and treatment. These changes have transformed cardiology from a field in which the diagnostician relied upon a stethoscope and the main treatments consisted of digitalis, quinidine, and bed rest. Now there is a wide variety of diagnostic procedures, and treatments range from delicate operative techniques to implanted artificial pacemakers, steadily emitting square-waved stimuli. Because of this continuing change in the field the cardiac patient is changing too.

The most commonplace symptom of anxiety is an awareness of the heart beat. We call this *palpitation*. The human individual cannot control his heart's beat, and he is hardly ever aware of its action. However, when something is wrong with the heart, or when a person is very anxious, he becomes quite aware of his heart's activity, and there is little question that his life is affected by the new awareness. Thoughts about the heart or heart disease are associated with feelings about personal vitality, hopes of survival. The heart is further associated emotionally with the capacity to be aggressive and with the ability to experience love and affection. In short, each of the three essential drives is clearly connected with and dependent upon one's perception of one's own heart and cardiac function. These are the drives of self-preservation,* aggression, and sexuality. The healthy expression of these drives will usually be affected by the knowledge that something is wrong with the heart. On the other hand, in the person *without* heart trouble, a complaint about precordial pain or fears of a coronary attack may *substitute* for conscious expression of conflicts about sexual feeling or aggression. In other words, the process can go both ways. When a patient is told he has heart disease, he will almost always experience fears of loss of life or vitality and he will feel a degree of impending

---

* The group of self-preservative drives (p. 54) being here considered as one.

frustration of sexual and aggressive drives. Patients with known heart disease will usually be conscious of fears of death and will express these concerns directly. The idea or suspicion (in some cases, superstition) that heart disease means frustration of sexual and aggressive impulses will usually not be conscious nor very evident clinically. A common outcome is that the energy blocked by the neurotic frustration of aggressive and sexual drives will be shunted into the self-preservative drive(s), thus increasing the concern about death. The augmented and unrealistic fears of death from heart trouble tend to mask the feelings of frustration of sexual and aggressive drives. It should be clear that this self-imposed frustration, acting to increase fears of death, is not a logical outcome, but rather a neurotically generated feeling that the impairment of heart function indicates the loss of sexual and aggressive capacities.

A 39-year-old short, muscular and peppery store manager suffered a serious myocardial infarction. His recovery was uneventful, and about six weeks after the attack he returned to work. He had been an ambitious and resourceful man, whose salesmen, driven by his threats and scornful goads, had repeatedly won competitions between the stores in his chain. He had hated vacations and loved the dark store at night, as he worked over the adding machine and plotted to push sales even higher.

Some of the postcoronary change in the personality of this patient can probably be imagined. He returned to work, but he felt like a robot without the vigor and aggressiveness he had before. He arrived punctually but felt he should have stayed home. He took an hour for lunch and left exactly at five. He did not dare the pleasures of the store after hours. Instead of driving his salesmen, he meticulously picked at their reports and grumbled over costs and expenses. Instead of goading his employees he was quiet and sullen but subject to tantrums. He grew listless over "loss leaders" and all the rest of the intricate strategy of fighting for the buyer.

At home he was withdrawn from his wife and taciturn with the children. He felt his wife wished he would stay at the store as in the past, that she did not want him around and that she had lost her affection and sexual desire for him. Just before beginning psychotherapy he dreamed of a rabbit on a busy urban street darting frantically and dangerously through the traffic. He felt the rabbit was himself.

The therapeutic work brought out the guilt which he had always managed to conceal before his illness. After the coronary he expected that expression of *any* kind of aggression would bring another attack. This fear was rapidly generalized to include almost all activity so that he became immobilized to prevent the end of his life. He felt he was less than half the man or person he had been and his long-suppressed shame or guilt over wishes for closeness returned to increase the feeling of inadequacy and frustration of wishes for affection. It required about a year and a half of psychotherapy for the restoration of at least part of his former drive and effectiveness.

This man suffered mainly from inhibition as a response to serious cardiac illness. A second type of response often appears in the hospital. The cardiac patient may react with the defense of *denial*, and he may go further to behave as though the coronary attack, or other difficulty, had not occurred. He will then find it necessary to resist the physician's advice on diet, activity, or medication since to accept these treatments admits the fact of the illness. There may be a wide variation in the degree of this reaction. On the other hand, the degrees of inhibition and unrealistic immobilization during and after heart disease may be very extensive too. Some patients may become invalids as a psychological reaction to a coronary attack or cardiac decompensation. A striking example of this occurred in the writer's experience to a 35-year-old contractor who had for years suffered a "cardiac neurosis." He had prevailed upon physicians to obtain an electrocardiogram 23 times, claiming he was sure he had had a coronary seizure. For 22 times the record was normal. On the twenty-third occasion, to the internist's consternation, the electrocardiogram revealed a large anterior infarct. The patient recovered well as far as electrocardiographic records would reveal, but he was an invalid anyway. When efforts were made to alter this reaction, he responded very slowly.

Another interesting set of responses has occurred since the advent of intracardiac surgery. Most patients with chronic cardiac disabilities resulting from congenital heart disease or chronic valvular disease have responded to surgical repair with renewed ambition, hope, and vigor. However, there is a group who have not responded in these ways and an even larger group whose responses have not been as strongly hopeful and vigorous as could be expected from the changes in their physiological status. For many patients the rather thoroughgoing and sudden alteration of heart function afforded by surgery has meant a major shift in psychological integration. Many patients unwittingly do not welcome this new way of life, and they unconsciously resist it by developing new somatic or emotional symptoms. One can empathize. Having accepted and adjusted oneself to the way of life of the invalid or disabled, it might not be easy quickly to prepare oneself not to be an invalid or disabled and to assume all the privileges and responsibilities of relatively good health. This situation of finding oneself abruptly relieved of an illness when it was expected to go on and on is nature's ironic contrast to the immobilization caused by fear of recurrence or aggravation of a cardiac condition.

In summary, the reaction of giving in to invalidism or partial immobilization and the contrasting neurotic response of complete denial of cardiac illness depend psychodynamically upon the heart's emotional meaning, its associations with deep affection and longing for others, with fear of the destructive power of one's own hostility, and with concerns for vitality and self-preservation.

Neuro-musculo-skeletal Systems

The above subtitle, a poor phrase, fractured and festooned with hyphens, is intended to indicate the discussion will turn to some of the illnesses which affect motility. Paraplegia is the most obvious and stark example of these. In addition to the considerable handicap and its social significance each individual will have inner problems to manage when he has suffered spinal cord injury and a loss of lower motor neuron function. Nearly the whole array of psychological problems we have been discussing are possibilities here. Conflict over body-image and over feelings of limitation in expression of affection and aggression are strong possibilities presented in individual patterns by different patients. There is no question that the paraplegic begins a new way of life and requires a thorough reorganization of the manner of coping with inner strivings and with the environment. The effectiveness of this new adaptation will depend upon the patient's own resources and the kind of help he gets from others. Some rehabilitation centers for paraplegics use the management of vital functions as an index of both psychological and physiological readaptation. They say that when the patient has re-established a form of bladder and bowel control, he is ready to begin home visits.

The syndrome of *Parkinsonism* affecting a few young people but many more older patients is a vivid example of interacting somatic and psychic systems. The symptoms of rigidity, tremor, gait disturbance, facial mask, and the loss of vocal power make the body a prison for the mind and its energies. Relapses and remissions correlate with mood and emotional reactions to life situations in these patients. The relations between emotional control and the basal ganglia have not yet been completely charted. A young Parkinsonian patient once said to the author, "Almost always I have to talk like this (a soft whisper), but when I get mad, then I TALK LIKE THIS!" Parkinsonian patients invariably seem to be over-controlled emotionally. Whether this damping of feeling is a guard against useless rage over their plight, a direct result of the disorder of the basal ganglia, or a reflection of the basic cause of the disorder is not known. It is fairly well known among patients afflicted with the syndrome that alcohol provides relief, yet the author has not known a patient who will touch it after the first try, perhaps fearing addiction or dangerous loss of emotional control.

Among the other illnesses affecting motility are the various forms of *arthritis*, which can impose slight to very serious degrees of limitation. We know from clinical studies of these patients and from study of patients who must be bedfast because of *fractures* of hip, vertebra, and skull that conflicts over regression to a state of having to be cared for can be devastating to the consistency and assurance of self-image. These limitations are also damaging to the confidence of relationships with others. The type of person whose motility and muscular ability is essential to his adaptation will suffer deeply and have less inner strength to deal with the enforced regression which bed rest or other limitations impose.

Genitourinary Syndromes

Two examples of somatopsychic interactions will be briefly discussed in this section. First, the genitourinary system includes some glands of internal secretion, and the interplay of emotion and conflict with endocrine supplies is an important part of over-all psychobiological integration. A somatic illness which affects or requires the removal of ovaries or testes will have several direct endocrine effects upon psychological adjustment. These changes are due to the loss of endocrine secretions. However, the direct endocrine effect should not be overemphasized since the feelings about the removal are also important. In some of the preceding sections there has been discussion of the anxiety about the loss of sexual and reproductive organs as a result of surgical treatment.

With the aging of our population there are increasing numbers of older men who require prostatic, bladder, and urethral surgery. The feelings about the self and the concern about interference with sexual and excretory functions are important considerations for the treatment of the aging male.

Special Senses: Blindness and Deafness

Both of the problems to be considered in this section are associated with extensive practical psychological and social problems. Each of these handicaps requires specialized attention for readaptation to the way of life of the blind or deaf. The physician is only part of the team aiding in the rehabilitation of these patients.

For a beginning understanding of the psychological impact of blindness we need to remember two facts. One is that the eyes are organs for taking in. The taking in of a vast multiplicity of sensory images is a constant function of the healthy eye. A wide and rich range of pleasurable taking-in, as well as many other life-preserving functions and everyday business, is dependent upon efficient visual function. Some of this taking-in, most of the life-preserving functions, and some of the everyday business can, under favorable conditions, be adequately served by other sensory channels, but there is one function that is especially difficult to change. The eyes are extremely important for interpersonal relations. The other person's visual image is taken-in in a love relationship. The object of fondness is brought close by the mind's retention of his or her visual image and thousands of memories stored via visual channels. The loss of sight blocks the capacity to refresh the visual element of the mind's representation of the other person. For most blind people memories remain visual, but new relationships and the changes in old ones now require a shift to other senses. There is a communicative function too. Consider two popular songs of quite different eras.

> Your eyes are the eyes
> Of a woman in love.

> Drink to me only with thine eyes
> And I will pledge with mine.

There are thousands more.

Also the eyes are the means of testing reality, of establishing whether a mental image exists in outside reality or is only a figment of the imagination. A simple clinical test can demonstrate this function. When a patient is slightly confused, when his hold on reality is tenuous, he may be asked to close his eyes and the eyelids are then rubbed gently. Visual images will be produced, often of a quite well-formed and vivid nature. Patients who are blinded temporarily because of surgical treatment of the eye will be made anxious after a time by the flood of vivid visual imagery which they know to be unreal. The permanently blind person has to try to find other means to this constantly necessary function of reality testing to determine whether an image exists outside or is only in the mind.

A dressed-up and sophisticated hostess is introducing a guest to an older woman wearing an uncertain smile. The hostess says, "I want you to meet our Aunt Madge. She's deaf as a post and a hell of a bore." This situation appeared in a *New Yorker* cartoon at least 20 years ago. It describes the social position of the deaf person and reflects upon the inner experience of the person who has lost hearing. Once again, the impairment of this special sense leads to a separation from others and from the outside world requiring a shift to the use of other senses to bridge the gap. Often the impairment in capacities for interpersonal relations and the tendency to feel separated from others seem greater in the deaf person than in the blind. This impression may be accounted for by the degree to which social relations depend upon vocal communication. Though it is not a fact established by statistical investigation, it appears that deaf people are inclined to paranoid ideation. This clinical impression is consonant with the difficulties in reality testing which might be expected with the defect in a special sense. A tendency to suspicions about what people are saying could grow to delusional proportions if the capacity for testing the suspicions were lacking.

Dermatological Syndromes

The skin serves as protective barrier, as a sensory organ, and as part of the secretory-excretory systems. It functions in the expression and control of emotions too. The skin is usually conceived to be the part of the person presented to the rest of the world. The appearance and texture of the skin are felt to convey aspects of the personality. This emotional association of skin qualities with psychological qualities is especially operative when there is an affliction of the skin. The tremendous self-consciousness when the skin is scaling, crusted, weeping or discolored by inflammation or other disorder is an indication that the person feels devalued. Often skin patients will facetiously refer to themselves as "lepers." Patients who present these alterations of exposed portions of the skin not only feel less attractive but feel that their personalities are showing their less desirable aspects. An adolescent with acne may say, "This filth is coming out of me." It is strange but understandable that a person with an eczematous eruption of the forearm, wrist and hand feels more embarrassed and uncomfortable when it is thought to be noticed by others, than a patient with a plaster cast covering the same area. There is an instant sensitivity reawakened in the skin patient that others would not want to touch or be touched by skin that is diseased. This feeling of shame and injury over the wishes for contact with others goes a long way toward explaining the special meaning of skin afflictions.

Patients with chronic skin ailments fall clearly into two groups. Some patients almost defiantly seek exposure of their skin lesions. They subject other people to the sight of them, thereby testing and retesting their capacity to show fondness or repugnance toward the person with the illness. Other patients take flight, withdraw and conceal themselves as though they were outcasts and hideously pitiful. Thus the feelings about the appearance and meaning of skin disorders tend to revive childhood attitudes and behavior relevant to self-esteem and the acceptance of others.

Itching and scratching cycles are also in close interaction with psychological events. Unquestionably the intensity of itching of any skin disorder varies with emotional states; the reverse is also true. An itch can be worse in conflictual situations, and the itch itself can measurably affect levels of tension. Cycles of itching and scratching may have a pleasurable, libidinous quality. It is frequently noted clinically that these cycles mount to a crescendo and come to an end with the patient exhausted and sweating. Here the parallel is with an autoerotic experience. The cycles may also have an aggressive meaning in which the indulgence of an urge to scratch is felt as defiant behavior. The forbidden scratching is thought to be rebelliousness against parents, doctors and others, while at the same time, it is a self-injurious, self-tearing activity. (Except for the recognition that the doctor is opposed to the scratching, these significances are usually not conscious.)

The following sequence is not uncommon. A minor skin ailment is the cause of an itch. The itch brings about a scratching. The itching and scratching acquire libidinous and/or aggressive meaning through unconscious associations (perhaps involving the mechanism of displacement). The cycle may then continue, autonomous of the original skin ailment. Many difficult skin problems begin in this fashion from a condition which would not be at all difficult to treat by itself.

Endocrine Disorder: Diabetes Mellitus

Every form of adaptation in man, healthy or ailing, requires the participation of endocrine systems. Thus one can be sure, although all the patterns are not yet known, that endocrine secretion is an element or a pathway in all forms of illness, "physical" and "mental." For the purposes of this discussion, let us take a condition, referred to elsewhere in this book in which the illness is known to be the result of a disorder of endocrine functioning, i.e., diabetes mellitus.

The psychological sequences in the diabetic arise from two facets of the natural history of diabetes, the illness itself and the customary treatment. The psychological effect of the illness is profound and subtle. The diabetic finds that he has the illness from tests of his urine and blood. The symptoms have probably been insidious. Possibly the patient has heard on radio or television, "There are thousands of people in the United States today who do not know they have diabetes. Perhaps you are one of them." The whole thing is very deep and mysterious. The feeling of a debilitating process, of a subtly accelerated dying, is added to by the symptoms of fatigue, weight loss, unreasonable hunger and thirst. The idea of relentless debilitation is reinforced by the knowledge that "once a diabetic, always a diabetic." The feeling in reaction to this knowledge of the nature of the illness is that something uncontrollable and invisible is going on inside. One could even doubt that the reassuring doctor knows what he is talking about. This feeling about an inner process one had not considered possible before appears to lead to an increase of needs directed towards the outside. The hunger, then, is not only for food, but for emotions as well, and the demands for attention and fondness from others increase. These needs will usually encounter opposing motives in the personality, and various forms of inner conflict will develop. However the reaction is handled, the enhanced need of the diabetic for supplies of many sorts from the outside is the driving force of the reactions to the illness.

The nature of treatment for diabetes further complicates the somatopsychic sequences so often associated with the illness, and the so-called "complications" of diabetes are added factors in the psychological responses to this way of life.

The diabetic develops a complex relationship with his conscience (in relation to the new responsibilities his malady entails). He is often told that he must follow a diet, that certain foods and certain quantities of food are restricted. Usually he must be the judge of selection and quantity. Secondly, the diabetic is told that he must administer to himself a medicine—a procedure which is a little painful and certainly inconvenient. Thirdly, he is often instructed to test his urine once or more each day.

Any of these three responsibilities can put the patient in the position of evasion, bribery, and suffering of punishment from the conscience. Some irresponsibility toward diet, urinalysis and medication can represent a revival of childhood deceptiveness toward parents. This deception is now practiced toward the physician and the patient's own conscience. A few diabetic patients acquire a tendency towards irresponsibility in other fields, having bribed their consciences by being very good diabetic patients adhering strictly to the instructions. They feel they have gained special privileges and allowance by being so faithful to their doctor's advice. A third group of patients work out their expiation of guilt feelings or indirectly express hostility by subjecting themselves to acidosis and coma. A variant of the latter behavior is the reproachful diabetic who starves himself or overtreats himself into hyperinsulinism. The "brittle" diabetics and the young diabetics present the three types of problems with especial acuteness.

The long-term treatment of the diabetic requires careful attention to the strength and weaknesses of the person involved. A perfectly good conventional treatment program can be sabotaged through being used (without conscious intent) by the patient to further neurotic solutions. The type of therapeutic program designed to treat the blood and urine of the diabetic will in the long run be much less effective than the treatment designed for the whole patient.

Pain and Phantom Phenomena

How is one to understand the meaning of a patient's statement that he is suffering pain? This situation, so frequent and commonplace in the practice of medicine, is actually very complex and often loaded with ambiguity in that neither doctor nor patient can have a sense of validation, consensual validation. The conscientious doctor struggles to be sure about the intensity and quality of the pain. He suggests some of the old and tried medical words to the patient; is the pain "throbbing," "stabbing," "dull," or "shooting"? The patient finds none of these words very applicable or helpful and tries some of his own. Often these do not jibe with the doctor's experience, and the patient begins to question whether the doctor appreciates the kind and degree of pain he is suffering. There is a vast amount of negotiation and transaction in the whole field of medicine over this area of ambiguity, over what type and how much pain the patient is feeling, and then, sadly and wearily and sometimes heatedly, over the question of whether or not the patient "really" feels pain. At least one can give a nearly unqualified answer to the last question. In the vast majority of instances he does feel pain. There is little need to question the fact; there is need to understand the meaning of the fact, of the statement that something opposite to pleasure is being felt. (Even if the patient is lying, i.e., malingering, it is safe to say that something opposite to pleasure is at least threatening and serving as the motivation for the complaint. See Chap. 5.)

Once the present author, then in military service, was called at 3 A.M. to the bedside of a young soldier.

Dr. T.: You say that you are in pain. Where is the pain?
Soldier: All over.
Dr. T.: All over, that's impossible! It's got to be somewhere.
Soldier: Why did you come, if you don't believe me? It's all over my body.
Dr. T. (in exasperation): Well, let's see if that is really true. Do you hurt at the very tip of your nose?
Soldier (thinking for a while): Yes, I hurt at the very tip of my nose too.

A bit triumphant, the doctor prescribed aspirin and went back to bed. The patient had been forced to break the rules. He was not giving a well phrased and feasible complaint. The culture and the community of medical sciences say complaints should be localized and should fit some schematized concept of the body, etc. The patient, in his need to speak of his feelings, violated the rules and made himself inarticulate. The truth is that, in an important sense, he *did* have pain. He *did* want the doctor at 3 A.M. He was communicating a feeling, a state, a sense of something very much the opposite of pleasure. What it was remains unknown. The point is that a description of pain is an inarticulate communication from within a person to the outside. The message always has meaning. We are sometimes deaf to it and more often puzzled by it.

Thomas Szasz describes three levels of communication about pain.

1. The first level is biological. It is entirely within one person in which a signal is received at a central part of the body, the brain, from another part. The signal indicates a threat to the integrity of the body and may call for instant action. The generation of the signal is entirely spontaneous and is not greatly influenced in intensity or quality by factors outside of the person. (It may be, though, that threshold can be influenced.) There is no question of validation and no misunderstanding of the messages at this level.

2. In the second level two persons are involved. The message from a body part has been received centrally and then an effort is made to transmit the message to another person, usually for the purpose of obtaining help. At this level problems of validation enter, and different concepts of the body held by the subject of the pain and by the observer complicate the message.

3. At the third level of communication the body reference is lost. The communication is purely a plea for help or a reproach to the observer. Often an effort is made to make the complaint more concrete, credible, and more within the rules of the culture by the unconscious selection of a body part as a vehicle for the communication.

Most communications about pain in the practice of medicine are a composite of levels one, two, and three; that is, the pain has body reference, is difficult to validate, is complicated by differing body concepts, and is a plea for help beyond the wish for relief of pain and assistance for the threat to body integrity. (The communication is also for help with a problem in living or emotional conflict as well as a response to physical pain.) One can begin diagnosis by recognizing the state of pain the patient is experiencing and figure from that point the more exact meanings of the communication.

The phenomena of phantom limb and phantom pain are interesting and, though common, always surprising findings in medical and surgical practice. The term, "phantom," implying a ghost of some living thing now departed is well-chosen because that is exactly what it is. When considered, though, it need not be surprising. Rather, one would expect every amputee to report the sensation since it is true that the central neurons and the mental representation of the amputated limb remain a part of the individual. They are not excised with the limb. The neural circuits for the limb and the extensive memory system remain intact with all of the associated emotions and thoughts.

It is necessary, then, to understand the persistence of the feeling of the amputated limb and also the onset of pain, sometimes excruciating pain, in the location of an amputated extremity. The persistence of the phantom phenomenon is quite clearly a form of denial of the loss of the body part. It is a kind of mourning that goes beyond the expected duration, and it is a reluctance to give up the cherished part of the self. The pain is the discharge of feeling over the loss. The latter is contradictory from a logical point of view, but it is a compromise solution from an emotional point of view. That is, the pain is the expression of feeling over the loss of the part, but it also denies the loss of the part because the presence of pain assures the patient that the extremity is not gone, else how could the patient feel pain from it.

SUMMARY AND IMPLICATIONS

The extended discussion of the surgical patient included an assertion that a truly *objective* consideration of surgical problems would indicate that the illness is acquired by and the treatment performed upon a whole, living human being. Since one is dealing in surgical practice with a system as volatile and complex as the human animal, the doctor's predictions, his plans, and his methods of diagnosis and treatment—in fact, the entire design of the practice of medicine and surgery—should attempt to make order out of emotional processes and patterns of thinking, as well as out of anatomic structure and physiologic processes.

Nearly everyone going through an illness, an operation, and period of convalescence will demonstrate at least some small break in the otherwise even flow of feeling and adjustment to life situations. The exaggerations of these minimally conflictual responses are the "neurotic" reactions to phases of the surgical experience. These disturbances have been considered with regard to their sources in feelings about the body and the mind's image of the body and from the viewpoint of the self and the self-image. The excitation of conflict and the dynamic reactions to it in a surgical situation have been explored, and consideration has been given to the appearance of anxiety, fear, and depression in a person having an operation.

It has been advocated that a truly therapeutic program be based upon a kind of total balance sheet, which would determine at the end of convalescence how many ways the patient is better as against how many ways he is worse. If the patient's balance sheet shows that there has been surgical improvement but also that the trauma of the experience has severely impaired psychological adaptation, then the treatment has been only a qualified success. Feelings of tension and depression postoperatively are strong indicators that adaptation has in some ways been weakened. In such cases it is likely that a less effective, neurotic compromise is in the making. Often this compromise involves the surgical illness in a complex fashion, making the operative results less beneficial to the patient.

Little has been said in this section about treatment. The writer's desire has been to increase the capacity for an empathic attitude toward the patient facing a surgical experience, by offering clinical and research data organized into some principles which can inform the expectations of the doctor towards patients in surgery. The improved ability for empathic understanding of his patient's experiences will enable the doctor to make fuller use of his relationship with the patient toward the goal of comprehensive treatment. The methods of *supportive treatment*, described fully in Chapter 13, will be most useful in combination with the everyday contacts between physician or surgeon and patient.

The best advice for the doctor sensitive to the needs of his surgical patients is that which a riding instructor is apt to give his pupils: hold the reins loosely but firmly. The doctor can be permissive, can even help the patient express himself and give vent to some of his feelings, but through his strength, stability, and authority, he can retain the needed degree of control and help the patient regain (or maintain) his integration. An overly tight hold on the patient, his emotional expression, and his behavior will make him frustrated and exhausted from the surging inner forces. A too permissive, loose hold will bring conflict out too strongly and too rampantly, and this will be frightening, even destructive. Through his relationship with the patient, his understanding, and his supportive techniques, the doctor can help the patient to a sense of control over the expression of feeling and over his conflict and defensive reactions to them. The patient should sense that he is, in large measure, contributing to the control of things, rather than merely being controlled.

In addition to its discussion of the surgical experience, this chapter has taken up some other examples of the interaction between somatic and psychological systems. The conditions discussed in the latter section have in common the direction of interaction. Disturbances arise in somatic systems and affect associated ideational and emotional components of the total organism. The presentation of some common physical illnesses has shown that the somatopsychic interaction is sure to occur when there is physical illness; one needs only assess the intensity and quality of the psychological reactions. A second general principle is that certain conflict areas, certain emotional problems and certain attitudes have special associations with certain areas and parts of the body, so that there is a range of predictability regarding the type of problem to be expected when a physical illness occurs.

Bibliography

1. Browning, J., and Houseworth, J.: Development of new symptoms following medical and surgical treatment for duodenal ulcer, Psychosom. Med. *15*:328, 1953.
2. Menninger, K.: Polysurgery and polysurgical addiction, Psychoanal. Quart. *3*:173, 1934.
3. Titchener, J.: Surgery as a Human Experience, New York, Oxford Univ. Press, 1960.
4. Ulett, P., and Gildea, E.: Survey of surgical procedures in psychoneurotic women, J.A.M.A. *143*:960, 1950.
5. Zwerling, I., Titchener, J., Gottschalk, L., Levine, M., Culbertson, W., Cohen, S., and Silver, H.: Personality disorder and the relationship of emotions to surgical illness in two hundred surgical patients, Am. J. Psychiat. *112*:270, 1955.

Suggestions for Further Reading

Deutsch, H.: Psychoanalytic observations in surgery, J.A.M.A. *154*: 509, 1954.

Grinker, R. R., and Robbins, F.: Psychosomatic Case Book, New York, Blakiston, 1954.

Hackett, T. P., and Weisman, A. D.: Psychiatric management of operative syndromes: 1. The therapeutic consultation and the effect of non-interpretive intervention. 2. Psychodynamic factors in formulation and management, Psychosom. Med. 22:267-282 and 356-372, 1960.

Janis, I. L.: Psychological Stress: Psychoanalytic and Behavioral Studies of Surgical Patients, New York, Wiley, 1959.

CHAPTER 8

Introduction to Principal Psychiatric Disorders. Organic Brain Reactions

INTRODUCTION

Organic and Functional Illness

In psychiatry, as in other areas of medicine, it has long been customary to distinguish between *organic* and *functional* forms of illness. The traditional definitions run about as follows: *An organic disease is one in which the etiology necessarily involves morbid alterations in structure. A functional disease is one in which the etiology does not involve structural change and its symptomatology is based primarily upon unhealthy responses of the patient.* An example of an illness of the first category would be *dementia paralytica* (p. 282), and of one of the second category would be *dissociative reaction* (p. 322).

It was long recognized that there were some disease states (including psychiatric ones)—those called *toxic*—that did not fit perfectly into either category. An example of this would be alcoholic intoxication. Whereas there may be structural damage in toxic conditions, this is often not the case in the ordinary sense of the term (and, of course, it is not the case in mild alcoholic intoxication). However, because of clinical similarities and because the etiological agent is a specific, identifiable chemical substance, it is customary to group the toxic brain reactions with the organic, rather than with the functional conditions.

While the differentiation between organic brain disorders and functional psychiatric diseases remains of practical value—and will be followed in this book—it is important to realize that the distinction cannot be a simple, and certainly not an arbitrary, matter. As has been stressed repeatedly, the organism is an indivisible unit; nothing can occur mentally which does not have its physiological concomitants. If one extends the concept of structure from the microscopic, through the electron-microscopic, to the biochemical and the electrophysiological, one finds the distinction between functional and organic begin to fade. For example, although it is impossible to say just what ultraminute molecular alterations within neurons may be involved in the establishment of memory traces, there is no question but that there are such alterations. In this sense, there are organic etiological components in all psychiatric disorders.

Psychosis and Neurosis

A second type of distinction, equally complex and subtle, which it will be necessary to keep in mind both during the ensuing discussion and in the chapters to follow is that between *psychosis* and *psychoneurosis (neurosis)*. The term, *neurosis*, corresponds approximately to the layman's expression, "nervousness." The term *psychosis* corresponds approximately to the commoner expressions, "madness" and "insanity." These are, however, no more than rough approximations, and will not do for the physician. Although, for the sake of convenience, one-sentence definitions of the two types of conditions will be attempted presently, it should be conceded at the outset that these definitions will be approximations also. Therefore, it may be well to indicate in tabular form at this point the principal points of distinction which may be made between the two conditions from various points of view.

PSYCHOSES	NEUROSES
1. Socially speaking,	
A psychosis is a severe disorder of the mind, preventing or seriously interfering with the patient's relationships with other persons and with groups. Vocational, social, and sexual adjustments are markedly impaired and may be completely blocked.	A neurosis is a less severe disorder of the mind. Social, vocational, and sexual adjustments are often impaired, but they are not, as a rule, prevented.
2. Etiologically speaking,	
A psychosis may be brought on by organic (including toxic) factors, or by psychological factors, or by a combination of the two.	A neurosis is brought on by psychological factors, i.e., by the *meaning* (to the individual) of whatever stress elements are operating, rather than by the direct physiological effects of the stress. It is always a "functional" disorder.

PSYCHOSES	NEUROSES

3. Descriptively speaking,

A psychosis involves severe disorganization of the various personality functions: perception, memory, judgment, motor activity, etc. Psychotics are usually not aware of the fact that they are psychiatrically ill. (They lack *insight*.)	A neurosis involves decreased efficiency of one or more functions, but much less disorganization of them. Neurotics are usually aware that they are psychiatrically ill. (They have *insight*.)

4. Clinically speaking,

Psychoses are usually characterized by the presence of one or more such specific symptoms as *delusions, illusions*, and *hallucinations*.*	Neuroses are not characterized by delusions or hallucinations; illusions are infrequent. The clinical picture includes one or more specific symptoms such as *conversions, phobias*, and *obsessions*.†

5. Therapeutically speaking,

Psychotics usually require hospitalization, at least at the outset of treatment. Many modalities of treatment may be valid.	Neurotics usually do not require hospitalization. Psychotherapy is usually the treatment of choice.

6. Dynamically speaking,

There is a serious impairment of the executive functions of the personality. Reality-testing is more or less obviously faulty. Previously suppressed and repressed conflicts between deep-seated impulses and the executive functions are mobilized. There is a grave impairment of the ability to relate to objects.	There is a partial impairment of the executive functions, but the major capacities remain intact. The neurotic attempts to deal with conflicts largely by suppression and repression. The ability to relate to objects is affected, but not gravely impaired.

On the basis of these considerations, a practical definition of psychosis may be attempted, as follows: *A psychosis is a severe mental illness, involving a grave impairment of the executive functions of the*

---

* These symptoms will be defined in the course of the present chapter.

† These symptoms will be defined in Chapter 9.

personality, particularly with respect to reality-testing, and revealed by signs of a serious maladjustment to life.

A *psychoneurosis* may be defined as *a mild to moderately severe mental illness, in which the function of reality-testing is not gravely impaired, and in which the maladjustment to life is of a relatively limited nature.*

DELIRIUM AND DEMENTIA

A classification of organic psychiatric disorders will follow shortly, but let us begin by considering clinical illustrations of two syndromes, *delirium* and *dementia*, which appear with great frequency in such disorders; one or the other of these invariably is present in cases which are of *psychotic* proportions.

An elderly patient in moderate heart failure, resting in the Fowler position, is being examined by a medical student. While determining the physical findings, the student is talking with the patient, beginning to take the medical history. The patient's answers to the routine questions are clear and relevant.

The student has the patient lie flat in bed, intending to complete the examination and history-taking, but he is briefly called away from the bedside to answer the telephone. When he returns, he finds that the patient is confused, misinterprets the questions, and can no longer give clear answers. When the patient is again placed in the Fowler position and given oxygen, his mental status returns to normal.

F. D., a man 30 years of age, is on a medical ward with the diagnosis of lobar pneumonia. He is somewhat dehydrated and has a fever of 104°. Aside from the chest findings, fever, and an increased cardiac rate, the physical examination is essentially normal. There is a past history of mild, chronic alcoholism.

Routine treatment measures for pneumococcal pneumonia are instituted with the patient's full cooperation.

Toward evening of the first hospital day, Mr. D. becomes restless. When the nurse urges the patient to drink more fluids, he asks her for a glass of beer. In response to a few moments of quiet explanation, the patient accepts a glass of water and temporarily becomes calmer.

At 8:00 P.M., when receiving medication, Mr. D. appears tremulous and agitated and says that he is afraid that he will be late for work. Again a brief explanatory conversation is sufficient for the patient to abandon the idea.

Lights on the ward are turned down at 9:00 P.M. Shortly afterward the patient is seen by the nurse on duty to get out of bed and begin searching for something. In response to her question, Mr. D. says that his clothes have evidently been stolen, refers to the hospital as a "boarding house," and insists that he be provided with street clothes and be allowed to leave for work.

Within a few days of admission, unusual behavior of this sort ceases entirely and does not return.

Mr. H. M., a white widowed man, aged 75, is a management problem throughout his hospital stay. He has entered the hospital on the urology service for diagnosis and treatment of prostatic disease. The patient has lived in retirement for the past ten years, and has been given a good home and much careful attention by a daughter and son-in-law for the latter half of this period.

Mr. M. is a basically agreeable man, and he has been a person of some refinement, but he is completely unable to adjust to his new surroundings. He continually forgets that he is in a hospital and receiving treatment. He repeatedly pulls out his indwelling catheter and wanders up and down the corridors, sometimes only partly clad, asking for "Susie" and "Jim" (his children). At times he sits quietly, holding a newspaper or watching the ward television set, but he appears unable to understand what he is reading or watching. Occasionally, he mistakes medical and nursing students for his grandchildren. Depending upon his mood, he either asks friendly but irrelevant questions about their activities, or querulously insists that they summon one of their parents.

The first and second patients exemplify the condition of *delirium*; the third patient, that of *dementia*. *Delirium* may be defined as *an altered level of consciousness (awareness), often acute and in most instances reversible, manifested by disorientation and confusion, and induced by an interference (usually chemical) with the metabolic processes of the neurons of the brain*. In general terms, the immediate cause of delirium may be reduced to the following elements, acting singly or in combination: (1) a decreased supply of oxygen or other essential nutrients to the brain in the presence of a constant demand, (2) an increased demand for such factors in the presence of a fixed supply, and (3) an interference with the enzyme systems upon which the essential metabolic processes of the neurons depend.

Delirium is an extremely common condition in medical practice, often being overlooked in its milder forms. It is estimated that as many as 30 per cent of the acutely ill patients on the medical wards of a general hospital suffer from some degree of delirium during portions of any 24-hour period.

The transient delirium of the cardiac patient was evidently due to factor (1). With his overstrained heart, the additional effect of the supine position resulted in an inadequate supply of oxygenated blood to the brain.

The delirium of patient F.D. was in all probability due to a combination of factors (1) and (2). The pulmonary disease interfered with a thorough oxygenation of the blood at the same time that the high fever increased the metabolic demands of the cells of the brain (and other tissues).

Examples of the influence of factor (3) would be bromide, barbiturate, and alcoholic intoxications.

The condition of *dementia* is exemplified by the third patient, H. M. Dementia may be defined as a *chronic, typically irreversible, deterioration of intellectual capacities, due to organic disease of the brain that has produced structural changes (the actual death of neurons)*.

Classification of Organic Brain Reactions

In the official (A.P.A.) nomenclature, organic brain reactions are first classified as *acute* or *chronic* and then subdivided on the basis of a statement as to pathogenesis. *Acute* organic brain reaction is, for practical purposes, synonymous with *delirium*. Chronic organic brain reaction usually involves *dementia*, but it may often involve a long-lasting delirium, or a combination of the two.

Here is an outline of the more common diagnostic possibilities in organic brain reaction, based upon the official American Psychiatric Association nomenclature, slightly modified.

ETIOLOGICAL CLASSIFICATION OF ORGANIC BRAIN REACTION

1. **Infection**
    A. Intracranial
        (1) Syphilitic
        (2) Other: bacterial, viral
    B. Systemic
2. **Intoxication**
    A. Alcohol
    B. Medications
    C. Heavy metals (lead, etc.)
    D. Other
3. **Physical Trauma (to the head)**
    A. In connection with birth
    B. Other
4. **Circulatory Disturbances**
    A. Cerebral arteriosclerosis
    B. Cardiac failure
    C. Other
5. **Convulsive Disorders**
    A. Idiopathic
    B. Secondary to known physical factors
6. **Disturbances of Growth, Metabolism, or Nutrition**
    A. Senile brain disease
    B. Glandular disorders
        (1) Cretinism

(2) Addison's disease
(3) Simmonds' disease
(4) Other
   C. Nutritional Deficiencies
      (1) Pellagra
      (2) Beriberi
      (3) Pernicious anemia
      (4) Other
7. **Intracranial Neoplasm**
   A. Primary
   B. Metastatic
8. **Prenatal (constitutional) Influence**
   A. Mongolism
   B. Congenital Spastic Paraplegia
   C. Cranial anomaly
   D. Other
9. **Unknown or Uncertain Causes**
   A. Multiple sclerosis
   B. Huntington's chorea
   C. Pick's disease
   D. Other

Depending upon the intensity and the duration of action of the above etiological factors, most of them are capable of producing, first, delirium, and then, dementia.

As may be inferred from the clinical examples on pages 274 and 275, the basic syndromes of delirium and dementia have many common elements. In the following discussion, some of the principal phenomena of delirium will be considered, and the modifications of the symptom picture to be found in dementia will then be indicated.

Delirium

The essential symptom components of the syndrome of delirium may be said to be of a "negative" character, involving the *loss or impairment of certain functions of the personality*. Chief of these is an alteration in the patient's level of consciousness, such that the threshold of awareness is raised. As shown in the patient with pneumonia and even more strikingly in the patient with cardiac failure, the level of consciousness in delirium tends to fluctuate within short periods of time. This clinical instability is based upon the instability of the metabolic equilibrium. For example, the oxygen demand of the cortical cells at a temperature of 104° is quantitatively different from that at a temperature of 98.6°. The supply of oxygenated blood to the brain in a patient with cardiac failure may be decidedly different in a sitting position from what it is in a supine position.

The clinical changes are reflected in electroencephalographic* changes. Not only does delirium produce a characteristically disturbed electroencephalographic tracing, but the degree of disturbance correlates well with the degree of delirium noted clinically.

The primary or basic symptoms of delirium involve other significant functional losses: defects in orientation, in memory, and in judgment (as illustrated in the case of F. D., the patient with pneumonia).

In certain delirious patients, the symptoms are confined to the elements just mentioned. In such instances, the clinical picture may be a rather quiet one, particularly if the hospital setting is calm, orderly, and reassuring. If, in addition, it is also a busy setting, the condition of delirium may pass unrecognized. Specific questioning of the patient may be required to demonstrate his confusion and disorientation.

On the other hand, delirium is very often accompanied by other, more striking, although in a sense secondary, symptoms. Prominent among these are excitement and agitation. Combined with the confusion, the excitement may lead to impulsive and even violent actions of a quite inappropriate kind. Mr. F. D.'s behavior tended in this direction, but more serious examples are by no means rare.

After a prolonged bout of alcoholic intoxication, a patient was admitted to the hospital in *delirium tremens* (p. 292). He was thoroughly confused, agitated, and extremely anxious. When an orderly approached the bedside with an intravenous stand, the patient misinterpreted his intentions as hostile, leaped out of bed, and assaulted him.

A patient in cardiac delirium got out of bed while his nurse was out of the room. He was restless and intended to take a stroll. He stepped through a window instead of the door, and was saved from very serious injury only by the circumstance that his room was on the first floor of the hospital.

In both of the above examples, the general confusion of the patients probably involved *a specific misinterpretation of a sensory experience* (intravenous stand for a weapon; window for door). This symptom has the special name, *illusion*; it is frequent in delirious states. Illusions are not confined to visual misinterpretations; they are often auditory; less frequently they may involve other sensory modalities. The com-

---

* As the student may recall, the *electroencephalograph* is an instrument, based on the string galvanometer of Einthoven, for measuring very small changes in potential derived from the electrical activity of the neurons of the brain. An *electroencephalogram* is a record obtained by means of the electroencephalograph, a "brain-wave tracing."

monest example of auditory illusions are those involving frightening and personalized misinterpretations of low-voiced conversations at the patient's bedside, as for example, between doctor and nurse. (For this reason, such conversations should be avoided.)

A still greater departure from reality is manifested in the phenomenon of hallucination. A hallucination may be defined as *a sensory experience, occurring (in the absence of adequate reality-testing) on the basis of the subject's inner needs and fears, and independent of stimulation from the environment.* The well-known tendency of patients with delirium tremens to "see" nonexistent rats, snakes, and other biting animals is an illustration of this phenomenon.* In delirious states, hallucinations, like illusions, are most commonly visual. Next in frequency come auditory hallucinations; then, tactile. Other sensory modalities are only rarely involved.

Delusions are not common in delirium. A delusion may be defined as *a fixed idea, unconsciously motivated, which is contrary to the observed facts as these are interpreted by normal persons under the same external circumstances.* Like hallucinations, delusions derive from forces deep within the personality, unchecked by an adequate appraisal of reality. When they do occur in delirium, they are apt to be of a disconcerting nature, suspicious or persecutory, and to involve figures in the current environment.

An understanding of the phenomena of delirium must go beyond the clinical-descriptive and the neurophysiological levels to include a grasp of the psychological forces involved (the psychodynamics). To begin with, one can readily see that the acute interference with cortical metabolism exerts an effect upon the executive functions of the personality. This effect may be considered to have two principal aspects: (1) there is a lessened ability for perception, appraisal, and manipulation of the environment; i.e., the intellectual and sensorimotor functions are impaired; and (2) there is a lessened ability for control of the inner forces of the personality (impulses deriving from the basic drives and opposing forces emanating from the conscience). The symptom picture of patients with delirium may be comprehensively understood as resulting either simply and directly from these psychological aspects or from the interplay between them.

What were called the primary symptoms are, of course, the direct and immediate effects of the weakening of executive capacities. As a rule there is some partial awareness in the personality that its position

---

* In some instances there exist external stimuli for such sensory experiences in delirium tremens, e.g., a spot on the wall may be perceived as a spider. In such cases the experiences would be considered to be illusions.

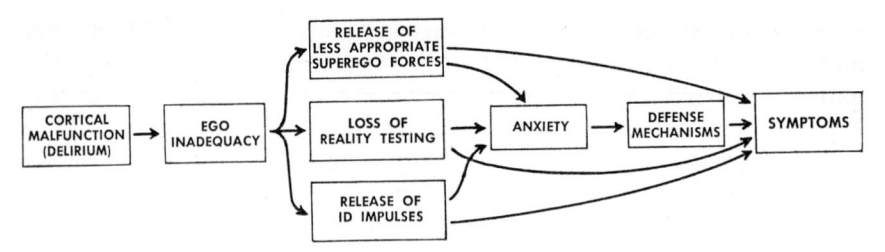

FIG. 2. Sequence of psychological events in the production of the symptomatology of delirium.

(its capacity to effect adjustment) has been fundamentally weakened. However dimly sensed, this situation is productive of anxiety. The anxiety is greatly reinforced (as indicated in the diagram) by the release from normal control of potentially disrupting inner forces: unacceptable impulses, on the one hand, and condemnatory, often inappropriate, conscience forces, on the other.

What were called the secondary symptoms are (1) direct expressions of the considerable anxiety, (2) direct expressions (modified by the weakened reality-testing) of the impulses and conscience forces, and (3) manifestations of the emergency defense mechanisms which the personality brings into action to cope with the anxiety and the disturbing impulses.

For example, patient F.D.'s asking for beer may be considered a direct expression of a drive (impulse); his attempts to get ready for work may be considered a direct expression of conscience forces (both being unchecked by consideration of the reality of his situation). The behavior of the patient with delirium tremens (p. 278) is best interpreted as being the result of his use of the mechanism of projection (p. 77) to cope with the release of hostile impulses within himself (i.e., he attributes his own hostility to the orderly).

In general, one may say of the illusions and hallucinations of delirious patients, that they are made possible by the characteristic loss of reality-testing. They are, however, the immediate result of the extensive use of certain specific defense mechanisms against anxiety and unacceptable impulses; of these mechanisms, projection is the most significant. The specific *content* of such symptoms is not dependent upon the delirium and only partially dependent upon the immediate environment; it is, in large part, dependent upon the premorbid personality of the patient, i.e., upon his significant life experiences.

As a matter of fact, if the premorbid personality of the patient has been an essentially healthy and mature one, the likelihood of there being florid secondary symptoms is greatly diminished. Even when the delirium is quite intense, such patients tend to show symptoms very largely consisting of the quieter, primary manifestations.

Dementia

As has been mentioned, the symptomatology of *dementia* (or of the *chronic brain reactions* generally) has a great deal in common with that of delirium. There is the same loss of intellectual functions (which, in extreme cases, may become almost total), the same inability to perceive, appraise, and respond adaptively to reality. There is the same loss of control over inner forces.

The points of difference are very largely traceable to the typically slower onset and to the greater chronicity of dementia. The slower onset makes a sudden release of marked anxiety less likely, and the greater chronicity affords the opportunity for the development of more complicated compensatory efforts (more elaborate use of defense mechanisms).

Thus an anxious excitement is uncommon in dementia, as is panicky behavior of an impulsive sort. On the other hand, if the dementia is chronic but not yet so extreme as to interfere with all thought processes, there are quite apt to be delusions (unlike the situation in delirium).

Another difference in the clinical picture of dementia from that in delirium is the absence or near-absence of fluctuations in the patient's level of awareness. This is what one would expect since dementia is produced by the actual death of brain cells, whereas delirium is produced by an interference with the function of the cells (usually reversible). This difference is reflected in the electroencephalographic tracings. This method of investigation is far more sensitive to disturbance of function than to loss of function; hence the electroencephalogram is often normal in dementia. Such minimal fluctuations in awareness as are occasionally to be found in cases of dementia are due to a co-existing delirium.

SPECIFIC ORGANIC BRAIN REACTIONS

The general features of delirium and dementia which have just been presented are to be found in nearly all instances of organic brain reaction. To a very large degree they are independent of the etiology of the individual case. With this material as background, it is now possible to consider the pathogenesis and clinical findings of a number of specific organic brain reactions without undue repetition. The underlying diseases productive of these psychiatric conditions will, in many instances, be studied in other courses (neurology, internal medicine, pediatrics). In this chapter, consideration will be given to representative sample of these disorders: dementia paralytica, delirium tremens, arteriosclerotic dementia, organic brain reaction with convulsive disorder, and post-traumatic personality disorder.

Dementia Paralytica (General Paresis)

This disease may be defined as *a chronic meningo-encephalitis of syphilitic origin, resulting, if untreated, in a progressive dementia and paralysis and ultimately in death.*

Case histories of patients with this disease show considerable variation, particularly in the early stages. The following history is illustrative of the principal clinical features.

Mr. W. B., aged 42, the proprietor of a small grocery store in a rural area of one of the Appalachian states, was brought, rather unwillingly, to the hospital by his wife and brother. The presenting complaint, offered by the relatives, was of irresponsible behavior, which included impulsive extravagance and the making of unrealistic business plans.

The recent history was as follows: Mr. B. had been, on the whole, a good husband and a rather popular member of the little community in which he lived. He had always "had his faults"; he was sometimes careless with money, extending credit too readily ("it made him feel like a big shot"), and he was given to a fairly acceptable type of boasting (chiefly about exploits at hunting and fishing).

Mrs. B. said that, over the past year, there had been a series of changes—at first, seemingly minor ones—in her husband's personality. He had become forgetful. He was restless and irritable on occasion. At other times his mood would change abruptly and he would be boisterously cheerful for no apparent reason. The patient had begun spending quite beyond his income, buying lavish sports items for himself and expensive gifts for his wife, children, and friends. This trend had culminated, two days before admission, in his purchase of a luxury automobile on credit, whose cost exceeded his annual income. During the past several months, the patient had begun to neglect his store, but spent a great deal of time driving from one little neighboring town to another, "looking for business locations." The patient's wife had first been a little amused, then puzzled, and then frightened and angry, but had not known what to do about the matter. Her determination to take action had been crystallized by the car purchase and a conversation which had occurred in her presence the following day between Mr. B. and the town banker. As they were coming out of church, the patient had attempted to solicit a large loan. He had become more excited as he spoke, finally reaching the point of incoherence.

Direct examination of Mr. B. yielded the following positive findings: a tremor of the protruded tongue, a faint slurring of speech on test phrases (as "Methodist Episcopal"), contracted, slightly irregular pupils, reacting sluggishly to light, and generally hyperactive deep reflexes.

The patient's mood was basically one of inappropriate euphoria, edged by resentment at his relatives' insistence on his having a medical evaluation. Intellectual functioning was distinctly impaired: the patient made frequent errors in simple mathematical calculations and was often unable to answer questions requiring a degree of abstract thinking. Mr. B. was quite distractible and showed marked difficulty in retention and recall of simple facts given him by the examiner.

In the unstructured portion of the interview, the patient's content of thought had to do with his ambitious and ill-conceived plans "to build a chain store empire." Only with considerable difficulty could Mr. B. be persuaded to give an approximation to a medical history. Two relevant statements were eventually made: the patient had had a syphilitic chancre in his youth, and, during the past year, he had been much troubled with headaches.

Mr. B. was admitted to the hospital, where a spinal puncture was performed. The cerebrospinal fluid pressure was at the upper limit of normal. There were 30 white cells (lymphocytes) per cu. mm. The protein content was elevated with a disproportionate increase in the globulin fraction. A Lange's colloidal gold curve determination was 5555444332. The cerebrospinal fluid Wassermann test was strongly positive (as also was the blood Wassermann).

In late stages of the disease, the neuropathology of dementia paralytica is rather striking. Gross examination reveals a somewhat shrunken brain with the convolutions exceptionally well defined. The loss of brain substance is essentially confined to the anterior two thirds of the hemispheres. There is a thickening and opacity of the membranous coverings of the brain, especially marked over the frontal lobes and the vertex. Microscopically, there is evidence of a diffuse inflammatory process involving the meninges and the smaller blood vessels. The leptomeninges are infiltrated with lymphocytes and plasma cells, as are the perivascular spaces of the small vessels and the capillaries of the cerebral cortex. The changes in the cortical parenchyma are diffuse, being most severe in the frontal and temporal regions. Actual destruction of neurons, particularly ganglion cells, is likely to be extensive; so much so, in fact, that there may be numerous small areas in which no neurons can be found. Glial proliferation is marked. With the use of a special silver stain, the infectious agent, the *Treponema pallidum*, can be demonstrated.

Like *tabes dorsalis* and *gumma*, dementia paralytica is a late (a so-called "tertiary") manifestation of syphilitic infection. It is most important to keep in mind the natural sequence of events in the pathogenesis of this disorder. In the very early stages of syphilis, the treponema spreads from the chancre through the lymphatics of the skin to the small blood vessels. A septicemia ensues, with generalized dissemination of the organisms. It is at this point, during the stage of "secondary eruption" involving the skin, that the treponema invades the central nervous system (i.e., two to six weeks after the primary lesion). Positive cerebrospinal fluid Wassermann tests can be obtained in a large majority of all cases of untreated or inadequately treated syphilis at some period within the first two years of infection.

By contrast, if cerebrospinal fluid tests for syphilis are performed after a lapse of ten or more years, the results are negative in a considerable majority (about three-fourths) of cases, regardless of treatment. Of the remainder, only a small proportion will develop dementia paralytica. All in all, it is estimated that from three to five per cent of patients contracting syphilis will later be so afflicted if untreated. (The percentage is somewhat smaller if there has been inadequate treatment.) The average period of time between the primary lesion and the onset of dementia paralytica is somewhere between 10 and 20 years.

The interesting question as to what factors subsequent to the original treponemal invasion determine the pathogenesis of dementia paralytica (or, for that matter, other forms of syphilitic involvement of the central nervous system) remains unanswered. On the other hand, the clinical lesson is perfectly clear: once a patient is diagnosed as syphilitic, he must be kept under periodic medical observation, regardless of treatment given, until a negative cerebrospinal fluid Wassermann reaction has been obtained. (See, however, p. 286.)

As in the case of W.B., psychological symptoms are usually the first to be noted in dementia paralytica—although, characteristically, not by the patient, himself. Common early complaints include headache, irritability, fatigue, impaired concentration, and sleep disturbances. One or another subtle neurological difficulty will usually have preceded psychological abnormalities, but may go unnoticed by patient and family. Eye signs of some sort are present in essentially all cases. The classical eye syndrome is known as the *Argyll Robertson* pupil. In this syndrome, the pupils are constricted, unequal in diameter, and irregular in outline. The pupillary light reflex is impaired or absent, while that of convergence is normal. The basis for these abnormalities has been thought to be a lesion in the fibers of the peri-aqueductal region of the midbrain which conduct impulses from the pretectal region to the nucleus of the oculomotor nerve.* (The corticomesencephalic fibers serving accommodation, taking another course, are not affected.)

As has been noted, the infection induces progressive destruction of

---

* It now seems equally likely that the principal lesion is in the iris of the eye itself (Langworthy and Ortego).

cortical neurons. As the cortex begins to be affected, an interference with coordinated voluntary motor function develops, first becoming noticeable in the smaller muscles. Hence it is that slurring of speech and tremor of the tongue and lips appear early, as does a shakiness in handwriting.

As the disease progresses, both psychological and neurological abnormalities become more severe and extensive. The psychological symptoms have, as a universal feature, the indications of a progressive dementia (i.e., the primary or "negative" characteristics, mentioned on p. 281). If the disease remains untreated, this aspect becomes so extreme as to involve complete loss of all intellectual functions, rendering the patient entirely helpless, even apart from the motor difficulties.

Long before this point is reached, there are, typically, certain other personality changes. Quite often, as in the case of W.B., premorbid personality traits will become exaggerated (carelessness becoming recklessness; boasting becoming grandiosity). In other instances, there will be qualitative, rather than merely quantitative, alterations in the personality. A timid person may become aggressive; a sexually inhibited person, promiscuous. Such overt changes are to be understood as release phenomena (p. 280); long-standing, repressed tendencies find overt expression as the executive functions of the personality are weakened through the organic damage to the brain.

In addition to such alterations in temperament and behavior, there may be more striking symptoms, suggestive of one another of the functional psychoses: *depression* (p. 341), *mania* (p. 351), *paranoia* (p. 390), or *schizophrenia* (p. 360). Even apart from neurological and laboratory findings, however, the differential diagnosis from functional psychoses does not ordinarily prove difficult, since the latter conditions do not involve a true dementia.

Patient W. B.'s ideas regarding the expansion of his business bordered on the delusional. Delusions of one kind or another are quite frequent in dementia paralytica; their content depends upon the basic personality make-up of the patient. Delusional ideas of an expansive, grandiose nature are particularly frequent, developing, at least in part, as a reaction of the personality to its obscure sense of being weakened by the illness. Hallucinations and illusions are not common in dementia paralytica.

In untreated cases, the muscular weakness and lack of coordination become progressively severe. Convulsions are apt to occur (in about three-fourths of the cases). Sooner or later, the patient becomes completely helpless: incontinent, unable to feed himself, and, ultimately unable even to swallow. In such instances—exceedingly rare at the present time—death usually results from marasmus with an aspiration pneumonia. If untreated, the disease is uniformly fatal within a period of about three years.

TREATMENT OF DEMENTIA PARALYTICA. The treatment of dementia paralytica involves both chemotherapeutic and psychological aspects; i.e., one treats the infection and one also treats the patient. Penicillin is the drug of choice for treatment of the infection. The usual routine is a daily dose of 1,000,000 units of procaine penicillin, given intramuscularly in divided doses, for a period of two weeks. In vitro, the *Treponema pallidum* is ordinarily highly sensitive to penicillin; the same is true in vivo provided that a high and rather even blood level is maintained.

Following a course of penicillin, the effects are gauged by serial studies of the patient's cerebrospinal fluid. Theoretically, the objective is to return the cerebrospinal fluid to normal in every respect. Actually, penicillin reverses the so-called "paretic formula" in the cerebrospinal fluid in the following order: white cell count, protein, gold curve, and serological reaction. It may require years to reverse the serological reaction, and indeed a positive serological test *may* be no more than a biochemical relic after successful therapy. Provided that all of the other features have returned to normal, one need not be greatly concerned with its persistence. Particular attention is given to the white cell count. If it has not returned to normal (under five leukocytes per cu. mm.) within six months, a second course of penicillin is given. The same procedure is followed, with a third course being given at the end of another six months, if necessary. It has been shown (Dattner) that the syphilitic infection can be eliminated in all cases through the repeated use of penicillin.

It should be realized that, unless the diagnosis is made and chemotherapy instituted very early in the course of the disease, the patient does not become well the moment the last organism has been destroyed. (In the case of Mr. W. B., for example, a six weeks' period of hospitalization was required.) As indicated in the diagram on page 280, the interference with cortical function has produced a disequilibrium of the personality. The executive forces of the personality have been weakened, various inner forces have been released, and a variety of pathogenic defense mechanisms have been called into play. The restoration of inner harmony requires time, and quite often, psychiatric assistance.

The principles governing this aspect of treatment are essentially the same as they would be if the psychological symptoms had developed in the absence of a brain infection. (See Chapters 13 and 14.) Thus, sedation may be required for insomnia, tranquilizing agents for excitement, electroconvulsive therapy for manic or severe depression reactions, etc. In addition, a supportive (p. 440) or relationship (p. 450) psychotherapy is often indicated to facilitate the patient's readjustment.

The degree of improvement which is possible depends largely upon the extent of destruction of brain tissue. If it has been great, there may be irreparable intellectual damage, in which case the patient must be helped to stabilize at a less ambitious level of adjustment than he had known before the illness. If it has been only slight, sufficient compensation (in the neurological sense) may take place to permit a full psychological readjustment, a return to the status quo ante. (This was true of Mr. W. B.)

The extent of improvement, however, also depends upon the premorbid personality structure of the patient. If this has been an essentially sound one, a satisfactory readjustment is favored; if there has been a pre-existing *neurosis* or other psychiatric illness (or the potentialities for it), the possibilities for a good functional recovery are more limited, even in the face of only mild to moderate cortical damage.

Largely as a result of the advent of penicillin, there has been a decided decrease in the incidence rate of dementia paralytica. For this reason, there is some tendency for physicians to think less promptly than formerly of this condition as a diagnostic possibility. Yet in view of the correlation of degree of possible improvement with the extent of irreversible brain damage in dementia paralytica, promptness in establishing the diagnosis and in instituting treatment is most important.

Arteriosclerotic Dementia (Psychosis with Cerebral Arteriosclerosis)

This condition may be defined as a *dementia, usually of old age, primarily based* upon irreversible degenerative changes in the blood vessels of the brain that interfere with the supply of oxygen and other nutrients to the neurons.* (It may be helpful for the reader to review, at this point, the material on psychological problems of old age, pp. 121 to 123.) As a corollary to the increasing life-span of the population, this disease is one of the few major psychiatric conditions in which the incidence is currently on the increase. Since a great many patients with this disorder do not reach psychiatric attention (many, indeed, not requiring it), an accurate estimate of its incidence is not possible, but if one includes mild forms, it is certainly great. Nearly 20 per cent of all first admissions to state psychiatric hospitals are diagnosed as having arteriosclerotic dementia.

The clinical picture of this disorder, in moderate form, is exemplified

---

* It is well, however, to keep in mind that brain arteriosclerosis may exist without dementia.

by Mr. H. M. (p. 275), the patient admitted for treatment of prostatic disease. The age of H.M. is somewhat atypical; although the age at onset of the illness is subject to considerable individual variation, the average age is about 60 years.

The manner of onset characteristically is rather insidious, but this feature may be altered by either of two circumstances. (1) In addition to the generalized atherosclerotic changes, the patient may experience a small stroke at a point of minimal circulation. (2) The patient may be called upon to make a rapid adjustment to some new situation. Whether the personality is suddenly weakened as a result of increased organic brain damage or whether it is suddenly called upon to increase its adjustment efforts, the net effect is often the same: the acute development of a relative inadequacy of mental resources, with the appearance of frankly psychotic symptoms. (The second possibility is exemplified in the case of Mr. H. M. whose adjustment showed a marked deterioration on his being admitted to the hospital from a sheltered home situation.)

Among the early indications of arteriosclerotic dementia are an impairment in the ability to concentrate, a fatigability at mental tasks, a decrease in general initiative, mild memory defects, irritability, and restlessness. To a varying degree, there is apt to be an awareness on the part of the patient that he is less alert and mentally fit than hitherto, and his awareness brings with it anxiety and shame and hence defensiveness. There is often an element of depression also, which tends gradually to increase as the disease progresses.

For a considerable length of time in the course of arteriosclerotic brain disease, there is apt to be a significant element of delirium along with the dementia. Perhaps the diminution in cerebral blood quantity and quality and the diminished permeability of the vessel walls bring about a state of anoxia and semistarvation of the cortical neurons preceding their actual destruction. It appears, moreover, that in the early stages the diminution in blood flow is due not entirely to a thickening of the walls of the vessels, but that it may, in part, be due to shifts in body demands, as in peripheral vasodilatation. These factors—the lowered functional capacity of large numbers of neurons which are still viable and the reversibility of one aspect of the vascular inadequacy—are likely to be responsible for the phenomenon of fluctuation in mental ability, which is, for a time, characteristic of patients with arteriosclerotic dementia. (This fluctuation, when fairly marked, is a point of differential diagnostic value, serving to help distinguish arteriosclerotic dementia from another diagnostic category in the official nomenclature, *psychosis with senile brain disease*. The latter condition is considered to be due to primary degenerative changes in the neurons themselves. It is about half as common as arteriosclerotic dementia. The conditions may coexist. Under present therapeutic limitations, the differentiation is primarily one of academic interest.)

Although one typically finds arteriosclerotic changes in the blood vessels of the eye grounds in arteriosclerotic dementia, positive physical findings are of only limited value in making the diagnosis. On the other hand, careful neurological and laboratory studies are decidedly indicated in order to rule out such conditions as *dementia paralytica* and *psychosis with brain tumor*.

As in dementia paralytica, the clinical picture of the developing illness is much influenced by the premorbid personality of the patient. If the individual's inner conflicts have not been severe, if his adjustment to life has been fundamentally a healthy one, the symptoms of his illness, to a large extent, will remain those of a "negative" sort, i.e., the loss of certain abilities. The likelihood of this being the case is enhanced if the environment is favorable, if the patient's situation is such that he receives a reasonable amount of affection and consideration and is not called upon to adapt to altered circumstances and to solve new problems.

Even under favorable conditions, however, the clinical picture of advancing dementia is complicated by the emotional *regression* which takes place. As noted in the discussion of problems of aging (pp. 121 to 123), a certain amount of regression is a rather usual feature of even a healthy old age, being a defense against certain inevitable anxieties of this period. If the individual's childhood has been a healthy one, the childishness of old age, whether hastened and accentuated by arteriosclerotic dementia or not, is not apt to be found objectionable, even though it exhibits such characteristics as rapid, mild alterations in mood, distractibility, talkativeness, an increase in self-centeredness, a mild obstinacy, and some slight disregard for social conventions.

However, if the patient's adult personality has been conflict-laden, or if the childhood toward which he regresses was a very stressful one, then, as the dementia intensifies, he is forced increasingly to utilize more pathogenic defenses, such as denial and projection. As in dementia paralytica, this circumstance results in the production of more florid symptoms, including delusions and hallucinations.

A picturesque and touching symptom frequently noted in arteriosclerotic dementia (and in various other organic brain reactions as well) is *confabulation*. This symptom is akin to delusion, but a bit more specific. Confabulation may be defined as *the filling in by the patient of memory gaps with detailed but inaccurate accounts, derived from fantasy, of his activities during the period in question*. The symptom is an (unconsciously motivated) attempt to ward off the anxiety and shame which are stimulated by the patient's failing memory and confusion. It is analogous to a healthy person's telling "a white lie" to cover up some point of embarrassment, but it differs in that it is actually believed by the patient at the time. Here are two examples, one mild and the other more severe.

A young woman and her grandmother are going out for the afternoon. The latter excuses herself and goes upstairs, intending to get a small present she has been keeping for her granddaughter. She forgets her purpose and returns without it. When asked what she has been doing, she replies that she had to brush her coat.

On the psychiatric service, an elderly man, suffering from a dementia on the basis of arteriosclerotic changes plus the toxic effects of mild but very chronic alcoholism, is asked (inappropriately) where he has spent the previous evening. After a moment of bewilderment, his face brightens and he replies, "Oh, I was with a bunch of the fellows at Joe's Bar. We were drinking beer and watching the fights on TV."

The neuropathological findings in cerebral arteriosclerosis vary considerably. There is no close correlation between the degree of cerebral damage and the clinical severity of the dementia*—another indication of the importance of the patient's fundamental personality organization in producing the symptoms. At autopsy, in cases in which the sclerotic process is widespread and advanced, a diffuse loss of brain substance is apparent. The convolutions of the brain show irregular outlines. Numerous areas of atrophy may be evident. In coronal sections of the hemispheres, one frequently sees an enlargement of the ventricular system, indicating that a passive expansion has taken place as the mass of brain tissue has diminished. Microscopically, one sees the fatty degeneration of the intima of the cerebral vessels with secondary increase in connective tissue. One notes that many of the neurons have undergone atrophic changes involving a deposition of lipids. There are numerous rarified areas in which the neurons have died, with varying degrees of glial replacement.

TREATMENT OF ARTERIOSCLEROTIC DEMENTIA. There is no etiologically based treatment of cerebral arteriosclerosis. Nevertheless, it is often possible to effect a considerable improvement in the patient's clinical status through a combination of therapeutic techniques. Indeed, since the clinical picture may be looked upon as the result of an interplay between the organic damage and psychological factors (causing an exaggeration of the common problems of old age), the use of certain psychological techniques may, in a sense, be considered to have an etiological basis.

---

* A partial exception to this statement is the relationship which exists between lesions in the hippocampus and memory loss.

If the patient is hospitalized, milieu therapy (p. 497), occupational therapy (p. 510), recreational therapy (p. 512), and supportive psychotherapy (p. 440) should all be employed. The first objective is to establish a meaningful contact with the patient, to get through the barrier established by his confusion, misunderstanding, and, quite often, suspicion. One attempts patiently to convey a considerate acceptance of the patient, despite the regressed basis on which he is likely to be functioning. It is often surprising and gratifying to see the degree of functional improvement which is possible notwithstanding the unchanged neuropathological state. Initially, one utilizes the resources of the hospital setting to create a sense of security and to gratify the patient's regressive needs. Gradually one offers, in as nonthreatening and persuasive a fashion as possible, increasingly mature types of gratifying experiences. Through the supportive relationships with understanding, noncritical personnel, and later with other patients, one may often be able to win the patient back from the considerable social isolation into which he has withdrawn. Occupational and recreational therapies further reduce tension by affording opportunities of sublimation (p. 75) of various sorts. From his study of the patient's personal history, the psychiatrist learns what the patient's most useful patterns of adjustment have been, and the re-establishment of these is fostered.

In many instances, hospitalization will not have been required; in many others, the patient will regain sufficient functioning capacity to return to his home. In both of these situations, the physician endeavors to work with the immediate family of the patient (and often with appropriate social agencies), to provide the understanding and the hope which enable such persons to meet the needs of the patient, to allow the patient a degree of latitude in his behavior, and to provide the required emotional support.

Psychological measures can often be supplemented—not replaced—by chemotherapeutic measures. For example, the judicious use of one or other of the tranquilizing agents (p. 455) may be of considerable value in reducing the anxiety and restlessness which are often prominent features. Delusions and hallucinations, if present, may also respond to such medication. Sometimes it is of value to combine the administration of a mood elevating drug (p. 459) or a mild central nervous system stimulant with the use of a tranquilizer, thus trying to allay the elements of fatigue and depression which are so often present.

The truth is that despite the continuing lack of a definite treatment for the arteriosclerosis, it is the rule, rather than the exception, that the patient's lot can be greatly improved, the clinical progression of his disease delayed, and its manifestations favorably altered.

Delirium Tremens

This condition is a serious complication of chronic alcoholism, and a rather frequent one if the alcoholism is severe. (Alcoholism itself is discussed on pp. 405 to 414.) The following excerpt from a case history illustrates some of the principal features.

Mr. G. S., aged 38, a bachelor, was brought to the hospital in an excited and confused state. The brief history obtainable from the friend who accompanied him was as follows: The patient had been a very heavy drinker for about ten years. Although functioning well below his potentialities, he had managed to remain employed for the most part. Three days before admission, G. S. had been discharged from his job and had immediately gone on a drinking spree, which had continued almost uninterruptedly. The afternoon of admission, the patient had fallen, in the presence of his friend, sustaining a Colles' fracture. He was taken to a neighborhood doctor, who had set the fracture and instructed the friend to take him home, get him to bed, and stay with him until he became sober.

This course was followed, but soon G. S. became tremulous and displayed mounting apprehension. Within a few hours, he became wildly confused. He repeatedly jumped out of bed, endeavored to continue drinking, and twice started to leave the house in his pajamas. He had fleeting moments of recognition, in which he understood where he was, with whom, and why, but for the most part, he was disoriented and did not recognize his friend.

Toward evening the patient began to experience visual hallucinations, and these persisted in the hospital. The hallucinations were of a frightening nature, consisting of the distorted shapes of "huge lizards with open mouths."

The precise etiology of delirium tremens is not certainly known. It is rather specifically related to the excessive consumption of alcohol; with the exception of the barbiturates (which are chemically related to alcohol), no other toxic agents are known which will produce the syndrome. Furthermore, it is dependent upon the heavy consumption of alcohol over a period of years. Delirium tremens seldom occurs in a person who has been an alcoholic for less than five years; more commonly, the duration of the alcoholism at the time of the first episode of delirium tremens is eight to ten years or more.

Unlike most other complications of severe alcoholism, delirium tremens is not due to avitaminosis (or to any other deficiency of nutritional intake), even though it is rather common for the patient to be malnourished. It appears to be the direct result of a prolonged interference by the alcohol with the metabolism of the neurons.

For a long time it was strongly believed that delirium tremens was usually precipitated by the abrupt cessation of heavy drinking in an habitual drinker. The weight of evidence then began to suggest that this was unlikely. It is true that a history of cessation of drinking shortly before the onset of hallucinations is often obtained, but this sequence has been thought often to be due to the fact that the premonitory symptoms (beginning confusion, disorientation, restlessness, anxious excitement) induced the patient to stop drinking. At the present time, there is some difference of opinion on this point. The most plausible view is that whereas abrupt cessation of drinking may contribute significantly to the onset of the syndrome, it is not a necessary feature.

Some concurrent event often appears to act as a precipitating factor in bringing on the delirium: physical trauma (as in the case of G. S.), an infection, or some form of psychic trauma.

The reason why some severe alcoholics repeatedly experience episodes of delirium tremens while others never have such an experience is not known. There exists the possibility that something in the personality make-up of the subject is a prerequisite for this particular type of toxic reaction to develop.

In recent years, with prompter diagnosis and with the advent of potent new therapeutic agents (the tranquilizers), the full-blown picture of delirium tremens is seen less frequently than before. Often treatment can be instituted while the condition is still a rather quiet affair, with good chances of eliminating the more florid features entirely. In such cases, the diagnosis is made on the history of alcoholism, including a recent or current bout of hard drinking, on the general features of an anxious delirium, and if there is a question, on the elimination of other etiological factors.

In the clinical picture of a fully developed delirium tremens, hallucinations are apt to be prominent. Visual hallucinations predominate. Auditory hallucinations are much less conspicuous; when they occur, they are fragmentary—as opposed to the more frequent and more extensive auditory hallucinations of another, less common complication of chronic alcoholism, *alcoholic hallucinosis.** Tactile hallucinations are fairly frequent, being perhaps related to the paresthesias which are often present. Illusions are very often experienced (p. 278).

Typically, the patient's mood is one of considerable anxiety; periods of depression are also quite frequent. The patient's behavior is, in general, impulsive and unpredictable.

The findings on physical examination are somewhat variable, de-

---

* Acute alcoholic hallucinosis is the only other disorder resulting from alcoholism which, like delirium tremens, is not due to a nutritional deficiency. In this condition, the physical manifestations of delirium tremens are absent as is the intellectual impairment.

pending upon the severity of the reaction, the presence or absence of concurrent physical illness, and the patient's general pre-morbid condition. As a rule, there is the odor of alcohol on the breath (although this is certainly not always true, since the episode may occur as long as several days after the last drink). The conjunctivae are injected. The pupils tend to be dilated and unstable in size. There are tremors of the tongue and lips and, more often than not, of the extremities as well. The speech is slurred. The pulse rate is always, and the temperature is usually, elevated.

There are no pathognomonic laboratory findings, but albuminuria is quite common.

In a rather high proportion of cases, some type of respiratory infection is present. The signs and symptoms of such a condition may be obscured to a degree by the more striking features of the delirium, but since a complication decidedly increases the gravity of the situation, it must be carefully sought.

TREATMENT OF DELIRIUM TREMENS. The treatment of a patient with delirium tremens should always be carried out in a hospital, for the sake of the constant surveillance which can be offered there. The patient should be attended by a nurse, by an experienced nurse's aid, or by a reliable member of the family at all times. In this way, impulsive, self-destructive actions, born of anxiety and disorientation, can be prevented or stopped, and, by the attendant's pointing out the realities of the situation, the frightening illusions and hallucinations can be reduced. If it is impossible for any reason to give the patient this amount of individual attention, he at least should be placed on an open ward as near the nurse's station as possible. A patient with delirium tremens should never be left alone in a private room.

The room (or corner of the ward) should be well lighted as another means of improving the patient's contact with reality. Dark or dimly lighted rooms increase the likelihood of disturbing illusions (e.g., mistaking shadows for sinister objects) and of visual hallucinations. Ideally, the room should be basically quiet, but it is often helpful for the person in attendance to attempt to talk with the patient, in this way preserving contact and offering reassurance. If conversations are necessary among personnel within earshot of the patient, they should be clear and distinct. Whispered consultations (between doctor and nurse, for example) should be scrupulously avoided to prevent the patient's suspicious misinterpretation of what he is able to hear.

Physiologically speaking, the problem is to restore the patient's metabolic equilibrium. The preponderance of medical opinion is that further alcoholic intake is contraindicated. If there is any evidence of infection, this should be treated promptly and with exceptional vigor.

Other measures depend upon the severity of the patient's delirium. If a degree of cooperation is possible, the patient is given a high fluid intake by mouth, and a high protein, high carbohydrate, low fat diet. If cooperation is, for the time being, not possible, the metabolic requirements are given through a stomach tube and parenterally (with every effort being made that such procedures be carried out in as non-threatening a manner as possible).

Mechanical restraints are to be avoided if at all possible. (Usually they can be avoided if the patient is properly attended.) Some chemical means of calming the patient is nearly always required. In most instances, the drug of choice is one of the phenothiazines (p. 456). Convulsions ("whiskey fits") occur in delirium tremens with sufficient frequency to make the administration of an anticonvulsant drug (e.g., dilantin) a routine preventive measure in some hospitals.

Delirium tremens can be a fatal disease. Apart from the effects of a serious intercurrent infection, death occurs from vasomotor collapse. If, despite the treatment measures outlined above, the patient's condition worsens, adrenocortical steroids and oxygen inhalation are administered.

Occasionally (as is also true of other deliria), a chronic mental illness of psychotic proportions appears as a sequel to severe delirium tremens. Such a psychosis may be either of an organic nature (e.g., *Korsakow's psychosis*, a form of dementia largely brought on by a secondary vitamin deficiency) or of a functional nature (e.g., *schizophrenic reaction, paranoid reaction*). In the latter instance, the subsequent treatment would not be affected by the mode of precipitation.

It may be mentioned at this point that severe chronic alcoholism, apart from clear-cut episodes of delirium tremens, may lead to a condition of simple dementia. The syndrome may present only general features, being diagnosable on the basis of the history and the exclusion of other dementing diseases. Sometimes there occurs a chronic psychotic state which is a blend of the features of a dementia with paranoid features.

Chronic Brain Syndrome Associated with Convulsive Disorder (Idiopathic Epilepsy)

A thorough discussion of the epileptic disorders is in the province of neurology, but a brief presentation of idiopathic epilepsy is in order here because of the psychiatric implications. The syndromes of epilepsy may be defined, simply, as *a group of clinical conditions produced by an abnormal excessive neuronal discharge within the central nervous system*. Although there is evidence that heredity can be a significant factor in the etiology of these conditions, this does not appear to be invariably the case. Furthermore, statistics indicate that nearly 10 per cent of the general population have electroencephalographic abnormalities similar to those found in epilepsy, whereas the overall incidence of the clinical disorder is but 0.5 per cent. In other words, even if it could be demonstrated that gene-born factors are a necessary cause in the production of epileptic disorders, it seems unlikely that they could be a sufficient cause.

It appears improbable that there exists any neuropathological basis for idiopathic epilepsy within the range of conventional microscopic techniques. It appears equally improbable that even long-standing epilepsy produces significant cerebral damage, per se.

While there are actually many shades of variation in the clinical syndromes of epilepsy, for the purposes of a brief presentation, it is of value to adhere to a consideration of the three principal types: *grand mal, petit mal,* and *psychomotor seizures (psychomotor equivalents).*

GRAND MAL SEIZURES. Characteristically, although not invariably, a grand mal seizure is preceded by premonitory symptoms called the "aura." This phase is of varying duration, lasting from seconds to days. It involves abnormal sensations, often visceral, which the patient himself usually comes to recognize as the prelude to a convulsion.

The next phase, one representing a state of decerebrate rigidity with loss of consciousness, is often ushered in by an involuntary, inarticulate vocalization, the "epileptic cry." If the aura has been absent or very brief, or if it has gone unrecognized or ignored, the patient will fall at this point. In the *tonic phase*, the trunk is in an extended position with the arms and legs adducted and the feet in plantar flexion. The eyes remain open; the pupils are dilated; the corneal and light reflexes are absent. Respiration is suspended, and the patient becomes cyanotic.

The tonic phase persists, on the average, for 15 to 30 seconds, and it is succeeded by a *clonic phase* of about double that duration. The clonic phase is characterized by an alternation, at first rapid but gradually slowing, between the marked generalized tonus of decerebrate rigidity and complete muscular relaxation. Respiration is resumed in the form of a series of automatic gasps, determined by the alternate contraction and relaxation of the thoracic musculature. Urinary and fecal incontinence may occur; the patient may bite his tongue involuntarily; and foamy saliva may appear on the lips.

Following the generalized convulsion, there is a period of deep muscular relaxation, characterized by transient neurological abnormalities (as, for example, fixation of the pupils to light and a Babinski sign), but otherwise resembling a profound sleep. Most commonly, the patient does not immediately regain consciousness, but actually sleeps for a period of time (varying from minutes to hours). The patient may awaken feeling drowsy and with a headache, but he may awaken feeling exceptionally well. Of course, the latter is not the case if injuries have been sustained during the seizure (tongue-biting, undue muscular strain, sprain, fracture, etc.). Furthermore, there may be a reaction of anxiety, shame, and/or guilt secondary to the patient's conscious recognition of what has occurred. The patient is, however, completely amnesic for the period of the seizure, itself.

There is considerable variability, in any given case, as to the length of time between seizures, and there is a still greater variability in this respect between one patient and another. Some individuals may experience but one or two seizures in a lifetime. With other persons, it may happen that a series of convulsive episodes will occur in rapid succession, perhaps separated by as small an interval as is measured in minutes. In such situations—called *status epilepticus*—recovery of a normal level of consciousness between seizures becomes impossible. Confusion during the intervals becomes marked. Usually there is a decided rise in body temperature. The patient becomes exhausted and eventually comatose. If a remission cannot be brought about rather promptly, death may ensue.

During a seizure, the electroencephalogram indicates a massive increase in the voltage of the brain waves. A single tracing taken during symptom-free periods need not reveal any abnormality; hence serial electroencephalograms are often necessary. Eventually tracings will show evidence of bursts of high-voltage activity, indicating the (abnormal) synchronous electrical discharge of large numbers of neurons.

PETIT MAL SEIZURES. The clinical picture of *petit mal*—in the great majority of instances, a disorder of childhood—is very different from that just described. A single episode lasts from one to about 30 seconds. During this period, the subject loses awareness of himself and his surroundings, and if he is engaged in any activity, he is likely to stop it. The eyes ordinarily remain open, but are unseeing. If the episode lasts but a few seconds, it may pass unnoticed by both the subject and any observers who may be present. If it lasts longer—or if it happens to occur at a critical moment, as in the course of a delicate activity or a serious conversation—it is apt to be noticeable, but it may be misunderstood. To the observer, the attack may appear to be mere absentmindedness. To the subject, the attack is felt as a disconcerting gap in his experiencing of events.

On the average, petit mal seizures occur with much greater frequency than grand mal. It is not unusual for an individual afflicted with this condition to experience attacks many times a day. As in grand mal, there is ordinarily a total amnesia for the seizure periods. (Infrequently, episodes of petit mal may occur so nearly continuously as to produce an extended period of confusion. This condition is termed *status epilepticus in petit mal*.) It is a curious fact that, in some cases, episodes of petit mal can be halted by a strong external stimulus, as for example, shouting the patient's name.

The electroencephalographic tracing of a patient experiencing petit mal attacks is characteristic, consisting of marked elevations in voltage of very brief duration alternating with longer-lasting, more moderate elevations, the so-called "spike and dome" pattern.

PSYCHOMOTOR SEIZURES. The third principal form taken by convulsive disorders (much less common than the other two) is that of *psychomotor seizures (psychomotor equivalents, temporal lobe epilepsy, twilight states)*. This type is practically never seen in children; it is sometimes erroneously diagnosed in children, being confused with partial seizures (a form of grand mal). Psychomotor epilepsy is often ushered in by an aura, similar to that in cases of grand mal. It is of highly variable duration, lasting from a few minutes to a few days. Typically, the patient becomes a sort of automaton, retaining control of his motor apparatus, but losing the ability to exercise his habitual judgment regarding his activities. In this state, the patient may carry out rather complicated behavioral sequences of a sort quite foreign to his personality when consciously integrated. (For example, the patient may leave home, obtain transportation, and travel aimlessly to a distant city.)

This condition is potentially an exceedingly dangerous one. Without warning, the patient may enter an enraged state, the "epileptic furor," in which he may lash out savagely at anyone in his environment in the complete absence of provocation. (This is, however, particularly likely to occur if attempts are made to restrain the patient.)

As in grand mal and petit mal, the patient is subsequently totally amnesic for events occurring during the attack.

The electroencephalogram is almost always abnormal during such an episode, although the nature of the abnormality varies. Serial electroencephalographic studies during a period of clinical normality will usually yield evidence of a dysrhythmia.

PSYCHOLOGICAL FACTORS IN PRODUCTION AND DIAGNOSIS OF EPILEPTIC ATTACKS. Psychological factors need to be taken into account (1) in the production of epileptic attacks, (2) in the differential diagnosis, and (3) in the treatment. The first and second of these aspects will be briefly discussed here, and the third will be mentioned under the next subheading.

There is a good bit of evidence to suggest that chronic emotional tensions tend to increase the frequency of grand mal attacks. It also appears likely that individual attacks can be triggered by a sudden increase in such tensions. This effect is probably nonspecific in the main, but the commonest sequence of this sort is one in which a grand mal attack is immediately preceded by the mobilization of anger (only partly conscious) due to a sense of unjust restriction or constraint.

Episodes of petit mal are well known to occur with greater frequency in settings in which the subject feels bored. The significance of this correlation is not clear, although it is known that children with petit mal tend to measure a bit higher intellectually than their peers who are free from the disorder.

Diagnostically speaking, two important problems in differentiation are: (a) grand mal seizures from hysterical convulsions (conversion reactions), and (b) psychomotor seizures from dissociative reactions.

Electroencephalographic studies, if they are thorough, are of great help in both problems. It is, however, important to realize that they may not be conclusive. A single normal electroencephalographic tracing proves nothing. Repeated normal tracings, with the utilization of various technical procedures to bring out latent dysrhythmias, constitute strong evidence against the existence of an epileptic disorder. On the other hand, positive electroencephalographic findings, while they point in the direction of an epileptic disorder, do not actually prove it. For one thing, as has been mentioned, about 10 per cent of the population can show, at times, a degree of cerebral dysrhythmia (whereas only 0.5 per cent of the population experiences clinical epilepsy). For another, the existence of a cerebral dysrhythmia is no guarantee against the simultaneous occurrence of a conversion reaction.

The differentiation of a grand mal seizure from an hysterical seizure on purely clinical grounds may be a matter of weighing probabilities also, but since the weight of the various factors is cumulative, it is usually possible to arrive at a definite opinion. In general, one can say that the following clinical features argue for a grand mal seizure as against an hysterical seizure (conversion): (a) the absence of a clear-cut precipitating event, (b) the occurrence of an aura, (c) falling at the onset of the seizure in such a way that the subject is bruised or otherwise injured, (d) the occurrence of seizures when the patient is alone, (e) the sequence of well-marked tonic and clonic phases, (f) the total duration of the seizure being less than two minutes, (g) tongue-biting during the seizure, (h) urinary and/or fecal incontinence during the seizure, and (i) fixation of the pupils to light and a Babinski sign immediately after the seizure. (Of these points, tongue-biting, fecal incontinence and the neurological findings in the immediate post-convulsive phase are particularly weighty indications favoring the diagnosis of epileptic seizure.)

The strongest argument for the diagnosis of conversion reaction exists when the episode can be psychologically formulated (p. 317), i.e., when a detailed evaluation of the patient indicates that the behavior is symbolically meaningful. Even this argument, however, is not ironclad since an epileptic seizure, like other organic symptoms, may *acquire* a symbolic meaning which played no part in the pathogenesis.

The differentiation of a psychomotor seizure from a dissociative reaction rests principally upon the following points: (a) the electroencephalographic findings, (b) the aura, (c) the reaching of a state of furor (which may or may not occur in the course of a psychomotor seizure, but which has no real counterpart in dissociative reaction), (d) a history of convulsive seizures, and (e) the absence of the clear-cut (although unconscious) motivational features of a dissociative reaction (p. 322).

TREATMENT OF EPILEPTIC DISORDERS. The treatment of epileptic disorders involves both chemical and psychological components, and it varies, depending upon the syndrome presented and the personality of the patient. Three families of drugs are of primary value: the barbiturates, the hydantoins, and the "diones." One or another member of these groups of drugs is efficacious in the control of seizures in most instances. All of them, however, are capable of producing undesirable side-effects in susceptible individuals, and the drug of choice, in any particular case, may have to be established on the basis of repeated trials.

At the present time, Dilantin, one of the hydantoins, is the drug most often chosen to initiate the treatment of grand mal epilepsy (as well as that of most of the minor seizures other than classical petit mal). Dilantin can cause a marked hypertrophy of the gums, particularly in children, and for this reason may have to be replaced. Mesantoin (of the same chemical family) may be substituted; it, however, will occasionally produce a severe skin eruption. Phenobarbital and Mysoline are the other drugs of particular effectiveness, but in heavy doses, phenobarbital may produce considerable drowsiness, and Mysoline, an undesirable sense of fatigue.

It is the exceptional case of grand mal in which one of these agents will not produce a considerable therapeutic effect without (or with a tolerable minimum) of the unwanted side-effect. In such an instance, the usual procedure is to use two of the drugs in combination, since the therapeutic effect is additive, while the side-effect is much less likely to be so.

The regulation of the dosage of these preparations is an important matter. It should be guided not merely by a sustained period of clinical observation, but by a series of electroencephalographic studies. The objective should be to bring the patient as close as possible to a state of both clinical and neurophysiological normality.

In the treatment of petit mal, the drug of choice is Tridione, an oxazolidinedione. In most instances, this drug is markedly effective. If it is not, another member of the same chemical family, such as Paradione, may occasionally be helpful. Sometimes it is necessary to add phenobarbital to an oxazolidinedione to achieve the maximum therapeutic effect. (Since Tridione and Paradione can be quite toxic, it is sometimes necessary to substitute phenobarbital.) Occasionally the addition of racemic amphetamine in small doses is also of value.

The chemotherapy of patients with psychomotor seizures usually involves a combination of a hydantoin with an amphetamine, most often, Dilantin and Dexedrine.

The psychological aspects of the management of patients with epileptic disorders is of considerable importance. Indeed, instances are known in which intensive and prolonged psychotherapy was a prerequisite to improvement. Such a course is, as a rule, unnecessary, but for optimum therapeutic results, it is usually necessary to take into account certain emotional responses of the patient. In addition, particularly since the onset of the disorder is predominantly during childhood and adolescence,* it is usually necessary to deal with emotional responses of the patient's family as well.

Despite the vigorous and extensive educational efforts of the past several decades, convulsive disorders, particularly in the grand mal form, continue to elicit disturbing emotions. Quite often, epilepsy is perceived by patient and family as a kind of disgrace. The patient is apt to feel anxious about and deeply ashamed of his difficulty; the parents share these feelings and, in addition, are apt to feel a sense of guilt and often (although this is usually unconscious) a degree of anger at the patient.

In untreated cases and in cases which have received some chemical treatment, but in which these various emotions have not been brought into the open and dealt with, patterns of interaction are very likely to be set up between the patient and his family and between the patient and other figures in his environment which contribute as much (or more) to his maladjustment as do the seizures per se. In fact, a vicious cycle may be set up in which the seizures lead the parents to adopt a morbid way of handling the total situation, a way which heightens inner tensions in the patient to the point of increasing the frequency of the seizures. The patient's anxiety and shame at his illness are accentuated at his sensing of the family's negative reactions, and a deep rift may

---

* All cases combined, in three instances out of four, idiopathic epilepsy has its onset before the age of 21 (Lennox).

develop between patient and family, making helpful communication difficult or impossible. The family's disturbing emotions may lead them, on the one hand, to place numerous restrictions on the patient's life, and on the other, to pamper him excessively. The restrictions tend to interfere with the patient's social development and the parental pampering tends to stimulate the patient's dependency needs unduly and to reduce his initiative. In these various ways, the very psychological factors which have been clinically noted to increase the likelihood of seizures—a rebellion against constraint and an oppressive sense of boredom—are enhanced.

It is clearly the physician's responsibility in the treatment of a convulsive disorder to do everything in his power to prevent the development of such a situation (if the patient is seen at the outset) or, if it has already developed, to restore a healthier atmosphere. The patient and the family should be encouraged to express openly to the doctor their disturbing emotions. Certain measures of a supportive, reassuring, and educational nature can then be used. It can be emphasized that the development of the disorder is not anyone's fault. It can be stated categorically that a convulsive disorder, in itself, does not lead to any sort of deterioration of the brain. It can be brought out that the potentiality of developing a seizure—in the presence of sufficiently strong stimulation—is built into the human nervous system and so exists in everyone. It can be emphasized that with a proper adjustment of medication and with the family's learning to adopt a relaxed attitude the prospects are good for the patient's being able to lead an essentially normal life.

In milder cases and in cases in which the family is already responding to the illness in a mature fashion, adequate anticonvulsant medication alone may yield satisfactory results. In most instances, however, it is indicated to review carefully the patient's and the family's reactions to the illness and to offer opportunity for the ventilation of emotions as well as clarification of specific issues. Counselling and adjustment of the medication go hand in hand. A lowering of the tensions in the household will usually make the medication more effective, and increasing control of the seizures through medication tends to help the family relax, as their anxiety and feelings of guilt are reduced.

Speaking generally, there are very few restrictions which need interfere with a well-controlled epileptic's having a normal pattern of childhood and adolescent experiences. Nearly all ordinary social, cultural, and athletic pursuits may be followed. (Some exceptions: swimming should be confined to shallow water in the company of a good swimmer; driving a car should be postponed until it is established that seizures are completely controlled during waking hours.)

It is well established that a particular kind of diet (the "ketogenic diet") may have an anticonvulsant effect, and there is a strong general impression that certain matters of general hygiene, such as getting plenty of sleep, are of considerable value. Yet the possibility of reinforcing the family's anxiety and need to control the situation and the patient's sense of undue constraint by advocating such measures must be carefully weighed against their intrinsic benefit in any given case.

In the older psychiatric and neurologic literature, reference was frequently made to what was called the *epileptic personality* and to a condition, developing after the disorder had been in existence for a number of years, called *epileptic deterioration* or *epileptic dementia*. Characteristics of the epileptic personality were said to be dullness, sullenness, irascibility, self-centeredness, and various antisocial tendencies. The psychosis of epileptic deterioration was described as a condition in which comprehension, memory, and other intellectual processes were impaired and emotional responses were blunted. There was said to be a considerable degree of withdrawal from the figures in the patient's environment, with a breakdown in the ability to communicate.

Nowadays, reference is seldom made to "the epileptic personality" and *psychosis with cerebral dysrhythmia* ("epileptic dementia") is diagnosed less frequently. It appears that the former condition is largely in the nature of an artifact, and the latter, partially so. When the patients are under proper treatment, the personalities of epileptics show nearly as much variation as do those of a comparable group of nonepileptics. Under adequate treatment, including regulation of the social environment, psychosis with cerebral dysrhythmia seldom develops.

While it is still plausible that the underlying causes of epilepsy *may* ultimately produce a dementia, it seems evident that the fundamental neurophysiological difficulty has less to do with the development of an abnormal personality or with a psychotic mode of behavior than have the psychological responses of the patient, or his family, and of society, to his experiencing repeated seizures.

Another factor in this altered picture appears to be that formerly a certain proportion of cases diagnosed as "epileptic dementia" or "deterioration" were actually instances of chronic barbiturate intoxication (and, at an earlier date, of chronic bromide intoxication). With the diminished and more careful use of such medication, this element has declined, and with the development of electroencephalography, it is more easily recognized.

Psychiatric Disorders Associated with Head Trauma

There is a tremendous range as to severity and as to details of the symptom-picture among psychiatric conditions following trauma to the head. There is, further, an interweaving of organic and functional components which is often quite subtle and complicated. A thorough elucidation of the pathogenesis of certain syndromes following head trauma is best reserved to the field of neurosurgery, but a number of points of psychiatric relevance may be presented here.

Possibly the most important statement to be made in the present context is one in the nature of a caution or reservation: among lay persons, undue and misleading significance is apt to be attached to the experiencing of head trauma, however slight, in evaluating the subsequent development of psychiatric illness. This phenomenon appears to have two principal bases. On the one hand, the head (like the eyes, the genitals, and women's breasts) is a part of the body which has exceptionally great emotional significance. That is to say, a great deal of an individual's self-esteem, of his narcissism (p. 99), whether normal or excessive, is involved in the preservation of the integrity of this part of the body. Regardless of physical consequences, any injury to the head is apt to be perceived as a serious threat. On the other hand, the attributing of subsequent personality difficulties or symptoms to a minor head injury (something which nearly everyone has experienced at one time or another) is a rather effective way in which patients and particularly patients' relatives may divest themselves of the sense of responsibility which might otherwise attend a consideration of intimate details of the personal history.

This is not at all to say that mention of injury to the head should be disregarded, or even that the physician should not, on occasion, seek to elicit it. Such an episode may be of key importance in making the correct diagnosis of a psychiatric and/or neurological disorder, as in some of the conditions to be mentioned below. The point is that, in most instances, the etiological inquiry should not stop with the elucidation of this aspect, nor linger upon it any longer than is necessary.

It is important to recognize that a blow to the head may involve no physical damage whatever and yet play a part in the etiological sequence leading to a psychiatric syndrome. A prime example of such a situation occurs when the blow (usually in association with other circumstances of a disturbing nature) triggers a *traumatic neurosis* (pp. 151 to 153 and pp. 308 to 310), a disorder which, in turn, may activate a true *psychoneurosis* or *psychosis* (pp. 272 to 274). In cases of this kind, it is the *meaning* of the victim's experience—which need not depend upon pathophysiological or structural alterations—which constitutes the trauma.

Physical alterations of the brain associated with trauma to the head are usually considered in three categories: *(cerebral) concussion, contusion,* and *laceration.* Concussion may be defined as *a transient state, of instantaneous onset, due to head injury that has momentarily changed physical conditions in the brain (especially pressure) without causing actual structural damage.* Contusion is *the condition in which diffuse, fine structural damage, such as the rupture of tiny blood vessels, has occurred in the brain as the result of head trauma.* Laceration is *the gross tearing or rupture of brain tissue.*

If the case is one of concussion only (as, for example, may often happen in the boxing ring or on the football field), the subject will experience a transient phase of unconsciousness, lasting from several seconds to several minutes, followed by a phase of from several minutes to several hours in duration, during which there is some degree of confusion and disorientation. (At this time, the patient suffers from a type of delirium.) Fairly often, the patient will remain amnesic for the event immediately preceding the loss of consciousness.

If the concussion has been quite mild, no treatment is indicated save informal observation over perhaps the next 24 hours. If it has been more severe (as judged primarily by the duration of the phases of unconsciousness and confusion), the conventional treatment is to place the patient at bed rest in the hospital with arrangements for routine checking of pulse, respiration, and blood pressure, and medical observation for the possible development of complications.

It is under the latter circumstances that the activities of doctors and nurses may inadvertently contribute to the production of unnecessary anxiety in the patient, anxiety which may result in the accentuation of symptoms or even in the patient's becoming something of an invalid (through the mobilization of neurotic defense mechanisms).

For example, repeated inquiries, made in a grave tone of voice, as to the presence of a headache (or its precise nature and location, if present) have been known to encourage the development of a persistent headache having no direct relationship to the physical trauma which was the basis for the hospitalization. It is thus important that determination of the vital signs should be made in as relaxed, casual, and unimpressive a fashion as possible, and that other observations be, for the most part, indirect. Such questioning of the patient as is really necessary should be done in a brief, simple, and matter-of-fact way. Undue restrictions on the patient's freedom of movement should be avoided.

If the physical injury has caused cerebral contusion and/or laceration, the clinical picture will ordinarily be much more severe and the diagnostic and therapeutic problems more complicated. Even here it is possible that the resulting syndrome may have a large psychogenic element, i.e., it may partake to a considerable extent of the nature of a *traumatic neurosis.* On the other hand, following the acute phase, it may consist largely or entirely of organically based symptomatology (e.g., *traumatic epilepsy*). It is commoner, however, for the clinical picture to involve a combination of organic and psychogenic elements. Various terms have been used to designate the chronic brain syndromes which are associated with brain trauma, of which the principal ones are *post-traumatic personality disorder* and *post-traumatic personality defect.*

The former syndrome is usually characterized by such symptoms as emotional instability, headaches, dizziness, irritability, vasomotor instability, a relative intolerance of external stimuli, impaired concentration, and an impairment of judgment and discrimination in their finer aspects. In other words, the syndrome combines features of traumatic neurosis with features of a mild dementia.

Post-traumatic personality defect is apt to involve similar features, but it is further characterized by a serious incapacitation in one or more specific functions (e.g., an apraxia or an aphasia).

A complication of the diagnostic—and therefore of the therapeutic—problem in the management of post-traumatic conditions is the circumstance that the question of compensation (often including litigation) may be involved. In that portion of the diagnostic appraisal which takes place after the acute phase, it may become important to attempt to distinguish between conversion reaction (p. 312), organically based symptom, and malingered complaint (p. 145).

Hypnotic techniques are sometimes of value here, but they must be used thoughtfully. If *loss of function*—let us say, visual impairment or paresis of the muscles of deglutition—can be restored under hypnotic suggestion, this is very strong evidence of a psychogenic etiology. On the other hand, if complaints of pain, discomfort, or paresthesia are removed under hypnosis, this does not constitute evidence as to etiology. (Hypnosis cannot make good the effects of the destruction of neurons, but it can suppress morbid stimulation, whether this be psychologically or neurologically based.) If the symptoms are malingered, the commonest finding is that the subject is refractory to the hypnotic procedure.

Aside from such neurosurgical measures as may be indicated (see reference at end of chapter), the therapeutic management of post-traumatic brain reactions involves a combination of the measures described under the treatment of dementia and traumatic neurosis (p. 308).

Suggestions for Further Reading

Arieti, S. (ed.): American Handbook of Psychiatry, Vol. 2, **Part 8:** Organic conditions, New York, Basic, 1959.
Wilson, S. A. K., and Bruce, A. N.: Neurology (3 vols.), pp. 535-553, 1402-1412, and 1609-1679, Baltimore, Williams & Wilkins, **1955.**

CHAPTER 9

The Neuroses

As the student has learned, in considering the etiology of most forms of illness it is useful to distinguish between *precipitating* and *predisposing* factors. Thus, in the case of Mr. M. (p. 186), one might say that constitutional factors having to do with his physiology of digestion plus the early development of oral-dependent needs somewhat in excess of normal, constituted the predisposing factors, while the inconsiderate behavior of his daughter-in-law and, possibly, dietary changes constituted the precipitating factors. The combination of the two sets of factors resulted in the development of the peptic ulcer. Characteristically there is a *complementary relationship* between precipitating and predisposing factors, such that the greater the contribution of the one set is, the less the contribution of the other set need be to produce the illness.

There are some forms of illness to which all human beings are predisposed, merely by reason of being what they are (members of a particular mammalian species). One example is degenerative disease of the vascular system. Of course, some individuals do not survive long enough to develop signs of such disease, and among those who do, there is great variation as to time of onset and severity.* Yet, no matter how favorable his life circumstances may have been, no human being reaches really advanced age without some indication of vascular degenerative processes.

Neurosis† is another example of a state of illness to which everyone is in some degree predisposed merely because he is a human being, a creature with a mind whose adaptive capacities are not unlimited trying to make his way in a very complex world. The extent of this predisposition, however, varies widely from one individual to another, and there is an equal range of severity among possible precipitating factors.

It is customary to differentiate between two classes of neuroses on the basis of the relative significance of precipitating and predisposing

---
* As there are racial and ethnic variations.
† For a definition of the term, see discussion on pp. 272 to 274.

factors. In the case of an essentially healthy personality succumbing to extraordinary environmental stress (physical, emotional, or a combination of the two) the illness is called a *traumatic neurosis*. (See pp. 151 to 153.) In the case of a personality which is basically rather unhealthy succumbing to mild or moderate stress (as judged by ordinary standards), the illness is called a *psychoneurosis*.*

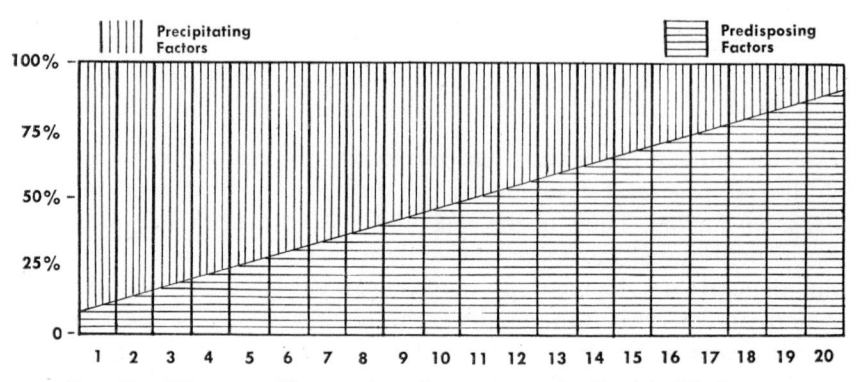

FIG. 3. Diagram illustrating the reciprocal relationship between precipitating and predisposing factors in the production of psychiatric illness. One could arrange a series of patients having the same symptom picture in the order of increasing proportion of predisposing stress to total stress. In the above series, Patients 1, 2 and 3 would represent typical traumatic neuroses, and Patients 18, 19 and 20 would represent typical psychoneuroses. (In civilian practice, the various psychoneuroses outnumber the traumatic neuroses by more than ten to one, a fact not represented in this diagram.)

TRAUMATIC NEUROSES

In ordinary civilian practice, it is somewhat unusual to see a patient who has been the victim of environmental stress of such severity as to bring on a traumatic neurosis. However, the occurrence of such natural disasters as fire, flood, earthquake, and hurricane, and sometimes of disasters on a smaller scale, such as automobile accidents, occasionally requires a physician to examine and treat patients suffering from traumatic neurosis. In military practice (during wartime) the incidence of this disorder is rather high. The following very typical example illustrates the condition.

H. R. was a young infantryman in a combat division during the Korean War. His personal background was not remarkable. His record

---

* When the term *neurosis* is used without qualification, it is ordinarily understood as referring to *psychoneurosis*.

at school and in the civilian job he had formerly held had been good. He was considered to be a competent soldier, and he had received two promotions during his 18 months in service. He had a friend, who was actually his closest buddy, but with whom he carried on a certain amount of rivalry.

The outfit was called upon to defend an advanced position against an enemy assault. In the course of the action, H. R. neglected to take cover promptly during heavy mortar fire, and he was saved from an exploding shell by his buddy, who threw him to the ground. His friend was killed instantly by the shell fragments.

H. R. lost consciousness at the explosion. Still in a dazed condition, he was later found by medical corpsmen and was removed first to a battalion aid station and then to a hospital behind the line.

The patient was found to have sustained no physical injury (beyond perforation of one ear drum), but he was completely incapacitated by the experience. He was sweating and tremulous. His blood pressure was labile, and his pulse rate tended to remain faster than normal. He was restless, unable to sit still for longer than a few minutes. He had lost his appetite and had to be coaxed and, at first, even assisted to eat. He showed a marked startle reaction: he would jump and become muscularly tense all over at any unexpected sound, however slight. On several occasions when there was a louder noise, such as a door slamming, he threw himself under the nearest bed. He was insomnic and required heavy sedation.

After several weeks these symptoms diminished in intensity, and other aspects of the traumatic neurosis became apparent. The patient was full of self-reproach, condemning himself for having been a poor soldier and having caused the death of his friend. He suffered from repetitive nightmares, in which he would relive the battle experience in vivid detail and from which he would awaken screaming.

Gradually, in response to a supportive treatment program that included talks with a psychiatrist, medication, and a rather heavy schedule of various planned activities, H. R. recovered. After two months, he was able to return to duty.

How is such a reaction to be explained? As a starting-point, one may recall the basic functional significance of mind: to effect adjustment (see pp. 29 to 31). In its executive aspects, the mind is called upon to bring about a continuing series of working compromises between the pressures exerted by the basic drives, the pressures exerted by the environment, and the pressures exerted by that inner monitor, the conscience. An increase in pressure from any of these quarters—if it is very great—can tax the executive functions of the mind beyond their capacities. If, in addition to being very great, the increase in pressure is also very sudden, the result can be not merely maladjustment, but a kind of inner choas. The subject is not merely in disequilibrium with his environment, but the executive faculties of his mind are thrown into a functional disarray. Continuing to speak figuratively, one may say that not only is the mind, for the time being, incapable of mastering the situation, it is incapable of *setting about the process* of mastering the situation.

Prior to the battle experience, H. R. was in a relatively good state of mental health. The executive faculties of his mind (perceptive, integrative, motor) were in good working order. Predisposition to entering a state of mental decompensation was minimal. The case history therefore illustrates the truth of the old saying, "Every man has his breaking point." The clinical picture shown by the patient can be understood as a series of incoordinated, emergency responses to overwhelming stress. They included fainting, hyperactivity of the sympathetic division of the autonomic nervous system, and a morbid and inappropriate hyperalertness (at the hospital). None of these early responses was really adaptive.* (Or, to express the situation somewhat differently, one might say that this was a case of "adaptation running wild.")

On the other hand, the nightmares, while painful and not immediately adaptive, were nevertheless among the first steps in the direction of a restored equilibrium. Studies of many such cases indicate that the nightmares represent an attempt to absorb the shock of the traumatic experience, to relive the experience in imagination over and over again until it can be integrated within the personality, thus achieving what has been called "a belated mastery" of the situation.

Ordinarily, in patients such as H. R., whose personalities have developed along essentially normal lines and are free from long-standing, powerful inner tensions, an effective adjustment is reestablished after a period of time. (The time can be shortened—as in the case of H. R.— by prompt treatment, but the readjustment would usually take place in any event.) On the contrary, if the personality has not reached a normal maturity, if it is chronically weakened by inner conflicts, then the overthrow of the executive functions at the moment of intense stress may allow these conflicts to get out of hand. In such a case, as the personality begins to rally from the trauma, it is called upon not merely to "get over" a recent bad experience, but to deal with the newly intensified inner conflicts. Frequently the personality is unable to do this, and the result is the development of a true *psychoneurosis*, a chronic emotional illness that is kept going from within.

THE PSYCHONEUROSES

As indicated in the diagram on page 308, the relative contributions to the illness of the predisposing factors (the personal immaturities

---

* To a limited extent, the fainting may be considered an exception to this statement, inasmuch as it protected the subject from receiving additional horrifying sensory impressions.

and the inner conflicts) and of the precipitating factors (the immediate traumatic events) vary by almost imperceptible degrees from one patient to another. Thus one can see that the designation of one emotional illness as a traumatic neurosis and another as a psychoneurosis, although clinically useful in the extreme cases, is actually arbitrary. An experience is traumatic, psychologically speaking, when it produces a stress which exceeds the solution-finding capacity of the individual personality at the time it takes place. In this broad sense, one can find a precipitating trauma at the point of clinical onset of a great majority of psychoneuroses if one looks carefully enough. (In instances where this seems not to be the case, a frequent explanation is that the pressure of one or more of the inner drives has mounted to the point at which quite ordinary external circumstances have become too much to manage. An example would be the onset of a neurotic difficulty in connection with the hormonal alterations at puberty.)

Just as there is no sharp demarcation between traumatic neuroses and psychoneuroses, so within the diagnostic category of psychoneuroses the various syndromes merge and blend. For the purposes of an initial presentation it is of value to select cases which come as close as possible to illustrating the various forms of psychoneurotic reaction "in pure culture." In considering the material which follows, however, it is important for the student to keep in mind that there has been this process of selection and that in actual practice it is very common to find that a psychoneurotic patient will not fall neatly into a single category.

Anxiety Reaction

In Chapter 3, the experience of anxiety was discussed and an example was given (p. 67) of a young patient experiencing an *anxiety attack*. The clinical picture, although usually a milder one, is quite similar to that of a traumatic neurosis. The major point of difference between the two conditions lies in fact that the anxiety attack has nothing to do with an external situation of real danger; it has to do with a sense of danger threatening from within the personality. This "danger"—in the case cited, the mounting pressure of sexual impulses—cannot be consciously identified by the patient, who regards his disturbing emotional state as inexplicable.

The term *anxiety reaction* refers to a more or less chronic emotional illness, characterized by the constant presence of a degree of anxiety which is in excess of normal, and, as a rule, by the development, from time to time, of actual anxiety attacks. Between these acute episodes, the anxiety may make itself known through such symptoms as restlessness, insomnia, irritability, general dissatisfaction and discomfort, and some impairment of the ability to concentrate.

If one reviews the whole clinical picture of this condition, one finds that the symptoms are divisible into two categories. The first comprises such elements as the feeling frightened, the increase in pulse rate and respiratory effort, the sweating, and the insomnia. All of these symptoms are direct manifestations of the anxiety, itself. The second category comprises such elements as the irritability and the impaired concentration. These symptoms are not expressions of anxiety, per se, but rather expressions of what might be called psychological fatigue. That is to say, so much of the energy of the personality is involved in the unconscious inner conflict (productive of the anxiety) that there is insufficient energy left over to deal with current situations gracefully or efficiently.

Depending upon the nature of these conflicts, the degree of repression which bars them from consciousness, and the general resourcefulness of the patient's personality, is the seriousness of the illness. An anxiety reaction may be quite amenable to treatment or it may be quite refractory.* In either case, however, there is a certain simplicity about the formation of its symptoms which is in contrast to the more elaborate phenomena seen in the other psychoneuroses.

Conversion Reaction

In its milder forms, this type of psychoneurotic reaction is fairly common; an understanding of this condition, in both mild and severe manifestations, is of considerable importance to physicians in general practice and in nonpsychiatric specialties, for it may be a source of real distress to the patient and it may offer differential diagnostic problems of some complexity.

As an introduction to a discussion of conversion reaction, or conversion hysteria, as it is sometimes called, one may consider the spontaneous somatic manifestations of any sudden affect. Let us take the everyday, normal phenomenon of blushing.

A group of highschool boys are telling sexual jokes. A lively but refined girl unexpectedly happens to join the group just as a story is being concluded whose implications are based on the double meaning of a key word. The girl blushes markedly as the "punch line" of the joke is reached.

The physiology of blushing involves skin changes depending on a rather sudden dilatation of the venules forming the subpapillary venous

---

* A preliminary statement about the treatment of the psychoneuroses will be offered at the end of the present chapter, with a more detailed explanation of various treatment modalities being given in Chapters 13 and 14.

plexus in response to an increase in blood flow coming through the arterioles of the skin. The latter vessels are primarily under sympathetic control. In blushing, cortical impulses are relayed to the hypothalamus, gain in momentum there, and are sent to a control center in the medulla oblongata, where they act on the midline portion of the center, exerting an inhibitory effect on the sympathetic outflow. In this way the ordinary degree of constriction of the skin arterioles is relaxed.*

Blushing occurs automatically and unconsciously, though in response to an ideational-emotional stimulus. It is only when afferent fibers bring information as to the alteration in skin temperature (seconds later) that the subject knows that he is blushing. As a matter of fact, at the present time, when "sophistication" is so highly prized among young persons, there is often a rather strong conscious wish not to blush.

Perhaps the most interesting feature of blushing is that it carries a message; it is (among other things) a form of expression and communication. Indeed, in most situations, including the episode just cited, blushing conveys a double message. These meanings can, in fact, be (approximately) translated into words. In the above illustration, the young girl by her blushing expresses some such idea as the following: "I am a proper young lady. My mind is not on sexual matters. You should not speak in this way in my presence." However, since it is perfectly clear to the subject and to the others that the blushing would have to have depended upon the joke's being understood, the reaction also conveys the message: "I am not so innocent. I get the point of your story."

As one can readily see, this line of interpretation of the significance of blushing involves nothing mysterious or subtle. In the situation just described (and the same would be true of most other sudden affective responses), the participants would intuitively understand all of this, and would probably act accordingly. That is to say, the boys would "kid" the girl about her blushing. If one of the boys were really quite fond of the girl and desirous of her good opinion, he might even blush, himself.

Further evidence of the correctness of this sort of interpretation of blushing derives from the fact that ordinarily blushing occurs only in the most conspicuous portion of the surface of the body, the face. (The area of the flush varies, however, from one individual to another and with the depth of the emotions aroused. In a sensitive person who is feeling deep shame, the flush may extend to involve the neck, upper chest, and shoulders.) Then, too, as one can verify from his own ex-

---

* Whether or not vasodilator fibers are involved is at present a moot point.

perience, blushing very seldom occurs in situations in which it cannot be seen (in the dark, or in talking over the telephone), even when the appropriate emotions are aroused.

Even simpler examples of the use of "body language" may be found in such common phenomena as spontaneous laughter or crying. In laughter, for example, what begins as a purely psychic experience (amusement) is automatically *converted* into certain physical effects: movements of the diaphragm, the glottis, facial muscles, etc. And, of course, laughter has a meaning: The situation is funny! As a matter of fact, the chief difference between spontaneous emotional expressions, such as laughing, crying, and blushing, and the primary symptom in a *conversion reaction* is that the meaning is conveyed in the former instances in body language that is common to everyone (or to all members of a given culture), whereas in the latter instance the meaning is expressed in a highly *personalized* body language that often can be translated only by someone who has been trained to do so.

Unless they are very frequent and intense, the physical expressions of the emotions are not considered symptoms. Yet consider how closely they parallel the following instances of conversion reaction.

A young man, who has had some experience with guns and who has thought that he would like to try hunting, is taken into the field by a friend who hunts. After tramping about for several hours, the men sight a deer. The novice is offered the first shot. He raises the rifle to his shoulder and finds that the index finger of his right hand has become stiff and cannot pull the trigger.

During basic training, a draftee is brought to the M.O.D. by his sergeant. Following a severe reprimand from an officer for having forgotten a portion of his equipment, the patient has developed a coarse tremor of his right forearm, making it impossible for him to salute properly. In any situation except that of saluting, the tremor is unnoticeable or absent.

In both of these instances it is rather easy to infer that psychological factors have produced a disturbance of innervation, a specific interference with motor function. Another common type of conversion symptomatology involves a similar interference with sensory function. Here is a more detailed example of such an instance.

C. L., a man in his early 20's, was brought to the receiving ward one evening by a neighbor. The young man had to be led into the room, and he announced to the nurse on duty that he had suddenly gone blind. The intern's examination revealed no physical abnormality either of the external structures of the eyes or of the fundi. Visual acuity was limited to light perception. A cursory general examination showed only normal findings.

When asked to relate the present illness, the patient did so in a manner that, although somewhat agitated, was nevertheless not so deeply disturbed as the doctor had anticipated in view of the condition.

C. L. mentioned that he had been at the hospital only that morning, when he had brought his wife home from the maternity ward. The couple had been married for just a year and had had their first child, a boy, several days before. The patient had taken the day off from work to be at home with his wife and baby. During the afternoon, he had felt somewhat nervous and tense, but had passed off these feelings as normal for a new father. He had been aware at times of a fleeting feeling of annoyance at his wife's required inactivity, but he thought of the day as a happy one in general and he was proud of his infant son.

C. L. had prepared supper and, after the meal, had asked his wife to play a game of cards. She agreed, but at just that moment the baby awoke and cried. Mrs. L. said she would nurse him, that the card game could wait. As she put the baby to her breast, the patient became aware of a smarting sensation in his eyes. He had been smoking heavily and attributed the irritation to the room's being filled with smoke. He got up and opened a window. When the smarting sensation became worse he went to the washstand and applied a cold cloth to his eyes. On removing the cloth, he found that he was completely blind.

After he had heard this story, the intern called the psychiatric resident. As it happened, the latter was quite lacking in experience, although not in self-confidence. After reviewing the history, the resident told C. L. in a very authoritative manner that there was absolutely nothing the matter with his eyes and that the only trouble was that he was jealous of the baby and did not want to see him suckled. He followed these statements with very strong suggestions that the patient's vision was returning. Within a few minutes, C. L. was able to see fairly well. At the same time he had become very distressed and agitated. He paced up and down restlessly, began sweating profusely, and complained of palpitation. He gave protestations of his love for his infant son, interspersed with fragmentary admissions that he had felt angry. The patient's anxiety continued to mount, so that rather heavy sedation was required. Ultimately, he was sent to the psychiatric service for observation and further treatment.

The following day the patient was found to have somewhat blurred vision. He expressed resentment toward the resident and doubts as to the validity of the statements that the latter had made. He was quite anxious and complained of headache and tremulousness. All other physical findings remained negative.

At this point, a course of psychotherapy was instituted, using less aggressive techniques than had been employed by the resident in the receiving ward. C. L. was able to leave the hospital after several days, but he remained in psychotherapy for more than a year. The visual symptoms disappeared rather promptly, with only very mild and fleeting exacerbations during the next several months. The therapy was essentially devoted to helping the patient recognize, understand, and deal with a number of personal problems which had troubled him (involved in the presenting illness, but having developed before then). C. L. derived considerable benefit from this treatment.

In the course of psychotherapy, the patient and the psychiatrist were able to confirm the interpretation that had been originally presented by the resident. C. L. came to realize, beyond question, that he had been deeply disturbed at the sight of his wife nursing the infant and, in fact, by the whole experience of becoming a father. He had been jealous of the baby—this was a difficult admission to make—and jealous on two distinct counts. One feeling was, in essence, a sexual jealousy, accentuated by his own sexual deprivation during the last weeks of the pregnancy. The other was a more childish kind of jealousy, a jealousy of the maternal solicitude shown the infant by its mother.

PSYCHODYNAMICS. It is important to recognize that in conversion reactions the difficulty is always central, never peripheral. In the first and second examples, the nerves, muscles, tendons, and bloodvessels of the finger and of the hand and forearm were in perfect working order. In the third example, there was no lesion involving the eye or the optic nerve. In the first example, there was a centrally determined inhibition of the flexors and stimulation of the extensors of the index finger. In the second example, there was a centrally determined, rhythmically alternating stimulation of flexors and extensors of the forearm. In the third example, there was a centrally determined inhibition of those portions of the cerebral cortex whose function it is to receive and interpret impulses arriving over the optic tract.

It is equally important to recognize that the symptoms are entirely genuine and develop apart from the conscious volition of the subjects. In the ordinary sense of the words one would say that in the first instance the young hunter wanted to shoot the deer; in the second instance the draftee wanted to execute the salute correctly; in the third instance, the young husband wanted to see and, in fact, came to the hospital to have his vision restored. It would be decidedly incorrect to confuse any of these examples with *malingering*, as is so often done. (Yet, as indicated on pp. 145 to 151, malingering also is neurotically motivated as a rule.)

Having said this much, it is necessary to add that most significant of all is the recognition that the conversion response—the spastic paralysis, the tremor, the blindness—is nevertheless a *motivated* response. Conversion symptoms indicate that unconscious motivations, more powerful than the conscious ones, have taken over control of the motor or sensory organs involved.

It happened that the difficulty disappeared spontaneously in the first example cited, and in the second example, it responded to superficial treatment measures. Therefore one can only guess the nature of the unconscious motivations which were in operation. It seems likely that some sort of guilty fear was primarily operative in the first example and a mocking hostility in the second.

In the third example, a thorough evaluation was made, and the etiological picture is therefore more nearly complete. One can discern quite clearly the major unconscious motivation of the young husband: the wish to blot out painful perceptions and thereby reduce his inner tension. The conversation symptom thus represents *an effort at adjustment*. In addition, one notes that the painful perceptions temporarily were *erased*, and that the tension temporarily *did subside* (the patient was found by the intern to be less upset than one would have supposed). Thus one can add that the adjustment effort was successful, to a degree. Of course, the price paid by the subject for this partial adjustment was inordinately high; the balance sheet of this internal transaction was decidedly unfavorable; hence the patient came to the hospital for treatment.

Like blushing and like the first and second example of conversion responses, the symptom of the blind patient conveys a meaning, translatable into words; in a kind of body language it says: "I do not want to see this (the act of nursing) take place!" As has been mentioned, a significant difference between the conversion phenomenon and blushing or other affective expressions, such as weeping or laughter, is that the conversion is highly individualized, not generalized or stylized as are the affective expressions, and hence not translatable without a special effort at understanding by examiner and patient.

This aspect of conversion symptoms, that they convey a meaning, is of considerable significance both in diagnosis and in treatment. Diagnostically speaking, it is a point of differentiation from anxiety neuroses on the one hand and from abnormal psychophysiological states ("psychosomatic diseases") on the other. In the description of the anxiety reaction it was pointed out that the various symptoms are either the direct expression of the emotional state or the result of psychological fatigue deriving from the excessive expenditure of energy on the internal conflict. The symptoms of anxiety reaction convey no meaning, *have no symbolic significance for the patient* (conscious or unconscious) in the sense that the conversion symptoms have. A very similar statement can be made about the psychophysiological disease states. For example, the elevation of blood pressure in the case of Mr. N., the essential hypertensive (p. 193), was not the expression of any hidden message. In fact, during the early stages of the disease, the existence of the hypertension was not only outside the patient's field of conscious awareness, it was not registered mentally *in any sense*. (It is true that when the patient's hypertension was discovered on routine physical examination, the elevation of blood pressure was of immediate clinical significance *to the company physician*, but this was a phenomenon in the physician's mind and was in no sense a communication from the patient.)

Confirmation of this important differential point is to be found in a consideration of what transpired between C. L. and the resident in the receiving ward. It will be recalled that the resident took the bold step of offering the patient *a translation of his symptom* from body language into the language of conscious ideas. To use a technical term, the resident *interpreted* the symptom. For reasons which are not entirely clear, but which may include such factors as the severity of the symptom, the authoritative manner of the resident, and the fact that the patient's personality was fundamentally not a very sick one, C. L. accepted the interpretation. To speak technically, he gained (a temporary) *insight*. From the long-range therapeutic point of view, the resident's interpretation was probably ill-timed. Nevertheless it was a true interpretation, and it had the effect of temporarily reversing the process by which the symptoms had developed, i.e., it *undid the repression* which was the psychological basis for the symptom. There can be no counterpart to this therapeutic maneuver in the case of a patient with hypertension. A psychotherapist may help a hypertensive discover his repressed anger, he may help him understand and alleviate his conscious though unexpressed anger, but he cannot (correctly) *interpret* the high blood pressure as being a substitute for, an expression of, or a defense against the anger.

In the example of blushing, it was pointed out that the bodily change actually expressed more than one meaning. The same is generally true of conversion symptoms (and of other psychoneurotic symptoms as well). In the first two examples, not enough is known of the subjects to demonstrate this point, but, in the example of hysterical blindness, material which came to light in the patient's psychotherapy shows this feature rather clearly. In addition to the significance already mentioned, the symptom was an expression of self-punishment for hostility and of reproach to the "faithless" wife (as she was unconsciously regarded at the time for her ministrations to the baby).*

Now, the existence of conflicts such as those which troubled C. L. is actually not an uncommon thing. Despite a wish for fatherhood, affection for the baby, and some degree of willingness to accept the privations of parenthood, many a new father—whether consciously or unconsciously—experiences *some degree* of jealousy and irritation toward the baby, particularly if it is a son. Thus the question arises as to what combination of factors could have made the conflicts of C. L. sufficiently intense to have required the strenuous use of repression and the development of a conversion symptom.

---

* The meanings of the conversion symptom are thus drawn from both sides of the neurotic conflict, i.e., from the side of the basic drives and from the side of the anti-instinctual forces (p. 75). The symptom is thus a compromise formation. This tends to be true of psychoneurotic symptoms in general.

A detailed exposition of the background factors—the predisposition—involved in the production of a conversion reaction is beyond the scope of this book, but certain factors may be mentioned briefly. Key elements in the case of C. L. turned out to be childhood jealousies (which had not been completely resolved) of his father and of a three-year-younger brother plus residual feelings of guilt because of the jealous resentment. In general, one may say that emotional problems dating from the family triangle period of development (pp. 99 to 108) are usually of central significance in the predisposition to conversion reactions. Problems from the later phase of the oral period (pp. 85 to 93) are often of significance also.

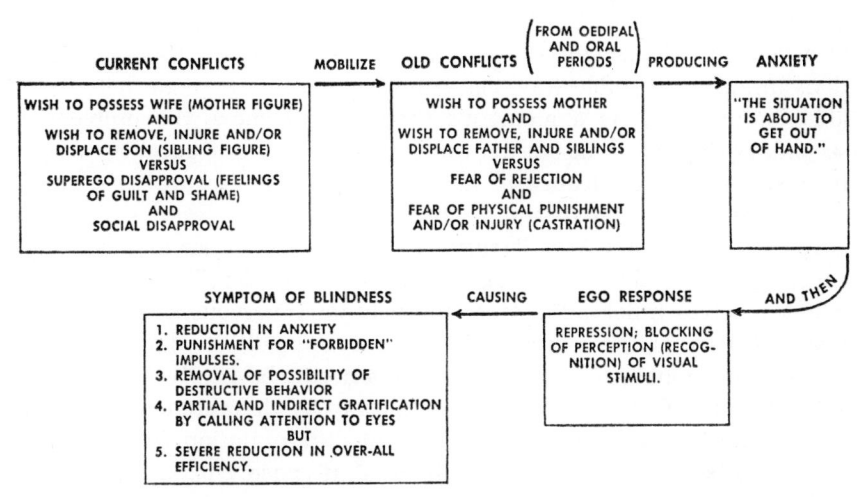

```
                                              (FROM OEDIPAL)
                                               AND ORAL
  CURRENT CONFLICTS      MOBILIZE  OLD CONFLICTS ( PERIODS )  PRODUCING    ANXIETY

┌─────────────────────────┐         ┌─────────────────────────┐         ┌─────────────────┐
│ WISH TO POSSESS WIFE    │         │ WISH TO POSSESS MOTHER  │         │ "THE SITUATION  │
│ (MOTHER FIGURE)         │         │          AND            │         │  IS ABOUT TO    │
│         AND             │         │ WISH TO REMOVE, INJURE  │         │  GET OUT        │
│ WISH TO REMOVE, INJURE  │         │ AND/OR DISPLACE FATHER  │         │  OF HAND."      │
│ AND/OR DISPLACE SON     │         │ AND SIBLINGS            │         │                 │
│ (SIBLING FIGURE)        │         │        VERSUS           │         │                 │
│       VERSUS            │         │ FEAR OF REJECTION       │         │                 │
│ SUPEREGO DISAPPROVAL    │         │          AND            │         │                 │
│ (FEELINGS OF GUILT AND  │         │ FEAR OF PHYSICAL        │         │                 │
│ SHAME) AND              │         │ PUNISHMENT AND/OR       │         │                 │
│ SOCIAL DISAPPROVAL      │         │ INJURY (CASTRATION)     │         │                 │
└─────────────────────────┘         └─────────────────────────┘         └─────────────────┘

         SYMPTOM OF BLINDNESS      CAUSING      EGO RESPONSE          AND THEN

┌────────────────────────────────┐           ┌─────────────────────┐
│ 1. REDUCTION IN ANXIETY        │           │ REPRESSION; BLOCKING│
│ 2. PUNISHMENT FOR "FORBIDDEN"  │           │ OF PERCEPTION       │
│    IMPULSES.                   │           │ (RECOGNITION) OF    │
│ 3. REMOVAL OF POSSIBILITY OF   │           │ VISUAL STIMULI.     │
│    DESTRUCTIVE BEHAVIOR        │           │                     │
│ 4. PARTIAL AND INDIRECT        │           │                     │
│    GRATIFICATION BY CALLING    │           │                     │
│    ATTENTION TO EYES           │           │                     │
│           BUT                  │           │                     │
│ 5. SEVERE REDUCTION IN OVER-ALL│           │                     │
│    EFFICIENCY.                 │           │                     │
└────────────────────────────────┘           └─────────────────────┘
```

FIG. 4. Sequence of psychological events in the case of C. L.

A final word may be said about the adjustment value of conversion symptoms. As we have seen, there were certain temporary values inherent in the symptoms of blindness, itself. Not only did it afford expression to certain feelings, but it temporarily solved a disturbing situation (and possibly prevented the patient from having taken some impulsive step of an aggressive nature which he would have later regretted). Such inherent adjustment values are referred to as the *primary gain* of the neurosis. They are unconscious. It should now be added that a further development can take place. Suppose, for example, that C. L.'s wife had been angry with him and partially estranged from him, but that the onset of his blindness had made her become very affectionate and considerate. Or, alternatively, suppose that the soldier's arm tremor had developed under highly stressful circumstances not of his own making, with the result that he had been awarded a discharge and material compensation for a service-connected disability. Either of these developments might also be considered to be "advantages" accruing from the neurosis. However, they would not be inherent in the illness, itself, but would have resulted from *responses to the illness* on the part of figures in the environment. Such results are termed the *secondary gain* of a neurosis. They are, ordinarily, fully conscious. Not being a part of the neurosis itself, the secondary gain can have no part in the pathogenesis. Thus it would be completely incorrect to say, for example, that C. L. developed the conversion symptom of blindness "to get attention from his wife." (A type of mistake which is made with great frequency, perhaps because it is often easier for all concerned to perceive the secondary gain than it is to perceive the primary gain.)

However, the element of secondary gain may assume considerable—and sometimes even decisive—significance in determining the course of a neurotic illness since it may tip the scale of the patient's motivations in an unfavorable way, i.e., it may make illness seem more desirable than health. As a moment's thought will show, the problem of secondary gain is by no means limited to the class of psychoneuroses; it may assume significance in almost any disease (regardless of etiology), particularly if it becomes chronic.

SYMPTOMATOLOGY AND DIAGNOSIS. The range of symptoms which can be produced by conversion reactions is considerable. Any effector which receives innervation from the voluntary nervous system can be involved. Any of the exteroceptive sensory modalities: sight, hearing, smell, taste, touch, temperature, and pain can be involved. It is considered doubtful if organs innervated solely by the autonomic nervous system can be involved (another point of differentiation from "psychosomatic" diseases), but it is quite likely that sensory experiences mimicking those of visceral pain can be on a conversion basis. The differential diagnosis of conversion reaction can thus be one of considerable difficulty, as is illustrated by the following case.

A 17-year-old girl was admitted to the medical service from the receiving ward, to which she had been brought by her mother with the complaint of "lockjaw." The physical examination showed moderate trismus and a slight, generalized hyperreflexia, but was otherwise negative. The patient was tense, somewhat agitated, and very anxious. No history of a recent injury, even a trivial one, could be obtained. A moderate-sized dose of tetanus antitoxin had been administered in the receiving ward, but the diagnosis was considered to be in doubt.

An emergency psychiatric consultation was requested. The psychiatrist hypnotized the patient, who proved to be a very good subject, promptly entering a rather deep trance. Relaxation of the muscles of the jaw was suggested, and the suggestion was almost immediately effective. The patient was then interviewed, and the following material was obtained. On the previous night the patient had had her first date with a young man who had a reputation for being "wild." Toward the end of the evening, he had introduced the girl to "French" kissing. She had become very upset, and insisted on returning home immediately. She went immediately to bed. During the night she was troubled by bad dreams. She awakened in the morning with sensations of tension in the muscles of her jaw, and shortly thereafter began to experience trismus.

During the trance, a posthypnotic suggestion was given to the effect that the patient's jaw muscles would remain relaxed. When the patient was awakened, it was found that this suggestion was effective. A tentative diagnosis of conversion reaction was made and the patient was transferred to the psychiatric service.

Within three hours, the muscle spasms returned. The trismus became more severe than before. General rigidity of the muscles of the neck, back, and extremities began to develop. The patient was then given intensive treatment for tetanus; she survived, but went through a most critical course of this disease.

The differential diagnosis of conversion reactions has a number of aspects. It goes without saying that, when possible, specific organic disease should be ruled out by appropriate techniques. In weighing probabilities, it is of value to remember which organs and functions of the body are likely to be affected by conversions, which are unlikely to be affected, and which cannot be affected (e.g., most visceral functions). It is important to realize that, in conversion reactions, it is *the patient's conception of his body* (his "body-image"; see Chap. 7) and not the finer details of anatomical fact, which is of paramount importance. For example, in the case of hysterical anesthesias and paresthesias, the distribution of the abnormality does not conform to the functional areas served by a specific tract in the spinal cord, but to a gross concept such as "the hand," "the arm," "the ankle." (From this circumstance are derived the expressions "stocking anesthesia" and "glove anesthesia.") The same principle often holds true for motor abnormalities. Thus, in the first and second examples of conversion reactions, no single neurological lesion could account for the spastic paralysis of the index finger or the gross intention tremor of the forearm.

Sometimes the speed of the onset is of value in the diagnosis, since the conversion symptom tends to appear rapidly and all at once. (This is by no means an absolute rule.) Thus, in the case of hysterical blindness, the suddenness of onset, combined with the fact that both eyes were affected, practically eliminated from consideration any organic affliction of the eyes.

The patient's attitude toward his symptom is often of considerable diagnostic value. As has been noted, it is characteristic of the conversion hysteric that his attitude is one of greater calmness than is wholly appropriate. (A feature that was noted in the case of blindness, but whose absence in the case of tetanus was one of the few points against the diagnosis of conversion reaction.) This feature of *relative* calmness toward the presenting complaint has been designated "la belle indifférence" of the hysteric.

As was brought out in the discussion of the case of blindness, this calmness is (in large part) based upon the circumstance that the symptom has adjustment value for the patient; it is an attempt at solution of an internal conflict, and one which is ordinarily at least partially successful. For the positive diagnosis of conversion reaction, it is necessary to demonstrate this solution-seeking feature. Closely related to this point is the one that conversion symptoms have a meaning, translatable into words if it can be grasped. (It was the presence of this feature, more than any other, which was responsible for the mistake in the case of the girl with tetanus.) As a matter of fact, this feature could be called pathognomonic but for the fact that, in exceptional cases, the meaning may become attached to the symptom *after* the latter has begun to develop. In such cases, one may correctly use the greatly overworked expression, "an hysterical overlay."

Dissociative Reaction

This phenomenon was, for a long time, combined with conversion reaction in a nosological entity called "hysteria." Although the two types of reaction are clinically quite different, there was some justification for the combination inasmuch as not infrequently both reactions appear in the same individual as manifestations of neurotic illness and both reactions depend for their production on the intensive use of the mechanism of repression. Here are two clinical examples of a form of dissociative reaction.

An attractive young girl, rather dramatically dressed, was brought to the receiving ward by a taxicab driver, who stated that after entering his cab at the airport the girl had seemed utterly confused, being unable to give a destination or even to give her own identity.

There were no abnormal physical findings. The patient was disoriented as to time, place, and person although not as to situation; that is to say, she realized that she was in a hospital and that she was mentally ill in some way. She was cooperative in the examination, but completely unable to relate events in her personal life prior to her having stepped into the cab. There was no anterograde* amnesia: the patient retained memory of the events of the ride to the hospital and events occurring in the receiving ward. In fact, aside from the loss of memory and a mood of mild anxiety and depression, the mental status findings were normal. The girl gave indications of being well educated; her fund of general information was for the most part quite adequate although she could not say how she knew these things. She even could express opinions on certain subjects (preferring one form of music, literature, athletics, to another) although she could not recall the experiences upon which the opinions were based.

In the patient's purse were an airplane ticket, showing that she had

---

* Amnesia is usually classified as *retrograde*, loss of memory for events preceding a certain point in time, or *anterograde*, loss of memory for events occurring since a certain point in time.

arrived on the morning plane from an Eastern city, and a driver's license giving her name, Miss K. B., her age, 19, her address, a fashionable suburb of the city from which she had departed, and her physical description. In response to questions, the patient could only say that the name and address sounded vaguely familiar; she had no sense of their belonging to herself. As the questions continued, she became increasingly anxious without knowing why.

Miss B. was admitted to the psychiatric service, given reassurance and small doses of a tranquilizing drug, and otherwise left undisturbed. By the following morning, isolated fragments of her memory had begun to return. For example, she realized what her name was and the name of her native city. She had a scattered recall of events in her life, although this did not include any recent or intimate events.

At this time, with the patient's somewhat hesitant agreement, she was given sodium pentothal intravenously and interviewed while under the influence of this drug. A technique of free-association was used, taking some of the facts which Miss B. had already remembered as starting points. Within half an hour, the amnesia had cleared completely. The purpose of the airplane trip had been a rendezvous with a twice-divorced man of 30, of whom the girl's parents violently disapproved. With the recovery of this memory, Miss B. became, for the first time, very upset, and she began to weep.

J. F. was brought to the city hospital by the police. He had been arrested on the charges of disorderly conduct and carrying a concealed weapon. At the police station, he was unable to answer routine questions.

In the receiving ward, the patient was found to be almost completely amnesic. He had evidently been drinking, but analysis of a blood sample indicated that there was insufficient alcohol in his system for ordinary intoxication.

In this instance, the amnesia wore off spontaneously within a period of 18 hours. The patient then recalled that he had been in a tavern, had gotten into a violent argument with an acquaintance whom he disliked, had run home and gotten a revolver, and was making his way back to the tavern when he "blacked out."

One can see that in dissociative reactions repression operates in a more widespread and generalized fashion than in conversion reactions. In the latter condition, the effect of repression is limited to keeping unconscious certain specific perceptions, wishes, and impulses (and thus interfering with perceptual and motor functions). In the former, the use of repression walls off from the subject's consciousness massive blocks of mental material, with the result that the patient's sense of identity and his orientation to his world are seriously affected.

It is significant, however, that an amnesia is almost never complete (if of any appreciable duration). Even in a case such as that of Miss K. B., in which the amnesia was quite severe, a good bit of mental material remained: for example, matters of information and of taste. Although this aspect was not explored fully, there doubtless also remained something in the way of skills, attitudes, and even ambitions. The usual rule is that the repression spares those aspects of the personality which are not involved in or associatively linked to the precipitating conflict.

Since the ability remains to work, to experience emotions, to retain current impressions and to learn from them, one can see the possibility that, if the amnesia persists for a really long period of time, the individual could continue to exist with his somewhat altered personality, to develop along modified lines, and in fact, to "build a new life" for himself. This condition is called a *fugue state*. It is not of common occurrence, and if it is discovered, either through coincidence or through a relaxation of the repressive forces and a lifting of the amnesia (months or even years later), it usually receives wide publicity. Since it is typical of human beings to have potentialities for more than one style of living and of personal development, the new pattern of adjustment need bear little surface similarity to the old.

As a result of repression operating against certain aspects of the personality and sparing others, the condition known as *dual* or *multiple personality can arise*. This form of illness resembles that of fugue state, but differs from it in that, instead of a single and relatively long-lasting change from one sense of identity and pattern of adjustment to another, there is an alternation (sometimes very frequent and rapid) between two or more identities and patterns. The classical scientific description of such a condition is Prince's *The Dissociation of a Personality*. More recently, Cleckley's *The Three Faces of Eve* and the motion picture based on his book present a portrayal of this type of mental disturbance. In fiction, the best known and very imaginative example of this phenomenon is Robert Louis Stevenson's *The Strange Case of Dr. Jekyll and Mr. Hyde* (1886).

Another phenomenon which stands in a close relationship both to amnesia and to conversion reactions and which is of great clinical significance is one of the forms of *syncope* or *fainting*. As the student doubtless knows, this syndrome can arise from a variety of causes: cardiac asystole, sudden hypotension, hyperventilation, etc. One of the commoner causes, particularly in women, is the sudden and massive use of repression, resulting in a temporary complete (or nearly complete) loss of the faculty of awareness. Typically, this form of fainting occurs at a dramatic moment; typically it occurs in the presence of other persons, and typically it is not productive of physical injury. Unless there is some complicating factor (such as marked fear or hyperventilation), there are no positive physical findings.

As was shown to be the case with conversion reactions, it is clear that amnesia and the other forms of dissociative reaction represent an *attempt at adjustment*. In the first example, the patient was struggling with impulses of an erotic nature; in the second, with hostile, destructive impulses. Presumably, in both instances feelings of anxiety and guilt were opposing the discharge of the impulses. (In the first instance, shame may also have been operative.) The amnesia temporarily solves the conflict situation, since the elements of the conflict are forgotten and the carrying out of the disturbing impulses is prevented.

Phobic Reaction (Anxiety Hysteria)

A *phobia* may be defined as *the dread of a specific object, act, or situation which is not realistically dangerous but has come to represent a danger*. To sharpen the definition a bit more, one should add that the object, act, or situation is *one which can, at least in theory, be avoided, with more or less vigorous effort*. Thus, fears of dying, of growing old, of breathing, of God, of the future, may be justified or unjustified, but cannot be true phobias.

Nearly everyone, at times, has had a mild phobic experience. An example is the slight tinge of fear which is so often felt on looking down from high places. "Stage fright" is another common example, and would not be considered pathological unless it were quite severe or recurrent.

The following case history illustrates the principal features of a phobic reaction.

Miss E. M., a woman of 22 years of age, was referred to a psychiatrist by her family physician for treatment of a set of severe phobias. The patient had a marked air of refinement and propriety; her potentially expressive features were, for the most part, rigidly controlled, as if she were striving for composure. She was dressed in an extremely subdued and conservative fashion that de-emphasized her femininity. Miss M. was accompanied to the psychiatrist's office by her widowed mother, a woman of domineering manner.

The present illness had begun about nine months before the consultation with the abrupt onset of a severe dread of elevators. The feeling was so intense that the patient had been constrained to avoid the use of elevators during this entire period. For the past several months, Miss M. had been unable even to contemplate taking an elevator without experiencing an anxiety reaction. In addition to the original fear, a number of others had made their appearance. First, the patient had begun to feel anxious when climbing stairs alone; then, when walking unaccompanied in any situation. Most recently, Miss M. had felt anxious whenever she left her home, unless accompanied by some adult, preferably her mother.

Despite her attempts to be cooperative, the patient's account of the onset of the initial symptom was, at first, quite unclear. As she told it, the anxiety reaction appeared "like a bolt from the blue" and did not seem to be related to any immediate stress situation. However, after a number of interviews the precipitating conflict could be elucidated.

At the time of onset, Miss M. had been doing secretarial work in a large business office, a position in which she took dictation from a number of salesmen and minor executives. Although intellectually competent and physically very attractive, the patient had always been extremely shy in any personal situation involving a man. She led a restricted social life and very seldom went out on dates. She functioned adequately, however, in most business and other group settings. While working for the firm, Miss M. secretly developed a romantic interest in one of the young executives, an interest that she scarcely acknowledged even to herself. She managed to banish it from her (conscious) thoughts entirely when she learned, in casual office conversation, that he was married.

The company offices were on an upper floor of a large downtown office building equipped with automatic elevators. One morning, arriving at work an unaccustomed few minutes late, Miss M. found herself alone in an elevator with the young executive. The man made a complimentary but slightly suggestive remark about the patient's dress. Miss M. blushed and became highly embarrassed, tense, and anxious. By dint of considerable effort, she managed to get through the day's work. The next morning, as she was about to enter the elevator, she experienced an attack of anxiety so severe as to verge upon panic. She left the building, walked about for nearly an hour, and then was able to return. This time she climbed six flights of stairs to the office.

During succeeding days the patient made several efforts to use the elevator, but she invariably found herself becoming too anxious to do so. She continued to use the stairs, and for several months was able to continue work in reasonable comfort, having taken this precaution. Eventually, the use of the stairs became as disturbing as that of the elevator. At this point, the patient was compelled to ask for a leave of absence, and she had not returned to work at the time of consultation.

At no point did the patient consciously associate her attacks of anxiety with the young executive. In fact, as she told the psychiatrist, she "no longer thought of him at all." Miss M. had no doubt that she was ill, but she considered the nature of her illness to be inexplicable.

Despite the patient's bewilderment, it is not difficult to discern that the inner conflict whose flare-up brought on the present illness involved sexual impulses on the one hand and a set of strong inhibitions on the other. (From the statement of the present illness alone, the nature of the inhibiting forces is not entirely clear, but seemingly the inhibitions were of long standing and had something to do with the patient's mother.) It is also clear that the conflict was unconscious; from the time the patient learned that the young man was married, she had not thought of being attracted to him.

To understand precisely how Miss M.'s symptoms were produced, it is necessary to examine closely the experience on the elevator. At this point, the setting, the presence of the young man, and his suggestive remark threatened to overcome the repression which had been in effect. Anxiety and shame seem to have been mobilized within the patient to oppose the breakthrough of erotic feeling, and since the threatening situation was, in reality, very brief, the patient managed to get through it. By plunging into her work, she staved off awareness of the emotional forces at work within her.

The erotic impulses did not cease to operate, however, and the following morning, as the patient approached the setting of the original temptation, they again pushed toward awareness. The patient was assailed with extreme anxiety, and at this moment the actual phobia began.

The anxiety indicates that there was unconscious recognition on the patient's part of something regarded as an imminent danger; this "something" was, of course, her own sexual impulses.* Yet, what Miss M. next consciously experienced was fear of something in the environment (the elevator). Thus one can say that, through the mechanism of *projection,* anxiety over an inner danger was transformed into fear of an outer danger. Note, however, that the fear attached not to the young man, but to the elevator, a realistically neutral object, one which came into the situation largely through coincidence. Thus, in addition to projection, the psychological technique of *displacement* can be seen to have been at work.

It is as if the patient's personality had made a sort of bargain or pact with itself, one in which a degree of reality-testing was sacrificed for the sake of finding a way out of the conflict situation. It is as if the patient had said to herself, "The danger is not created by my emotions, nor by the young man, but by the elevator. The elevator is what I fear. If I can just avoid it, I shall be safe."

This psychological transaction was of short-term advantage (from the patient's point of view), since one can get away from most external dangers, whereas one cannot get away from oneself. As a result of the psychological transaction, the sexual repression remained in force, and even the anxiety diminished greatly, since it had been transmuted into fear of the elevator, which the patient now avoided by climbing the stairs en route to and from work.

In cases such as this, the subsequent course of the neurosis depends upon the summation of two groups of factors: (a) the predisposing elements and (b) features of the current life situation. The predisposing elements derive from unresolved childhood conflicts of a nature similar to the current conflicts. If these old elements are only mildly or

---

* The expression "unconscious recognition" may seem strange, since recognition is ordinarily thought of as a conscious phenomenon. What is meant is that, although Miss M. remained unaware of it, a part of her personality was responding to the mounting pressure of her sexual impulses. This response was attended by a phase of anxiety. (Cf. the example of an anxiety attack on p. 67.)

moderately disturbing, they may again be brought under control by simple repression without the necessity of an indefinite prolongation of the phobic response. If there occurs some decisive change in the current environment such that the repressed strivings are no longer, so to speak, being tempted into consciousness, then the phobic reaction may also gradually subside.*

If, on the other hand, the childhood conflicts have been quite intense, and if the current situation remains one of drive stimulation, there is the continuing "danger" that the forbidden impulses will break through into consciousness and lead to action. In such circumstances, the phobic sequence tends to be repeatedly evoked. The personality's "bargain with itself" tends to assume larger proportions and thus, from the point of view of the whole personality, to become increasingly maladaptive. That is to say, the sacrifice of freedom of action becomes ever greater. (An additional factor which comes to be operative in some instances is that of shame attaching to the phobia itself, and leading the phobic individual to go to considerable lengths to hide his condition from other persons. See the case history of the malinger on p. 147.)

In the case of Miss E. M., the status of both the predisposing and the current elements militated against a spontaneous remission of the phobic reaction and, in fact, led to its further development. As it was eventually learned in the course of psychotherapy, the patient's oedipal experience had been an intense one, and, owing partly to the father's premature death, the conflicts it had engendered had been resolved to only a minimal degree.

Then, too, the current situation was unfavorable. So long as the patient was employed at the same firm, the temptation remained (the instinctual side of the conflict continued to be stimulated). So long as she made her home with her mother, who dominated and infantized her, the possibilities for excessive anxiety and guilt remained (the anti-instinctual side of the conflict continued to be stimulated).

It is important, however, not to form a general overestimation of the significance of current environmental factors in producing and perpetuating a phobic reaction. The crux of the matter is that one or more long-standing key conflicts are mobilized and exert deeply disturbing effects *without entering consciousness*. There was nothing in Miss M.'s recent experiences which could not, in theory, have been handled with more realistic techniques of adjustment if it had not been that her psychological defenses against anxiety from the unresolved childhood

---

* Neither of these possibilities is very common. To produce a clear-cut phobic reaction, the predisposition usually must be quite strong. Furthermore, a certain amount of *regression* (p. 75) attends the revival of the old problems, rendering the personality less well able to deal with them.

conflicts required that she remain largely unaware of what was actually taking place within her. If, for example, she had been able consciously to accept and to appraise her feelings toward the young executive, she could have resolved merely not to act upon them and to seek another love object. The experience in the elevator would then have been of only fleeting significance. Similarly, if she had been able to use her intelligence in evaluating the effect of her mother's influence upon her adult pattern of living, she could have made other living arrangements.*

In concluding this discussion of phobic reaction, it should be stated that erotic impulses are not the only ones which can be dealt with in this fashion. Hostile impulses are of equal—in men, of greater—significance. Frequently the neurosis develops as a result of conflicts involving both kinds of impulses simultaneously.

Compulsive Reaction (Obsessive-compulsive neurosis)

Blushing and the expressive innervations which accompany affective states were considered the normal counterparts to conversion reactions. Slips of memory, such as some of those discussed in Chapter 3, may be considered to stand in a similar relation to dissociative reactions, and various minor but irrational fears to be the counterparts to phobic reactions. Most persons can also find within their experience bits of behavior which correspond to *obsessions* and *compulsions*, the principal symptoms of the neurosis now to be discussed.

An obsession may be simply defined as *a thought, recognized by the subject as more or less irrational, which recurs persistently, despite the subject's conscious wish to avoid it.* There is an obvious and close connection between obsessions and compulsions, inasmuch as the preoccupation with the former can at times be dispelled (temporarily) only by the performance of the latter. A compulsion may be defined as *an act which is carried out, in some degree against the subject's conscious wishes, either to avoid the anxiety that would otherwise appear, or to dispel a disturbing obsession.*

Toward the normal end of the obsessive-compulsive spectrum of behavior, the phenomena blend into the area of habits, "manners," and minor worries. The common saying about someone showing an anxious irritability, "He must have gotten out on the wrong side of the bed this

---

* In this particular instance, the patient responded well to intensive psychotherapy. Quite early in the process she became able to appraise the unfavorable aspects of the current situation, and she changed her job and her living arrangements. Later, she became able to gain some awareness of the childhood conflicts, and to gain a greater degree of freedom from their influence. She continued to have a mildly phobic personality (p. 400), but, by and large, she remained free of symptoms.

morning," is indicative of the compulsive force of an unimportant habit. So is the maintenance of correct table manners by an individual who is ravenously hungry. (See discussion of muscle-training, pp. 93 to 99.) A child may be showing compulsive behavior when, in the course of a walk, he touches every telephone pole or fence-post that he passes. Compulsive tendencies are indicated when an adult is made slightly uncomfortable by unemptied ashtrays or by pictures hanging a bit askew. A mild obsession is exhibited when a student, having taken an examination, keeps thinking about a particular question which he may have missed and "cannot get it out of his head." The term obsession is misused when it is made to refer to a consciously acceptable goal or objective, as in the expression "he was obsessed with the idea of getting ahead," or "achieving a lofty social status was an obsession with her."

The following excerpts from a case history illustrate the principal features of a full-blown obsessive-compulsive neurosis (compulsive reaction).

W. D., a married man of 42, the father of two children, the treasurer of a medium-sized business concern, was referred to a psychiatrist with the presenting complaints of "nervousness" and unremitting insomnia.

In the initial interviews it could be seen that the patient was exerting a considerable, and an outwardly successful, effort at self-control. He spoke in an articulate and rather unemotional manner; he was quite reserved and, although generally precise in his statements, he only gradually found it possible to give the pertinent details of his symptoms.

For the past six months, Mr. D. suffered from the illogical but frequently recurring thought that his wife was becoming ill or might even be dead. At first, and oftener than not even at the time of consultation, the thought appeared just as a thought, i.e., it was not accompanied by strong emotion. It was, however, persistent. When the thought occurred to Mr. D. at his office, he would "try to argue with himself about it." Often such efforts were ineffectual, and he then had to seek reassurance by telephoning his home and speaking with Mrs. D. During the past several weeks, he had averaged four such calls per day. Since Mrs. D. was rather active socially, about half of the time she would not be at home. In such instances, Mr. D. had to choose the alternatives of trying to reach her wherever she might be or of continuing to be harassed by the unwanted thoughts.

The couple slept in twin beds, and, during the night, Mr. D. would find the thoughts of his wife's illness or death entering consciousness, not to depart until he had switched on the lamp at the bedside table and made certain that his wife was resting normally. Mrs. D. generally had accepted the telephone calls without undue protest, but she had begun to complain rather sharply about the switching on of the night lamp, a procedure which often interrupted her sleep.

In addition, Mr. D. had developed an elaborate routine of "safety measures" which he had to follow each evening before retiring if he were to be spared severe anxiety. He had always been a somewhat cautious person, but he had recently begun to make thorough rounds of his rather large house, checking the locks and all the doors and windows and checking all of the gas and electric appliances. Often, after he had done this and retired to the bedroom, he would begin to doubt the thoroughness of his survey and would then lie awake, worrying until he had repeated it.

Mr. D. had, in the course of time, established a good reputation at his firm, being considered conscientious, meticulous, with a fine eye for detail, and the ability (based upon painstaking thought) to foresee various possible contingencies. (He was not a lively or a flexible person and had initially had some difficulty in finding his proper niche, but once he had gotten into the treasurer's office, his temperament fitted the job requirements very well.) Recently, however, the patient had been investing so much energy in his various symptoms that, suffering from chronic fatigue and impairment of concentration, he was beginning to make errors at his work, something which had never happened before in his career and which caused him considerable shame.

Mr. D. entered an extended period of very intensive psychotherapy, from which he eventually derived considerable benefit. In the course of this treatment, the development of his neurosis was rather thoroughly elucidated. Among the relevant factors in his recent and current life, the following were of especial significance.

The patient had always been a cautious, methodical person, actually having some difficulty in "letting go" socially or in recreation. He had not married until his middle thirties, having wished first to make himself financially secure. His wife was three years younger than he. She came from a family of some social prominence and had rejected several previous suitors as not being up to her rather exacting standards. The patient was of humbler origin, but at the time of their marriage Mrs. D. had begun to fear becoming "an old maid." There was a certain amount of affection, if not passion, between the two—in the initial interviews the patient consistently spoke of his wife in terms of high regard —but in the half-year preceding the outbreak of his symptoms Mr. D.'s adjustment was adversely affected by two circumstances.

The couple had two children, a boy and a girl, whose ages at the time of the consultation were five and three years, respectively. The little boy had suffered from birth with allergic difficulties and at the age of four began to experience asthmatic attacks. By the time of the consultation, these had begun to abate, but for a time his illness had placed rather heavy demands upon his mother, particularly in the evening when most of the attacks occurred. Mr. D. (unconsciously) experienced considerable resentment at this encroachment upon his and his wife's normal schedule.

The other circumstance was a marked business recession, reversing the trend of Mr. D.'s income which had been one of a steady increase. The patient's self-esteem and sense of security had rested heavily upon his business success, and were thus directly threatened. Probably of still greater importance (and of this the patient was not conscious at the time of his illness) was anxiety lest his wife become seriously disappointed in him and turn against him, since his prospects of attaining the expensive style of living which the couple had set as their goal were dimmed.

One can readily see that obsessive-compulsive neurosis is a more serious, a more deeply-seated, and a more complicated form of neurotic illness than those we have previously considered. What can one discern of the psychological forces involved in its production?

As is the case with the other psychoneuroses, the symptoms of obsessive-compulsive neurosis are to be interpreted as an effort at adjustment, an effort at handling inner conflict(s). From the story of Mr. D., one can see that the impulses representing one side of the current conflict were hostile ones. Mr. D. was angry at his wife, feeling neglected by her, unsure of her affection, and to an extent, controlled by her (her habitual expensive tastes). The other side of the conflict involved at least two components. Fear of losing the gratifications he did obtain from his wife restrained the patient from any open show of hostility. More than this, a sense of guilt was present which operated to oppose any conscious recognition of the angry feelings.

Now as to the defense mechanisms whose use underlay the actual symptom production. First one can detect an unmistakable childishness in the patient's behavior. There is something highly inappropriate to Mr. D.'s outward status as a competent adult in the anxious phone calls seeking reassurance and in the ineffectual, "fussy" behavior of checking and rechecking the locks. One can therefore say with assurance that an element of *regression* (p. 75) is present. Next one can not overlook an aspect of the patient's behavior which can properly be called one of solicitude (albeit an unnecessary and misguided solicitude), the frequent inquiries about his wife's health. In the same vein were the favorable remarks about his wife which the patient made early in the psychotherapy. This contrast between surface behavior and the underlying emotional position (hostility) indicates the use of *reaction-formation* (p. 77).

The disturbing thoughts about Mrs. D.'s illness or death were unaccompanied by any strong affect (if the compulsion to telephone were resisted, it is true that anxiety would develop, but that is another matter). The same was true of the patient's initial presentation of his difficulties. Thus one discerns the operation of the mechanism of *isolation* (p. 79). Inasmuch as the obsessional ideas were nevertheless basically hostile, one is led to consider the solicitous telephone calls as an example of *undoing* (p. 79).

These several mechanisms—regression, reaction-formation, isolation, and undoing—are the cardinal defenses which underlie the clinical picture of obsessive-compulsive reaction. All of them are present as a rule, although they are combined in varying proportions in different patients.

As in the case of phobic reaction, there is a tendency for the underlying conflict to increase in intensity, for the patient's personality to become ever more extensively involved, and for the symptom-complex to dominate the patient's life, rendering him a psychiatric casualty unless the external pressures are drastically reduced or unless vigorous treatment is instituted. Once the neurosis has gotten well under way, a moderate improvement in the environmental situation alone is often insufficient to reverse the morbid process. In the case of Mr. D., such a favorable change had begun to occur—the improvement in the health of the patient's young son—without any corresponding change in the patient's psychiatric condition.

This circumstance is largely because the process of regression tends to mobilize long-standing unconscious conflicts from early childhood (primarily from the muscle-training period) which, once roused, operate with a certain amount of independence of the actual, current situation.

It is not indicated to go more specifically into the predisposing factors involved in the production of obsessive-compulsive neurosis in a book designed for the nonspecialist, but a final point should be made with respect to the behavior pattern in the fully developed illness. A typical feature of the case of Mr. W. D. was that, notwithstanding the various desperate efforts of the personality, the basic hostility was not thoroughly contained. Resentful impulses continued to threaten to break into awareness and to find overt expression. As a matter of fact, they did find a certain amount of expression: the telephone calls afforded the patient's wife a degree of embarrassment and inconvenience, and the switching on of the night lamp prevented her getting a restful sleep, finally eliciting her sharp objection. This phenomenon, in which unacceptable drives, despite vigorous efforts directed against them by another portion of the personality, break into awareness or expressive action, is technically termed *the return of the repressed.*

Neurotic Depressive Reaction

Nearly everyone has experienced, at times, transient periods of low spirits ("blue spells") in response to adversity. Such an experience may be regarded as the normal analogue to a neurotic depression and merits consideration as an introduction to the latter problem.

A "normal depressive episode" is characterized by a certain mood, one of sadness, often tinged with anxiety and involving an outlook which may be described as pessimistic. One's thoughts tend to center around the precipitating circumstances and to be rather nonconstructive. Typically there is a period of relative inactivity; one senses a disinclination for one's usual pursuits; if these must be followed, it is with a sense of extra effort. Concentration may be difficult; there may be a vague feeling of restlessness and, possibly, of irritability; there may be an inclination to weep. There may be mild changes (in either direction) in one's appetite and in one's inclination to sleep. The most significant inner change is characteristically a lowering of one's opinion of himself (the "low down'" feeling of the blues songs).

The circumstances producing such a reaction are ordinarily such as involve a disappointment or a loss: failure in an examination, delay in winning a promotion, loss of a pet animal, loss of a business opportunity. Sometimes they involve a sense of (moderate) shame or guilt: one has mishandled a situation or has behaved badly in some fashion. The cause-and-effect sequence is, for the most part, quite conscious; one knows "what is the matter" with him.

Characteristically, the reaction is self-limited. A lightening of mood and a return of one's normal perspective appear hand-in-hand. As the sadness begins to wear off, one perceives that the situation is remediable after all; a more realistic glimpse of the situation favors a return of ordinary good spirits. The whole process of restoration is accelerated if, as often happens, the external situation takes a turn for the better, but it is not dependent upon mere good fortune. If the situation tends to remain the same, one begins planning to do something about it: to work harder, to correct the mistake, to make amends. A "spell of the blues" of this normal variety lasts a matter of hours or days, or at the most, a few weeks.

A neurotic depressive reaction has important similarities to such an experience, but it is a more complex as well as a more serious phenomenon.

Mrs. R. L., aged 23, the wife of an attorney newly established in practice, was evaluated for the complaint of "nervousness." Her symptoms were of two months' duration and of increasing severity. They included a persistent mood of anxious low spirits, with occasional crying spells and, less often, outbursts of ill temper provoked by trifles. The patient, who was quite well physically, had become mildly anorexic, particularly for the evening meal, and had sustained a weight loss of five pounds. She had experienced a marked decrease in sexual interest.

There had been no overall slowing down in the patient's activities—in fact, she had "tried to keep busy"—but there had been a shift in emphasis. Mrs. L. had been quite active socially and had begun to take an interest in community affairs; during the past two months she had declined a number of invitations, had issued none herself, and had taken to spending more time at home. She made some efforts at recreation, but these tended to be solitary efforts and were not productive of relaxation. The relationship with her husband had gradually become rather strained.

Mrs. L. was reticent about disclosure of the event which had triggered her depression (and had at first hoped for some form of treatment which would not involve personal discussions), but she was perfectly aware of what the event had been. She and her husband had but recently come to live in the city in which her illness had developed. As soon as they were established, she had made application for membership in the Junior League. Immediately before the onset of her "nervousness," she had learned that her application had not been approved.

On the other hand, the patient could not understand the severity of her reaction, nor why she had been unable "to bounce back" from the disappointment. A series of anamnestic interviews yielded background material which bore upon this point. Mrs. L. was the only child of a widowed mother, a rather selfish woman who had used her daughter as a source of vicarious gratification. Mother and daughter had never been really close. Although the mother had been quite generous to the patient in material ways, she had given her the impression that her good opinion depended very largely upon certain aspects of the patient's performance. In the patient's early years, great stress had been placed upon good manners and obtaining good grades in school. During adolescence the emphasis was shifted to social accomplishments and "knowing the right people." Mrs. L.'s mother had been somewhat opposed to the patient's marriage, considering Mr. L. to be of a lower social stratum.

Thus one sees that in a neurotic depressive reaction—unlike the situation in a normal depressive reaction—the intensity and duration of the patient's distress, and particularly the lowering of his self-esteem, are out of proportion to the precipitating event (objectively viewed). The emotional status is only to be explained by reference to the patient's personality as it was constituted at the time of the stress. There are two personality features which strongly predispose to the experiencing of a neurotic depression. One of these is a basic insecurity and uncertainty of one's personal worth, needing to be more or less continuously allayed by reassurance coming from without (i.e., from figures in the environment). The other is a morbidly punitive conscience, ready to go into action at any hint of hostile behavior (or possibly even at the mobilization of hostile thoughts) directed at key figures in the individual's life. Oftener than not, both features can be discerned to be in operation in the production of a neurotic depressive reaction although one is apt to be of greater significance than the other in any given instance.

In the case of Mrs. L., the first feature was of primary importance. Failure to win the official approval of the new circle of acquaintances toward whom her aspirations were directed meant to the patient that her long-standing doubts and fears were actually justified, that she was not a worthwhile person. Just below this sequence of thought was the more serious one that she had also forfeited her mother's approval and love. The second feature was also contributing to the severity of the reaction. Unconsciously the patient perceived her failure to win formal social recognition as a hostile act against her mother, and this was the basis for rather harsh conscience reproaches.

In Chapter 5 there was a discussion of the nature and effects of grief and mourning. It was mentioned that, if pre-existing inner conflicts interfere with the usual process of mourning, serious consequences may ensue. One of these is the development of a depression, which may be of either neurotic or psychotic (p. 341) intensity. The commonest personality factor tending to the production of such a result is the existence in the bereaved of signficantly ambivalent feelings toward the deceased.

Hypochondriasis

This syndrome is no longer given an official diagnostic category. As a matter of fact, even among doctors and nurses, the terms, *hypochondriasis* and *hypochondriac* have always been used quite loosely, usually with an implication of dislike. They are likely to be applied to almost any patient whose complaints become annoying, particularly if these complaints are not related to obvious physical lesions.

In reality, the syndrome of hypochondriasis, in a clear-cut and fully developed form, is a rare condition. It is also a very serious one, appearing to occupy a position in the border zone between neurosis and psychosis. Clinically, this form of illness may be defined as *a severe, morbid preoccupation with the state of one's own body, tending to be chronic, and manifested by unremitting physical complaints and a lack of interest in one's environment.*

There still exists a slight question as to whether or not actual physical alterations, emotionally based, may be a regular feature of this condition. Since the basic drives of persons afflicted with hypochondriasis are severely inhibited, the possibility exists that the resulting inner tensions may produce obscure functional disturbances of various organs. However, even if such alterations do exist, they are manifestly inadequate to account for the intensity of the patient's complaints. To explain this intensity, one must consider the psychological factors involved.

In the clinical discussions thus far presented, it has been mentioned that the chronic inner conflicts which predispose to anxiety reaction, conversion reaction, and phobic reaction are largely derived from unsolved problems of the family triangle period of development. Those predisposing to obsessive-compulsive reaction derive in large part from an earlier period, that of muscle-training. Patients developing hypochondriasis may also have conflicts deriving from these periods, but in addition and more fundamentally they have conflicts stemming from a still earlier period. As a result of these primitive disturbances, individuals predisposed to hypochondriasis experience difficulty in establishing meaningful relationships with others. The onset of the clinical illness is usually associated with a situation that threatens these weak relationships still further.

Without going into undue theoretical detail, it can be said that the fundamental psychological mechanism underlying the development of hypochondriasis is a severe regression, one considerably further reaching than the regressions which occur in the neuroses previously considered. From the standpoint of basic drives and emotions, the position of the hypochondriacal patient becomes rather like that of late infancy. Like the infant, the hypochondriac is quite aware of the figures in his environment, but he is not able to give to them emotionally. His position is quite *narcissistic* (p. 99). As a result of the marked regression, a large portion of the libido of the patient has been withdrawn from environmental figures and reinvested in various parts of his own body. It is this phenomenon which is responsible for the intensity of the patient's interest in the state of his bodily organs; it differentiates his complaints from the physical complaints of other neurotic patients.

Whereas the emotional regression in hypochondriasis is extensive, it does not affect all aspects of the personality equally. Intellectual ability is quite intact, and the executive (ego) functions in general, while impaired, are not lost. The ability to determine reality remains to a considerable extent. Clinically speaking, this factor marks the principal difference between hypochondriasis and a functional psychosis. For example, a given physical complaint of a hypochondriacal patient may at times be alleviated by such measures as explanation, reassurance, and suggestion. This is not the case with a similar complaint representing an actual (psychotic) delusion (p. 279). However, as one would suppose from the above sketch of the psychological factors underlying the hypochondriac's symptoms, such relief is, as a rule, extremely shortlived. As with other neurotic symptoms, those of hypochondriasis represent an attempt at adjustment. Hence, if they are interfered with by such superficial measures (and the patient is left with nothing to take their place), they either return shortly in their original forms or are replaced by other symptoms of equal severity.

As a matter of fact, while such an approach is of some theoretical interest, it is quite often therapeutically incorrect, since it may signify to the patient that he is not understood and thus it may actually further estrange him from the doctor. The proper approach is to accept the patient fully with his complaints and to endeavor to earn his trust and confidence. If a good relationship can ultimately be established, then there is the hope of coming to understand the patient sufficiently to be of help in meeting some of his more fundamental needs.

If the syndrome of hypochondriasis is suspected, a psychiatric evaluation is indicated. In its milder forms, this condition may be treated by various supportive measures, including psychotherapy, on an outpatient basis. In some instances, this treatment can be carried out by the family physician. One rarely expects a "cure" in the sense of enabling the patient to become symptom-free, but one may have the reasonable hope of assisting the patient to effect a moderately good overall adjustment. In more severe forms, the condition usually requires hospitalization and its treatment then, in many ways, resembles that utilized for various forms of schizophrenia (Chaps. 11 and 14).

PROGNOSIS AND TREATMENT OF THE PSYCHONEUROSES

As will be understood from the examples which have been offered in this chapter, the range of symptom-producing maladaptations which comprise the classical psychoneuroses is so great that it is difficult to make general statements about prognosis. If one were to include such phenomena as far-spaced, fleeting spells of anxiety, transient minor conversions, and the commoner mild phobic manifestations, he might say that the majority of human beings experience psychoneuroses *at one time or another*. The corollary would be that the prognosis is generally good, both for symptom remission and for a state of reasonable well-being after the episode. Furthermore, such a statement could be made independently of considering the effects of treatment.

On the other hand, there are instances—such as of Miss M., the young woman with a phobic reaction, and of Mr. D., the man with a compulsive reaction—in which, apart from intensive psychiatric assistance, the prognosis is quite poor, whether for symptom remission or for any sort of "learning to live with" the symptoms.

One generalization which can be made with some assurance is that, other factors being equal, the less the etiological contribution of the predisposing elements, the more favorable is the prognosis. Since predisposition involves significant emotional and learning experiences during the individual's earliest and most formative years, a closely related—though not identical—generalization is that, whatever the symptoms, the greater the personality's total resources (intelligence, specific talents, capacity to sublimate, etc.), the more favorable the prognosis.

A third generalization has to do, not directly with the patient, but with his situation, including both the specific precipitating factors and other factors bearing upon the patient's general well-being. Insofar as any of these elements have to do with the development or perpetuation of the neurosis, the more modifiable the situation is, the better the prognosis.

Present-day treatment of the psychoneuroses involves three principal modalities: psychotherapy (pp. 436 to 450 and 478 to 497), environmental manipulation (pp. 514 to 515; also portions of Chap. 14), and chemotherapy (pp. 452 to 460).

Unless the illness partakes to a considerable extent of the nature of a traumatic neurosis, i.e., unless predisposition is of minimal significance, a cure in the dual sense of (a) complete alleviation of symptoms and (b) deep-going alterations of the personality, removing the specific vulnerabilities to subsequent episodes, requires either intensive psychotherapy of an "expressive" or "uncovering" nature (p. 484) or, in the more severe instances, psychoanalysis (pp. 484 to 489).

If the morbid reaction appears to be very largely the product of the precipitating events, or if for any reason, it appears highly impractical to think in terms of appreciable personality revision, treatment would probably be by a combination of a "suppressive" (pp. 436 to 440), a "supportive" (pp. 440 to 450), or perhaps, of a "relationship" type (pp. 481 to 484) of psychotherapy with thoughtfully considered environmental manipulation.

The place of chemotherapy in the treatment of the neuroses now appears to be assured, but its precise definition is not yet generally agreed upon. There is reason to believe that these drugs ("tranquilizers," "psychic energizers," etc.), exerting a powerful effect upon the patient's affective life, may obscure or confuse important psychological issues. Therefore they are seldom used in the course of a psychoanalysis and not often used in the course of an intensive psychotherapy having as its objective the acquisition of insight. On the other hand, they may very properly be used as part of a therapeutic approach having symptom removal or alleviation as its basic objective. At times, they also have a place in the initial phase(s) of treatment of a patient for whom psychoanalysis or intensive psychotherapy is contemplated, but whose clinical condition at the time of the initial evaluation is such as to interfere seriously with his participation in the more ambitious forms of therapy. (Examples: a serious anxiety reaction, verging on panic, or a neurotic depression of unusual intensity.)

The use of chemotherapeutic techniques as the sole modality of treatment of a neurotic reaction is nearly always to be deplored. Not only are the patient's chances of a good symptomatic recovery increased by the personal support which can be conveyed only through interviews, but the shifts in the balance of psychological forces within him can be followed in this way and no other. Even if the patient were to have received the correct initial diagnosis, to place him upon some form of chemotherapy and then neglect psychotherapeutic contacts would be similar to diagnosing a severe respiratory infection, placing the patient on an antibiotic, and thereafter neglecting to evaluate the shifting signs and symptoms.

The question as to when a patient experiencing a neurotic reaction should be treated by the family physician and when he should be treated by a psychiatrist has been touched on in Chapter 5 and will be discussed at greater length (along with related questions) in Chapter 13. The original diagnosis is, however, of critical importance to the therapeutic management (not merely the clinical diagnosis, but an appraisal of the intensity of the reaction and of the assets and liabilities of the personality in general); hence, if there is any doubt in the family physician's mind, a psychiatric consultation is clearly indicated, even if it were to be decided later that treatment should remain in the hands of the referring doctor.

Suggestions for Further Reading

Abse, D. W.: Hysteria *in* Arieti, S. (ed.): American Handbook of Psychiatry, New York, Basic, 1959.

Freud, S.: A General Introduction to Psychoanalysis, pp. 268-283, Garden City, New York, Permabooks (Doubleday), 1953.

Lindner, R.: The Fifty Minute Hour, New York, Rinehart, 1955.

Maslow, A. H., and Mittelmann, B.: Principles of Abnormal Psychology, ed. 2, pp. 431-453, New York, Harper, 1951.

CHAPTER 10

The Functional Psychoses Part 1: The Affective Reactions

At the present state of medical knowledge, the designation of certain psychotic syndromes as functional (i.e., primarily psychogenic; see p. 271) must be somewhat tentative, reflecting a weighing of probabilities and a placing of terminological emphasis rather than being an absolute statement. There is, of course, no doubt that such an entity as a purely psychogenic psychosis can exist: a clear-cut example can be seen in *panic state*. In the case of certain major psychoses, however, the evidence is still quite incomplete although it is being very actively accumulated and sifted at the present time. The psychiatric conditions which are currently considered as the major functional psychoses are *affective reactions* (depressive or manic), *schizophrenic reactions*, and *paranoid reactions*.

Of these disorders it can be said that: (1) they involve no pathognomonic histological alterations, either of the central nervous system or elsewhere in the body; (2) there is very strong evidence for the etiological significance of psychological factors; (3) with the probable exception of paranoid reactions, there is some evidence, weaker than that for psychological factors but whose precise weight is difficult to assess, for the etiological significance of organic factors (including hereditarily determined elements) in the form of subtle metabolic derangements; and (4) there is no necessary conflict between the two lines of evidence since there is good reason to believe that the etiology of these disorders is complex (multifactorial).

AFFECTIVE (PSYCHOTIC) REACTIONS

Depressions of Psychotic Intensity

Clinically speaking, depressive reactions appear to form a continuum, ranging from "blue spells" through mourning reactions and neurotic depressions to psychotic depressive reactions, including those of a recurrent or cyclic nature. (It is suggested that the student review the material on pp. 130 to 134 and pp. 333 to 336.) The following case history is illustrative of the principal features of a psychotic depression, showing both the similarities to and the differences from the milder forms of depressive mood alterations.

Mr. T. S., aged 40, married and the father of three children, was hospitalized after a consultation between his family physician and a psychiatrist. In the hospital, if left to his own devices, he would spend most of his time sitting on a chair by the side of his bed, moaning and wringing his hands. His facial expression was one of the deepest dejection, and his eyes were reddened from weeping. At times he would get up and pace the floor heavily. All of his postural muscles seemed to sag, giving him the appearance of a much older man. Mr. S. was anorexic and, if left to himself, would not eat. He was severely constipated. He tended to ignore his personal appearance and hygiene completely. He was insomnic although appearing to be very fatigued.

As a rule, Mr. S. would not speak unless spoken to, but occasionally he would address another patient or a member of the ward staff. At such times he would usually blame himself in the harshest terms for having "ruined his family," saying that he did not deserve to live. Now and then, paradoxically, he would express fears of dying, saying that he was certain that he had some incurable physical disease, the nature of which the doctors were concealing from him.

The physical and laboratory findings were essentially negative except for indications of rather marked recent weight loss and mild dehydration.

The patient was unable to give an adequate history of the present illness, but Mrs. S. gave a rather full statement which included the following relevant material. The couple had been married for 12 years, and the marriage, for the most part, had been reasonably satisfactory. Mr. S. was the proprietor of a small business; he worked hard and was a good provider. He was a careful, conscientious, and methodical person, very fair in his dealings with others. He placed great emphasis upon routine and was disconcerted by departures from it. He seldom took a vacation, and when he did, he was apt to become restless after a few days, finding it difficult to relax. He was lacking in a sense of humor although he tried to be a good sport about things. His business judgment was usually sound, but he was evidently an insecure person, for he seldom expressed confidence in himself.

About three months before the present admission, Mr. S. had experienced a minor business reverse. A month later, while he was still endeavoring to cope with this situation, his mother died of a heart attack. The patient was terribly distressed. He appeared to grieve deeply. He was restless and agitated. He became anorexic and increasingly insomnic. For a time he strove to carry on his business, but he was quite ineffectual, and had had to turn the management over to an assistant. At first the family had interpreted his condition as one of deep mourning, but they realized that something more serious was taking place as his self-reproach became increasingly intense and unrealistic. (He spoke of himself as having thrown away the family resources and having caused his mother's death and the impoverishment of his wife and children.) Mrs. S. had become increasingly frightened, but had not known what to do. When the patient had begun to speak of himself as not deserving to live, his wife had sought medical assistance.

As may be judged from this description, the characteristic clinical findings in psychotic depression are striking and readily recognizable. The mood is one of profound melancholy and dejection. Anxiety is nearly always present in some degree and it may be very great, manifesting itself in word, manner, and overt agitation. Although it tends to be masked by the pervasive sadness, a touch of hostility toward figures in the environment can usually be discerned (primarily in the patient's inconsiderate behavior).

Mr. S.'s appearance and manner were typical. The psychotically depressed patient is apt to be completely neglectful of his appearance. His whole manner is indicative of extreme distress. His facial expression is apt to be relatively immobile, although it may show a grievous animation. Typically the forehead is transversely furrowed, the nasolabial folds are accentuated, and the corners of the mouth droop. The patient's gaze, for the most part, is fixed downward. The postural muscles sag, giving the patient the appearance of being older than he is. Aside from movements expressive of agitation, all that the patient does is done heavily and slowly.

The patient's stream of talk is retarded and, typically, greatly diminished. The content of thought is monotonous and appropriate to the mood. Typically there is a great deal of bitter self-reproach, some of it of a frankly delusional character (i.e., the patient accuses himself of grave offenses which he has not committed). Frequently there are also delusions about the patient's physical state; ideas that his body, particularly the viscera, are being consumed by cancer or some other ominous disease are frequent. Pleas and demands for reassurance are often made; if the conventional responses are given, they are unavailing or make the patient feel worse.

At one point early in his hospital stay, Mr. S. was engaged in conversation by a well-intentioned but inexperienced nursing student. The patient had heaped reproaches on himself, and the student had countered by saying that she knew he was a good man and had tried hard to do his best for his family. The patient became rapidly more distraught and continued to vilify himself, saying, "No one knows how I am suffering. Do you really think I am fit to live?" The student became tense and, unconsciously, somewhat irritated.* She strove to conceal her feelings

---

* The student's irritation very likely was not merely in response to a feeling of professional helplessness, but in response to a subtle feature of the patient's words and manner, i.e., a curious kind of conceit. It is very often true that the psychotically

by making sympathetic comments. Mr. S. then burst into tears and began to strike his head with the palm of his hand.

Hallucinations are quite uncommon in psychotic depressions; illusions are occasionally noted (but may be difficult to distinguish from delusions). If these phenomena occur, their content is in keeping with the patient's general mood and content of thought. For example, one patient had the illusory impression that an oxygen administrator was an instrument for his torture (actually "seeing" it in this way).

It has been conventional to group a number of findings noted in psychotically depressed patients as "the vegetative signs of depression." These findings are: (1) anorexia, (2) loss of weight, (3) constipation, (4) insomnia, (5) amenorrhea in women, and (6) what is called "morning-evening variation." Actually, the term "vegetative" lacks accuracy, but the list retains significance as being fundamental to the diagnosis of psychotic depression. "Morning-evening variation" refers to a change in the intensity of the patient's symptoms during the course of the day. It is typical of psychotic depression for the patient's mood and whatever other symptoms are present to be at their worst in the early morning hours and to ameliorate somewhat by afternoon or evening. The point can be of some diagnostic significance, for it tends to differentiate psychotic from neurotic depressions. In the latter condition, if there is a diurnal variation, it is usually from better to worse. (Cf. R. L.'s loss of appetite for the evening meal, p. 334.)

An aspect of the psychotically depressed patient which is of great importance both practically and theoretically is the potentiality for suicide. The self-condemnation of such patients is frequently not confined to thoughts and words, but finds expression in overt acts of a self-destructive nature.* The risk is great and warrants prompt hospitalization with more or less continuous surveillance until the patient is well out of the depression. The period of greatest risk is usually not, as one might suppose it to be, when the patient appears clinically the most depressed, but shortly afterward, when it looks as if recovery has begun. The reasons for this circumstance are not entirely clear. One plausible explanation is that when the patient is at lowest ebb he lacks the energy to carry out a suicidal act, whereas later on, while he may still be in a mood to destroy himself, he may have more energy at his disposal.

In this country, at the present time, one no longer observes the full natural course of a psychotic depression. However, before the advent of

---

depressed patient, far from being humble or submissive, flaunts his misery, not minding in the least if others are upset thereby. (The misery is nevertheless entirely genuine.)

* Severely depressed patients are apt to furnish shattering disproof of the old saw that "people who talk a lot about suicide never commit suicide."

electroconvulsive therapy (p. 475) and mood-elevating drugs (p. 459), it was established that most periods of psychotic depression tend to be self-limited (in this respect resembling milder episodes of depression). Barring death from suicide or the effects of malnutrition, after a period of months, or sometimes of one or more years, the patient would usually experience a gradual return to his previous level of adjustment. The susceptibility to further episodes—a matter which is not appreciably affected by treatment of the psychotic reaction, per se—depends upon factors to be discussed presently under the question of etiology.

In the case of Mr. S., it is evident that the major precipitating event of his psychosis was the death of the patient's mother. Indeed, the case was selected for presentation because it illustrates with especial clarity the relationship between psychotic depression and ordinary mourning.* As the student will recall from Chapter 5, in mourning the personality is faced with a complex problem of adjustment. On the one hand, there is the loss (or at least a profound sense of loss) of the affection and the emotional support of the deceased. On the other, there is the disquieting effect inevitably produced when inner strivings are suddenly deprived of an object. As described on page 132, the "work of mourning" consists largely in efforts within the bereaved's personality to "let go" emotionally of the now hopeless yearnings toward the deceased. This process involves a temporary intensification of memories of the deceased and a gradual (and, of course, partial) detachment of libido from these memories, thus freeing it for new attachments or the strengthening of (other) existing attachments. The development or strengthening of these attachments completes the process of mourning and results in the re-establishment of a state of adjustment.

The whole work of mourning, as has been said, may be further complicated by the effects of conscience. If the relationship between the bereaved and the lost emotional object (the deceased) has been fundamentally sound, these effects are very mild. If it has been significantly ambivalent (p. 95), the work of mourning is interfered with, and the emotional crisis is prolonged and intensified.

In instances, such as the case of Mr. S., in which mourning passes over into psychotic depression, the relationship with the deceased has typically been highly ambivalent, and accordingly *the conscience activity becomes extreme.* In most such instances—and this was true of Mr. S.—the negative components of the emotional strivings directed toward the deceased are in large part unconscious.

Mr. S.'s father and an aunt were interviewed in an attempt to obtain the patient's early personal history. In the father's judgment, the pa-

* A relationship which is of great theoretical significance, but is often far more obscure than in this case.

tient's early relationship with his mother had been "quite satisfactory" although "not free and easy." H. S. was described as a "dutiful and conscientious son." The aunt mentioned some more specific points, including the fact that the patient had been "a feeding problem" at around the end of his first year, and she felt that the patient's mother in his early childhood had been "impatient for him to grow up."

At a later stage in the patient's course of treatment, projective psychological tests (p. 542) were administered, and they proved to be consistent with the fragmentary material obtained from the father and aunt. They indicated that the patient continued to have strong (unconscious) yearnings for maternal love of a sort appropriate for an infant plus a deep-seated (also unconscious) anxious hostility toward women, particularly mother-figures. The conscious attitudes were ones of affection and compliance.

As a result of this third factor, the harsh disapproval of conscience, there is an immediate further lowering of the individual's self-esteem (well below the point which is typical of a state of mourning and which is reached out of a normal sense of loss). A state of acute psychological emergency develops, which the personality is unable to deal with by ordinary techniques of adjustment. As a result, the regular process of mourning cannot be carried on, and a severe regression (p. 75) ensues, in which the personality experiences a retreat to the emotional position of infancy.

The influence of the conscience blocks any expression of the subject's hostility in its original form, i.e., toward the deceased. The mounting pressure of hostility is dealt with by the mechanism which has been called "turning against the self" (p. 79). In other words, all of the negative emotions which had originated in the relationship with the lost object now become manifest in the form of self-condemnation.*
This development constitutes the final blow to the subject's self-esteem, which is virtually annihilated.

To repeat and summarize, one can say that *the devastation of a patient's self-esteem in psychotic depression has (typically) three sources: a sense of loss, severe disapproval of conscience, and a turning inward of hostile impulses which had originally developed toward the lost object.*

The question may naturally arise as to why the patient's hostility

---

* An important psychoanalytic concept underlying what has been expressed in this and the preceding paragraph is that, in connection with the arrest of the process of mourning, the subject *introjects* (p. 78) certain characteristics of the lost object, particularly hated characteristics. As a result of the ensuing partial identification with the object, *the subject comes to hate that part of himself which is now equivalent to the object.* Evidence tending to support this view is the clinical observation that quite often inappropriate accusations which the depressed patient makes against himself turn out (on close study of the family history) to fit much more closely some aspects of the behavior of an important figure in the patient's early life (who in the current situation is, or is equated with, the lost object). See discussion on p. 133.

should become intensified under just these circumstances. The answer has three components: (a) unconsciously, the patient interprets his loss (in the specific instance we have been considering, the actual death of the loved-and-hated object) as a rejection, (b) the heightened memory activity tends to stimulate long-standing, though latent, hostile impulses, and (c) the regression activates infantile sources of anger toward the object.

Various aspects of the treatment of psychotic depressions will be presented in a later chapter, but the following episode may be considered at this point as an illustration of some of the dynamic factors in the illness.

Shortly after the experience involving the nursing student, Mr. S. was conducted, rather against his will, to the occupational therapy room (p. 462). Nothing attracted his interest, and he asked the therapist to be allowed to return to his room, saying that his presence would only spoil the enjoyment of the others. The therapist spoke to Mr. S. in a kind manner, but with extreme firmness, saying that, whether he was sick or not, there was some work that needed to be done. She gave the patient some sandpaper and told him to remove the paint from a piece of hospital furniture that was to be restored. The patient complained bitterly, maintaining that he would be sure to make a failure of the work, but finally he complied. He worked fitfully, with frequent pauses, during which he would point out how poorly he was doing.

Having often participated in the treatment of depressed patients, the occupational therapist felt quite comfortable with Mr. S., and she merely reminded him in a courteous but businesslike way that the furniture was needed and would have to be finished somehow. The patient became absorbed in his work as he continued. Eventually he sanded with an almost fierce vigor. On returning to the ward, Mr. S. complained about the therapist, but for the first time he ate a portion of his meal on his own initiative.

Much can be learned about severe depression from consideration of an episode of this sort. One of the chief points to be noted is *the redirection of the patient's hostility*. The therapist's firmness in confronting the patient with a task to be done enabled him to turn a small portion of his hostility outward again, away from himself and onto a figure in the environment (thus effecting a transient and partial reversal of the process by which he had become ill). This slight gain was immediately utilized in getting the patient to apply himself to a task. The nature of this task—one which required vigorous muscular effort in overcoming mechanical resistance—was such as to allow a slight draining off of the (redirected) hostile energy, i.e., it was a sublimation (p. 75).

The task had other features which gave it therapeutic value: it was activity of a monotonous, tiring sort, and it was activity which would benefit the hospital. In other words, it had implications of penitence and restitution. These aspects offered the patient a bit of relief from the harassment of his conscience.

It should, incidentally, be pointed out that the chief therapeutic principle illustrated in the example of Mr. S. and the occupational therapist —the value of the redirection outward of the depressed patient's hostility —is also applicable to other situations. It frequently happens, for example, that when an antidepressant drug (p. 459) is taking effect the patient will express anger toward the doctors and nurses who are in attendance upon him. Since this anger is not objectively justified, it is often responded to with suppressive and rejecting attitudes by the professionals. It is important to see that such responses work in opposition to the beneficial effect of the drug, and may neutralize it altogether. Such inconsistent management is especially likely to occur when the patient is afflicted with some organic disease as well as depression and therefore is being treated on a medical or surgical unit. In the nonpsychiatric setting, undue reliance is apt to be placed upon the purely pharmacological effect of the medication, and the integrally related effect of the patient's relationships is too easily disregarded.

Returning now to the main thread of the discussion, one can probably see with reasonable clarity how a psychotic depression can develop, under certain circumstances, from a bereavement followed by a disturbed mourning reaction. It is obvious, however, that a decided majority of psychotic depressions are not immediately preceded by an actual bereavement. The question naturally arises as to how one is to account for such instances.

In seeking an answer, it must be remembered that even in cases such as that of Mr. S. in which a bereavement has taken place, it is primarily the bereaved's *sense of loss* and *sense of guilt*, rather than his actual loss and "objective" guilt, which are critical. That is to say, in his adult life Mr. S. was not dependent upon things that his mother actually said and did so much as he was upon what she meant to him; nor was his sense of guilt dependent upon his having mistreated her, but rather, upon buried hostile impulses toward her.

This being the case, it need not come as a surprise to learn that the precipitating circumstance for a psychotic depression in many instances is not a serious actual bereavement, but merely an event which symbolically represents a bereavement. Such happenings as the death of a neighbor or a distant relative or an important public figure may trigger a depression. So may the loss of a pet animal, of a job, or of a piece of property. So may an emotional estrangement from some figure of significance in the patient's life, or geographical removal from such a figure.

In all such instances, if one is in a position to study in depth the thoughts and emotions of the depressed patient, one can discern that the precipitating event has caused the patient to relive an experience of severe bereavement with all of the complications described in the case of Mr. S.

Is it then necessary, for the production of a psychotic depression, that the individual *at some previous time in his life* have experienced the actual loss of a highly significant (loved-and-hated) figure? No, not literally. It is true that in some instances a person experiencing a psychotic depression will be found to have experienced the loss of his mother or of a mother-figure in infancy, and that the precipitating event in adult life will be found to represent the original loss. This sequence of events is, however, the exception and not the rule.

What is much more commonly found is that the original experiences, predisposing to the later development of a psychotic depression, constituted *the psychological equivalent of a bereavement*. That is to say, neither the precipitating event nor the predisposing circumstances need involve an actual, physical loss; both may involve an overwhelming *sense of loss*.

Typically, what has happened is that the relationship between the individual, as an infant, and the figure upon whom he is most dependent, usually his mother, for a time was sufficiently disturbed to have had an impact similar to that which would have been produced by the mother's actual death. It appears that the period between one-half and one and one-half years of age is especially critical in this respect. As the student will recall from Chapter 4, during this period the infant is still almost completely dependent upon the mother for love and, indeed, for life itself. Moreover, as contrasted with the first several months of life, there is a considerable and an increasing recognition of the mother during this period, first as a discrete object (or group of objects) and then as a person. Given the urgency of the infant's needs and their focusing with increasing clarity upon the person of the mother, one can readily see that if the mother is unable to meet these needs, the effect upon the infant can be very severe. From the point of view of an infant who is allowed to go unnourished—physically or emotionally—for repeated periods (even brief ones) during this developmental phase, the mother might as well be dead.

It is not to be thought, however, that this disturbance need be a very obvious affair (to an observer). It may be so, but more commonly it is a subtler estrangement.

Sometimes the sequence of events appears to be as follows: There is an initial period of perhaps as long as one year in which the infant's needs are adequately met, followed by a rather abrupt and decisive change in the attitudes of the parents (and particularly the mother) in the direction of increased demands and expectations, of a premature insistence upon the infant's moving into childhood. The infant is made to feel that his supply of support and affection is contingent upon his meeting the demands and expectations. Great insecurity is thus created and hostility is stimulated, which, since it cannot be expressed, is turned inward and is felt as a primitive analogue of what would be called a severe sense of guilt in an older child or an adult.

Various circumstances usually come gradually into play to bring about a partial alleviation of the situation: the small child begins to achieve a performance level which brings the necessary minimum of parental approval, other figures enter the scene, making some contribution to the child's sense of security. Yet the harm may have been done, and the individual may retain a vulnerability which will predispose him to a seriously morbid reaction in later life, whenever the old conflicts are sufficiently revived.

As will be remembered from the material on page 346 there was good reason to believe that some such sequence had taken place in the infancy and early childhood of Mr. T. S. Presumably, this period in the patient's early life was less traumatic, on the whole, than is often the case with a person developing a psychotic depression, inasmuch as the onset of the psychosis required precipitating events (the business reverse and the death of the mother) of greater magnitude than is often found. Yet one can see that Mr. S.'s illness was, after all, less of a special case than at first appeared. In psychotic depression, as in other forms of psychiatric illness, there is a complementary relationship (p. 307) between predisposing events and precipitating events. If the one set of circumstances have been quite severe, the other need only have been mild or moderate for the production of the illness.

It should be mentioned at this point that, if the immediate circumstances are extremely traumatic, very little or even nothing may be discernible in the way of remote predisposing events. Clear-cut examples of this type of situation are rarely found in ordinary civilian practice. They were discovered, however, in appreciable numbers in prisoner-of-war and concentration camps during World War II. These subjects had experienced extreme and sustained environmental stress, involving severe physical privations and traumata and all sorts of humiliations and indignities. As a result of the unusual severity and duration of these blows, some prisoners reached the point of feeling utterly worthless and helpless. In such cases, guilt feelings were not necessarily a decisive factor in the production of the depressive syndrome; self-esteem had collapsed under the impact of unendurable current happenings.

In psychotic depressions of the sort just mentioned, if the individuals survive the experience and then, in a less stressful environment, recover their previous level of adjustment, they are not especially prone to further episodes of depression. On the other hand, persons who have developed psychotic depressions in the absence of overwhelming environmental stress may, after clinical recovery, remain psychologically vulnerable to subsequent psychotic episodes.

Strange as it may seem at first thought, patients who are subject to recurrent episodes of a mood disturbance of psychotic intensity may, in one instance, experience a reaction of the sort we have just been considering (depression), and in another, experience a reaction of equal severity which may assume a quite different clinical form, a form characterized by an intense and unrealistic elevation of spirits, *mania*. The interrelationship of these two syndromes and the bases for the recurrence of psychotic episodes of either sort will be discussed shortly, but first it will be well to present an example of the second syndrome.

Manic Reaction

The following excerpt from a case-history illustrates some of the principal features of mania.

As seen on the ward the morning after admission, Mrs. L. J., aged 38, presented a striking picture. She had been too excited to eat breakfast, but after gulping a cup of coffee she had taken several daisies from the centerpiece on the table and entwined them in her hair. She paced briskly up and down the hallways singing snatches of popular songs, and she paused briefly from time to time attempting to get other patients and personnel to join in the singing. Her eyes were bright, her cheeks flushed; she looked youthful and quite pretty, despite a general carelessness in her attire.

Mrs. J. took the initiative in greeting everyone she encountered, patting the women on the back in a familiar manner and putting her arms around the men. It was, however, almost impossible for personnel to maintain a conversation with her. She responded with smiles and laughter to most remarks addressed to her and often talked volubly, but she was too distractible to give attention to any one subject for more than a moment. If an effort was made to detain her or to hold her attention, she would break away with a transient flash of anger.

A brief excerpt from the patient's stream of talk was as follows: "How do I feel? I feel with my hands. How do you feel? No, seriously, everything's wonderful. Couldn't be better. Going 'From Bed to Worse,' Benchley said." (Laughs.) "Really, honey, this is a marvelous place you've got here, mar-ve-lous. 'Marvelous *Vel.*' I really must shampoo my hair."

Mrs. J.'s talk was full of personal references, including comments (having no factual basis) about her extensive wardrobe, purchased from the couturier utilized by the President's wife, and fragmentary plans for a world cruise on which her younger sister and family were supposedly to be her guests.

In the course of the diagnostic evaluation and subsequent treatment of Mrs. J., a full background history was obtained, of which two features may be mentioned here. (1) The present illness had begun about ten days prior to admission upon the patient's having received the information that an ambitious volunteer-service project of which she had been chairman had failed to gain the approval of the community agency on which it depended. (2) Her initial response had been one of low spirits and irritability, lasting two or three days and then giving way to a mood of unusual cheerfulness, accompanied by various erratic activities and gaining in intensity until it reached the reckless and irrational gaiety shown on admission. On the previous day, the patient had stopped at a travel agency where, despite her confusion, she had arranged passage for five on a luxury cruise at a cost which was wildly beyond the family's means.

One sees that the symptom-picture of mania is, in many ways, the direct opposite of that in psychotic depression.

The patient's mood is one of a florid gaiety; on brief exposure, it is rather infectious. The facial expression is, for the most part, joyous. Muscular tone is high; the patient's movements are speeded up (sometimes very markedly so); his step is resilient, and his appearance is more youthful than befitting his calendar age.

There is a great relaxation of ordinary inhibitions, a disregard for social conventions. All motor activity tends to be increased. In early stages and in mild forms of the disorder (*hypomania*), the appetite and libido are increased, and the patient may eat and engage in sexual activity with an avidity quite beyond his usual pattern. As the tension mounts, the patient's actual performance in these areas decreases. The excitement appears to be too great to allow sustained attention even to ordinarily gratifying activity. As in the case of Mrs. J., the expression of the drives is shown in allusions and gestures rather than in accomplishment.

The type of speech illustrated in the case-history (or, speaking more strictly, the ideational activity underlying it) is known as *flight of ideas*. There are swift changes in topic, with most lines of thought not being pursued to a conclusion as in ordinary conversation. Notice, however, that each idea is connected with the preceding one by some intelligible association. The speech of the manic is sometimes witty and often verges on the witty, lacking only the ingredient of an underlying intellectual discipline. It is a strange way of talking, having as an important function the discharge of inner tension, but nevertheless remaining partly in the service of communication.

Delusions, shifting rather than fixed as to content, are common in mania, and as in the case of Mrs. J., they are typically of a grandiose nature. The patient thinks of himself as being very wealthy, powerful, handsome, sexually irresistible, etc. The precise form of the delusional ideas is largely dependent upon the pre-morbid personality. Fleeting ideas of persecution are not uncommon.

Hallucinations and illusions are not the rule, but their presence is compatible with the diagnosis of mania. When present, their content is consistent with that of the delusions.

If the reaction is allowed to continue untreated, the patient experiences severe physiological strain. Ideational and motor activity are accelerated to the point at which the minimum needs for food and rest cannot be met. Before the advent of modern therapeutic methods, manic patients at the height of their excitement occasionally died of sheer exhaustion.

Despite the dramatic clinical differences of the two syndromes, psychotic depression and mania, their relationship has long been recognized. Weighty evidence of the connection was found in the long-term study of patients afflicted with mood disorders. Such case-histories showed that quite often the same individual would at one period experience a depressive reaction and at another period, a manic reaction. Some instances were noted in which the two syndromes even alternated in a fairly regular fashion. Some were discovered in which a patient passed directly from a depressive reaction to a manic reaction without an intervening phase of clinical normality. The reverse phenomenon was also recorded. Of much greater frequency was the finding that a full-blown reaction of either sort would be ushered in by a transient (and milder) reaction of the other sort. (A circumstance exemplified by both T. S. and L. J.) A final clinical point was the finding that, insofar as precipitating circumstances could be made out,* they appeared to be of the same general sort: a disappointment or loss (actual or symbolic).

Given an individual whose personality is predisposed to the development of a mood disturbance of psychotic proportions and given precipitating circumstances of the sort which have been mentioned, what determines the direction which the patient's responses will take? When will the resulting syndrome be that of mania and when that of psychotic depression? The answer is not yet fully known. Evidently, in the case of many persons predisposed to a psychotic mood disorder, there is a considerable degree of potential instability in the personality. That is to say, not only are the predisposing inner conflicts intense, but they involve a rather even balance of opposing forces. The precipitating circumstances serve to upset this precarious equilibrium, and a brief period of inner turmoil ensues, in which hostile and other impulses struggle against feelings of loss, of guilt, and of shame. If (for

* Sometimes they cannot be discerned with any assurance.

whatever reasons) the instinctual impulses win out for the time being, the result is the manic syndrome; if the anti-instinctual forces win out, the result is the depressive syndrome.

Recurrent Affective Psychotic Reactions (Manic-Depressive Psychosis)

We may now return to the consideration of a related problem introduced on page 351, the phenomenon of *recurrence*. Whereas some individuals may experience but a single episode of a psychotic mood disturbance, either depression or mania (more commonly the former), others may experience repeated episodes of one or the other syndrome or of both. Here again the full answer is not known. Insofar as purely psychological factors are concerned, one can say, in general, that the predisposing factors (traumatic experiences of late infancy and early childhood) are likely to have been more severe in patients who experience repeated psychotic episodes than in those who have a single such experience.

Related to this circumstance is the common finding that patients in the former group—long before the onset of the first psychotic episode, as well as later on during periods of clinical remission—tend to experience mood swings in excess of normal. One can often detect in the fundamental personality make-up of such individuals the tendency toward exaggerated affective responses which are manifest in extreme form in the clinical illness. (This type of personality is referred to as *cyclothymic*.)

Another element seemingly has to do with the nature and the extent of the inner healing which takes place as the patient returns from a given psychotic episode to clinical normality. To resume for a moment the analogy between mourning and depression, one may say that in some instances (particularly those in which intensive psychotherapy is used) the patient is able to obtain a greater degree of freedom from the torturing emotions which, even when latent, made him susceptible to the psychotic reaction.* (He accomplishes something corresponding to the "work of mourning" in the case of ordinary bereavement.) Insofar as this development takes place, the likelihood of subsequent episodes of a psychotic mood disorder appears to be reduced. In other instances, recovery from the psychotic reaction appears to involve merely a re-establishment of the pre-existing personality defenses, leaving the patient as vulnerable as before to chance circumstances capable of mobilizing the old conflicts in all of their original intensity. In such cases there is a strong likelihood of subsequent psychotic episodes.

---

* In terms of the footnote to page 346, one would say that the patient is able to give up some of the disturbing introjects.

Before mentioning current trends of thought with respect to the possible significance of *organic* etiological factors, it is necessary to refer to some problems of nomenclature. For the sake of coherence, that portion of the official (A.P.A.) nomenclature dealing with the "functional psychoses" is given below. It will also be referred to in the subsequent discussions of *schizophrenic reactions* and *paranoid reactions*.

DISORDERS OF PSYCHOGENIC ORIGIN OR WITHOUT CLEARLY DEFINED PHYSICAL CAUSE OR STRUCTURAL CHANGE IN THE BRAIN

Psychotic Disorders
Disorders Due to Disturbance of Metabolism, Growth, Nutrition or Endocrine Factors
    Involutional psychotic reaction
Disorders of Psychogenic Origin or Without Clearly Defined Tangible Cause or Structural Change
    Affective reactions
        Manic depressive reaction, manic type
        Manic depressive reaction, depressive type
        Manic depressive reaction, other
        Psychotic depressive reaction
    Schizophrenic reactions
        Schizophrenic reaction, simple type
        Schizophrenic reaction, hebephrenic type
        Schizophrenic reaction, paranoid type
        Schizophrenic reaction, catatonic type
        Schizophrenic reaction, acute undifferentiated type
        Schizophrenic reaction, chronic undifferentiated type
        Schizophrenic reaction, schizo-affected type
        Schizophrenic reaction, childhood type
        Schizophrenic reaction, residual type
    Paranoid reactions
        Paranoia
        Paranoid state
Psychotic reaction without clearly defined structural change, other than above

The conditions which have thus far been discussed in this chapter fall under the subheading, *Affective Reactions*. The diagnostic term *manic-depressive reaction* is taken to mean *a psychotic disorder characterized by recurrent episodes of marked melancholia or elation, with appreciable loss of reality-testing, and accompanied by retardation or hyperactivity respectively*. The key word is, of course, *recurrent*. Given a patient who has previously experienced at least one psychotic mood disturbance (of either sort) from which he has made a full clinical recovery, the formal diagnosis is usually not difficult to make. On the other hand, if the patient under observation is experiencing his first psychotic affective reaction, there may be a serious question as to the appropriateness of the term *manic-depressive* with its implication of recurrence.

Since classical mania rarely appears as a single, isolated episode, this syndrome is ordinarily classified as *manic-depressive reaction, manic type* even if it is the first manifestation. If the syndrome is one of profound depression, the diagnostic decision rests on the psychiatrist's judgment as to the likelihood of recurrences. This, in turn, means an evaluation of the patient's basic personality make-up, with a weighing of the relative significance of predisposing and precipitating factors. If the former appear to be preponderant—and particularly if the patient's personality is of the cyclothymic type—the likelihood of recurrences is relatively great, and the term *manic-depressive reaction, depressive type* is used; if the precipitating factors appear the more significant, the likelihood of recurrences is much less, and the term *psychotic depressive reaction* is used.

The question of predisposing factors on a hereditary basis arises only in connection with manic-depressive reactions (i.e., not in connection with an isolated psychotic depressive reaction). Expert opinion is divided as to the nature, the significance, and, to an extent, even as to the existence of such factors. A detailed discussion of this controversial point is beyond the scope of this book, but the position which is currently the most widely held may be briefly summarized as follows. Predisposition to the development of manic-depressive psychosis appears to be a complex matter, always involving experiential factors and sometimes involving constitutional factors. The latter are believed to be hereditarily transmitted. Since the disorder does not appear in accordance with the laws of simple Mendelian inheritance, the hypothetical genic factor must be complex or weakly dominant.

Just as there is a complementary relationship between predisposing factors and precipitating factors in the production of any given episode of an affective psychosis, so there appears to be a complementary relationship between constitutional and experiential factors in the development of the predisposition. It is not difficult to see how this could be the case. If an infant is born without innate vulnerabilities of personality, his early experiences must be quite unfavorable to be significantly *traumatic*, i.e., to lead to the development of a predisposition to psychosis. If, on the other hand, an infant is born with innate vulnerabilities of personality, then his early experiences need be only slightly unfavorable to constitute significant traumata and thus to favor the development of a predisposition to psychosis. Evidently the "innate vulnerabilities" of which we have been speaking are quite specific, since, for example, the hereditary backgrounds of patients with manic-depressive reactions and of patients with schizophrenic reactions are not the same (when they are discernible). The nature of the specificity is, however, not known.

Involutional Psychotic Reaction

This condition, which receives a special heading in the official nomenclature, may be defined as *a psychotic reaction, primarily depressive in character, but usually with some paranoid features, commoner in women than in men, and occurring in association with involutional changes* ("change of life").

This syndrome was originally separated from other forms of psychotic depression because it was believed that biochemical alterations of the menopause (and probably of the male climacteric as well) were directly involved in its pathogenesis. The idea has never really been substantiated, and it is, in fact, open to serious question. It appears quite possible that every human being who lives through the period of sexual involution is temporarily placed under additional biological stress, but such a possibility scarcely justifies a separate diagnostic category for psychiatric disorders occurring during this period. It appears more likely that "involutional psychosis" is a form of psychotic depressive reaction (probably not of manic-depressive psychosis), having as its major precipitating factor the *meaning*—to the individual—of the total experience of involution. Recognizing the significance of a sense of loss in the production of depressions, it is not at all difficult to see how this could be the case (see pp. 119 to 121).

State hospital statistics indicate that there has been a decline in the incidence of manic-depressive reactions in the United States over the past 30 years. The reasons for the change are not thoroughly understood. It has been suggested that altered cultural conditions may be involved, and also that more efficacious methods of treatment may lessen the chances of a recurrent psychosis. To some extent, the newer figures may reflect trends in diagnosis, e.g., that, in questionable cases, a diagnosis of schizophrenic reaction is being made in a higher proportion of instances than formerly. As a rough approximation, the student may take the incidence figure of 10 per cent as representing the combined first-admission rate of all of the psychotic mood disorders, with the diagnostic category of manic-depressive reaction contributing about one-third of the number.

TREATMENT OF AFFECTIVE PSYCHOSES

The treatment of mania and of psychotic depressions is, of course, a matter for the psychiatrist. Specific measures will be discussed in detail in Chapter 14, but mention of the principal modalities may be briefly made at this point.

Prompt hospitalization is always indicated. In the case of the psychotically depressed patient, special precautionary measures must be taken to prevent suicidal acts. In both depressed and manic patients, attention must be given to the patient's basic nutritional and hygienic needs.

The treatment of mania and depression was revolutionized in the 1930's by the introduction of electroconvulsive therapy (p. 475). By this means the duration of the actual psychotic episode can nearly always be reduced from a matter of months or years to a matter of a few weeks. More recently, the use of chemotherapeutic agents, "tranquilizers" (p. 455) in mania and mood-elevating drugs in depression (p. 459), has supplanted electroconvulsive therapy to a considerable extent, yielding comparable results. Other therapeutic measures used in connection with psychotic episodes are: milieu therapy (p. 497), occupational and recreational therapies (p. 509), and supportive psychotherapy (p. 440).

Through these various means, the treatment of any given episode of a manic or a psychotic depressive reaction has become quite efficacious. The more difficult, and fundamentally the more important, task of effecting some modification of the underlying conflicts which limit the patient's adjustment and which may render him susceptible to further episodes can only occasionally be accomplished. No thoroughly satisfactory technique or combination of techniques for achieving this end is yet known. The method offering the patient the greatest possibility of reaching a state of lasting health is intensive psychotherapy (p. 484) or a modified form of psychoanalysis (p. 484), begun during a period of clinical remission. There is, however, mounting evidence that the more modest objective of assisting the patient to maintain his pre-psychotic level of adjustment (avoiding subsequent psychotic episodes) can often be attained through the use of chemotherapeutic agents plus supportive psychotherapy.

Suggestions for Further Reading

Abraham, K.: Notes on the psycho-analytical investigation and treatment of manic-depressive insanity and allied conditions (1911) *in* Selected Papers of Karl Abraham, London, Hogarth, 1927.

Arieti, S.: Manic-depressive psychosis *in* Arieti, S. (ed.): American Handbook of Psychiatry, Vol. I, New York, Basic, 1959.

Bellak, L.: Manic-Depressive Psychosis and Allied Conditions, New York, Grune, 1952.

Freud, S.: Mourning and melancholia (1917) *in* Collected Papers of Sigmund Freud, Vol. 4, London, Hogarth, 1925.

CHAPTER 11

The Functional Psychoses Part 2: Schizophrenic and Paranoid Reactions

SCHIZOPHRENIC REACTIONS

A look at the official nomenclature of the functional psychoses (p. 355) is likely to create something of a false impression with respect to "schizophrenic reactions." It may appear that here is a well-defined disease entity, having a number of well-defined clinical variations. The truth is that the term is used to cover various (seemingly) related morbid reaction-patterns, the pathogeneses of which are complex, almost certainly multifactorial, and differing from one patient to another. To a considerable extent, the diagnosis itself remains a descriptive one.

Taken together, schizophrenic reactions (or "the schizophrenias") constitute one of the greatest of all medical problems, being comparable in scope, in the United States today, only to neoplastic disease and degenerative cardiovascular disease. Almost certainly there are more unhospitalized than hospitalized schizophrenics, yet it has been estimated that, at any given moment, one out of every four hospital beds in this country is occupied by a schizophrenic patient.

The following excerpts from case-histories indicate something of the clinical range of these disorders and furnish a basis for a discussion of the common elements.

W. G., a handsome, athletic-looking youth of 19, was admitted to the psychiatric service on the referral of his family physician. The boy's parents said, on admission, that within the previous several months there had been drastic changes in their son's behavior. He had been an adequate student in high school, but had had to leave college recently with failures in all subjects. He had been a star at various nonteam sports—swimming, weight-lifting, and track—winning several letters, but now he took no exercise at all. Although always careful about his health, he had almost never had physical complaints; within the past several weeks he had repeatedly expressed vague complaints about his head and chest, which, he said, indicated that he was "in very bad shape." During the past several days, the patient had spent most of his time sitting in his room, staring vacantly out of his window. He had become (quite uncharacteristically) careless about his personal appearance and habits.

While there was no doubt but that serious recent changes had taken place, further conversation with the parents indicated that the patient's childhood and adolescent adjustment had not been a healthy one. He had always been painfully shy except when in highly structured situations and had gotten to passing a good bit of his free time alone (often working out with the weights). Despite his athletic achievements, he had no really close friends. Although he tended to conceal his emotions, he had been rather prone to misunderstandings, often seeming to have taken offense where none was intended.

The personnel of the psychiatric service found it difficult to converse with the patient; an ordinary diagnostic interview was impossible. For the most part, the boy volunteered no information. He would usually answer direct questions, but he was apt to do so in a flat and toneless way, devoid of emotional coloring. Frequently the answers were not actually responsive, i.e., they lacked a logical connection with the questions. Observers often found it taxing to record their conversations with the patient. After a period of speaking to him, they would find themselves wondering just what the conversation had been about.

Occasionally the patient would use some very odd turn of phrase, as when he characterized his social activity at college as "completely indistinguishable." At times the disharmony between the content of the patient's words and his emotional expression was striking. For example, in speaking sympathetically of an acute illness that had rendered his mother bedfast during a portion of the previous fall, the boy giggled constantly.

At times, W. G. would rapidly become agitated and then would speak with a curious intensity. On one such occasion he spoke of "electrical sensations" and then of "an electrical current" in his brain. On another, he revealed that when lying awake at night he would often hear a voice repeating the command, "You'll have to do it." The patient felt that he was somehow being influenced by a force outside himself to commit an act of violence—as yet undefined—toward his parents.

W. G. had mixed ideas about his hospitalization. On the one hand, he regarded himself as perhaps being dangerously ill physically and needing medical attention. On the other, he could not dismiss the idea that the hospitalization represented some sort of plot against him, engineered by his parents, perhaps with the collusion of the family doctor and, possibly, of one of his instructors at college.

R. S. was a 22-year-old airman, who was brought one evening to the admitting ward of the nearest military hospital by the police. They reported that they had picked him up after being summoned to a bar, where the patient was smashing furniture and fighting with strangers in a wildly uncoordinated fashion.

R. S. continued to struggle all the way to the hospital. In the admitting ward he was sporadically assaultive, but when freed from restraint and merely observed, he would, for the most part, confine his ceaseless activity to pacing back and forth at one end of the room, pounding on the wall, and flexing and extending his arms in a manner suggestive of an automaton.

The patient would not answer questions, nor did he address any actual person in the room. From time to time, however, he would stop his activity abruptly and stand with one hand cupped to his ear, as if straining to hear something. On several occasions, he would then speak in a loud but hoarse tone of voice. These utterances came in bursts, starting very abruptly and stopping in the same way, in response to no observable external stimulation. The words were fairly distinct, yet the content was unintelligible. Again there was the impression of a machine being turned on and off. An excerpt from the patient's stream of talk at such a period was as follows: "Coming, coming, coming. Black men. Red men. Bones and bones. Bastard bones. Under the bed, under the table, under the water. Cover the cursing heavens. Eventual, eventually, more eventually. Bastard bones."

There was at first the diagnostic question of the patient's behavior representing some form of pathological intoxication, but there was no odor of alcohol and a blood alcohol determination was negative.

The patient was given an intravenous injection of a tranquilizing agent and a protracted bath in a tub of warm water. He appeared to become very drowsy and was then helped into bed.

The following day on the psychiatric ward, the clinical picture was quite different. The patient was mute and remained in bed until roused by the nurse and orderly, whose assistance in dressing he accepted in an awkward and mechanical fashion. He then sat motionless in a chair, with his features devoid of expression. When addressed by personnel, he did not respond save for an occasional grimace.

R. S. had carried an identification tag, by means of which it became possible to contact his Air Force unit and then his family. It was learned that the patient had left his assigned base on a three-day pass to attend his sister's wedding (in the city where hospitalization occurred). His condition on leaving the base was not remarkable. He had arrived home on the morning of the wedding day. Despite the preoccupation of the family, it was noticed that he appeared "tense and confused." He had left the wedding party after the ceremony and had evidently walked the streets until evening, when he had entered the bar from which the original call to the police had been made.

Mr. J. T., aged 43, for nearly 20 years had operated the elevator in a warehouse of a small manufacturing concern. He had never consulted a physician, but was evaluated in connection with a routine medical examination required of all employees at the time of a change in management.

Aside from an extraordinary leanness and a general inattention to personal hygiene, the patient was quite normal physically. He answered the ordinary questions in an unvarying monotone that contrasted oddly with a broad grin which traversed his features at frequent intervals. The patient had lived alone at the local Y.M.C.A. for many years. He had no friends. His recreation consisted of occasional solitary walks into the countryside.

Mr. T. subsisted entirely upon a liquid diet. His explanation of this peculiarity was quite vague, consisting of a reference to "a throat infection as a young man," which had left him unable to swallow solids without discomfort. He had the idea (of nearly delusional intensity) that his throat had "shrunken."

With respect to the chronicity of the psychotic reaction in these three examples, it may be said that W. G.'s psychosis persisted as a clinical entity for about nine months. What the natural history of the disorder might have been, cannot be said, for W. G. was given intensive treatment (involving several modalities) in the hospital for six months of this period, followed by prolonged out-patient psychotherapy. R. S. recovered from his very acute psychotic reaction within five days, before any therapeutic measure could have exerted much effect. He was separated from service with a recommendation for follow-up treatment. A year later it was found, upon inquiry, that this patient had not acted upon the recommendation, but he had remained clinically well. J. T. was given no recommendation. He continued at his job and, so far as is known, received no treatment. The duration of his psychotic reaction cannot be stated with accuracy, but it was estimated to have been present for at least as long as his term of employment at the warehouse (i.e., about 20 years).

The diagnostic term *schizophrenia* was introduced by the great Swiss psychiatrist, Eugen Bleuler. Its derivation is from two Greek words (*schizo* and *phren*), meaning "split mind" or "split personality." The expression refers to a seeming discrepancy between content of thought and expression of emotion which is very often noted in schizophrenic reactions.* (Examples: W. G.'s giggling when speaking of his mother's illness and J. T.'s grinning when answering routine questions about his medical history.)

On the basis of his extensive clinical observations, Bleuler divided the manifestations into two categories: "fundamental symptoms" and "accessory symptoms."[2] The fundamental or primary symptoms he believed—and the belief has widespread current acceptance—to be present in some degree in all schizophrenic reactions. The chief symptoms in the fundamental group may be listed as: (1) a disturbance in affectivity (emotional responses), (2) a disturbance in the relationship to reality and hence in thought processes, and (3) a basically

---

* Thus "split personality" is to be clearly distinguished from "dual personality," which is an entirely different phenomenon. The latter is discussed on p. 324.

ambivalent attitude toward significant objects and acts. The second item is usually subdivided, as follows: (2a) the thought disturbance, per se, and (2b) a resultant disturbance in communication (speaking and writing).

Bleuler's "Four A's"

Traditionally, these four characteristics have been termed *affective inappropriateness, autism* or *autistic thinking, associative looseness,* and *ambivalence.* They have come to be taught as "Bleuler's Four A's." Because of the value of this format as a memory device, it will be retained in the following preliminary discussion.

Affective Inappropriateness

Even to the nonprofessional observer, it is quite typical for the schizophrenic's emotional status to seem inappropriate to his stream of talk (and often to his immediate situation as this is judged by ordinary standards). This feature contributes greatly to the impression of strangeness, of queerness, which is so generally received of the schizophrenic.

The considerable impact exerted by an expression of emotion which is out of keeping with the concurrent ideational expression has been used by actors for particular effects. Thus, the great comedian, Eddie Cantor, would occasionally enact scenes in which he would relate a piece of obviously bad news in a cheerful voice between bursts of laughter. In these instances, the audience would have been given to understand in advance some coincidental basis for the euphoria (e.g., the speaker had inhaled "laughing gas"), and the effect would be intensely comic. On the other hand, Richard Widmark, in his remarkable portrayals of psychopathic criminals, achieved a disturbingly sinister effect through the technique of giggling in connection with cruel behavior or the expression of cruel thoughts. In the former instance, the effect was softened by the comedian's having provided a (superficially) rational basis for the behavior. In the latter instance, the effect approached much more closely that often produced on an observer by schizophrenic patients; it was not merely startling, but conveyed the anxiety-laden impression that the subject was operating on a set of premises quite alien to those which (seem to) govern conventional behavior.

The inappropriateness of the schizophrenic's affective responses may be quantitative or qualitative, or sometimes both. W. G.'s giggling and J. T.'s grinning seemed qualitatively inappropriate. R. S.'s fury in the bar and in the receiving ward seemed both quantitatively and qualitatively inappropriate.

While schizophrenic patients may, at times, give way to strange and even violent expressions of emotion, the commonest form of affective deviation from the normal seen in this condition is a pervasive *apathy*. W. G., for example, displayed apathy when staring out of his window for hours on end. R. S., on the day after his hospital admission, was extremely apathetic; so much so, as to seem almost inanimate. Apart from his peculiar grin, J. T. displayed no form of emotion and presumably had not done so for years.

Autistic Thinking

Clinical observation of the speech and other behavior of schizophrenics indicates—as do psychological tests—that the thought processes of such patients are characteristically quite different from those of normal adults. The word *autistic* is derived from the Greek *autos* (self), and autistic thinking may be freely defined as "self-centered thinking" or "thinking which is (fully) intelligible only to the self." Since the self-concept and the concept of reality are interdependent, it is also correct to say that autistic thinking is based upon an inadequate relation to reality (see p. 86 ff.). Reference is intended to the *manner* of thinking, not to the conclusions reached. Thus, for example, if one member of a group expresses an opinion which differs from that of all other members, such an opinion is not necessarily autistic.

Autistic thinking utilizes processes not found in the conscious, waking mind of a normal observer, but regularly found in dreams (and the more fanciful types of daydreams), in deliria, under conditions of extreme fatigue, in the thinking of infants and very small children, and in the thinking of very primitive peoples, though to a considerably lesser extent. It is a kind of thinking in which objective considerations —considerations of time and place, of possible and impossible, of whole and parts, of self and not-self—have little weight, and in which subjective considerations—wishes and fears—have great weight.

The difficulty experienced by an observer in attempting to understand what a schizophrenic is thinking, i.e., what is signified by his speech and actions, should not lead to the inference that the speech and actions are meaningless. On the contrary, to the patient they are full of meaning. It is merely that the activities of the schizophrenic, verbal and nonverbal, are often primarily in the service of self-expression, of the release of inner tensions, rather than in the service of communication with other persons.

With study and experience and the close observation of an individual patient, it often becomes possible for the psychiatrist to "decode" the message, so to speak, and to enter temporarily into communication with the patient. Here are two examples of successful efforts of this kind.

A beautiful, intelligent but extremely ill schizophrenic young woman, the wife of a medical student, was stalking about her room on the psychiatric service the morning after admission. She was speaking wildly of "savages with spears." The psychiatrist had noted, in the morning report, that on the previous night the patient had been so hyperactive as to have required parenteral sedation. Since she had been completely unable to cooperate in the procedure, the nurse in attendance had required the assistance of two aides, one of them a swarthy male.

The psychiatrist made the assumption that the patient was referring to this episode, and he asked her directly if this was not the case. The patient replied, quite intelligibly, that it was. The psychiatrist said that he knew how distressing such an experience must have been. He assured the patient that the personnel deeply regretted the occasional necessity of such treatment measures and had resorted to them as a last-ditch device to prevent the patient from driving herself to utter exhaustion. Though still angry at first, the patient spoke rationally for several minutes, saying that she resented the indignity of the procedure and felt it unjustified, since she had wanted to accept the medication quietly but simply could not.

Some days later, the same young woman was noticed to be pounding her pillow, muttering obscenities, and repeatedly using the phrase, "the all-seeing eye." The head nurse knew that a visit from the patient's mother was expected that day, and despite the fact that the patient had occasionally called her mother's name, she wondered if the patient's behavior might not be an expression of hostility to and fear of her mother.

The nurse informed the psychiatrist, who thought that the interpretation might well be correct. He asked the patient if she were not upset at the prospect of a visit from her mother. The patient immediately confirmed the idea, and expressed relief when the doctor told her that the visit would be postponed indefinitely.

Associative Looseness

This figurative term refers to the relative lack of conventional, logical connections ("associations") between successive items in the stream of talk of many schizophrenics. An extreme example is the excerpt from the verbal productions of patient R. S. (p. 362). When associative looseness is this pronounced, it is virtually impossible for even a trained observer to grasp the meaning of what the patient is saying. In milder examples, the interviewer may have the experience mentioned in connection with W. G., i.e., he may be able to sustain some sort of conversation with the patient, yet come to the eventual recognition that he and the patient have not been in very meaningful communication.

As one can readily infer, associative looseness is a behavioral manifestation of the previously mentioned schizophrenic characteristic, autistic thinking. Even in such a disturbed form of speaking as that of R. S., it is not to be considered that there is no connection (for the patient) between the successive thoughts, but rather that the connections are of an extremely subjective nature, not to be understood by ordinary logic.

There is a superficial similarity between looseness of association and the phenomenon of *flight of ideas*, seen in mania (p. 352). For diagnostic purposes, it is important to distinguish between the two. Apart from the quality of the patient's mood (which is unmistakably gay in the case of the manic patient, but not in the case of the schizophrenic), the distinguishing feature is that the links between the successive ideas are usually comprehensible to the observer in the manic's stream of talk, but not in the schizophrenic's.

Ambivalence

Ambivalence, it will be recalled, is the term designating the simultaneous experiencing by the subject of contradictory attitudes or emotions toward a given object, act, or situation. This phenomenon is more highly developed in schizophrenic disorders than in any other condition. It is, in fact, typical for the schizophrenic to experience a powerful admixture of hatred and fear with a primitive kind of love toward those figures for whom one might expect to find only the latter emotion. (An example would be W. G.'s feelings toward his parents.) The simultaneous operation of strong, conflicting mental forces can also be inferred (and, in certain psychotherapeutic situations, confirmed by the patient's subjective report) to be influencing the motor behavior of schizophrenic patients. For example, some of the awkwardness and retardation which are displayed at times by schizophrenics can be the result of an ambivalence about the activity in question.

Accessory (Secondary) Symptoms

As is apparent from a consideration of the case material thus far presented, schizophrenic patients experience a more or less marked impairment of the processes of reality-testing. They may be unable to distinguish objective data from inner strivings and fears, true perceptions from fantasy-bred images. As is true in the case of delirious patients (pp. 279 to 281), this circumstance permits the occurrence of certain phenomena of a rather florid nature, *delusions and hallucinations*.

Examples of delusions are: W. G.'s ideas that he had some severe affliction of his head and chest and that hospitalization was part of a plot being carried out against his better interest; R. S.'s impression (not stated, but to be inferred) that the strangers in the bar were his enemies; and probably J. T.'s belief that his esophagus had shrunk to the point that it would not allow passage of solids.

Examples of hallucinations are: W. G.'s hearing of voices commanding him "to do it" and, perhaps, whatever subjective experience underlay his complaint of "electrical sensations" in his brain; also, R. S.'s presumably auditory experiences (when he seemed to be listening intently).

Delusions and hallucinations are common in schizophrenic reactions. Any of the sensory modalities may be involved in schizophrenic hallucinations, but the auditory sense is involved with a considerably greater frequency than any of the others. (In the interests of memorization, auditory hallucinations may thus be added to the list of "A's" although not a "fundamental symptom.")

There are borderline phenomena, essentially of the nature of delusions and hallucinations yet less striking, for which special descriptive terms are usually employed. These phenomena consist in thoughts or sensations of change or of unreality, involving either the patient's own body or objects in his environment.* In early or mild cases of schizophrenia, the patient may refer to these thoughts or sensations in a somewhat tentative fashion. Ideas of bodily change are usually referred to as "feelings of depersonalization"; ideas of some alteration in the environment are referred to as "feelings of unreality" or "feelings of estrangement."

Clinical Syndromes

As indicated in the classification of functional psychoses on page 355, it is customary to divide schizophrenic reactions into a number of subgroups. It would be incorrect to place a great deal of emphasis upon these syndromes, for they are not sharply demarcated and afford few correlations with what is known about schizophrenic etiology. On the other hand, it is not unusual to encounter quite classical examples of the various syndromes, and when this is the case, certain prognostic and therapeutic inferences can be drawn.

Four of the subgroups have been recognized since the turn of the century: *catatonic type, paranoid type, simple type,* and *hebephrenic type*. These syndromes will now be discussed in moderate detail. The remaining subgroups—*schizo-affective type, acute* and *chronic undifferentiated type, childhood type,* and *residual type*—will then be briefly reviewed.

* In quite mild form these manifestations may occasionally be found in psychoneuroses also.

Catatonic Type

This syndrome is exemplified by the airman, R. S. (p. 361). Of the four classical subgroups, catatonic reaction, or *catatonia* as it is sometimes called, has the earliest age of onset (commonly the late teens or early twenties), and it is the likeliest to have a very acute onset. (With respect to the duration of the psychotic reaction, however, the case of R. S. was atypical; in the absence of vigorous treatment measures, a much longer duration is the rule.) For reasons which are not clear, but which may be related to the acuteness of onset and the drastic nature of the reaction, catatonic schizophrenia has the best prognosis of the four original subgroups.

Catatonia may involve either of two clinical forms, or both forms in quick succession, as in the case of R. S. In their more extreme manifestations, these forms are called *catatonic excitement* and *catatonic stupor*, respectively.

In catatonic excitement, the patient is apt to behave in a wild and unpredictable fashion. Motor activity may be almost ceaseless for long periods of time; the patient's behavior may be marked by a cold and furious intensity, or by stereotyped, robot-like movements. As in manic excitement, the patient may appear to be impervious to fatigue, but in the absence of therapeutic intervention, he may actually exhaust himself to a dangerous degree.

In catatonic stupor, the patient becomes extremely inactive; in fully developed stupor (a phase which is rarely seen nowadays), he may abandon all forms of voluntary motor activity. He may sit silent and absolutely motionless or lie motionless upon his bed, sometimes in the so-called "fetal position." He may appear absolutely indifferent to and unaware of bodily functions, being involuntary of urine and feces and requiring tube or parenteral feeding.

Actually, there are many gradations of intensity in both phases. In a phase of mild excitement, the patient's motor activity may be confined to a restless agitation. In the quiescent phase, there may be no more than a generalized retardation and awkwardness in the performance of actions. On direct examination of the nonexcited catatonic patient, one may be able to demonstrate the phenomenon called "waxy flexibility" (*cerea flexibilitas*). It is usually desirable to attempt to elicit this sign in a fashion which is as inconspicuous as possible. One such way has long been described as follows: With the patient seated, the physician stands slightly to one side, takes the patient's arm by the wrist, and elevates it while appearing to take the pulse. After a few moments, the arm is released. If the patient is catatonic, the arm frequently will not return normally to the resting position, but will remain for an appreciable period of time in the awkward raised position. To generalize, one may say that the sign of waxy flexibility consists in the patient's retaining, over long periods and without apparent fatigue, an odd position or attitude into which his body, or a part of it, has fallen or has been placed by the examiner. It is not to be thought that there is any intrinsic difficulty in the motor system of the patient. Under such conditions it is not that he cannot move his body; it is that he cannot *will* to move it. (The difficulty is related to the pervasive ambivalence of the schizophrenic previously mentioned.)

A related and somewhat more severe manifestation of catatonia occurs when the examiner is able to elicit an automatic, stereotyped sort of mimicry of his own words or gestures from the patient (*echolalia* and *echopraxia*).

Hallucinations, particularly auditory hallucinations, are common in both forms of catatonic schizophrenia.

As one may suppose, there can arise a differential diagnostic question involving, on the one hand, catatonic excitement and mania, and on the other, catatonic stupor and psychotic depression. In such cases, the most reliable clinical criterion is the physician's estimate of the patient's affective state. If one receives an impression of an infectious gaiety or of an oppressive sadness and despair, he can be reasonably certain that the condition is one of mania or depression, respectively. If one's predominant impression is neither of joy nor sorrow but of coldness and strangeness, the condition is very likely to be one of catatonic reaction.

Paranoid Type

Of the cases of schizophrenia that come to medical attention, the largest subgroup is paranoid schizophrenic reaction. (Both W. G. and the young woman described on page 366 were diagnosed as paranoid schizophrenia although certain catatonic features were also present.) The onset of a paranoid reaction is typically rather gradual, and it may be extremely so although an acute onset is by no means rare. The age at onset tends to be greater than in the other subgroups; it is not unusual for paranoid schizophrenia to make its first clinical appearance in the late thirties. The prognosis is variable, but tends to be less favorable than that of catatonic reaction although more so than that of hebephrenic reaction or that of simple schizophrenia.

The most characteristic clinical feature of paranoid schizophrenia is a sustained and extreme suspiciousness. This trait is sooner or later revealed in most of the patient's relationships although it may be much more apparent in some than in others. Typically the patient's mistrust reaches clearly delusional proportions ("delusions of persecution"). W. G., for example, thought that he was being plotted against by his parents and his physician. The young woman patient was convinced that her mother was spying on her.

The idea expressed by W. G. that he was being mysteriously influenced by some external force is also a common one in this condition. Sometimes the delusions have primarily to do with ideas of bodily change, perhaps brought about by the "persecutors."

The delusional ideas vary considerably from one patient to another (and from one phase of the illness to another) with respect to what might be called "sharpness of focus." That is to say, the delusions may attach almost exclusively to a single key figure in the patient's life; they may involve a small group of persons, or they may be quite diffuse. Often some organization may be named as the "enemy": a religious, political, or social group ("the Masons"; "the Catholics"; "the Communists"; etc.).

Hallucinations are also frequent and they tend to be consonant with the delusions. The patient may hallucinate threatening voices, warning voices, or (like W. G.) voices of command.

With respect to the content of the delusions and hallucinations, there often tends to be a shift in emphasis in the course of the disease. In later stages, the patient may experience "delusions of grandeur." This term has previously been applied to a symptom found in mania (p. 352), but the two cases are not quite the same. In paranoid schizophrenic reaction, the delusions are more bizarre, as a rule, and they lack any quality which could be called joyful. The patient may believe that he is some awe-inspiring military, political, or religious figure, or that he is supernatural or even divine. The hallucinations in such a phase may be to the effect that the patient is receiving some special messages of tremendous importance. (Sometimes grandiose delusions and hallucinations may be present when the patient first comes to medical attention. When this is the case, however, it not infrequently means that the disorder has been quietly present for a considerable length of time.)

In considering cases of paranoid schizophrenia, one can distinguish between clinical features which are schizophrenic in a general sense (apathy, associative looseness, etc.) and features which are specifically paranoid (inability to trust, an active suspiciousness, delusions of persecution, etc.). Sometimes cases are encountered in which the specifically paranoid features are far more prominent than the general features of schizophrenia. There is some question as to how such patients should be classified: should they be considered to constitute merely an atypical form of (paranoid) schizophrenic reaction, or should they be considered as a separate nosological entity? Further material relevant to this question will be presented in the section on *paranoid reactions* (p. 390 ff.).

Simple Type

In the purest form, this syndrome is considered to involve the primary ("fundamental") characteristics of schizophrenia, but not the secondary symptoms. (Most psychiatrists, however, would probably consider patient J. T. to belong essentially to this subgroup.) It is the least conspicuous of all the schizophrenic syndromes. It is very likely the most numerous, although statistics on its incidence are not reliable since patients suffering from this type of reaction may never come to psychiatric attention.

The onset of simple schizophrenia is typically very gradual; indeed, it may be difficult to tell at what point a *schizoid* ("schizophrenialike") personality (p. 400) becomes clinically psychotic and warrants the diagnostic label of simple schizophrenic reaction. Delusions and hallucinations are never prominent in this condition, and often they are altogether absent. Odd quirks of behavior, which society is likelier to regard as mere eccentricities rather than as symptoms of mental illness, are frequent. There is typically an absence of close human relationships.

As in the case of J. T., the life patterns of simple schizophrenics are indicative of the seriousness of their emotional handicaps and of the ineffectual nature of their adjustment efforts. Although the majority of such persons spend most of their lives outside of the hospital, they tend to gravitate to certain occupations or niches in which interpersonal contacts are either very few or very superficial. They become tramps, vagrants, prostitutes, migratory workers, or performers of tasks that are very simple and routine or of such a nature as not to involve close cooperation with others.

Hebephrenic Type

This syndrome is generally considered to be the most malignant form of schizophrenia, the least responsive to therapeutic measures. The onset is usually gradual. Before the advent of intensive milieu therapy (p. 497) and of the tranquilizing drugs (p. 455), it not infrequently happened that, if a patient of one of the other schizophrenic subgroups was quite unresponsive to existing treatment measures and remained in hospital for an extended period of time, his symptom picture would gradually assume hebephrenic features.

Delusions and hallucinations are prominent in this condition, and they are apt to be of an especially bizarre nature. Visual hallucinations are frequent, much more so than in other forms of schizophrenia. While not necessarily seclusive, the patient is utterly self-centered, showing a complete disregard for the conventions which ordinarily regulate human behavior. He may, for example, eat with his fingers, masturbate openly, resist wearing clothes, and urinate and defecate at inappropriate times and places. While the significance of the observation is open to a variety of interpretations, it is true that suggestions of an organic component to the disorder are particularly evident in hebephrenia (acne, obesity, seeming endocrine disturbances).

Schizo-affective Type

While it is not difficult, as a rule, to distinguish any of the classical forms of schizophrenic reaction from a manic or a psychotic depressive reaction, there are instances in which the clinical picture partakes simultaneously of schizophrenic and manic or depressed features. Such a patient, while suffering from the disordered thought processes associated with schizophrenia, may experience either exaltation or profound dejection and despair instead of apathy.

It appears likely that, for the most part, this condition was diagnosed formerly as manic-depressive reaction. When the opportunity was afforded for methodical long-term observation of such patients, however, it often was found that the manic-depressive elements gradually became less prominent (in successive psychotic episodes or phases) and the schizophrenic elements more so. With the advent of electroconvulsive therapy (p. 475) in the late 1930's, it was noted that when such patients were treated by this means the manic or depressive elements usually disappeared, leaving in many instances, a relatively clear picture of one or another form of schizophrenic reaction.* Another bit of evidence as to the essential nature of this reaction was made available by the increasing use of projective psychological tests. Such studies tended to show that the condition had more in common with other schizophrenic reactions than with manic-depressive reactions. For these various reasons, the condition has come to be classified under the former heading.

Of the schizophrenic reactions, the schizo-affective type is generally considered to have the best prognosis.

Acute and Chronic Undifferentiated Schizophrenic Reaction

It has been noted that the two examples of paranoid schizophrenic reaction utilized in the present discussion were marked by some

* If, in any given instance, all evidence of psychosis disappeared in response to a relatively short course of E.C.T., there would be the strong likelihood that the case was one of manic-depressive psychosis.

catatonic elements. To this observation one may add that J. T., the simple schizophrenic, probably showed some paranoid elements. The truth is that the clinical features presented by any given schizophrenic patient oftener than not are a blend of the symptoms of more than one of the traditional syndromes. While it is still customary, for purposes of clinical classification, to use the diagnostic term which indicates the most conspicuous features of the patient's symptom-picture, the overlapping is a good indication that the various types do not represent anything so fundamental as separate, discrete disease entities.

It happens not infrequently that the symptomatology of a schizophrenic patient is one in which features of several of the subgroups are closely intermingled, with none being particularly conspicuous. In such instances, the term *undifferentiated schizophrenic reaction* is used, with the qualification *acute* or *chronic*, as the case may be.

Childhood Schizophrenia

It is well recognized that schizophrenic reactions may take place before puberty. Because of the natural immaturity of the personality in such circumstances, there are some special clinical features, and a separate diagnostic classification is used. To preserve the proper setting for the discussion, childhood schizophrenia will be considered in the chapter on child psychiatry (Chapter 15).

Residual Type

This diagnostic label is applied to patients who have experienced a schizophrenic reaction, from which they have recovered sufficiently to effect an adjustment outside the hospital, while continuing to manifest some of the less florid characteristics of the disorder. The value of this classification is primarily administrative.

ETIOLOGY

Even the few glimpses of schizophrenic reactions which have been offered in the present discussion may suffice to give some indications of the great range of cases which may receive this diagnosis, of the marked variations as to type of clinical picture and as to severity and duration of the psychosis.

Actually, the range is even greater than has thus far been indicated. At one extreme might be a soldier who, in connection with some harrowing battle experience, develops an acute but relatively mild catatonic reaction lasting perhaps 24 to 48 hours and disappearing essentially without treatment, never to recur. At the other extreme might be a patient who was a behavior problem since infancy, whose mode of adjustment became overtly psychotic at puberty, and who, at the age of 30, is a seemingly deteriorated and completely withdrawn person on the chronic ward of a state psychiatric hospital, despite extended trials of psychotherapy, shock therapy, and several forms of chemotherapy.

Contrasts such as these are sufficiently bewildering, but as one turns to the question of etiology the obscurity appears to deepen even further. Consider, for example, the matter of early environment. Whereas a patient whose schizophrenic illness follows an ominous course is *typically* the product of an obviously unhealthy and emotionally destructive family, this is not always the case. A severe schizophrenic may come from a family whose relationships and behavior, while not actually healthy, have yet not been so destructive as to stand out markedly from the relationship and behavior of many other families that have not produced schizophrenics. (See, however, p. 384.)

The situation is similar with respect to heredity. It is quite common to find a history of mental illness in some form in the family background of a schizophrenic, and it is not at all uncommon to find a history of schizophrenia, yet in a certain proportion of instances there is no history of diagnosable psychiatric illness.

In attempting to render such impressions comprehensible, a number of psychiatrists, particularly European psychiatrists of a generation ago, postulated the existence of a condition which they termed *nuclear* or *process schizophrenia*. They used these designations to indicate what they believed to be a central or core group of patients, showing the cardinal features of schizophrenia early in life and in severe form, in whom the etiology included significant (although unspecified) somatic elements and who could not be cured nor markedly helped by any form of treatment then known. Patients showing a schizophrenic syndrome, but who were not a part of this nuclear group, were considered to have developed a similar clinical picture on an essentially psychogenic basis (*reactive schizophrenia*).

This hypothesis was never proved. It encountered the following quite serious clinical objection: Given the opportunity to study carefully a large number of instances of schizophrenic reaction, one invariably finds that they form an unbroken continuum from the mildest, most fleeting reactions, scarcely needing treatment, to the most severe and chronic, almost untreatable cases.

Nevertheless, in recent years the idea has again received attention in connection with some of the newer researches on the organic aspects of schizophrenic etiology, and it remains entirely possible that it contains an element of truth (see p. 378).

Organic Factors

HEREDITY. It is easy to see some of the difficulties which have beset investigators of possible hereditary aspects of schizophrenic disorders.

For one thing, the criteria for diagnosis are not hard-and-fast; they involve as yet unavoidable subjective elements, and thus they differ, sometimes appreciably, from one psychiatric center to another.

Then, too, it is an extremely difficult matter to eliminate environmental variables from any genetic investigation. For example, one line of inquiry has been to study the relatives of patients unquestionably suffering from schizophrenia and try to determine if there is any clear correlation between incidence rate of the disease and degree of consanguinity. Kallmann,[10] a leading investigator of the genetics of schizophrenia, has followed this sort of approach (among others) and has found that in the series; uniovular twin, full sibling, half sibling, step sibling, there is a definite correlation between incidence of schizophrenia and degree of consanguinity to the original schizophrenic patient. Yet in this and in similar studies it nearly always (and quite naturally) turns out that closeness of kinship is paralleled very closely by similarity of early environment. That is to say, identical twins are more likely to be treated similarly by their parents and other significant figures than are ordinary siblings; full siblings are more likely to be treated similarly than are half siblings, etc.

It is possible to imagine a definitive sort of naturally occurring experimental situation, one in which hereditary factors would be identical and environmental factors distinctly different: identical twins, one of whom is known to be schizophrenic, who have been raised apart from birth. If a number of such cases could be studied, and if it were to be found that the incidence of schizophrenia in the "second" twins was definitely higher than the incidence of schizophrenia among other full siblings of known schizophrenics when the children have been raised together, the significance of genetic factors would be shown to be of cardinal importance.

If, however, one considers the odds against such a combination of circumstances occurring and coming to medical attention, one is not surprised to learn, as Jackson puts it, that "an exhaustive search of American and European literature of the past forty years has uncovered only two such cases."[9] As a matter of fact, one of the two cases is of questionable value, since the twins were not separated until in their ninth month (and, as will subsequently be discussed, there is a considerable likelihood that the significant emotional traumata predisposing to the development of schizophrenia can at least begin to exert their effect well before this time).

This entire area of investigation remains in a state of flux. The evidence for the significance of a genetic factor in the development is suggestive rather than demanding of credence. Yet it is rather strongly suggestive, and one could probably obtain a fair measure of agreement to the proposition that there can (but need not always) exist an inherited predisposition, of varying strength, to the development of some type(s) of schizophrenic illness.

At the present time, it would be (1) more difficult to obtain agreement as to the precise nature of the hereditary mechanism, and (2) impossible to obtain agreement as to the nature of the predisposition thereby produced. With respect to the first point, it may be said that the consensus of the geneticists is against a polygenic form of inheritance and wavers between favoring a recessive Mendelian factor and a dominant factor "of reduced penetrance." Various aspects of the second point will be treated in the ensuing discussion.

CONSTITUTION. It has long been attempted to correlate schizophrenia with various characteristics of a constitutional nature, including some quite gross anatomical characteristics. Much of this material is obviously of no value; some of it is interesting but puzzling. For example, it has been clearly shown (Kretchmer, Sheldon) that there is a decidedly higher incidence of the so-called *asthenic* body type* among schizophrenics than among the general population.[11, 13] The significance of such observations is, however, not known.

ENDOCRINE STATUS. There have been many attempts to shed light upon schizophrenic etiology through studies of the endocrine glands.[8] One of the incentives to this type of investigation has been the recognition that the onset of clinical schizophrenia frequently coincides with a period of grossly altered endocrine activity (puberty, postpartum periods, menopause). The early finding that certain physiological, particularly homeostatic, responses of perhaps two thirds of hospitalized schizophrenics are somewhat altered from the normal added hope to this inquiry. It was repeatedly noted, for example, that the response in blood pressure of such schizophrenics to an injection of epinephrine involves a slowing down both of the departure from and of the return to the normal resting level.

By and large, however, these efforts have been disappointing. Certainly there is no significant correlation between any of the well-established endocrine disorders and schizophrenia. Yet these studies have been the precursors of more recent biochemical investigations which hold promise. (See Biochemistry, below.)

PATHOLOGY. For a long time—and until quite recently—a considerable controversy was maintained as to whether or not there existed histopathological changes in the brain pathognomonic for schizophrenia. At the present time, however, it is generally accepted that

---

* Characterized by small shoulders, a flat chest, relatively long extremities, and underdeveloped musculature, giving an angularity of profile.

there are no structural changes of a specific nature within microscopic range.

BIOCHEMISTRY. Unquestionably, one of the most exciting areas of research in the entire field of the etiology of schizophrenia is currently the biochemical. Data are accumulating with a rapidity which makes the drawing of extensive conclusions hazardous, if not impossible. No attempt will be made to present here a comprehensive survey of this material, but some of the principal lines of investigation can be indicated.

One of the major approaches to the subject has been through the production of *experimental psychoses* through biochemical means. It has been known for a long time that the administration of any of a number of substances in quite small amounts can produce transient psychotic reaction in human subjects. Certain of these substances produce syndromes bearing a rather strong resemblance to some schizophrenic reactions. *Mescaline* is one of the older of these drugs; *lysergic acid diethylamide* (LSD) has been widely used more recently. For example, feelings of unreality and visual and auditory hallucinations may be produced in this manner in previously normal subjects.

Interest in approaching the immense problem of schizophrenic etiology through the study of drug-induced psychoses has been enhanced by several considerations. One of these is the realization of the similarity in chemical (molecular) structure between some of the psychotogenic agents, such as mescaline and LSD, and some of the (naturally occurring) neurohumoral amines, particularly adrenalin and serotonin. (See diagram.)

Mescaline

Adrenalin

Adrenolutin

LSD

Serotonin

Adrenochrome

Another point of interest has been the repeated demonstration that the more striking symptoms of such biochemically induced psychoses can often be suppressed by the administration of some of the recently discovered drugs (notably the "tranquilizers") which exert a similar effect on actual schizophrenic symptoms.

Expectations have been stimulated further by reports of a more specific nature. For example, Hoffer and his associates have reported that *adrenochrome*, an unstable derivative of adrenalin that is normally present in minute amounts in skeletal muscle, can produce schizophrenialike reactions when injected into normal subjects intravenously.[6,7] Heath and his co-workers have reported the isolation of a protein (called *taraxein*) from the blood plasma of schizophrenics which, when injected into the blood stream of nonschizophrenics, produces symptoms of the disease.[4,5] However, these research leads and others of a comparable nature are, at the present time, in need of additional confirmation and exploration.

Research activity in this general area (the biochemical investigation of schizophrenia) is so vigorous, reports are so numerous, and hopes naturally so high, that a few words of caution may not be out of place to the student or nonpsychiatric physician who may be doing some independent reading or contemplating some form of investigation in the field.

Consider the principal propositions which one finds in this portion of the literature. (1) Substance X is found in the body fluids or tissues of a majority of schizophrenics; whereas it is not found (or not found in comparable concentrations) in nonschizophrenics. (2) Substance Y (whatever its derivation), when introduced into normal subjects, produces a syndrome indistinguishable from some schizophrenic syndrome. Sometimes one finds these propositions combined; that is to say, (3) substance X is uniquely found in schizophrenics and, when given to nonschizophrenics, will produce the clinical picture of the disease.

Apart from a number of serious technical problems, there is one general and outstanding difficulty in evaluating any instance of proposition (1). Given an individual who is unquestionably schizophrenic and given some biochemical finding (or biophysical finding) that is consistently abnormal, which is the cart and which is the horse? Or, to continue the metaphor, are both elements really carts, being drawn by a horse as yet unseen? Research methodology is becoming ever more stringent in matters such as this, yet in all studies which begin with patients having the established disease, one must be careful of unwarranted inferences. There is no question but that to be schizophrenic is a major psychological experience; it is altogether likely that it is a major experience physiologically as well. Horwitt has admirably said: "Comparing data from blood samples of schizophrenics and normal people is like comparing samples from soldiers on the battlefields and people in a relaxed, basal condition."

One of the difficulties in accepting proposition (2) unreservedly is that, in most instances reported, the patients with experimental psychoses tend to show two characteristics not typically associated with naturally occurring schizophrenia: (a) signs of toxic psychois (i.e., signs of delirium), and (b) some concurrent recognition of the unrealistic nature of their experiences (some *insight*).

Psychological Factors

Since the turn of the century, a good bit of information gradually has been gained with respect to psychogenic aspects of the schizophrenic disorders. As is true of organic aspects, a detailed presentation of the material is beyond the scope of this book, but the principal features may be summarized here under three headings: predisposing factors, precipitating factors, and psychological mechanisms in operation during the actual clinical illness.

PREDISPOSING FACTORS. Although the point has not been made specifically in preceding chapters, a consideration of the various types of functional psychiatric disorders which have been presented will show that, in a general way, there is a correlation between the severity of the type of illness and the age at which the predisposing psychological traumata were experienced. It appears that, other factors being equal, the earlier the traumatic experiences occur, the more serious the subsequent psychiatric illness will be.

Consider, for example, the following diagnostic categories, listed in the order of increasing severity: conversion reaction, compulsive reaction, psychotic depressive reaction. The predisposing experience (original traumata) of the patient with conversion reaction will ordinarily have occurred chiefly during the family-triangle period of development; those of the compulsive patient, during the muscle-training period; those of the depressed patient, during middle and late infancy.

It is generally agreed that schizophrenic reactions comprise the most severe of the functional psychiatric disorders. One would therefore expect that the predisposing traumatic experiences of schizophrenics would have begun during the earliest months of life. This expectation frequently appears to have been borne out. Historical material strongly suggests in many instances that the patient's basic trauma has been a disturbed mother-infant relationship in which a primitive and powerful impression of rejection has been conveyed to the infant. (See the material on the earliest stages of personality development, p. 85 ff.)

An important point here is that the traumatic experiences often appear to have begun before the point at which the rejecting mother can be clearly perceived by the infant as a separate object, with the result that the whole environment comes to be dimly perceived as hostile and threatening. As a result, the basic personality structure is impaired, particularly in its executive aspects (p. 71). The self-concept becomes a disturbing one, and the differentiation between self and not-self is made and retained with greater difficulty.

The early traumatic situation also exerts an effect upon the development of the basic drives, particularly of the libido. Since it is (in some fashion) repelled by the first natural love object, the mother, the libido of the preschizophrenic never becomes so firmly directed outward—toward objects—as does the libido of the individual with more favorable early experiences. The preschizophrenic remains more narcissistic (emotionally self-centered) and exists in a less meaningful contact with objects.

While of such fundamental importance to personality development, the relationship between a mother and her infant is a subtle and complex phenomenon (see p. 87). If the mother is basically healthy, secure in her femininity and uninhibited in her maternal inclinations, there is a naturalness in all of her interaction with the baby which is difficult to describe, let alone analyze scientifically. When things are not right between mother and baby—as in the infancy of the preschizophrenic—it may be equally difficult for the observer to be precise in his description and in his analysis of the difficulty. If, in addition, it is necessary to reconstruct this vital portion of personal history long after the fact (as has, for the most part, been the case in the study of schizophrenia), the difficulties are further magnified.

It appears that the precise nature of the early traumatic experiences varies. It is not to be thought that some gross and obvious rupture between mother and infant is the rule. Such situations are noted fairly often in the early life histories of schizophrenics. Sometimes the traumata have been glaring, as for example when a mother dies in childbirth and the infant is reared by a harsh and indifferent substitute. Much more often, however, the difficulties have been subtler. Frequently the mother has been well-intentioned, but lacking in maternal warmth. She may have performed all of the tasks of motherhood correctly, but has done so anxiously, perhaps with inner resentment, and out of a sense of duty rather than as a natural expression of her own instincts.

It is worth stressing that the timing of these early disturbing experiences in the infant's life may be decisive. Human development, being to a large extent conditioned by heredity, tends strongly to proceed according to a schedule. What is accomplished easily and naturally at one period may not be capable of accomplishment at a later period. For an analogy, one might consider skeletal development. Nutritional deficiencies during intrauterine life or the first months of infancy exert effects upon the development of the bones at a very critical period. Subsequent vigorous attempts to provide the necessary nutrients to compensate for the early deprivation are certainly worthwhile, but the odds are against a complete reversal of the maldevelopment. The life history of the organism has moved on, and other aspects of the developmental process now receive a natural priority. For an example, more clearly in the realm of psychology,* consider the acquisition of language. Whatever the tongue is in which verbal communication with the child is carried on during the first several years of life, this is almost surely to be the one in which he can express himself the most naturally in later years. An equal period of time, spent as a young adult, in mastering a new tongue will very seldom provide an equal facility of idiom and delicacy of accent. To bring this analogy even closer to the case in point, one might compare a child whose early years have been spent in an environment in which grammatical errors and slovenliness of pronunciation are the rule with one whose exposure, from the beginning, was only to correct usage. What the latter child acquired almost effortlessly, the former will be able to acquire as an adult, even under very favorable conditions, only with great difficulty and, oftener than not, incompletely.

In the case of the preschizophrenic infant and child, there is always the possibility that experiences subsequent to those of the earliest months of life may be more favorable.† The mother's confidence may increase, her anxieties diminish, or her resentment subside, and accordingly she may become more capable of genuinely maternal responses. Then, too, the infant's social horizons expand: other figures than the mother—father, grandparents, siblings, etc.—come to be recognized and assume significance. This development furnishes the possibility that fresh supplies of emotional nutrients (to hark back to the first analogy) become available. Or (to recur to the linguistic analogy), one may say that fundamental aspects of the human message— affection, trust, respect—begin to come across in clear accents.

If such favorable developments take place, some degree of repair of the effects of the early trauma will occur. If the repair is marked, the subsequent experiencing of a schizophrenic reaction may well be

---

* And in which the determining factors, although inevitable, are largely experiential.

† Even apart, that is to say, from the early experience of intensive psychotherapy, which can favorably alter the entire balance of forces.

averted although ordinarily there will remain a certain amount of personality damage (see Chap. 12). Often the degree of repair is such that the child's personality development can continue up to a point, but considerable vulnerability remains, with the result that a clinical psychosis may develop at some later date in response to relatively mild stress.

Fairly often the preschizophrenic child will appear to progress through postinfancy developmental periods—muscle-training, family-triangle, latency—in a manner which is not markedly different from that of the average child. In this respect, however, appearances are usually deceptive. Despite the conformity in overt behavior, it usually turns out that the inner meaning of the principal developmental experiences has been quite different for the preschizophrenic than for the healthy child. Because of the fundamental personality weaknesses (derived from early traumata and any constitutional limitations which may have been present) the preschizophrenic child finds the usual problems of each developmental phase more difficult to solve than does the healthy or even the neurotic child. Then, too, as another result of the fundamental weaknesses, the preschizophrenic child is apt to interpret many of his developmental experiences in a highly unrealistic and overpersonalized fashion (i.e., autistically). Another way of putting this would be to say that because of his morbid orientation to life, the preschizophrenic child experiences certain situations as problems which are not experienced in this way by the normal child.

As a result of these severe handicaps, there is apt to be further traumatization of the preschizophrenic despite the various favorable environmental modifications which often take place. This course of events is largely responsible for the frequent finding that adult schizophrenics are beset with inner conflicts deriving from all developmental levels (a situation different from that seen in most neurotics, even when severely ill).

Within recent years, schizophrenia and the preschizophrenic state have received increasingly early recognition (see Chap. 15). As a result, material such as that just presented, which was originally based very largely upon reconstructions of the life histories of adult schizophrenics, has received a degree of confirmation and also some amplification from observations made much closer in time to the significant traumata.

One concept of considerable value in elucidating the development of a predisposition to schizophrenia is that which Bateson, Weakland, and their associates have termed "the double-bind hypothesis."[1] These investigators have studied the problem from the point of view of communication specialists. They have found that very often there is, from the beginning, a considerable degree of ambivalence toward the child on the part of one or more key figures (most significantly, the mother), as a result of which the child is, more or less continuously, being given conflicting behavioral cues. For example, the mother may convey one sort of message to the child with her words (let us say, one of approval and encouragement), while conveying quite a different sort of message with her facial expression, gestures, or tone of voice (perhaps one of irritation, anxiety, or dismay).

It is the persuasively reasoned belief of these investigators that a profound sense of insecurity and confusion are thus developed in the child, which have a great deal to do with his subsequent inability to relate trustingly to other persons and with his estrangement from his environment, as well as with his difficulty in integrating his own thoughts and feelings.

It has long been the impression of many clinicians who have worked with schizophrenics that other members of the patients' families (father, mother, siblings) also were apt to show signs of being poorly, or at least peculiarly adjusted. Furthermore, it was noted in the course of treatment of schizophrenics in the hospital that contacts with members of the family (during a pass or an extended visit) were fairly often attended or followed by set-backs in the patient's course of recovery. Until recently the other members of the family seldom received psychiatric evaluations unless their personal difficulties reached clinical proportions. More rarely still were the families of schizophrenics studied as units. Within the past dozen years, however, serious attention has been given to observation of the young schizophrenic as part of a family group and observation of the family as a social unit.

The number of families which have been intensively studied in this manner—by investigators such as Bowen, Lidz, and Jackson—is still not large, and as one would suppose, the data are quite complicated.[3, 12, 13] A well-substantiated impression, however, appears to be this: whatever the facade presented by the family to the casual observer, and whether or not the family's individual members (other than the schizophrenic patient) are diagnosably ill, the family itself—as a group, a social unit—tends to be a sick one.

Certainly it is rarely a happy one, although its members often attempt to conceal this fact. Details vary, of course. The parental marriage tends to be an unhappy one, often with undue rivalry, often with threats of separation, explicit or implicit, often with an enrollment of the children (patient and siblings) on the side of one parent against the other. The mother is fairly often described as being over-protective, over-anxious, aggressive, yet basically cold and distant. The father, in a number of instances, has been described as passive and insecure in his masculinity.

It must be admitted that all this is rather nonspecific, yet one can readily believe that the tendency toward withdrawal from reality, which is such an important aspect of schizophrenia, is decidedly favored by the unwholesome atmosphere. Furthermore—apart from whatever additionally may be deduced with respect to pathogenesis—it is clearly implied that in many instances treatment of the schizophrenic should involve serious efforts to assist key members of his family.

PRECIPITATING FACTORS. Considered as objective events, the circumstances which constitute the current stress contributing to the onset of a schizophrenic reaction (in the clinical sense) cover a wide range. Sometimes they may be very intense and acute, of a nature which might well produce some type of emotional illness even in a nonpredisposed individual. Sometimes they may be very inconspicuous and chronic. (Sometimes, for practical purposes, they may be undiscoverable. In such instances, one usually can establish the fact of an exceptionally strong predisposition.)

Because the preschizophrenic is already (in many instances) perceiving his world in a somewhat autistic fashion, it is extremely difficult to sort out predisposing from precipitating elements with any assurance. Under present limitations of understanding, it is necessary to speak in quite general terms. One knows, however, that schizophrenia most characteristically develops in adolescence or early adult life and in a situation calling for a new or an increased adjustment effort. The "situation" may primarily involve inner changes (e.g., hormonal alterations of puberty) or environmental changes (e.g., new relationships). Quite often, the sequence appears to be about as follows. In connection with developing adolescent relationships, with marriage, or with parenthood the preschizophrenic finds himself in a situation calling for *close interaction* with another human being, interaction of a sort different from that to which he has been accustomed. His chronically weakened personality (particularly the ego) is unable to deal with the problems involved in such a relationship. He may be called upon to love or to assume some other significant type of interpersonal initiative, and he cannot do so. Hostile and deviate sexual impulses of a primitive (infantile) nature may be mobilized, impulses which cannot be controlled by ordinary psychological measures. In such a crisis, the personality falls back upon desperate defense techniques, the use of which involves the appearance of the clinical psychosis.

PSYCHOLOGICAL (DEFENSE) MECHANISMS. Of these defense techniques, the most outstanding is *regression*. The regression occurring in schizophrenia is the most profound and the most extensive to be found in any of the functional psychiatric disorders. The most profound in the sense that the retreat of certain aspects of the personality goes all the way back to the earliest phase of infancy; the most extensive in the sense that a great many (or sometimes all) of the personality functions are affected.

The effects of the massive regression may be summarized under two headings: effects upon the patient's basic drives, particularly the libido, and effects upon the executive functions of the personality (the ego).

The effect upon the libido is that this complex drive loses anything approximating an adult organization or even a childhood organization (as is characteristic of psychoneuroses). In fact, to speak a bit figuratively, the libido very largely gives up its attempts to find gratifying objects in the environment and comes to be focused on the patient's own person (his body and his self-concept). Like the small infant, the patient becomes extremely narcissistic. There are also regressive alterations in the individual's hostile-aggressive urges which are apt to be very strong and which now assume characteristics of early infancy.

Of the effects upon the executive functions of the personality, the most significant is the loss of the ability to determine reality. In some instances this loss may be rather circumscribed, i.e., it may involve an inability to test reality in certain specific areas only. More commonly it is widespread, and in severe cases it may be almost total, with the result that the patient's position in this respect comes to resemble that of the newborn infant.

Earlier in this chapter (p. 365) we have indicated that it is the loss of the capacity for reality testing (along with the greatly heightened narcissism) which is responsible for the autistic thinking of the schizophrenic. This loss also makes possible the development of such florid symptoms as delusions and hallucinations. Viewed from this standpoint, the existence of a delusion indicates that the individual has become unable to differentiate between certain of his own more intense thoughts and objective reality. The existence of a hallucination indicates that he has lost the ability to differentiate between certain memory traces of sensory experiences and the actual, current sensory experiences themselves.

As the student will recognize, these same confusions exist for the normal person when he is asleep and dreaming. Indeed, schizophrenic states have sometimes been referred to as "waking dreams."* While this comparison is not without value in attempting to conceptualize

---

* They could not be referred to as pleasant dreams, except in the most regressed cases, however. Contrary to widespread lay opinion, the schizophrenic, even if quite withdrawn, seldom finds peace. One of the reasons for this is that the infancy to which he regresses has rarely, if ever, been a happy one.

the plight in which the schizophrenic finds himself, it has distinct limitations. Two of the more significant differences come quickly to mind. Whereas the normal individual relinquishes his hold on reality voluntarily in the process of going to sleep (as shown by the usual ability to awaken very rapidly when it is important to do so), the schizophrenic has fallen a victim to powerful disruptive forces beyond his control. Whereas the normal individual does regress in dreams and the aims and objects of his drives may become childlike, the regression ordinarily stops far short of the position reached in the schizophrenic, a position in which clear-cut external objects may be largely given up (and even the mental representations of them become inaccessible).

Since schizophrenic delusions and hallucinations, like those in organic brain reactions and like the phenomenon of dreaming, involve an attributing by the subject of his own inner experiences to the outside world, one can readily see that the immediate psychological mechanism underlying these symptoms is that of *projection.*

Thus one can say that the combination of massive regression with the use of projection is largely responsible for the delusions and hallucinations of the schizophrenic. As was mentioned in the case of these symptoms in organic brain reactions, the precise content of the delusions and hallucinations is dependent upon details of the life history of the patient. In a general way, however, the content of certain delusional and hallucinatory experiences is directly affected by the regressive alterations in the patient's libidinal and hostile aims and objects. The same is true of certain related clinical findings (p. 368), such as feelings of unreality, estrangement, and bodily change.

Some specific examples may be helpful in clarifying these points.

Patient W. G., the 19-year-old individual athlete, experienced vague symptoms referable to his head and chest. He spoke of "electrical sensations in his brain."

J. T., the elevator operator, was convinced that his throat was "shrunken."

Another schizophrenic patient told his doctor that his head and heart "had become larger." His heart "had strength enough to pump the blood of four men."

Still another patient, in speaking of his environment, complained that the furniture in his study at home had somehow changed. He used such expressions as "artificial," "unreal," "like a stage setting," in attempting to describe the change.

In considering the meaning of the last-mentioned patient's experience, it may be of value to recall just what is involved in the normal experiences of recognition and familiarity, experiences which are such a constant feature of everyday life as seldom to receive conscious appraisal. Suppose that one has a favorite easy chair, into which he sinks with a sigh of relief after a hard day's work. Recognition of the chair, familiarity with it, and a positive feeling about it are based in considerable measure upon numerous associations (memories), perhaps largely preconscious and in part unconscious, that connect the piece of furniture with one's life, giving it, in a sense, "substance." In this chair (for example) one had sat caressing the puppy he had been given for Christmas. In this chair one had studied for a difficult examination, which meant completing college with a good record. In this chair one had opened and read love letters. And so on, and so on.

Now suppose that the most meaningful portion of all of these associations, namely the emotions and the drive-satisfactions, were lost, were completely unavailable. Would not the chair seem altered and unfamiliar, perhaps unsubstantial? This is, in effect, the situation in which the schizophrenic finds himself. As a result of the withdrawal of the libido from the objects of the environment, associations such as those mentioned above become meaningless. The weakened personality (specifically, the ego) notes that something is terribly different, but *it misinterprets the difference.* Not being able to appraise what has inwardly taken place (since the processes of the illness have been largely unconscious), the patient *judges the difference to represent an external change.* He begins to think of himself as behaving rationally in a world that has gone crazy.

There is another side to the difficulty. As was mentioned, the libido that is withdrawn from objects in the environment becomes attached, so to speak, to various aspects of the patient's own person (as does also much of the aggression). Thus there comes to be a marked (and sometimes rather sudden) increase in the emotional significance of the patient's body. Here again, *the weakened personality makes a misjudgment, interpreting a subjective change as an objective one.* The patient's impression is that mysterious changes have taken place in his body or parts of it. On this basis arise complaints such as those of W. G. about his brain, or J. T. about his throat, and of the other schizophrenic about his heart.*

This turning inward of libido and aggression which have previously been directed toward objects, amounting to a hyper-investment in vari-

---

* Such confusions are of the essence of those it is reasonably certain are experienced by young infants (see pp. 86 to 87). Hence it would be correct to say that they are manifestations of a regression to a primitive ego state, one preceding recognition of the boundaries of the self and preceding any stable investment of the libido or aggression in external objects.

ous aspects of the self, may also give a schizophrenic patient a feeling of enormous importance, and thus contribute to the formation of (other) delusions, either grandiose or persecutory, which place him at the center of things.

TREATMENT

The diagnosis of schizophrenia always warrants referral to a psychiatrist for a full appraisal and, in most instances, treatment by the psychiatrist. Oftener than not, treatment will involve an extended initial period in the hospital. Since the range of conditions labeled schizophrenic is broader than that of manic-depressive conditions, it turns out that even though schizophrenia can be much the more serious reaction, the therapeutic management is more variable. In long-standing, mild, static conditions, such as that exemplified by Mr. J. T. (p. 362), no active treatment may be indicated. In some comparable situations, treatment of a supportive nature by the family physician under psychiatric supervision may be sufficient.

Ordinarily, however, treatment will begin with hospitalization and will involve several of the modalities mentioned in connection with the treatment of the affective psychoses: milieu therapy, occupational and recreational therapy, chemotherapy, and psychotherapy. Electroconvulsive therapy should occupy but a minor place in the treatment of schizophrenic reactions (see p. 476).

Since schizophrenic reactions tend to be sustained rather than episodic, it is difficult to compare treatment results with those in the affective psychoses. However, a great majority of patients, if seen at or close to the onset of their schizophrenic reactions, can be helped appreciably.

In estimating the prognosis of a patient experiencing a schizophrenic reaction, the following factors may be taken as relatively favorable indications: (1) an acute onset; (2) an onset in which current stresses are clearly distinguishable and significant; (3) absence of a family history of the disorder; and (4) a history of a period during which a reasonably effective adjustment to life has been made.

Perhaps 80 per cent of schizophrenics can achieve a degree of recovery sufficient for them to leave the hospital and effect some kind of adjustment on the outside (for a variable period of time). As in manic-depressive psychosis, the crucial question is whether or not a permanent clinical remission can be obtained. With increasing knowledge of psychotherapy, of milieu therapy, and of chemotherapy, the proportion of such remissions is increasing to a significant and hopeful degree although data are not sufficiently clear to permit any exact statement. The proportion of such patients of whom it would be proper to speak of a "cure" in the sense that the fundamental personality difficulties underlying the psychotic reaction have been markedly alleviated is, of course, much smaller. Up to the present time, psychoanalytically oriented techniques of intensive psychotherapy are the only known means of effecting this end. These techniques cannot be offered on a large scale, and even then they are fully effective in only a minority of instances.

PARANOID REACTIONS: PARANOIA AND PARANOID STATE

While paranoid reactions are given a separate heading in the official nomenclature and (at least, in the case of paranoia) have long been recognized as a psychiatric disease entity, the conditions have such close similarities to paranoid schizophrenia that many clinicians believe that they should be regarded as varieties of the latter.

There are several clinical differences between a classical case of paranoia and one of paranoid schizophrenia. The age of the patient at onset is, for example, likely to be greater in paranoia, with the most typical age being in the early forties. Less of the personality appears to be involved in paranoia than in most instances of schizophrenia, with the result that some paranoid patients may give a superficial impression of near-normality. In general, the patient's emotional responses seem to be more appropriate. Aside from the specific delusional material, there may be little evidence of autistic thinking. Hallucinations are absent. As in paranoid schizophrenia, the delusions are characteristically of a persecutory nature, but they differ from those of the former condition in that they are *more highly organized*. The delusions of the classical paranoiac have considerable internal consistency, forming a closely knit system. That is to say, there is a kind of logic about the delusional material, such that, if the patient's first erroneous premise is accepted, the rest of the material appears to follow rather naturally. Hence it not infrequently happens that a paranoiac may win over other persons to his delusional way of thinking. It seems quite likely that a number of founders of religious sects and cults and of extremist political systems have been afflicted with paranoid psychoses.

The principal clinical basis for believing that paranoia is to be considered a variant of paranoid schizophrenia lies in the fact that patients can be found to show every gradation of symptomatology from a clinical picture in which an isolated delusional system is (aside, perhaps, from certain morbid character traits) essentially the only symptom, to one in which persecutory delusions are accompanied by all of the basic symptoms of schizophrenia. Of course, this observation does not prove the point. It could be objected that there is no basis for supposing that paranoid patients would be immune to schizophrenia in varying degrees of severity, nor is there any basis to suppose that schizophrenics would not often think in a highly paranoid fashion.

At the present time, the question remains unsettled. It may be that paranoid psychosis is merely a variant of paranoid schizophrenia, or it may be that it is a purely psychogenic disorder, which may exist by itself or which may form a part of the more severe and complicated disease process which is schizophrenia.

PARANOIA

Here is a case history illustrating many of the features of paranoid psychosis in its most classical form (paranoia).

Major H. N., aged 40, married but childless, was referred to the psychiatric service of an army hospital for thorough evaluation by order of his commanding officer. The patient was quite certain that he was not ill in any way; he had no presenting complaints in the ordinary sense. He was hurt and angry that his colonel "had so little confidence in his intelligence" as to send him to the psychiatrist.

Aside from the material to be presented in detail below, the examination of the patient's mental status revealed few abnormalities. Major N. was of above-average intelligence. His sensorium was perfectly clear. His emotions were, in general, quite appropriate to his content of thought. There was no evidence of neurotic symptomatology, nor of hallucinations or illusions. In ordinary conversation the patient created quite a favorable impression, speaking in a reasonable and perfectly coherent manner and giving courteous attention to the remarks of others.

Major N. was a career man and had been in the service for 20 years. Most of this time he had been a noncommissioned officer, reaching the rank of master sergeant. About two years before the psychiatric consultation, the patient had been promoted from the ranks after taking an examination, and because of his age, had been given a majority. H. N. held an administrative assignment and, until recently, had always been credited in his efficiency reports with being exceptionally conscientious and giving meticulous attention to detail. Within the past six months, however, some falling off in efficiency had been noted. The patient had been recently described as preoccupied and forgetful.

Major N. was at first quite reserved in speaking to the psychiatrist about personal matters and particularly about his recent difficulties, but eventually he related the following story. About a year ago, a new officer, Captain L., had been assigned to a job in the patient's office. This man was a good-looking, intelligent, and rather aggressive ("cocky") person. He was a West Pointer, about ten years younger than the patient and came from a distinguished military family. Initially, Major N. had taken a liking to the newcomer ("In fact, I loved him like a brother"), and had taken special pains in orienting him to his job and to the post. The two officers developed an off-duty friendship as well, and often stopped in the club together for a round of drinks. Occasionally, Major N. would invite the captain, who was unmarried, to his home for dinner.

The patient told the psychiatrist, "All of my troubles began then." He related that Captain L. and his own wife had been greatly attracted to one another and had become lovers. He accused the captain of arranging secret meetings with his wife, some of which were "taking place right in my own home." He also accused Captain L. of "spreading ugly rumors" about him at the club. When pressed for details, Major N. at first said merely that the captain was making malicious remarks "about my lack of education." Eventually the patient added that the "rumors" were to the effect that he was a homosexual.

During the interviews, it was noticeable that the patient spoke with mounting intensity. It was of great importance to Major N. that he convince someone of the truth of his beliefs. In his attempt to do so, he related further details which he said constituted "positive proof" that his wife and the captain were "guilty as charged." Several weeks earlier the major had noticed that his wife was making their coffee stronger than usual. He had not understood the reason for the change at first, but soon came to the conclusion that Mrs. N. was using the coffee to "cover up the taste of a sedative" that she was giving him at their evening meal. The major suspected that his wife wanted him to sleep soundly so that she could "entertain her lover" in the guest room. To trap the "guilty pair," the patient had secretly sprinkled flour on the doorsill before retiring. On several occasions he had arisen early in the morning and found markings in the flour that, he felt certain, were the captain's footprints.

Major N. had thereupon resolved to kill Captain L., when "a good opportunity" presented itself. He had taken to carrying his service revolver, loaded, in his brief case. It was the discovery of this weapon that had led the patient's commanding officer to make the referral. (It appeared that the patient was not without some wish to be deterred from his planned course of violence, for the discovery was made on an occasion when he had carried the brief case into the colonel's office.)

Sufficient outside information was available to establish beyond question the delusional nature of the major's ideas regarding the activities of his wife and Captain L. However, when Mrs. N. was interviewed, certain additional points of interest were brought to light. Mrs. N. was an attractive, well-educated, rather strikingly dressed woman, nearly 12 years younger than her husband. She was frank enough to characterize the marriage as being largely one of convenience (for herself). Mrs. N. categorically denied any indiscretion of the sort with which she had been charged by her husband—a denial substantiated by other sources—but she volunteered the information that, in her heart, she had been attracted to Captain L. and had "played up to him" slightly when they met socially.

A six months' period of treatment in a military hospital was not successful in bringing about a recovery. The precise content of the patient's delusional ideas shifted slightly and the patient's actual behavior was reasonably well controlled, but otherwise there was no change. At this point, Major N. was separated from service on medical grounds and transferred to a Veterans Administration Hospital.

Dynamically speaking, it is clear that *projection* is the defense mechanism of primary importance in the production of the symptoms of paranoia (and, as will be seen, of milder paranoid reactions, as well). The fact that certain ideas assume a delusional intensity—with the implication that reality testing has been impaired—is evidence that a considerable *regression* is also involved, although, as indicated by the relative intactness of the personality in many aspects, the regression is not so massive as is usually the case in schizophrenia.

Since personality function is better preserved, on the whole, in paranoiacs than in (other) paranoid schizophrenics, the delusional material can often be more readily understood and the meaning of the projections better demonstrated. In the case of Major N., it is reasonably clear that the principal drives which the personality was striving to master by the use of projection were ones of a hostile, destructive nature. The original (childhood) sources of Major N's. hostility are not demonstrable on the basis of the case history which includes no information about the patient's formative years. However, recent and current stimuli are readily discernible. It is plain that the patient felt inferior to and envious of both the new officer and his wife. In addition, he felt rather at the mercy of these individuals in his career and in his home life. It is also plain that the patient had a strong conscience (he was described as conscientious and had a reputation for honesty). Under these conditions, direct awareness of the hostile impulses was not possible for him.

Through the mechanism of projection, the intolerable feeling, on the verge of welling up into consciousness, "I hate them (and wish to injure them)" was altered into the conscious thought, "They hate me (and betray me)." Once the projection had become consolidated, once it had been fully accepted by the personality, it became possible for some of the patient's hostility to be consciously recognized and even acted upon, since hostile behavior could then be regarded as in the nature of self-defense.

Hostile, destructive impulses, often of a quite primitive nature, are the principal strivings with which the personality has to deal in paranoid psychoses. Next in importance and frequency among the troublesome and forbidden impulses in these conditions are strivings of a homosexual nature. In the case of Major N., this element can also be discerned with considerable clarity. At the beginning of the patient's relationship with the new officer, Major N. experienced a definite attraction to him and became his "buddy." As was true of the hostile impulses, the sexual impulses were blocked from awareness. As they became stronger through the continued association and threatened to break into consciousness, they were dealt with through *reaction-formation*. Thus the unconscious feeling, "I love (desire) him," was transformed into the opposite, "I hate him." As was previously noted, however, the patient's conscience would not tolerate this feeling either; therefore it was transformed through the further use of projection into the idea, "He hates me." This final conviction, then, stemmed from two sources: one was the projection of a basic, original hostility, and the other was the projection of a secondary hostility, the product of a preceding reaction-formation.

Both of the psychological sequences which have just been described are very common in patients with paranoid psychoses. It is little wonder that the persecutory delusions of a paranoiac acquire a fixed intensity rarely equaled in other disorders.

Paranoid States

This diagnostic term is used for psychotic conditions in which the principal clinical feature is the presence of one or more delusions of a paranoid nature, but in which (a) the general features of schizophrenia and (b) a high degree of organization of the delusions are absent. These conditions are often short-lived and not infrequently represent a reaction to a realistically severe stress. The predisposing elements in such patients are considered to have been far less severe than in the schizophrenias or in classical paranoia; or, to put this in another way, the personalities of such patients appear to be fundamentally stronger than is the case in the major psychoses.

Mr. K. F., a semiskilled laborer, aged 34, married and the father of two children, was severely injured in a hunting accident. As a result of a temporary incapacitation, he lost his job. A period in the hospital on the surgical service was followed by a protracted convalescence at home. The patient's wife found employment to eke out the family's meager savings. For the first time in the marriage, the patient found that he was sexually impotent. Under these circumstances, Mr. F. developed the delusional idea that his wife was having sexual relations with customers at her place of work. His accusations were severe and bitter.

Toward the end of the period of convalescence, the patient confided his troubles to the family doctor, who referred the couple to a family service agency (p. 461). While evaluative interviews were still in progress, the patient regained his strength and found a new job, similar to the one he had previously held. His sexual potency returned within a couple of weeks, and the delusion vanished.

Treatment measures for paranoid reactions are closely comparable to those for schizophrenic reactions. Classical paranoia is very seldom modifiable in any fundamental way, although some degree of "social recovery" can be achieved more often. Since such patients are potentially dangerous, treatment should always be undertaken in the hospital. If the psychiatrist succeeds in establishing a reasonably good relationship with the patient, it may become possible to continue treatment on an office basis. The patient should remain under psychiatric observation for the duration of his illness.

Paranoid states are much more amenable to treatment; this is especially likely to be true if, as in the case cited, the psychotic reaction is traceable to a clear-cut environmental factor which can be modified.

References

1. Bateson, G., Jackson, D. D., Haley, J., and Weakland, J. H.: Toward a theory of schizophrenia, Behavioral Sciences 1:251, 1956.
2. Bleuler, E.: Dementia Praecox or the Group Schizophrenias, translated by Joseph Zinkin, New York, Internat. Univ. Press, 1950.
3. Bowen, M., Dysinger, R. H., and Basamania, B.: The role of the father in families with a schizophrenic patient, Am. J. Psychiat. 115:1017, 1959.
4. Heath, R. G.: A biochemical hypothesis on the etiology of schizophrenia in Jackson, D. D. (ed.): The Etiology of Schizophrenia, New York, Basic, 1960.
5. Heath, R. G., Leach, B. E., Cohen, M.: Relationships of psychotic behavior and abnormal substances in serum in The Effects of Pharmacologic Agents on the Nervous System, Proceedings of the Association for Research in Nervous and Mental Disease, Vol. 37, p. 397, Baltimore, Williams & Wilkins, 1959.
6. Hoffer, A., Osmond, H., and Smythies, J.: Schizophrenia: a new approach. II. Result of a year's research, J. Ment. Sci. 100:29, 1954.
7. Hoffer, A., and Kenyon, M.: Conversion of adrenaline to adrenolutin in human blood serum, Arch. Neurol. Psychiat. 77:437, 1957.
8. Hoskins, R. G.: The Biology of Schizophrenia, New York, Norton, 1946.
9. Jackson, D. D. (ed.): The Etiology of Schizophrenia, New York, Basic, 1960.
10. Kallman, F. J.: The genetic theory of schizophrenia, An analysis of 691 twin index families, Am. J. Psychiat. 103:309, 1946.
11. Kretchmer, E.: A Text-book of Medical Psychology, Translated by E. B. Strauss, London, Oxford, 1934.
12. Lidz, T., Cornelison, A. R., Fleck, S., and Terry, D.: The intrafamilial environment of the schizophrenic patient, Psychiatry 20:329, 1957.

13. Lidz, T., Cornelison, A. R., Fleck, S., and Terry, D.: Marital schism and marital skew, Am. J. Psychiat. *114*:241, 1957.
14. Sheldon, W. H., Stevens, S. S., and Tucker, W. B.: The Varieties of Human Physique, New York, Harper, 1940.

Suggestions for Further Reading

Arieti, S.: Interpretation of Schizophrenia, New York, Robert Brunner, 1955.
Auerback, A.: Schizophrenia: An Integrated Approach, New York, Ronald, 1959.
Bellak, L.: Dementia Praecox, New York, Grune, 1948.
Bleuler, E.: Dementia Praecox or the Group of Schizophrenias, translated by Joseph Zinkin, New York, Internat. Univ. Press, 1950.
Freud, S.: Certain neurotic mechanisms in jealousy, paranoia, and homosexuality *in* Collected Papers of Sigmund Freud, Vol. 2, London, Hogarth Press, 1924.
Jackson, D. D.: The Etiology of Schizophrenia, New York, Basic, 1960.

CHAPTER 12

Personality Disorders

Taken together, the *personality disorders* unquestionably comprise the largest group of psychiatric conditions. For reasons which will become apparent as the discussion proceeds, persons in this category are seldom referred to a psychiatrist early and may never be referred at all. In one connection or another, however, they are seen in general practice and in the practice of the nonpsychiatric specialties with great frequency. When one hears remarks by experienced general practitioners and internists, such as "half of my practice is composed of neurotics," one can be certain that the category of personality disorders is primarily responsible for the statement. Examples of this type of disorder which have already been presented—in other contexts—include those on pages 145 and 250.

It may be worthwhile to restate at this point the conventional medical definitions of *sign* and *symptom*.* A symptom is considered to be *a departure from the normal in function, appearance, or sensation, experienced by the patient and indicative of disease.* A sign is more objective, being considered to be *a departure from the normal in structure or function, either naturally existing or elicited by the examiner and directly perceptible by him.*

All of the psychiatric and psychophysiological disease states which have been considered in the four chapters preceding this one have plainly been characterized by signs or symptoms or both. The elevated blood pressure of the essential hypertensive (p. 193), the paralysis, the tremor, and the blindness of the conversion hysterics (pp. 314-316), and the fixed pupils of the patient with dementia paralytica (p. 282) are all obvious signs of illness. The amnesia of the patients with dissociative reaction (pp. 322-323), the anorexia of the depressed patient (p. 342), and the somatic delusions of the schizophrenic patient (p. 360) are obvious symptoms of illness. Moreover, in most of these instances the sick person recognized the sign or symptom as an indication that some-

---
* As given in Dorland's *Medical Dictionary*, slightly modified.

thing was wrong with him (although he may not have understood the nature of the difficulty).

It is usually quite otherwise with the class of patients now to be considered. Patients with personality disorders do not offer presenting complaints (do not have symptoms) in the usual sense of the term; nor does examination of such patients disclose isolated, discrete signs of illness in the usual sense.

On what basis, then, does *personality disorder* become a nosological entity? The definition provides the first step toward an answer. *A personality disorder is a form of psychiatric illness in which the subject's inner difficulties (neurotic conflicts, or in some instances, "psychotic conflicts") are manifested, not in specific symptoms, but in an unhealthy pattern of living.*

In the course of the discussion of conflict (p. 69), it was brought out that essentially all human beings have neurotic conflicts, and still earlier (p. 34), it was indicated that perfect health—and therefore a completely healthy pattern of living—is actually an ideal, rarely or perhaps never achieved. It accordingly becomes clear that the diagnosis of personality disorder must be a relative matter, involving questions of degree. A patient with such a disorder is the victim of relatively severe inner conflicts which manifest themselves in a relatively unhealthy pattern of living.

It should be clear that an expression such as "a relatively unhealthy pattern of living" implies a decidedly subjective element in the diagnostician. Whereas certain departures from conventional behavior, e.g., the sexual perversion called *sadism* (p. 416), would be considered indicative of a personality disorder by nearly all trained observers (and most laymen), other behavior patterns, e.g., membership in an extremist political group, might be considered normal or healthy by some observers and abnormal or unhealthy by others, depending upon their own points of view. In general, it is important for the physician to refrain from using diagnostic terms in a polemical fashion, to refrain from labeling behavior as "sick" merely because he does not approve of it.

Before going on to a consideration of the pertinent clinical material, it may be well to review the concept of *personality* and to note the function of character "traits" in an individual's adjustment effort. Personality has been defined (on p. 31) as *the whole group of adjustment techniques and equipment which are characteristic for a given individual in meeting the various situations of life.* It includes such aspects as tastes, attitudes, ways of looking at things, ways of doing things; it includes the preferential and habitual utilization of certain defense mechanisms (rather than others). When one speaks of the "traits" of an individual's personality—whether these be healthy or unhealthy—one is speaking of matters having an altogether greater stability and constancy than have "symptoms" of an illness.

Like symptoms, however, the development of character traits may be considered as an approach to the solving of adjustment problems. There are advantages and disadvantages to handling one's conflicts in this way. The principal advantage is that, being in considerable measure a once-for-all affair, adjustment through the development of a character trait is economical. That is to say, it does not require much in the way of a continuous expenditure of mental energy, whereas the formation of a series of symptoms—or even the making of a series of voluntary decisions—may consume a great deal of energy. The principal disadvantage is that a character trait, being relatively permanent, imparts a certain *rigidity* to the personality. Having become habituated to a certain way of responding whenever a given problem or conflict is involved, an individual finds that his over-all choices of action have decreased.

To illustrate these points, let us consider an extremely simple, mildly humorous, hypothetical situation. Let us say that an individual has suffered a severe attack of indigestion on an occasion when he has eaten seafood and drunk milk at the same meal. Let us say, further, that he has had a strong liking for both types of food. The "problem" then is, how to handle such situations in the future? A solution through symptom-formation would occur if the person (without conscious intention) were to develop mild nausea whenever he were subsequently served this combination. A solution through the establishment of a character trait would occur if he (without conscious intention) were to develop a simple aversion to one or the other food or merely to the idea of eating them at the same meal. A *rational* solution would be to make inquiries or cautious experiments or to consult a physician to determine whether or not there was any cause-and-effect relationship between the food combination and the gastric upset.

Note that the solution through the establishment of a character trait would leave the individual from that time onward with a slightly narrowed choice of diet, whereas the symptom might wear off in time, and the rational approach might indicate that the ill effects had come from some other source. On the other hand, so far as the specific "problem" was concerned, both symptom-formation and the rational approach might involve a greater psychological effort.

One way, then, of looking at *personality disorders* is to view such patients as having acquired, by reason of unfavorable early experiences, a set of character traits which, though originally of some adjustment value, have exerted a limiting and a warping effect. Certain anxieties are held in check by the morbid traits—although the patient is never fully conscious of this fact—but the price is an increased rigidity of the personality, the loss of a degree of freedom.

To come now to the clinical material, consider the following example, based upon a case history which has already been presented (p. 330). Suppose that one had had the opportunity of examining Mr. W. D., the patient with obsessive-compulsive neurosis, at some point in his life prior to the outbreak of his clinical illness. Would he, at such a point, have been psychologically well? He would have been free of classical obsessions and compulsions. On the other hand, there were certain features of his adjustment, certain characteristics of temperament ("traits") which could scarcely be considered indicative of good health. He was a rather subdued, cautious, inflexible, and overcontrolled person who found it difficult to relax and have a good time. He was sufficiently insecure to have put off marriage until his midthirties, and when he did marry, his choice was not based "on the heart," but on objective considerations. If one had been called upon to make a psychiatric diagnosis of Mr. D. at such a time, one could have used the designation of "neurotic personality—compulsive type—reasonably well compensated."

As another illustration, one might consider the case of Miss E. M., the patient with phobic reaction (p. 325). Suppose that she had been examined psychiatrically shortly before the onset of her clinical illness. Again, there would have been no actual symptoms, yet the patient's style of living would have been obviously an unhappy and incomplete one. Her sexual life (in the usual sense) was nonexistent, and her social life extremely restricted. Her dress and manner was suggestive of a woman seriously on guard against any expression of her femininity. Her dependence upon her mother exceeded that of a healthy adolescent. The diagnosis at this point could have been that of "phobic personality" or possibly that of "hysterical personality" (both being subheadings of "neurotic personality").

As a third example, take the case of Major H. N., the paranoid patient (p. 391). There is no question but that his actual psychosis had its beginning within a year of the incident of the loaded pistol. Yet, here too, a thorough psychiatric evaluation of the patient at any period of his adult life would probably have disclosed evidence of a characterological type of illness. Depending upon the relative prominence of rigid, formalized, ritualistic behavior on the one hand, and cautious, humorless, suspicious behavior on the other, the patient might have been diagnosed either as "compulsive personality" or as "paranoid personality" (a subheading under "psychotic personality").

Similarly, if the schizophrenic patient of page 360 had been evaluated during his adolescence, his shyness, seclusiveness, and eccentricity would probably have warranted a diagnosis of "schizoid (schizophrenialike) personality."*

To re-emphasize a point made earlier in the present discussion, it should be stated that a diagnosis of personality disorder is not made merely upon the inference or even upon the demonstration that an individual is beset with one or several neurotic conflicts. Neurotic conflicts are the common lot of humanity. The diagnosis is made only when the intensity of the conflict(s) is such as to result in a style of living which is clearly unhealthy, in which basic gratifications are blocked or (as will be further discussed) are sought in ways which deviate appreciably from the normal. Thus, Miss M., before the onset of her clinical illness, would have been diagnosed as having a personality disorder not because she had unsolved and unconscious sexual and dependency conflicts, but because these conflicts affected her attitudes, manner, and behavior rather seriously.

Now suppose that the life situation of one of the individuals referred to on the preceding pages had taken a different, a more favorable course before the occurrence of what we have called the precipitating circumstances (of the clinical illness). Suppose, for example, that Mr. D.'s firm had suffered no reverses and that his young son had remained in good health. Under these conditions—and barring future misfortunes of a comparable sort—Mr. D. might never have experienced a frank psychoneurosis. His neurotic personality, on the other hand, in all probability would have remained such throughout his adult life.

The point is that if individuals with personality disorders encounter life situations which are moderately favorable or even neutral, they may continue to be able to effect some kind of working adjustment, i.e., the personality disorder may persist without the development of symptoms. If such individuals encounter unfavorable life situations, there is always the possibility of "decompensation" into a clinical psychoneurosis, psychosis, or psychophysiological disease state. On the other hand, for any fundamental amelioration of the personality disorder to take place, dramatically favorable life experiences or intensely favorable experiences in psychotherapy are required.

---

* It is not to be thought, however, that every neurosis and psychosis is preceded by a phase in which the patient suffers from a personality disorder having certain features closely resembling characteristics of the subsequent clinical illness. For example, pre-psychotic personalities of both manic-depressive and schizophrenic patients are often of the compulsive type. Indeed, the "pre-morbid" personality features of an individual who subsequently experiences a neurosis or psychosis may, at times, not be sufficiently remarkable to warrant a diagnosis of any sort. (In such instances, however, the precipitating events leading to the clinical illness will be found to be very strong.)

A discussion of treatment must be postponed, but it may be of interest, at this point, to cite an example of the impact of a highly favorable life experience on a sick personality. The illustration can serve also as an introduction to another form of personality disorder. In real life, intensely moving experiences of precisely the right sort to exert a healing effect upon a given individual are, of course, uncommon. Turning to imaginative literature, Alexander[1] called attention to the example given below. The illustration is in Victor Hugo's *Les Misérables*.

Jean Valjean, the ex-convict and man of hatred, fresh from the prison galleys, is given food and shelter by the saintly Bishop of D. During the night, Valjean runs off with a basket of silver (among the few touches of luxury in the austere household). He is apprehended by the gendarmes and returned to face charges. The bishop, understanding the severe deprivation and injustice which have made Valjean what he is, indicates that the silver had been given to Valjean, and thereupon presents him with two silver candlesticks in addition, saying, "I purchase your soul for God." The hardened outcast is overwhelmed. There follows a brief period of wavering, after which Valjean is never again the same, becoming a man of generosity, kindness, and courage.

Jean Valjean is illustrative of a type of personality disorder other than those which have thus far been considered. That is to say, his condition was not one resembling a specific neurosis or psychosis minus the overt symptoms, as were those of the previous examples. He was not suffering from a "neurotic personality" or a "psychotic personality," but from a third (related) type of disorder which is called "sociopathic personality disturbance" (in older psychiatric terminology, "psychopathic personality").

It will be helpful at this point to introduce the official (American Psychiatric Association) system by which the personality disorders are formally classified.

PERSONALITY DISORDERS

1. Personality Pattern Disturbance ("Psychotic Personality")
    A. Inadequate personality. (Characterized by inadequate responses to intellectual, emotional, and social demands. They are neither physically nor mentally grossly deficient on examination, but they do show inadaptability, ineptness, poor judgment, lack of stamina and social incompatibility.)
    B. Schizoid personality
    C. Cyclothymic personality
    D. Paranoid personality

2. Personality Trait Disturbances ("Neurotic Personality")
   A. Emotionally unstable personality. (The individual reacts with excitability and ineffectiveness when confronted with minor stress, and his relationship to other people is continuously fraught with fluctuating emotional attitudes, because of strong and poorly controlled hostility, guilt, and anxiety.)
   B. Passive-aggressive personality
   C. Compulsive personality
   D. Other (phobic, hysterical, etc.)
3. Sociopathic Personality Disturbance ("Psychopathic Personality")
   A. Antisocial reactions. (Chronically antisocial individuals who are always in trouble, profiting from neither experience nor punishment, and maintaining no real loyalties to any person, group or code. They are frequently callous and hedonistic, showing marked emotional immaturity, with a lack of a sense of responsibility, lack of judgment, and an ability to rationalize their behavior so that it appears to be warranted, reasonable and justified.)
   B. Dissocial reaction. (Individuals who manifest disregard for the usual social codes and often come into conflict with them, as the result of having lived all their lives in an abnormal moral environment. They may be capable of strong loyalties.)
   C. Sexual deviation (specify)
   D. Addiction
      (1) Alcoholism
      (2) Drug (specify)
4. Special Symptom Reactions*
5. Transient Situational Personality Disorders. (An acutely unhealthy response to a serious stress situation by an individual without apparent underlying personality disorder. Sometimes used as synonymous with traumatic neurosis.)

Actually, no system of classification of the personality disorders has yet been devised which is thoroughly satisfactory, primarily because personality, itself, is such a complex concept. It is far more difficult to say what a *person* is really like than it is merely to create a diag-

---

* This category—which includes such items as "learning disturbance," "speech disturbance," and enuresis—need not be considered in the present context since these conditions are ordinarily encountered by the physician in children and so will be discussed in Chapter 15.

nostic category based upon the presence of certain specific manifestations of maladjustment. In the official nomenclature, categories 1 and 2 are chiefly derived from the similarity of certain personality disorders to certain (descriptive) categories in the areas of neurosis and psychosis respectively. Category 3 is a hodgepodge, including two subcategories (A, B) which make some attempt to say what the patient is like, and two other subcategories (C, D) which are dependent upon singling out a conspicuous behavioral feature.

Another, and more basic, attempt at classification, which the reader will encounter in some psychiatric and most psychoanalytic literature,[2] derives from a consideration of the developmental history of the individual rather than from clinical descriptive features. In this system, the personality disorders are categorized according to the *fixation point* (p. 92) at which the individual's emotional development has been arrested. Thus, a person who is beset in adult life with emotional problems deriving from the nursing period of development would be called an *oral personality*; one whose problems derive chiefly from the muscle-training period would be called an *anal personality*; one whose problems derive from the early phase of the family-triangle period, a *phallic personality*, etc.

There is a considerable overlapping—although not a complete one—between this system of classification and that based upon the similarity of particular personality disorders to overt neuroses and psychoses (official nomenclature, categories 1 and 2). Thus, the three examples just mentioned would, to a degree, correspond to *cyclothymic personality*, *compulsive personality*, and *hysterical personality*, respectively. Since, however, the psychoanalytic type of classification is based upon critical early life experiences pertaining to the *etiology* of subsequent illness, rather than to the surface (clinical) manifestations of such illness, its terms also overlap with those in category 3 of the official nomenclature. Thus, many subjects of *alcoholism* and the (other) *addictions* may also properly be termed *oral personalities*; many *homosexuals* may be considered to be *anal personalities*, etc.

A good bit remains to be said about the *neurotic personality* (category 2), particularly in its subtler manifestations, but first it may be well to discuss some examples of patients from category 3, since the material from the preceding several chapters is less applicable to these disorders than to the ones in categories 1 and 2.

Problems involved in the syndrome of chronic alcoholism will be given very extended consideration at this point, in view both of the great prevalence of this condition and of the illumination which a careful study of it can shed upon personality disorders in general.

ALCOHOLISM

As was mentioned in the discussion (pp. 171 to 173) of mild forms of this condition, alcoholism is a very widespread medical problem. It is said on good authority* that there are upwards of 5,000,000 alcoholics in the United States at the present time. Only a small minority of these persons come to psychiatric attention; a considerably larger number come to the attention of the general practitioner, the internist, or of any physician who is in the status of a friend of the family involved. (Many others do not come to medical attention at all, except in the late stages of some complication.)

The definition of alcoholism adopted here is a functional and therefore a somewhat inexact one. As mentioned on page 172, alcoholism may be said to exist when an individual's intake of alcoholic beverages affects him in ways which interfere appreciably with his adjustment to life (vocational, social, sexual, etc.). Individual variations in metabolism and in psychological defenses absolutely preclude any attempt to define the condition in quantitative terms referable to alcoholic intake.

In recent years, there has been a vast amount of propaganda to the effect that "alcoholism is a disease." If one must oversimplify, it is a good deal better, no doubt, to consider alcoholism primarily as a disease rather than as a sin or a crime. Nevertheless, if one is to be scientific, he must insist that alcoholism is not "a disease." That is to say, it certainly is not *a* disease.† It is best considered as a prominent manifestation of one of a number of psychopathological states, the commonest being some form of personality disorder. Much of the discussion which follows has particular relevance to alcoholism as a manifestation of a personality disorder of category 3, but the truth is that alcoholism may be a manifestation of underlying psychopathology of category 1 or 2 or of still other conditions (frank neuroses or psychoses).

Here are excerpts from the case histories of two alcoholics, illustrative of some of the principal clinical features and also of the wide variations as to the nature of the psychological factors involved and the severity of the underlying personality disorder.‡

---

* Statistics of the National Council of Alcoholics, Inc., New York (1959).

† Thinking of the literal meaning of the word, one may add that alcoholism is usually not a *dis*-ease, either. That is to say, to the alcoholic his drinking is seen as a means of trying to achieve a comfortable state rather than as something which is, per se, uncomfortable.

‡ In older terminology, these cases would probably have been designated as two different forms of alcoholism. J. Y. would have been called "a symptomatic alcoholic"

J. Y., a distinguished-looking man of 54, sought admission to the hospital (through his internist), realizing that he was in a state of incipient delirium tremens (p. 292). By the use of appropriate medical measures, the impending attack was warded off. In connection with planning the treatment of the alcoholism itself, a psychiatric consultation was suggested and readily accepted.

The patient had been a rather hard drinker since his college years. He was an insurance salesman and a very successful one, having a number of large corporations as clients and having achieved an annual income of about $40,000. He had been until recently an ardent sportsman, his principal avocations having been tennis, boating, and hunting. During most of his adult life, the patient's drinking had interfered neither with work nor with recreation. It had, however, slowly increased over the years. Just prior to the circumstances leading to his "present illness," his intake was approximately a pint of whiskey per day. During all of this period, Mr. Y's general health had been good.

About four years before the present admission, the patient had begun to develop arthritis. Despite conventional treatment measures, the disease progressed to the point at which the patient's recreational pursuits were considerably inhibited. It was recommended that his alcoholic intake be curtailed, but Mr. Y. was unwilling or unable to implement this recommendation.

The patient had married in his early twenties, and the couple had raised two children, both of whom had married and established their own homes. Mrs. Y. had been a capable and quite feminine person, who had shared a number of social and community interests with her husband. About a year before the present admission, she had died suddenly of complications arising from pneumonia contracted while on a yachting trip with her husband.

From this point on, the tempo of Mr. Y.'s drinking increased markedly. His arthritis worsened, and the patient became something of a recluse. He continued to put in appearances at his clubs, but he avoided company and often drank heavily while at home alone. He went to his office irregularly, and seldom called on clients. The inevitable financial reverses contributed further to his despondent mood.

Mr. Y. had no illusions as to the seriousness of his situation, and had thought more than once of trying to do something about it. The threatened onset of delirium tremens overcame his lingering resistance to seeking medical help for his alcoholism. On the basis of preliminary interviews, psychotherapy was recommended, along with certain other measures, and the patient readily accepted the recommendation.

---

and F. T., "an essential alcoholic." By this device it was originally intended to distinguish between those alcoholics whose condition was considered to be the result of clear-cut emotional and/or physical trauma and those in whom no such trauma could be made out. It has become apparent, however, that this type of distinction is an artificial one. There will have been severe emotional trauma in both instances. In the "symptomatic" alcoholic it is largely recent trauma (and therefore readily perceived by an observer); in the "essential" alcoholic, it is remote (predisposing) trauma. The distinction retains some prognostic value, however, inasmuch as treatment of the "symptomatic" alcoholic is more often successful than treatment of the "essential" alcoholic.

F. T. was a 23-year-old semiskilled laborer, currently unemployed. The evaluation which yielded the following material was obtained during a hospital admission for bronchitis and bronchopneumonia, during the course of which the patient experienced an episode of delirium tremens.

Mr. T. was the second in a family of seven children and of very limited means. There was chronic, severe dissension between the parents, the father being a spree drinker and the mother a long-suffering whining person, of little basic warmth and with inadequate personal resourcefulness to meet her difficult situation.

The patient was a disciplinary problem from early childhood. Although of at least average intelligence, he did poorly at school, failed a grade, and left school at the age of 17 to join the army. He had already begun to drink, and in service his drinking had led to administrative difficulties. On one occasion he was sentenced to 30 days in the post prison for being A.W.O.L. while intoxicated. Shortly afterward, the incident was repeated, and this time the patient was given an "undesirable discharge" from service.

F. T., then 19, returned to his home town, but lived at a boarding house. He worked sporadically for building contractors, losing several jobs either because of coming to work intoxicated or of missing work for the same reason.

In a consideration of the etiology of alcoholism it is necessary to keep in mind the fact, mentioned on page 405, that despite its status as an "official" diagnosis, alcoholism is not a disease entity in the usual sense of the word (not in the sense of acute bronchitis or even in the sense of conversion reaction). As a matter of fact, it is incorrect to speak of drinking, itself, even as a *symptom* of disease, if the term is used in its strictest sense. For one thing, alcoholics very seldom complain of their drinking. For another, taking a drink (or several drinks) cannot really be called a symptom since this act is a more or less regular occurrence among large numbers of entirely healthy persons. Finally, there is little evidence to suggest that an alcoholic need develop a significant *physical* dependence upon alcohol[*] in the sense that a narcotic addict develops a dependence upon his drug (see p. 414).

As with other character disorders, so with the alcoholic: it is his pattern of attempted adjustment (actually, of maladjustment) to his life situation which is indicative of underlying psychopathology; specifically, the manner, the frequency, and the purpose of his drinking. (Of course, alcoholic intoxication involves a symptom complex, and so do various states which result from the chronic overuse of alcohol, such as delirium tremens and Korsakoff's psychosis, but these are secondary matters, not the alcoholism, per se.)

---

[*] This is not to say that a physical dependence cannot develop; it can (as indicated by the occurrence of convulsions upon the withdrawal of alcohol). It is merely to say that alcoholism as defined on p. 405 need not involve a physical dependence.

Perhaps the best way in which to express the situation of the alcoholic is somewhat as follows: The alcoholic is one who is psychologically ill; he suffers from severe inner conflicts (neurotic or psychotic); as one of his defense measures, he comes to rely upon an excessive intake of alcohol; this measure tends to cause a further impairment of his adjustment and to bring about a number of secondary symptoms.

The idea that there is usually an organic (perhaps hereditary) basis for alcoholism is a popular one. Since the idea tends to make any deep sense of personal responsibility unnecessary, it is especially popular among alcoholics themselves, as well as among those whose behavior might be considered to have played a part in the development of the disorder (parents, spouses). It is, however, also held by a number of serious investigators, whose interest is scientific. Yet, despite extensive efforts, the theory that there exists any gene-borne predisposition to alcoholism remains unproved. About the most that can be said along the organic line is that individual metabolic peculiarities in the adult (which, in turn, may prove traceable to experiential factors) have been described in some alcoholics. Against the idea of an hereditary influence is the fact that children of alcoholic parentage, when reared in foster homes from an early age, do not develop alcoholism with any greater frequency than does the general population.

Two other forms which have been taken by theories of organic etiology, and which have received considerable publicity, are: (1) that alcoholism is based upon an allergic hypersensitivity, and (2) that it is based upon a hypofunction of the adrenal cortex. As the student doubtless knows, allergenic substances fall into a very brief list of chemical categories (proteins, polypeptides, polysaccharides, or substances which form proteins in the body) of which alcohol is not a member. Therefore the allergic hypothesis was inherently very improbable. The bulk of evidence appears to be against it.[4]

Concerning the etiological involvement of the adrenal cortex, it may be said that this idea remains in the realm of unlikely speculation. One quite significant observation in this connection is that the incidence of alcoholism is no higher among persons afflicted with disease of the adrenal cortex than it is among the general population. (On the other hand, there is no question but that the continued overuse of alcohol may contribute, on occasion, to the development of endocrine disturbances.)

Notwithstanding these several considerations, there are significant pharmacological aspects to the study of alcoholism. Alcohol is unquestionably a depressant of cellular function, and one to which neurons are particularly susceptible. To be specific, the action of alcohol in anything less than the most massive doses (i.e., in doses producing blood levels under 300 mg. per ml.) is to block synaptic transmission.[3] This effect is achieved by a disturbance of energy stored in phosphate bonds and probably through the production of an accumulation of acetylcholine in the brain. (In still higher concentrations, alcohol interferes directly with intracellular oxygen metabolism.) Still more importantly, the functional inhibition exerted by alcohol acts in a distinctly selective fashion. The phylogenetically newest (the "highest") brain centers are affected first. Thus, the cortical association areas (and portions of the cerebellum) are the first to show functional impairment from alcoholic intake. Since these cortical centers normally exercise control of lower centers (thalamus, hypothalamus, etc.), ingestion of alcohol has, up to a point, largely the effect of releasing the lower centers.

The psychological effects of drinking alcohol, and hence the psychological aspects of alcoholism, correlate with the pharmacological aspects. Since, however, the psychological phenomena are (also) dependent upon the past experiences of the individual subject, there is no simple, one-to-one correlation. Many things are happening at once, psychologically speaking, and the clinical phenomena of an individual's becoming intoxicated are only to be comprehended by a consideration of the various forces involved and their mutual interaction.

There may first, for example, be a simple reduction in alertness, or in anxiety, shame, guilt, or a combination of these elements. Eventually there will be an impairment in judgment and orientation. There may be a mobilization of erotic impulses, hostile impulses, and/or dependency cravings.

The picture becomes further complicated in two ways: (1) the pharmacological effects of drinking are accompanied by effects deriving from the *meaning* of the drink, of the act and manner of drinking, and of the setting in which the drinking occurs, and (2) the "primary" elements—reduction in anxiety, impairment of judgment, mobilization of impulses, etc.—interact with one another to produce various secondary effects. These points may be illustrated by specific examples.

(1) Various impulses expressive of dependency cravings may be released by drinking and thus press toward some form of overt action. At the same time, the *meaning* of the act of drinking may be essentially one of gratifying dependency needs and thus create a tendency for *in*action. What an alcoholic might do under such circumstances could largely depend upon the balance between these opposing tendencies.

Numerous experiments have been performed to illustrate the significance of the setting and manner of alcoholic intake. If, for example, a group of subjects, sitting quietly in an experimental laboratory, receive by intravenous injection an amount of alcohol equivalent to the ingestion by mouth of several cocktails, their subsequent behavior will usually be quite different from that at an office party in which the oral route has been used.

Naturally occurring illustrations of the influence of cultural factors are to be found in the variations in incidence of alcoholism among racial, religious, and national groups, as well as between the sexes. In the United States, for instance—possibly as a residual effect of frontier days—hard drinking often has such implications as toughness, virility, or a rebellion against the established order. These implications very likely have something to do with the statistical fact that the ratio of male to female alcoholics in this country is approximately six to one.

To illustrate point (2), one may consider the following not uncommon sequence. Given an individual who is chronically anxious because of buried hostile impulses, the initial effect of a period of heavy drinking may be simply a nonspecific reduction in the sense of anxiety. As the latent hostile impulses begin to be released from the inhibiting forces and to make themselves known, however, the anxiety may be so stimulated by them as to return with redoubled force, despite the initial dulling effect.

An additional element in the sequence of events making up the total phenomenon of alcoholism has to do with reactions to the errors of omission or commission that are apt to be made while the individual is under the influence of alcohol. That is to say, in addition to the chronic personality difficulties with which the alcoholic has to cope (and which have led to his excessive drinking), there are, as a rule, fresh, acute problems to be faced after a bout of intoxication, problems which have arisen as a result of his behavior during the intoxicated period. However difficult the situation seemed before any given period of excessive drinking, it usually seems (and quite often is) still more difficult afterward. Thus the patient's distress and maladjustment and, correspondingly, his need to drink tend to become constantly greater.

Both the similarities and the differences between drinking in the normal person and drinking in the alcoholic deserve further illustration and consideration. Let us take, as a hypothetical subject, a physician coming home tired after a heavily scheduled day at the office and hospital, a day in which there have been a number of frustrating situations and the development of a certain amount of tension and anxiety. The emotional position of the physician on arrival at his home may be rather complex. He may be somewhat "on edge," perhaps not in the best of spirits; he desires to enjoy his family, but may not immediately be in a position to meet their emotional needs, to relax to a point at which the give-and-take of family life is easy and pleasant. Suppose that our physician is able to pause and drink a cocktail with his wife before dinner. He may now experience some elevation in mood; his anxiety and irritability may be reduced; he may become more affectionate and relaxed. He finds himself able to dismiss from his mind the frustrations of the day. On the other hand, certain desired and favorable memories (of pleasant family doings, for example) return more easily to his mind.

The ingestion of alcohol has thus served our physician as a means to an end. The effectiveness of this means is partly intrinsic (chemical) to be sure, but to understand the need to resort to it and the details of its effects, it is clearly required that one take into account the subject's past experiences, both recent (the events of the day) and remote (past favorable experiences with home and family, including the family of childhood).

It is easy to note the similarities between such an episode and its background and sequences in which an alcoholic drinks. The differences may need to be specified. To begin with, it may safely be assumed that the frustrations of the physician's day gained a part of their impact on the basis of previous unfavorable experiences. In the case of the alcoholic, this "sensitization" to disappointment is tremendously magnified. A current frustration need only be a quite minor one (by ordinary standards) to evoke serious amounts of anxiety and hostility and to reduce the self-esteem to dangerously low levels. Next, it was pointed out that the physician's readjustment after taking the drink was fostered because there was a backlog of favorable memories to be revived. In the case of many an alcoholic, this backlog is very slight; in severe instances (as Mr. F. T., on p. 407), it may be practically nonexistent. There may be essentially no warm, reassuring memories of home and family, of friendship, security, and comfort.

As a result, the alcoholic feels required to drink far more—and more often—than the normal subject. Soon the element mentioned on page 408 enters the picture: each bout of drinking causes behavior leading to repercussions which ultimately increase the state of frustration, of bitterness, and of a morbidly low self-esteem.

Certain features of the treatment of patients suffering from alcoholism are best discussed in the general context of psychiatric treatment measures (pp. 481 to 489 and 473 to 475). There are, however, other aspects of treatment which are properly discussed at this point, since they illustrate important psychological features. At the outset it may be said that, in most cases, treatment of an alcoholic patient should be undertaken by the general practitioner or internist only in consultation with a psychiatrist, and in severe cases (to speak more precisely, in cases with severe underlying psychopathology), the psychological aspects of treatment should be placed in the hands of the psychiatrist with the referring physician retaining the management of the physical complications, if these are present.

Of cardinal importance in treatment is the point already stressed, that *the patient does not perceive his drinking as a true symptom*. He may give lip-service to the idea, but whatever he may say, the alcoholic has a deep conviction to the contrary. He may view with dismay certain sequellae of his drinking—job loss, marital strife, financial and legal complications—but alcohol, itself, is usually viewed as a balm, as the one true source of relief from the devastating anxieties and the maddening frustrations which are ever hovering in the background, threatening to break into awareness. The true feelings of an alcoholic who is threatened with having to stop drinking are comparable to those of a patient with intractable pain who is told that there are to be no more morphine injections.

Yet it is scarcely feasible to undertake treatment unless the patient is in a state of abstinence. If it is an aim of treatment to give the patient *insight* (p. 318), abstinence is of obvious and fundamental importance since, otherwise, the patient tends to oscillate between two positions, both unfavorable: either he is under the influence of alcohol, in which case his judgment is too clouded for him to be accessible, or else he is in a state of "hangover," in which his restlessness, turmoil, and pseudoremorse are too great to allow serious introspection.

Even if the therapeutic plans do not involve an attempt to offer extensive personal insight, it is nevertheless highly important for the patient to remain in a state of sobriety. Without it, the repeated cycle of rash indulgence and fervid "repentance" obscures realistic objectives. Moreover, his behavior during periods of intoxication renders the patient's entire position (vocational, marital, social) too unstable to permit serious planning.

For these reasons, the treatment of serious, chronic alcoholism is often best undertaken in the hospital (preferably a psychiatric hospital or hospital-unit). Hospitalization gives the degree of environmental control needed to ensure abstinence and also makes possible a greater degree of emotional support than is usually possible in an out-patient setting. When hospitalization is not feasible—or, in milder cases, where it is not indicated—there are other possibilities which may be utilized to give some assurance of an initial period of sobriety. One is the existence of some combination of external circumstances which temporarily strengthen the patient's resolve (as the impending attack of delirium tremens, in the case of Mr. J. Y.). Another is the administration of a specific drug* which renders the ingestion of alcohol impossible.

If a period of continuing sobriety cannot be fully ensured, it is, at the least, necessary, for any hope of success, to ensure that the alcoholic patient will appear regularly for his psychotherapy sessions.† If the patient has been functioning sufficiently well to have retained a job and if he happens to work for a company with reasonably enlightened personnel policies, it is often possible to enlist the company's cooperation in bringing pressure to bear favoring the patient's regular attendance. In such instances, the firm can place the patient on probationary status with the stipulation that retention of his job is contingent upon faithful attendance at his therapy sessions.

The essential objective of the first phase of psychotherapy of an alcoholic is the difficult one of enabling the patient to perceive that his drinking is what it is: a defense, born of desperation, against the pressure of *internal* conflicts. If this objective is achieved, the therapy becomes similar to that of a psychoneurosis. Yet the therapy is not really the same, for the patient's recognition of the meaning of his drinking still does not mean that it is, per se, as distressing as are many psychoneurotic symptoms. Still, if the first step is achieved, the physician has at least gained the patient's conscious cooperation for the therapeutic effort.

This initial therapeutic problem—getting the patient to regard one or more traits of character and the resulting behavior as *symptomatic*, as a *loss of freedom*—is a critical one in the treatment of nearly all of the personality disorders.

It is significant that a similar recognition is deemed an absolute prerequisite to being helped by the nonmedical organization, Alcoholics Anonymous, which has had the greatest success in helping alcoholics. After making the frank avowal that his drinking has not been really voluntary but out of an inner necessity, the newcomer to "A. A." pledges not to drink, accepts certain guiding principles of an essentially religious nature, and is then immediately involved in the organization's efforts to help other alcoholics. Since Alcoholics Anonymous is entirely composed of former alcoholics, it is in a position to offer a large measure of understanding and support to the newcomer, as well as sources of identification and group-feeling which can go a long way toward restoring his self-esteem, thus relieving inner pressures. While it in no way replaces psychiatric consultation, Alcoholics Anonymous is a legitimate resource to which the physician may turn for collabora-

---

* This drug is tetraethylthiuram disulfide, commercially known as Antabuse. It is discussed in the second chapter on treatment measures (p. 473).

† Or for A. A. meetings or other therapeutic measures.

tion in the treatment of alcoholics whose underlying psychopathology is relatively mild.

The treatment of chronic alcoholism is obviously a difficult matter. Among the minority of patients who cooperate in the therapeutic effort for a reasonable length of time (i.e., for more than a few months), the fraction who can be helped to a significant degree is about two-thirds.

With any other treatment than a thorough psychoanalysis—which is to say in the great majority of cases—it is misleading to speak of a "cure" in the sense that the patient gains sufficient self-understanding and personal maturity to be able to handle alcohol in a normal fashion. For practical purposes, much the wisest course is to encourage the patient never to drink again.

NARCOTIC ADDICTION*

The incidence of this disorder is far smaller in this country than is that of alcoholism, in some measure, perhaps, because of the stringent legislation against it. Recent estimates[4] of the number of narcotic addicts vary rather widely, ranging from 60,000 to 1,000,000; an average estimate would, perhaps, be of around 200,000. (The Harrison Narcotic Act is considered by some authorities also to have affected the incidence of the condition in another way—which would be an interesting example of the influence of cultural factors upon the forms of psychiatric illness. Whereas in the early 1900's before passage of the Act, the ratio of men to women addicts was approximately one to three, it is currently approximately four to one.)

The principal drugs comprising the category of narcotics include opium in various forms (unrefined, laudanum, paregoric, and pantopon), opium derivatives (dilaudid, codeine), and synthetic opiates (demerol, methadone). Marijuana is legally included with the narcotics, but it is quite a different drug, and though widely used, has little addictive potentiality. Cocaine is also included and it has a definite addictive potentiality, but it is not widely used. The present discussion will be confined to a consideration of the use of the opiates.

Two closely interrelated phenomena associated with the taking of opiates, which tend to distinguish this addiction from most instances of alcoholism, are *tolerance* and *(physical) dependence*. In the pharmacological sense, there is relatively little tolerance to alcohol. Habitual heavy drinkers often show a pseudo- or psychological tolerance. This is primarily due, however, not to an alteration in metabolic processes, but to an increased ability to dissemble the effects of a mild degree of intoxication. On the other hand, the physiological tolerance which can

---
* The reader is advised to review the introductory discussion of addiction on p. 166 to p. 169.

be built up for morphine and related drugs is a remarkable phenomenon. Whereas in the nonaddict a dose of 120 mg. of morphine can easily be fatal, it has been experimentally demonstrated that, over a period of time (weeks to months), a tolerance can be developed such that a daily dosage of 1,200 mg. produces no physiological ill effects. It is a remarkable fact—again unlike the case of alcoholism—that severe addiction to morphine, over a long period of time, produces no appreciable damage to bodily tissues. (It is, of course, true that a great many addicts develop physical disease of one sort or another as an *indirect* result of their addiction—e.g., syndromes of malnutrition, skin diseases—but such an outcome depends ultimately upon psychological factors and not upon the toxicology of the opiates.)

The phenomenon of dependence is strikingly manifested by the syndrome which ensues when an addict is deprived of his drug (*withdrawal syndrome*). In addition to psychological symptoms (primarily of an anxious and depressive nature), there is a well-marked group of essentially physiological symptoms, including pupillary dilatation, muscular twitching and tremors, "goose flesh," lacrimation and sneezing, and more or less profuse sweating. If the addiction has been severe, if the withdrawal has been abrupt and complete, and if no medical measures are taken to combat the reaction, the syndrome may go on to include fever, vomiting, dehydration, abdominal distress, and general prostration. Aside from the occasional production of convulsions ("whiskey fits") on sudden withdrawal and the limited role of such withdrawal in the production of delirium tremens in severe alcoholics whose condition is very chronic (p. 292), there is nothing really comparable in the case of alcoholism.

As is true of alcoholics, however, drug addicts suffer from a variety of underlying psychiatric disorders, including various sorts of personality disorders, serious psychoneuroses, and psychoses, particularly depressions. (Incidentally, since morphine is the more powerful drug—and because of its special psychopharmacological characteristics—one finds not infrequently that an addict will have first been an alcoholic; the reverse development is almost never seen, although an addict will often drink heavily if temporarily unable to obtain his drug.)

The effect of the opiates is clearly different from that of alcohol. There is no phenomenon comparable to the release of impulses taking place under moderate doses of alcohol. The opiates seem to act to allay the basic drives: hunger, libido, aggressive-hostile urges, and dependency strivings. In addition, they tend to allay anxiety and excitement, and to relieve pain, if this is present. In the normal or near-normal personality, the effect of an isolated or occasional dose of an opiate is primarily sedative.

Patients addicted to narcotics may spontaneously acknowledge addiction and request drugs from the physician. Oftener the drugs will be requested under the guise of some medical contingency. When patients do not admit addiction, certain symptom patterns may be suggestive of the illness. For example, periods of restlessness, irritability, and anxiety are followed rather suddenly by periods of contentment or even euphoria. With other patients the diagnosis can be made on the basis of unexplained needle marks and scars. At times, the only method of diagnosis may be isolation of the patient from a source of the drugs —not an easy procedure—followed by observation for signs of an abstinence syndrome.

Addiction can be produced in any human being, but if the basic personality structure is essentially normal—supposing the addiction to have been experimental or accidental—the likelihood of a cure, after withdrawal, is very good. In a considerable majority of actual cases, however, the basic personality to begin with is seriously disturbed. The temptation to revert to the solace of narcotic addiction is therefore very great, and the rate of cure among addicts is far from satisfactory.

Narcotic addiction is reportable to the federal authorities, and, except in the mildest cases, its treatment is carried out by specialists in Public Health Service hospitals designed for this purpose.

SEXUAL DEVIATION

This diagnostic category (officially, another subheading under *sociopathic personality* disorder) is a broad one; like alcoholism and drug addiction, the category is based upon the presence of a conspicuous behavioral feature and is indicative of etiology only to a limited extent. Specific examples of sexual deviation are: *homosexuality* (by far the commonest), *sadism* (sexual pleasure in inflicting pain), *masochism* (sexual pleasure in experiencing pain or humiliation), *voyeurism* (sexual pleasure in looking at the body of another person), *exhibitionism* (sexual pleasure in exposing one's body or a part of it to the gaze of another person), and *fetishism* (direction of the principal sexual interest to a body part—sometimes an unusual one—of another person or to an inanimate object associated with a body part.)

From the standpoint of libidinal development (p. 55), one may say of sexual deviation that while the *source* of the sexual drive remains normal (in the vast majority of instances), there is an alteration from the normal adult pattern with respect to the *aim* or the *object* or both. This alteration may be primarily based upon a fixation or upon a regression or, more commonly, upon a combination of the two.

The following excerpts from the case history of a male homosexual are illustrative of some of the principal features of this type of deviation.

Mr. B. K. was a 30-year-old bachelor who came to the psychiatrist, self-referred, with the presenting complaint of overt homosexuality of 12 years' duration. (As a secondary complaint there were some mild compulsive features.) He was a tall, lean man, prematurely graying but rather athletic looking, immaculately and smartly dressed, with a certain fastidiousness of manner. (His internist reported him to be in good health and completely normal physically.) His occupation was that of men's buyer for a large department store.

The patient had never been completely satisfied with a homosexual adjustment although he had known no other in adult life. His immediate conscious motivation for seeking psychiatric help had several components. (1) A recent promotion at work had led him to understand, somewhat to his surprise, that his performance was highly regarded and that he was in line for an eventual executive position at the store. His career advancement, however, would require him to be socially active along conventional lines. (2) As a result of evening college courses in psychology, he had come to realize that his sexual condition was not, as he had for the most part surmised, primarily a constitutional matter, but one which at least theoretically was amenable to treatment. (3) Within the past several months he had developed a sincere friendship, having faintly romantic overtones, with a young woman who worked at the store. He found himself able to imagine the possibility that this relationship might lead to love and marriage. The thought frightened but intrigued him.

Preliminary interviews yielded the following historical information. The patient was one of three children, having an older and a younger sister (both now married). His father, dead some two years, had been an immigrant from Eastern Europe and a butcher by occupation. He had worked fairly steadily, but was a chronic alcoholic and had never gained for the family an economic status much above that of mere subsistence. He had not been a destructive person at heart, being at times capable of a degree of warmth and even playfulness (especially when the children were quite small), but when he was drunk he was a frightening figure and physically abusive.

The patient's mother was a native-born American, being 12 years younger than her husband, whom she married when only 17. She was an attractive woman, but for the most part, an unhappy one. She did not love her husband, resented the family's lack of social advancement, and though not devoid of affection for her children, found the cares of motherhood burdensome. She was something of a "nagger" although afraid of her husband when he was intoxicated. She never spoke well of him. She was fond of the patient in her own way, and behaved rather seductively toward him at times, kissing him on the lips and stroking his hand when she talked to him.

B. K. had an essentially normal infancy; toilet training had been early and vigorous. He had become nocturnally enuretic at about age three, but regained bladder control by the age of seven. He became an exceptionally neat child.

During the war years, the father worked at a defense plant in a city about 100 miles distant from the one in which the family lived. Thus, from the age of 11 until the age of 14, the patient would see his father only on occasional week-ends. At times during this period and occasionally later on, the patient's mother would use him as an escort when she went to bingo games or the movies.

B. K. was shy and socially awkward as a boy. He was a good student, particularly in English and in art, which had been his mother's favorite subjects. In high school he continued to get good grades, wrote for the school magazine, and became fairly proficient at tennis. Through these activities he made a number of friends, but he went out seldom, being painfully conscious of his poor socio-economic status. He thought occasionally of dating during these years, but he seldom had pocket money and often felt that his appearance was scarcely presentable. He had dated a girl only three times during his four years of high school, feeling quite uncomfortable on these occasions. He recalled being very self-conscious, finding it difficult to make conversation and impossible to seek any physical intimacy.

In his teens the patient was more than once approached by homosexuals, but he never acceded to their propositions. His first overt homosexual experience (apart from some episodes of mutual masturbation in childhood) was at age 18 while in the army. During the ensuing 12 years the patient had had a variety of homosexual contacts. At first his partners had usually been older men; more recently they had been younger than he. As a rule, his partners were decidedly effeminate. At one period, soon after leaving service (with an honorable discharge), the patient experienced a homosexual love affair. The romance was broken up by the patient when he discovered that the man he loved was unfaithful. Following this experience, Mr. K. was moderately depressed for about six months.

Toward the end of this period, the patient had enrolled at college under the G. I. Bill. He had taken three years of a business course, became interested in retail merchandising, and left school at the end of his junior year to take a position with the firm where he was currently employed. At the time he sought psychiatric help, Mr. K. had just completed work for his degree by taking courses in evening college.

The patient had realized that his interest in homosexuality was somehow waning, but being thoroughly occupied with work and with school, and continuing to regard himself as socially inept, he had made no real efforts at heterosexual contacts. Chance had thrown him and the previously mentioned young woman together, inasmuch as they were assigned to work on a series of sales campaigns. Much of this work took place after store hours under rather informal circumstances. On several occasions the patient had taken the girl to dinner at a nearby restaurant. As it happened, she was an attractive and warmhearted person, of a lively intelligence, but refined and not at all forward. To his surprise, the patient had found that he was not very ill at ease with her.

Following the evaluation interviews, Mr. K. was offered and promptly accepted a trial of intensive psychotherapy. During this treatment, it was possible to gain considerable understanding of the pathogenesis of his sexual deviation. (The following account is not, however, an exhaustive explanation.)

The patient had, in his earliest years, some tendency to turn to his father (and hence to males) for comfort and affection since his mother was not very capable of giving to small children in a maternal way and since his father, despite his erratic behavior, was actually the warmer of the two parents.

To this predisposition were added the effects of an intense and unfortunate type of oedipal experience. Because of the mother's seductiveness (born of her own unhappiness), the patient's sexual attraction to her during the family-triangle phase of development was quite strong. These feelings were opposed by an unusually great fear of the father. The strength of this fear had several sources: the father's occupation, the disturbing impression created when he was intoxicated, his physical abusiveness, and the mother's physical fear of him. Along with the patient's fear of his father there did not develop a corresponding respect since the father was not really a strong person and, particularly by the mother's standards, was not a success in life. (In short, the father was of little use to the patient as a model.)

As a result, the tendency toward a normal subsidence of the oedipal conflicts was counterbalanced. The patient dealt with his attraction to his mother by an emotional regression to an earlier level, burying his wish to possess her beneath the wish to please her, to receive from her in a childish way, and to be like her (thus taking himself out of the "competition" with father).

Since the family was not devoid of healthy elements and since the patient was constitutionally sound and, in fact, a talented person, B. K.'s latency period experiences were not unfavorable, and there remained the possibility that puberty might have afforded him the opportunity of a belated resolution of some of his problems. This chance was, however, minimized by the circumstances of the father being away from home much of the time and the mother thrusting the patient into the father's place. The anxiety and sense of guilt thus mobilized prevented any emotional step forward at this time, and the patient became emotionally fixed in a homosexual pattern although his shyness and considerable maternal supervision prevented his acting upon this orientation, or even realizing it fully, until he got away from home. In the male society of military service, he began to act, for the first time since middle childhood, upon the homosexual impulses.

The healthier aspects of the patient's personality asserted themselves even under these circumstances, however. Mr. K.'s choice of sexual partner was largely confined to effeminate men, i.e., to men who were (unconsciously) perceived in some measure as tomboyish women.

Several events of the patient's recent life combined to stir him emotionally, and to instigate his personality to make tentative efforts, so to speak, to pick up the developmental threads where they had been dropped. One of these appears to have been the death of his father, which freed him from a degree of (unconscious) anxiety about heterosexual strivings. Another was the patient's success in business, a circumstance which led to an increase in self-confidence and won him the approval of significant male figures (the executives of the company). Finally, there was the timely meeting with the emotionally healthy young woman at the store. This girl, quite different from the patient's mother, was genuinely friendly, unselfish, not dissatisfied, not demanding, and interested in the patient for his own sake.

These events gave the patient motivation to seek professional help. He persevered in the psychotherapy, being seen three times weekly for a period of four years. Toward the end of this period, the patient was able to marry the young woman. Her affection and admiration were further incentives toward gaining maturity. The patient completed psychotherapy with an essentially masculine orientation toward life.

The significance for any individual patient of his homosexuality—and hence the treatability of the condition—depends upon the nature of his major conflicts and the point in his personality development to which he is fixated or to which he has regressed. In the case of Mr. B. K. there may have been a degree of fixation to a quite early libidinal position, i.e., to a period in infancy in which he may have turned to his father for the satisfaction of oral-dependent yearnings. However, the principal etiological factors were regressive ones, occurring later in his course of development. The initial regression was an attempt to deal with the excessive anxiety engendered by the family-triangle situation during the age period of about three to six years. Some further personality development then occurred, but the regression was repeated as a response to the anxieties of puberty. Thus, the emotional position of the patient at the time he sought treatment was partly that of the muscle-training period and partly that of latency (the stages to which the regressions had taken him). Aspirations toward a higher level of maturity had never been eliminated, however, and had become moderately active in the period immediately preceding psychotherapy.

From a review of the material on the development of the libido (pp. 57 to 58) it will be clear that, in general, *the elements of sexual behavior that are called "deviate" in adults occur regularly in infants and young children.* In the instance of homosexuality, it has been noted that mutual exploration of the genitals by two or more children of the same sex, often with some efforts at mutual masturbation, is a very common phenomenon of the latency period, a phase which is also characterized by a preference for association with members of one's own sex.

Voyeuristic and exhibitionistic activities of small children are so common as not to require illustration here. Sadistic and masochistic activities are less frequent, yet it is wholly probable that all children express such drives at times. For example, it is likely that all small children, if they have pets, will "tease" them at times; similarly, if they have dolls or stuffed animal toys, they will take pleasure in spanking or behaving cruelly to them on occasion. When a small brother and sister struggle together, half seriously and half playfully, the inflicting and receiving of small degrees of pain in a setting which also has (unconscious) erotic implications may be considered a rudimentary sort of sadism and masochism.

The significance of the skin as an erotogenic zone has been mentioned (p. 58). Sensual experiences involving strong stimulation of the skin are thought often to play an important part in the development of masochism. In mild form, as in the example cited below, masochistic phenomena which involve being slapped or spanked are quite common.

Cathy, aged four, was very fond of her father, with whom she had, generally speaking, a good relationship. She was a somewhat mischievous child, playfully provocative although quite capable of showing warmth. Now and then she would tease her father—to draw attention to herself and away from the other children—perhaps breaking a minor household rule in some conspicuous fashion. Occasionally she would receive a spanking as a result. Both father and daughter would be only half serious about the offense and punishment. In fact, during the spanking it was difficult to tell from her squeals if Cathy were laughing or crying.

The perversion, fetishism, has as its normal childhood counterpart the pleasure derived from close contact with some inanimate object (as a pillow, a blanket, or furry toy) which has been closely associated with the receiving of parental affection.

Thus one may say that a degree of predisposition to the subsequent development of sexual deviations is universally present, deriving from the sexual constitution of human beings plus certain very common early experiences. If the developmental course is essentially normal, these tendencies, as has been described (p. 58), become subordinated to a heterosexual genital orientation. Various traumata of childhood, however, may interfere with this process, blocking the normal developmental course and leading to the abnormally heightened significance of one of these early modes of partial gratification.

It is most important to recognize that the vast majority of persons with sexual deviations are entirely normal anatomically and physiologically. Efforts to treat such conditions hormonally or chemotherapeutically in any fashion are at the least wasted and may be harmful.

To an even greater extent than is true of alcoholism and narcotic addiction, the treatment of sexual deviation has been clouded by legalistic and moralistic approaches. This is not to say that there are not legal, ethical, and religious aspects to the problem of sexual deviation, but it is to say that the only sound way to a genuine understanding of and therapeutic planning for such conditions is to recognize them as psychological developmental anomalies. The truth is that individuals and society are made anxious by sexual deviation and therefore tend to respond punitively and often irrationally to persons thus afflicted.

The only form of treatment of any value in the sexual deviations is intensive psychotherapy or psychoanalysis. The initial therapeutic problem is the same as the one pointed out in the case of alcoholism, namely, the patient's orientation toward his sick behavior. Fundamentally, the patient's conscious attitude toward his deviate sexual experiences is that they furnish his principal source of gratification. The idea that a mature heterosexual orientation is productive of a greater and more substantial pleasure may be intellectually accepted, but it cannot be deeply felt as a rule. (In this aspect, the homosexual patient whose history was presented was a partial exception.) Nor is the patient initially aware of the extent to which he has been driven and limited to his deviate form of sexual activity by powerful anxieties.

For the family physician who is consulted* about such problems, the first issue is whether or not, by means of patient listening, a nonjudgmental approach, and a matter-of-fact persuasiveness, he can win the patient's conscious cooperation in seeking the assistance of a psychiatrist. Once referral has been made, the technical point upon which the therapy will stand or fall is, again, whether or not the psychiatrist can enable the patient to see that his behavior is truly symptomatic, not merely disapproved of by society. This is very difficult to achieve. Among patients who persevere in their efforts at accepting therapy, the proportion who can be helped is similar to that in the case of alcoholism.

NEUROTIC PERSONALITIES

Far more numerous than patients whose sexual behavior is overtly deviate are those having somewhat similar inner conflicts, but in whom there is no conscious inclination toward a deviate sexuality and in whom the psychopathology is manifested in subtler, though consistent, traits of character. For diagnostic purposes, such individuals would be placed in category 2, *personality trait disturbances* ("neurotic personalities").

T. M. was a bachelor, aged 62. Although a successful professional man (an accountant), his life had been a very quiet one. He had made

---

* If he has not been consulted, but has merely become aware through his own observations of the existence of a patient's sexual deviation, it would usually be correct not to do more than indicate a willingness to discuss the subject since the patient's motivation for any sort of change would presumably be minimal.

his home with his widowed mother until her death at an advanced age. He had never been engaged, nor in love, and had very seldom dated, even as a young man. His social activities had largely been limited to occasional games of bridge with men friends. An important exception was his interest in church activities. He had served for many years as teacher of a boys' class in Sunday School, and he was very fond of cooking for church suppers and outings. A principal hobby interest, confided to his close friends, was needlepoint.

Mr. M. had an appearance rather like that of Dicken's Mr. Pickwick. He had a shy sense of humor (primarily of an "anal" nature), and a naïveté in most matters not directly concerned with his work. He was a kindly, gentle person and a very conscientious one, being well liked in the community. He warmed to praise, particularly that of the minister or of the elders of the church.

One sees some similarities between T. M. and B. K., but also important differences. T. M. never sought psychiatric treatment, and so one cannot be sure of the elements which shaped his personality. Nor is there any diagnostic term which fits with precision. If one were to invent a term, one might call T. M. a "homosexual personality."

In an analogous way, there exist other personality disorders, in the general category of neurotic personalities, having some degree of correspondence to the various sexual deviations, but in whom manifestly deviate erotic behavior is absent. Of these, the most numerous and the most significant is the *masochistic personality* (or "moral masochist," as the condition is sometimes called).

One form which may be taken by individuals with this type of neurotic personality is that of operation-proneness (p. 242). Another form is illustrated by the following excerpts from a case history.

Mrs. C. W. was a drab, inconspicuous, "mousey" little woman of 40, who received a psychiatric evaluation at an out-patient clinic in connection with a diagnostic work-up for obscure visual complaints. She worked as a bookkeeper for a small business concern. She was actually rather intelligent and quite competent at her work, but although she had been with the firm for eight years, she had never requested nor received a raise. She seemed to be frequently imposed upon, finding it necessary to do a good bit of overtime work for which she very rarely received additional compensation. At times she would complain bitterly to her friends about the injustice, but never made representations to her employer.

Mrs. W. had married at the age of 22. Her husband was an alcoholic and ne'er-do-well, who was often abusive to her, sometimes physically so. He died when the patient was 30, of injuries sustained in a tavern brawl, leaving Mrs. W. with three small children. The patient remarried two years later. Her second husband, a much older man, was in poor health at the time and was known for his bad temper. He later suffered a mild stroke and had been a semi-invalid for three years preceding the evaluation of the patient.

What is one to say of such a person? Or of Mr. M., the elderly bachelor? In the conventional medical sense, they may very seldom have been ill. Yet, in a basic sense, it is nearer the truth to say that they have never been really well. Since their very early years, when their personality patterns took shape, they have been constrained to lead incomplete, frustrated lives, achieving only limited gratifications and paying a heavy price for them. Since such individuals, because of the extreme chronicity of their problems, tend to come into some kind of equilibrium with their worlds, tend to find situations, niches, fitting in with their neurotic needs, the fact of their basic illness may be obscured to casual observers. They may even be the objects of praise. Thus, Mr. M. was praised for his devotion to his mother, and Mrs. W., for being a source of strength to her husband and children.

On the other hand, they may also be the objects of criticism, disappointment, and even dislike, arising out of misunderstanding. The masochistic personality, if not promptly recognized, may be a troublesome problem to any physician he may happen to consult (the consultation being not for his masochism—of which he is unaware—but for conventional medical reasons). Such an individual's need to experience discomfort and pain, to be misunderstood and mistreated, to be shamed or punished, to misinterpret events in ways unfavorable to himself, may be factors which seriously complicate the medical management.

As has been mentioned, the masochism in some instances may lead the patient to operation-proneness. In many other instances, medical problems of a less dramatic nature arise. Whatever the presenting complaint—and whether the patient makes the most of it or preserves a martyrlike calm—the physician is apt to receive an impression of considerable distress, and may therefore initially make a special effort. Later on, when, despite this effort, the patient appears to find diagnostic and therapeutic measures difficult and/or painful, and when the results of treatment seem equivocal because of the patient's continued suffering, the physician is apt to experience a reaction of disillusionment and hostility. This response is often unconsciously gratifying to the patient, who indeed may be subtly quite provocative, and matters may go from bad to worse.

If, however, on the basis of the personal history or of the patient's manner and attitude during the various phases of the initial examination (pp. 6 and 10), the physician can discern the psychiatric aspect of the patient's difficulties, the situation can often be somewhat better managed. It is not that the patient's masochism can be readily altered, but that the physician can make some allowances and provision for it. For example, he may find it best to avoid giving the usual amount of reassurance since this technique is often disconcerting to the masochist (running counter to the need to suffer). He can adopt and maintain a courteous but matter-of-fact attitude. Within himself, he can face realistically the prospect that the patient may continue to have symptoms of one kind or another, despite the correctness of conventional diagnostic and therapeutic measures. In this way, the physician can spare himself the subsequent negative reaction. As a result, in later stages of treatment, the patient's masochism will be less stimulated, and his response to the therapy of his presenting illness will be the maximum of which he is capable.

Under such circumstances, the physician may frankly recognize (to himself) the advisability of sustained professional contact with the patient, including various forms of symptomatic treatment, having as its object not the elimination of the patient's complaints but the provision of interest and support sufficient to enable the patient to maintain his equilibrium. If the patient is young, if the masochism is severe, or if, whatever its severity, it interferes with needed therapeutic measures, psychiatric referral is indicated.

References

1. Alexander, F., and French, T. M.: Psychoanalytic Therapy, New York, Ronald, 1946.
2. Fenichel, O.: The Psychoanalytic Theory of Neurosis, New York, Norton, 1945.
3. Himwich, H. E.: Brain Metabolism and Cerebral Disorders, Baltimore, Williams & Wilkins, 1951.
4. Nyswander, M.: The Drug Addict as a Patient, New York, Grune, 1956.
5. Robinson, M. W., and Voegtlin, W. L.: Investigation of an allergic factor in alcohol addiction, Quart. J. Stud. Alcohol. *13*:196, 1952.

Suggestions for Further Reading

Freud, S.: Some character-types met with in psychoanalytic work (1915) *in* Collected Papers of Sigmund Freud, London, Hogarth, 1925.
Freud, S.: The psychogenesis of a case of homosexuality in a woman (1920) *in* Collected Papers of Sigmund Freud, London, Hogarth, 1924.
Karpman, B.: The Sexual Offender and His Offenses, Washington, D.C., Julian Press, 1954.
Kruse, H. D. (ed.): Alcoholism as a Medical Problem, New York, Hoeber-Harper, 1956.
Menninger, K. A.: Alcohol addiction *in* Man Against Himself, New York, Harcourt, Brace, 1938.
Nyswander, M.: Drug addictions, *in* Arieti, S.: American Handbook of Psychiatry, New York, Basic, 1959.

CHAPTER 13

Psychiatric Treatment Measures, Part 1. Measures Suitable for Use by the Nonpsychiatrist

John A. MacLeod, M.D.

As in other medical specialties, clinical problems in psychiatry can be divided into those of major and minor natures. Also as in other special fields, minor problems in psychiatry are more numerous than major. This chapter recognizes that "minor psychiatry," like "minor surgery," can and should be practiced by the general practitioner, internist, or other nonpsychiatric specialist.

COMMON MISCONCEPTIONS ABOUT TREATMENT BY THE NONPSYCHIATRIST

At times the suggestion that psychiatric tools be added to the repertoire of the nonpsychiatrist arouses a somewhat wearied response. Such weariness does not ordinarily spring from denial that many patients' sufferings are born of emotional tensions. On the contrary, many practitioners today are quite sensitive to functional disorders. The weariness is more likely to result from certain misconceptions about what they can do effectively and about the time and energy required to treat such disorders.

That It Takes Too Much Time

A tradition has been established that psychological treatment, and especially planned psychotherapy, entails an expenditure of time which most medical practitioners could not afford in their day-to-day work.

The prevalent arrangement in formal out-patient psychotherapy is a regularly and frequently scheduled 45- to 50-minute interview. For the sorts of psychotherapy to be practiced by the nonpsychiatrist, this arrangement is inappropriate. These sorts are principally suppressive and supportive psychotherapy. By *suppressive* and *supportive* are meant those therapeutic attitudes and maneuvers which work toward a restoration of an adequate intrapsychic equilibrium rather than toward personality reorganization and growth.* In these approaches patients can very often be seen briefly (for 15 or 20 minutes) and infrequently (once a week or less). Thus appropriate psychological treatment for many patients is seen to require amounts of time consistent with the maintenance of heavy professional schedules.

That It Involves Intimate Doctor-Patient Relationships

It is simply not true that psychological treatment necessarily involves the physician in intense and potentially uncomfortable relationships with patients. Many physicians prefer that patients confine their reports to physical signs and symptoms, feeling that a widened scope of inquiry will lead to discussion of highly personal matters with which they are unprepared to deal. Though a continuing treatment relationship can and should develop to the point where the patient can speak freely of his emotions and personal problems and can consider how such factors may influence his health, the physician is in a natural position of leadership and can learn to manage the treatment arrangements in the way he thinks appropriate. The variables in the situation which can be most readily adjusted are the frequency and duration of office visits.

That It Demands Exploration of the Unconscious

Conscientious treatment of an emotional problem does not necessarily demand a deep-going, "uncovering" type of psychotherapy, one designed to bring unconscious forces into the patient's awareness. The existence of such a misconception is a by-product of the tremendous impact which psychoanalysis has had upon psychotherapy. The truth is that patients with functional problems can very often benefit from a psychotherapy primarily designed to help them through some especially stressful experience of limited duration. If the physician chooses his cases properly, he can help patients with an impressive frequency to rally from relatively disabling symptomatology.

---

* The terminology and much of the thinking regarding psychiatric treatment are derived from Levine. For further details, see Levine's chapter in *Dynamic Psychiatry* and his book, *Psychotherapy in Medical Practice*. (Suggestions for Further Reading.)

That Every Patient Is Really Suited for Intensive Psychotherapy

This notion is quite unsound, as a listing of some of the prerequisites for major psychotherapy will show. For a person to receive substantial benefit from an intensive psychotherapy, there must be a capacity to fulfill regular appointments, a tolerance of considerable tension and delay (in resolving problems), some ability to control antisocial or self-destructive impulses, a recognition of the meaningfulness of communicating thoughts and feelings, the ability to communicate in this way, and a potential for developing considerable powers of self-observation. One can readily see that all of these qualifications are not often to be found. In most instances, an unintensive psychotherapy is the appropriate one. This psychotherapy may be managed by a nonpsychiatrist.

That Extensive Specialty Training Is Required of the Physician

It is, of course, true that a certain amount of knowledge and graded experience is prerequisite to an effective use of psychological techniques, but the acquisition of appropriate knowledge and experience for treatment of minor psychiatric problems is not really so formidable an undertaking as it may appear to be. After all, the physician's awareness of the importance of emotional and environmental factors *in every illness* is one of his most valuable tools (Chap. 6). Beyond such awareness, the physician should develop a comfortable style of talking with patients; he should maintain a sharp weather eye on the limits of his psychotherapeutic techniques, and he should recognize that in psychiatric work, as in other medical practice, he must often be satisfied with improvements rather than cures. If a physician is especially challenged by psychological work and desires to augment his skills, he should arrange for continuing supervision by a fully trained and experienced psychiatrist.

TREATMENT ARRANGEMENTS

A convenient aspect of the chief psychological tool, talking, is that no specialized equipment is necessary. Medical office, examining room and hospital room are all suitable for the conduct of an interview. All such facilities allow patient and physician to be comfortable and provide the privacy freeing the patient to discuss personal matters to the extent that he desires and that the physician judges prudent. (See Chaps. 1 and 5).

Most physicians regularly allocate more time for initial than for follow-up visits. Initial visits range from 15 or 20 minutes to an hour or two. Time provisions of this order usually enable the doctor to gain tentative impressions and to plan the patient's treatment. If it appears that a major source of the patient's problem can be traced to emotional or environmental stresses, a portion of the first appointment can readily be allotted to investigative interviewing.

Follow-up visits in general medical work come to 15 minutes or less. If the doctor intends a psychotherapeutic approach, a minimum of 10 or 15 minutes should be set aside for a patient visit. Experience has shown that it is exceedingly difficult to conduct an interview in a shorter time without leaving the patient with a feeling that the doctor is in a hurry. The opening phases of a conversation, the middle business period, and the closing moves can seldom be fitted into less than 10 minutes.

INTERVIEWING

The word "interviewing" has acquired something of a magical connotation. It suggests that something difficult is involved and that mysterious talents are going to be necessary. In psychiatry, "interviewing" is simply conversation as a means to understanding an individual's problems. Insofar as such talking can convey a natural, everyday feeling, it will be rewarding to patient and doctor alike.

Many doctors feel awkward in introducing the idea to their patients that emotional factors are important in the patient's problem. Such awkwardness is today almost always unnecessary since the novelty of the idea that physical symptoms can be influenced by psychological stresses has worn off. The simple question, "How have things been going generally?" is usually received with no surprise and no feeling that the doctor is intruding. Such an introductory remark by the doctor as, "I have a feeling that you have been carrying a good bit of tension," can lead to a valuable review of the patient's current responsibilities and feelings.

As has already been noted, every physician should develop and select his own repertoire of interviewing techniques. A common error of beginning physicians is to ask too many questions and to ask them too rapidly. Though the doctor must be direct and searching, the patient requires time to think, to respond, and to make his own contribution to the diagnostic inquiry. On the other hand, it is obvious that lengthy silences in the interview will only create anxiety in the patient and doctor which will complicate their common task.

Since interviewing is a cooperative venture, it naturally follows that any measures enhancing communication will move patient and doctor closer to their goal. One measure which doctors are inclined to overlook is the use of everyday language. Almost always it is possible for the doctor to discover everyday words which will adequately convey medical questions and information. Usually the avoidance of technical terms in speaking to patients requires a conscious effort on the doctor's part. It is, of course, inappropriate for him to talk down to patients whom he knows to be reasonably well-informed on medical matters.

An additional move which will enlist the patient's cooperation is to ask him how he understands his situation and symptoms. Many patients have thoughtful and valuable replies. When common sense and intuition of patients are overlooked, the oversight reduces the resources which can be brought to bear on treatment problems.

Usually the questions and treatment by the physician should be confined to the patient's present situation. It is important for the doctor to focus on feelings, symptoms and events in reality rather than on dreams and fantasies. When the patient talks freely of old fantasies, dreams and past life, there is a chance that the old problems and feelings will be unnecessarily revived, a development which can interfere with the work at hand.

It is important that interviews not be terminated abruptly. There should routinely be some indication by the physician as to his thinking and planning with regard to the patient's problems. The closing phase of the interview should also include discussion of future appointments and the management of medication. Always there should be an opportunity for the patient to express his feelings about what he has talked of.

DIAGNOSTIC THINKING

As in all his work, the physician is thinking diagnostically while he is conducting the interview portion of his examination. It would, of course, be unusual for the nonpsychiatrist to carry out a formal *mental status examination*, but he should certainly review the elements of this examination as he is interviewing his patient. These elements include at least six areas of psychological functioning: (1) action, (2) mood, (3) thought processes, (4) intelligence, (5) recent memory and retention, and (6) personality.

1. ACTION. From a scrutiny of the patient's behavior and appearance in the medical examination and from the patient's account of his daily activities, the physician may uncover abnormalities which have a bearing on the clinical impression. The neatness of the patient's dress, the mobility of the facial features, restlessness or agitation in the patient's movements are objects of appropriate observation. (See material on pp. 5 to 6.)

2. MOOD. A general evaluation of how depressed, elated, anxious or angry the patient is, is intended here. Have there been suicidal

thoughts? Is the manifest mood of the patient consistent with his life situation or is there some inappropriateness of feeling?

3. THOUGHT PROCESSES. Is the patient's speech presented in an orderly way with the associations logically linked? Does the patient make sense in his account of symptoms and problems? Are there unusual preoccupations, suspicions, obsessional ideas, delusions or hallucinations?

4. INTELLIGENCE. The patient's manner of speaking, his school and work record will all give information suggesting the level of intelligence. If the physician is in doubt, he can ask a few simple questions regarding current events or the solution of sample life problems, or he can request a description of some current interests of the patient.

5. RECENT MEMORY AND RETENTION. Patients will usually give evidence of memory function during the normal course of an examination, but recent and remote memory should be specifically tested if there is any reason to suspect a brain disorder.

6. PERSONALITY. Some general impressions as to whether the patient is dramatic or inhibited, impulsive or measured, isolated or gregarious, dependent or independent, aggressive or passive, will have importance in the doctor's clinical thinking. These impressions will provide leads as to the type of difficulties the patient is likely to have and as to how the doctor should plan his management of the patient.

Diagnostic Groups

As a framework for his diagnostic thinking the doctor should keep in mind five broad diagnostic groups: (1) normal, (2) mentally deficient, (3) neurotic (this general group to include both the neurotic reactions and the personality disorders), (4) psychotic reactions, and (5) organic brain disease.

The criteria for defining each of these categories have been extensively covered in previous chapters, but a brief résumé may be convenient at this point.

1. NORMALITY. Initially the statement can be made that many patients in an office or hospital practice should be thought of as "normal" psychiatrically. Such an impression is justified if patients are experiencing no remarkable anxiety, neurotic or psychotic symptoms, are recognizing their appropriate need for medical care, are cooperative in making use of such care, and are apparently managing their lives so that they and the people around them are gaining reasonable satisfactions from living. If the physician correctly makes the diagnosis of "normal as of this time," he will have smooth sailing. A note of warning and caution should be sounded, however. Only the briefest of illnesses can be experienced without the patient encountering the frus-

trations and regressive pulls which almost routinely create in the patient the somatopsychic problems complicating medical care. The veteran practitioner is not startled to see his patient, mature and responsible before the onslaught of illness, become, albeit temporarily, obviously neurotic and self-centered. Such developments merely substantiate the contention of this book that psychological normality is a relative judgment which can hold only for a given time.

2. MENTAL DEFICIENCY. In most practices there are infrequent occasions for dealing with mentally defective patients. Usually such a diagnosis has been made in childhood as a result of retarded development, unusual behavior problems, or failure to progress in school. The particular problems of any individual with limited emotional and intellectual development will be experienced in caring for the mentally defective patient. These problems include poor personal hygiene, accident proneness, variable but often poor impulse control, poor tolerance of stress, and difficulty in cooperating with the physician. The difficulty the mentally defective patient has in cooperating with his physician usually necessitates that the doctor work through some other responsible family member or friend. The poor tolerance of stress in mentally defective patients is demonstrated clinically by rather prompt and marked disorganization of the personality in response to rather mild or moderately stressful life experiences. It is not unusual for mentally defective patients to develop, transiently, psychotic symptoms when physical illness or any other life experience which creates a disequilibrium is encountered.

3. NEUROTIC REACTIONS. In the group of neurotic reactions is included (for present purposes) the psychophysiologic, autonomic and visceral disorders, the psychoneurotic disorders, the personality disorders and the transient situational personality disorders. This group consists of the largest number of psychiatric patients who will be seen by the nonpsychiatrist. Almost always it will be correct for the nonpsychiatrist to plan to work with patients in this group in a continuing way, employing the measures to be described in this chapter.

4. PSYCHOTIC REACTIONS. Included in this grouping are the schizophrenic reactions, the paranoid reactions, and affective disorders of psychotic proportions. If the practitioner seriously suspects that his patient is experiencing one of these reactions, psychiatric consultation should be arranged before the doctor assumes a continuing responsibility for the patient.

5. ACUTE AND CHRONIC BRAIN SYNDROMES. Comprehensive discussion of these clinical states already has been presented (Chap. 8). At this point it is sufficient to say that the appropriate evaluation, whether medical, neurological or psychiatric, must precede any

planned psychotherapeutic approach to patients with brain syndromes. Psychological approaches are very important in the treatment of patients with organic brain disease. The general physician will find the treatment measures to be described useful in his work with patients with organic brain disease. It is, of course, necessary that a patient's organic deficit be taken into account in determining the level and complexity of any psychological work.

Some of the challenge inherent in diagnostic work can be illustrated by a brief consideration of such a common symptom as headache.* This symptom can be part of a neurotic reaction, as for instance, the tension headache of an anxiety reaction. It can appear as a symptom of a psychotic reaction, the headache being part of a paranoid patient's delusions of persecution. Finally, headache is a well-known symptom in a number of organic brain syndromes. The importance of early definitive thinking toward a clinical diagnosis is demonstrated by the different treatment approaches to each of the three broad categories, neurotic and psychotic reactions and organic brain syndromes.

To conclude this review, one may note that problems stemming from mental deficiency (pp. 541 to 546) should be handled by a nonspecialist unless serious psychopathology continues for more than a few days; difficulties of a neurotic variety can usually be managed without referral to a psychiatrist; while diagnostic impressions of psychotic reactions or organic brain syndrome should suggest consultation before the nonpsychiatrist assumes responsibilty for long-term management.

Diagnostic thinking can be productive of more than clinical impressions. As in the rest of medicine, so in psychiatry one looks for etiological factors not reflected in the clinical diagnosis. In medicine generally the factors considered are infectious agents, toxic influences, metabolic disturbances, degenerative processes, neoplastic growths, nutritional deficiencies. Even when disorders are thought to be "functional," such factors should be scrutinized carefully as possible causative agents. More often than not, however, this scrutiny will be unrewarding, since the usual etiological factors in functional disturbance are changes in the balance of forces within the personality and between the personality and the environment.

Dynamic Diagnosis

One method for surveying this balance of forces is to look for recent or relatively recent changes in the resources of the personality. These resources can than be judged as to their adequacy for handling recent external or environmental stresses. The evaluation of the forces cur-

---

* Only entities of psychiatric significance are considered here.

rently operating within the personality and between the personality and the environment is usually referred to as a *dynamic diagnosis.* Some clinical examples will demonstrate this type of approach.

The wife of a graduate student, a 28-year-old mother of three children, was examined because of multiple somatic complaints and the report of a "terrible nervousness" which was interfering significantly with her general functioning and with her sleep. She was experiencing real trouble in keeping up with her household duties and especially with the care of her five-month-old infant. The patient had had no recent physical illnesses, and physical evaluation during the present examination revealed no significant problem. During the evaluation the patient mentioned her concern about being able to manage a move to a distant city in two or three months when her husband would have finished his studies and be starting on a new job.

This problem could be further elaborated but there is sufficient information to hypothesize as follows. This woman is still in the postpartum period when mild depressions are common and when the new mother's energy resources have not returned to normal. Any external stresses have to be met with less than the usual supply of energy. Two such stresses can be identified. The care of the new baby represents a new external stress, and without question the approaching move with its separations from the familiar and its introduction of the new and strange is a severe challenge. The patient shows in her experiencing of "terrible nervousness" and in her many somatic complaints that the combination of reduced inner energies and heightened external demands has created a disequilibrium.

A 52-year-old married man was seen because of abdominal cramping with intermittent diarrhea of several weeks' duration. A thorough evaluation failed to produce a definitive diagnosis although the working diagnosis of "colitis" was settled upon with the impression that this disturbance was of a functional nature. In a review of recent events it was learned that during the past six months the patient had failed to receive an anticipated promotion. During the same period the patient's mother had died after a chronic illness.

Here again, one finds a combination of dynamic factors leading to a functional disturbance. This 52-year-old man can be thought of as deeply involved in handling the transitions of an involutional period of life. These transitions, usually involving both environmental and internal issues, make substantial demands on the energies so that the involutional years should be regarded as one of the more vulnerable periods of life. During such a time this patient has had to meet two stress experiences, the failure to achieve promotion and the loss of his mother, and has not found it possible to handle these life problems without a mild imbalance demonstrated by the appearance of the bowel symptoms. Incidentally, it may be noted that the death of an elderly family member, even one who has been expected to die shortly, still poses the problem of working through the loss. Such "grief work" always strains the integrative capacity of the personality.

Genetic Diagnosis

Complementary to the dynamic diagnosis, the appraisal of the recently operating forces, is the *genetic* diagnosis*, the appraisal of the longer range forces, those influences which have been operating throughout the patient's life or for many years. As in most of medical practice, attention is appropriately concentrated on the more currently active forces although "past history" should to some extent be brought out. The influence of these past strengths and weaknesses in the patient's background can be fitted into the clinical evaluation. An extensive correlation of early life experiences with present psychopathology is, however, a task usually requiring time and special experience beyond that available to the nonpsychiatrist.

Some of the common factors which should usually be considered are: the number of siblings and the patient's place in the rank order of the siblings, the occurrence of important family moves, the separation of patient from significant family members by death or illness, the quality of the relationships within the family, the incidents of physical illness in the patient or other family members, evidences of effective functioning on the part of the patient in such areas as school and sports, indications of early problems such as persistent neurotic symptoms or behavior disturbances.

There should be no question in the physician's mind that early life experiences mold the later patterns of energies available to his patient and the form in which these energies are marshalled to the task of maintaining an adaptation. As clinical experience accumulates, the genetic approach to the understanding of human problems becomes ever more fruitful.

As impressions regarding clinical, dynamic and genetic diagnosis take form, the physician becomes ready to relate these impressions to the available treatment possibilities.

TREATMENT THINKING

The most useful categorization of treatment approaches is one which takes into account a progression of treatment goals ranging from relatively urgent suppressive procedures to long-term uncovering techniques. From the material already presented it is clear that the non-

---

* In this context, "genetic" means "pertaining to formative factors," not "gene-borne."

psychiatrist will most need experience in techniques which do not include goals of extensive uncovering or insight. The four-category approach to treatment planning—centering on forms of psychotherapy—to be presented here includes: (1) suppressive approach, (2) supportive approach, (3) relationship approach, (4) insight or uncovering approach.* The suppressive and supportive approaches will be presented in the greatest detail.

Suppressive Approach

The diagnostic impression which leads to plans for a suppressive approach is the presence of severe symptoms—whether reactive to internal or environmental pressures—which the individual is judged unable or unprepared to deal with through bringing his basic conflicts into awareness. In fact, the physician decides in such instances actively to side with the repressing and suppressing forces of the personality. This approach is used in the treatment of incipient or arrested psychoses or in the severe neuroses where the legitimate goal is not a solution of neurotic conflicts. The goal of a suppressive approach is to assist the patient to regain or maintain a shaky equilibrium through the use of such techniques as persuasion, direct instruction, reassurance, and avoidance of too highly charged material. A number of examples are in order.

A young man was seen who reported obsessive ruminations about bizarre physical ailments which he felt to be the result of his frequent masturbation, an activity concerning which he was deeply guilty. The patient's medical history included the occurrence of a psychotic episode of some months' duration and a difficult adjustment since his return to his family and to his work following hospitalization.

The correct decision in this clinical situation is to avoid any special discussion of masturbation or even any extended general reassurance as to the physical harmlessness of this practice. Rather the physician should listen, but not permit too lengthy a dissertation, and then guide the discussion to a review of the patient's family and job activities, in other words, to more neutral material. In fact, there are times when the physician needs to be actively uninterested, even to the point of changing the subject, in material which he feels is too pathological for the patient to talk about.

The above clinical example represents work with a "borderline patient," a patient whose adjustment is precarious and whose personality resources are so limited that a psychotic illness is a distinct possibility.

---

* See Levine's chapter on psychiatric treatment in *Dynamic Psychiatry*.

Such a precarious adjustment can, however, continue in balance for years unless unusual environmental traumata are encountered. Suppressive psychotherapy is especially tailored to assist individuals with seriously defective ego functioning, that is, patients whose integrative energies are barely up to the task of maintaining an equilibrium within the patient and between the patient and his environment.

There are hazards in the application of suppressive techniques. It is easy for the patient to interpret the physician's frequently casual response to his concern as a lack of interest or even as a blanket rejection. As is well known, patients with severe emotional problems are apt to have had all too much indifference and rejection in their lives and are often but too ready to seize on additional evidence seeming to support their contention that the world is an unfriendly place. To neutralize this effect of his planned suppressive techniques, the physician must rely upon his basic therapeutic attitude. If this attitude is one of warmth and genuine interest in the patient, the physician's position is fundamentally a strong one, and there need be no serious concern. But a word of caution must be included here, as well, for it would be a mistake for the physician to "summon up" his warmth and interest and force a smile onto his face for the purpose of reassuring his patient. Planned displays of interest can occasionally be important, but the element of genuineness must exist, or again the patient may be confronted with a confirmation of his thesis that no one really cares. Clearly the physician's own sense of security and of a capacity to be helpful is deeply involved in his therapeutic work. As a final caution, surprising as the idea may appear, there are some emotionally disturbed patients who are unable to tolerate warmth in their relationships. When the physician senses that he is working with such a patient, he may need to curb his friendliness and interest and be more matter-of-fact and professional in his mien than would naturally be the case.

There may be some surprise at the indication that borderline patients or patients who have had psychotic reactions, currently in remission, are thought of as comprising part of the patient load of the nonpsychiatrist. It is, however, true that many such patients can be cared for by the nonspecialist. In fact, a number of quite disturbed patients experience greater comfort in the "more medical" atmosphere of the nonpsychiatrist's office and can better tolerate a continuing professional relationship there than if they were seeing a psychiatrist.[2] *However, the physician should feel free to use psychiatric consultation in planning the care of such patients, particularly if he is uncertain as to the diagnostic formulation.*

Another example of suppressive technique is as follows:

The 37-year-old father of six children reported that he was plagued by obsessive thoughts of damaging his children, or of damage occurring to them, to the point where he had found it necessary to remain at home in order to reassure himself that no injury befell family members. Although the thoughts regarding his damaging his children had been experienced intermittently for several years, it was only recently that the concern about the children's safety had become continuous and had led to the patient's remaining home. A scrutiny of the patient's past functioning failed to reveal substantial evidence of personality strength. The decision was made to deal initially with the patient's problems in a suppressive way, using the procedure of universalization or generalization. The doctor began by observing to the patient that all parents at one time or another have aggressive or upsetting thoughts regarding their children and that such thoughts are more or less to be expected at times.

It is clear that such a technique does not encourage the patient to explore the deeper significance of the obsessive thoughts. Such generalization *can* be employed as a preparatory step to inquiring further with the patient into the less apparent significance of obsessive thoughts, but when the treatment decision has been to emphasize a suppressive approach this further inquiry would not be pursued. The physician's conservative handling of such a clinical problem need not dim his eyes to the indications for referral of the patient to a psychiatrist. If, after a time, the patient fails to become more comfortable regarding his thoughts or if he experiences mounting anxiety with serious doubts as to his ability to cope successfully with his thoughts and impulses, a specialist's help is indicated.

There will be many occasions when the physician is able to correlate a recent event in the patient's life with the development of disturbed thinking. For instance, it is quite possible that this father of six children was responding to the most recent birth in his family by developing, unwittingly, thoughts that more demands for support would be coming his way at the same time that there would be less care and attention for himself. Such thoughts are usually accompanied by hostile feelings toward the offending object, in this case the children. In such a situation it would be appropriate for the physician to speak in a supportive way to the father about his growing family, possibly noting the demands the family makes on the father, and ways in which such demands might be met.

It should be noted in this clinical example that, even though the physician recognizes the patient's wish to damage his children, he does not inform the patient of the deeper meaning of his obsessive thoughts. Further, if there is discussion regarding the growing family and the demands which it is making on the father, the discussion can take place without reference to the patient's chief complaint. The avoidance of such a linkage is consistent with the doctor's decision in using a suppressive approach; the patient is not prepared to recognize his hostile feelings or to handle them in a more conscious way.

The use of supportive techniques along with the suppressive approach in this case is recognition of the fact that there may be considerable overlapping of approaches during any treatment.

One of the more frequent applications of suppressive techniques is in the treatment of "hypochondriacal" patients. Hypochondriasis is no longer a nosological entity but refers to those patients who are unusually preoccupied with their bodies and chronically manifest a variety of physical complaints, usually without somatic basis. Although seriously handicapped psychologically, such patients do not usually represent emergencies, but often are seen in a continuing way by their physicians.

A 45-year-old married woman was seen by her doctor because of a number of somatic complaints of a somewhat vague character but nonetheless persistent and preoccupying. Although various parts of the body seemed afflicted, the patient focused her concern on her abdomen where she reported a nonspecific pain and a "blowing up with gas." Physical evaluation of the symptoms did not provide any explanation in the way of organic disease. After ruling out the major possibilities of organic disease, the physician did not persist in the organic investigation since he had made the working diagnosis of a hypochondriacal condition and correctly judged that a persistent pursuit of organic causes would but serve to increase and fix the patient's preoccupation with her body, a preoccupation which was already posing a serious handicap to her successful functioning. After making his decision the doctor utilized the suppressive technique of evincing as little concern as possible regarding the symptoms and the patient's general body functioning. At the same time the doctor briefly but clearly showed interest in other areas of the patient's life, thereby countering the patient's disabling tendency to over-invest emotionally in her body.

The decision to use such a suppressive approach must often be made in the face of continuing somatic symptoms after a conscientious appraisal has failed to produce evidence of physical disease. Techniques of this sort are not always happily responded to by hypochondriacal patients, who receive gratifications through their concern with physical illness. However, the doctor's continuing goal is to enable the patient to grow toward more independent and healthy functioning, and the more he can encourage hypochondriacal patients to direct their energies outward to other people and to the world, rather than toward themselves, the greater is the possibility of such patients finding healthier gratification. As in the previous case, if recent events in the patient's life, such as, for example, the loss of a loved relative, seem related to the symptoms, there should be some discussion of the feelings and thoughts around the event, but as little attention as possible should be devoted to the hypochondriacal problem itself.

Supportive Approach

A supportive approach comprises all those therapeutic attitudes and maneuvers which work toward the restoration of psychic equilibrium rather than toward personality growth and maturation. In some contrast to those leading to a suppressive approach, the diagnostic impressions leading to a supportive approach more often suggest significant personality strengths even in the presence of moderate to marked psychopathology. There is less frequently the feeling that a fragile adjustment exists and oftener the impression that the patient has a capacity to manage some anxiety and perhaps benefit from becoming aware of a combination of forces which have created his distress. So with a supportive approach the physician does not side with the repressive and suppressive forces of the personality as he would be doing in a suppressive approach. On the other hand, a supportive approach does not include extensive investigation of essentially unconscious forces and thoughts, nor does it involve a detailed investigation of past events and influences. The primary focus of this approach is on the currently or recently influential events or forces which are available to the patient's awareness but which the patient has not brought together into a reasonably coherent picture of his recent life experiences and his responses to them.

One should not conclude that the physician must himself form such a comprehensive picture of the patient's recent life and then discuss it with the patient. Often the physician will find it more appropriate to act supportively without directly discussing matters which appear to have caused the patient's dysfunction. How direct the discussion should be primarily depends on the doctor's assessment of the patient's capacity to use information about his emotional and psychological functioning that has previously escaped his attention. Generally speaking, however, doctors tend oftener to err in the direction of caution than of boldness in judging a patient's capacity to discuss such matters.

One special consideration of which the physician should be aware is that the patient may, in fact, be avoiding confrontation of certain information because of its threatening or unpleasant nature. If the doctor sees that such avoidance is blocking the patient's recognition of what appears obvious, he can assess more carefully the seriousness of the threatening material and, on the basis of this assessment, better plan his work with the patient.

If, as has been postulated, the patient does not wish to know more about the factors which have led to his functional disturbance, if, indeed, he prefers a degree of suffering with his functional discomfort, what forces can be brought to bear which will enable him to deal more effectively with reality? The patient is not consciously planning, of course, which experiences he will allow to enter his field of awareness or to which he will deny access. The mental operations which are being discussed are not performed at the level of consciousness but rather at a preconscious or unconscious level. Nevertheless, since some force in the patient has determined that an experience is too threatening or unpleasant for him to handle, it seems clear that an alliance of forces will be necessary for the patient to handle such experiences more effectively and more realistically. The alliance which is very often useful is the one in which doctor offers patient understanding and support sufficient for him to manage the threatening situation. The word, "sufficient," is important here since too much support for a patient can limit the opportunities of the patient for discovering capacities to work things out on his own.

The physician should realize that a doctor-patient relationship takes time to develop. If the doctor perceives that difficult matters require discussion, he should ordinarily not proceed with this discussion during an initial visit. Rather, he should plan follow-up visits. When he and the patient are better acquainted, a more appropriate time will have arrived for the patient to rely on his doctor during a discussion of the threatening material.

The doctor need not (and should not) think of the doctor-patient relationship as he thinks of the usual social relationship. Patients come with many preconceptions endowing the physician with power and understanding equal to any task. While remaining aware of the unrealistic aspects of such expectations, the physician utilizes them, since they often make possible the more rapid development of the relationship than could occur in most other situations.

Some of the time limits of a supportive approach can appropriately be indicated at this point. As has been noted, a supportive approach assumes, with respect to "the restoration of a psychic equilibrium," that there previously has been healthier functioning. With most patients the use of a supportive approach means that the doctor anticipates a return to this status quo ante within the relatively brief period of a few weeks or perhaps months. However, the doctor should not be surprised or dismayed to discover that a sizeable group of his patients need continuing professional contact of indefinite duration. This group of patients consists of the more than usually dependent individuals who actually are unable to function autonomously for a sustained period because of limitations in their early life experiences. In a way, these patients should be regarded as chronically ill, but capable of leading essentially happy lives so long as there exists the opportunity for intermittent contacts with an important figure such as their doctor. An analogy may easily be drawn with the chronic cardiac patient who is usually well compensated but who requires occasional modifications in his treatment regime, and who should be seen in office visits with some regularity over an extended period of time.

There will be numbers of patients who require an on-going supportive approach. In such medical situations the doctor knows that improvements in clinical conditions are, more often than not, disappointing in extent and fleeting in duration. This knowledge need not dampen the physician's enthusiasm for such treatment. It does require that he be relatively satisfied in working with patients who offer limited and long-term goals.

The need for extended care of the chronically distressed patient can lead to a difficulty in treatment. This difficulty involves the frequency of visits. The tendency of many patients to become dependent on medical care may result in their requesting appointments of unnecessary frequency. The physician must be careful to provide conscientious help without creating a situation in which the patient is tempted unduly to employ his illness for the purpose of various secondary gains (p. 319). Too great secondary gains will tend to fix the symptom picture, even in the face of the patient's experiencing considerable discomfort.

A number of clinical situations will be sketched for the purpose of exemplifying the supportive measures available to the physician.

A 60-year-old woman, separated from her husband for many years and living alone, was seen because of "bad nerves." Getting the history was difficult because of the patient's asthmatic condition, her speech frequently being interrupted by spells of wheezing and coughing. During her wheezing episodes the patient would use an inhalator which she carried in her purse. The doctor observed that she would frequently exhale when she squeezed the inhalator so that little medication was taken into the lungs. The patient reported that her "bad nerves" took the form of a terrible fear of being alone and she told of the various arrangements she had made so that she would be in touch with people. She then gave an account of recent experiences with her two grown children amounting to family explosions, which resulted in the patient's only daughter refusing to talk to her. Past history indicated that the patient's asthma had been under relatively good control until the recent family turmoil. Previous medical investigation had shown no infectious or allergic causation of the asthma.

From this information the conclusion can be drawn that the patient previously had been able to make a relatively stable adjustment. Her difficulties should probably be thought of as belonging in the neurotic area of psychopathology. It can be anticipated that she will be able to cooperate to some extent in efforts directed toward understanding more of the background of her functional problem although her present need for symptoms is graphically demonstrated by her breathing against the medication in the inhalator. Therefore, the pace of discussion with the patient will probably be a quite deliberate one. It is most important for the patient that the doctor indicate some plan for the medical management of the patient's asthmatic symptoms and that he state that a continuing professional contact is needed. The patient's primary fear appears to be that she will be abandoned and, even though the physician recognizes the basic irrationality of such a fear at the patient's time of life, he should specifically counter this fear by arrangements which manifestly demonstrate his intention to work with the patient. The doctor should not be startled if such a patient "tests out" his intention to care for her by being moderately provocative in a way designed to stimulate the doctor to reject her. Such provocativeness should be handled as comfortably as possible. It should not be interpreted by the doctor as representing anything more than additional evidence of the patient's uncertainty about acceptance. With such a patient the prognosis can be considered favorable for the immediate relief of symptoms although there is likelihood that recurrent asthmatic symptoms will be experienced which will require similar management.

Some of the psychologically supportive techniques for the care of this 60-year-old woman may be enumerated. Several of them are traditionally regarded as "physical methods," but (in addition) they have direct psychological impact. (See Chap. 14, pp. 469 to 470.) To begin with, a history and physical examination have been accomplished which assure the patient that she is in the care of an interested, conscientious physician. Next, medicinal treatment has been planned, a circumstance which not only indicates that specific symptoms are to be treated, but also that emotional needs are to be gratified. Further, the patient has been reassured that something can be done about her condition and that her treatment requires that she be in continuing contact with her doctor. In this continuing contact, the doctor satisfies some of the patient's basic needs to be cared for. More than this, the doctor is recognizing some of the patient's neurotic, unrealistic needs, and for the time being, he is satisfying some of these less reasonable needs through his comfortable management of her provocative behavior and by his stating that a continuing professional contact is required. Thus, he counters the patient's concern about isolation.

The opportunity might develop for employing treatment measures beyond the ones already suggested. As was noted, there is reason to believe that this patient can cooperate in efforts to understand some of the background of her functional disturbance. In subsequent visits the medical setting may first provide a chance for the patient to ventilate her hurt and angry feelings about the recent family turmoil. Such ventilation in itself can significantly reduce the pressure under which the patient is laboring. The doctor needs to judge how much expression of aggression and anger to permit in such ventilation since many patients become depressed or develop additional symptoms if they are encouraged or permitted to reveal precipitously an unusual amount of negative feeling. Often a patient's reciting recent upsets and hurts result in enough "steam blown off" to allow disruptive relationships to be resumed. On the other hand, the doctor may perceive that the patient's family relationships present problems of such gravity that the patient cannot be expected, either because of her personal limitations or because of the degree of environmental disturbance, to manage these relationships adequately. In this event the physician should consider the advisability of talking with other members of the family to explore their capacities to revise their attitudes toward the patient. The position and authority of the physician may well be the deciding factor in bringing a discordant family into better balance.

A problem of a recently married young man demonstrates additional supportive approaches.

Walter R., a 22-year-old college senior, came to his doctor with the chief complaint of impotence. The discussion quickly revealed that this young man was experiencing a definite anxiety reaction with manifest symptoms of palpitation, excessive perspiration and shortness of breath. The patient reported that he had married 10 months previously and that his sexual adjustment was initially satisfactory. From the beginning, however, other aspects of the marriage had not gone smoothly, and there had been definite strife between the patient and his wife. More recently, the patient had found himself sexually impotent, at first occasionally, and then quite consistently. The patient said that when he did find it possible to have sexual relations, his wife was either disinclined or definitely fearful of the sexual act. There was no question in the couple's mind about their wish to continue the marriage.

A review of the previous history established that the patient had always been in good health and had not suffered from any significant emotional difficulty. During all of his college career his work had been at least adequate. Examination confirmed the initial impression that this young man was in good physical health.

In talking things over with the patient, the doctor observed that there was real fear that some disastrous illness was in process. He informed the man very firmly that no such illness existed and that he definitely anticipated that the patient would be able to have a normal sexual life.

The doctor also commented that new demands and adjustments were a part of marriage and that its "honeymoon period" was frequently a stressful one. The patient agreed that the past 10 months had been rather rough. He had thought that these stresses might be related to his sexual difficulty, but had not been able to feel convinced about such an association. The doctor informed the patient that very often tensions such as he and his wife were experiencing resulted in temporary sexual difficulty. The doctor said it was also likely that the patient's wife was undergoing a change in her responsiveness because of the tension under which the couple had been living.

The doctor then stated that he felt that the reported symptoms of palpitation, perspiration and shortness of breath were those associated with anxiety and should be regarded as temporary. He added that, although the approaching graduation of the patient would require a number of new adjustments, he felt confident that the patient would be able to handle this transitional period. At the end of the appointment the doctor suggested that this was a period when the patient and his wife, more than usually would want to talk things over together. He suggested that the patient see how things went along for 2 or 3 weeks and then give the doctor a call and make another office appointment.

As was the case with the previous patient, this man came to his doctor with considerable evidence of personality strengths. Yet the experiences of recent months had somehow resulted in his decompensating to some extent and developing an anxiety reaction with the symptom of functional impotence. The doctor proceeded with a rather active, supportive approach, based on his diagnostic impression of a neurotic type of reaction occurring in a young man of good basic personality resources, the reaction being caused by recent stresses related to marriage and approaching graduation. Of course, the doctor had assessed the patient's physical condition before planning his talk with this man.

In this talk the doctor used a number of supportive techniques which have broad application in medical practice. In reassuring the patient about the functional nature of the disturbance the doctor employed an authoritative, firm approach. Similarly, the doctor confidently expressed the expectation that the patient's symptoms were temporary. Such reassurances can be extremely effective in offering the patient sufficient emotional support that there is relief of anxiety and therefore symptomatic improvement.

Also in the doctor's comments is suggestion therapy. The doctor has suggested that the patient's symptoms soon will be alleviated. The doctor has decided already that his patient has essentially good emotional resources and should be able to manage most life stresses. Naturally, for a doctor to use such suggestive treatment appropriately he should himself be convinced as to the soundness of his prediction. Effective suggestion therapy requires that the patient already have the view that his doctor is a reliable, helpful and authoritative person.

From this case study it is clear that the doctor has given his patient some valuable information about how basically healthy people react to stress and anxiety. As much as possible the doctor should share such knowledge with his patients. Frequently, doctors are too conservative in their assessment of how much information of a medical or psychological nature they can offer to their basically healthy patients. Of course, doctors have to be careful that the information given to patients is within their capacity to understand and not of a nature to cause excessive anxiety.

Still another technique which the doctor made use of was the giving of guidance and advice. Many doctors are reluctant to use such a technique because of an understandable hesitation about "running other people's lives." Guidance and advice should not remove a patient's responsibility for handling his life. In this case study the doctor gives the advice that the present period in the patient's life is one during which the patient and his wife should talk things over together more than usually. The doctor has decided that the couple's relationship is sufficiently strong that they can tolerate and make use of the intimacies which he is suggesting and that most likely such closeness will help work out their problems rather than be disruptive. From this observation it is clear that the doctor has been careful not to give advice which is beyond the capacity of his patient to use.

As much as any other factor, a supportive therapy depends on the doctor's being a strong and reliable figure with whom an identification can easily be made. In the case example the doctor's comfortable, nonanxious handling of the patient's problems does much to make the doctor, in the patient's eyes, an ideal, mature figure. The doctor is at ease in his position of a strong, grown man. The young man very much needs to see that there are such grown-up men since one of his present anxieties is about being an adult male rather than a growing boy. Almost always it is necessary for a positive relationship to exist between the doctor and patient before the patient will be able to look upon the doctor as a model. In order to foster such a positive relationship, the doctor will need to control any critical feelings or competitive strivings he may experience. For instance, in all probability, it would have been a serious error for the doctor to remind his patient of his growing responsibilities and tell him to straighten out quickly. Or again, it would have been a mistake for the doctor to imply that the patient should be a little ashamed of his sexual impotence, that he should be more of a man (i.e., more like the doctor). Such techniques, because of the critical and sharply competitive themes involved, inevitably arouse negative feelings to the point where they alienate the patient from the doctor or at least reduce the positive influence of the doctor-patient relationship.

A third clinical case is of supportive work with an older patient.

Mrs. T., a 70-year-old widow, had been living for a number of years with her daughter's family. When brought to the doctor by the daughter Mrs. T. reported that she had felt a decreasing interest in food and in the world generally for the past year. She also complained of increasing difficulty in moving around because of pain in various joints, and she commented that any effort seemed to make her surprisingly short of breath. The daughter told of her mother's being much more quiet, of her having lost considerable weight, and of her having a problem recently with constipation. The daughter had noted no other physical or mental changes, except that her mother had stopped seeing her old friends. The doctor knew from his previous care of Mrs. T. that she had been in essentially good health prior to the past year and was on no regular medication.

During his examination the doctor observed the signs of recent weight loss with some evidence of malnutrition. He also discovered signs of arteriosclerotic cardiovascular disease with a somewhat enlarged heart and one to two-plus ankle edema. The joints of both upper and lower extremities showed evidence of moderate arthritic changes, but no signs of an active inflammatory process. The doctor found Mrs. T. rather listless and apathetic, a condition which was in contrast to her previously more animated moods. There were no other remarkable changes in the mental status.

In reviewing the recent past with the patient and her daughter, the doctor was unable to uncover any events which provided an explanation for the change in Mrs. T.'s state of health.

After this initial examination the doctor's diagnostic impression was that Mrs. T. was experiencing a definite depressive reaction with no clear precipitating event other than her aging. He did not feel that there was any indication of organic brain disease. The doctor also recognized that Mrs. T. had decompensated arteriosclerotic cardiovascular disease and that the development of this problem probably contributed to the gradually increasing depression. In his thinking the doctor accounted for weight loss, malnutrition and constipation as essentially secondary to the depressive illness. The declining vigor and depression from which the patient was suffering had made more definitely symptomatic the chronic and inactive arthritis which had been present for years.

In working out his treatment plan the doctor came to the conclusion that Mrs. T. needed the concentrated diagnostic and treatment services of a hospital. He therefore admitted her to a medical floor and arranged for the appropriate diagnostic examinations, which confirmed his initial impression. He initiated treatment of the patient's cardiac condition, including digitalization. During the hospitalization the doctor also prescribed soaks in warm baths twice a day, partly in order to alleviate the joint discomfort, but also as a form of hydrotherapy to improve the patient's spirits.

The patient responded promptly to the attention and interest of the hospital staff and to the medical regime. She became more alert and conversational, but seemed uncertain how to engage her new energies. The doctor asked the hospital's occupational therapist to talk with the patient. The occupational therapist found Mrs. T. eager to take up an old skill, knitting, an activity that was made possible by the diminished joint discomfort. But, even further, the therapist learned that Mrs. T. loved to play cards and was able to arrange a number of card games during the hospitalization.

The positive response of the patient to these activities alerted her doctor to encourage their continuation after discharge. In further discussions with the daughter, the physician learned that the patient had been keeping pretty much to her own room and had fallen into quite an irregular pattern of meals and sleep. He advised Mrs. T.—and requested the daughter to support the advice—that there should be a regular living pattern, with three meals a day, even though one or two of these were light, and with regular hours for sleep. He also stressed the importance of Mrs. T.'s being with her friends more and of keeping up with her usual activities, such as church. He suggested that the patient capitalize on her enjoyment of card playing, to broaden her circle of friends and acquaintances.

After a period of about two weeks in the hospital, the doctor discharged Mrs. T., to be followed at regular intervals in his office. Her appetite was much improved; she had begun to gain back a few pounds; her physical vigor had returned; the constipation and joint discomfort were no longer causing distress. With her improved emotional and physical well-being, it looked as though Mrs. T. would follow her doctor's recommendations.

There may be an impression that Mrs. T.'s doctor provided no more than the expected medical care, the care of "the whole patient." This is indeed true. The point is that, if such care is provided, some psychological measures will be routinely included.

The first of these measures (in the above instance) is hospitalization. Mrs. T. probably could have been diagnosed and treated as an out-patient, but the doctor decided that the support of the hospital environment and the opportunity to be away from whatever stresses existed in her home were over-riding considerations. It is a common experience in medical practice to find that appropriate hospitalization in the manner discussed avoids the occurrence of more serious emotional and physical decompensation. On the other hand, the doctor must exercise careful clinical judgment since many patients benefit more from being challenged to struggle actively with adjustment problems and would be deprived of this challenge by hospitalization. As in all medical activity, potentially beneficial treatment measures are attended by some risks. The primary risk accompanying hospitalization is that the stay will be so long as to encourage the patient to become excessively dependent. Such a development would certainly interfere with the patient's moving toward a healthier and more mature adjustment.

A fact which is easily overlooked is that the physical treatment of any illness usually is regarded by the patient as a demonstration of being given to, of interest and of support. There are occasions when a patient's need to be given to is appropriately met by the prescription of medication even when minimal pathophysiological indications exist. With the patient being discussed, treatment of the cardiac condition and arthritis would definitely be felt as an emotionally supporting experience, though the patient recognizes that the primary purpose of the medication and physical treatment is to alleviate physical disease. As her physical distress is alleviated, the patient will feel even more emphatically that she has been dealt with in a very kindly fashion. Physical treatment of such obvious deformities as disfiguring scars, seriously decayed teeth, or orthopedic conditions can have an even more direct supportive effect on the patient than is seen here.

Modern medicine has largely by-passed a proved remedy for many aches and pains of the psyche and of the soma by neglecting to use warm baths or hydrotherapy. This ancient prescription should be regarded as lying within the area of generally supportive measures. When the physician is caring for an agitated or tense patient, advising soaks in warm baths should certainly be kept in mind. Depressed patients, when they are not agitated, less frequently benefit from such baths. However, the patient just described was emotionally in need of being physically cared for, and the baths provided this therapeutic experience in addition to whatever easing effect they had on the joint symptoms.

Several of the supportive measures utilized by this physician can be regarded as essentially occupational therapy. In fact, the physician was able to consult an occupational therapist, a specialist whom all well-staffed hospitals should provide. Patients who have been isolated or preoccupied with themselves need outside interests to which their energies can be attached. Occupational therapists are skilled in discovering and developing such interests, here exemplified in the knitting and card playing. Often enough, occupational therapy leads to the growth of serious hobbies or even vocations. Here the doctor concentrated on increasing Mrs. T.'s possibilities of diversion and entertainment. Appropriately, he focused on Mrs. T.'s renewing friendships and establishing new ones, so that remobilized energies could once again be invested in a healthy and gratifying way. (See further discussion of occupational therapy on pp. 510 to 512.)

Finally, Mrs. T.'s doctor recognized that a minimum of organization is necessary so that life may proceed in a comfortably productive, nonanxious fashion. The recommendation that regular meals and sleep be arranged was the doctor's way of encouraging compulsive defenses as an important contribution to a healthier adjustment. It will be seen that the doctor has focused on assisting the patient to invest her interest in her environment rather than increasingly withdrawing into herself. The patient's use of withdrawal and isolation can be identified as her use of unhealthy and maladaptive defenses.

In reviewing this brief presentation of *supportive techniques* the reader will observe that the physician has seldom discussed his deeper understanding of the patient's emotional functioning, but has made use of such understanding in treatment. In most medical work the open discussion between doctor and patient of such deeper understanding results in the development of a more complicated doctor-patient relationship than is desirable or fruitful.

Relationship Psychotherapy

Although all of the doctor's work with patients recognizes the importance of the doctor-patient relationship, the term *relationship psychotherapy* is used to indicate a type of therapy which hinges to an unusual degree on this relationship. Frequently the patient will be seen at short intervals and over a long period of time, so that the psychological work is intensive. Detailed correlations are attempted between early life experiences and present-day problems. Through the treatment experience the patient is offered a novel opportunity to examine his way of doing things and to ponder whether there might be healthier and happier ways to manage his life. In contrast to the suppressive or supportive approach, the use of relationship psychotherapy indicates that the doctor has decided to work with the patient toward a goal beyond the restoration of psychic equilibrium, the goal being further personality growth and maturation. From this description it is clear that the conduct of a relationship psychotherapy requires specialized training and experience beyond that acquired by any but the exceptional nonpsychiatrist. Clinical problems meriting such an approach should always be referred to a psychiatrist for an initial appraisal and usually for treatment.

Expressive Psychotherapy

An expressive psychotherapy, working toward insight and using uncovering techniques, is the most intensive psychological treatment short of psychoanalysis (which may be considered a special form of expressive psychotherapy). This type of treatment will be discussed in detail in the following chapter.

THE DOCTOR-PATIENT RELATIONSHIP

Transference

From the discussion covering treatment approaches it has been abundantly evident that the doctor can anticipate that all of his patients, at one time or another, will react to him in a somewhat unrealistic way and that some of them will occasionally respond in a quite irrational way. Such reactions may take the form of unexpectedly hostile, dependent, seductive, or competitive behavior. Under certain conditions, these reactions are to be expected even in the "healthiest" of people. These unrealistic responses usually can be understood as representing the patient's method of relating to some early significant figure in his life (see pp. 487 to 489). The term *transference* is used of these reappearances of old experiences and techniques. Almost always it is correct for the nonpsychiatric physician to respond to such behavior in his patients in as comfortable and casual a way as possible, offering no interpretive remarks regarding the significance of the transference behavior.

Counter-transference

Just as there are occasions when patients, in their contacts with the doctor, manifest behavior which has to do with the past and with people other than the doctor, so doctors should be alert for parallel manifestations in themselves in response to their patients. These universal, yet illogical, responses in the physician have been termed *counter-transference*. Some of the more common counter-transference reactions for which physicians should scrutinize themselves can be quickly reviewed.

In this regard, the problems relating to dependency challenge the doctor. The doctor is aware that he must discover the fine line between healthy and necessary gratification of his patient's basic needs and "over-feeding" which would prevent the patient's developing in independent, illness-free ways. A doctor should question himself if he notes that his patients almost always remain in the hospital longer than other patients with similar pathology. On the other side, he should take a close look at himself if he discovers that he infrequently hospitalizes patients or hospitalizes them very briefly for conditions for which other physicians are more or less routinely prescribing in-patient care. In office work with chronic disease states, the doctor, in reaction to repeated visits with slight demonstrable improvement, may be conscious that he is impatient, or angry, to the point where it interferes with his work. Finally, the physician may discover that he is unable comfortably to discontinue a patient's appointments when a condition has cleared.

Another sensitive area can be a physician's excessively sharp reactions to a patient's competitiveness or rebelliousness, behavior which inevitably will be encountered during medical work. Of course, no doctor is able to establish and maintain an adequate working relationship with all patients. Such an expectation is unrealistic. Yet, if a doctor becomes aware that he is having persistent irritations with a particular type of patient, or with a number of patients, this awareness can be put to very good use by the doctor's wondering just what may be going on in himself which could contribute to or provoke these reactions.

A discussion of counter-transference would be incomplete without mention of one further problem with which doctors have to struggle. Patients come to physicians to be helped. When the indicated help has been provided, the doctor should discharge his patient. If the doctor does not discharge his patient, a situation exists in which the doctor's needs, rather than the patient's, are being gratified. The patient may have an unusual medical condition no longer meriting follow-up but interesting to the doctor; the doctor may have come to value his friendship with the patient; the doctor may worry that the patient will be angry if the doctor discharges him. All these are common enough situations. Yet considerable alertness is required if the physician is to be sure that he is serving his patient's needs rather than his own. (As the Hippocratic Oath states, "In every house where I come, I will enter only for the good of my patients.") A doctor should not be self-depreciating in discovering repeatedly that he has human needs. What is necessary is that he maintain self-scrutiny and control so that these needs are met in a way which does not interfere with the highest conduct of his professional work.

COMMONLY USED PSYCHOPHARMACOLOGICAL AGENTS

In recent years there has been a tremendous acceleration in the development of drugs which alleviate "emotional symptomatology." These newer drugs fall mostly into the *tranquilizing* group of medications. They join the older sedatives and stimulants as drugs of central nervous system action* with which the nonpsychiatrist should be familiar in his handling of the problems of "minor psychiatry."[5] More recently, a new group of drugs, *antidepressant agents*, has been discovered. These drugs are also ones with which the nonpsychiatrist should be familiar although there is some question as to how frequently they should be used in general medical practice.

---

* The tranquilizers and antidepressants are more selective in their action than the sedatives and stimulants and hence of much greater theoretical interest.

A reminder is appropriate as to the nonspecific action of these psychopharmacological agents. In contrast to many drugs, such as penicillin and other antibiotics which have a direct action on the etiological agent of a given infection, the group of psychopharmacological drugs acts in a symptom-alleviating fashion but seems not to have any direct affect on the underlying psychopathology. There may be exceptions to this generalization, such as the possibility that some of the new antidepressants, e.g., *imipramine,* may interfere directly with a neurophysiological mechanism having to do with the production of depression. However, the generalization is a fairly sound one. The physician should not be under the impression that he is curing an illness when he prescribes the medications being discussed.

The doctor should have particular symptoms in mind when he prescribes one of these agents. As in the treatment of infections the doctor should have actual evidence of the character of the infectious agent in order to prescribe an appropriate antibiotic, so in the use of psychopharmacological agents the doctor should have a clear conception of the form emotional symptoms are taking, such as depression, agitation, insomnia, in order that the appropriate drug can be used. Such definitive use of these medications will reveal them to be staunch assistants in the doctor's therapeutic work.

The fact that these psychopharmacological agents are assisting rather than principal agents of the doctor's work is important to realize. Many physicians are uncomfortable in treating patients unless they are prescribing some medication. The corollary of this observation is that many patients feel that they have received inadequate care unless some medication has been prescribed. Indeed, many patients are so dependent in their orientation that they *do* require something physically and concretely from the doctor in order for the doctor's treatment to be effective. But many other patients do not have such needs, and the doctor can be comfortable in using a supportive approach and no medication in the treatment of a functional disturbance. At no time should the physician offer aid on the principle that the prescribed medication stands alone as effective treatment. The therapeutic action of any drug is based not only on its pharmacological potential, but also on the status of the doctor-patient relationship.

The number of possible choices in this area of medication makes it impossible for doctors to be thoroughly familiar with every drug. All doctors know that every effective drug is capable of causing some side reactions and offers some potential hazards. Therefore, after studying the possibilities, the doctor acts most wisely in selecting one or two drugs in each category of medication and concentrating on these. By now it has become clear that the arrival of every new psychopharmacological agent is attended by so many conflicting reports as to its effectiveness and hazards that the wise course for every practitioner is to employ only those agents which have had a thorough clinical evaluation over an extended period of time.

The matter of side reactions presents a real problem in assisting patients to understand what they can expect of the medication. Some side reactions, such as the insomnia caused by some stimulants, should be explained to patients, but so many people develop side reactions on the basis of suggestibility that many doctors find the best method of assuring that the medication is being used in a safe way is to have frequent follow-up visits after medication is initiated. The doctor prescribes the medication with a minimal explanation as to side reactions. This conduct follows the principle that no medication should be taken in a continuing way without the patient's maintaining contact with a physician.

The long-continued use of any psychopharmacological agent should suggest the need for psychiatric consultation. Quite possibly such a consultation would result in the nonpsychiatrist continuing to care for the patient, but the prolonged use of these medications does suggest that the patient has psychological problems which are not responsive to treatment approaches available to the nonpsychiatrist. In addition, the protracted use of these medications can create a situation in which the patient is addicted, either psychologically or physiologically, a development which would certainly limit the doctor's ability to move his patient toward a healthier adjustment.

With the medications under consideration, as in the entire field of pharmacology, the doctor must always write his prescription so that there is as little chance as possible for the patient to use the medicine in a self-destructive way. The instructions for the use of the medicine should be clear and should be reviewed with the patient. The amount of medicine in any given prescription should not be of a dangerous quantity.

Sedatives

BARBITURATES. Doctors have accumulated the greatest experience in the use of barbiturates for the purpose of sedation. This group of drugs offers a selection of agents providing short to long-acting sedation.

Phenobarbital, the longest acting of the group, is used where prolonged sleep is desired. The dosage for sleep is 0.1 Gms. an hour before sleep. Phenobarbital can also be used for reducing tension and anxiety during the day in the smaller dosage of 0.032 Gm. t.i.d., although a number of patients will find themselves somnolent enough with this dosage schedule that it will have to be reduced.

Nembutal and *Amytal* are moderately short-acting barbiturates, usually given for sleep in dosages of 0.1 to 0.2 Gm. The shorter acting barbiturates will produce less of the "hangover" feeling which accompanies the use of phenobarbital. If there is a problem with early morning waking, then the larger dosage schedule should be employed with Nembutal and Amytal.

Seconal, 0.1 Gm., is best prescribed when there is difficulty in getting to sleep. Seconal has the shortest action of the commonly used barbiturates.

NONBARBITURATES. There are now a large number of short-acting, nonbarbiturate sedatives which have been especially helpful when patients have problems in getting to sleep. The most widely used of these preparations are methylparafynol (Dormison), 0.25 Gm.; glutethimide (Doriden), 0.5 Gm.; and methyprylon (Noludar), 0.2 Gm.

A sedative which was formerly heavily relied upon is chloral hydrate, 0.65 Gm. This drug is especially helpful to and well tolerated by older people.

Alcohol in the form of wine and whiskey is frequently very effective in providing mild sedation in the evening.

Although the incidence of skin problems and toxic psychoses as a result of uncontrolled use has placed bromides rather in disfavor among doctors, this medication should still be kept in mind when a change in a sedation routine is indicated and when the doctor can be assured that good supervision of the medication will be maintained. The prescription of bromides by doctors for daytime sedation has largely disappeared.

Tranquilizers

The present period remains a time of such rapid proliferation of new tranquilizing agents that it is not feasible to attempt to present a comprehensive survey of the available medications. Those agents which have had thorough clinical evaluation are presented in Table 1, where a division is made between the "major tranquilizers" and the "minor tranquilizers."

The primary indications for the use of a major tranquilizer are the symptomatic treatment of excitements, emergency treatment of acute psychotic breaks, long-term treatment of chronic refractory schizophrenia, and maintenance therapy of psychoses in remission. From this list of indications it is clear that the major tranquilizers are used in serious psychiatric disorders and that their continued use should only be maintained if there has been a psychiatric consultation. The contraindications to the use of the major agents are mild anxiety, coma or severe central nervous system depression, any condition in

TABLE 1. COMMONLY USED PSYCHOPHARMACOLOGICAL AGENTS[4]

Generic Name	Trade Name	Daily Oral Dose Range (mgs)
MAJOR TRANQUILIZERS*		
Phenothiazines (in order of increasing potency)		
chlorpromazine	Thorazine	60-1600
thioridazine	Mellaril	40-1000
triflupromazine	Vesprin	30-400
prochlorperazine	Compazine	15-200
thiopropazate	Dartal	10-150
perphenazine	Trilafon	4-64
trifluoperazine	Stelazine	2-40
fluphenazine	Prolixin; Permitil	1-20
Rauwolfia Alkaloids		
reserpine	(many)	0.5-12
MINOR TRANQUILIZERS		
acetophenazine	Tindal	20-80
hydroxyzine	Atarax, Vistaril	30-100
mephanoxalone	Trepidone	600-1200
meprobamate	Equanil, Miltown	600-1200
methaminodiazepoxide	Librium	10-100
phenaglycodol	Ultran	800-1200
PSYCHOMOTOR STIMULANTS		
Amphetamines		
amphetamine	Benzedrine	5-20
dextroamphetamine	Dexedrine	5-15
metamphetamine	(many)	2-15
Miscellaneous		
deanol	Deaner	25-100
methylphenidate	Ritalin	10-60
pipradrol	Meratran	1-7
Combinations		
benactyzine & meprobamate	Deprol	2-4 tablets
dextroamphetamine & amobarbital	Dexamyl	2-3 tablets
ANTIDEPRESSANT DRUGS		
Monoamine Oxidase Inhibitors		
isocarboxazid	Marplan	10-30
nialamide	Niamid	15-200
phenelzine	Nardil	10-75
tranylcypromine	Parnate	20-30
Iminodibenzyl Derivatives		
amitriptyline	Elavil	75-150
imipramine	Tofranil	75-225

* Synonymous with *neuroleptics* in the classification of Kalinowsky and Hoch.

which hypotension would be seriously detrimental (i.e., myocardial infarction), severe liver insufficiencies, and epilepsy or history of convulsive disorders. In patients who are experiencing mild anxiety, the major agents may be useful, but often the side effects are intolerable to mildly ill patients. All of the phenothiazines are believed, at the present time, to act in essentially the same way. In contrast to sedatives, such as barbiturates, the phenothiazines are selective inhibitors having their major influence on the brain stem and only in very large doses on the cortex. They do not produce the initial disinhibition (excitement) characteristic of barbiturates and alcohol which inhibits brain stem and cortex simultaneously. Although the pharmacology of the agents in this group is quite similar there are minor distinctions. (a) chlorpromazine produces more drowsiness; (b) perphenazine produces less drowsiness and side effects; (c) trifluoperazine produces less drowsiness; (d) prochlorperazine produces mild stimulation.

A review of the side effects of the major tranquilizing agents is instructive as it emphasizes the care with which these agents must be administered.

SIDE EFFECTS OF MAJOR TRANQUILIZING AGENTS

1. Central nervous system
   a. Drowsiness, usually diminishes after one week, more marked with chlorpromazine, can usually be controlled with amphetamine.
   b. Temperature variations, usually in evenings.
   c. Extra-pyramidal symptoms (akinetic or hyperkinetic parkinsonism) in 10-15 per cent of patients in large doses. May be managed with methanesulfonate (Cogentin).
   d. Meningismus or tic-like syndrome especially involving musculature of neck and jaw (particularly perphenazine).
2. Cardiovascular
   a. Hypotension, usually orthostatic, lasting 1-4 hours (particularly with chlorpromazine, thioridazine, and prochlorperazine). If severe, may be treated with shock blocks, norepinephrine, fluids, etc.
3. Autonomic
   Dry mucous membrane.
4. Gastroenteric
   a. Increased appetite in 40 per cent.
   b. Allergic obstructive jaundice in 1 per cent (with temperature elevation, abdominal pain, nausea, vomiting, jaundice). Treat by withdrawal of drug. Jaundice often does not recur if the

same or another phenothiazine is begun after initial jaundice has receded (2-3 weeks).
    c. Constipation.
 5. Skin
    a. Pruritis over extremities.
    b. Increased susceptibility to sunburn.
    c. Angioneurotic edema.
    d. Morbiliform eruption.
 6. Respiratory
    Nasal congestion (48 per cent).
 7. Musculoskeletal
    Muscular weakness—mild.
 8. Endocrine
    a. Increased libido in women; decreased in men.
    b. Swelling of breasts, lactation, menstrual abnormalities.
 9. Urinary
    Urine sometimes becomes deep orange at high dosage.
10. Hematologic
    Agranulocytosis. The most serious complication. Incidence is 1 in 5,000 to 10,000 patients. Treat with antibiotics, steroids.
11. Psychological
    Depression.

The Rauwolfia alkaloids, of which reserpine is the best known, may also be classified in the major tranquilizing group. These drugs have also been used in both psychoses and neuroses, but they are slower to act and more erratic in their effectiveness than the phenothiazines. At the present time the Rauwolfia derivatives are much less frequently used than the phenothiazines in the treatment of emotional disturbances.

Of the minor tranquilizers, meprobamate and phenaglycodol are the ones which are most frequently used. The indications for their use are mild anxiety states, particularly when accompanied by muscular tension and when sedatives are indicated in out-patients who may use drugs to attempt suicide. The lethal dose of both of these medicines is very large. The contraindications to their use are those patients with an easy tendency toward addiction. Physiological addiction to meprobamate and phenaglycodol can result from prolonged administration of moderate to large doses. Severe withdrawal symptoms result from abrupt termination of large doses.

Stimulants

Amphetamine (Benzedrine), dextroamphetamine (Dexedrine), metamphetamine (Desoxyn and others) are well known for their favorable effect on such symptoms as fatigue and mild depression. Unfavorable side effects of these medications are their tendency to produce sleeplessness, restlessness and sometimes anxiety. To a certain extent these undesired effects may be neutralized by the addition of small doses of a sedative or a tranquilizer. Because of the value of both the relaxant barbiturates and tranquilizers and the stimulating amphetamines, these drugs have been combined for the treatment of mild depressions. The most commonly used combinations are benactyzine and meprobamate (Deprol) and dextroamphetamine and amobarbital (Dexamyl). These combinations work well with some patients, but with others it it more helpful to prescribe the drugs separately since the dosage of each can be adjusted independently to fit the needs of the individual patient.

More recently developed stimulants include deanol (Deaner), methylphenidate (Ritalin), and pipradrol (Meratran). All these agents are of some value in mild depression. However, the drugs already mentioned as stimulants are better known and are effective in the treatment of mild depression either by themselves or in combination with a barbiturate or tranquilizer.

Antidepressants

All of the drugs listed in Table 1, under the heading antidepressants, have had extensive clinical trials and are known as effective antidepressant agents. However, recent opinion is growing to the effect that amitriptyline and imipramine are not only safer than the monamine oxidase inhibitors, but are also more effective as antidepressant drugs.[1,5] It is also known that the amine oxidase inhibitors potentiate opiates, atropine derivatives, barbiturates, ganglionic blocking agents, corticosteriods, and antirheumatic compounds. Other complications are not infrequent in the use of monoamine oxidase inhibitors. These attributes of the amine oxidase inhibitors limit their usefulness and their range of therapeutic application. Amitriptyline and imipramine are not innocuous compounds. However, in contrast to the enzyme inhibitors, they do not potentiate most of the commonly used drugs, so they can be administered conjointly with whatever other medicine the depressed patient requires. Clinical experience with these medications has demonstrated them to be especially safe for protracted administration, offering little physical or psychic hazard to the patient. The use of these medications should be confined to moderate to severe depressive reactions. Almost certainly a nonpsychiatrist should arrange for psychiatric consultation if he is seriously considering the use of one of these antidepressant medications.

Placebos

Many times a physician will wish to respond to a patient's need to be given something, either with or without physiologic justification, and will think of prescribing a *placebo*.[3] It is perhaps questionable as to whether it is ever justified to give completely inert preparations as a treatment measure. In any event, almost always the doctor will have sufficient conflict about prescribing such inert preparations that this conflict will be communicated to the patient either consciously or unconsciously. As has already been mentioned, the effect of any medication is influenced in important ways by the doctor-patient relationship. Therefore, when a patient receives such placebo medication, with the doctor feeling that he is being other than straightforward with his patient, the medication is not likely to be wholly effective. There may well be times, however, when the doctor is genuinely interested in gratifying his patient rather than manipulating him, and in such instances inert placebos may relieve symptoms.

COLLABORATIVE AND ANCILLARY APPROACHES

With the development of new techniques and increased community resources, the treatment of the "whole patient" not infrequently goes beyond the scope of the physician's direct experience and available time. Doctors no longer feel that they have performed inadequately when they see the need for outside help, but rather they welcome the assistance of other disciplines. The major resources will be covered in this section. The coverage is not intended to be exhaustive and hardly does justice to the contribution these collaborative and ancillary approaches provide.

As has been noted repeatedly therapeutic moves must be carried out with the recognition that they are attended by certain hazards. The chief hazard in the use of a collaborative approach is that the doctor-patient relationship may be disrupted. It is of crucial importance that the patient understand that the doctor is not "putting him off" when the suggestion is made that additional help is indicated in the management of the patient's difficulty. The doctor should always make it clear that he is continuing his medical responsibility and interest and will want to work with whatever professional or agency is coming into the picture.

In arranging for additional help the doctor should be careful to be specific with the patient about what information will be shared with other people. Naturally the doctor is aware that he is not free to talk about his patient without the latter's specific permission. In the patient's acceptance of the idea that additional help will be arranged is implied a realization that some general discussion regarding his problem will be required, but the continuing positive development of the doctor-patient relationship is fostered only if the doctor demonstrates that confidential matters will not be discussed with other people.

Social Casework

The qualified caseworker has had two years of specialized education in a professional graduate school of social work and supervised field work in an approved agency comparable to a medical internship. The casework tradition is that workers continue to progress in experience with supervision, much as doctors continue their professional development in residency training. Even with a rapidly increasing number of trained social workers, the demand continues to exceed the supply of academically qualified people with the result that there are many social workers employed, especially in welfare agencies, without full training. Most private agencies, such as family service agencies, have fully trained workers. Social workers are also employed in hospitals and medical and psychiatric clinics.

Many people still associate the idea of social work with some type of charity activity with emphasis on helping those who are in financial need. Modern social casework is not primarily involved with the giving of financial help except in public welfare agencies. Today's social workers are skilled interviewers with a knowledge of psychodynamics, of family dynamics, and of community resources. This knowledge enables the social worker to help people help themselves and their relatives. Social workers in such settings as family service agencies assist families or individuals in the solution of individual adjustment and family relationship problems. Such problems may include marriage difficulties, parent-child relationships, unmarried motherhood, budgeting and financial management problems, and those difficulties associated with illness or aging. In particular, when the doctor encounters an emotional problem of minor severity or a family difficulty which does not require ongoing medical supervision, he should definitely think of referral to a family service type of agency.

Psychologists

A trained psychologist should have a Ph.D. degree if he is working independently. Vocational counseling is one important area in which the physician may find the help of a psychologist of great value. A psychologist engaged in vocational counseling will be experienced in correlating information gained from various psychological tests with the skills and personality qualities which a wide variety of vocations require. His work involves skill in interviewing and in counseling techniques.

Another area of psychological activity which should be familiar to the nonpsychiatrist is that of the *clinical psychologist*. A qualified clinical psychologist has a Ph.D. degree plus an internship or equivalent experience in a Department approved for training in clinical psychology. This professional renders service through the use of clinical psychological tests; he initiates or participates in research and teaching, and he may conduct psychotherapy of certain emotional disturbances. Although there is very active discussion of psychologists engaging in psychotherapy, the consensus of psychiatrists is that such therapy should be safeguarded by medical consultation. Clinical psychologists do not have medical degrees and therefore cannot be expected to have adequate knowledge of the psychosomatic or somatopsychic sequences which need to be understood during psychotherapeutic work.

Visiting Nurse Associations and Public Health Nurses

The increasing participation of visiting nurses and public health nurses in the out-patient care of psychiatric problems, both minor and major, is a very positive development. A number of communities now have programs in which much of the posthospital follow-up of discharged patients is carried out by visiting nurses. For the nonpsychiatrist such nursing care can be of valuable assistance in his treatment of some psychiatric disturbances. The older patient who becomes depressed when left too much on his own may be helped to avoid a serious depression by the occasional visits of a nurse for the purpose of attending to minor medical needs. The distraught mother of a large family, who feels overwhelmed with the arrival of yet another baby, can be helped to maintain her shaky equilibrium through the visits of a nurse to assist in the baby's care and, incidentally, to help the mother maintain the basic household routines. In almost every chronic illness a visiting nurse can render a medical service and in addition can help reinforce the fragile emotional adjustment which so often accompanies chronically ill states.

Occupational Therapy

Occupational therapy has become a distinct profession with the therapist being a graduate of an accredited university that offers a program in occupational therapy leading to the degree of bachelor of science. The therapist's educational program includes a special focus on a study of the arts and crafts and on both the physical and the psychological aspects of rehabilitation. It includes a 9- to 12-month field placement in the areas of children's services, tuberculosis or cardiac services, physical disabilities services, and psychiatric service. A registered occupational therapist has taken a licensing examination from the Committee on Hospital Standards of the American Medical Association. Most occupational therapy is conducted in hospitals for the purpose of supervising the occupational therapy of patients in collaboration with the doctor in a manner which facilitates over-all therapeutic progress. "Occupational therapy is a rehabilitative procedure guided by a qualified Occupational Therapist who works under medical prescription, uses self-help, manual, creative, recreational and social, educational, prevocational, and industrial activities to gain from the patient the desired physical function and/or mental response."*

Occupational therapy may be prescribed by the doctor for one or more of the following purposes: (1) as specific treatment for psychiatric patients (see pp. 510 to 512); (2) as specific treatment for restoration of physical function, to increase joint motion, muscle strength and coordination; (3) to teach self-help activities, those of daily living, such as eating, dressing, writing, the use of adaptive equipment and prostheses; (4) to help the disabled homeworker readjust to home routine with advice and instructions as to adaptations of household equipment and work simplification; (5) to develop work tolerance and maintenance of special skills as required by the patient's job; (6) prevocational exploration to determine the patient's physical capabilities, interests, work habits, skills and potential employability; and (7) a supportive measure in helping the patient accept and utilize constructively a prolonged period of hospitalization or convalescence.

Most of the occupational therapist's work is carried out in hospitals, but there are opportunities in larger communities for out-patients to receive this kind of assistance.

Physiotherapy

Large numbers of doctors have equipped their offices so that they are able to apply a number of physical techniques to the treatment of patients in their practice. Diathermy and ultrasonic equipment is found in many medical offices. Numbers of doctors have had special training and experience in physical medicine, and there are increasing numbers of trained physiotherapists who do not have medical degrees, but who practice with medical supervision. Many patients with minor psychiatric problems can make use of the assistance which physical medi-

---

* This definition and the seven objectives which follow have been taken from an officially adopted statement by the World Federation of Occupational Therapists, Copenhagen, Denmark, August, 1958.

cine offers. The fact that there is a large psychological component to whatever pathology is presented does not rule out the helpfulness of these methods. Such problems as chronic and disabling muscular soreness, retarded convalescence after an injury, difficulties accompanying the use of limb prostheses, and problems subsequent to cerebral vascular accidents are but a few of the conditions which should suggest the use of physiotherapy.

Recreational Therapy

There are relatively few trained recreational therapists, and such therapists' activities are essentially confined to hospital work. The doctor should be aware of the various community resources which can help his patient recreationally. Agencies such as family service agencies, YMCA, and public recreation commissions can give detailed information about any local area's facilities. Special age group activities, such as those of Golden Age groups, are also implied by the term, recreational therapy.

Educational Therapy

Much of a doctor's work with a patient, aside from direct medication or surgical intervention, can be considered a form of education. But the expression *educational therapy* refers to a doctor's referral of a patient to a qualified teacher for special instruction in a particular subject as part of a total treatment effort. Also, a doctor, especially in working with a young patient, may encourage the patient to seek further education so that the opportunities in life will be broadened. Many communities have adult education groups which offer an educational opportunity as well as enjoyable use of leisure time. If the doctor seriously desires that his patient seek further educational opportunities, he may well want to use a vocational counselor.

Vocational Rehabilitation

Many professional groups participate in rehabilitation work. Each state in the United States has a division of Vocational Rehabilitation, and the Veterans Administration offers comprehensive services. In many communities private nonprofit agencies provide rehabilitation services or sheltered workshop conditions. If the doctor is uncertain as to what local services are available, his medical society or the local family service agency will prove helpful.

A number of general hospitals have developed rehabilitation services in recent years. In this country the Department of Physical Medicine and Rehabilitation of the New York University College of Medicine at Bellevue Hospital under Dr. Howard Rusk's leadership was probably the first such service. This service's emphatic orientation has been that rehabilitation work should commence at an early point in any illness which has the possibility of becoming chronic. If chronic problems become fixed, any rehabilitative effort will be much more difficult.

The Clergy

Traditionally the clergy has provided help in times of sickness and need as part of their pastoral care. Today many clergymen have become especially interested in the help their counseling can provide to people with minor emotional difficulties. Increasing numbers of clergymen have had special training and experience in counseling techniques. Therefore the doctor can look to many clergymen for collaborative work which will add to the effectiveness of his patient care.

Lawyers

Doctors not uncommonly find that their patients present anxieties and disturbances secondary to life problems having to do with legal questions. Such problems may be accident suits, difficulties arising from the settlement of estates, business questions, questions of responsibility after a divorce, and the nature of responsibility for an incompetent family member. Although it may seem self-evident that legal advice is needed, the doctor will find that many patients are surprised and grateful that it is suggested.

CONSIDERATIONS INVOLVED IN PSYCHIATRIC CONSULTATION

At a number of points in this chapter and elsewhere in this book psychiatric referral has been discussed. A systematic presentation of the referral process may now be helpful. Referral involves preparation of a patient for psychiatric consultation, the indications and contraindications for such consultation, and expectations of gain from the consultative work.

Whenever a doctor has concluded that a psychiatric consultation will be helpful, the need for this consultation should be presented in a straightforward way. It is improper, for example, to present the psychiatrist as a neurologist. The doctor can tell his patient that there are emotional concomitants to all disease which need to be understood in order for the most effective treatment to be planned. The doctor can be emphatic in acquainting the patient with the fact that a psychiatric referral in no way indicates the presence of a serious mental illness (if the patient is thought not to have one). He can similarly acquaint the patient with the lack of stigma attending a psychiatric consultation or psychiatric treatment. *Such direct preparation and explanation on the doctor's part is often of critical importance if the consultation is to have a constructive outcome.* Many doctors find that it is very helpful to have a preliminary telephone discussion with the psychiatrist to whom they will be referring the patient to assure further that the referral will be conducted in a smooth and positive fashion.

The procedure of the psychiatric consultation should be outlined for the patient. The psychiatric interview will usually last approximately 50 minutes. The interview consists of talk, with a number of questions being asked of the patient. To the extent that the patient is able to talk freely and frankly the value of the consultation will be enhanced. The patient should be reassured that there will be communication between the referring doctor and the psychiatrist, unless there is some unusual situation which legislates against such communication.

Since so much of this book is a discussion of psychiatric problems, the indications for psychiatric consultation can be presented briefly in outline form. The commonest clinical situations meriting consultation are:

1. Somatic symptoms without physical basis or somatic symptoms which are inadequately explained by the physical disease which is present, particularly when such symptoms have not responded to the doctor's use of a supportive approach. Some of the common conditions presenting in this way are anxiety reactions, conversion hysteria, depressive reactions, hypochondriacal states, and paranoid conditions with somatic delusions.

2. Somatic illnesses with emotional complications which have not responded to a supportive approach. An instance of this type of problem would be the patient with myocardial infarction who develops a persistent depression.

3. Illnesses generally considered as emotional or functional in etiology but often handled in a general practice. An example of such a problem would be the alcoholic patient who has not responded to a supportive approach.

4. Illnesses in the category of "psychosomatic disease" where psychiatric consultation about the management of the patient is often valuable. Conditions such as duodenal ulcer, bronchial asthma, and hypertension will be included in this category.

5. Patients who appear to be "accident prone."

6. Patients for whom decisions regarding surgery involve the possibility of emotional complications, i.e., polysurgical patients, patients thought likely to develop postoperative psychoses, patients of an age group usually thought to be vulnerable emotionally to surgical procedures (see Chap. 7).

7. Patients for whom the diagnosis of a psychotic reaction is part of the differential diagnosis.

8. Patients who present as suicide risks.

9. Patients presenting problems of addiction.

10. Patients presenting sexual difficulties which the nonpsychiatrist feels require psychiatric help.

11. Patients with persistent sleep disturbances which are not the result of organic pathology. This group might be placed under 1, but there are so many patients with such problems that separate mention is made.

12. Patients with unexplained personality changes. Clinical conditions such as acute and chronic brain syndromes and incipient schizophrenia are most often responsible for such unexplained personality changes.

13. Patients in whom the doctor-patient relationship has become such a problem as to interfere with the patient's getting well or with the doctor's being able to help the patient. Special importance is given to the patient who has a history of getting along badly with several doctors. It is unlikely that such patients can benefit from medical treatment until they have had some psychiatric help.

14. Patients and families who have developed difficulties related to the placement of family members outside the home. For instance, patients who are emotionally unable to follow through on indicated placement of mentally defective children, chronic invalids, senile family members.

15. Patients with epilepsy for which the pharmacological management of the illness has not sufficed to maintain reasonable control.

16. Patients presenting problems in an essentially nonmedical way —behavior problems in children, marital problems, persistent occupational problems, any variety of character disorder complaints such as repetitiously self-defeating behavior.

When there is a manifest need for psychiatric consultation, there are very few contraindications for carrying through on a referral. The primary contraindication is the presence in the patient of such a degree of hostility and resistance to the idea of referral that it is clear that no benefit would be derived from efforts to encourage such a referral. The doctor's hope can be that over a period of time the patient and he can work toward a psychiatric consultation.

The nonpsychiatrist can reasonably expect a substantial amount of information to result from a psychiatric consultation, and, as in all consultation work, the referring doctor can anticipate prompt communication between himself and the psychiatrist. If possible, this communication should include a person-to-person conversation or a telephone conversation. An adequate consultation report should include a general discussion of the clinical situation, a diagnostic formulation, including a differential diagnostic discussion of the clinical diagnosis, and a brief presentation of the psychiatrist's thinking regarding the dynamic and genetic diagnosis. On the basis of his formulation the psychiatrist will be able to make suggestions regarding the future management of the patient, outline anticipated problems in the doctor-patient relationship, indicate the need for psychopharmacological agents, discuss the need for further diagnostic studies, or recommend continuing psychiatric treatment.

References

1. Ayd, F. J.: A critique of anti-depressants, Dis. Nerv. Syst., Vol. 22, Sec. 22, Suppl., May, 1961.
2. Heine, R. W., and Trosman, H.: Initial expectations of the doctor-patient interaction as a factor in continuance of psychotherapy, Psychiatry 23:275, 1960.
3. Hofling, C. K.: The place of placebos in medical practice, G.P. *11*: 103, 1955.
4. Kapp, F. T., and Gottschalk, L. A.: Drug therapy *in* Spiegel, E. A. (ed.): Progress in Neurology and Psychiatry, New York, Grune, 1962.
5. Lehmann, H. E.: Tranquilizers and other psychotropic drugs in clinical practice, Canad. M. A. J. 79:701, 1958.

Suggestions for Further Reading

Ayd, F. J.: A critique of anti-depressants, Dis. Nerv. Syst. Vol. 22, Sec. 22, Suppl., May, 1961.
Castelnuovo-Tedesco, P.: The twenty-minute "hour": an experiment in medical education, New Engl. J. Med. 266:283, 1962.
G. A. P. Report, No. 39: The psychiatrist's interest in leisure-time activities, August, 1958.
Lehmann, H. E.: Tranquilizers and other psychotropic drugs in clinical practice, Canad. M. A. J. 79:701, 1958.
Levine, M.: Psychotherapy in Medical Practice, New York, Macmillan, 1942.
Levine, M.: Principles of psychiatric treatment *in* Alexander, F., and Ross, H. (eds.): Dynamic Psychiatry, Chicago, Univ. Chicago Press, 1952.
MacLeod, J. A., and Middelman, F.: Wednesday afternoon clinic: a supportive care program, Arch. Gen. Psychiat. 6:56, 1962.
Novey, S.: The technique of supportive therapy in psychiatry and psychoanalysis, Psychiatry 22:179, 1959.
Szasz, T. S., and Hollender, M. H.: Contribution to the philosophy of medicine: basic models of the doctor-patient relationship, A.M.A. Arch. Int. Med. 97:585, 1959.
Whitehorn, J. C.: Understanding psychotherapy, Am. J. Psychiat. *112*: 328, 1955.

CHAPTER 14

Psychiatric Treatment Measures, Part 2. Measures Suitable for Use by the Psychiatrist

GENERAL REMARKS

In presenting an organized summary of psychiatric treatment measures, one thinks of two basic principles: (1) the differentiation of measures which are *definitive* (which attack the etiology of the disorder in question) from measures which are *symptomatic* (that remove or relieve a given symptom without necessarily affecting the etiology), and (2) the differentiation of measures which are *chemical or physical* in essence from measures which are essentially *psychological.*

Yet any division of the methods of psychiatric treatment into categories must remain somewhat arbitrary. What the psychiatrist is ultimately to treat—whether directly or indirectly—is, of course, the mind. It follows from the definition of mind given quite early in this textbook (p. 29) that mental illness, of any sort, is illness which affects the subject as a whole, as a functioning unit. If one considers the differentiation of physical-chemical from psychological measures, keeping these definitions in mind, one sees that no description of a physical or chemical technique is complete without a consideration of its psychological implications, and by the same token, that no description of a psychological technique is complete without a consideration of the physiochemical aspects involved.

From the complexities of the human mind it also follows that the differentiation of definitive from symptomatic measures is difficult and cannot be a hard-and-fast one. A series of intensive occupational therapy sessions, for example, can be used at times to provide a "corrective emotional experience" (p. 402), i.e., to reverse, in part, the effects of early traumatic experiences, and thus it can be a definitive treatment measure. Along the way, however, it may afford symptomatic relief of a secondary feature of the patient's illness, such as restlessness. For another example, consider a supportive psychotherapy (p. 440). Such a series of interviews may be undertaken purely for the purpose of affording the patient symptomatic relief. Yet if in the course of the therapy a deep-going identification with certain healthy features of the therapist's personality happens to occur, the psychotherapy will turn out to have been, at least in some aspects, of the definitive variety.

For purposes of discussion and study, however, the advantages of organizing the subject matter, utilizing the two principles mentioned, outweigh the difficulties and inaccuracies. One may profitably approach the subject of psychiatric treatment on the basis of the following rough outline (which is by no means exhaustive).

TREATMENT MEASURES*

1. Techniques Primarily Physical or Chemical
    A. Definitive measures
        a. Anti-infectious agents (p. 286)
        b. Replacement of nutritional deficiencies (p. 295)
        c. Replacement of hormonal deficiencies
        d. Certain neurosurgical techniques (p. 306)
    B. Symptomatic measures (May or may not affect etiology)
        a. Chemical
            (1) Stimulants (p. 458)
            (2) Sedatives (p.454)
            (3) Anticonvulsants (p. 300)
            (4) Tranquilizers (p. 455)
            (5) Insulin
            (6) Antidepressants (p. 459) (p. 358)
            (7) Antabuse (p. 413)
        b. Physical
            (1) Electroconvulsive therapy (electroshock therapy)
            (2) Physiotherapy (p. 463)
            (3) Psychosurgery
2. Techniques Primarily Psychological† (Most of these therapeutic measures may be used in either a definitive or a symptomatic way, depending upon circumstances.)

---

* Treatment measures discussed in other chapters are indicated by placing the page reference in parentheses behind them; if the measure has been discussed in the chapter immediately preceding this one, the reference is in italic.

† The various terms used under this heading which have not already been explained will be clarified in the present chapter.

A. Individual psychotherapy
    a. Suppressive psychotherapy (p. *436*)
    b. Supportive psychotherapy (p. *440*)
    c. Relationship psychotherapy (p. *450*)
    d. Expressive ("uncovering") psychotherapy
    e. Psychoanalysis (p. 85)
    f. Hypnotherapy (at any of the five levels)
    g. Play therapy (at any of the five levels)

B. Group psychotherapy
    a. Homogeneous groups (various levels)
    b. Heterogeneous groups (various levels)
    c. Psychodrama
    d. Ward meetings (including patient government)

C. Milieu therapy
    a. Ward (hospital) atmosphere
    b. Attitude therapy
    c. Environmental manipulation within the hospital

D. Activity therapy
    a. Occupational therapy (p. *462*)
    b. Recreational therapy (p. *464*)
    c. Educational therapy (p. *464*)
    d. Other (bibliotherapy, music therapy, etc.)

E. Indirect measures
    a. Working with and through family, friends, clergymen, employers (p. *465*)
    b. Manipulation of the external environment (recommending or arranging job changes, housing changes, vacations, changes in routine, etc.)

As stated in Chapter 13, and exemplified by it, a third way in which to divide therapeutic procedures used in psychiatric illness is to follow the example of surgery and speak of "major" and "minor" procedures; in this case, of "major psychiatry" and "minor psychiatry." Here, too, circumstances alter cases; there can be few clear dividing lines. In a general way, the reader is to consider any of the measures discussed in the preceding chapter (and indicated in the outline by the italic page references) to be suitable for the well-informed nonpsychiatrist under appropriate conditions. In the discussion which occupies the present chapter, these measures will not, for the most part, be given further consideration. In other respects, the order of the outline will be followed, with the exception that items under 1.A will not be discussed since they will have been presented in other courses (internal medicine, neurology, surgery).

PHYSICAL AND CHEMICAL THERAPIES PRIMARILY SYMPTOMATIC

Insulin

This hormone has two principal applications in the treatment of psychiatric difficulties: in small doses it acts as a sedative and serves to increase the appetite; in large doses it produces coma. The first of these applications is suitable for many situations that are by no means confined to the psychiatrist's practice. Many different types of patients, suffering from mild to moderate anxiety and anorexia in combination, will benefit symptomatically from the administration of from 5 to 15 units of regular insulin hypodermically about 20 minutes before meals.

Insulin coma therapy, originated by Manfred Sakel, then of Vienna, and first described in 1933, is a far more elaborate procedure and has a quite different objective. In this technique, the patient is invariably hospitalized on a psychiatric unit. Breakfast is withheld on the mornings of treatment, and the patient is given increasing doses of regular insulin every treatment morning until hypoglycemic shock is produced. Once deep coma has been achieved, it is usual for the patient subsequently to enter the comatose state with smaller doses than the one originally required. A full course of insulin coma therapy ("insulin shock therapy") involves the production of from 40 to 80 comas, usually at the rate of five or six a week.

Because of the physical hazards and the important psychological implications of this form of treatment, much is required of the psychiatrist and nurse in the way of knowledge, skill, and experience. Insulin shock should only be administered by a team of specialists in the technique.

Insulin coma therapy is much less widely used than was the case 15 years ago although very recently there has been a slight renascence of its use. Current opinion about its special merits is by no means uniform, but tends to reserve use to the treatment of certain schizophrenic reactions. In view of the hazards and inconvenience of the therapy, it is further restricted in most of the centers using it to those patients who have not responded to, or for one reason or another, are not considered suitable for tranquilizing agents, electroconvulsive therapy, or a combination of milieu and psychotherapy.

It is difficult to arrive at a satisfactory evaluation of the efficacy of insulin coma therapy in schizophrenia. For one thing (p. 360), there is good reason to believe that schizophrenia is not a single, sharply defined disease, but a symptom-syndrome whose etiology varies. Thus it is natural that some schizophrenic patients are more amenable to one type of therapy and others to another. Furthermore, there are variations in the technique of administering insulin coma, not only with respect to physical and chemical factors, but especially with respect to the type and intensity of the psychological techniques that are used concurrently. Finally, there are differences from one psychiatric center to another in the criteria and the terminology used in describing the results of treatment.

It is still believed in some quarters, however, that insulin coma therapy, particularly when reinforced by generally sound principles of in-patient treatment, is of definite value for some schizophrenic patients. It appears capable of bringing about a remission of psychotic symptoms in more than 75 per cent of schizophrenics who have been clinically ill for less than six months and in more than 25 per cent of patients who have been clinically ill for longer than six months. Some few of these patients—no one is certain as to exactly what percentage—will never have a subsequent episode of overt psychosis. Most of them will have relapses, especially if further therapeutic efforts are not made.

Antabuse

This chemical agent has been mentioned (in the chapter on Personality Disorders) and identified as tetraethylthiuram disulfide. It is a so-called "enzyme poison" and is not unique among drugs used in psychiatry inasmuch as certain of the psychopharmacological agents also act in this fashion. It is, however, unique in that it lies latent in the system, not exercising any appreciable effect unless the foreign substance, ethyl alcohol (or some closely related substance such as a barbiturate) is introduced.

In the case of Antabuse, the enzyme rendered inactive is one required for the metabolism of alcohol. As a result of the Anatabuse effect, the chemical breakdown of alcohol in the body is arrested at a stage that is normally a very fleeting one, the stage at which acetaldehyde is formed. A relatively large amount of the latter, quite toxic, substance is thus formed. The "Antabuse reaction" is, in fact, acute acetaldehyde poisoning.

The usual therapeutic procedure is to make certain that the patient has not been drinking for at least 24 hours (and is in reasonably good physical condition), and then to administer repeated doses of Antabuse over a period of several days until the desired blood level has been built up. (Usually requiring the administration of 1 Gm. of Antabuse—in tablet form—for three or four successive days.) Then this level can be maintained by a smaller, maintenance dose (usually, 0.5 Gm. daily).

Antabuse is both absorbed and excreted slowly; as a rule, therefore, at least two or three maintenance doses must be omitted before the patient can drink without becoming violently ill, and six or seven days before he can drink in comfort. While a person is on Antabuse, the amount of alcohol needed to produce nausea, vomiting, palpitation and general prostration is very slight: an ounce of whiskey or half a glass of beer is usually sufficient.

Recalling the material presented on alcoholism, the reader may well ask, if an alcoholic has sufficient ego strength (strength of purpose) to take a daily dose of Antabuse, knowing its effects when combined with alcohol, would he not have enough strength to stop drinking without the drug? Certainly the question is pertinent. In many instances an alcoholic who has made unsuccessful attempts to stop drinking without assistance will also be unsuccessful on an Antabuse regimen. However, it is at this point that various other psychological factors come into play, making the situation somewhat more hopeful.

The time element is the simplest of these factors. Since the ingestion of his daily Antabuse tablet requires only a moment, while the resulting protection persists for a period of at least several days, one can see the possibility that the defective self-control of the alcoholic can thus (artificially) be rendered more nearly adequate. If, for a single moment out of each day, the patient feels sufficiently free from anxiety and hostility to take the medication, he is ensured of many hours of protection, whereas without Antabuse he is forced to wage a more intensive and perhaps continuous inner struggle against the impulse to drink.

More significant in the long run is the emotional support that one attempts to give the patient along with the medical regimen. If the doctor is sincere, respectful, noncondemning, but firm, in time the patient may come to regard the medication as a gift, rather than as a threat or punishment. If, furthermore, there is a person in the patient's immediate environmen whom he respects and trusts, this figure is often brought into the treatment plan and made responsible for administering the daily dose of Antabuse. Such a technique often helps give the alcoholic the feeling that he is not alone in the fight, that his friends really want to help him, and this makes it a bit easier for him to accept the treatment plan.

In the preceding sentence, the accent should be upon the last word, *plan*. Antabuse does not constitute treatment for the alcoholic; it is one technique which in connection with others—and particularly with sustained contact with the physician—makes up a course of treatment. Thus, while it is proper for a psychiatrically oriented internist or general practitioner to utilize Antabuse, this use should only be in conjunction with a good over-all understanding of the case and willingness to follow it closely.

Electroconvulsive Therapy

This form of treatment was introduced in 1937 by Cerletti and Bini, Italian psychiatrists. In its original form, the procedure consisted of attaching electrodes to opposite sides of the patient's forehead and then using a special type of transformer (the "shock machine"), sending an alternating current of electricity (50 to 60 cycles per second, at a potential difference of about 100 volts, for 0.1 to 0.5 seconds) through the head. Ordinarily this procedure causes an almost instantaneous loss of consciousness, followed by a grand mal type of seizure with both tonic and clonic phases.

Many technical modifications of this procedure have been introduced over the past 25 years, of which several have gained general acceptance. One of these is the use of premedication, consisting usually of atropine and a barbiturate, for the purposes of anesthesia and of decreasing oropharyngeal secretions. Another is the use of a drug such as succinylcholine chloride (Anectine) to block the myoneural junction (i.e., to block the transmission of impulses from the motor nerves to the skeletal muscles). This technique allows all of the central nervous system features of a convulsion to take place, while markedly reducing the actual muscular spasms. (One of the relatively few complications of unmodified electroconvulsive therapy is the rather frequent production of strains, sprains, and—less commonly—fractures from the excessive muscular tensions.)

Another series of modifications has had to do with the position of the electrodes and with the amount, the type, and the timing of the current. It was soon learned that with the proper modifications the shock machine can be used to produce effects other than convulsions of a classic sort. For example, it can be used to stimulate selected portions of the brain. Since this effect is immediate and can be quite carefully graded, it is sometimes of great value in the treatment of profound drug intoxications (e.g., barbiturate coma as the result of a suicide attempt). The current can also be administered in such a manner as to produce loss of consciousness with a minimum, sustained quivering of the muscles, rather than a typical grand mal seizure. This type of treatment, ordinarily of from 3 to 5 minutes in duration, is called *electronarcosis*.

Electroconvulsive therapy (abbreviated as E. C. T.) has been used in the treatment of a wide range of psychiatric conditions. As with insulin coma—although less stringently so—current general opinion tends to restrict the use of this form of therapy to a rather small group of patients. Electroconvulsive therapy has been shown to be most effective in the treatment of psychotic depressions, where its results are usually striking.

Quite often the vegetative signs of depression begin to ameliorate after as few as two or three treatments. A full course of electroconvulsive therapy for a patient with a psychotic depression usually consists of from 10 to 15 treatments. Initially, treatments are ordinarily given at a frequency of three times a week; during the later phase of therapy they are spaced at greater intervals. Hospitalization of the patient depends primarily upon his clinical condition, rather than upon the therapy he is receiving as in the case of insulin treatment. In more than 80 per cent of psychotic depressions, a full remission of the depressive symptoms is obtained. Prepsychotic morbid personality characteristics are, of course, unaffected.

The next best results with E. C. T. are obtained in mania, as one would suppose from the close relationship between mania and psychotic depression. In the former reaction the results are not quite so favorable as in the latter, but they are sufficiently good as to warrant consideration of this method of treatment.

Among patients with schizophrenic reactions, electroconvulsive therapy has proved often effective in the symptomatic treatment of the catatonic and schizoaffective subgroups. Catatonic excitement and stupor frequently yield to E. C. T., and the affective component (euphoria, depression) of schizoaffective reactions usually disappears. The number of treatments needed to produce these results is similar to that needed in psychotic depression or mania. The more basic features of the schizophrenic reaction (ambivalence, autistic thinking, etc.) usually persist. If one attempts to influence these symptoms by E. C. T., a much longer course of treatment (30 to 60 shocks) is required, and even then the results are very uncertain. As a rule, the most that can be hoped for from such a course is a rather brief period of symptom remission.

No psychiatric disorder other than the ones just mentioned has responded in a consistently favorable way to electroconvulsive therapy although it has been widely tried. A qualified exception to this statement is that E. C. T. can usually afford specific relief from the undesirable affective features which may complicate an organic psychosis, such as dementia paralytica.

After a single electroconvulsive treatment, the patient usually experiences a brief period of mild confusion (i.e., a transient sensorial impairment). When a series of shock treatments (at a frequency of several times a week or oftener) is given, the sensorial impairment tends to become cumulative. Actually, the patient develops an artifically induced organic brain reaction. As a rule, these symptoms are rather mild, and they disappear with time. Even after a relatively long course of E. C. T., it is quite unusual for organic symptoms to persist for more than a few weeks or at most, a few months, after the last treatment.

Largely due to recent developments in the fields of chemotherapy and of milieu therapy, electroconvulsive therapy is being used with considerably less frequency than was the case five years ago. It is still in wide use, however (unlike insulin coma therapy) and because of the rapidity and power of its effects and the absence of physiological side effects (other than the organic syndrome), it bids fair to remain upon the therapeutic scene for some time.

Psychosurgery

This term is inclusive of all operative procedures on the central nervous system, undertaken in the absence of physical lesions (or at least independently of them), designed to affect the patient's psychological state. In other words, it is exclusive of such intracranial neurosurgical procedures as the removal of a meningioma or the repair of an aneurysm.

The founder of modern psychosurgery is Egas Moniz, a Portuguese neurosurgeon and neurophysiologist, who first published his work in 1936. The original operation came to be known as "prefrontal lobotomy." In this procedure, a large proportion of the fiber paths connecting the anterior portions of both frontal lobes with the rest of the central nervous system is severed. Since the pioneering work of Moniz, many new operations of a similar type have been devised. The procedure that has been performed by far the greatest number of times is the "transorbital lobotomy" of Freeman and Watts. This operation does not require burr holes (in the skull): the approach to the frontal lobes is made through the thin medial walls of the orbital cavities. The psychosurgical operation involving burr holes in greatest recent favor has been the one known as the "Grantham procedure," after its originator.

To make a broad generalization, one may say that the aim of most psychosurgical procedures is to reduce anxiety or other overpowering affects (as, for example, rage). Since this aim can now usually be achieved in a simpler, safer, and reversible fashion through the use of drugs, psychosurgery is rarely considered unless the newer methods have failed (not merely when used alone, but when used as part of such over-all treatment measures as those discussed on pp. 497 to 515).

When other methods have failed, psychosurgery is still considered in a few instances. Diagnostically speaking, these patients are usually in the categories of chronic schizophrenic reaction, severe, chronic obsessive-compulsive reaction, and severe hypochondriasis. A further prerequisite to lobotomy is a personal history indicating that the patient has, at some time in his past life, managed to make a moderately satisfactory adjustment. It must be remembered that in psychosurgical procedures one can only take something away from the patient's mental life; one cannot add anything. If the personality's resources have always been inadequate to effect a working adjustment, it is most unlikely that they will become adequate following psychosurgery.

TECHNIQUES PRIMARILY PSYCHOLOGICAL

Individual Psychotherapy

The term *psychotherapy* is used in a variety of ways. In the broadest sense, it actually becomes synonymous with the expression "psychological treatment measures" and refers to any treatment technique which strives for its effects through an approach to the patient as a person, as an integrated functioning unit. Psychological treatment measures fill a very wide range. For example, they do not necessarily even involve direct contact between the patient and the therapist. (One may treat a small child indirectly through counselling his parents.)

In the narrow sense, the one used in the present discussion as well as in the previous chapter, psychotherapy refers to a certain kind of direct relationship between one or more patients and a professional person, the therapist. Relationships are apt to have such complex and elusive features as to be very difficult to define simply and precisely, and the psychotherapeutic relationship is no exception. Perhaps no thoroughly satisfactory definition exists, but for practical purposes it is worthwhile to review briefly some of the typical and more important features.

As indicated in the previous chapter, individual psychotherapy typically consists in a series of private contacts between patient and therapist, during which communication is established and maintained primarily through verbal channels and in which, as Levine has simply put it, the therapist endeavors "to provide new life experiences which can influence the patient in the direction of health."*

As was also brought out in Chapter 13, the characteristics of a good parent-child relationship and of a good friend-friend relationship have pervasive similarities to those of psychotherapeutic relationships. Levine† has drawn a moving and informative parallel between the attitude of a good parent and that of a good psychotherapist. (Notice

---

* Levine, M.: Psychotherapy in Medical Practice, New York, Macmillan, 1943.
† Levine, M.: Principles of psychiatric treatment *in* Alexander, Franz and Ross, Helen (eds.): Dynamic Psychiatry, Chicago, Univ. Chicago Press, 1952.

how closely this fits with what the highest type of physician expects of himself in general.)

. . . the therapist would like his attitude to include all the attitudes that can characterize the helpful parent or older sibling. A good father is not too supporting; the therapist must not be. A good father sets limits to unacceptable behavior; so must the therapist. A good father can point out mistakes; so can the therapist. A good father is not frightened by threats; nor is the therapist. A good father can be firm without hostility; so should the therapist. A good father expects a growth in self-reliance; and so should the therapist. A good father is not always good and can make mistakes; the same goes for the therapist. A good father need not try to be the perfectly good father or completely well adjusted with his children; nor need the therapist with his patients.

The question naturally arises, Are there any truly unique characteristics of the therapeutic relationship? The answer is not an easy one. At the present state of knowledge, it appears most nearly correct to say that, while no single feature of the therapeutic relationship is unique, the combination of features is essentially so. The "how" of psychotherapy is dependent upon this combination of features.

There are, it is true, certain aspects of a good psychotherapist's knowledge, motivations, and behavior which are at least quantitatively different from those of the great majority of figures to whom the patient will have been called upon to relate.

The first of these applies with equal force to the psychotherapist who is a psychiatrist and the psychotherapist who is an internist, general practitioner, or other broadly informed specialist. It may be expressed as follows: *The therapist's legitimate strivings with respect to the patient and to the (psycho) therapeutic situation are few and relatively simple in contrast with the motivations the patient has encountered in most other figures.* For example, wishes and impulses such as the following—common enough in nonmedical relationships— have no legitimate place in the psychotherapist's mind: to judge or to be judged, to impress, to overawe, or to frighten, to compete or to submit, to seduce, or to be seduced. Even certain wishes of a sort which, while not desirable, are yet not actually uncommon in other aspects of medical practice, such as those to please, to be liked or loved, to be admired, or otherwise to gratify pride through the patient, are out of place in a psychotherapy unless they are of the mildest intensity, since they may interfere with the therapist's perception and judgment as well as distort the therapeutic relationship (at least for the patient).

Ideally, the psychotherapist wishes: (a) to understand the patient, and (b) to help him achieve a more effective adjustment to life. If the psychotherapy is other than supportive or suppressive (as delineated in the preceding chapter), the psychotherapist will have some wish for the patient to understand himself better. The deeper-going the therapy is, the more significant becomes this wish of the therapist, but it always remains subordinate to (b). If, as is the case in a majority of instances, the psychotherapy is part of a private medical practice, the therapist will, of course, wish (c) to receive material compensation for his services. *These three items essentially comprise the list of the effective psychotherapist's strivings in the treatment situation.* Of course, since he is a fallible human being, the therapist never fully achieves this simplicity of motivation, but it should be his continuing striving to do so. Notice how much simpler these strivings are than, for example, those that often influence parental behavior.

The second special aspect of an effective psychotherapist may be expressed by saying that he should be *equipped to achieve a more thorough understanding of the patient than can be reached by the figures in the patient's other relationships (at least, the nonprofessional ones).* Particularly should this be true of the preconscious and unconscious psychological factors, for the perception of which the psychotherapist should have cultivated a special sensitivity. There are quite permissible degrees in the depth and pervasiveness of this capacity for understanding. For example, there is no reason for a competent internist-psychotherapist to feel that he should duplicate the capacity of the psychoanalyst (any more than that the latter should feel that he must equal the former's grasp of physiology and pathophysiology). Yet, through such measures as his medical school psychiatry courses and clinical experience, study of technical books such as this one, reading of psychiatric articles in current journals, and above all, the continuous, unbiased observation of human nature, the nonpsychiatric psychotherapist should make it a point to have acquired an appreciably greater understanding of psychological matters than the well-informed layman or the physician not interested in doing psychotherapy. Experience in doing a certain amount of psychotherapy (comparable to some of the examples presented in the previous chapter) under psychiatric supervision is of great value and, in fact, is a necessary prerequisite if the psychotherapy is to be other than suppressive or supportive.

The third special aspect of a good psychotherapist is one which was illustrated very early in this book (pp. 47 to 48), namely that he should *know himself considerably better than does the average person.* (It might well be added that he should know himself better than those physicians need to who are not interested in doing psychotherapy.) Self-knowledge is certainly of value in all of medicine and in much of the rest of life, but it is of the greatest importance in psychotherapy for only the awareness of his own quirks and biases enables the therapist to discount their effects in appraising the patient's responses and to reduce the possibility of their getting in the way of treatment objectives.

It is of considerable practical value to differentiate various "levels" of psychotherapy, as noted in the previous chapter and recognized in the outline on page 471. In this context, "levels" does not refer to the duration or the seriousness of the treatment effort (nor necessarily to the length or frequency of the individual interviews), but primarily to the extent to which preconscious and unconscious material is encouraged or allowed to enter the patient's consciousness and become clarified and integrated into the personality as a result of the therapy.

The first two levels of psychotherapy, the suppressive and supportive, are, as has been indicated in the previous chapter, the most widely used of all. They will not be discussed further in the present chapter. Psychotherapies at the remaining levels and the highly specialized techniques of psychoanalysis and hypnotherapy will be considered in turn.

RELATIONSHIP PSYCHOTHERAPY. The terms, suppressive and supportive, are rather obviously descriptive of the techniques used in (or with) these types of therapy, but the term *relationship* requires some clarification, since by definition every direct mode of psychotherapy involves a relationship between patient and therapist. Perhaps the simplest way to begin is by mentioning again that the relationship, particularly in its conscious aspects, is here, to an exceptional degree, at the center of things. The therapist strives to maintain an interested, understanding, and nonjudgmental attitude, incorporating the various features mentioned in the paragraph quoted on page 479. He is realistic, unsentimental, and endeavors to help the patient appraise his own behavior and environment correctly. He will not approve of destructive or unhealthy components in the patient's behavior, but will nevertheless convey a fundamental acceptance of the patient himself as a human being with worthwhile potentialities.

In the setting of the therapy—which at this level generally takes on the characteristics of regular interviews of standard length—a significant interaction gradually takes place between patient and therapist. In addition to deriving benefits described in the previous chapter under the heading of suppressive and supportive approaches, the patient is given the opportunity for two other sorts of therapeutic experience. One is the considerable chance of making a (partial) identification with the therapist, to adopt certain of the latter's adjustment techniques, and to come to look at certain aspects of life from his (relatively) healthy standpoint. The other is the occurrence, from time to time in connection with the patient's current behavior and the material discussed in treatment, of what Alexander has called a "corrective emotional experience" (illustrated on p. 402 by Alexander's example of Jean Valjean).

The advantages of an opportunity for healthy identifications do not require explanation. The only point to be mentioned in this connection is that it is the greater intimacy of the topics suitable for discussion in a relationship psychotherapy which is primarily responsible for the greater opportunity for identifications. In a relationship therapy, patient and therapist *share more* than they are apt to do in therapies at suppressive and supportive levels.

The working of a corrective emotional experience is further illustrated by the following excerpts from case histories, one involving an out-patient and the other an in-patient.

G. L. was in psychotherapy for a combination of mild but chronic colitis and obsessive-compulsive personality difficulties. The patient treated time with the precision he would use in counting money or writing a check. On one occasion, despite genuine and considerable effort, he arrived at his appointment ten minutes late—an extraordinary thing for him—markedly uneasy at having kept the physician waiting. Without being self-depreciatory, the latter made light of the incident, knowing that the patient had been affected in a seriously adverse way by overstrenuous early training in neatness, cleanliness, and punctuality. The patient was dumbfounded, having expected some form of retaliation from the doctor. The net effect of the episode was slight, but clearly and lastingly beneficial, as shown in the patient's being from that point on somewhat more relaxed in the sessions than he had previously been able to be.

R. B., an 18-year-old boy, was hospitalized for long-term treatment of a severe personality disorder of a mixed type, having exhibitionism as a major feature.

The patient's mother, it was learned, had been rather flirtatious toward him (as a small boy), but fundamentally rejecting. R. B. had a deep-seated ambivalence toward women. He had great (largely unconscious) feelings of guilt over both his erotic and hostile impulses toward them. One of his behavior patterns had been to exhibit his penis to young girls in a menacing fashion, causing them to become frightened and to run. Because of his guilt feelings, the patient tended to neglect precautions for his own safety, and he had been caught and legally punished prior to hospitalization.

In the psychiatric hospital, R. B. at first behaved in a rather unobtrusive manner. He was assigned to a psychiatrist for an exploratory period of psychotherapy, but aside from this relationship he remained fairly aloof from personal contacts. Gradually, however, he developed an attachment to the psychiatric charge nurse.

One evening when it had been necessary for this nurse, despite her senior status, to work on the 3 to 11 shift, R. B. approached her after the other patients had retired and exposed himself to her, muttering aggressively. The nurse, who was exceptionally well trained and emotionally mature, remained perfectly calm and self-possessed. She did not cry out, run, or assume a threatening attitude. She asked the patient in a courteous but quite firm manner to dress himself properly. She followed up by saying that if he were lonely or frightened or angry, there were better ways of expressing these feelings than by his routine of exhibitionism.

The patient was much taken aback by the charge nurse's composure. He responded by compliance, with a mixture of gratitude and anxiety. Since he was restless and insomnic, the nurse gave him a cup of hot chocolate and conversed with him for a few moments before suggesting that he return to bed.

No striking change in the patient's general psychological status seemed to result, but in retrospect, it became clear that the incident had constituted a turning-point in the direction of health.*

While the second vignette was highly dramatic, the first illustrates the fact that this outward characteristic is not always a necessary one. What is needed in the therapist is an understanding of the specific early traumata of the patient and a keen sense of timing in the execution of his key responses. On the other hand, generally considerate, healthy, mature behavior on the part of therapeutic figures usually carries with it some possibility of at least mildly corrective experiences for patients since all neurotic conflicts are in part based upon childhood experiences in which the responses of key figures were in some fashion immature, unhealthy, and self-centered.

In contrast with suppressive and supportive treatment, relationship psychotherapy (like expressive therapy and psychoanalysis) has the aim of helping the patient advance in maturity and emotional stability *beyond his best previous adjustment.* It may be thought of whenever the patient needs extensive help, but is well enough to form a close working relationship. One may eventually conclude that a fuller solution to the patient's residual early conflicts is called for, in which case expressive psychotherapy or analytic therapy will be required.

It is a more difficult matter to offer an opinion as to the suitability of relationship psychotherapy as a treatment modality of the nonpsychiatrist than it is to offer an opinion about the suitability of therapy at the other four levels. With respect to suppressive and supportive therapy, one can say with assurance that many a nonpsychiatric physician should equip himself to do this kind of work. With respect to expressive psychotherapy and psychoanalysis, one can say with assurance that, without intensive psychiatric training in the one case and psychoanalytic training in the other, the nonpsychiatrist should

---

* The nurse was not a psychotherapist of the patient in the strict sense, yet her continuing relationship with him and her own considerable ability enabled her to carry out the corrective experience (in this instance) just as might be done in an organized psychotherapy.

not attempt to use these methods. Regarding relationship psychotherapy, perhaps the soundest position is that there are several prerequisites additional to those mentioned for doing the less ambitious types of psychotherapy: (1) an innate suitability of temperament; (2) some formal training in psychotherapy; and (3) frequent contacts with a psychiatrist of a consultatory-supervisory nature, particularly to ensure the necessary recognition of *transference* and *counter-transference* problems (p. 451 ff).

EXPRESSIVE PSYCHOTHERAPY characteristically includes most of the features of a relationship therapy, but goes beyond it in including "the goals of a greater awareness (on the part of the patient) of the determinants of the illness, and emotional reorientation, and a more mature perspective with regard to these determinants, an increase in ego capacity and strength, and more specific and central corrective experiences."*

In this form of treatment there exists a considerable range with respect to the depth at which patient and therapist work. At one extreme would be a therapy in which the patient would be encouraged to verbalize freely and fully—using a technique in essence like that of ordinary conversation—thoughts, feelings, worries, and problems of which he is already aware, but in which no special attempt would be made to get at unconscious material. At the other extreme would be a therapy in which, in addition to conversational methods, special techniques would be employed to facilitate the release and expression of material which had been repressed or otherwise warded off from consciousness. (The utilization of such techniques would bring the therapy close to psychoanalysis, the next method to be described.)

Expressive psychotherapy requires more of both patient and therapist than the methods previously discussed. Of the patient, it requires that he be emotionally strong enough to bear successfully the initial stress of the new insights (as well as the stress of waiting for the insights to occur). Of the therapist, it requires that he be discerning enough to understand the essentials of what is going on in the therapy, both in an over-all way and from hour to hour, and to exercise an even keener sense of timing (as to which trains of thought to encourage and which to discourage or subordinate) than is needed in the previously described types of therapy.

PSYCHOANALYSIS. Like "psychosomatic" the term *psychoanalysis* is one about which the student may have some understandable confusion, for it has been subject to widespread careless usage. Actually the word is correctly used to designate (1) *a method* of (a) psychotherapy and

---

* Levine, M.: Principles of psychiatric treatment *in* Alexander, Franz and Ross, Helen (eds.): Dynamic Psychiatry, Chicago, Univ. Chicago Press, 1952.

(b) of psychological research, and (2) *a body of facts and theories* of human psychology.

Both the method and the body of knowledge represent the work of Sigmund Freud and his followers. Freud, as the student very likely knows, was a renowned Viennese neurophysiologist, neurologist, and psychiatrist, who lived from 1856 to 1939, and was the first to demonstrate scientifically the power and the modes of operation of unconscious forces in the personality.* The facts and many of the theories of psychoanalysis have come to form the core of dynamic psychiatry as it is being taught in this country today; much of this material has been presented in this book. Our present concern, however, is with the method.

As with other branches of medical science, certain trappings have come to be associated with psychoanalysis. Through popularization of them in motion pictures, in the theatre, and on television, the general public has become thoroughly familiar with them. Everyone knows, for example, that in analytic treatment sessions the patient lies on a couch, so placed that he cannot observe the therapist but the therapist can observe him. Nearly everyone knows that analytic treatment is intensive and prolonged (with 45- or 50-minute sessions at a frequency of four to six times a week, often lasting several years), and therefore expensive. Many persons realize that such treatment can be performed effectively and legitimately only by therapists who have had rigorous special training.

While matters such as the physical positions of patient and therapist and the frequency and duration of treatment are not unimportant, they by no means constitute the essence of psychoanalysis. Just as expressive psychotherapy may be thought of as an extension of relationship therapy, psychoanalysis may be considered as an extension of expressive therapy (while still retaining certain features of relationship therapy).† *The salient feature of psychoanalysis is that the unconscious determinants of the patient's personality and behavior, including those factors which have arisen in his earliest years, are explored and clarified with a thoroughness not approached in other methods of psychotherapy.*

Various techniques are utilized to facilitate the exploration and clarification. The so-called "basic rule" of psychoanalysis is the seemingly simple one that, unless he is instructed otherwise, the patient is

---

* See Jones' biography of Freud in Suggestions for Further Reading.

† It is worth mentioning as a matter of historical fact, that the actual development occurred in the reverse direction: the technical and theoretical understanding gained through psychoanalysis has made possible scientific psychotherapy at more superficial levels.

to communicate with the analyst through the process of *free-association*. As mentioned earlier (p. 85), in this process the patient strives, to the limit of his ability, to avoid conscious direction of his thoughts, thus allowing his stream of talk to represent the spontaneous play of his thoughts, much as in a reverie or daydream. Under these conditions, preconscious and unconscious forces in the personality tend to reveal themselves with gradually increasing clarity. The analyst is relatively passive (overtly) in the sense that he does not attempt to direct the patient's mental productions (for the most part) and does not advise or counsel, confining himself largely to giving close attention, asking occasional questions, and, when he deems it helpful, offering interpretations of the material (suggestions as to the basic meaning of what the patient is thinking, feeling, or doing).

In addition to free-association, various other means are utilized to facilitate awareness and comprehension of hitherto unconscious forces. For example, such slips of the tongue and of behavior as naturally occur from time to time (and actually tend to occur with greater frequency in the treatment situation) are examined by analyst and patient for the light they shed upon unconscious motivations and feelings. Similarly, the patient is encouraged to report his dreams, which, when carefully studied, reveal wishes and fears that are kept out of waking consciousness by repression. (The study of dreams has formed one of the cornerstones of psychoanalysis and hence of dynamic understanding of the personality. This subject is, however, too complex for adequate treatment here.)

Although the foregoing account may be sufficient to suggest that psychoanalysis is not an easy psychological transaction for either patient or analyst, it falls short of indicating the nature of the principal technical difficulty. The problem may be summarized in this way: The emotional illness for which the patient has sought treatment has arisen on the basis of his using pathogenic defense mechanisms to avoid the experiencing of keen anxiety (and related negative feelings). In psychoanalytic treatment, the patient is asked to relax, and, to an extent, to relinquish the use of these mechanisms, at least to the point of seeing, with the analyst, the ultimate nature of his inner conflicts. Therefore, the very motivations which have led to the development of the illness come into action (unintentionally) to oppose the work of the treatment. Only through the development of a strengthening relationship to the analyst and through keeping in mind the ultimate benefits to be derived from the treatment, can the patient gain the courage to lay aside his illness-producing defenses sufficiently to get a look at his basic problems. This appraisal then, hopefully, brings the opportunity of the patient's utilizing his intelligence and judgment in beginning the solution of his problems; a partial solution is further strengthening, allowing more therapeutic work to be done; and so on.

MORE ABOUT TRANSFERENCE. One highly significant aspect of the patient's relationship to the analyst and a quite fundamental aspect of psychoanalytic treatment has to do with the phenomenon which, as has already been mentioned, is called *transference*. This phenomenon was the discovery of Freud. While fully exploited therapeutically only in psychoanalysis, it occurs (in varying degrees of intensity) in every psychotherapy and, in fact, in all other (childhood and adult) relationships as well. (See references on pp. 451 to 452.)

Transference may be defined as (1) *the attributing by the subject to a figure in his current environment of characteristics first encountered in some figure of his early life,* and (2) *the experiencing of desires, fears, and other attitudes toward the current figure which originated in the relationship with the past figure.* Since the phenomenon is entirely subjective, it would be more accurate to say "impressions first received of some figure in early life" than "characteristics first encountered."

Transference, *as a process*, always occurs unconsciously and automatically, arising out of the inner needs of the subject. Accordingly, while it may be facilitated by any coincidental similarities between the current figure and the past figure, transference is always in some measure *inappropriate* (to the current figure and/or to the real situation) and sometimes markedly so. The *effects* of transference may, at times, be largely conscious; the subject may remark (inaccurately), for example, that a figure in his current life is "just like" a figure from the past.

The episode on page 482, involving the exhibitionistic patient and the psychiatric nurse, may be viewed as an illustration of transference, in which the patient was not at all aware of the process and only partly aware of the effects. The nurse, however, realized that the patient's responses to her were taking place (in part) on the basis of a "mother transference,"* and she was greatly assisted in her own responses by this realization. In the first place, her general understanding that there was a strong transference element in the patient's motivations made it unnecessary for her to take personal offense at his behavior. Secondly, the more specific realization that the transference sprang from certain unwholesome aspects of the patient's early relationship with his mother guided the nurse in her specific responses to the unconventional, aggressive-erotic behavior.

---

* In describing the transference of a patient in psychotherapy, one endeavors to specify the nature of the feeling or attitude involved and the figure in the patient's early life toward whom it was first experienced.

A number of excerpts from case histories offered earlier in this book will, on re-examination, be found to illustrate the influence of a transference element. For example, the young doctor (p. 44) who felt an "instinctive" dislike of swarthy older men was *transferring* to such persons feelings which had originated in the early unpleasant relationship with his father's cousin. In this example, the transferred attitude was so clearcut, so automatic, and so obviously irrational, that the young man realized, even before entering psychoanalysis, that it required explanation.

Oftener than not, transference phenomena occurring outside of psychotherapy are subtler, less conspicuous than in the example just cited. Everyone has experienced something of the sort and, if the reader will reflect carefully, he will probably be able to think of one or more instances in which his responses to some figure of his current life have clearly been influenced by transference elements. One rather reliable clue to the existence of transference factors in a relationship is the rate at which one's attitude toward the other person takes form. Love, hate, or any other attitude that springs into being more or less "at first sight," before one has had the opportunity to get to know the object of the feeling, is almost always influenced by transference factors.

Since transference is a universal phenomenon, it is experienced by therapeutic figures toward their patients as well as by patients toward their therapists. Primarily for the sake of convenience in discussion, such feelings on the part of therapists toward their patients are usually referred to as "counter-transference." (See discussion on pp. 451 to 452.)

In the psychoanalytic situation, the patient's transference feelings and behavior become a very important focus of treatment. The development and the eventual full clarification of such phenomena give a special power and depth to this form of psychotherapy. As one can readily believe, it is far more effective to explore a neurotic conflict through a consideration of emotions and impulses being consciously experienced at the time (within the therapeutic hour) than it is to work primarily with emotions whose existence can only be inferred or with the memories of emotions or even with emotions being experienced but far past their peak of intensity.

In therapeutic situations other than psychoanalysis, an awareness of transference phenomena in general and of the specific transference expressions in the patient with whom one is working is also of major importance. In such instances (aside from the deeper forms of expressive psychotherapy), the objective is usually not the giving of conscious insight to the patient on this score, but, rather, the utilization of such knowledge to guide one's responses to the patient, to make them more fully therapeutic.

HYPNOTHERAPY. Hypnosis has been twice mentioned in earlier portions of this book, once in connection with experimental evidence of the existence of unconscious mental forces (p. 42) and once in connection with differential diagnosis and (as it proved) palliative treatment of the young patient with tetanus (p. 320). No attempt was made to define hypnosis in those references and, indeed, the fact is that despite the antiquity of the phenomenon, there remains even today, some question as to its scientific definition. A simple, rather crude definition might be as follows: *Hypnosis is an artifically induced state, somewhat akin to sleep, in which the subject enters so close a relationship with the hypnotist that the suggestions of the latter become virtually indistinguishable from activity of his own ego.* A more scientific definition is that *hypnosis is a state in which a portion of the ego functions with a certain autonomy as a subsystem or subagency of the mind, experiencing a regression which places it in the control of the hypnotist.* To speak a bit figuratively, one might say that in hypnosis the over-all ego lends a portion of itself, an organized portion, to the hypnotist; while the loan is in force, this portion is the hypnotist's agent in controlling the behavior of the subject; when, however, it becomes really important to the over-all ego to do so, the loan may be recalled (see below). Hypnosis thus constitutes an example of a (temporary and partial) *regression in the service of the ego* (which, as a whole, desires to be hypnotized). It thus bears comparison not only with sleep but with certain waking activities in which a serviceable regression takes place, such as becoming engrossed in a game or in some sport.

Before discussing the therapeutic applications of hypnosis, it may be of value to clear away certain rather common misconceptions of this psychological experience. (1) Hypnotizability is not a rare characteristic of human beings. In theory, at least, it may be a universal characteristic; in practice, with the use of sufficient time and the initial assistance of sedative drugs, a decided majority of individuals can experience some degree of hypnosis. (2) Hypnotizability is not indicative of a "weak will" (minimal ego strength), nor of a limited intelligence. As a matter of fact, a normal or superior intelligence and a generally strong ego can be assets in the process of induction, since a considerable effort at concentration is involved. (3) In the normal or near-normal individual, there is no risk of the hypnotic state's persisting indefinitely, once induced. Should the hypnotist leave the subject in a trance state, the latter will eventually fall into a natural sleep and then awaken in his normal psychological state. (4) Except under the most extreme and artificial conditions, the normal or near-normal hypnotic subject cannot be induced to violate his habitual standards of conduct to any appreciable degree (the superego is not overthrown or deprived from access to the main body of the ego). Should a suggestion be given during the trance which would require such a violation for its execution, the subject tends to waken spontaneously. (The "loan" is "recalled.")

On the other hand—and despite the point of comparison mentioned above—hypnosis is no parlor game. It should always be considered a scientific procedure, and hypnotherapy should be considered a medical procedure. Certain risks are involved in the experience. Accordingly, the hypnotherapist will need special training to be able to appraise these risks soundly and take appropriate measures if the patient becomes disturbed as a result of the procedure. For example, if there is reason to believe that the patient's ego is fundamentally quite weak, hypnotherapy may be contraindicated since the experience of induction may prove to be an excessive strain. Similarly, if it appears likely that the patient will misinterpret the hypnotic experience in an erotic fashion (as a sexual advance, either heterosexual or homosexual), one must take precautions against such a misinterpretation or select some other therapeutic technique.

It should be emphasized that hypnosis, per se, like free-association in the waking state, is but a *technique*. It is used to implement some form of treatment and is not a treatment in itself. (In the felicitous expression of H. Rosen, "patients with emotional disease, if hypnotized, are to be treated not *by*, but *under* hypnosis.") That is to say, all the work of diagnosis, of defining objectives, and of making a decision as to the correct level of psychotherapy in any given case, must precede a consideration of what the technique of hypnosis may have to contribute to the efficacy of the therapeutic program. A hypnotherapy can be carried on at any of the levels which have been described. (The usual procedure is for a portion of every interview to be conducted with the patient in the trance state, with the remainder being handled in the usual fashion.)

To illustrate the technical modifications introduced with the use of hypnosis, examples will be given of hypnotherapy at a suppressive level and hypnotherapy at an expressive level.

In a suppressive hypnotherapy, the usual objective is the removal of a given symptom or of a given bit of symptomatic behavior. To generalize, one might say that this approach is suitable for patients in whom the symptom is consciously quite unpleasant and the underlying neurosis (or neurotic personality) is relatively mild. For instance, various minor disturbances of the sort usually thought of as undesirable habits may be reduced or entirely suppressed. Examples would be excessive smoking, moderate overeating, "nervous" clearing of the throat, and minor speech difficulties. In some cases the symptom remission must be maintained by hypnotic sessions—in which the suggestions are repeated and reinforced in various ways—continued over a long period of time, or perhaps indefinitely, although at a very low frequency.

The young man with the conversion symptom of blindness (pp. 314 to 316) might have been treated symptomatically under hypnosis. To avoid the error of the over-ambitious therapist in the receiving ward, one would have had to proceed at a gentler and more leisurely pace. In a series of hypnotic sessions over a period of several days, suggestions might have been given with increasing strength and directness that the patient's vision would return. In the meantime, various types of supportive measures, such as reassurance and practical advice as to handling the problems of a new father, would have been offered, both in the trance and in the waking state. *No interpretations would have had to be given.* Under these conditions, it might well have turned out that the patient could have relinquished the symptom of blindness without undue stress and resumed his previous level of adjustment. (As in the actual case, however, the patient would still have benefited from a subsequent period of expressive psychotherapy, and this should be recommended.)

When hypnosis is used as an adjunct to an expressive psychotherapy, it may be useful in a number of ways. For example, the feeling of alliance with the hypnotist may be used to facilitate the lifting of certain repressions of the patient (if they are only moderately strong) by appropriate suggestions given during the trance. In this way, memories of past traumatic experiences can be brought into consciousness and considered by doctor and patient. Subsequently, it often becomes easier for the patient to recall the same material in the normal waking state, at which time he may be able to understand the experiences and their effects and to gain some degree of inner mastery over them.

As another example, the hypnotherapist may suggest to the patient in the trance state that he will dream in a relatively undisguised way about a given subject. Such a suggestion is very often followed, and the resulting dream may give the therapist an enhanced understanding of the patient's conflicts in this area. (Depending upon the patient's psychological status at the time, this understanding may be conveyed to him or it may be postponed.)

Mention of the lifting of repression under hypnosis leads naturally to a few words about hypnoticlike states induced primarily by the use of drugs. In such therapeutic efforts, the drug of choice is usually Pentothal sodium or Amytal sodium, administered by slow intravenous injection with the patient lying down. This technique of treatment has been used fairly extensively in military psychiatry; its principal application is in the treatment of traumatic neuroses (pp. 308 to 310). In these cases, the patient is seen not long after the traumatic event(s). Under the drug, he is encouraged to recall vividly the entire traumatic experience that has brought about the neurosis (the memory of which has been in large part repressed). With the help of the drug and the suggestions of the therapist, the recollection is apt to become so realistic to the patient as to constitute a reliving of the experience. (This type of vivid recall with the expression of emotion[s] appropriate to the original situation is termed *abreaction.*) At each such reliving, the patient's ego becomes more nearly able to master the anxiety and the fear mobilized by the original trauma. It is assisted in this task by the active support and reassurance given by the therapist. After a number of such sessions, normal ego control of the personality is often reestablished, bringing an end to the traumatic neurosis. This method of treatment is called *narcosynthesis.*

Interest in hypnosis has increased markedly during the past 15 years among the general public, among physicians, among members of allied disciplines, and among members of quasi-professional groups. It is not unusual to find hypnosis used, in one way or another, by psychologists, dentists, osteopaths, chiropractors, and faith-healers. This practice is to be deplored—not because the technique is so difficult, but because it tends to be used without the dynamic and clinical understanding of the patient which is a necessary safeguard. It is hard to form a good estimate of the percentage of cases suffering untoward psychological results from the indiscriminate use of hypnosis, but it is a certainty that on occasion severe morbid reactions are thus precipitated. Apart from legitimate research, the use of hypnosis should be restricted to members of the medical profession, and further, to those who have met the requirements for carrying on suppressive and supportive psychotherapies and who, in addition, have had a course of formal instruction in hypnotic techniques.

PLAY THERAPY. Since this form of therapy is primarily a means of the psychiatric treatment of children, its discussion will be deferred until the following chapter.

Group Psychotherapy

Just as any good relationship between two persons contains many of the elements of an individual psychotherapy, so does any well-knit group, working effectively under a competent leader toward a common purpose, contain many of the elements of a group psychotherapy.

When a unit is formally organized for psychotherapeutic purposes, it typically consists of from four to, perhaps, twelve patients, plus one or two professionals. (In general, the size of the group is inversely proportional to the intended depth of the therapy.) If there are two professional figures, they may be co-leaders (co-therapists) of the group, or one may be the leader and the other secretary (recorder). Frequently the group is conducted by a single professional person, who then assumes the task of keeping the record. The frequency and duration of the meetings vary from one group to another, but, ordinarily, not so widely as in an individual psychotherapy. Typically, meetings are held at a frequency of once or twice weekly, and they last from 45 minutes to 1½ hours. (Once agreed upon, the frequency and duration are kept constant.)

The principal function of the group therapist has often been compared to that of a catalyst in a chemical reaction. It is the therapist's task to regulate the rate at which the interactions take place between the various members of the group and between every individual member and the group as a whole. Sometimes the therapist serves as a resource person, supplying relevant information. He may exercise some direction over the areas being explored by the group. He does this by raising appropriate questions, summarizing what he takes to be the group's consensus, and occasionally by offering tentative interpretations, either of the behavior (verbal and otherwise) of the group or of any member of it. This activity of the therapist is carried out in a relatively unobtrusive manner, so as not to interfere with the natural processes of the development of group spirit or of expression, learning, and developing insight on the part of the group and its individual members.

If there is a recorder, he ordinarily remains silent during the group session, confining himself to making careful observations of what is going on within the group and writing down these observations in a careful but inconspicuous fashion. The therapist and the recorder (or the two therapists) meet privately between regular sessions of the group to review the occurrences of the latest meeting, to look for trends of thought or emotion continuing to develop through a number of meetings, and to compare opinions as to the dynamic significance of what the various members of the group said and did. If a therapist is conducting a group unassisted, he must allow a comparable period of time between sessions to reflect upon what has taken place. (So much activity of psychological significance is apt to occur in a group session that such a regular reviewing of material is necessary if the therapist is to keep abreast of developments.)

The bulk of opinion is that group psychotherapy is not suitable for working at the very deepest psychological level for a number of reasons, one of which is that discussion naturally tends to take precedence over free-association; but it is a therapeutic method of considerable range and flexibility. The experiences of the members can be intense and productive.

There is a moderately common misconception that group psychotherapy is used largely for reasons of economy, i.e., that in this way one or two therapists can treat a considerably larger number of patients than they could otherwise do, and that therefore the cost per patient is much reduced. Actually, economy is one of the less important reasons for recommending group therapy, being appreciable only when a single therapist can handle a rather large group, i.e., when the therapy has quite limited goals.

Patients are assigned to psychotherapeutic groups primarily because of the specific characteristics of this mode of treatment. With certain patients these characteristics offer definite advantages over individual psychotherapy. For example, it may be of marked value for a somewhat withdrawn guilt-laden patient to hear others express some of the very conflicts which have troubled him so deeply and which he has felt were uniquely his. For another example, consider a patient who experiences great difficulty in relating individually to authority figures, but who feels moderately comfortable with his peers. Such a person, whatever his (other) conflicts, may express himself far better in group psychotherapy than in individual psychotherapy, since in the group situation most of the therapy is carried on in discussion and other forms of verbal interchange with fellow patients and, further, the patient may feel that he has the support of the group in his relationship with the therapist(s).

Since group therapy can provide experiences of a sort different from those of individual therapy, it is often helpful to arrange for a patient to have both types of treatment, either in succession or concurrently. In the latter case, the patient's experiences in the group may be productive of both inner and overt responses that can be very profitably explored in the individual psychotherapy sessions.

Many different types of groups can be organized, depending upon the functions to be served, the level at which the work is to be carried on, and external circumstances. Some groups, especially those that serve a research as well as a therapeutic purpose, are by design quite homogeneous. For instance, a group may consist entirely of young male alcoholics, or of the wives of alcoholics, or of young female schizophrenics. Apart from any research function, it may be decided to form a homeogeneous group when the therapy is intended to be primarily on a suppressive or supportive level, since many of the same ideas would then be helpful to a majority of the group.

It is commoner, however, for the group to be rather heterogeneous, as for example, the patient population of a convalescent unit, or a group having a clinical diagnosis in common, but of both sexes, a wide age range, and different stations in life.

Whatever the composition of the group, an important factor in the success of the therapy is that the membership be rather stable. While the loss or gain of one or two members is not apt to interfere with the group's progress—and may even prove stimulating—it is necessary that a sizeable nucleus of the membership remain the same throughout the therapy, in order that a "group spirit" can develop and continuity in the work be maintained.

PSYCHODRAMA. This variation of group psychotherapy has sufficiently distinct characteristics to warrant brief separate consideration. As ordinarily carried out, each session begins with the enactment by selected members of the group (more or less in rotation) of some conflict situation in human relations. Examples might be: a young girl brings home to dinner a boy friend of whom her parents disapprove; a man is detected in some legal but unethical act. All of the acting is extemporaneous and the lines are improvised. Following the episode, group discussion takes place, with all of the members of the group participating. The discussion may take as its focus the various aspects of the situation enacted, the interpretation of his role given by any of the participants, the presentation of similar real-life experiences of any of the members of the group, etc.

In the early sessions of such a group, the selection of the episode to be portrayed and the "casting" are usually done by the therapist. Later, these functions are taken over by members of the group, and the therapist's contributions are largely confined to those associated with the standard form of group psychotherapy.

The selection of psychodrama over the conventional type of group therapy is not so much a matter of clinical considerations as it is of the temperament of the therapist and the aptitudes of the group. The greater element of structure in this form of therapy allows the group to proceed somewhat less impeded by unavoidable alterations in the membership.

WARD MEETINGS constitute a form of supportive group psychotherapy especially adapted to residence in a hospital (not necessarily a psychiatric hospital). Here the membership is usually composed of the regular patient population of a given unit. As in the other forms of group psychotherapy, a psychiatrist is ordinarily the group leader although this position is sometimes taken by the charge nurse (on a psychiatric unit) or the physician-in-charge (on a nonpsychiatric unit). Sometimes the other physician or the nurse may serve as co-leader with the psychiatrist, or one may serve as leader and one as recorder.

Unlike most other forms of group psychotherapy in which the therapeutic intent is obvious and explicit, the ward meeting serves certain practical purposes of organized group living ("administrative" purposes, in a very broad sense); its therapeutic function is therefore subtler. The ward meeting has as its natural initial focus the discussion of matters pertaining to life in the hospital: diet, physical facilities, treatments, routines, privileges, restrictions. If matters are discerningly handled, the group will gain in confidence and cohesiveness, and will usually begin to touch on feelings about one another and about hospital personnel. Complaints, both realistic and unrealistic, naturally come to the fore; so do feelings of each patient about certain aspects of his illness.

Since the members of such a group live together, they start off knowing more about one another than is the case with the members of many other groups, and many insights (in a superficial sense) can develop from sessions having as their original or nominal focus some practical ward matter. How far such sessions should be encouraged or allowed to move in the direction of greater depth is a matter of the discretion and the experience of the leader. (An increase in frequency of meetings, the exclusion of observers, and the asking of well-timed provocative questions by the therapist tend to favor a greater depth; a decrease in frequency, invitations to observers, and the offering of reassurance and generalizations by the therapist tend to favor a lessening of depth.) If the group is suitable and interested and if the tensions are not too great, the interaction may come to approximate that which develops in group psychotherapy sessions unencumbered by administrative matters.

A variation of the ward meeting which has come into increasing use, particularly on long-term psychiatric treatment units, is "ward government" or "patient government." In this situation, patients, usually although not necessarily of a convalescent ward, are encouraged to elect a fixed number of representatives, of whom one serves as presiding officer ("ward president" or "ward chairman"). These representatives serve in a variety of ways, most of which could be grouped under the general headings of interpatient communication and functioning and liaison with personnel.

The presiding officer is typically in charge of the ward government meetings. As a rule both patients and personnel attend the meetings, but, perhaps with the exception of the psychiatrist in charge ("ward manager"), the personnel do not participate in the proceedings unless called upon to do so. The ward manager may serve as an auxiliary group leader, allowing the elected presiding officer the maximum responsibility of which he is capable.

Ward government meetings are applicable to a somewhat narrower range of situations than the conventional ward meetings presided over by the doctor and/or nurse, since they require the patient population to be more stable and less autistic if there is to be any smoothness of operation. On the other hand, ward government meetings fit a wider range of situations than those ward meetings which come to approximate an expressive group therapy, since the interchange is geared to deal with problems on a conscious, rational, and practical level.

Ward government meetings offer two advantages over the other type of ward meeting, both stemming from the greater overt activity and responsibility of the patients. (1) Such meetings can contribute to an enhanced self-esteem deriving from identification by the patient body with their representatives. (2) They can favor a lessening of the guilt feelings which are often stimulated by the passive-dependent position of the hospitalized patient.

In view of the distinct contributions of the two types of group sessions, the ward (psychotherapy) meeting and the ward government meeting, psychiatric hospitals tend increasingly to encourage both types. In such situations, the ward government meeting transacts the bulk of administrative matters of the unit and the psychiatrist-led ward meeting assumes the functions of a conventional group psychotherapy.

Milieu Therapy

Milieu is used here in its original sense (from which Claude Bernard coined his famous expression, *le milieu interieur*), that is to say, *environment*. *Milieu therapy* thus means "treatment by means of the environment." In particular, it refers to psychiatric treatment through the encouragement and/or manipulation of certain features of the hospital environment. As the reader will understand, the topic is a large one and requires discussion under several headings.

WARD ATMOSPHERE. There is a saying that health, like disease, is contagious. A health-promoting ward atmosphere is, in general, one in which certain characteristics (one is tempted to say, virtues) associated with the behavior of mature, well-adjusted persons are pervasively manifest. There are a number of ways in which these characteristics could be expressed; and any brief list would be incomplete. The ones selected here may nevertheless convey something of the essence of a therapeutic hospital or ward atmosphere; they are: respectfulness, courtesy, dignity, calmness, security, and freedom.

Ideally, these qualities would be shown (or offered) by all to all. In practice they must be shown first by personnel to one another and to patients. In time, as a sign of returning health, they will be shown by patients; first, as a rule, to personnel, and then, most importantly, to one another. For the sake of simplicity in the following discussion, the relationship of personnel to patients will be given primary consideration.

As was indicated in the discussion of individual psychotherapy, the relationship between a therapeutic figure and a patient has much in common with that between a parent and a child or between an older and a younger sibling (p. 479). With all of this country's sentimentality regarding children, it is a point too often forgotten that they should be shown *respect*. The good parent shows respect for his children as human beings, respect for their individualities, respect for their potentialities. The pleasures of parenthood should, in major part, be not possessive but *functional*. That is to say, there should be enjoyment of functioning as a healthy adult in the activities of parenthood. Vicarious pleasure in the children's realization of their own aspirations is legitimate; vicarious pleasure that requires the children to realize the parents' specific ambitions should be unnecessary. The good parent does not require the constant admiration and approval of his children; he is capable of acting in their best interest even in situations in which their immediate response is disappointment or resentment. In a quite analogous way, the good doctor (or nurse) is not possessive of the patients in his care. (If the expression, "*my* patients," is used a great deal, it is usually a sign that all is not quite as it should be.) He is glad to see them develop whatever healthy relationships they can with other patients and with personnel. The good doctor enjoys his profession and does not, for the most part, require any *particular* response from patients to maintain his self-esteem.

However unpleasant, regressed, or "deteriorated" the patient may be, the good doctor will respect him as a human being having certain potentialities, perhaps largely unrealized. While he will not accept certain aspects of the patient's *behavior*—those destructive to himself or others—he tries to accept him as a person. He will not hesitate to act in a way likely to draw the patient's immediate displeasure—such as refusing an insistent request—if his judgment tells him that to do otherwise would not be to the patient's benefit. To do otherwise would also indicate a lack of respect.

Despite almost universal lip-service to it, genuine *courtesy* is one of the more difficult qualities with which to suffuse a ward atmosphere. It is difficult of achievement largely because it requires considerable flexibility as well as knowledge of varying social usages. The same behavior which spells courtesy to some patients makes other patients ill at ease.

A slatternly appearing young woman with a severe personality disorder referred to herself by the nickname "Mickey" and strove to be treated as a dirty child, despite largely unconscious strivings toward a more generally acceptable role. A slight but distinct improvement was noted when ward personnel, at the psychiatrist's instigation, made a thoroughly persistent effort to address her as "Miss ——."

An elderly Negro, who had lived almost all of his life in the rural deep South and had been almost untouched by recent cultural developments there, was accustomed to a relationship with white persons in which his attitude of deference was met with support and protection from them. When he happened to be hospitalized in a Northern city for organic brain disease, he was regularly addressed by personnel as "Mr. ——." Eventually the staff realized that this usage was incomprehensible to him; he appeared tense and vaguely suspicious in response to it, as if there were some kind of a trap. He became more relaxed, and achieved better spirits when the personnel, putting aside some of their own feelings, began to address him as "Ben."

Dignity is not to be mistaken for the impersonal hyperprofessionalism so often associated with the white lab coat or the starchy nursing uniform. As a matter of fact, the latter attitude, where it is a manifestation of anything more than an ill-founded habit, is usually a product of professional and personal insecurities. True dignity is based on a healthy self-esteem, on compassion, and on a respect for the work in which one is engaged.

Mrs. D., an elderly woman, had been for several months a patient at a grossly understaffed state hospital, where, because of her uncommunicativeness, disheveled appearance, soiled clothing, and continuous driveling, she had been placed on a "back ward," staffed by inadequately trained attendants. Trials on chemotherapeutic agents had not altered the picture greatly.

When Mrs. D. became acutely ill of an intercurrent infection, she was transferred to one of the active medical wards, where diagnostic problems were concentrated. This unit was more adequately staffed, and Mrs. D. came under the care of a nurse whose innate graciousness and dignity were reflected in the atmosphere of the unit. By the time the acute illness had been diagnosed and treated, a noticeable change had taken place in the patient's general behavior. Although still a bit confused at times, the patient was pleasant and communicative. On one occasion she was heard to say, "I can't describe it right, but nowadays I feel human again. I feel like a lady."

Calmness is an important quality which is often misunderstood. It is not so much a matter of externals as of internals. It involves an inner serenity, and the patient who is on a ward where the personnel have this quality tends to absorb the feeling that there is hope, that time may be on his side, that life can be worthwhile and reality acceptable once more. Calmness is a sureness of action, based on serenity, that assists anxious, distressed patients to feel reassured and comfortable.

The episode involving the psychiatric charge nurse and the exhibitionistic patient, related on page 482, strikingly illustrates the value of calmness. Regardless of the depth of the nurse's theoretical understanding, she could not have helped the patient if she had become frightened or otherwise upset or if she had permitted the ward to become disturbed.

Obviously, a sense of *security* should exist in the doctor, nurse, and other personnel, should pervade the ward, and should be communicated to patients. A fundamental requirement is that personnel feel the strength of mutual support, particularly emotional and intellectual support. This condition can be developed only through good communication and active, continuous planning among staff members, with the knowledge that every member's contribution is appreciated by the others. Security also is favored if the personnel do not allow their desire to be liked by the patients to lead them into offering excessive "privileges" (activities and opportunities for which the patients are not yet ready), or into a reluctance to impose limitations on potentially harmful behavior.

On the basis of security plus the other values which have just been described, the ward atmosphere can be invested with a sense of *freedom*. Of the various characteristics, this one has come, at least in recent years, to be the best understood. The therapeutic variety of freedom is the basis for much of the progress which psychiatric patients can make in the hospital, and hence it constitutes one of the more important portions of the rationale for hospitalization. (Indeed, it would have been placed first on the present list, except for the importance of indicating that it is made feasible in large part by the other characteristics.)

The principal point for reflection is this: The more seriously ill psychiatric patients—whatever the etiology of their disorders—have come into an imbalance with their immediate (outside) environments. This imbalance contributes to the illness and tends to interfere with recovery. In addition to whatever internal conflicts are present, there are external conflicts. Figures in the environment are almost inevitably responding in nonconstructive ways to the patient's symptoms or symptomatic behavior. Very often a vicious cycle is established: the patient behaves in unacceptable ways because he is ill; society responds negatively to the unacceptable behavior; the negative responses favor a worsening of the illness, inasmuch as they are a further source of stress. (See discussion of epileptic patient and family on pp. 301 to 303.)

The intramural freedom which is possible in the hospital often breaks this vicious cycle.

ATTITUDE THERAPY. On the basis of a health-promoting ward atmosphere, the more subtle and specific forms of milieu can take place. Of these, one of the most important is termed "attitude therapy."* In the course of previous discussions, several examples of this treatment technique have been given. In the chapter on affective psychoses, examples were offered of the correct (p. 347) and incorrect (p. 343) use of attitudes. The attitude of the occupational therapist could be called "kind firmness"; that of the inexperienced nursing student, "sympathetic indulgence." The anecdote of the nurse and the exhibitionistic patient (p. 482) is illustrative of a therapeutic attitude which might also be called "kind firmness," but which is perhaps closer to one describable by some such phrase as "matter-of-fact friendliness" since its outstanding feature was the nurse's imperturbability.

Even from these few examples, one can see that ordinary intuition and a kind heart—assets which carry personnel far in the creation of a wholesome ward atmosphere—must be supplemented by scientific training and experience for the application of an effective attitude therapy. For instance, the sympathetic attitude of the nursing student toward the depressed patient was perfectly natural, as was her irritation as the incident proceeded; perfectly natural, but not therapeutic.

Ordinarily, the details of an attitude therapy are not planned—cannot be scientifically planned—until the patient has been in the hospital long enough for the personnel to have become reasonably well acquainted with him; for the psychiatrist to have conducted his initial interviews, for the clinical psychologist to have performed his tests, for the psychiatric nurse to have made her observations, and for the psychiatric social worker to have interviewed the family. At this point, a staff meeting is usually held, at which members of all the disciplines present their data. The clinical diagnosis is reviewed, a dynamic diagnosis† is made, and treatment plans are formulated.

A major part of these plans has to do with the management of the hospital experience itself. A decision is reached (subject to periodic

---

* This form of treatment has been most fully developed at the Menninger Hospital, Topeka, Kansas, under the leadership of Dr. William C. Menninger. Most of the present discussion is based upon the author's experience at the Menninger Hospital plus further experimentation at the Cincinnati General Hospital.

† The term *dynamic diagnosis* refers to "an understanding of the forces that currently are operating in the production of the patient's difficulty." (Levine, M. *in* Alexander, Franz and Ross, Helen (eds.): Dynamic Psychiatry, Chicago, Univ. of Chicago Press, 1952.)

review and to revision on the basis of further experience with the patient) as to how the hospital stay, in all its many aspects, should be structured in order to exert the maximum therapeutic effect. To do this, the staff must arrive at a tentative conclusion as to the relative importance of the patient's various inner conflicts and as to the point in his system of psychological defenses at which the hospital team will have the best chance of effecting a healthy modification. Despite the complexity of most psychiatric illnesses, experience has shown that it is nearly always best, for hospital management purposes, for the team to concentrate its general efforts on *one principal line of approach* at any given period; otherwise the possibilities for inconsistent handling and misunderstanding become too great.

As a rule it is a good procedure for the basic approach to be thought out to the point at which it can be expressed in a phrase or short sentence, which is then written on the order sheet, serving as a reminder that all of the separate treatment techniques which may be decided upon should conform to it, or at least not be at variance with it. Examples: "the re-establishment of socially acceptable compulsive defenses," or "offering of relief from a sense of guilt."

One of the more important ways through which the basic approach to a patient is carried out is the prescription by the psychiatrist in charge (with the collaboration of the other members of the hospital team) of certain attitudes to be used—as a general rule and barring special situations—by all personnel in their contacts with the patient. It usually has been found helpful to be quite definite in the statement of these attitudes.

Attitudes can be rather complex phenomena, but for the purposes of an attitude therapy they may be considered as involving three closely related components: (1) an emotional component, (2) a degree of activity, and (3) certain expectations. These several components require a brief clarification.

1. Naturally one's innermost *emotional responses* to patients vary considerably, depending upon one's own personality, upon that of the patient, upon immediate circumstances, and upon the depth of one's understanding. Some of these responses will be fully appropriate to the patient and to the professional relationship; others will be inappropriate to one or the other or both; i.e., they will be responses which leave out of consideration one or more of the real aspects of the total situation. (Thus, the responses of the nursing student to the depressed patient were, perhaps, appropriate to the patient merely considered as a person in distress, but were not appropriate to the circumstances of the illness nor to the professional relationship.) In the prescription of an attitude,

the assumption is made that inappropriate responses will be denied overt expression.

In general, it may be said that if one's self-knowledge and personal security are of respectable proportions, then his inappropriate *negative* feelings (i.e., "counter-transference" feelings such as anger, envy, and fear) are apt to be of only mild intensity. Such disturbing emotions can be further reduced through the opportunity, at management conferences, for achieving a rather deep-going understanding of the patients. Therefore, in speaking of the emotional component of a prescribed attitude, one usually assumes that whatever destructive feelings may exist can be brought under control—if they are not so already—through techniques, such as staff discussions, which do not affect the patient adversely. The emotional component in a prescribed attitude involves various fundamentally positive feelings (friendliness, compassion, hope, confidence) and the extent to which they are to be made evident to the patient. The latter aspect should be altered to fit the circumstances. Thus, an inhibited, emotionally starved patient may thrive on an attitude of unmistakably warm indulgence. On the other hand, a morbidly sensitive, suspicious patient, afraid of emotion in any form, may misunderstand such an attitude and may respond more favorably to one of casual friendliness.

2. *Degree of activity* refers to the technical point of finding the therapeutically correct balance between the amount of initiative that can be assumed by the patient and the amount of initiative that should be assumed by personnel in building the relationship and carrying on the therapeutic program. For example, a patient who is markedly withdrawn may be quite incapable of reaching out emotionally toward personnel. In such a case, it often would be correct for the personnel to be quite active, to go much further than halfway to make contact with the patient. Yet another patient may be fighting desperately for a sense of control, may need to feel that he is the active one; here it would be correct for the personnel to be a good bit more passive, to wait courteously for the patient to make overtures rather than to make the overtures themselves.

3. In this context, the term *expectations* is intended to refer not so much to what one can predict about a patient's behavior as to the extent to which one plans to guide that behavior. For example, an attitude of indulgence would imply that, within broad limits of safety, one is to offer little or no interference to the patient's spontaneous activities and make every effort to comply with his requests and demands. Such an attitude would be appropriate for a patient who has come to fear, hate, and continuously misunderstand his environment and who has re-

gressed to a point at which socially acceptable techniques of relieving inner tensions are impossible for the time being. On the other hand, a prescription of kind firmness indicates a readiness to offer considerable interference if necessary. It would be of far greater value to a patient whose hostility requires (and is amenable to) redirection, either away from himself and onto features of the environment (as in severe depressions) or away from inappropriate features of the environment and onto appropriate ones (as in certain personality disorders).

Because it is so important that there be no confusion or misunderstanding among personnel and that there be a uniformity and consistency in patient management, it is necessary that the attitude recommended for a particular patient be not merely stated (at the conference) but defined. In some settings, such definitions are worked out from the beginning at the conference in which the attitude is prescribed; in others, a list of the more useful attitudes has been thought out, defined in writing, and made available to all the personnel, so that the conference can merely select an attitude by name (after thorough discussion), knowing that it will be interpreted similarly by everyone.

Depending upon the precision and subtlety with which they are defined, a varying number of attitudes can be delineated. Given a reasonable breadth of interpretation, the following six attitudes have been proved adequate to cover the needs of a majority of patients:* (1) *indulgence,* (2) *active friendliness,* (3) *passive friendliness,* (4) *matter-of-factness,* (5) *watchfulness,* and (6) *kind firmness.* To convey a better idea of what is expected of personnel in an attitude therapy, these attitudes will be briefly defined.

The prescription of an attitude of *indulgence* indicates that an unusual amount of flexibility is called for in dealing with the patient's adherence to his therapeutic routine. It does not, of course, change the patient's status with regard to any written orders dealing with precautions and the use of privileges. It does mean that a certain amount of divergence from his schedule (diet, activities, nonessential medications, etc.) is to be gracefully accepted. Unnecessary "issues" are to be avoided; harmless favors are to be granted, even if some little inconvenience is involved.

In *active friendliness,* the word "active" indicates that ward personnel are to assume the initiative in making friendly overtures and showing a special interest in the patient. It should perhaps be emphasized that this attitude does not imply manifestations likely to be construed

---

* These designations and the definitions that follow are taken, with slight modifications, from A Guide to the Order Sheet (mimeographed form), The Menninger Foundation, Topeka, Kansas, 1950. This material is discussed in Menninger, K. A., A Manual for Psychiatric Case Study, New York, Grune, 1960.

as intimate or seductive by the patient. The quality and the quantity of interest and/or affection shown should be controlled at all times and adjusted to meet the therapeutic needs of the patient.

The attitude of *passive friendliness* differs from the one just described in that here the personnel wait for the patient to take the initiative in many aspects of the relationship (not, of course, in matters determined by ordinary courtesy or ward routine). The personnel should make it clear that they are available to the patient and they should preserve contact with him, but should not force attention upon him. Once the patient has assumed the initiative (sometimes a slight cue is all that should be awaited), the friendly response should quickly follow, but as in "active friendliness," it should remain consistent with therapy.

The attitude of *matter-of-factness* has in it an element of casualness, but is without any implication of lack of interest. It means that, apart from the underlying, quiet, sustained friendliness which is a part of all therapeutic attitudes, the personnel are not to respond with (overt) emotion to whatever pleas, apparent distress, or maneuvers the patient may present. Attempts at direct reassurance are to be avoided.

The prescription of *watchfulness* is appropriate when any aspect of the patient's total condition is such that he requires essentially continuous observation. "Watchfulness" always implies a thoroughness of execution, but it can involve widely varying degrees of conspicuousness. Ordinarily, if there is no statement to the contrary, it is understood that the watchfulness is to be maintained in as unobtrusive a manner as possible. In all cases, it is of importance that this attitude be carried out with special attention to courtesy.

The prescription of *kind firmness* requires that a feeling of assurance be conveyed to the patient by the personnel that they understand exactly what is to be done (i.e., in the various aspects of the therapeutic program) and that they expect their requests to be carried out. The nurse's statements, in particular, should be direct, clear, and quietly confident (but never overbearing or challenging). Consistency is of especial importance here. The degree of physical constraint to be used (as necessary) to implement this order should be specified at the time it is given.

Whether more or less permanent definitions such as those just described have been worked out or whether the attitudes are rephrased and redefined at the conference table for each individual patient, the question is occasionally raised as to how a prescribed attitude can be "genuine." This question is, in some respects, analogous to one occasionally raised with regard to the validity of formal prayers, pledges, and oaths (e.g., the Lord's Prayer; the Pledge of Allegiance to the Flag of the United States). How can an attitude be genuine, it is asked, if it is not entirely individual and spontaneous? How can a prayer be genuine if it is offered in the words of another? *The answer in both cases is that the genuineness is primarily a function of the understanding and the motivation of the subject.* In everyday experience, the principle is not difficult to grasp. If one spanks a rambunctious small boy for crossing a busy street before he has developed sufficient judgment to do so safely, the genuineness of the action is not lessened by its conventionality nor by the absence of spontaneous anger in the spanker. Probably the key quality in personnel who are implementing an attitude therapy is *understanding*. In the examples involving Mr. T. S., the psychotically depressed patient, both the nursing student (p. 343) and the occupational therapist (p. 347) were primarily motivated by the wish to alleviate the patient's misery; no doubt both student and therapist felt an inward sympathy. The therapist, however, had the understanding to adopt the constructive attitude of kind firmness, whereas the student had not had the opportunity to develop this degree of understanding.

ENVIRONMENTAL MANIPULATION WITHIN THE HOSPITAL. Manipulation of the hospital environment may not be required in some instances and in others be a rather complex affair. There are a number of subheadings under this general category of therapeutic effort, of which only two will be reviewed here: (1) regulation of what might be called the patient's "geographic range," and (2) regulation of the patient's contacts with other persons.

1. As with other measures of treatment, the question of the amount of geographic freedom to be allowed a given patient should be approached on the basis of an appraisal of his individual needs, his strivings, his psychological defenses, his strengths, and his areas of vulnerability. This aspect of treatment is capable of as many degrees of refinement as is attitude therapy. The major possibilities can be listed as follows: (a) confinement to one room (seclusion), (b) restriction to an acute psychiatric ward, (c) restriction to a convalescent psychiatric ward, (d) outside privileges to certain hospital areas, attended, (e) outside privileges to the hospital grounds, unattended, (f) privileges to go off grounds for limited periods, attended, and then (g) unattended (passes), and (h) unlimited privileges of movement.

Here are two examples to illustrate the impact upon therapy of variations in the geographic limits of movement, as well as the range of this aspect of treatment.

A patient was being treated in the hospital for severe neurotic difficulties, of which agoraphobia* was a prominent symptom. Fairly soon

---

* A morbid dread of open or solitary places.

the patient became quite comfortable so long as her activities were confined to the hospital grounds (which was initially the case at the psychiatrist's order). There came a time in the therapy when it became correct to give her—and to encourage her to use—off-ground privileges, unattended. This action resulted in an immediate (partial) return of the phobic response, but as a result of the therapeutic work already accomplished, the patient in the course of time and subsequent interviews was able to obtain further insight into and mastery of the specific conflict productive of the phobia. Continued venturing outside became an adjunct to this portion of the therapy.

An 11-year-old boy with a serious personality disorder was being treated in a child psychiatric unit. Rage reactions, in which the patient would become assaultive to other patients and to the personnel, were conspicuous features of the illness. It was found that the patient benefitted greatly from being confined to his room at the first sign of violence, with his doctor or nurse in close supervision. Occasionally the patient would actually be held in the doctor's arms (i.e., restrained) during such a period. It became clear that the boy was actually terrified of his own aggressive impulses and—despite his initial angry protests—gained important reassurance from the knowledge that he could be helped to gain control and would not be permitted to wreak serious harm upon others in the meantime.

2. In a somewhat comparable way, there exist many possible variations as to the time, the place, and the character of the social interaction that the patient is encouraged or permitted to have with other persons. These "other persons" fall into three categories: hospital personnel, other patients, and visitors. In general, it may be said that the sicker the patient, the more selective should the staff be in prescribing his contacts with others. If the patient is extremely ill, sometimes his only contacts should be with carefully chosen experienced personnel (since only they can carry out the proper therapeutic attitudes with assurance). The majority of patients, however, may be permitted spontaneous association with the personnel and the other patients on the unit. The patients who are least ill may usually be permitted to receive visitors in the same fashion as do nonpsychiatric patients.

Probably the greatest possibilities for mismanagement in this area lie in the inadequate regulation of the patient's contacts with relatives. In a well-regulated psychiatric unit, these associations are never left to chance, to the discretion of a seriously ill patient, or even to the discretion of a doctor or nurse who merely happens to be on duty at the time. Some of the most serious behavioral flare-ups to be seen in the psychiatric hospital occur during or immediately after unplanned interviews between patients and relatives (or "close friends").

As is true of all of the other significant aspects of the patient's life in the hospital, contacts with relatives and with other figures significant in the patient's preadmission life should be given thoughtful consideration at the staff conference, and thereafter should be regulated in accordance with the therapeutic objectives developed at the conference. It is worth emphasizing that the patient's most serious interpersonal difficulties are nearly always with the very figures to whom he has been, in the obvious but superficial sense, "the closest," i.e., mother, father, wife, children, employer. In other words, his illness is apt to have arisen, at least in part, on the basis of conflicts with the very persons who are so often on hand at the visiting hour.

The situation is further complicated by the fact that patients frequently ask to see visitors out of unhealthy motives, as for example, unrealistic feelings of guilt or of obligation. (The same is true of visitors asking to see patients.) Thus, while it is nearly always correct to allow the patient to decline to see any visitor, it is usually not good planning for the patient to have automatic permission to see all visitors. A comprehensive statement regarding the patient's contacts with other persons should include specific comments as to who may visit, and as to where, how often, and under what circumstances the visits may take place.

Obviously, if the patient is to resume his place in society following successful treatment, he will usually be called upon to resume his various outside relationships. Both for this reason and out of consideration for the distress and anxiety so often experienced by relatives and close friends of a psychiatric patient, these individuals should never be ignored or treated with indifference merely because their visits to the patient may be contraindicated for any given period. It is part of the work of the psychiatric social worker (p. 461) to interview such persons (after consultation with the patient's psychiatrist), to offer them whatever explanation and counsel may be helpful, and, in many instances, to draw them into the treatment planning.

The therapeutic planning should include specific consideration and specific statements regarding the patient's contacts with other patients and with personnel. In the case of other patients, the statement should specify whether these contacts should be encouraged, discouraged, or left entirely to the patient's option. In the case of the personnel, the statement should indicate the approximate amount of time to be spent with the patient and, if it is thought to make a difference in the therapeutic effort, the particular member or members of the staff who should be designated to this assignment (charge nurse, staff nurse, a particular attendant).

THE NIGHT HOSPITAL AND THE DAY HOSPITAL. The primary function of the "night hospital" is a transitional one. The term does not refer to a special institution, nor even (as a rule) to a special unit, but rather to a particular arrangement whereby certain patients regularly spend the equivalent of the ordinary working day outside the hospital, while continuing to make their home in it.

The purpose of this arrangement is to facilitate the convalescent patient's making a good work adjustment (or, sometimes, a good home adjustment) while continuing to receive the support and many of the other therapeutic benefits of the hospital milieu. Ordinarily the patient, with the assistance of outside contacts of his own plus those of social service (if needed), will have obtained employment or re-employment and will be developing an adjustment to the work situation while deferring his full readjustment to the social (including family) aspects of his life on the outside. During this phase the patient continues to participate in all phases of his hospital program taking place before he leaves in the morning and after he returns in the afternoon.

Among the advantages of this arrangement are the reduction in economic pressure on the patient who begins again to earn a living, and the fostering of independence and a healthier self-esteem.

The "day hospital" may also be used transitionally, but it may be used in lieu of full-time hospitalization in certain instances (i.e., from the beginning). Like the night hospital, the day hospital may involve merely a special arrangement for use of the facilities of the full-time hospital units or it may involve a comparable unit of its own.

In the initial discussion of hospitalization it was pointed out that the use of the day hospital should be considered when those factors having to do with *bringing the patient into* a certain type of situation are paramount and those having to do with *removing the patient* from certain other situations are of minor importance.

Since the costs of day hospitalization are appreciably less than those of full-time hospitalization, the day hospital shares with the night hospital the value of reducing the financial burden upon the patient and his family. It has the especial merit, in many instances, of being less stimulating of the patient's dependent needs and thus less apt to foster the further regression which often accompanies full-time hospitalization. In addition, it obviates the necessity of a partial break in and subsequent restoration of family relationships.

Typically, the day patient spends six to nine hours, five to six days a week, in the hospital, participating actively in a therapeutic program, while continuing to make his headquarters at his home.

Activity Therapy

The separation of activity therapy from milieu therapy is distinctly arbitrary, inasmuch as the settings, the personnel, and the activities involved in this aspect of treatment all form part of the therapeutic environment. The principal rationale for discussing certain treatment measures under this separate heading is that they have become fields of specialization for the relatively new professions of occupational, recreational, and educational therapists. These major subdivisions of the field have received mention in the preceding chapter, and therefore the present discussion will be brief, confining itself chiefly to the bringing out of certain technical points especially applicable to the situation in which these subdivisions are welded together under psychiatric direction to form integral parts of the treatment program in a psychiatric hospital.

OCCUPATIONAL THERAPY. It has been known for a long time that most patients tend to improve more rapidly if they are kept occupied than if they are ignored or allowed to remain idle. This is particularly true of most psychiatric patients since they so often lack the confidence and the initiative to seek constructive activity spontaneously. However, it has been only since the development of modern dynamic psychiatry that occupational therapy has become a scientifically based, highly refined method of treatment for the emotionally ill patient.

When there are special indications—as, for example, in the case of a highly autistic patient or a patient whose behavior is in some fashion quite disturbing to other patients—occupational therapy can be offered on a completely individual basis (i.e., in a one-to-one relationship involving a single patient and a single therapist). However, the great bulk of occupational therapy takes place in a group situation. Therefore, the work of the occupational therapist has a number of similarities to that of the group psychotherapist (pp. 492 to 495). Of course, no attempt at giving interpretations is made.

The more nearly unique features of occupational therapy arise from two circumstances: (1) the patient's interest is centered in an activity, and (2) the particular activity in which any given patient is involved has been selected, as a rule, for quite specific psychological reasons.

The first of these points has been brought out in the discussion of the preceding chapter. The only aspect requiring emphasis here is that, through occupational therapy, the patient is offered a *nonverbal* means of expression. Even in the case of a patient who has no special difficulty in talking, the additional behavioral outlets offered in occupational therapy give a new dimension to treatment. In the common case of a patient who is unable to communicate effectively in a verbal manner (e.g., a disorganized or severely inhibited patient), occupational therapy may at first be the only possible route of expressing drives and making contact with other persons.

Perhaps the aspect of occupational therapy which is technically the most interesting has to do with the second point, the utilization of specific forms of activity to achieve specific effects upon the conflicting psychological forces within the patient. With careful thought and the proper collaboration among members of the therapeutic team, the prescription of occupational therapy activities can be made almost as precise as the prescription of medications. (The occupational therapist is more active than the pharmacist, however. Whereas the latter receives instructions to prepare and dispense a certain drug, the occupational therapist is informed that it is desired to produce a certain *effect,* and it is usually part of her function to select the proper activity.)

The example of the occupational therapist and the depressed patient (p. 347), which has illustrated several other points, also shows the value of selecting a specific activity. As a matter of fact, based upon an understanding of the basic drives and the defense mechanisms, psychiatrists and occupational therapists have worked out a large number of correlations between specific activities and specific psychological effects. Here are two further illustrations.

A neurotic patient had regressed, in the face of severe problems of the family triangle period of development (remobilized in early adult life), to an adjustment in which the attitudes and defenses (reaction-formation, isolation, undoing) typical of the muscle-training period were prominent. Her behavior had assumed a decidedly compulsive character; she seemed rigid, constricted, inhibited, over-cautious. During the hospital phase of a protracted period of treatment, there came a time when she began to move psychologically in the direction of maturity. At this point it was felt that she should be encouraged to give up her compulsive techniques and seek means of greater self-expression. Accordingly the occupational therapist supplied her with materials for painting and sculpture. The patient was actively encouraged to use her own creativeness, to strive for broad, sweeping, dramatic effects and not to worry over painstaking, minute detail. Her initial efforts along these lines were accompanied by considerable anxiety, but with support she was strong enough to face this reaction, and in her individual psychotherapy she was able to use her occupational therapy experiences as the basis for developing further insight.

Quite the reverse technique was used with a schizophrenic patient. It had been learned that this man's prepsychotic personality had been strongly compulsive, but that he had nevertheless made a moderately effective life adjustment prior to the onset of schizophrenia. In this case the therapeutic objective was not a thoroughgoing reorganization of the patient's personality, but a return to his prepsychotic status. Therefore, the occupational therapy prescription was to "help the patient rebuild compulsive defenses." The occupational therapist assigned the patient to the task of sorting and classifying a collection of minerals (to be used in the child psychiatry division). Stress was placed upon the carefulness and the exactness with which the project was to be carried out. Praise was given for meticulous accomplishment. This measure proved of considerable value in assisting the patient to resume the compulsive defenses which had stood him in good stead before his psychotic reaction.

RECREATIONAL THERAPY. By "recreational therapy," particularly within the hospital setting, is meant a *program* of activities somewhat analogous to the occupational therapy program: a program in which specific activities are recommended for specific patients on the basis of psychological understanding. It will, perhaps, be sufficient to point out the wide range of effects that can be achieved through this means.

With respect to the degree of the patient's activity, a good recreational program offers a graded series of experiences. At one extreme would be the merely passive role of spectator at a game or contest, in which the patient would benefit through vicarious participation (partial release of tensions through observation of and some measure of identification with the active participants). At the other extreme would be some highly active role, such as playing a vigorous game of tennis. Activities such as croquet, shuffleboard, and volleyball would provide intermediate stages.

Similarly, a recreational program offers a series of experiences graded with respect to the amount and the overtness of expression afforded to the hostile-aggressive and libidinal drives. Hiking or swimming are activities in which some angry tensions can be "worked off," but in a limited and quite indirect way. At the other extreme would be activities such as boxing, wrestling, fencing, or punching a heavy bag.

All degrees of competitiveness can be accommodated in recreational activities, as can all degrees of cooperativeness. An example of a noncompetitive and noncooperative activity would be the solitary practicing of a golf stroke. An activity both highly competitive and highly cooperative would be tennis doubles or contract bridge. Team games such as volleyball and baseball also fit into this category.

Singing, dancing, and playing a musical instrument are examples of possibilities allowing the sublimated expression of libidinal impulses. Ward parties of various kinds offer opportunities for the gratification of social needs.

Attributing specifically masculine or feminine qualities to activities is largely a cultural matter. Nevertheless, once established, such attributes can be made use of in an activity program. Thus, an activity such as practicing ballet would be suitable for an individual needing a feminine type of expression, whereas weight-lifting or boxing would offer a masculine type of expression.

In general, recreational therapy places a somewhat greater emphasis upon the needs of patients as groups, whereas occupational therapy tends to retain a somewhat greater emphasis upon the needs of patients as individuals. A qualified recreational therapist takes the lead in helping to plan for parties, social clubs, movies, and various social programs. Shopping, outings in town or visits to scenic areas and educational institutions are also planned by the recreational director for groups of patients, since these activities offer many opportunities for spontaneous group socialization and individual social expression.

EDUCATIONAL THERAPY. The expression "educational therapy" refers to instances in which it is arranged for the patient to receive instruction from a qualified teacher in a specified subject as a part of the total treatment effort. There are two principal reasons for such a procedure: (1) to enhance the patient's self-esteem in a legitimate way, and (2) to supply information which will directly enhance the patient's adjustment efforts. The latter purpose includes various types of vocational preparation, but it also includes instruction in subjects of a more personal nature. The example of educational therapy given below illustrates both (1) and (2).

In the late stages of the successful treatment of a schizophrenic young girl, it was felt that the patient's progress in social adjustment would be enhanced by instruction in the principles of dress and grooming (matters which she had been too ill to master during adolescence). One of the staff nurses on the psychiatric service had been a professional model before entering nursing. It was arranged for this nurse to spend regular periods of time with the patient in which they discussed hair styles, selection and wearing of clothes, and principles of effective make-up. Nurse and patient tried various experiments that resulted in the patient's markedly improving her appearance and gaining in poise and self-confidence.

Indirect Measures

This topic has been repeatedly illustrated in connection with some of the clinical discussions earlier in the book, and so, although it includes therapeutic measures of great usefulness, it may be dealt with briefly here. The subject lends itself to a division into two categories, depending upon whether the object is to modify the behavior of certain persons who are of importance to the patient or to alter the patient's environment without directly affecting the behavior of any person in it.

WORKING THROUGH FAMILY, FRIENDS. In some instances, principally in child psychiatry (Chap. 15), the therapeutic effort may be conducted mainly or even entirely through psychotherapy of a counselling-supportive nature offered to the figure upon whom the "patient" is primarily dependent. It is much commoner, however, for work with the family or other significant figures to be undertaken as a supplement to direct work with the patient.

One of the chief indications for this measure has to do with the gravity of the patient's condition and the limitations of the therapeutic aims. If the patient is so severely ill that direct therapeutic efforts of ordinary scope are likely to achieve only quite modest success (as when a patient is helped to a recovery from an acute schizophrenic reaction, but is left with a strongly schizoid or paranoid personality disorder), the best possibility of avoiding a subsequent psychotic episode may be to help those responsible for the patient's welfare to a greater understanding of his condition and of the effects of their behavior upon it.

Other indications have to do not so much with the gravity of the patient's condition as with the nature of certain specific situations with which he has to deal.

A responsible professional man, aged 30, married and with two children, entered out-patient psychotherapy for impotence. After a period of treatment, the patient gained a certain amount of insight into his emotional conflicts and gained in general self-confidence, but he remained partially impotent. Both the doctor and the patient considered it likely that the patient's sexual behavior would become normal if it were not for immature and hostile features of the wife's behavior.

Despite her destructive behavior and although she was essentially asymptomatic clinically, the patient's wife was sincerely interested in making a success of the marriage. Accordingly it was advised that she undergo psychotherapy. This was done, and after a time her behavior became more considerate and gracious. The husband regained his potency, and the marriage eventually became a reasonably successful and comfortable one.

Other indications arise when a patient in psychiatric treatment is faced with realistic problems that are outside the doctor's sphere of competence—for example, questions of a religious or a legal nature—but that are intertwined with his own emotional difficulties. In such cases it is important that the efforts of the psychiatrist and those of the other professional person do not come into needless conflict. To this end it may become advisable for the lawyer, the clergyman, or the other specialist to be informed and perhaps counseled with respect to the patient's emotional status. (Unless the patient has been legally declared incompetent, such a step is never taken without his permission.)

MANIPULATION OF THE EXTERNAL ENVIRONMENT. Nowadays the physician is apt to think with a complacent smile of the many environmental changes recommended on an empirical basis or sometimes in sheer desperation by physicians of a generation or so ago. Yet the truth is that on the basis of modern dynamic understanding such recommendations can occasionally be made quite legitimately, with genuine assurance that they will enhance the patient's chances for recovery Such a favorable result is particularly apt to occur when the advised change is likely to remove the patient once and for all from excessive contact with persons or situations which overtax his adjustment capacity and when it will also provide ample opportunity for experiences capable of gratifying his fundamental needs.

A young man had compiled an enviable record in the army, reaching the rank of major during his wartime tour of duty. Although he liked the stability and the security of military life, with its fixed patterns of responsibility and authority, its well-organized social activity, and its automatic provision for the future, he was influenced by family pressure not to apply for a regular commission but to enter the business world.

Several years later the patient had become a struggling young business executive, and he had developed stomach symptoms likely to be the precursors of a peptic ulcer. One of the principal contributions that a brief period of psychotherapy made to the patient's subsequent well-being was to enable him to recognize some of his dependent needs, to realize the soundness (for him) of his original career plan, and to stand up against the influence of his relatives. The patient applied for and received a commission in the regular army, and he has remained symptom-free.

Suggestions for Further Reading

Alexander, F., and French, T. M.: Psychoanalytic Therapy, New York, Ronald, 1946.

Brenman, M., and Gill, M. M.: Hypnotherapy, New York, Internat. Univ. Press, 1947.

Freeman, L.: Fight Against Fears, New York, Crown Publishers, 1951.

Frank, J. D.: Group Therapy in the Mental Hospital, Monograph Series No. 1, Washington, D. C., American Psychiatric Association, Mental Hospital Service, 1955.

Jones, E.: The Life and Work of Sigmund Freud (3 vols.), New York, Basic, 1953-1957.

Levine, M.: Psychotherapy in Medical Practice, New York, Macmillan, 1942.

―――: Principles of psychiatric treatment *in* Dynamic Psychiatry, Alexander, F., and Ross, H. (eds.): Chicago, Univ. Chicago Press, 1952.

Maslow, A. H., and Mittelmann, B.: Principles of Abnormal Psychology, rev. ed., pp. 179-296, New York, Harper, 1951.

Menninger, K. A.: The Human Mind, ed. 3, Chapter 5, New York, Knopf, 1945.

―――: A Manual for Psychiatric Case Study, New York, Grune, 1960.

Stanton, A. H., and Schwartz, M. S.: The Mental Hospital, New York, Basic, 1954.

Weiss, M. O.: Attitudes in Psychiatric Nursing Care, New York, Putnam, 1954.

CHAPTER 15

Psychiatric Disorders of Childhood and Adolescence. Mental Retardation

CHATHAM GLENN CLEMENTS, M.D.

Many of the symptoms that bring children* to a doctor have emotional disorders as their principal cause. Similarly, the stress of illnesses and operations that children undergo may cause various types of emotional decompensation. Since differentiation of the various emotional disorders and more definite techniques for dealing with each have become possible, training in this area has taken on a new interest for physicians. Many symptoms and emotional disorders have a close link with the phase of development through which a child passes, and thus this link offers a natural system around which to organize one's thinking, one which emphasizes the aspects of immaturity, growth and change that are so important in understanding the child and adolescent. This is the approach used in this chapter.

THE CONSTITUTIONAL BASELINE

Observation in any newborn nursery will demonstrate how different the reaction patterns of healthy infants are. Some babies are tense and cry easily. Others are placid and relaxed. Child care that takes the variations of temperament into account will get the optimal response from the child. The infant with a weak sucking reflex will need small but frequent feedings. The robust one will take larger feedings and then will go longer between feedings. A baby that wakes up slowly

---

* For purposes of clarity the child will be referred to as "he" when both male and female are meant. This allows the pronoun "she" to designate the mother.

needs a mother who won't hurry him. Sudden loud behavior would be disturbing to this type of child. Most parents are flexible and adapt intuitively to their babies but early mishandling occurs when mothers don't understand the child's individual patterns. Help from the physician in understanding the constitutional baseline so that a reciprocal mother-child rapport can be achieved is preventive medicine of the first magnitude.

SYMPTOMS OF THE FIRST YEAR (ORAL PHASE)

Emotional disorders of the first year usually present one or several of the following symptoms: abnormal crying, feeding, thumbsucking, sleeping, depression and gross abnormal personality development.

Abnormal Crying

Crying should be regarded as abnormal if it persists in an otherwise healthy baby despite relief of physical distress (hunger, cold, wet diapers, etc.) and despite the presence of the mother. Possible emotional causes include: (1) chronic ignoring of "signal" crying of the infant until the infant is overwhelmed and frantic. Such handling blocks development of a sense of trust that tides the infant over the absence of the parents. Indeed, the infant develops fear each time it has to separate from parents and cries excessively when put on its own. (2) Oversolicitous behavior of parents can lead to similar crying, but for the opposite reason, namely, that the baby is never required to master the minimal stress of separating. (3) Overtense, jerky physical handling or rejecting attitudes and harsh physical treatment (inappropriate slapping, spanking) may also lead to anxiety and crying.

Disturbances of Feeding

Infants may develop disturbances of feeding even in the absence of physical causes and formula difficulties. They may refuse to eat, may develop abdominal cramps, colic, vomiting, and in extreme cases, may become cachectic due to emotional stress. If the infant has no appetite and is nauseated, he communicates this by refusing to eat, or by eating and then vomiting. If mothers can allow such a child to be "off its diet" when not feeling well, then the original cause will not be compounded by anger arising from forced feeding. However, a primary need of mothers is to have a baby that looks well, so loss of weight may produce an exaggerated reaction in certain oversensitive mothers.

Colic is a good example of the emotional factors in a feeding disturbance. The baby with colic will cry in a spasmodic fashion as if having abdominal cramps. Feeding, holding and formula changes bring only temporary relief. The formula apparently agrees with the baby the greater part of the day so is hardly at fault. Usually the colic begins in the evening and lasts for 3 to 8 hours. Typically, colic begins in the infant's first month and lasts until the third or fourth month and then gradually disappears. The baby is said to "grow out of it." The genesis of the difficulty may be due to the immaturity of the infant's gastrointestinal tract combined with tension developing between an anxious mother and her child. The fact that mother and infant are more fatigued at the end of the day, or that father on returning home adds his worries to the family load, are often factors. Once the pattern is started, the mother's anticipation of the difficulty recurring increases her tension, which she transmits unwittingly to the infant. Reducing the mother's tension so as to permit her to deal with the colic matter-of-factly is the treatment of choice.

An extreme form of feeding difficulty that used to occur was called marasmus. In this syndrome a baby, often in a well-managed hospital setting, would quit eating, become cachectic and die. Rene Spitz,[8] while working in such a hospital, discovered this was a severe depression brought on by the baby not having an individual mothering figure. A cubicle to itself, with three different nurses in a 24-hour span and still different ones on the weekends, could provide the best medical and physical care, but could not meet the emotional needs of the baby. The treatment of marasmus is to put the baby in the sole care of a good mother figure. Interestingly, infants were found to be more vulnerable to this form of depression in the last half of their first year of life than in the first half, which would seem to indicate that the younger infants are more involved just in coping with their basic physical needs, whereas the older ones, having a more stabilized physiological base, participate in and soon develop needs for meaningful love relationships. (See discussion of etiology of depression, p. 349). Although today marasmus, like any infectious disease for which there is a specific medicine, should not be allowed to develop, it illustrates clearly the life and death quality of the emotional needs of infants. Lesser, and usually reversible, degrees of this form of depressive reaction (*anaclitic depression*) are seen whenever infants are separated from their mothers. Observation of this has led to provisions being made in hospitals for mothers to room-in with infants, for more frequent visiting of the younger hospitalized child, and for physicians to see that adequate plans for mother substitutes are made whenever infants are without their mothers, no matter what the cause of the separation.

Appreciation of the emotional factors in feeding disturbances has led to a reinstatement of "demand feeding" as the feeding schedule of choice. With "demand feeding" the infant adjusts both the amount and the time between feedings. As his capacity increases in both areas he can be relied on to take a sufficient amount of food and to lengthen the interval between feedings, provided that he is secure and happy and offered enough satisfying food. Later on, the mother should use her judgment to see that the child eats a balanced variety of foods, and gradually subordinates most of his individual wishes about meals to family patterns.

Excessive Thumbsucking

Nowadays there is a much more permissive attitude among parents and pediatricians concerning thumbsucking. The change parallels recognition of a child's need for sucking beyond feeding requirements as well as an awareness that this activity brings relief from other tensions. However, when it is excessive or continues into latency years it is a symptom indicating that all is not harmonious (else why the need for self-administered reassurance?). The physician should explore the care of the child to see whether modification of some parental patterns or meeting of certain emotional needs is indicated. Although it would seem advisable to do nothing about thumbsucking while a child is actively dealing with developmental or other problems (bowel training, or hospitalization, for instance), positive nonpunitive parental efforts to understand and modify thumbsucking are indicated. When it is excessive, the child should be helped to find more adequate ways to cope with his problems.

Pediatricians have found that most babies who suck approximately 20 minutes per feeding seldom develop excessive thumbsucking. The holes in nipples or bottles should be kept small enough, or the air vent should be sufficiently compressed, to permit this length of time. In the case of breast feeding, the infant should be kept on one breast long enough to meet his sucking needs before switching to the other breast. Some babies will suck their thumbs no matter what precautions have been taken, and if it has been ascertained that adequate child care is provided, further concern about this habit should be minimized.

Sleep Disturbances

When infants are brought to the doctor for a sleep disturbance, it is usually reported that the infant either cries and resists the mother's leaving the room at bedtime or he becomes excessively alarmed if he awakens during the night. These infants are often fearful at other times as well and have difficulty letting mother out of sight, as when left alone with a baby-sitter.

Exploration of the patterns of child care usually gives some clues. For example, delayed, reluctant handling may generate a sense of distrust in infants accounting for the apprehensiveness whenever the parent is out of sight. Later on, abrupt weaning, or early rigid bowel training are also possible sources of difficulty leading to sleep disturbances. Or the parents may have left the baby with a "sitter" for several weeks due to business, health or vacation, and the baby on their return is noted to be overclinging and to have a sleep disturbance, illustrating again the wish of the infant for one special person to care for it. Another cause may be the mother's own anxiety about the dark. Such a mother would have difficulty in being casual and reassuring at bedtime.

Night lights, open doors, or staying with the baby long enough to reassure him are general measures that often bring relief. When the symptom persists and is part of an overt neurotic or psychotic reaction in the child, more extensive help, as with psychotherapy (in the older child), may be necessary. In other situations where the mother may be unable to handle the problem due to her own neurotic difficulties, a sleep-in maid or governess who would be more or less permanently available during the critical infant years, may be necessary.

Gross Personality Disorders

That psychoses could develop in children under one year of age may come as a surprise to many, yet frequently the psychological damage in schizophrenia is reported as traceable to ambivalence about trusting the mother and to trauma in the "oral" phase. Also constitutional or hereditary defects may bring about an ego so weak that the infant cannot master even the ordinary frustrations of life. A deficiency of mothering as in marasmus, may lead by way of a psychotic depression to death, or it may stop short leaving a residual psychosis. Severe disturbances in the mother (postpartum depression, personality disorders, etc.), may lead to grossly inadequate or disturbed child care so that reality testing by the infant is blocked or severely impaired.

Two types of psychoses begin in the first year of life. They are rarely diagnosed at this age since most of them become conspicuous in connection with later developmental problems. These types are the autistic and the symbiotic psychoses. In the autistic group the child doesn't attempt to gratify his needs by way of meaningful relationship with others. Instead he resorts to a few stereotyped isolated activities, personalized fantasies, rubbing or manipulating himself or chosen objects, and a compulsive need for sameness to maintain his emotional equilibrium. Behavior toward people is as if they are inanimate objects. In contrast, the symbiotic psychotic child never separates his self-identity from a fused identity with his mother. In failing to take this step, reality testing is impaired since the child attempts to cope with his world by clinging solely to the symbiotic relationship. The autistic child gradually moves toward a symbiotic position. Because he relates so poorly to others his contact with people is reduced to the few adults who have to care for him. He then becomes more and more anxious if they threaten to leave and in this situation he may demand strongly that the parents stay close although he does not seek to cling to them. Similarly, the symbiotic child, as he grows older, cannot have his demands for close contact met endlessly, so he is forced to develop other patterns, but since he, too, can't relate in a give-and-take fashion with peers, he has to turn more and more to autistic and self-centered patterns.

By the age of latency, if untreated, these psychoses require years of the most highly skilled psychiatric effort in psychiatric institutions, and even then the result is apt to be marginal. Ideally, treatment should be preventive, especially where experiential factors seem to predominate in the genesis of the syndrome, and the correction of emotionally toxic situations should be attempted as early as possible before irreparable damage is done. The psychoses are so involved they should be referred to the child psychiatrist.

PROBLEMS OF THE MUSCLE-TRAINING (ANAL) PHASE

Emotional disorders arising in this phase come mainly from conflictual experiences with parents as the child learns to use his developing muscle systems. Walking, manual dexterity, talking, and sphincter control make many new experiences possible for the child. Handicapping conditions in any of these areas would leave distinguishable imprints on the child. Similarly, parental handling can have marked effects, i.e., excessive curtailing of a child's motility could lead to inhibition in motility patterns as well as inhibition in many other areas, or poor handling of a rebellious child could lead to excessive challenging of authority or restrictions. Usually these areas develop naturally with parents meeting the child's needs for optimal motility or gradual bowel training within appropriate limits. When this occurs, a self-image develops in the child of his being a physically competent, communicating individual.

Symptoms arising in this developmental phase are: (1) Failures of training—soiling and enuresis, (2) physiological disturbances—constipation, diarrhea, and (3) personality pattern disturbance—excessive rebelliousness and excessive conformity.

Failures in Training

Parents who have never made sufficient demands, or parents who have dominated without considering the child's wishes, or parents who have made inconsistent efforts, are apt to have difficulty helping their children to become trained. Whatever its etiology, prolonged soiling or wetting always leads to secondary emotional complications for the child. School and peer group relationships are jeopardized as the child becomes the object of teasing and ridicule. The soiler or wetter ends up avoiding invitations to visit back and forth with potential friends or to take trips. His sense of shame affects his whole personality. Also the parents may feel that they are failures, which then could lead to anger and the conclusion that the child is willful and should be "broken." With the passing of the optimal time for starting training (usually one to two years old; roughly, soon after the child begins to walk) the pattern becomes more and more difficult to change.

SOILING is often a difficult symptom to treat since it arouses many mixed feelings in parents and in children which interfere with an objective handling of the training. Since the parents will ordinarily have used reaction-formation (p. 77) in connection with their own anal interests, it is difficult for them to feel empathy with the child's task of getting trained. Excessive disgust over cleaning diapers or changing sheets may lead to extra pressure regardless of the capacity or responsiveness of the child. In contrast the child has no comparable investment in training. He waves goodby to his feces in the toilet. If his diapers permit, he will play with the feces. The anus's being an erotic zone lends itself to more interest in its function and more resistance to others' interference. Furthermore, the child is now old enough to have a will of his own and with his bowel and bladder functions discovers mother can't make him perform unless he cooperates. Therefore, he can frustrate or please her depending on his mood. Mothers who first get their child in a mood for cooperation, and then make a legitimate demand for performance within the capacity of the child will initially elicit success on a basis of pleasing mother and then later, success because the child wills it. This turns into self-confidence as bowel control becomes a mastered skill.

ENURESIS by definition refers to involuntary wetting, but in ordinary usage it tends to be limited in reference to nocturnal wetting. It is a symptom brought about by many factors both physical and psychological. Physical factors such as congenital malformations and inflammation of the bladder must be considered and ruled out in the differential diagnosis of enuresis. *However, most cases (9 out of 10 or perhaps higher) are psychological.* These can be divided into two groups, (1) faulty training leading to habit disorder, and (2) a neurosis of which enuresis is a part.

Like training for bowel control, success of this training depends on the parents' first establishing a positive rapport with the child which leads him to attempt to become trained. The parent must avoid making issues out of the failures, while at the same time keeping the child at the task of attemping mastery of his bladder. Overpermissive attitudes give little incentive for the child to master the instinctual wish not to bother with control. In some cultures, enuresis can be ignored due to primitive living conditions until identification with older brothers and sisters accomplishes the task. In our culture, however, the optimal time for *beginning* training is when the child first has the capacity for control (see above), which is an appropriate time even from the child's side. Since pediatricians see soiling and wetting problems in the training period, the chance for preventive steps rests primarily on their shoulders. Enabling parents to be effective in training their children without overreacting is of great psychological value. Treatment of enuresis resulting from poor habit training primarily involves work with the parents; and in most instances will be carried out by pediatricians. Where the enuresis continues from force of habit despite the child's obvious embarrassment, use of certain drugs should be tried. Amphetamines, imipramine or meprobamate have been reported the most useful. Electric sounding devices that are triggered at the start of wetting are also useful, *but only with a child who is cooperative and wants to master the problem.* Without his consent the efforts will lead to further battles, and should not be used.

In a neurosis in which enuresis is a part of the symptom-complex, the enuresis may be a conversion symptom, or part of a character defense, or a regressive phenomenon. Enuresis as a substitute for an overt conflict typically occurs a year or more after a child has been adequately trained. For instance, conflict over birth of a sibling may lead to regression of a trained 4-year-old who then becomes enuretic, or conflicts in the oedipal phase may lead via regression or via conversion to enuresis. An interesting study[4] of this latter type of enuresis revealed that the enuresis in the boys symbolized passive behavior as a defense against fear of their fathers for their oedipal strivings. By contrast, in girls the enuresis symbolized a very aggressive act which served as an expression of aggressive-masculine strivings and a denial of castration fears. Treatment of this form of enuresis requires psychotherapy of the child, as well as collaborative therapy for the parents.

Physiological Disturbances

CONSTIPATION in a child is often the result of overly harsh or guilt-provoking handling during training. The child may at first fear an "accident" and in an attempt to control his bowels, develop constipation. Parents then, either from worry about the constipation or from being thwarted, proceed to get stricter and add the use of laxatives, suppositories and enemas. The child may respond by further covert or open resistance, and chronic constipation ensues. In some cases this may proceed to impaction. Corrective work with parents by the pediatrician is indicated in those situations where the child and parents are involved in a battle of wills. If the child develops a neurosis involving dirt and feces which then leads to constipation, psychotherapy for the child will also be required.

DIARRHEA may be caused by inconsistent, rejecting parental patterns of handling. Characteristically, the diarrhea may be touched off by an angry scene between child and parent. This usually subsides as the child matures. However, a review of children with ulcerative colitis reveals this type of background history, so prevention of this type of response is important.

Personality Pattern Disturbances

As mentioned before, parent-child conflicts centering around motility, aggressiveness and bowel control can leave a decided imprint on the child's personality. Some parents may be able to meet the needs of the dependent child but be unable to tolerate well the emergence of a will and aggressiveness. Parents may then become more controlling and domineering. A more passive or fearful child may then retreat and become anxious and overconforming. A more aggressive child may respond by fighting back harder and become more and more stubborn. Alternatively, in the face of aggressiveness in the child, parents may become overpermissive which may lead to the child becoming still more aggressive and nonconforming. No matter how permissive parents attempt to be, at some point the aggressiveness of the child has to be challenged, and if let go too far, the situation may evoke much harsher punishments than would have been necessary earlier which then results in a very inconsistent form of discipline.

EXCESSIVE REBELLIOUSNESS arising from either extreme of parental handling, leads to the child's not learning to share and cooperate in social situations. Aggressive insistence by a child on his own pleasure will not be tolerated well by the peer groups and eventually will lead to a clash, which in the eyes of the child is probably seen as rejection. Excessively aggressive behavior will isolate a child from socializing experiences with peers and adults just as surely as failure to master any other crucial developmental task. Aggressive behavior is the commonest referring symptom in most Community Psychiatric Clinics. When referred, the children usually are of school age and have failed to adjust to their peer group as well as having failed to develop a capacity to sit and study. Families that have trouble handling the aggressiveness of a child need help as much with this emotional disorder as do those whose child has a clearcut neurotic symptom. With older children collaborative psychotherapy is indicated. With the one- to three-year-olds, helping the parents to provide amply for the child's needs, to tolerate the child's aggressive self-expression (absorbing what needs to be absorbed, channelling, and limiting what should be limited), will prevent many future disasters.

EXCESSIVE CONFORMITY results in some children who have been overly dominated by their parents and in some excessively sensitive children where only minimal but probably subtle pressures have been used. The way in which experiences affect the child has to be the final gauge of their severity for the child. The resulting excessive self-control leads to inhibition of even normal, healthy activity. These children abandon their curiosity for safe, defensive patterns. Energy is used to placate adults and peers, and the child becomes overly good, essentially timid and nonspontaneous. In some children controls become so important that resurgence of unacceptable impulses may lead to the development of compulsivity, obsessive preoccupations and the use of rituals even at this age (1—3 years old). Again work with the environment is needed for the milder cases in this group and psychotherapy for the more severe group.

PROBLEMS OF THE OEDIPAL PHASE

Roughly between the ages of two-and-one-half or three and six further physical, emotional and intellectual development enables the child to understand many of the social complexities of his environment. The numerous questions, often quite penetrating, asked by three-year-olds usher in this phase.* Whereas previously the child has had a limited, egocentric view of the family, as if he and the mother were the central axis, now he comes to realize that mother and father form the central axis, and he forms but a peripheral connection to each. If there are siblings the ties seem further subdivided. Although sibling rivalry is not new at this age, it now poses the social question of who loves whom the best.

Also observable in this phase is the gradual transfer of interest from other body areas to the genital area. This may be due, in part, to a slight hormonal change combined with an interest in urination and to erotic feelings arising from touching the genitals. In any case, at this age most children switch from such forms of auto-erotic (self-gratifying) pleasures as thumbsucking, retaining stools, etc., to masturbation. Some, of course, just add masturbation to their armamentarium. The child connects these erotic feelings with love for the parents and even with babies being born. Soon this complex of feelings leads to the

---
* The reader should now review the portion of Chapter 4 on personality development in which a fuller presentation of oedipal phase is presented (pp. 99 to 108).

development of rivalry towards the parent of the same sex and amorous, possessive feelings towards the parent of the opposite sex. In boys this is rather uncomplicated in its beginnings, in that the primary dependent relationship is with mother and the libidinal strivings are also towards her. In girls, however, the primary dependent relationship is also with mother and therefore is at odds with her libidinal strivings which would lead her to compete with mother for father and risk the loss of her dependent security with mother. That most girls demonstrate rivalry with mother anyhow points to the strength of these strivings. These strivings increase until they reach an intensity at which the wishes in their unmodified form become quite anxiety provoking, as well as being markedly opposed to all of the positive feeling the child has for the parent of the same sex. The child as yet thinks in a very primitive, concrete manner. He fears that such strivings, if known, would lead to banishment from home or to genital castration. That castration fear is so universal indicates that genital, erotic feelings are much more than casually involved in the child's mind with his oedipal strivings (although not in the sense of adult sexuality). Repression of the unacceptable portions of these strivings relegates them to the unconscious and brings relief from the anxiety. When this occurs, the child is described as entering latency. Where the repression is accomplished by positive feelings for both parents, and without seductive stimulation by the mother or excessive punitiveness by the father, the repressing experiences with the parents are mild. This permits the formation of a flexible personality structure which can allow the resurgence of conflictual ideas in later life without raising the anticipation of disaster. However, difficult resolution of the oedipal strivings will leave the child vulnerable to the recurrence of anxiety whenever the strivings reawaken. The symptom neuroses seen at this time and in later years are the next line of defense that develops if oedipal anxiety re-emerges from the repressed state.

The emotional disorders of this period reflect the increasing complexity of the child's personality. Quite a variety of symptoms (excessive fear, immaturity, masturbation, peeping and exhibitionism) and syndromes (early personality patterns, symptom neuroses) occur.

Excessive Fears

Excessive fears arise in this developmental phase even in apparently well adjusted children. Transient day or night fears may occur. Occasional nightmares may occur. When these are infrequent the physician should check that child care is appropriate, i.e., not overstimulating or punitive. If no gross emotional conflict is observable he should reassure parents of the developmental aspects of the anxiety. A careful evaluation of the psychological factors in the handling of the child is indicated in states of fears. If parents are making unwitting mistakes and can correct them upon their being pointed out, then much can be accomplished by the physician. For instance a mother may respond to a son's nightmare (which may be symbolic of his fear of father for wishes to usurp father's place) by taking him to her bed for reassurance. Perhaps father leaves to sleep elsewhere. This allays the fear of the terrified child while he is awake, but adds fuel to the unconscious conflict. Time spent by both parents assuring the child, talking out his fears and getting him to go back to sleep in his own bed would present him with the reality of a secure mother-father bond which provides for him but does not accede to his wishes. This would be frustrating of the oedipal strivings, but very reassuring to his over-all security in the family. However, if the anxiety is excessive with frequent night terrors, or excessive panic about many routine life situations, and on direct examination the child is excessively frightened, then a neurosis with anxiety as its principle symptom must be considered. Treatment would require extensive psychotherapy in a collaborative setting.

Immature Responses and Regression

Where previous developmental tasks have not been mastered a child won't mature emotionally in other areas either in a consistent fashion. For example, if battles about bowel control are still continuing in the six to nine-year-old, the child would remain preoccupied with the battle for control aspect of his relationship with parents and people and wouldn't move on to the love relationships that usually would preoccupy him in the oedipal phase. Instead of becoming generous and developing the capacity to share, the child continues to be on guard lest others take away his prerogatives or try to control him. This hypersensitivity would then pervade all the areas of his personality so he wouldn't move on to the self-confident stage that allows him to learn from others without experiencing this as a narcissistic blow. This interferes with play with others of his chronological age and with the development of the curiosity so necessary if the four to five-year-old is to expand his horizons to the world outside the family. This child will also cling too much, cry too easily, have temper outbursts over trivial incidents and in general react like a two-year-old, which in fact is the level of emotional adjustment at which he is operating. Some parents will ask for help in getting the child over the immaturity especially as the age for enrolling in school approaches.

Another child might have progressed into the oedipal phase when conflicts or experiences frighten him into a retreat to the immature patterns of earlier years. Because this immature reaction represents a set-back he is said to have "regressed" in contrast to the previous type which would be due to being "fixated." The children who regress can often be helped more rapidly as their problem is a more current one. However the conflict is often repressed and in the unconscious so insight psychiatric help may be required. Resolution of the conflict permits the child to resume functioning at his normal age level. In contrast a child that has to overcome a problem of a previous developmental phase will require a more protracted treatment because (1) the problem has had time to become more rigidly entrenched and (2) when the problem is worked through the child is found to be far behind his peers in emotional maturity. The optimal time for mastering the next task of maturation has passed, the peer group probably will continue to reject the child because of his immaturity (his wanting to play in the sand when they want to play guns, etc.) It will therefore be necessary to continue supportive therapy through a catching-up phase.

A four-year-old boy and his mother were referred for psychiatric consultation by the pediatrician for severe constipation after two episodes of impaction. The family wouldn't consistently follow the recommendations of the pediatrician, and more intensive therapy seemed indicated. In a family-focused psychotherapy it was found necessary to give more time to the parents in helping them work through their inconsistent attitudes about bowel training which at first were quite oppositional, with the mother being over-permissive, and infantilizing, and the father being harsh and disgusted that the boy required so much help in this matter. The boy did not reveal any fear of toilets, nor did he give any indication that retaining stool was connected to identification with mother in subsequent pregnancies that she had. He was predominantly stubborn, and extremely controlling. After some six months of therapy the boy began having his own bowel movements at his own time, and was extremely proud of it. He wanted it saved until both parents had seen and praised him for it—which was permitted if it was near time for father to return from work. After self-regulation was well established another six months of therapy was required to undercut his tremendous need to control everything that concerned him. He would want to build projects which were appropriate but would require adult assistance which he couldn't permit except in the most disguised fashion. His inability to share and take turns with other five-year-olds was on the borderline of being a behavior disorder. It was only when parents and the nursery school teacher were reminded of his maladjustment of over a year previous that the strides he had made became apparent. Therapy with this boy will continue until the boy reaches the approximate capabilities of his age group.

Excessive Masturbation

As described earlier a major shift of interest to the genital area occurs in this phase. This shift, along with the increased erotic sensations in the genitals, leads to much more handling and touching of them. There is no cause for concern if at the same time the child is happy, spontaneous and relating well. In most instances helping the child to avoid touching himself too much in public is all the instruction that should be given. Concern about masturbation should arise when it becomes excessive and is in conjunction with a withdrawal from participation and activity that would be normal for the age. The excessive masturbation then is serving the purpose of allaying tensions arising from internalized or interpersonal stresses (oedipal conflicts, sibling rivalry, exclusion by friends, rejection by parents). When these situations are better resolved the child returns again to his usual round of activities, and masturbation dwindles to a casual and more appropriate frequency.

When parents bring a child to the physician for excessive masturbation, he should explore the situation. If the parents do not accept a child's normal needs in this regard, they should be counselled to tolerate much of the masturbation, and to limit their interference at most to helping the child be discreet. Attention should be given to whether the mother is over-stimulating the boy by too much holding, bathing, etc., and to whether the father is being too harsh and punitive in his relationships with the boy. No masturbation, especially not compulsive masturbation, should be handled by parental comments of disgust or threats such as restriction of hands or cutting off of hands or genitals. Such threats will increase the amount of anxiety over castration which then increases the need to touch the penis for reassurance that all is intact. The threats will tend to corroborate the fears of the child that such events occur. Circumcision, even for medical reasons, should be postponed at this age unless absolutely necessary, because of the psychological preoccupation with castration. If parents cannot respond to direct recommendations and if the masturbation is but one symptom of a more general neurosis, referral for psychiatric management should be made.

Peeping and Exhibitionism

Looking at things and being curious about them is part of a healthy child's interest in his environment. In the oedipal phase this is bound to extend to all the marvels of life including the difference in the size of adults and children and their body parts, the anatomical differences between the sexes, the changes in the body of the mother or other women during pregnancy, and the birth of siblings. If information about these facts is withheld or obviously distorted by parents, the child will strive to find out secretly by *peeping*. On the other hand, overstimulation of sexual curiosity in children by parents may lead to an exaggerated peeping. Such overstimulation may result from parents not taking precautions to prevent precocious exposure to adult sexual relations. Where the adult sexuality is combined with quarreling or sado-masochistic interchanges and an inadequately soundproof door intervenes, the likelihood of the child's going to great lengths to find out what is happening is only natural. Another mechanism causing peeping in boys is connected with seeing a girl in the nude and fearing that her body is proof that there is actual castration. Often, as a defense, a boy will invent the idea that he saw a penis anyway (denial). He doesn't really believe his defense, so he goes on peeping over and over to reconvince himself that there isn't such a thing as castration. Since he is not really looking, the question remains unsatisfactorily answered in his mind, and a repetitive pattern of peeping develops. Insight into his misconception about the anatomical differences between the sexes will resolve this pattern.

Exhibitionism stems from a need to deny ideas of physical inferiority (as a child in comparison to an adult) or of castration. Exhibiting the penis by boys and the nude body of girls at this age is an attempt at self-reassurance about these fears. Gentle setting of limits and offering other proof of the child's adequacy constitute the treatment of choice.

Early Personality Pattern Disturbances

In the symptoms described earlier the defensive nature of regression or symptom formation has been apparent. Some children handle oedipal anxiety by adopting certain characteristic modes of behavior which demonstrate a fusion of assertive and defensive drives.

"TOMBOYISH" BEHAVIOR in girls is basically an attempt to deny the difference between boys and girls because of the child's misconception that the biologic endowment of the female is inferior to that of the male. This impression arises from experiences with and attitudes held by parents. If unmodified, this solution of oedipal problems results eventually in a personality disorder when the girl grows to be an adult. There is a continuation of a strong masculine identification and at the same time an excessive competitive drive toward men. By denying her true biologic nature, the girl makes an adjustment to femaleness leading to an adult adjustment in which she feels out of place in many relationships with women and men and especially as a wife and mother.

Similarly, boys may develop "SISSY" BEHAVIOR which is basically an unconscious attempt to deny oedipal rivalry with father. In exchange for being passive there is the hope that father will not be provoked to an antagonistic position. Oftentimes this behavior then provides a disguised excuse (being too helpless to be on his own) for staying close to mother. A continuation of this behavior leads to a self-image of being an inadequate, impotent male. In adult life this interferes with assuming the male role comfortably, and in extreme cases may lead to a deviation of sexual role.

Childhood Psychoneuroses

As mentioned earlier, excessive fears from oedipal conflicts may lead to an anxiety reaction which is a true psychoneurosis. In such a case, repression of the direct fear has occurred. During the oedipal period the other mental mechanisms available to adults (such as reaction-formation, displacement, projection) are present or develop, and symptom neuroses similar to those previously described in adults (Chap. 9) occur. True phobias in this age group are seen regularly in any psychiatric clinic, as are conversion and obsessive-compulsive reactions. Phobias in children are apt to involve concrete objects such as animals or machines instead of the more abstract, disguised situations seen in phobic reactions in adults, such as heights, elevators, small spaces, or crowds. In children conversion responses are apt to involve tic formation, some forms of stuttering and a certain form of enuresis. Compulsive rituals and obsessive preoccupation with "bad thoughts" (sexual, hostile) are occasionally seen. Although the mental mechanisms are the same as with adults, the reaction and the handling are quite modified. Mainly the child tries to cling and stay close to its mother. He doesn't view his condition as a neurosis but as an actual fear. The child is bound by his dependent needs to his parents whom he feels he should please or fear. The immaturity of the child's ego makes a marked difference in his attitude toward getting help. A child for instance cannot be freed from inhibitions that developed as a protection from certain dreaded parental attitudes until those attitudes on the parents' part are modified, which then permits the child to risk a more assertive approach in that area. Thus working with parents is mandatory in the treatment of children and for this reason "collaborative therapy" in which parents and child are seen is recommended. The physician can do much to help the family provide a less stressful environment in these families although treatment of these problems should include insight psychotherapy for the child.

Psychosomatic Disorders

Psychogenic factors have been found to play a fundamental role in the genesis of the psychosomatic disorders of children (feeding difficulties, food fads, obesity, nervous vomiting, colitis, constipation, bronchial asthma, and allergies). The mechanisms are similar to those in adults with the variations in children being parallel to those variations described for psychoneuroses, namely the immaturity and dependent nature of the child.

Psychotic Disorders

Psychotic children may come to the physician's attention at this age, but, interestingly, already the impression will be that the basic trauma preceded this age. The failure to play and develop into the oedipal pattern (i.e., the overt pattern typical for this period) raises concern in the minds of parents who previously had been glossing over their child's "different" behavior. These children will show uneven ego development, bizzarre ideation, poor reality testing, excessive fear, abnormal behavior and marked difficulty in relating to people. Collaborative treatment (involving one or both parents as well as the child) over a number of years, with the child being in an institutional setting some of this time, is usually indicated.

PROBLEMS OF THE LATENCY PERIOD

The latency period is roughly the period between the ages of 6 and 12.* This phase begins after the child resolves the pregenital and oedipal tasks of the earlier years. With this achievement, which is gradual and uneven, there is a redirection of psychic energy from a preoccupation with his relationships in the family to the task of mastering the skills and knowledge required by the world outside the family. Now more abstract learning becomes possible and a start is made toward achieving goals by reliance on his own industry rather than on parental help. With this shift the child becomes ready for school. Also he becomes able to adapt productively to a wide assortment of adults other than his parents, and to become comfortable in a much larger peer group. Despite the tremendous differences between the 6- and 12-year-old, the psychological strivings are essentially similar and the preoccupation is primarily with developing what are called "tool skills" (precise academic knowledge, handskills, sports, etc.). The personality changes are very gradual during this period, and are concerned more with the development of existing mental structures than their modification. One modification that does occur comes by way of participation in the peer group. The rigidity and primitiveness of the infantile superego is gradually softened by the many experiences shared with peers. To find friends who face life with as limited a fund of knowledge gives a child a comfortable yardstick against which to measure himself. Children, by comparing ideas, gradually discover that different adults

---

* The reader should review the material on latency in Chap. 4 (pp. 108 to 111).

view matters differently. The child's view that his parents' knowledge and authority is absolute is gradually modified. This change then allows the child to be more tolerant toward his own independent views than previously. At this stage group loyalties do not supplant family loyalties but are added to the total experiences so vital to maturation. Later, in adolescence, the ties to peers become a more critical influence, which may lead either to increased stabilization or to disruption.

Although the disorders reviewed for the previous phases may become apparent in this age also, they will not be rediscussed here, since the clinical picture and the dynamics are essentially the same. Immaturity, neuroses, psychosomatic disturbances and psychoses do arise in this age group. In fact, most children brought for help with these disorders are of this age because the problem, which has been tolerated in the home, cannot be tolerated in the classroom. However, discussion here will be limited to those symptoms that arise more specifically in connection with the tasks of this age. These are: school problems and behavior disorders. For the sake of clarity, the school problems will be subdivided into motor restlessness, reading disabilities, learning disabilities, and a reluctance to attend school.

School Problems

Failure to progress in school can be the result of an emotional disorder or it can be a stress that causes other emotional problems.* The child who doesn't keep up with his peers will develop secondary problems from his discouragement and loss of self-confidence. Being consistently at the bottom of the class sets in motion a downward spiral of loss of interest in school, less effort and still less achievement. Any child who has a choice would drop out of activities in which he does badly consistently, but this, of course, is not permitted with school. As a consequence, steps by the adults concerned are necessary to restore self-confidence, motivation and the capacity to learn. Repeating a year with the chance for an increased number of successful efforts, and special tutoring to bring the child up to the class level are educational approaches that are very useful if the child then can have the successes that he needs in order to stay motivated.

EXCESSIVE MOTOR RESTLESSNESS combined with a short attention span is frequently seen in children. Since school requires that the child be able to substitute desk work for free play for a considerable number of hours in a day, this restlessness interferes greatly with school tasks. A constitutional factor and sometimes organic, neurologic factors may be the basis for the hyperactivity; however, emotional factors also can

---
* It can also be a result of mental retardation, a condition which will be discussed at the end of this chapter (pp. 541 to 546).

lead to such responses. Parents who irritate and confuse children by inconsistent and accusatory behavior, who cannot tolerate much pressure without "blowing up" or walking out on the situation or resort to too harsh physical punishment, will make it difficult for a child to be calm and relaxed around home. The restlessness is then a reflection of chronic fear combined with the child's poorly modified infantile aggressive patterns. Needless to say, learning is adversely affected by such patterns. These situations point to the need to focus on the family in any thorough approach to emotional problems of children.

READING DISABILITY is probably the most frequently seen school problem. An estimated ten per cent of all students of average or better intelligence read so poorly that their school adjustment is jeopardized as a consequence.[7] Inadequate motivation, lack of opportunity at the optimal time to start reading, and emotional problems of all categories can impair the capacity to read. Such factors provide the bulk of these cases. Gross organic brain damage is suspected in a group designated as having a "primary reading retardation." In this group there is marked difficulty in dealing with written words and written symbols although intelligence is normal and no measurable evidence of neurologic damage is found (by present techniques of testing, clinical examination, x-ray, EEG).

LEARNING DISABILITIES are usually part of a more extensive psychological problem. Learning is impaired sometimes in a more general and at other times in a more circumscribed area. Negativistic attitudes (conscious or unconscious) towards parents may extend to all adults including teachers, in which case all learning may be difficult. Anxiety about developmental or home problems may interfere with concentration while in the classroom and thereby affect all areas of learning. Curtailment and prohibition of aggressiveness in the name of discipline may so inhibit a child that he can't pursue his class subjects with sufficient aggressiveness or he can't pursue an idea in a group or with a teacher sufficiently to understand it. A child who has developed an exaggerated sense of guilt about sexual curiosity may attempt to master this conflict by blocking all curiosity which then blocks his capacity for general learning. Sometimes anxiety or guilt can be limited to specific areas of learning, for instance development of a block on subjects concerning health and the body because of the proximity to fear or guilt about sexual curiosity, or failing arithmetic because one's father is an accountant or mathematician and the subject is reacted to in the unconscious as too competitive. (These mechanisms are repressed and the child is not deliberately planning them.)

RELUCTANCE TO ATTEND SCHOOL. A fear of leaving home to attend school is seen with considerable frequency. The child is often preoccupied with a fear that mother will have a fatal accident or be attacked while he is gone from home. Typically the child is a good, conscientious child who has been overanxious about school performance. At the start of the difficulty there are usually various signs of anxiety such as sleep disturbances, various fears, and often anxiety dreams. On arising on a school day the child complains of stomach cramps, often won't eat breakfast, and fears he will vomit on the bus or in the school. The symptom rapidly subsides if the child is permitted to stay home. It doesn't occur on the weekend. Forced attendance at school often leads to a surprisingly violent scene from these ordinarily overly good children, which indicates the degree of anxiety present. However, secondary problems of getting behind in his studies compounds the anxiety for these conscientious children. If the child isn't overwhelmed, mobilization of the parents to get the child to return to the classroom despite some anxiety prevents the many secondary complications. Referral for insight psychotherapy should be made in all those situations where the anxiety is great.

Refusal to attend school due to inconsistent parental management gives quite a different picture. The child isn't anxious, and the parents can't be aroused particularly in their child's behalf. The child is often defiant and negativistic. He expects to win out over authority by some means and uses his ingenuity to devise methods to get his way, as if it is a big game.

The Behavior Disorders

Behavior is the first method of communication between child and parent, and precedes the use of words. Infants will signal fear, anger and pleasure, etc., by their behavior. Inevitably then behavior becomes the vehicle for the expression of the more complex interpersonal and intrapsychic conflicts of children and adults. The child who is eager to please can dress rapidly, perform chores graciously and produce neat homework. The child who is angry can dawdle or use overtly defiant aggressive behavior.

One form of negativistic antisocial behavior is an outgrowth of a hostile inconsiderate parent-child relationship. With time this tends to become more characterological in its patterning which then extends to all authority figures—school, police, etc. The oppositional interaction of the parent and child is often very easy for outsiders to see even when neither side is able to see the provocativeness of its own behavior.

Another form of behavior disorder is typically parallel to a symptom neurosis where the emotional conflict is repressed and unwittingly becomes acted out in behavior. To the untrained the behavior may seem like purely antisocial and delinquent behavior. The need to get caught and punished for a "lesser crime" is often apparent in these instances.

An eight-year-old boy who was openly the mother's favorite would reciprocate by bringing flowers to the mother. He made up stories to account for the flowers, but these were not very plausible. Mother was so pleased with the attention from him that she never really questioned him. One day he left his notebook in the florist's shop from which he had been taking the flowers. The florist rightly connected the series of thefts with the boy and irately spoke to the boy's father, who was a barber in the shop next door. Father was furious and beat the boy harshly, viewing the behavior as further evidence of the boy's delinquent tendencies and his being spoiled by his mother. This was one of a series of episodes in which the boy was caught and punished by his father for stealing (rather than for his oedipal fantasies, which were the major crime with which he was struggling in his unconscious and for which he sought punishment, albeit without being aware of it).

In another form of behavior disorder the pathology is limited in a given child to one area, such as stealing, fire-setting, running away, sexual acting out. In these homes parents seem able to provide adequate training and limits in all areas save those in which the symptomatic behavior occurs. Closer examination of the parents reveals an unresolved conflict in the same area, and the ineffective handling and even subtle encouragement to act out in this area is the specific cause of the child's delinquency. This permissiveness of parents toward specific antisocial pathology has been well described as a reciprocal interaction brought on by a lacuna in the parents' superego.[6]

JUVENILE DELINQUENCY is antisocial behavior which leads to referral to the courts, and, as such, may have multiple etiological bases. Most instances have mechanisms such as those described above. However, it is useful to consider also sociological factors (gangs, peer groups, minority group psychology) and biological factors (mental retardation, psychomotor epilepsy) as well as the dissocial behavior brought about by emotional disorders. The treatment will obviously be quite different if delinquent behavior is part of a group phenomenon or is a symbolic acting out of a neurotic conflict. A multifaceted[1, 2] approach based on diagnosis and dynamic understanding is necessary to handle the many etiological bases of juvenile delinquency.

PROBLEMS OF ADOLESCENCE*

Adolescence is a period of rapid physical growth including rapid sexual maturation. Mental processes and emotional controls do not automatically mature in step with the physical changes, and the result-

---

* Adolescence, as used here, is coextensive with puberty and adolescence, as listed on p. 82 and discussed on pp. 111 to 118.

ant imbalances give this period its characteristic fluctuating quality. The physical maturity gives the adolescent the drive to attempt more complex adult behavior. This may lead to a premature renunciation of any dependent position, which then may take the adolescent beyond his capacity for independent action. He is likely then to reverse himself and regress to a more dependent and childish position than he has assumed for years. At the same time he is likely to project his difficulty onto parents, a maneuver which "saves face" in his own eyes and with his peers. ("They should have stopped me," or the reverse, "they never let me do things my way.") Just the same there is a continuous and rapid maturation going on which permits the mastery of many increasingly difficult situations, and this fact should not be overlooked. Inappropriate behavior or effect should not be excused just on the basis of adolescence being a difficult time. As a matter of fact, appropriate, fair responses from those in charge are never more important than at this age. Adults should offer a dependable relationship without requiring the adolescent to assume any unnecessarily dependent position. Most advice can be given as a sharing of experience without demanding that the adolescent respond like a latency-age child.

The main psychological tasks that arise during this period[3] are: (1) a revision of the childhood superego which is by now outgrown in many areas, (2) acceptance and internalization of standards acceptable to the adult world, (3) acceptance of biologically determined sexual identity, and (4) some narrowing of vocational interests toward an attainable goal. Between the first and second steps listed above is a period when the adolescent is likely to behave quite erratically. He will have dismantled parts of his previous standards for conduct and as yet will not have replaced them with an adequate regulating system. Besides, he does not want advice from adults since he is trying to do without that very aspect of his previous adjustment. Peer morality and "other influences" are brought in to fill the void. In the meantime, the individual is more apt to make mistakes and to head off on poorly thought-out tangents than at any other time. But the willingness to experiment and try different approaches is a necessary part of the growth of any individual who aspires to attain an independent self-identity. The adults involved should provide the tolerance for some healthy deviation from their set patterns without rejection of the adolescent.

The psychopathology of this period that links specifically with these stresses can be described under the following headings: (1) imbalance of maturation, (2) psychoneuroses, (3) personality disorders, (4) borderline states, and (5) psychoses.

Imbalances of Maturation

The sudden growth spurt that occurs in adolescence often leads to full physical development without time for emotional and mental processes to keep pace. Nearly any seventh grade will have a 12-year-old boy who has suddenly become six feet tall. Adults then tend to think the tall boy should be more mature than the smaller 12-year-olds, whereas often he is temporarily least well adjusted just because of the stress of the change in size. Suddenly he may be bigger than his parents, and it then becomes difficult to ask for the care and love he is used to from these parents who are now physically smaller.

PRECOCIOUS SEXUAL DEVELOPMENT throws its burden on an ego even less ready than that of the typical adolescent. Boys will occasionally enter puberty at nine to ten years of age and girls even earlier. This circumstance often leads to the child's isolation, since he feels too different to be comfortable with his peers and usually will not be accepted by the 13- or 14-year-olds who are comparably developed.

One such boy pointed out that, since he couldn't get a license for a motor scooter, go on dates, or get jobs like those of the 14-year-olds who looked like him, and since he couldn't fit in with kids his age as the play of 10-year-olds seemed awfully juvenile, he had withdrawn and turned to hobbies to fill in his time. He also developed excessive masturbation followed by sufficient guilt to lead to cessation of the masturbation and the development of the compulsive rituals for which he was referred. Fortunately, after a few years of isolated adjustment, he was able to re-establish himself in a peer group slightly older than himself and then to resume more active, outgoing behavior.

DELAYED SEXUAL DEVELOPMENT can cause an equal amount of distress to the adolescent. As the peer group matures, leaving him underdeveloped, the question in his mind of what has gone wrong compounds the normal self-doubts and fears of inadequacy that are latent in all children. If this is reinforced by neurotic guilt over some sexuality or masturbation, he may fear that he has suffered some serious physical damage. The anxiety may then be repressed and reappear in any of a number of ways; for example, it may reappear either as a diffuse chronic anxiety or as a somatic neurosis such as a cardiac neurosis or as a personality pattern of overly conforming, noncompetitive behavior.

ANOREXIA NERVOSA is a serious disorder in girls which is precipitated by pubertal changes. Usually the girl has used "tomboy" defenses through childhood, indicating a masculine identification and problems with femininity. Beginning of the secondary sex changes, such as would ordinarily force an abandonment of the "tomboy" defenses in the less neurotic girl, arouses in these girls a counter-drive not to grow up. In an attempt to turn back the clock, the girl avoids all the food that she possibly can in hopes of avoiding the natural physical development. Often the actual onset of anorexia follows a date on which the first harmless kiss occurs. Misconceptions of oral impregnation are often found at the base of these situations.

One 14-year-old girl with anorexia developed a highly complicated conscious reason for watching her weight. She feared if she became overweight and then dieted she would develop abdominal lines which would mislead others to surmise they were from pregnancy—"striae gravidarum." When she first came for psychiatric consultation she looked cachexic and had pitting ankle edema, essentially famine edema.

These situations can proceed to such extents that hospitalization and tube feeding may be necessary. They should be managed in collaboration with a psychiatrist.

Psychoneuroses

Psychoneuroses in adolescents closely resemble those seen in adults. Often, however, this is the first such occurrence whereas adults with a neurosis recall a neurosis in adolescence or childhood. However the picture in adolescence is sufficiently parallel to that of adults that no further elaboration need be made.

The incidence of suicide attempts increases rapidly during this age. In latency, overt suicide attempts occur so rarely as to be virtually nonexistent. Occasionally a child will make a dramatic gesture, mimicking parental behavior. But children who have difficulty can ask for help and receive it without "loss of face." In adolescence more problem solving is attempted and "loss of face" is felt so much more acutely as to make it nearly impossible for some adolescents. Fortunately most attempts stop short of fatality, probably because the adolescent has an underlying will to live that is also at its peak.

NEUROTIC BEHAVIOR DISORDERS, including juvenile delinquency, in adolescence have a different quality from that seen in the latency group. Often the behavior may be precipitated more by the adolescent's need to prove himself or to demonstrate his independence of authority than by serious deprivation or clashes with parents. Mild authoritarian stands on the part of adults may release a need in the adolescent to overassert himself. Genuine understanding, along with real and not arbitrary limits, is still needed. Also indicated is a demonstrated willingness on the part of adults to negotiate, no matter what has developed. At the same time the capacity for destructiveness is now practically of adult proportion, so consequences become more serious. Stealing cars is certainly a more serious offense than stealing bicycles. If a car is wrecked, much more damage may occur. Gang fights may seriously injure someone. The runaway goes much farther and acts out more. The adolescent is often in danger of serious self-destructive behavior. Promiscuity and criminal behavior may entail such danger that placement (in an institution) for protection from himself may become urgent.

Personality Disorders

Toward the end of adolescence the personality settles into an equilibrium which is the result of the many internalized experiences the adolescent has had as a child as well as the modifications made in the course of adolescence. The personality becomes relatively stabilized into its characteristic patterns and traits. If the patterns are too defensive and inflexible they are designated as a "disorder." Masochistic, sadistic, hysteric, compulsive, passive-aggressive patterns are some of the constellations that may result.

Borderline States

"Adolescent turmoil" is a term used in a variety of ways by different authorities in psychiatry. Most often it is used to designate a temporary psychotic picture, with fleeting hallucinatory experiences, chaotic personalized ideation, and suspiciousness of paranoid proportion. However this state carries a more favorable prognosis than if the picture were presented in an adult. Stabilization, as in a hospital, allows the ego to regain mastery over the surging id conflicts. With this, the adolescent returns to his previous equilibrium which in most instances is a relatively healthy adjustment or perhaps one involving some form of personality disorder. Often the turmoil is precipitated by sexual conflicts, such as a latent homosexual wish leading to a state of panic. Instead of being acted out, a regression to the syndrome described occurs.

Psychoses

Schizophrenia is seen with moderate frequency in adolescence. It presents a picture parallel to that seen in adults, with the various types —simple, catatonic, hebephrenic, paranoid, and mixed being distinguishable. "Dementia praecox," now an obsolete term, was at first applied to schizophrenia that had its onset in adolescence. It used to be regarded as having an extremely poor prognosis, but with the development of the physical therapies, the chemotherapies, as well as advances in milieu therapy and psychotherapy, there is, at present, more optimism about working with this group than with adults who develop a comparable degree of schizophrenic regression.

PSYCHOLOGICAL ASPECTS OF MENTAL RETARDATION

In a brief discussion of mental retardation and its links with the psychiatric disorders of childhood the primary focus will be limited to the psychological aspects of the condition. Some 60 syndromes having mental retardation as one of the signs have been described. The sociological and management aspects of retardation are both large fields in themselves. (See Suggestions for Further Reading at the end of this chapter.)

The problem of mental retardation affects many individuals and will occasionally be brought to the attention of most physicians. Diagnosis and management of the retarded patient as such, however, tend to fall to the pediatrician, psychiatrist, and general practitioner. Approximately one out of 70 live births is a retarded child with an I. Q. below 75. This means that over 2,000,000 persons in the United States are retarded. It is estimated that 10 per cent of this group are seriously enough retarded to warrant institutional care. The group with I. Q. ratings in the 50-70 range are regarded as "educable," which means that they can learn to handle simple arithmetic. They can be trained to work productively in supervised settings. Persons with I. Q.'s in the 30-50 range are regarded as "trainable," which means that they can be taught to manage their personal hygiene and to do simple, closely supervised tasks. In many instances these accomplishments will enable them to be managed at home, or if they are in an institution, will enable them to be partially self-sufficient. Those with I. Q.'s of 30 or below will require round-the-clock supervision, and, for them, institutional management is clearly indicated. Management of the severely retarded child can be very disruptive of family life. Those who evaluate such patients should explore the adjustment of the total family, especially if other children are in the home.

Etiology

The etiology of mental retardation exemplifies the complexity of the whole problem. Steady advances have been made in the understanding of many of the 60 known syndromes, and where specific causes have been discovered, specific preventive or treatment measures have often been successful. Examples are: certain infections (congenital syphilis), endocrine disturbances (hypothyroidism), metabolic errors (phenylketonuria), and noxious agents (x-rays in the first trimester of pregnancy). Unfortunately the group of syndromes with known causes accounts as yet for only 8 per cent of the total; nonetheless it represents the kind of scientific approach that is needed in any basic dealing with the problem. Recent advances in the fields of cytology, chromosomes and embryology hopefully will lead to the discovery of more of the specific causes and then to the appropriate treatment or preventive measures. Some authorities estimate that as many as 40 per cent of the remaining 92 per cent may be retarded due to a combination of limited hereditary endowment with early cultural or social deprivation. Definitive studies to prove or disprove this contention are difficult to design. Eventually they must be done, and in the meantime it is clear that coping with sociological factors must be attempted.

Making the Diagnosis

The need for thoroughness in making the definitive diagnosis of mental retardation is evident when one considers the many different etiological possibilities. Furthermore, a thorough evaluation is needed to convince parents who may otherwise be justifiably unwilling to accept such a serious diagnosis. If a physician does not have the time or feel competent to evaluate all of the various aspects of the situation himself, he should make referrals for the appropriate studies, or the family should be alerted to the possibilities of retardation and then a referral of the child to a specialist or to a diagnostic clinic should be made.

When retardation is suspected, an evaluation should cover at least the following points.

1. History. This should be a thorough history, not only of the symptoms and signs but of the physical, social and psychosexual* development of the child. The parents' history, the family history, and family interaction should be explored. The school record and a report of the social adjustment in school should be obtained.

2. Physical and Neurologic Examinations. Besides the routine examinations, hearing should be carefully evaluated, especially in the many cases where no clear cause of retardation is discovered.

3. Laboratory Tests. X-ray, electroencephalographic, endocrine, and metabolic studies should be done as indicated.

4. Psychological Tests. A battery of psychometric tests (tests to determine I. Q.) as well as projective tests (tests to determine personality patterns and dynamics) should be done in all cases.

5. Psychiatric Evaluation. Referral for a psychiatric appraisal should be made where emotional conflicts are observed.

The differential diagnosis between psychiatric syndromes and mental retardation is not always easy. To be objective, one should attempt to evaluate both the psychological and the organic pathology of all children

---

* *Psychosexual* refers to the rate and manner of progression through the various stages of libidinal development, as described in Chap. 3.

in whom retardation is suspected. The retarded child will have had certain emotional stresses in being different from his peers and siblings. Inability to compete on an equal footing may lead to a sense of failure, much teasing and some isolation from his peer group. Also if the retarded child undergoes traumatic emotional experiences, he will respond with neurotic or psychotic defenses as would better endowed children.

It is naive to assume that the presence of organic factors rules out psychological factors or vice versa. Of 250 consecutive referrals for admission to a custodial institution for severely retarded children, 35 proved to have purely psychologic problems and 89 had such significant auditory, visual and other physical handicaps as to warrant their return home for further rehabilitative efforts.[5] Conversely of 328 consecutive admissions to a psychiatric ward for adolescents, 103 had I. Q.'s of 75 or below.[8]

Differential points to keep in mind include the following: 1. The longitudinal history of the retarded child will usually reveal a delayed development in all areas of functioning. This gradually will appear to become more severe as the slower rate of development causes an ever-widening gap between the retarded child and the more rapidly developing average child. In contrast the history of the emotionally disturbed child will usually give a picture of relatively normal progress until the onset of difficulty, when there is usually an erratic or uneven pattern of development. Certain skills or areas of intellectual functioning will be interfered with and others will not. For instance, a child may block on aggressive or sexual material but remain quite facile with arithmetic. However, this is not always a differential point, since a psychotic reaction or a severe neurosis may impair all functioning, leaving only the history of good developmental progress preceding the onset of the disorder as the primary clue indicating emotional factors. Then one is left to decide such questions as whether the history is colored by the parents' distortions and whether some such factor as a mild encephalitis could have produced such drastic results.

2. The diagnosis of a psychosis or a neurosis is a specific diagnosis and requires certain historical and clinical findings to support it. (See the discussions of psychoses and neuroses both in this chapter and in those dealing with adult disturbances.) A thought disorder of some magnitude will be noted in the psychotic child. He is apt to express ideas of a highly personalized, magical nature. Affective disturbances will affect the pattern of relating. Ambivalence will be marked and should be apparent in many of the child's constructs and in his overt behavior. Sufficient evidence of the psychotic defense aspects of the mental mechanisms should be observed before a diagnosis of psychosis is made. In contrast, the retarded child will not display such findings

unless he has developed a psychosis as well as being retarded. The diagnosis of a child with a neurosis will be based on the observation of neurotic defenses used to cope with an emotional conflict. These same mental mechanisms are available to the retarded child, so again this factor does not necessarily differentiate the two. The effort to differentiate should be based rather on attempting to assess whether the two entities are present concomitantly and whether the poor intellectual functioning that confuses the picture is the result of a neurosis in an (otherwise) adequately endowed child or due to some degree of retardation. Differentiating clues will arise from the history, psychological testing, and the clinical examination.

3. Problems of neurotic behavior (personality disorders) are frequently seen in the retarded population. The Juvenile Courts report an incidence of retarded children among those brought to them that is four to five times as high as the over-all incidence. This statistic is thought to be due to the retarded child's being less clever in avoiding the law, as well as his being likelier to gravitate to delinquent groups because of their relative simplicity of structure. Being continually frustrated by repeated failures when left "to sink or swim" with their brighter peers, they drift into antisocial groups. Of retarded children, the ones most frequently misjudged belong to this behavioral group. Being aggressive and often talkative despite a limited vocabulary, they first arouse the anger of the authorities. On testing them, one is surprised to discover that they are functioning in the retarded range. It then becomes apparent that they have been misjudged in many other situations, i.e., in schools and social situations where their lack of performance has been attributed to a blameworthy attitude toward authority.

Management

The emotional maturity and intellectual capacity of the parents of a retarded child should be evaluated by the physician before attempting to discuss management of the child with them. Occasionally parents may not be aware of the nature of the disorder, although secretly they may fear such a possibility. The emotional reaction of the parents to the diagnosis of mental retardation will often complicate the task of diagnosis and management since mental retardation is still dreaded in our society. This will be one of the main psychological aspects of the entire problem. The parents' reactions will be based on their emotional makeup, in this case how they react to a difficult situation. Mature parents will be able to accept the retarded child as he is and will follow constructive measures in dealing with the problem. They also will be able to accept the limits of professional help, and not search endlessly for elusive cures. Other parents may defend themselves against the fact of their child's retardation by illogically denying this reality. They may cling to the idea that nothing is wrong and that the child is just a "late bloomer." Still others may have a need to project the blame onto some nebulous organic factor as if failure to prove a cause would make them guilty. These neurotic responses may lead the parents to go from doctor to doctor or specialist to specialist searching for someone to say that their child isn't retarded. They may seriously deplete their financial resources as well as neglect themselves and the upbringing of their other, better endowed children. With this in mind the physician should attempt to help them understand their frustration and even their anger at having a child with such a handicap. The parents need the opportunity to ventilate their conflict without being judged or made to feel guilty. They need time and emotional support to work through their rejection, guilt, or other conflict before they can face their difficult reality.

Parents have become genuinely depressed when the handicapped child has been placed too suddenly, as if this move has been interpreted by them as proof that they had really rejected a helpless, innocent infant. Other parents have been too guilty to place a child and have gone to heroic extremes for years, giving up all of their other activities and sacrificing their other children in order to manage a child who is not trainable. Helping parents to achieve a more mature attitude may require a number of appointments. Nonetheless the physician who is able to help them accept the reality of the situation early in the process will prevent much of the anguish and emotional conflict that can develop. In some instances referral of the parents for more extensive counselling, as for example, by a social or psychiatric agency, may be necessary.

Good management of the retarded child from the psychological standpoint should include the provision of those emotional experiences that are essential for any child's development: security, love, discipline, and recognition of progress and capacity. Play and school experiences outside the home that are within the retarded child's capacity are often more difficult, but not impossible to provide. The child should not be protected to an unrealistic degree although often intelligent protection can be offered to a greater extent than parents realize. A variety of school classes geared to the various capacities of retarded children is now provided in most large cities. The advantage to a slow learner of being in a slow learners' or ungraded class is considerable. Otherwise, the inevitable "scape-goating," teasing, and failures will add a severe strain to his emotional adjustment. Some playgrounds and camps are similarly geared to the retarded child's capacity and should be used.

In essence, the parents should be advised of all of the available community resources. Most adjustment problems can be handled by adequate programming with the parents utilizing the available help. If, however, an emotional disorder such as a frank neurosis develops, the problem should be referred for psychotherapy, as would be done for any child.

Summary

While there are important special features, nevertheless the psychological aspects of mental retardation have much in common with those of children of average intelligence. The psychopathology seen in retarded children is similar to that seen in other children. The retarded child may well have emotional and social conflicts superimposed upon the retardation. These problems can be diagnosed and approached as with individuals of average intelligence, making allowances for the retardation. A careful evaluation of the history, of clinical, laboratory and psychological findings is needed to make the definite diagnosis of retardation. Many parents will have difficulty in accepting the diagnosis of mental retardation, and an evaluation of their capacity to understand and cope with the situation should be made. The parents should be offered appropriate emotional support and understanding by the physician to enable them to face the problem realistically. In some instances, one or both parents may benefit from referral for more extensive counselling in the management of the child, or for psychiatric help, if a depression or frank emotional disturbance develops.

Bibliography

1. Bovet, L.: Psychiatric Aspects of Juvenile Delinquency, Geneva, Switzerland, World Health Organization, 1951.
2. Eisler, K. (ed): Searchlights on Delinquency, New York, Internat. Univ. Press, 1949.
3. Gardner, G.: Psychological problems of adolescence *in* Arieti, S. (ed): American Handbook of Psychiatry, New York, Basic, 1959.
4. Gerard, M.: Enuresis: a study in etiology *in* Gerard, M. (ed): The Emotionally Disturbed Child, New York, Child Welfare League of America, 1957.
5. Gibson, R.: Survey of special types encountered in mental deficiency clinics, Am. J. Ment. Defic. 58:141, 1953.
6. Johnson, A.: Juvenile delinquency *in* Arieti, S. (ed): American Handbook of Psychiatry, New York, Basic, 1959.
7. Rabinovitch, R.: Reading and learning disabilities *in* Arieti, S. (ed): American Handbook of Psychiatry, New York, Basic, 1959.
8. Spitz, R.: Hospitalism: an inquiry into the genesis of psychiatric conditions in early childhood *in* Psychoanalytic Study of the Child, Vol. 1, p. 53, New York, Internat. Univ. Press, 1945.

9. Toolan, J. M.: Differential diagnosis of mental deficiency in adolescents, Am. J. Ment. Defic. 59:445, 1955.

Suggestions for Further Reading

Aichhorn, A.: Wayward Youth, New York, Viking Press, 1951.
Gerard, M.: The Emotionally Disturbed Child, New York, Child Welfare League of America, Inc., 1957.
Redl, F., and Wineman, D.: Children Who Hate, Glencoe, Ill., Free Press, 1951.
Toolan, J. M.: Differential diagnosis of mental deficiency in adolescents, Am. J. Ment. Defic. 59:445, 1955.

Index

Abreaction, 492
Activity therapy, 509-513
Addiction, 166-176
  narcotic, 414-416
    definition, 166-168
    dependence, 414
    tolerance, 414
  polysurgical, 243
  psychodynamic factors in, 168-169
Adjustment, definition, 29-31
Adolescence, 114-118
  "adolescent turmoil," 540
  borderline states, 540
  imbalances in maturation, 538-539
  problems of, 536-540
  psychiatric disorders of, 516-540
Adrenalin, 378
Adrenochrome, 378-379
Adrenolutin, 378
Affective inappropriateness, 364-365
Affective reactions, 341-359
  depressions, 341-351
  nomenclature in, official, 355
  recurrent, 354-357
    definition, 355
Affects and surgical experience, 240-251
Aggression, 61-63
  developmental course, 63
Alcohol, habituation to, 171-173
  hallucinosis, 293
Alcoholism, 405-414
  essential, 405
  meaning of drinking in, 409
  symptomatic, 405
Ambivalence, 95
  schizophrenia and, 367
  surgical experience and, 240-251
Amnesia
  anterograde, 322
  retrograde, 322
Amphetamines, 456
Amytal, 455
Anger, chronic, 197

Anhedonia, 164
Anorexia nervosa, 538
Antabuse, 473-475
Antidepressants, 452
  discussion, 459
  habituation and, 174-176
  listing of, 456
Anxiety, 66-68
  attack, 311
  hysteria. See Phobia
  postoperative, 253
  preoperative, 253
  reaction, 311-312
  surgical experience and, 251-255
Apathy and schizophrenia, 365
Appointment of, making of, 4
Apprehension and surgical experience, 251
Argyll Robertson pupil, 284
Arteriosclerosis, cerebral, and psychosis, 287-291
Arthritis, 260
Associative looseness, 366-367
Asthma, bronchial, 200-206
Attention
  ego and, 72
  infancy period and, 86
Attitudes
  attitude therapy, 501-506
    degree of activity, 503
    emotional responses, 502-503
    expectations, 503-504
  muscle training period and, 95
  patients'
    body, and surgical experience, 233-235
    laboratory procedures, 13
    toward illness, 2
    toward physicians, 2
  physicians'
    malingering and, 150-151
    physical examinations, 11-12
Autistic thinking, 365-366

Awareness, levels of
  concept, 38-48
    application to patients, 45-47
    application to physician, 47-48
    resistance to, 38-39
    evidence of, 39-45
    slips and errors, 39-42

Backache, 158-161
  psychologic factors causing, 160-161
  psychophysiological treatment, 159-160
Barbiturates, 454-455
Bereavement, 130-134
Biochemistry and schizophrenia, 378-380
Bleuler's "four A's," 364-367
Blindness, 261-263
Blushing, 116
Body
  attitudes toward, 233-235
  narcissism, 234
Body-image, 233-235
  conversion reaction and, 321
Boredom, 165-166
Brain
  disease, senile, and psychosis, 288
  mind and, 30
  organic reactions, 271-306
    classification, 276-277
    specific, 281-306
  syndromes
    chronic, with convulsive disorder, 295-303
    diagnosis, 432-433
  tumor, and psychosis, 289
Bronchial asthma, 200-206

Calendar, "perpetual," 43
Cardiovascular disease, 256-260
Case history, 6-10
Castration fear, 104
Catatonic schizophrenia, 369-370
  excitement, 369
  stupor, 369
Cerea flexibilitas, 369
"Change of life," 119-121, 357
Childhood, psychiatric disorders of, 516-540
  schizophrenia, 374
Chorea, Huntington's, 128
Classification
  brain, organic reactions, 276-277
  measures for use by psychiatrist, 470-471
  mental retardation, 541
  personality disorders, 402-403
  psychoses, 355

Clergy and treatment, 465
Colic, 517-518
Colitis, 210-212
Colon, irritable, 210-212
Compensation
  fears of surgery and, 223
  malingering and, 149-150
Compulsion, definition, 329
Compulsive reaction, 329-333
Concussion, definition, 304-305
Confabulation, 289
Conflict, 64-65
  "endopsychic," 65
  libido and, 56
  neurotic, 69
  realistic, 69
  resolution in latency period, 109
  self-preservative drives and, 56
  types of, 69
Conformity, excessive, in children, 525
Conscience
  depression and, psychotic, 345
  effectiveness of, 37-38
  formation of, 68
  severity of, 37
  superego and, 73
Constipation in children, 523-524
Constitutional baseline, 516-517
Consultations, 19, 437
  considerations in, 465-468
Contusion, definition, 305
Conversions, 273
Conversion reaction, 312-322
  malingering and, 146
  psychodynamics, 316-321
  symptomatology and diagnosis, 320-322
Convulsive disorder and chronic brain syndrome, 295-303
Counter-transference
  definition, 451-452
  psychotherapy, relationship, 484
Counterphobia, 250
Courtesy and therapy, 498
Crying, abnormal infantile, 517
Cyclothymic personality, 354

Day hospital, 508-509
Deafness, 261-263
Death and surgical experience, 251-255
Defense mechanisms, 74-80
  schizophrenia and, 385-389
  surgical experience and, 235
Delinquency, juvenile, 536
Delirium, 274-281
  definition, 275
  sequence of events in production of, 280

Delirium—(Continued)
  tremens, 278, 292-295
Delusions, 273
  definition, 279
  schizophrenia and, 367
Dementia, 281
  arteriosclerotic, 287-291
    definition, 287
    differential diagnosis, 289
  definition, 276
  epileptic, 303
  paralytica, 282-287
    definition, 282
Denial
  cardiovascular disease and, 259
  definition, 76-77
  surgical experience and, 235
Dependence, physical, 167
Depression
  affective psychotic reaction and, 341-351
  anaclitic, 518
  dementia and, 285
  surgical experience and, 251-255
Depressive equivalents, 244
Depressive reaction
  involutional, 120
  neurotic, 333-336
  psychotic, 356
Dermatological syndromes, 263-264
Development
  early periods, study of, 83-85
    direct observation, 83-84
    experimental regression, 84
    mental illnesses studies, 84-85
    psychotherapeutic techniques, 85
  periods. *See specific periods*
  personality, 82-129
  physiological, 82-83
Deviation, sexual, 57, 416-422
  in children and infants, 420
Diabetes mellitus, 128, 264-265
Diagnosis
  action, 430
  conversion reaction, 320-322
  diagnostic thinking, 430-435
  differential
    dementia, arteriosclerotic, 289
    malingering, 145-148
  disclosure of, 15-17
  dynamic, 433-435, 501
  genetic, 435
  groups, 431-433
    brain syndromes, 432-433
    mental deficiency, 432
    neurosis, 432
    normality, 431-432
    psychosis, 432

Diagnosis—(Continued)
  headache, 153-154
  intelligence, 431
  mental retardation, 542-544
  mood, 430-431
  personality, 431
  procedures, 6-17
  recent memory and retention, 431
  thought process, 431
Diarrhea in children, 524
Dignity and therapy, 499
Disgust, 69
Disillusionment in family triangle period, 106-107
Displacement, 80
  phobic reaction and, 327
Dissociative reaction, 322-325
Doctor-patient relationship, 451
Dread and surgical experience, 251
Drives
  basic, 49-64
    aim, 53
    forces opposing, 65-69
    listing of, 54
    manifestation of, 49-64
    object, 53
    source, 53
  sadistic, 79
  self-preservative, 52-54
    libido and, 55-60
  sexual-social. *See* Libido
Drug addiction. *See* Addiction
Dysrhythmia, cerebral, and psychosis, 303

Echolalia, 370
Echopraxia, 370
Educational therapy, 464
  discussion, 513
Ego, 71-73
  defense mechanisms. *See* Defense mechanisms
  formation capacity for 71
  ideal, 74
  infancy period and, 86
Electroconvulsive therapy, 475-477
Electroencephalography, 278
Electronarcosis, 475
Emotional forces and surgical experience, 240-251
Endocrine disorders, 264-265
Endocrine status and schizophrenia, 377
Energy, 70
  "psychic," 70
Enuresis, 522-523
Environmental manipulation
  external environment, 514-515
  within the hospital, 506-508

Epilepsy
  idiopathic, 295-303
    definition, 295
    epileptic dementia, 303
    epileptic deterioration, 303
    epileptic personality, 303
    psychological factors in attacks, 298-300
    seizures
      grand mal, 296-297
      petit mal, 297-298
      psychomotor, 298
    traumatic, 305
  temporal lobe, 298
Equilibrium, 29
Equivalents
  bereavement, in psychotic depression, 349
  depressive, 244
  psychomotor, 298
Erectores pilae, 65
Errors, behavioral, 39-42
Ethology, 51
Etiology
  brain, organic reactions, classification, 276-277
  mental retardation, 541-542
  neurosis, 272
  psychosis, 272
  schizophrenic reactions, 374-389
Examination
  mental status, 430
  physical, 10-13
Exhibitionism, 416
  family triangle period and, 101, 529-530

Fainting, 324
Family
  influences of, 123-127
  maladjustments, 138-139
  members, aiding therapy, 513-514
Family triangle period, 99-108
  achievements of, 99-100
  boys, changes in, 100-106
  girls, changes in, 106-108
  personality pattern disturbances, 530-531
  problems of, 525-532
Fatigue, 162-165
  treatment, 164-165
Fear, 65-66
  castration, 104
  excessive, and family triangle period, 526-527
  surgical experience and, 252
Feeding disturbances in infants, 517-519

Fetishism and sexual deviation, 416
Firmness and therapy, 505
Fixations
  definition, 92
  family triangle period and, 106
  maturity period and, 118
  muscle training period and, 98
  personality disorders and, 404
Flight of ideas, 352, 367
Fractures, 261
Free-association, 44
  definition, 85
  discussion, 486
Freedom and therapy, 500
Friendliness and therapy, 504-505
Friends and therapy, 513-514
Frigidity, transient or situational, 143-145
Frustration
  hostility and, 62
  infancy period and, 90
Fugue state, 324
Functional illness, 271

Galactosemia, 128
Gargoylism, 128
General practice, psychiatric problems in, 130-181
Genitourinary syndrome, 261
Genuineness and therapy, 506
Grand mal seizures, 296-297
  clonic phase, 296
  tonic phase, 296
"Grantham procedure," 477
Graves' disease, 212-216
Grief, 130-134
Group therapy, 492-497
  ward meetings, 495-497
Guilt
  depression and, psychotic, 348
  feelings of, 68
Gumma, 283

Habituation, 166-176
  alcohol, 171-173
  definition, 167
  psychodynamic factors in, 168-169
  tobacco, 169-171
Hallucinations, 88, 273
  definition, 279
  schizophrenia and, 367
Hallucinosis, alcoholic, 293
Hate and surgical experience, 240-251
Head pain, 153-158
Head trauma and psychiatric disorders, 303-306

Headache, 153-158
  diagnosis, 153-154
  incidence, 153-154
  migraine, 154-155, 216-218
  pathogenesis, 153-154
  "psychogenic," 157-158
  tension, 155-157
Health. See Mental health
Hebephrenic schizophrenia, 372-373
Hepatolenticular degeneration, 128
Heredity
  influences of, 127-129
  schizophrenia and, 375-377
History
  case, 6-10
  family, 9
  social, 9
  variations in, 6-7
Homeostasis, 29
Homosexuality, 56, 416
  male, 58
  "normal childhood," 110
Hospital
  day, 508-509
  night, 508-509
Hospitalization
  discharge after, 24-26
  environmental manipulation during, 506-508
  psychological aspects of, 20-24
Hostility, 61-63
  depression and, psychotic, 346
    redirection of hostility, 347
  developmental course, 63
  infancy period and, 90
  surgical experience and, 240-251
Hunger, 52-54
Huntington's chorea, 128
Hypertension, essential, 193-200
Hyperthyroidism, 212-216
  mechanisms involved in, 214
  treatment, 216
Hypnosis, 42-43
  definition, 489
Hypnotherapy, 489-492
Hypochondriasis, 246, 336-338
  definition, 336
Hypomania, 352
Hysteria. See Phobia

Id, 70
Identification, 78
  family triangle period and, 105
  hyperthyroidism and, 214
Identity, sense of, 235
Idiocy, amaurotic familial, 128
Illness
  functional, 271

Illness—(Continued)
  mental. See Mental illness
  organic, 271
  patient's attitude toward, 2
Illusions, 273
  definition, 278
Iminodibenzyl, 456
Imipramine, 453
Imitation, 78
  family triangle period and, 105
Impotence, transient or situational, 141-143
Inappropriateness, affective, 364-365
Incorporation and grief, 133
Indulgence and therapy, 504
Infancy period, 85-93
  personality disorders, gross, 520-521
  symptoms of, 517-520
Insight, 273
  alcoholism and, 412
  schizophrenia and, 380
Instincts, 51
Insulin, 472-473
Internal medicine, 182-221
Internalization, 68
Intelligence and diagnosis, 431
Interviewing, 7, 429-430
Introjection
  definition, 78-79
  depression and, psychotic, 346
  family triangle period and, 105
  grief and, 133
  infancy period and, 89
Involution, period of, 119-121
Involutional reaction, psychotic, 357
  definition, 357
Isolation, 79
  compulsive reaction and, 332

Juvenile delinquency, 536

Korsakow's psychosis and delirium tremens, 295

Laboratory procedures, 13-15
  attitudes and test results, 14
Laceration, definition, 305
Latency period, 108-111
  behavior disorders, 535-536
  problems of, 532-536
Lawyers and treatment, 465
Learning disability in latency period, 534
Libido, 55-60
  developmental course of, 55
  self-preservative drives and
    differences, 55-60
    similarities, 55

554 Index

Lobotomy, 477
Love
  abilities and, 36-37
  surgical experience and, 240-251
LSD, 378
Lysergic acid diethylamide (LSD), 378

Malingering, 145-151
  compensation problems, 149-150
  conversion reaction and, 316
  definition, 145
  diagnosis, differential, 145-148
  physicians' attitudes toward, 150-151
  "secondary gain," 146, 149-150
Mania and dementia, 285
Manic-depressive reaction, 354-357
  definition, 355
  depressive type, 356
  manic type, 356
Manic reaction, 351-354
Marasmus, 518
Marriage maladjustments of, 136-138
Masochism, 58, 80
  moral, 423
  sexual deviation and, 416
Masochistic personality, 423
Masturbation, excessive, in family triangle period, 528-529
Matter-of-factness and therapy, 505
Maturation, imbalances in adolescence, 538-539
Maturity, period of, 118-119
Mellaril and sexual drive, 143
Menarche, 113-114
Meningo-encephalitis, 282
Menstrual cycle, psychological aspects of, 113-114
Mental deficiency
  diagnosis, 432
  heredity and, 128
Mental health, 32-38
  criteria
    objective, statistical, 33-34
    psychological, 35-38
    subjective, 34
  general health and, 32-34
Mental illness
  malingering and, 145
  study of, 84-85
Mental retardation, 541-546
  classification, 541
  management, 544-546
Mental status examination, 430
Mescaline, 378
Migraine, 154-155, 216-218
Milieu therapy, 497-509
  attitude therapy, 501-506
  day hospital, 508-509

Milieu therapy—(*Continued*)
  definition, 497
  environmental manipulation in hospital, 506-508
  night hospital, 508-509
  ward atmosphere, 497-501
Mind, 28-29
  definitions of, 29-31
  executive faculties of, 71
    defense mechanisms and, 75
  organization of, 69-81
Models, parental, 105
Monoamine oxidase inhibitors, 456
Motivation, 49-64
  definition of, 49
  muscle training period and, 96
Mourning, 130-134
Mucous colitis, 210-212
Muscle tension and backache, 159-160
Muscle training period, 93-99
  personality pattern disturbances, 524-525
  physiological disturbances, 523-524
  problems of, 521-525
  training failures, 521-523

Narcissism
  body, 234
  hypochondriasis and, 336
Narcosynthesis, 492
Narcotic addiction. *See* Addiction
Needs
  dependency, 63-64
  gratification of, 38
Nembutal, 455
Neurasthenia
  definition, 162
  symptoms of, 162-165
Neuro-musculo-skeletal systems, 260-261
Neuroleptics, 456
Neurosis, 307-340
  adolescent, 539-540
  childhood, 531
  definition, 274
  dementia and, 287
  diagnosis, 432
  etiology, 272
  head trauma and, 304
  obsessive-compulsive, 329-333
  precipitating factors, 307-308
  predisposing factors, 307-308
  primary gain, 319
  prognosis, 338-340
  psychosis distinguished from, 272-274
  reaction. *See specific reactions*
  secondary gain, 319-320
  traumatic, 151-153, 304-305, 308-310
Neurotic personality, 404, 422-425

Neurotic reactions and surgery, 231-255
Night hospital, 508-509
Nocturnal emissions, 112
Normality and diagnosis, 431-432
Nurses
    public health, 462
    visiting nurse associations, 462

Obesity, 176-180
Object, definition of, 273
Obsessions, 273
    definition, 329
Obsessive-compulsive neurosis, 329-333
Occupational therapy, 462-463
    discussion, 510-512
Oedipal period, 101
    See also Family triangle period
Office visit, initial, 4-6
Old age, period of, 121-123
Oligophrenia, phenylpyruvic, 128
Organic illness, 271
Overeating, reasons for, 178-180

Pain
    head, 153-158
    phantom phenomena and, 265-268
    psychologic mechanisms and, 161-162
Palpitation, 257
Panic, 66
    state, 341
Paranoia, 391-394
    dementia and, 285
Paranoid reactions, 341, 390-395
    delirium tremens and, 295
    nomenclature in, official, 355
    projection and, 78
Paranoid state, 394-395
Paranoid type, schizophrenia, 370-372
Paresis, general, 282-287
Parkinsonism, 260
Peeping and family triangle period, 529-530
Peptic ulcer, 186-193
Periods of development. *See specific periods*
"Perpetual calendar," 43
Personality
    anal, 404
    attributes of, 32
    cyclothymic, 354
    defect, post-traumatic, 306
    definition of, 31-32, 398
    development, 82-129
        phases of, 85-123
    disorders, 397-425
        adolescent, 540
        classification, 402-403

Personality, disorders—(*Continued*)
        definition, 398
        infants and, 520-521
        latency period, 535-536
        post-traumatic, 306
        vocational maladjustments and, 135-136
    disturbances
        pattern
            family triangle period, 530-531
            muscle training period, 524-525
        trait, 422
    epileptic, 303
    masochistic, 423
    neurotic, 404, 422-425
    oral, 404
    phallic, 404
    rigidity, 399
    sociopathic, 416
    split, 363
Perversions, 57, 416-422
Petit mal seizures, 297-298
Phantom phenomena and pain, 265-268
Phenobarbital, 454
Phenothiazines, 456
Phobia and phobic reaction, 147, 273, 325-329
    definition, 135, 325
    "job," 135
Physical dependence, 167
Physical examination, 10-13
Physician, selection of, 3-4
    See also Attitudes
Physiological development, 82-83
Physiotherapy, 463-464
Placebos, 460
Play therapy, 492
Polysurgical addict, 243
Practice, general, psychiatric problems in, 130-181
Preconscious, 42
Presenting situation, 1-3
Primary gain in neurosis, 319
Projection
    definition, 77-78
    family triangle period and, 103
    phobic reaction and, 327
    schizophrenia and, 385
    surgical experience and, 235
Psychiatric problems in general practice, 130-181
Psychiatry
    major, 471
    minor, 471
    surgery and. *See* Surgery
Psychoanalysis, 484-487
    results of, 43-45

556 Index

Psychodrama, 495
Psychodynamics
   conversion reaction, 316-321
   definition, 130
Psychologists, 461-462
   clinical, 462
Psychology
   basic concepts, 28-32
   criteria in, 35-38
   fundamentals of, 28-81
   problems in, common, 1-27
Psychomotor equivalents, 298
Psychomotor seizures, 298
Psychomotor stimulants, 456
Psychoneurosis. *See* Neurosis
Psychopharmacological agents, 452-460
   long-continued use of, 454
Psychopathic development, 113
Psychosis
   adolescent, 540
   arteriosclerosis and, cerebral, 287-291
   brain disease and, senile, 288
   brain tumor and, 289
   childhood, 532
   definition, 273-274
   delirium and, 274, 295
   dementia and, 274
   diagnosis, 432
   dysrhythmia and, cerebral, 303
   etiology, 272
   experimental, 378
   functional
      affective reactions, 341-359
      nomenclature in, official, 355
      schizophrenic reactions, 360-390
   head trauma and, 304
   Korsakow's, and delirium tremens, 295
   manic-depressive, 354-357
      definition, 355
      depressive type, 356
      heredity and, 128
      manic type, 356
   neurosis distinguished from, 272-274
   trauma and, 356
Psychosomatic
   definition, 183-186
   disorders, childhood, 531-532
   medicine, 182-221
Psychosurgery, 477-478
Psychotherapist and self knowledge, 480
Psychotherapy
   expressive, 450, 484
   group, 492-497
      ward meetings, 495-497
   individual, 478-492
      motivations of therapist, 479
   intensive, results of, 43-45
   relationship, 450, 481-484

Psychotherapy—(*Continued*)
   study of early periods and, 85
   See also Treatment
Psychotic reactions. *See* Psychosis
Puberty period, 111-114
Pupil, Argyll Robertson, 284

Rationalization, 80
Rauwolfia alkaloids, 456
Reactions. *See specific reactions*
Reaction-formation
   compulsive reaction and, 332
   definition, 77
   latency period and, 111
   muscle training period and, 95
   paranoia and, 394
   surgical experience and, 235
   ulcer and, peptic, 192
Reading disability in latency period, 534
Reality, appraisal with accuracy, 36
Rebelliousness, excessive, in children, 524-525
Recreational therapy, 464
   discussion, 512-513
Regression
   compulsive reaction and, 332
   definition, 75-76
   dementia and, arteriosclerotic, 289
   experimental, 84
   family triangle period and, 106, 527-528
   hypnotic, 43, 489
   muscle training period and, 97-98
   paranoia and, 393
   phobic reaction and, 328
   schizophrenia and, 385
   ulcer and, peptic, 190
Repression, 41-42
   definition, 76
   degree, of, 42
   ego and, 72
Respect and therapy, 498
Restlessness, excessive, in latency period, 533-534
Rigidity
   personality disorders and, 399
   reaction-formation and, 77

Sadism, 79, 398
   sexual deviation and, 416
Schizo-affective schizophrenia, 373
Schizophrenia. *See* Schizophrenic reactions
Schizophrenic reactions, 341, 360-390
   accessory symptoms, 367-368
   Bleuler's "four A's," 364-367
   catatonic type, 369-370
   childhood type, 374

Index

Schizophrenic reactions—(*Continued*)
  clinical syndromes, 368-374
  defense mechanisms, 385-389
  delirium tremens and, 295
  dementia and, 285
  derivation of term schizophrenia, 363
  etiology, 374-389
  hebephrenic type, 372-373
  nomenclature in, official, 355
  nuclear, 375
  organic factors, 375-380
    biochemistry, 378-380
    constitution, 377
    endocrine status, 377
    heredity, 128, 375-377
    pathology, 377-378
  paranoid type, 370-372
  process, 375
  psychological factors, 380-389
    close interaction, 385
    precipitating factors, 385
    predisposing factors, 380-385
  reactive schizophrenia, 375
  residual type, 374
  schizo-affective type, 373
  simple type, 372
  undifferentiated types, 373-374
School problems in latency period, 533-535
  attendance and reluctance, 534-535
Seconal, 455
"Secondary gain," 149-150, 319-320
  definition of, 146
Security and therapy, 500
Sedatives, 454-455
  habituation and, 173-174
Selection of physician, 3-4
Self
  definition of, 235
  loss of esteem in psychotic depression, 346
  sense of, 235
  surgical experience and, 235-240
  turning against, 79-80
Self-condemnation, 68
Self-image, 235-240
Separation, 130-134
Serotonin, 378
Sexual deviation, 57, 416-422
  children and infants, 420
Sexual development
  delayed, 538
  precocious, 538
Sexual education, problems of, 139-141
Sexual problems, mild, 139-145
Shame, feelings of, 68-69
Side effects of tranquilizers, 457-458
Sign, definition, 397

"Sissy" behavior, 530-531
Situational maladjustments, 134
Sleep disturbances in infants, 519-520
Slips, 39-42
Social casework, 461
Soiling by children, 522
Somatopsychic sequences, 255-268
Spastic colitis, 210-212
Split personality, 363
Status epilepticus, 297
  petit mal, 298
Stimulants
  discussion, 458-459
  habituation and, 174-176
  psychomotor, 456
Subconscious, use of term, 38
Sublimation, 59
  aggression and, 63
  definition, 60, 75
  hostility and, 63
  hypertension and, 197
  infancy period and, 89
  latency period and, 110
  muscle training period and, 96
Superego, 68, 73-74
  family triangle period and, 105
  formation, capacity for, 74
Supportive treatment, 269
Suppression, 80
Surgery and psychiatry, 222-225
  body and body-image, 233-235
  delay in seeking treatment, 230-231
  forces in the surgeon-patient relationship, 223-225
  neurotic reactions, 231-255
  self and self-image, 235-240
  surgical experience
    beginning of, 226-230
    modifying effects of, 225-226
Survival and surgical experience, 251-255
Symptoms
  conversion reaction, 320-322
  definition, 397
  infancy period, 517-520
  muscle-training period, 521-525
  psychiatric, 35
Syncope, 324

Tabes dorsalis, 283
Taraxein, 379
Tension
  headache, 155-157
  muscle, and backache, 159-160
  surgical experience and, 251
Terror, 66
Thioridazine and sexual drive, 143

Index

Thumbsucking, 519
Thyrotoxicosis, 212-216
Tobacco, habituation to, 169-171
"Tomboyish" behavior, 530
Toxic disease states, 271
Transference
  definition, 451
  discussion, 487-489
  psychotherapy, relationship, 484
Tranquilizers, 452
  discussion of, 455-458
  habituation and, 173-174
  sexual drive and, 143
  side effects, 457-458
Trauma
  head, and psychiatric disorders, 303-306
  psychosis and, 356
  traumatic neurosis. *See* Neurosis
Treatment
  affective reactions, 358
  ancillary approaches, 460-465
  arrangements for, 428-429
  backache, 159-160
  collaborative approaches, 460-465
  consultations, 19, 437, 465-468
  delay in seeking, 230-231
  delirium tremens, 294-295
  dementia
    arteriosclerotic, 290-291
    paralytica, 286-287
  diagnosis. *See* Diagnosis
  epilepsy, 300-303
  expressive psychotherapy, 450
  failure to improve, 26
  fatigue, 164-165
  hyperthyroidism, 216
  indirect measures, 513-515
    external environment manipulation, 514-515
    working through family and friends, 513-514
  interviewing, 429-430
  measures for use by nonpsychiatrist, 426-468
    common misconceptions, 426-428
      all patients suited for intensive work, 428
      intimate relationships involved, 427
      much time involved, 426-427

Treatment, measures for use by nonpsychiatrist, common misconceptions —(*Continued*)
      much training required, 428
      unconscious explored, 427
  measures for use by psychiatrist, 469-515
    chemical, 469-470
    classification, 470-471
    definitive, 469-470
    physical, 469-470
    psychological, 469-470
    symptomatic, 469-470
  neurosis, 338-340
  office, 17-20
  procedures, 17-26
  relationship psychotherapy, 450
  schizophrenic reactions, 389-390
  supportive, 269, 440-450
  suppressive approach, 436-440
  symptomatic, physical and chemical, 472-478
  treatment thinking, 435-450
  See also Psychotherapy
Treponema pallidum, 283
Triangulation and consequences of surgery, 226
Twilight states, 298

Unconscious
  defense mechanisms and, 75
  definition of, 42
  psychoanalysis and, 485
  use of term, 38
"Unconscious recognition," 327
Understanding and therapy, 506
Undoing and compulsive reaction, 332
Ulcer, peptic, 186-193

Vocational maladjustments, 134-136
  personality disorders, 135-136
  situational factors, 135
Vocational rehabilitation, 464-465
Voyeurism, 56, 58, 416
  family triangle period and, 101

Waiting to see physician, 5
Watchfulness and therapy, 505
Withdrawal syndrome, 415
Work, productive, 37